Tony Holland.
Dept of Psychiatry
Univ. of Cambridge.

Handbook of Eating Disorders

Handbook of Eating Disorders

Theory, Treatment and Research

EDITED BY

GEORGE SZMUKLER
CHRIS DARE

AND

JANET TREASURE
Institute of Psychiatry, London, UK

WITH A FOREWORD BY

PAUL E. GARFINKEL
Clark Institute of Psychiatry,
Toronto, Canada

JOHN WILEY & SONS
Chichester · New York · Brisbane · Toronto · Singapore

Other Wiley Editorial Offices

John Wiley & Sons, Inc., 605 Third Avenue,
New York, NY 10158-0012, USA

Jacaranda Wiley Ltd, 33 Park Road, Milton,
Queensland 4064, Australia

John Wiley & Sons (Canada) Ltd, 22 Worcester Road,
Rexdale, Ontario M9W 1L1, Canada

John Wiley & Sons (SEA) Pte Ltd, 37 Jalan Pemimpin #05-04,
Block B, Union Industrial Building, Singapore 2057

Library of Congress Cataloging-in-Publication Data

Handbook of eating disorders : theory, treatment, and research /
   edited by George Szmukler, Chris Dare, and Janet Treasure.
       p.   cm.
   Includes bibliographical references and index.
   ISBN 0-471-94327-4 (cased)
   1. Eating disorders.   I. Szmukler, George.   II. Dare,
Christopher.   III. Treasure, Janet.
   [DNLM: 1. Eating Disorders—therapy.   2. Eating Disorders–
–etiology.   WM 175 E1473 1994]
   RC552.E18E2842   1994
   616.85'26—dc20
   DNLM/DLC
   for Library of Congress   93–40625
                                                                CIP

British Library Cataloguing in Publication Data

A catalogue record for this book is available from the British Library

ISBN 0-471-94327-4

Typeset in 10/12pt Times by Dorwyn Ltd, Rowlands Castle, Hants
Printed and bound in Great Britain by Bookcraft (Bath) Ltd

Contents

About the Editors

G.I. SZMUKLER *Bethlem Royal and Maudsley Hospitals, London; and Institute of Psychiatry, De Crespigny Park, Denmark Hill, London SE5 8AF, UK*

George Szmukler is a Consultant Psychiatrist at the Bethlem Royal and Maudsley Hospitals, he was previously a Senior Lecturer at the Institute of Psychiatry, London, and later a Consultant Psychiatrist at the Royal Melbourne Hospital in Australia, where he directed an eating disorders unit. His major interests in the eating disorders include epidemiology, the evaluation of treatments, and some biological aspects.

C. DARE *Department of Psychiatry, Institute of Psychiatry, De Crespigny Park, Denmark Hill, London SE5 8AF, UK*

Christopher Dare is Senior Lecturer in Psychotherapy Research at the Institute of Psychiatry. He trained in psychoanalysis and child and adolescent psychiatry and developed interests in psychodynamic and family therapies for adolescent and young adult patients.

JANET TREASURE *Department of Psychiatry, Institute of Psychiatry, De Crespigny Park, Denmark Hill, London SE5 8AF, UK*

Janet Treasure runs the Eating Disorder Unit at the Maudsley Hospital and the Institute of Psychiatry, where she is a Senior Lecturer. She is actively involved in research into the aetiology and treatment of eating disorders.

Contributors

A. ANDERSEN   *Professor, Department of Psychiatry, University of Iowa, 500 Newton Road, Iowa City, IA 52242, USA*

P.J.V. BEUMONT   *Professor of Psychiatry, Department of Psychiatry, University of Sydney, Royal Prince Alfred Hospital, Camperdown, NSW 2050, Australia*

PATRICK CAMPBELL   *Consultant Psychiatrist, Royal Free Hospital, Pond Street, London NW3 2OG, UK*

MIREILLE COLAHAN   *Research Psychotherapist, Department of Psychiatry, Institute of Psychiatry, De Crespigny Park, Denmark Hill, London SE5 8AF, UK*

CATHERINE CROWTHER   *Psychotherapist, Department of Psychiatry, Institute of Psychiatry, De Crespigny Park, Denmark Hill, London SE5 8AF, UK*

PADMAL DE SILVA   *Senior Lecturer, Department of Psychology, Institute of Psychiatry, De Crespigny Park, Denmark Hill, London SE5 8AF, UK*

IVAN EISLER   *Senior Lecturer in Psychology, Department of Psychiatry, Institute of Psychiatry, De Crespigny Park, Denmark Hill, London SE5 8AF, UK*

MANFRED FICHTER   *Professor, Klinik Roseneck, Ludwig–Maximilians Universitat Munchen, Am Roseneck 6, 8210 Prien am Chiemsee, Germany*

CHRISTOPHER FREEMAN   *Consultant Psychotherapist, Royal Edinburgh Hospital, Morningside Park, Edinburgh EH10 5HF, UK*

PAUL E. GARFINKEL   *Director and Psychiatrist-in-Chief, Clark Institute of Psychiatry, 250 College Street, Toronto, Ontario M5T 1R8, Canada*

KATHERINE A. HALMI *Professor of Psychiatry, Cornell Medical Centre—Westchester Division, 21 Bloomingdale Road, White Plains, New York 10605, USA*

ANTHONY HOLLAND *Senior Lecturer, University of Cambridge, Services for People with Mental Handicap, Ida Darwin House, Fulbourn Hospital, Cambridge CB1 5EE, UK*

P. MCHUGH *Professor and Head, Department of Psychiatry and Behavioural Sciences, Johns Hopkins University Hospital, 600 North Wolfe Street, Baltimore, Maryland 21205, USA*

H. GETHIN MORGAN *Professor of Psychiatry, Department of Mental Health, University of Bristol, 41 St Michael's Hill, Bristol BS2 8DZ, UK*

GEORGE PATTON *Senior Lecturer, Department of Psychiatry, University of Melbourne, Centre for Adolescent Health, William Buckland House, Parkville, Victoria 3052, Australia*

K.M. PIRKE *Professor, Department of Psychoendocrinology, Centre of Psychobiology & Psychosomatic Research, University of Trier, Building D, PO Box 3825, 5500 Trier, Germany*

PAUL ROBINSON *Consultant Psychiatrist, Peter Dally Eating and Weight Disorders Unit, Gordon Hospital, Bloomburg Street, London SW1V 2RH, UK*

JANICE RUSSELL *Senior Lecturer, Department of Psychiatry, University of Sydney; and Director, Eating Disorder Unit, Concord Hospital and Northside Clinic, NSW 2050, Australia*

ULRIKE SCHMIDT *Consultant Psychiatrist, St Mary's Hospital, Praed Street, London W2 1NY; and Honorary Senior Lecturer, Department of Psychiatry, De Crespigny Park, Denmark Hill, London SE5 8AF, UK*

ROB SENIOR *Family Therapist, Department of Psychiatry, Institute of Psychiatry, De Crespigny Park, Denmark Hill, London SE5 8AF, UK*

J.A. SILVERMAN *Clinical Professor of Paediatrics, Columbia University, College of Physicians and Surgeons, 3 East 85th Street, New York 10028, USA*

PETER SLADE *Professor of Clinical Psychology, University of Liverpool, New Medical School, Ashton Street, PO Box 147, Liverpool L69 3BX, UK*

STEN THEANDER *Head of Anorexia Nervosa Unit, Department of Psychiatry, University Hospital, S-221 85 Lund, Sweden*

JANE TILLER   *Senior Registrar, Maudsley Hospital, Denmark Hill, London SE5 8AZ, UK*

GILL TODD   *Research Nurse Therapist, Department of Psychiatry, Institute of Psychiatry, De Crespigny Park, Denmark Hill, London SE5 8AF, UK*

STEPHEN TOUYZ   *Associate Professor of Psychiatry, University of Sydney, Head of Department of Medical Psychology, Westmead Hospital, Westmead, NSW 2145, Australia*

WALTER VANDEREYCKEN   *Professor of Psychiatry, University of Leuven, Leuvenselaan 85, B-3300 Tienen, Belgium*

A. WAKELING   *Professor of Psychiatry, Royal Free Hospital, School of Medicine, Pond Street, London NW3 2PF, UK*

Foreword

PAUL E. GARFINKEL
Clark Institute of Psychiatry, Toronto

Professor Gerald Russell's retirement in September 1993 has prompted his students and colleagues to organize this volume as a tribute to his distinct contribution to the understanding and treatment of the eating disorders over the past 30 years. I am delighted to provide a North American perspective on Gerald's influence. In the last 15 years, there has been an amazing convergence of European and North American approaches to the eating disorders, reflective in large measure of the work and perspectives of Gerald Russell.

To begin to appreciate the importance of the changes in our understanding, we need only turn back to 1962, when Gerald first wrote about anorexia nervosa. Recognition of the psychopathology of this disorder was poor; there was even uncertainty about the discreteness of the syndrome (Bliss and Branch, 1960). The endocrine complications were confined to knowledge of the amenorrhea and abnormalities of adrenal steroid excretion (Emanuel, 1956). Awareness of the complications was minimal. Treatment approaches were split into distinct psychoanalytic or somatic therapy approaches, and these did not take into account the special needs of these patients. There were no centres of excellence where treatment-resistant cases could be seen with sufficient frequency to provide additional advice. Bulimia nervosa was unheard of.

Thirty years later, progress has been made on many levels, and Gerald Russell has been at the centre of each advance. For example, his diagnostic criteria were the first to be widely used (Russell, 1970), and in many ways were the precursors to the

Handbook of Eating Disorders: Theory, Treatment and Research.
Edited by G. Szmukler, C. Dare and J. Treasure.
© 1995 John Wiley & Sons Ltd.

approach taken in the planned DSM-IV criteria (Garfinkel, 1993); he and his colleagues have carefully documented the hormonal and metabolic changes in anorexia nervosa (Russell, 1965, 1969; Beardwood and Russell, 1970) and they have alerted us to some of the complications of anorexia nervosa, especially the delayed puberty (Russell, 1983); the presence of neuropathies and myopathies (Alloway et al, 1985), cystic ovaries (Treasure et al, 1985), delayed gastric emptying (Robinson et al, 1987) and osteopenia (Treasure et al, 1986). The Maudsley Group have carefully followed up their patients and have provided detailed data on the 20-year course of anorexia nervosa. Gerald's work on the clinical features of the eating disorders has brought unusual recognition; he is probably the only modern psychiatrist to have a clinical feature named after him ("Russell's sign" in bulimia nervosa)—much to his chagrin!

While Gerald has made significant contributions at many levels, his influence on North American psychiatry has been greatest in four areas: (1) a treatment model for hospital-based weight restoration; (2) comparative treatment evaluations; (3) empirical assessments of psychopathology, especially body image; and (4) most importantly, the delineation of bulimia nervosa as an autonomous disorder.

In-Hospital Treatment of Anorexia Nervosa

The approach to anorexia nervosa in Toronto in the early 1970s was probably typical of most North American centres. The disorder was rare, so any one clinician saw few cases. When they presented, patients were almost always admitted to hospital and an extensive metabolic work-up was conducted. In Toronto, our approach to hospital care varied considerably. At first, influenced by the work of Hilde Bruch (Bruch, 1970), we provided a setting in which what the patient said was listened to and made the object of repeated exploration, with no emphasis on weight restoration. However, we became frustrated by our patients' resistance to weight changes. They would remain in hospital for long periods, develop some awareness of their psychological problems and yet continue to be emaciated. At about this time, a small series of articles began to describe operant conditioning in anorexia nervosa. We began to provide reinforcement for weight gain and published on this technique (Garfinkel, Kline and Stancer, 1973). However, we soon saw problems with this; we did not understand an optimal level or rate of weight gain; operant conditioning could be applied without sensitivity to a particular patient's psychopathology and often it became the entire focus of treatment, rather than one component of it. We also saw how limited the gains were, in terms of rapid relapse after discharge (Garfinkel, Moldofsky and Garner, 1977).

This frustration with treatment led us to the literature and Gerald Russell's excellent paper on multifaceted management (Russell, 1970) which later was expanded (Russell, 1981). Shortly after reading Russell's approach to management, I was invited to a small National Institute of Mental Health meeting on anorexia nervosa, held in Bethesda in 1976. It was here that I first met Gerald, listened to him speak and discuss the work of others. Three years later, I was able to visit the Institute of Psychiatry, the Royal Free and Friern Hospitals, where

Gerald was both a gracious and a thoughtful host. He visited Toronto in 1978 and 1981 and I returned to spend several months at the Institute of Psychiatry in 1986. Along the way, and after many discussions about treatment, our management approaches began to show increasing congruence, as is apparent in some of the Toronto group's writing on the subject (Garfinkel and Garner, 1982; Garfinkel, Garner and Kennedy, 1985). The Maudsley Hospital's emphasis on weight restoration , in a setting of emotional support, prior to psychological therapies, has now been widely accepted throughout North America and wherever anorexia nervosa is treated.

Comparative Treatment Evaluations

Many forms of treatment have been advocated for anorexia nervosa, but almost none has been subject to controlled evaluation. Without the results of careful investigations, clinicians are left to determine individual treatment decisions based on such subjective factors as their personal biases. All too often, clinicians have provided treatments according to their abilities, not necessarily in keeping with the patient's specific needs. We must increasingly develop a tailored approach to any individual's treatment, with our selections beginning with the least costly, least intrusive, effective type and work from there, according to the patient's needs. In order to provide such tailored treatments, we must understand the natural history of the eating disorders, conduct comparative treatment trials of the highest order and learn about predictors of response to treatments.

Since 1981, Russell and his colleagues have been engaged in a series of investigations aimed at developing and evaluating psychological treatments for the eating disorders. These have demonstrated the specific value of family therapy in young patients with anorexia nervosa, and its enduring benefits (Russell et al, 1987). Comparative trials of brief focal psychotherapy with family therapy, and of parental counselling with family therapy, are now being completed. Together they will provide the first substantive literature on the responses to specific treatments, and the foundations for a tailored approach to treatment for anorexia nervosa. They have served as a basis for treatment trials elsewhere and also document the great and long-term value of psychological therapies in anorexia nervosa.

Psychological Mechanisms

As I noted earlier, Russell's (1970) diagnostic criteria for anorexia nervosa were the first widely accepted ones; they highlighted three components: (1) a set of behaviours (aimed at achieving weight loss); (2) an endocrine disorder (amenorrhea in the female and loss of sexual potency and interest in the male); and (3) a characteristic psychopathology (a morbid fear of becoming fat). This latter feature has been the subject of much study.

In anorexia nervosa, there is a desperate avoidance of normal body proportions. The individual religiously follows certain guideposts in determining her weight:

what she has allowed as a reading on the scale; how certain clothes fit; and how she views and feels about her body. Bruch (1970) had earlier written on the importance of the body image in anorexia nervosa. Russell and his colleagues began to develop the first sophisticated measures of visual self-perception in anorexia nervosa (e.g. Slade and Russell, 1973). They were also able to demonstrate that the cognitive process of "what the scales show" is an important regulating feature (Russell, Campbell and Slade, 1975). While not an absolute diagnostic feature, how people see and feel about their bodies is clearly an important aspect of the eating disorders and this is closely related to such phenomena as self-esteem, pleasure with the body, mood and cognition. Russell's group has taken a valuable psychological construct and carefully studied it. In so doing, they have stimulated a great deal more research on body image, including the largely neglected affective dimension of this construct (Garfinkel et al, 1992). As a result, they have increased awareness of the clinical importance of these issues.

Delineation of Bulimia Nervosa

When Gerald visited Toronto in 1978, we chatted pleasantly for a while before he steered the conversation around to a particular topic: people who had the psycho-pathological stance of the anorexic, but who may or may not have reached low weight levels; these women engaged in binge-eating and purging. He became ex-cited, reached into his briefcase and brought out a manuscript that was then in press (Russell, 1979) and that was soon to become a classic. The Toronto group had been interested in anorexics who were "restricters" versus those who were "bulimic" and we reviewed our data on this for Gerald (Garfinkel, Moldofsky and Garner, 1980). Casper and Halmi were also examining this identical subject (Casper et al, 1980). Russell's paper quickly led to an appreciation of a larger group with bulimia nervosa; and this new disorder was rapidly incorporated into DSM-III in 1980. By the following year, Christopher Fairburn at Oxford was describing the value of cognitive–behavioural therapies for bulimia nervosa; many epidemiologic studies began to appear, as well as investigations examining mechanisms, sequelae and treatment effectiveness. In less than two years, psychiatrists throughout the western world recognized an important new disorder.

While this brief comment highlights an important aspect of Gerald Russell's aca-demic world, that of scholarship, this volume highlights a second related contribu-tion as well — his teaching. This handbook has been produced by Russell's students and all contributors have worked closely with him and have learned from him. All are now active in some aspect of treatment and enquiry about the eating disorders. And, all display a commitment to the care of these patients blended with a desire to learn more. The range of topics covered reflects the breadth of research conducted on Russell's units, and characteristically, the focus is not merely on what is known today, but also on how progress can occur in the future.

Gerald Russell has been a thoughtful clinician and scholar. For all of us, he has been a particularly effective teacher. He has taught us about the eating disorders in so many areas; and he has taught us about the fusion of science with humanity, to which many aspire yet few achieve. William Osler once described the teacher in this manner: "No bubble is so iridescent or floats longer than that blown by the successful teacher."

REFERENCES

Alloway, R., Reynolds, E.H., Spargo, E. and Russell, G.F.M. (1985). Neuropathy and myopathy in two patients with anorexia and bulimia nervosa. *J. Neurol. Neurosurg. Psychiat.,* **48**, 1015–1020.

Beardwood, C.J. and Russell, G.F.M. (1970). Gonadotrophin excretion at puberty. *J. Endocrinol.,* **48**, 469.

Bliss, E.L. and Branch, C.H.H. (1960). *Anorexia Nervosa: Its History, Psychology and Biology.* New York: Paul B. Hoeber.

Bruch, H. (1970). Instinct and interpersonal experience. *Compr. Psychiat.,* **11**, 495–506.

Emanuel, R.W. (1956). Endocrine activity in anorexia nervosa. *J. Clin. Endocrinol. Metab.,* **16**, 801–816.

Casper, R.C., Eckert, E.D., Halmi, K.A., Goldberg, S.C. and Davis, J.M. (1980). Bulimia: its incidence and clinical importance in patients with anorexia nervosa. *Arch. Gen. Psychiat.,* **37**, 1030–1034.

Garfinkel, P.E. (1993). Diagnosis and classification. In: K.A. Halmi (Ed.), *The Eating Disorders.* New York: American Psychopathological Association.

Garfinkel, P.E. and Garner, D.M. (1982). *Anorexia Nervosa: A Multidimensional Perspective.* New York: Brunner/Mazel.

Garfinkel, P.E., Garner, D.M. and Kennedy, S. (1985). Special problems in in-patient management. In: D.M. Garner and P.E. Garfinkel (Eds), *Handbook for Treatment of Anorexia Nervosa and Bulimia,* pp. 344–359. New York: Guilford Press.

Garfinkel, P.E., Goldbloom, D.S., Olmsted, M.P., Davis, R., Garner, D.M. and Halmi, K.A. (1992). Body dissatisfaction in bulimia nervosa: relationship to weight and shape concerns and psychological functioning. *Int. J. Eat. Dis.,* **11**, 151–161.

Garfinkel, P.E., Kline, S.A. and Stancer, H.C. (1973). Treatment of anorexia nervosa using operant conditioning techniques. *J. Nerv. Ment. Dis.,* **157**, 428–433.

Garfinkel, P.E., Moldofsky, H. and Garner, D.M. (1977). Prognosis in anorexia nervosa as influenced by clinical features, treatment and self-perception. *Can. Med. Assoc. J.,* **117**, 1041–1045.

Garfinkel, P.E., Moldofsky, H. and Garner, D.M. (1980). The heterogeneity of anorexia nervosa: bulimia as a distinct subgroup. *Arch. Gen. Psych.,* **37**, 1036–1040.

Robinson, P., et al. (1987) Delayed gastric emptying in patients with anorexia nervosa. *J. Physiol.,* **387**, 92p.

Russell, G.F.M. (1983). Delayed puberty due to anorexia nervosa of early onset. In: P.L. Darby, P.E. Garfinkel, D.M. Garner and D.V. Coscina (Eds), *Anorexia Nervosa: Recent Developments in Research.* New York: Alan R. Liss.

Russell, G.F.M. (1981). The current treatment of anorexia nervosa. *Br. J. Psychiat.,* **138**, 164–166.

Russell, G.F.M. (1979). Bulimia nervosa: an ominous variant of anorexia nervosa. *Psychol. Med.,* **9**, 429–448.

Russell, G.F.M. (1970). Anorexia nervosa: its identity as an illness and its treatment. In: J.H. Price (Ed.), *Modern Trends in Psychological Medicine,* pp. 131–164. London: Butterworth.

Russell, G.F.M. (1969). The neuro-endocrinology of human undernutrition with particular reference to anorexia nervosa. In: J. Vague (Ed.), *Physiotherapy of Adipose Tissue.* (Proceedings of 3rd International Meeting of Endocrinologists, Marseilles, 9–12 May 1968). Excerpta Medica Monograph Series.

Russell, G.F.M. (1965). Metabolic aspects of anorexia nervosa. *Proceedings of the Royal Society of Medicine,* **58**, 811.

Russell, G.F.M., Campbell, P.G. and Slade, P.D. (1975). Experimental studies on the nature of the psychological disorder in anorexia nervosa. *Psychoneuroendocrinology,* **1**, 45.

Russell, G.F.M., Szmukler, G.I., Dare, C. and Eisler, I. (1987). An evaluation of family therapy in anorexia nervosa and bulimia nervosa. *Arch. Gen. Psychiat.,* **44**, 1047–1056.

Slade, P.D. and Russell, G.F.M. (1973). Awareness of body dimensions in anorexia nervosa: cross-sectional and longitudinal studies. *Psycholog. Med.,* **3**, 188.

Treasure, J., Forgelman, I. and Russell, G.F.M. (1986). Osteopenia of the lumbar spine and femoral neck in anorexia nervosa. *Scottish Med. J.,* **31**, 206–207.

Treasure, J.L., Gordon, P.A., King, E.A., Wheeler, M. and Russell, G.F.M. (1985). Cystic ovaries: a phase of anorexia nervosa. *Lancet,* **2**, 1379–1381.

Preface

This volume marks the occasion of the retirement of Professor Gerald Russell. It is our tribute to his seminal influence on our understanding of the eating disorders. To do this we have organised a scholarly volume charting the achievements in the field over the past three decades, an epoch during which he was such an important leader. We know that a series of personal tributes along the lines of a traditional *festschrift* would be unwelcome to him; indeed they are unnecessary since his research and that of those associated with him speak for themselves.

Our aim has been to provide an up-to-date review of the eating disorders, anorexia nervosa and bulimia nervosa. Space does not permit a detailed account of these disorders. Rather we have asked the contributors to focus on the powerful ideas, hypotheses, or models which have dominated the field. The extent to which these ideas have supporting evidence, what they do and do not explain, and how they might be developed further are highlighted. The evolution of principles governing the treatment of these disorders is similarly treated. We invited contributors to take a broad view of their areas of special interest, to present arguments in favour of the best models, to challenge them with rigour, and to examine their implications for our patients.

The style of this volume, we hope, mirrors the approach exemplified by Gerald Russell. It is that of the clinician scientist—forever alert and faithful to clinical observation, discerning in its apparent mysteries explanations able to be fashioned into hypotheses for scientific testing, and forever maintaining a keen but critical eye on the implications of the results for the care of his or her patients. All of the contributors have been closely associated with him. Nearly all have worked with him in one of his units at various times over the past 30 years. All have imbibed his methods and strived to maintain his high standards. They have participated in a programme of research where findings have been shared by all, so that, for example, the family therapy has been informed by genetics and nutritional physiology, and investigations of follicular growth in the ovary have been sensitive to issues in psychosocial development and cognitive theory. Such interchange between disciplines has deterred any tendency to sectarian thinking or refuge in un-challenged ideas inhibiting further developments. Many of the contributors continue to work in the Eating Disorders Unit at the Institute of Psychiatry and the Maudsley Hospital. The current addresses of many of the others incidate that they went on to establish units of their own in the United Kingdom (Royal Free Hospital, Bristol, Liverpool, Westminster Hospital), Australia (Sydney and Melbourne), and the United States (Johns Hopkins).

The organisation of the book is a little unusual. We have tried to provide a framework which compelled the authors to clarify their ideas as far as possible and to see how far they might be pushed. We probably would all agree that the eating disorders are multifactorial in origin, but by asking contributors to explore discrete models to see how much they might explain, we hoped to arrive at a richer understanding of what "multifactorial" actually means. In the introductory section the editors prevailed upon Gerald Russell to allow us to include a paper by him examining the history of anorexia nervosa and bulimia which he recently presented at a conference at the Royal College of Psychiatrists. We invited comments on his ideas from two senior figures in the field, Sten Theander and Joseph Silverman. Katherine Halmi examines current concepts and definitions. The separation of causal influences in terms of aetiological versus maintaining factors (which are consequences of the disorders) was also planned as a spur to contributors to ask how our current models, involving different levels of abstraction, really explicate the origins of the eating disorders. Similar principles informed the section dealing with treatment, the editors hoping that the range and limitations of our key interventions would emerge, together with an appreciation of what they might tell us about the nature of the disorders. Then the difficult question of prevention is addressed. Finally, we include an evaluation of Gerald Russell's contribution by Walter Vandereycken, but wish to add that many colleagues offered to contribute personal tributes.

We hope this volume pleases its dedicatee and its readers as much as its preparation has pleased its compilers. In seeing the contributions as a whole, we have become even more keenly aware of Gerald Russell's influence, especially his ability to newly create what he saw, thus opening fresh directions for others to follow.

G.S.
C.D.
J.T.

Part I

Concepts and Definitions

Introduction to Part I

No-one has contributed more than Gerald Russell to the modern definitions of anorexia nervosa and bulimia nervosa. Arising out of an application of careful descriptive psychopathology, the criteria proposed by him in his accounts of these disorders in 1970 and 1979 have become the basis of current DSM and ICD classifications. We were therefore grateful when he agreed to the inclusion in this volume of a paper examining changes in anorexia nervosa through time in which he presents significant new views.

No classificatory system is free of fundamental assumptions about which observations are important and which are not, how a particular disorder is to be construed, what are the relevant areas for study, and what are the appropriate investigative techniques to be used. Recognising this, Gerald Russell notes the importance of "keeping the right balance between a cohesive diagnostic approach and a flexible aetiological frame of reference". He concludes that the psychological expression of anorexia nervosa is liable to change with time (and culture), and that the dread of fatness is a modern development in the psychopathology of the disorder. A consequence is that "a broader formulation of the psychopathology of the disorder may be called for" and that soon it may be "advisable to retreat from our cherished diagnostic criteria of anorexia nervosa, as there may be false precision in the current formulations of DSM-IIIR and ICD-10". The new formulation sketched by him requires that "the patient avoids food and induces weight loss by virtue of a range of psychosocial conflicts whose resolution she perceives to be within her reach through the achievement of thinness and/or the avoidance of fatness". (Some similar issues are addressed in Chapter 14 dealing with sociocultural models of the eating disorders.)

Almost in counterpoint to the paper by Gerald Russell is a discussion by Katherine Halmi of current concepts and definitions. The value of operationalised definitions of psychiatric disorders for research is indicated, and we see how these are altered and refined with advances in knowledge. For example, attempts have been made to accommodate the recognition that a "body image disturbance" is not as central as was formerly thought by now stressing some attitudinal and affective dimensions of body shape (for example, a role in the evaluation of self). Investigations of "comorbidity" between eating disorders and other psychiatric disorders may clarify influences on symptomatology and outcome. While specific definitions may become increasingly polished, it is impossible to escape from some fundamental questions raised by the classificatory exercise. The status of a proposed "new" category, "Binge Eating Disorder", raises the question of what constitutes an "eating disorder", or indeed a "disorder", in the first place.

Why are the eating disorders called "eating disorders"? The details of eating have been relatively little studied in patients with this appellation. Could attention, such as Dr Halmi's, to the definition of abnormalities in these behaviours lead to a reconceptualisation of anorexia nervosa and bulimia nervosa with broader application in time and place?

1

Anorexia Nervosa Through Time

GERALD F.M. RUSSELL

The burden of this contribution is that anorexia nervosa, and its offshoot bulimia nervosa, have become transformed during the course of recent decades. That psychiatric disorders change during the passage of time has for long been recognised (Jaspers, 1959; Hare, 1981). A similar view regarding the changeability of anorexia nervosa has already been expressed (Russell, 1984, 1985; Russell and Treasure, 1989). Apart from its historical interest, the malleability of anorexia nervosa merits close study by virtue of its significance for illuminating the causation of the illness.

The evidence in favour of the changeability of anorexia nervosa will be discussed under three headings:

1. changes in the psychopathology of anorexia nervosa
2. an increase in the incidence of anorexia nervosa since the late 1950s
3. a change in the form of the illness exemplified by the appearance of bulimia nervosa—a new eating disorder which is a variant of anorexia nervosa.

THE HISTORICAL POINT OF REFERENCE

In order to ascertain whether changes have occurred in anorexia nervosa, it is first necessary to define a suitable historical baseline to permit comparisons with later developments in the illness. Two different approaches may be discerned.

Handbook of Eating Disorders: Theory, Treatment and Research.
Edited by G. Szmukler, C. Dare and J. Treasure.
© 1995 John Wiley & Sons Ltd.

The medico-clinical approach defines the illness in terms of its clinical manifestations. If some of the clinical features are judged to be necessary for the diagnosis they become elevated to the rank of diagnostic criteria. In recent times the formulation of diagnostic criteria has become enshrined in systems of medical and psychiatric classification (the Diagnostic and Statistical Manual of Mental Disorders, e.g. DSM-III-R); the Classification of Mental and Behavioural Disorders (ICD-10).

The socio-cultural approach to causation differs from the more empirical clinical and diagnostic perspective, and views the illness as a response to prevailing social and cultural systems. This is the approach of the social historian Joan Jacobs Brumberg who regards anorexia nervosa primarily as the control of appetite in women responding to widely differing forces which may change during historical times (Brumberg, 1988). This approach has the merit of allowing flexibility in identifying anorexia nervosa in different historical settings; it carries the risk of excessive diagnostic latitude as is evident from this quotation:

> we should expect to see anorexia nervosa "present" differently, in terms of both predisposing psychological factors and actual physical symptoms.

Thus, she sets no limits on the possible variations in clinical "presentation".

In this discussion a balance will be sought between maintaining diagnostic rectitude and allowing for the effects of socio-cultural factors which mould the clinical manifestations of the illness. This is no easy matter, because the psychopathology of the disorder both influences the diagnosis, and is influenced by adverse psychosocial events and personality traits. It is, therefore, desirable to establish a clinical frame of reference, so consistent as to safeguard the diagnostic cohesion of anorexia nervosa, while at the same time sufficiently flexible as to allow for malleability in response to changing historical and socio-cultural influences.

For the historical point of reference it is best to choose the early 1870s when William Gull (1874) and Charles Lasègue (1873) formulated their clinical descriptions of anorexia nervosa and l'anorexie hystérique respectively. They both recognised a disorder associated with severe emaciation and amenorrhoea, inexplicable in terms of known causes of wasting. They were both extremely cautious about the nature or origin of the mental disorder, while at the same time recognising that there was a morbid mental state (Gull), a mental perversity (Gull; Lasègue) or hysterial anorexia (Lasègue). Their hesitations are best illustrated by quotations from their original articles:

> The want of appetite is, I believe, due to a morbid mental state . . . we might call the state hysterical without committing ourselves to the etymological values of the word, or maintaining that the subjects of it have the more common symptoms of hysteria. I prefer, however, the more general term "nervosa". (William Gull, 1874)

Lasègue echoed the same view of "perversion mentale" but also believed the disorder was hysterical in form.

> Après plusieurs mois . . . c'est à ce moment que va se dessiner la perversion mentale, qui à elle seule est presque caractéristique et qui justifie le nom que j'ai proposé faute de mieux, d'anorexie hystérique. (Charles Lasègue, 1873)

Neither Lasègue nor Gull drew attention to the psychological disturbance which appeared so striking to later observers: the patient's disturbed experience of her own body (Bruch, 1966), her "weight phobia" (Crisp, 1967) or her "morbid fear of fatness" (Russell, 1970). The explanation previously proposed for this apparent oversight on the part of Gull and Lasègue is that the psychopathology of anorexia nervosa has changed between the 1870s and the 1960s (Russell, 1985; Russell an Treasure, 1989). There is, moreover, a strong argument for accepting the original descriptions by Gull and Lasègue as containing the essence of anorexia nervosa. The modifications made by modern observers are mainly to the psychopathological content of the illness. They merely represent changes during recent historical times in response to those influences which have favoured the expression of the patients' sensitivities to the size and shape of their own bodies.

CHANGES IN THE PSYCHOPATHOLOGY OF ANOREXIA NERVOSA

The importance of keeping the right balance between a cohesive diagnostic approach and a flexible aetiological frame of reference can best be illustrated by the dangers of an imbalanced approach. Thus, an over-inclusive extension of the diagnosis of anorexia nervosa to chlorosis by Loudon (1980) ignored the fact that this illness occurred in working girls who were generally well nourished and had an iron-deficiency anaemia (Russell, 1993). Another example is the tragic case of the Welsh fasting girl, Sarah Jacob, who died following a reckless "watch" by a team of nurses from Guy's Hospital who ensured she had neither food nor drink (Cule, 1967). A diagnosis of anorexia nervosa can be excluded because an autopsy revealed she was not emaciated but had perished from water deprivation and renal failure (Cule, 1967; Russell, 1993).

On the other hand, it would be too restrictive to exclude well documented cases of self-imposed food avoidance from the diagnosis of anorexia nervosa, just because they failed to satisfy the modern criteria, in particular that of a morbid concern with body size and shape. Among these case descriptions should be included Catherine of Siena, as described by Rudolph Bell (1985) and David Rampling (1985), and Mr Duke's daughter depicted by Richard Morton (1689). We should also consider the patients with hypochondriacal ideas and beliefs ("une forme de délire hypochondriaque"), reported on by Louis-Victor Marcé (1860) and accepted by Silverman (1989) as true examples of anorexia nervosa.

The correct balance is probably the more cautious, open-minded approach adopted by Gull and Lasègue. The modern diagnostic criterion of morbid concern with body size is right for current times and socio-cultural mores, but should not be imposed on patients described during earlier historical times. Brumberg's amusing leap across several centuries captures well the necessary flexibility:

> In the earlier era (13th to 16th centuries) control of appetite was linked to piety and belief; . . . the modern anorectic strives for perfection in terms of society's ideal of physical, rather than spiritual beauty.

It follows that we should not imagine that the psychopathological content of the anorectics' preoccupations will in future necessarily remain fixed on the size and shape of their bodies. It also follows that anorexic patients in cultures very different from our own need not express their concerns in terms of their body weight. This has already been pointed out by Lee, Chiu and Chen (1989) when they described their anorexic patients in Hong Kong, with absent or only minor fears of fatness. They remind us that the desirability and pursuit of thinness are less intense in Hong Kong than in the West. This argument is taken further by Hsu and Lee (1993) who write:

> . . . by rigidly imposing the criterion of fear of fatness on patients from a different culture or era who do not particularly value slimness, we may well be committing a contextual fallacy (i.e. failure to understand the illness in the context of its culture).

Changes in the Socio-Cultural Ideal of Body Size and Thinness

We should not, however, forget the tenacity with which our own westernized anorexic patients cling to their morbid fear of fatness. There has been a move to reject the concept of a body image disturbance (Hsu and Sobkiewicz, 1991), perhaps in favour of the concept of "body disparagement". Neither of these concepts is satisfactory and we should stick rather to our patients' preferred language in which they express directly their self-evident dread of fatness or their satisfaction when they achieve thinness. Moreover, our patients' capacity for denial may be such as to conceal their fear of fatness. It is often more reliable to observe these same patients when they are placed in situations where they are required to gain weight, for example during an in-patient treatment programme. Their resistance to weight gain and their distress will often break through their self-protective denial.

It is difficult to establish the period(s) during the last century when westernized society began to invest great value in thinness. This was surely not during the last forty years of Pierre Renoir's artistic output (1880–1919). He had always tended to paint fulsome portraits of his female models. Renoir's tendency to enlarge his female nudes became more marked after 1900, reflecting his desire to move beyond his immediate experience of the model towards a vision of female beauty as an ideal of physical amplitude. His last great masterpiece, the Bathers, painted in 1918–19 was so criticised that the French National Museums were reluctant to accept it as a gift after his death. A contemporary critic, Georges Duthuit in 1923 described this composition as slack and overblown, because of its representation of outsize and curvaceous female nudes (House, 1985).

Fashions in thinness have been identified by the study of models shown in women's fashion magazines (Silverstein, Peterson and Perdue, 1986; Silverstein et al, 1986) and by ascertaining the thinness of contestants for Miss America Pageant (Garner et al, 1980). Silverstein and colleagues measured mean bust-to-waist ratios in *Vogue* and *Ladies Home Journal* models appearing in issues from 1901 to 1981. They assumed that these influential journals would reflect phases in women's acceptance or rejection of curvaceous figures. They found two periods when the bust-to-waist ratios had steadily diminished:

1. A very sharp fall in this measure of thinness between 1909 and 1929. Unfortunately, there are no statistics for the incidence of anorexia nervosa during this earlier period. The authors nevertheless associated this earlier phase of non-curvaceous trends in fashion with a reported fall in body weight among college students, and increased literary references to self-starvation in schoolgirls, college girls and office workers.
2. A more recent phase from 1949 to 1981, corresponding to the putative change and increase in anorexia nervosa.

Garner et al (1980) obtained the recorded weights of contestants for the Miss America Pageant from 1959 to 1978. In comparison with national norms (Society of Actuaries, 1959) the mean percentage of average weight was 87.6% for the period 1959–70, and 84.6% for 1970–78. These weights showed that "beauty" contestants averaged weights well below the national norm. A negative correlation was also found between year of entry and percentage average weight of –0.83 ($p<0.001$). This reflected an average decline in weight of 0.13 kg (0.28 lb) for each year during 1959–78. The authors concluded that there had been a clear shift towards a thinner ideal shape for women in western culture over the 20 years 1959–78. They also noted that these changes in ideal weight occurred within the context of increasing weight norms for the general population of young women.

How do the powerful social pressures, subsumed within the modern cult of thinness, exert their harmful effects in causing eating disorders? Vulnerable young women in particular respond to these pressures first by experimenting with weight-reducing diets, a common practice even among schoolgirls (Nylander, 1971). Some of them persist with harsh dieting which carries an established risk (Patton, 1988; Patton et al, 1990): anorexia nervosa is arguably but an extension of determined dieting. The social pressures which promote dietary restraint are multiple and Brumberg has produced an impressive list: books and magazines containing keys to calorie counting, the fashion industry catering preferentially for the slimmer figure, the film industry and television with their message that a svelte figure is associated with sexual allure and professional success, and the emphasis on physical fitness and athleticism. Brumberg goes further in extending her view of the social causes of anorexia nervosa by considering that it may be a form of feminist politics, or that it may even be "promoted" by health professionals and medical researchers in need of funding for their work. These last claims may be somewhat extreme, but otherwise her catalogue of powerful social determinants of anorexia nervosa is a convincing one.

Conclusions regarding pathoplasticity and its effects on the changing psychological expression of anorexia nervosa

The first conclusion is that the psychological expression of anorexia nervosa (its psychopathology) is liable to change. Its modern expression in our anorexic patients who speak of their dread of fatness is entirely congruent with today's cult of thinness. It can be deduced that modern societal pressures have determined the nature of our patients' preoccupations which are held obstinately and amount to overvalued ideas. These socio-cultural pressures exert a "pathoplastic" influence. This term requires definition. It was introduced by Birnbaum (1923) who applied it to causal factors which contribute to the structure of an illness. They certainly influence the psychological content of a psychiatric illness, but in addition may affect its "colouring" and its form (Shepherd, 1975). They may not amount to fundamental or necessary causes but can act as triggering agents. In anorexia nervosa there is evidence that socio-cultural influences exert a pathoplastic effect. The current fashionable emphasis in western society on the ideal for women to be slim plays a major role in determining the preoccupations and behaviour of afflicted patients. Thus, the psychological content of the illness has changed and revolves round a dread of fatness and the pursuit of thinness. It is likely that these same pathoplastic influences have contributed to the increased incidence of anorexia nervosa and shaped it into the new disorder of bulimia nervosa.

The second conclusion is that our anorexic patients' psychological preoccupation with body weight and size should not be viewed as immutable. The diagnosis of anorexia nervosa should not be rejected just because patients express different kinds of preoccupation. The dread of fatness is likely to be a modern development in the psychopathology of anorexia nervosa. It need not persist in future generations of anorexic patients. The time may be approaching when it will be advisable to retreat from our cherished diagnostic criteria of anorexia nervosa, as there may be a false precision in the current formulations of DSM-III-R and ICD-10. A broader formulation of the psychopathology of the disorder may be called for. Thus, it may suffice to establish that the patient avoids food and induces weight loss by virtue of a range of psychosocial conflicts whose resolution she perceives to be within her reach through the achievement of thinness and/or the avoidance of fatness. These conflicts will still include the dread of fatness, but may need to embrace the fear of sexuality and fertility, or the reluctance to acquire independence from the family, or some other as yet unpredictable issue.

CHANGES IN THE INCIDENCE OF ANOREXIA NERVOSA

There have been numerous epidemiological studies which have estimated the incidence of anorexia nervosa. In order to examine the thesis that the incidence of anorexia nervosa has risen over recent decades, it is best to review only those studies which have repeated surveys on the same population at successive intervals. This is possible with the surveys conducted in south Sweden, north-east Scotland, Switzerland, and Monroe County and Rochester in the USA (Table 1.1). In the first four of these serial studies the researchers applied the same methods to a similar population. Thus many variables were controlled for, leaving the passage of time as the main factor influencing the incidence of anorexia nervosa. In the first four of these areas a progressive increase in the incidence was found over successive years.

The Rochester study at first seemed to be an exception. Lucas et al (1988) failed to find an increase in the incidence of anorexia nervosa when more recent years (1965–79) were compared with former years (1935–49). They later recalculated

TABLE 1.1   The incidence of anorexia nervosa.

Area	Authors	Period	Annual incidence per 100 000 population
Southern Sweden	Theander (1970)	1931–40	0.08
		1941–50	0.19
		1951–60	0.45
North-east Scotland	Kendell et al (1973)	1966–69	1.60
	Szmukler et al (1986)	1978–82	4.06
Zurich canton	Willi and Grossman (1983)	1963–65	0.55
		1973–75	1.12
	Willi et al (1990)	1983–85	1.43
Monroe County,	Kendell et al (1973)	1960–69	0.37
New York State, USA	Jones et al (1980)	1970–76	0.64
Rochester, Minn., USA	Lucas et al* (1991)	1950–54	4.63†
		1980–84	14.20†

* Increase in incidence occurred principally in females 10–19 years old.
† Figures kindly provided by Dr. A. Lucas.

their data, extending the study to 1984 and separating female patients who fell in the 15–24 year age-band (61%) from the remaining (mainly older) patients. An increased incidence was found then in the younger group, when the incidence rates were plotted for each 5-year period from 1935–39 to 1980–84. These authors concluded that the increased incidence rates over successive half-decades reflected the greater vulnerability of the younger female subjects to adverse social factors. The incidence rates for the older group remained fairly constant over the successive 5-year periods.

Thus, there is persuasive evidence in support of a rising incidence of anorexia nervosa from the 1950s until the 1980s. Investigators who have identified this trend have attributed it to changes in culturally determined attitudes or behaviour patterns over time (Kendell et al, 1973; Szmukler et al, 1986). These findings also support the occurrence of change in anorexia nervosa over recent decades.

THE APPEARANCE OF BULIMIA NERVOSA

The new syndrome of bulimia nervosa was described and named as a variant of anorexia nervosa in 1979 (Russell, 1979). This is not to say that examples of this disorder had been missed by earlier investigators. The account of Ellen West by Binswanger (1959) is that of a young woman torn between the fear of fatness and constant preoccupations with food ingested in large amounts without achieving satiety. Wulff (1932) described alternations between the gorging of food associated with depression and the ascetic avoidance of food. Brusset and Jeammet (1971) reported on three adolescent women who developed bulimic episodes during the later course of anorexia nervosa. They also remarked on the alternation between periods of anorexia and bulimia. In spite of these early descriptions, it is almost certain that there occurred in the 1970s a sudden increase of cases of the disorder later named bulimia nervosa. Within a few years the incidence of bulimia nervosa exceeded that of anorexia nervosa (Fairburn, 1990; Hoek, 1991; Hall and Hay, 1991).

There are two alternative explanations for the sudden appearance of patients with bulimia nervosa:

1. The diagnosis was missed by clinicians prior to the description of bulimia nervosa in 1979, whereas there were as many patients as today.
2. The high frequency of bulimia nervosa has only occurred during comparatively recent times.

This second explanation is the more likely and is supported by two recent studies which provide us with tantalising glimpses into the past. The first study is by Kendler et al (1991). They interviewed 2163 female subjects from a population-based twin register in Virginia, USA. Among the 2163 twins, 32 were given a definite diagnosis, 28 a probable diagnosis, and 63 a possible diagnosis of bulimia

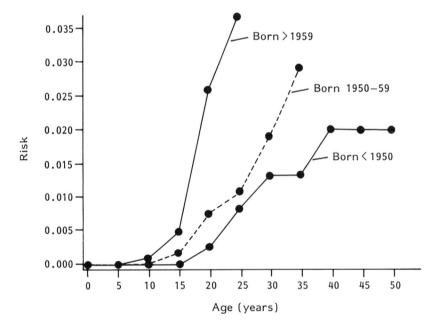

FIGURE 1.1   Lifetime prevalence of definite and probable cases of bulimia nervosa in three cohorts according to date of birth. The highest lifetime prevalence is shown in subjects with the most recent date of birth; the lowest lifetime prevalence is found in subjects with the earliest date of birth. The data are derived from Kendler et al (1991) and are reproduced by permission of the authors and the editors of the *American Journal of Psychiatry*. Copyright 1991 the American Psychiatric Association.

nervosa according to DSM-III-R criteria. The definite and probable cases were categorised together: their recognition led to the calculation of the "lifetime prevalence" of bulimia nervosa (the proportion of individuals who received the diagnosis at any time in their life).

The lifetime cumulative risk for definite and probable bulimia nervosa is shown in Figure 1.1 and represented by three curves for:

- patients born before 1950
- those born between 1950 and 1959
- those born after 1959.

The three curves look very different and demonstrate a cohort effect. The older subjects (born before 1950) were less likely to have had bulimia nervosa than the younger patients (born after 1960). The "lifetime prevalence" by the age of 25 could be calculated for all three cohorts from the published data of Kendler et al. Table 1.2 shows that the lifetime prevalence increased progressively according to the recency of birth for each of the three cohorts.

The conclusions of Kendler and associates are extremely cautious. They attribute the cohort effect to one of two artefacts producing low rates among the older subjects: they would have been less aware of bulimia as a disorder, or they were more likely to forget their bulimia.

Whereas Kendler's explanations are possible, it is more likely that the older subjects reported less bulimia precisely because bulimia nervosa was uncommon before the 1970s when they would have been of an age which nowadays is associated with a high risk for the disorder. In conclusion, this cohort effect would confirm the relative rarity of bulimia nervosa before the 1970s.

TABLE 1.2   The reported prevalence of bulimia nervosa by the age of 25 years in each of three age cohorts.

Cohort	Mean age* (years)	Prevalence by age 25
Born before 1950	42	0.8%
Born 1950–1959	33	1.1%
Born after 1959	24	3.7%

* Mean age when interviewed.
Data derived from Kendler et al (1991).

The second study is that of Lucas and Soundy (1993) only recently reported. They carried out a retrospective appraisal of cases that would have merited the diagnosis of bulimia nervosa (according to DSM-III-R), as recorded in the Mayo Clinic epidemiological archives. These records provide medical data for the entire population residing in Rochester, Minnesota (population 60 000 in 1985). The findings of Lucas and Soundy are summarised schematically in Figure 1.2. The solid line represents the incidence of bulimia nervosa among the female population.

1.   Before 1980 only a handful of cases were found and they were unusual (e.g. infants who had been overfed and overweight men).

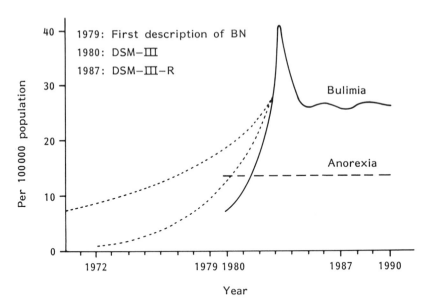

FIGURE 1.2   Schematic of the annual incidence of bulimia nervosa (solid line). The average incidence of anorexia nervosa over time is also shown. The lower dotted curve is derived from patients with bulimia nervosa identified by the author (Russell, 1979). The upper dotted curve represents an entirely hypothetical gradual increase in the incidence of bulimia nervosa before its recognition. The data are derived from Lucas and Soundy (1993).

2.   After the description of bulimia nervosa in 1979 and in DSM-III in 1980, there was a sharp rise in detected cases—altogether 100 females up to 1990. This figure can be translated into an incidence of 26.5 cases per year per 100 000 of the female population. This is twice the incidence of anorexia nervosa.

3.   The sharp peak in 1983 is attributed to a drug trial which led the researchers to "solicit" cases of bulimia nervosa. The authors conclude that there are usually undetected cases in the community and that their incidence rate is probably an underestimate. This is in spite of the Rochester figure exceeding that of other population surveys including that of Hoek (1991) (9.9 cases per year per 100 000 population). The peak age of ascertainment was from 15 to 19 years.

The question should again be asked: "Why did bulimia nervosa appear suddenly in the late 1970s?" Lucas and Soundy agree that their patients must have acquired the illness some time previously as many of them gave long histories. The dotted curves in Figure 1.2 represent speculations on the growing incidence of bulimia nervosa before it was recognised formally. The lower dotted curve fits in roughly with the rates of detection of patients in my own series, beginning in 1972. One can only guess that an earlier and less steeply rising incidence curve is more likely (e.g. the higher dotted curve in the figure).

These data fit in with the following conclusions:

1. Cases of bulimia nervosa certainly occurred before the 1970s, but much less frequently.
2. The description of the syndrome of bulimia nervosa must have facilitated the recognition of the characteristic clinical phenomena by physicians and psychiatrists.
3. It is possible, and worrying, that the description of the disorder also encouraged the appearance of the key behaviours in vulnerable young women who consequently acquired the illness as if by contagion.

SUMMARY

Anorexia nervosa is, without any doubt, an illness which has undergone major change. The time span for this change is uncertain but it is possibly in the range thirty to fifty years or longer. The evidence is threefold:

1. The psychological content of anorexia nervosa has changed into the expression by the patients of a dread of fatness. This change is congruent with societal attitudes which attribute great importance to thinness in women.
2. The incidence of anorexia nervosa in westernized nations has risen since the late 1950s, probably as a result of adverse socio-cultural factors.
3. Bulimia nervosa has appeared as a new variant of anorexia nervosa, possibly in the late 1960s and early 1970s, and has already exceeded anorexia nervosa in its incidence.

REFERENCES

American Psychiatric Association (1987). *Diagnostic and Statistical Manual of Mental Disorders*, 3rd edn revised (DSM-III-R). Washington, DC: APA.

Bell, R.M. (1985). *Holy Anorexia*. Chicago: University of Chicago Press.

Binswanger, L. (trans. by Mendel, W.M. and Lyons, J.) (1959). The case of Ellen West. In: *Existence: A New Dimension in Psychiatry and Psychology* (eds. R. May, E. Angel and H.F. Ellenberger), pp. 237–364. New York: Basic Books.

Birnbaum, K. (1923). *Der Aufbau der Psychose*, pp. 6–7. Berlin: Springer.

Bruch, H. (1965). Anorexia nervosa and its differential diagnosis. *Journal of Nervous and Mental Disease,* **141**, 556–566.

Brumberg, J.J. (1988). *Fasting Girls: the Emergence of Anorexia Nervosa as a Modern Disease.* Cambridge, Mass.: Harvard University Press.

Brusset, B. and Jeammet, P. (1971). Les periodes boulimiques dans l'evolution de l'anorexie mentale de l'adolescente. *Revue de Neuropsychiatrie Infantile,* **19**, 661–690.

Crisp, A.H. (1967). Anorexia nervosa. *Hospital Medicine,* **1**, 713–718.

Cule, J. (1967). *Wreath on the Crown: the Story of Sarah Jacob the Welsh Fasting Girl.* Llandysul: Gomerian Press.

Fairburn, C. (1990). Studies of the epidemiology of bulimia nervosa. *American Journal of Psychiatry,* **147**(4), 401–408.

Garner, D.M., Garfinkel, P.E., Schwartz, D. and Thompson, M. (1980). Cultural expectations of thinness in women. *Psychological Reports,* **47**, 483–491.

Gull, W.W. (1874). Anorexia nervosa (apepsia hysterica, anorexia hysterica). *Transactions of the Clinical Society of London,* **7**, 22–28.

Hall, A. and Hay, P. (1991). Eating disorder patient referrals from a population region, 1977–1986. *Psychological Medicine,* **21**, 697–701.

Hare, E. (1981). The two manias: a study of the evolution of the modern concept of mania. *British Journal of Psychiatry,* **138**, 89–99.

Hoek, H.W. (1991). The incidence and prevalence of anorexia nervosa and bulimia nervosa in primary care. *Psychological Medicine,* **21**, 455–460.

House, J. (1985). The bathers. In: *Renoir,* pp. 288–289. Arts Council of Great Britain.

Hsu, L.K.G. and Lee, S. (1993). Is weight phobia always necessary for a diagnosis of anorexia nervosa? *American Journal of Psychiatry,* October 1993.

Hsu, L.K.G. and Sobkiewicz, T.A. (1991). Body image disturbance: time to abandon the concept for eating disorders. *International Journal of Eating Disorders,* **10**, 15–30.

Jaspers, K. (1959). *Allgemeine Psychopathologie,* 7th edn (translated by J. Hoenig and M.W. Hamilton), pp. 732 and 742. Manchester: Manchester University Press.

Jones, D.J., Fox, M.M., Babigian, H.M. and Hutton, H.E. (1980). Epidemiology of anorexia nervosa in Monroe County, New York: 1960–1976. *Psychosomatic Medicine,* **42**, 551–558.

Kendell, R.E., Hall, D.J., Hailey, A. and Babigian, H.M. (1973). The epidemiology of anorexia nervosa. *Psychological Medicine,* **3**(2), 200–203.

Kendler, K.S., Maclean, C., Neale, M., Kessler, R., Heath, A. and Eaves, L. (1991). The genetic epidemiology of bulimia nervosa. *American Journal of Psychiatry,* **148**, 1627–1637.

Lasègue, C. (1873). De l'anorexie hystérique. *Archives Générale de Médicine,* **21** (April), 385–403.

Lee, S., Chiu, H.F.K. and Chen, C-N. (1989). Anorexia nervosa in Hong Kong: why not more in Chinese? *British Journal of Psychiatry,* **154**, 683–688.

Loudon, I.S.L. (1980). Chlorosis, anaemia and anorexia nervosa. *British Medical Journal,* **2**, 1669–1675.

Lucas, A.R., Beard, C.M., O'Fallon, W.M. and Kurland, L.T. (1988). Anorexia nervosa in Rochester, Minnesota: a 45-year study. *Mayo Clinic Proceedings,* **63**, 433–442.

Lucas, A.R., Beard, C.M., O'Fallon, W.M. and Kurland, L.T. (1991). 50-year trends in the incidence of anorexia nervosa in Rochester, Minn.: a population-based study. *American Journal of Psychiatry,* **148**, 917–922.

Lucas, A.R. and Soundy, T.J. (1993). The rise of bulimia nervosa. Ninth World Congress of Psychiatry, Rio de Janeiro, Brazil, 6–12 June. Abstract 544, p. 139.

Marcé, L.-V. (1860). Note sur une forme de délire hypochondriaque consécutive aux dyspepsies et caractérisée principalement par le refus d'aliments. *Annales Médico-psychologiques,* **6**, 15–28.

Morton, R. (1689). *Phthisiologia, seu Exercitiones de Phthisi.* London: Smith.

Nylander, I. (1971). The feeling of being fat and dieting in a school population. Epidemiologic interview investigation. *Acta Sociomedica Scandinavica,* **3**, 17–26.

Patton, G.C. (1988). The spectrum of eating disorder in adolescence. *Journal of Psychosomatic Research,* **32**(6), 579–584.

Patton, G.C., Johnson-Sabine, E., Wood, K., Mann, A. and Wakeling, A. (1990). Abnormal eating attitudes in London schoolgirls—a prospective epidemiological study: outcome at twelve-month follow-up. *Psychological Medicine,* **20**, 383–394.

Rampling, D. (1985) Ascetic ideals and anorexia nervosa. *Journal of Psychiatric Research,* **19** (2/3), 89–94.

Russell, G.F.M. (1970). Anorexia nervosa: its identity as an illness and its treatment. In: *Modern Trends in Psychological Medicine* (ed. J.H. Price), pp. 131–164. London: Butterworths.

Russell, G.F.M. (1979). Bulimia nervosa: an ominous variant of anorexia nervosa. *Psychological Medicine,* **9**, 429–448.

Russell, G.F.M. (1984). The modern history of anorexia nervosa. *Aktuelle Ernährungsmedizin,* **9**, 3–7. Stuttgart: Georg Thieme Verlag.

Russell, G.F.M. (1985). The changing nature of anorexia nervosa: an introduction to the conference. *Journal of Psychiatric Research,* **19** (2/3), 101–109.

Russell, G.F.M. (1993). The social psychiatry of eating disorders. In: *Social Psychiatry* (eds. D. Bhugra and J. Leff), pp. 273–297. Oxford: Blackwell Scientific Publications.

Russell, G.F.M. and Treasure, J. (1989). The modern history of anorexia nervosa: an interpretation of why the illness has changed. In: The Psychobiology of Human Eating Disorders: Preclinical and Clinical Perspectives (eds. L.A. Schneider, S.J. Cooper and K.A. Halmi). *Annals of the New York Academy of Sciences,* **575**, 13–30.

Shepherd, M. (1975). Epidemiologische Psychiatrie. In: *Psychiatrie der Gegenwart Forschung und Praxis, Vol. 3*, 2nd edn. (eds. K.P. Kisker, J.-E. Meyer, C. Müller and E. Strömgren), pp. 119–149. Berlin: Springer.

Silverman, J.A. (1989). Louis-Victor Marcé, 1824–1864: anorexia nervosa's forgotten man. *Psychological Medicine,* **19**, 833–835.

Silverstein, B., Peterson, B. and Perdue, L. (1986). Some correlates of the thin standard of bodily attractiveness for women. *International Journal of Eating Disorders,* **5**(5), 895–905.

Silverstein, B., Perdue, L., Peterson, B., Vogel, L. and Fantini, D.A. (1986). Possible causes of the thin standard of bodily attractiveness for women. *International Journal of Eating Disorders,* **5**(5), 907–916.

The Society of Actuaries (1959). Build and Blood Pressure Study, Volume 1, p. 16. Chicago, Il. Reproduced in *Geigy Scientific Tables*, 7th edn., 1970 (eds. K. Diem and C. Lentner), p. 711. Basle: Documenta Geigy.

Szmukler, G.I., McCance, C., McCrone, L. and Hunter, D. (1986). Anorexia nervosa: a psychiatric case register study from Aberdeen. *Psychological Medicine,* **16**, 49–58.

Theander, S. (1970). Anorexia nervosa: a psychiatric investigation of 94 female patients. *Acta Psychiatrica Scandinavica,* Suppl. 214.

Willi, J. and Grossman, S. (1983). Epidemiology of anorexia nervosa in a defined region of Switzerland. *American Journal of Psychiatry,* **140**, 564–567.

Willi, J., Giacometti, G. and Limacher, B. (1990). Update on the epidemiology of anorexia nervosa in a defined region of Switzerland. *American Journal of Psychiatry,* **147**, 1514–1517.

World Health Organization (1992). *The ICD-10 Classification of Mental and Behavioural Disorders: Clinical Descriptions and Diagnostic Guidelines.* Geneva: WHO.

Wulff, M. (1932). Lieber einen interessanten oralen symptomenkomplex und seine Beziehung zur Sucht. *International Psychoanal. Z.,* **18**, 13–16.

The Essence of Anorexia Nervosa: Comment on Gerald Russell's "Anorexia Nervosa Through Time"

STEN THEANDER
University Hospital, Lund, Sweden

In Chapter 1 we are given a personal view of the history of anorexia nervosa by a person who has dedicated a great deal of his life to this disorder and who is himself an integral part of its history.

A phrase from that chapter has been chosen as the title of this comment, the whole sentence being as follows: "There is, moreover, a strong argument for accepting the original descriptions by Gull and Lasègue as containing the essence of anorexia nervosa". Gerald Russell gives a review of the changes over time of the syndrome of anorexia nervosa. He repeatedly emphasises the need for "keeping the right balance" between, on the one hand, a strict clinical diagnosis, and on the other flexibility in regard of the effect of various aetiological factors. The idea is that factors like sociocultural pressures may exert a pathoplastic influence, thereby modifying the basic syndrome.

As always when Gerald Russell writes, the text is clear and easy to follow, and the message of the text seems to be readily understandable. However, it is worthwhile rereading the chapter as complex and far-reaching questions are raised, which are relevant not only for our ideas of anorexia nervosa, but also for our outlook on mental disorders in general and especially for making diagnoses. Even when

Handbook of Eating Disorders: Theory, Treatment and Research.
Edited by G. Szmukler, C. Dare and J. Treasure.
© 1995 John Wiley & Sons Ltd.

humbly put, these thoughts are deep and revolutionary as they question some of the cornerstones of today's diagnostic practice. This radical view is expressed in the following way: "The time may be approaching when it will be advisable to retreat from our cherished diagnostic criteria of anorexia nervosa, as there may be a false precision in the current formulations of DSM-III-R and ICD-10."

Russell's idea is that the basic syndrome—the essence of anorexia nervosa—is the clinical picture described by Gull and Lasègue, and that the recent developments of the syndrome, including the fear of fatness and the disturbed body image, might not be crucial or necessary elements of the clinical entity. Thus, those symptoms and signs which change over time might be regarded as secondary developments, and however much we may "cherish" them, they should be regarded as being of minor importance as a basis for understanding and explaining the illness. Instead it is those symptoms and signs which show continuity over time that should be regarded as fundamental.

In Oxford in 1868, William Gull pointed out that some tissue changes show "fidelity" (that is, continuity) and he stated that "the fidelity of the characteristics of a disease" may serve as a guide to diagnosis (Gull, 1868). Murphy (1983) expressed similar views, but without a strong conviction of their practical value for psychiatry in general. Murphy writes: "Some authorities believe that it should eventually be possible to distinguish the nature of mental diseases from the forms in which social forces cast them, that is, from the pathoplastic aspects, and then to attack the 'true causes' while ignoring such social variations."

One of Russell's ideas in his contribution to this volume is that the study of "the malleability of anorexia nervosa" may have "significance for illuminating the causation of the illness'. The approach which Russell indicates would mean that it is possible to sort out those symptoms and signs which are continuous from those that are changing; and, further, that the results of such an operation may contribute to clarifying the aetiology. In an enigmatic syndrome like anorexia nervosa this method of separating the continuous traits from the ephemeral variations provides a chance for extracting "the essence" of the syndrome, thereby helping to reveal "the true causes" in accordance with the formulation by Murphy.

Developing and expanding on Russell's idea, I have reviewed the early writings on anorexia nervosa, those of Gull and Lasègue, and also of Marcé, with the aim of identifying traits in these early descriptions which are still apparent in the syndrome today (Gull, 1874, 1888; Lasègue, 1873; Marcé, 1860). In this way I have tried to distill "the essence of anorexia nervosa" according to Russell's proposal. Those traits which show the greatest "fidelity" were in this way separated from those which have changed over time. In the identification of stable symptoms and signs, those which are directly a result of starvation, including amenorrhea, have been omitted. These are the results:

The Majority of Patients are Female

Marcé claimed to have seen a great number of these cases, and he described the patients as "young girls". Lasègue saw eight cases, all women. Gull wrote: "The subjects of this affection are mostly of the female sex", but added: "I have occasionally seen it in males at the same age."

The Majority of Patients are Young

Marcé tells us that the illness afflicts young girls at the period of puberty. Lasègue said that his eight patients were between 18 and 32 years of age. Gull said that patients are chiefly between the ages of 16 and 23.

The Main Symptom is the Refusal of Nourishment, the Non-Eating

Restriction of eating is the main symptom in anorexia nervosa. Many explanations of the non-eating have been offered, and are reflected in the terminology. Lasègue and Gull made a mistake when they selected the term "anorexia" as a descriptive name. Lasègue saw a difference between the attitude to food in anorexia nervosa compared with that of melancholic and cancer patients, but he was not able to propose a better name. Marcé gave a straightforward and simple explanation. His description of the syndrome was "une forme de délire hypocondriaque consécutive aux dyspepsies et caractérisée principalement par le refus d'aliments". He explained the non-eating as follows: It starts in some patients with "inappetency", and in others with dyspeptic problems. Later on: "These patients arrive at a delirious conviction that they cannot or ought not to eat". The term "delirious" would simply mean that the patient has a delusion. He says further that the patients' ideas about their symptoms develop into "a state of partial delirium", which in modern terminology would mean a partial or a monosymptomatic psychosis. Marcé complained about doctors who did not understand that the main problem is of a psychiatric nature; instead these doctors were preoccupied with treatment of the stomach. Marcé stated: "The stomach is well able to digest, and suffers only from want of food." And he continued: "It is the delirious idea . . . in which lies the essence of the malady; the patients are no longer dyspeptics—they are insane."

Gull had obvious difficulties in explaining the non-eating. He started with the term "apepsia", then "anorexia". In the beginning he used the term "hysterica", but changed his mind and used "nervosa", which he claimed was a "more general term". He used expressions like "a morbid mental state", "mental perversity" and "a perversion of the ego"; and he spoke generally about "persons of unsound mind". It should be remembered that Gull was not a psychiatrist, but a physician. Lasègue said that the term "anorexia" might be replaced by the term "hysterical inanition" (starvation). But he preferred "anorexia" as this term seemed to be more medical and less superficial. Lasègue described a similar development in the patient's way of thinking as did Marcé. They have a "conviction that food will prove injurious", which idea leads to refusal of all food. And this state will eventually develop into "that mental perversion . . . which justifies the name which I have proposed for want of better—hysterical anorexia".

The Emaciation may be Extreme and Life-Threatening

Speaking strongly in favour of anorexia nervosa being a true disease, that is, something different from mere dieting for aesthetic reasons, is its tendency to develop into a life-threatening condition. Both Marcé and Gull claimed they had seen patients who died of the illness. Marcé wrote: "Some of these sufferers . . . literally die of hunger". He also described patients who were "reduced to skeletons". Gull said that his experience "supplies one instance at least of a fatal termination". Both Marcé and Gull mentioned autopsies revealing no other cause of death than "the starvation alone". In contrast, Lasègue argued in favour of hysteria, claiming that these patients never terminate directly in death, but he obviously worried over their cachectic state and mentioned that hysteria may indirectly result in a fatal disease.

There is Also a Great Tendency to Recovery

All three of the early writers noted that patients may be fully recovered, including patients who were very ill. It is easy to understand that the doctors regarded the recovery as resulting from their treatment. Nowadays we are more aware that there is an inherent tendency in the eating disorders towards spontaneous healing.

The Patients Tend to Deny their Illness

Lasègue, especially, emphasised the patient's tendency to deny any problems: the patient is in ". . . a state of quietude—I might almost say a condition of contentment, truly pathological. Not only does she not sigh for recovery, but she is not ill-pleased with her condition . . .". This "indifférence" Lasègue saw as an hysterical trait. Gull, too, pointed out the patient's special attitude to her illness: one emaciated girl of 28.6 kg "persisted in walking through the streets" to Gull's house, and she "expressed herself as quite well".

The Reasons Given by the Patients for their Emaciation are not Constant

In the writings of Marcé, Gull and Lasègue I have nowhere found the motive of dieting aimed at reducing body weight. Gull may not have listened very closely to his patients. In one case he noted: "No account could be given of the exciting cause", and another girl is said to have starved herself "without apparent cause". Marcé mentioned that the girls have had "a precocious physical development" at the period of puberty, but it is not clear what he actually meant by this term or if the girls had complained. Lasègue was more psychologically oriented. He proposed several possible motives: for instance, "some real or imaginary marriage prospect", or "a violence done to some sympathy". Lasègue also tells us that after their recovery, he tried to obtain more information from his patients, but without good results. The most common answer to the question "Why did you not eat" was "I could not; it was too strong for me, and, moreover, I was very well".

Consistent with Russell's view, Regina Casper in her historic review of bulimia nervosa claims that the desire for bodily thinness appeared only gradually as a central issue (Casper, 1983). Dr Casper mentions another early author on anorexia nervosa, Dr Playfair, who in 1888 enumerated several "well-marked causes reacting on the nervous system". The following examples are given: "Study for some of the higher examinations for women now so much in vogue" and "domestic bereavements, money losses, disappointments in love, strain of overathletic work". Thus, many possible factors are enumerated, but nowhere is there any hint of a wish to become slim. A wish to reduce weight as an apparent motive appeared first around the turn of the century, and it is not until around 1940 that a desire to become thin is more regularly mentioned in clinical descriptions.

SUMMARY

The idea which Gerald Russell puts forward in his introductory chapter is that an historical view, aimed at the identification of continuous traits, would be a method of defining "the essence of anorexia nervosa", and, further, that this procedure may contribute to clarifying the aetiology.

The following traits of anorexia nervosa has been found to be continuous over time: the marked preponderance of females and young people among the patients; food refusal; the extreme, often life-threatening emaciation, but also the tendency to recovery; and the denial of illness. On the other hand, the patients' motives for their food refusal have changed.

It is not self-evident how these findings are to be interpreted. Seen in this perspective, the true reasons for the non-eating seem even more enigmatic and difficult to understand. The discussion must go on; and one hopes that Gerald Russell will show continuity and fidelity in his efforts by proceeding in the same bold and creative way, formulating questions and pointing out directions for future research.

REFERENCES

Casper, R.C. (1983). On the emergence of bulimia nervosa as a syndrome: an historical view. *International Journal of Eating Disorders,* **2**, 3–16.

Gull, W. (1868). The address in medicine delivered before the Annual Meeting of the British Medical Association, at Oxford. *Lancet,* **2**, 171–176.

Gull, W. (1874). Anorexia nervosa (apepsia hysterica, anorexia hysterica). *Transactions of the Clinical Society of London,* **7**, 22–28.

Gull, W. (1888). Anorexia nervosa. *Lancet,* **1**, 516–517.

Lasègue, C. (1873). De l'anorexie hystérique. English translation in: M.R. Kaufman and M. Heiman (Eds), *Evolution of Psychosomatic Concepts.* New York: International Universities Press, 1964.

Marcé, L.-V. (1860). Note sur une forme de délire hypochondriaque consécutive aux dyspepsies et caractérisée principalement par le refus d'aliments. English translation in: J.A.
   Silverman, "Louis-Victor Marcé, 1824–1864: anorexia nervosa's forgotten man. *Psychological Medicine,* **19**, 833–835.
Murphy, H.B.M. (1983). Socio-cultural variations in symptomatology, incidence and course
   of illness. In: M. Shepherd and O.L. Zangwill (Eds), *Handbook of Psychiatry,* Vol. 1.
   Cambridge: University Press.

Something New under the Sun: Comments on Gerald Russell's "Anorexia Nervosa Through Time"

JOSEPH A. SILVERMAN
Columbia University, New York, USA

What has been is what will be, and what has been done is what will be done; and there is nothing new under the sun.

Is there a thing of which it is said, "See, this is new"? It has been already, in the ages before us.

There is no remembrance of former things, nor will there be any remembrance of later things yet to happen among those who come after.

Ecclesiastes (1: 9–11)

Not so at all, writes Russell in his insightful essay. Things *do* change. Diseases change; symptoms change; people change. There is indeed something new under the sun. And what is new, according to Russell, is the fact that "anorexia nervosa and its offshoot, bulimia nervosa, have been transformed during the course of recent decades".

Perhaps the only constant factor in this ever-changing syndrome of anorexia nervosa (and its sister, bulimia nervosa) is that its victims are invariably psychiatrically vulnerable young women. This vulnerability is probably the single most common denominator in the pathogenesis of the eating disorders.

Handbook of Eating Disorders: Theory, Treatment and Research.
Edited by G. Szmukler, C. Dare and J. Treasure.
© 1995 John Wiley & Sons Ltd.

Russell makes the point that the transformation in eating disorders has occurred during the course of recent decades. In fact, the illness seems to have changed regularly over the past 300 years.

Morton's (1694) first patient, Mr Duke's daughter, presented in a marasmic state. By ruling out all of the then known causes of wasting, he declared her illness to be "a nervous consumption", due to "sadness and anxious cares". In essense, his was a diagnosis of exclusion.

Whytt (1764) described a case of "a nervous atrophy" in a teenage boy, and made a similar diagnosis by exclusion.

In 1860, Louis-Victor Marcé saw a group of patients, all female, who presented with gastrointestinal complaints associated with weight loss. Their dyspepsia presented in the form of "absence of appetite or by the uneasiness caused by digestion". Marcé wisely concluded that his patients' food avoidance was psychological in character: "In one word, the gastric nervous disorder becomes cerebro-nervous." He considered the illness to be "a hypochondriacal delirium". He wrote that "the patients are no longer dyspeptics—they are insane".

Thirteen years later, in 1873, Lasègue reported his findings. Some of his patients also had gastrointestinal complaints. He, too, wisely concluded that the problem was psychological rather than physical, and described the illness as "a hysteria linked to hypochondriasis".

At about the same time, Gull in London described similar cases and eventually concluded that the illness was due to "a morbid mental state" (1874). He later described it as "a perversion of the ego" (1888).

In summary, change occurred in our understanding of anorexia nervosa over two centuries to cause it to be described variously as:

- a nervous consumption (Morton)
- a nervous atrophy (Whytt)
- a hypochondriacal delirium (Marcé)
- a hysteria linked to hypochondriasis (Lasègue)
- a perversion of the ego (Gull)

As Russell clearly elaborates, the changes have continued.

Little needs be said about the increase in the incidence of anorexia nervosa since the late 1950s. The statistics speak for themselves, and the facts are indisputable.

Few comments are needed to deal with Russell's last points about bulimia nervosa. There is no question that bulimia nervosa occurred before the 1970s, but much less frequently. His seminal description in 1979 brought the diagnosis to the fore, and made the medical profession sit up and take notice of the illness.

Lastly, Russell ends his paper as he began it, stressing that eating disorders are usually found in vulnerable young women. As time passes, and vulnerability continues, we may expect to find other variants in the family of eating disorders.

REFERENCES

Gull, W.W. (1874). Anorexia nervosa (apepsia hysterica, anorexia hysterica). *Transactions of the Clinical Society of London,* **7**, 22–28.

Gull, W.W. (1888). Anorexia nervosa. *Lancet,* **1**, 516–517.

Lasègue, C. (1873). De l'anorexie hystérique. *Archives Générales de Médicine,* **21**, 385–403.

Marcé, L.V. (1860). Note sur une forme de délire hypochondriaque consécutive aux dyspepsies et caractérisée principalement par le refus d'aliments. *Annales Médico-psychologiques,* **6**, 15–28.

Morton, R. (1694). *Phthisiologia: Or, a treatise of Consumptions.* London: Smith and Walford.

Russell, G.F.M. (1979). Bulimia nervosa: an ominous variant of anorexia nervosa. *Psychological Medicine,* **9**, 429–448.

Whytt, R. (1764). *Observations on the Nature, Causes, and Cure of those Disorders which have been commonly called Nervous, Hypochondriac or Hysteric to which are Prefixed some Remarks on the Sympathy of the Nerves.* Edinburgh: Becket, DeHondt and Balfour.

2

Current Concepts and Definitions

KATHERINE A. HALMI
Cornell Medical Center, New York, USA

INTRODUCTION

Current concepts of the development of anorexia nervosa (AN) and bulimia nervosa (BN) are best represented by a multi-dimensional model (Figure 2.1) initially proposed by Lucas (1981), later expanded by Ploog (1984) and further developed here. AN and BN develop with dieting behavior (Fairburn and Cooper, 1984). To the dieting experience, the dieting individual brings a biological vulnerability, psychological predisposition, family influences and societal expectations. All of these antecedents to dieting behavior are discussed thoroughly in chapters throughout this book. Almost all women diet during their adolescent or early adult years (Nylander, 1971). However, very few go on to develop AN or BN. The mechanism that triggers this development is still unknown. There is increasing evidence that the biological vulnerability may be a susceptibility to dysregulation or dysfunction of neurotransmitter systems that regulate eating behavior as well as affect (Kaye and Weltzin, 1991). Eventually we should be able to decipher how much influence or what percentage of the variance is accounted for by biological vulnerability, psychological predisposition, family characteristics and societal expectations in the development of AN or BN. In these eating disorders physiological changes occur which induce mental changes and together they produce sustaining factors which perpetuate the aberrant eating behavior. Current findings of these physiological changes are presented in the chapters on biological models of the eating disorders.

Handbook of Eating Disorders: Theory, Treatment and Research.
Edited by G. Szmukler, C. Dare and J. Treasure.
© 1995 John Wiley & Sons Ltd.

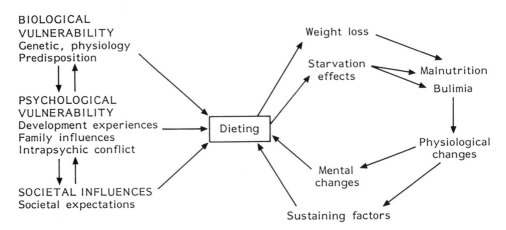

FIGURE 2.1   Multidimensional model for anorexia nervosa and bulimia nervosa, adapted from Ploog (1984) and Lucas (1981).

Current concepts and definitions are reflected in the changing classification of the eating disorders. In the first section of this chapter the proposed criteria for the North American Diagnostic and Statistic Manual IV for eating disorders and the rationale for these criteria will be presented.

Current concepts have been strongly influenced by studies of comorbid psychiatric disorders in eating disorders. Some of these studies led to theories of etiology of the eating disorders and even the proposal that they are not *sui generis*. The second section of this chapter will review and discuss the studies on comorbidity of both Axis I and Axis II psychiatric diagnoses with the eating disorders.

In the past decade more attention has focused on the complexities of eating behavior in the eating disorders. The third section of this chapter will present and discuss Blundell and Booth's concepts of eating behavior and the usefulness of these concepts as applied to AN and BN.

CLASSIFICATION OF EATING DISORDERS

In 1970, Russell proposed three criteria for the diagnosis of anorexia nervosa:

1. behavior that is designed to produce marked weight loss
2. a morbid fear of becoming fat, which is the characteristic psychological disturbance
3. evidence of an endocrine disorder which in the post-pubertal girl causes the cessation of menstruation.

Later in 1979, Russell proposed criteria for bulimia nervosa which consisted of:

1. a powerful and intractable urge to overeat, resulting in episodes of overeating

2. avoidance of "fattening" effects of food by inducing vomiting or abusing purgatives or both
3. a morbid fear of becoming fat.

The proposed diagnostic criteria for eating disorders in DSM-IV are presented in Table 2.1. It is obvious that the three criteria for anorexia nervosa proposed by Russell over 20 years ago are still embedded in the latest DSM criteria. An earlier version of criterion C for anorexia nervosa in DSM-III was described as a "body image disturbance". This resulted in many studies of a narrow definition of body image related to visual self-perception. Since these studies show that many anorectics do not overestimate their sizes, and that overestimation is not unique to those with anorexia nervosa (Lindholm and Wilson, 1988) the criterion was reworded in DSM-III-R to focus on attitudinal and affective dimensions of body image. Because this newly worded criterion of "overconcern with body size and shape" had significant overlap between AN patients and the general female population, it was revised in DSM-IV to emphasize the central concern of weight and shape in the evaluation of the self in addition to a reference to the denial of the serious consequences of weight loss. These two additions to the body dissatisfaction criterion should reduce overlap with the general population.

In response to numerous studies documenting reliable differences between anorectic patients who engage in bingeing/purging behavior and those anorectic patients who merely restrict food intake, the DSM-IV criteria have defined an AN restrictor type and an AN binge/purger type. Studies consistently demonstrated that impulsive behaviors including stealing, drug abuse, suicide attempts, self-mutilations and mood lability are more prevalent in anorectic-bulimics compared with anorectic restrictors. The anorectic–bulimics also have a higher prevalence of premorbid obesity, familial obesity, debilitating personality traits and a familial psychopathology (Casper et al, 1980; Garfinkel, Moldofsky and Garner, 1980; Andersen, 1985; Yellowlees, 1985; Strober et al, 1982; Eckert et al, 1987). There are important physiological differences between bulimic people who lose large amounts of weight and meet criteria for anorexia nervosa and those who never lose weight. For this reason patients who binge and purge and meet criteria for anorexia nervosa are diagnosed as anorexia nervosa, binge/purge subtype, rather than bulimia nervosa.

The criteria for bulimia nervosa are more arbitrary and more ambiguous compared with the criteria for AN. Although binge eating is a necessary diagnostic criterion for bulimia nervosa, there is no consensus on what constitutes a binge and what is acceptable as the minimum binge frequency for this disorder. Binge eating is therefore defined as eating more food than most people in similar circumstances in a similar period of time. The sense of losing control is a significant subjective aspect that occurs in binge eating and is present as a second part of criterion A for bulimia nervosa. The emphasis on a discrete time period in this criterion is to differentiate binge eating from continual 'snacking' throughout the day.

The diagnosis of bulimia nervosa will be subtyped into a purging type for those who regularly engage in self-induced vomiting or the use of laxatives or diuretics and a non-purging type for those who use strict dieting, fasting or vigorous exercise

TABLE 2.1   Eating disorders.

F50.0   ANOREXIA NERVOSA

A. Refusal to maintain body weight at or above a minimally normal weight for age and height, (e.g. weight loss leading to maintenance of body weight less than 85% of that expected; or failure to make expected weight gain during period of growth, leading to body weight less than 85% of that expected).
B. Intense fear of gaining weight or becoming fat, even though underweight.
C. Disturbance in the way in which one's body weight or shape is experienced, undue influence of body shape and weight on self-evaluation, or denial of the seriousness of current low body weight.
D. In post-menarchal females, amenorrhea, i.e. the absence of at least three consecutive menstrual cycles. (A woman is considered to have amenorrhea if her periods occur only following hormone, e.g. estrogen, administration.)

Specify type:

Restricting type: During the episode of anorexia nervosa, the person does not regularly engage in binge eating or purging behavior (i.e. self-induced vomiting or the misuse of laxatives or diuretics).
Binge eating/purging type: During the episode of anorexia nervosa, the person regularly engages in binge eating or purging behavior (i.e. self-induces vomiting or the misuse of laxatives or diuretics).

F50.2   BULIMIA NERVOSA

A. Recurrent episodes of binge-eating. An episode of binge-eating is characterized by both (1) eating, in a discreet period of time (e.g. in any two-hour period), an amount of food that is definitely larger than most people would eat in a similar period of time (taking into account time since last meal and social context in which eating occurred); and (2) a sense of lack of control over eating during the episodes (e.g. a feeling that one can't stop eating or control what or how much one is eating).
B. Recurrent use of inappropriate compensatory behavior to avoid weight gain; e.g. self-induced vomiting.
C. A minimum average of two episodes of binge eating and two inappropriate compensatory behaviors a week for at least three months.
D. Self-evaluation is unduly influenced by body shape and weight.
E. The disturbance does not occur exclusively during episodes of anorexia nervosa.

Specify type:

Purging type: These individuals regularly purge after binge-eating via self-induced vomiting or the abuse of laxatives.
Non-purging type: These individuals do not engage in self-induced vomiting or laxative abuse. Some may use compensatory methods of dieting and exercising.

F50.8   BINGE-EATING DISORDER

A. Recurrent episodes of binge-eating. An episode of binge-eating is characterized by both (1) eating in a discrete period of time (e.g. in any two-hour period), an amount of food that is definitely larger than most people would eat in a similar period of time (taking into account time since last meal and social context in which the eating occurred); and (2) a sense of lack of control over eating during the episode (e.g. a feeling that one can't stop eating or control what or how much one is eating).
B. At least three of the following behavioral indicators of loss of control are associated with binge-eating: (1) eating much more rapidly than normal; (2) eating until feeling uncomfortably full; (3) eating large amounts when not feeling physically hungry; (4) eating large

amounts of food throughout the day with no planned meal time; (5) eating alone because of being embarrassed because of how much one is eating; (6) feeling disgusted with oneself, depressed or feeling very guilty after overeating.

C. Marked distress regarding binge-eating or the struggle against binge-eating.

D. The binge-eating occurs, on average, at least twice a week for a 6-month period.

E. During an episode of illness, the individual does not meet criteria for bulimia nervosa and does not abuse medication (e.g. laxatives or diet pills) in an attempt to avoid weight gain.

F50.9 EATING DISORDER NOT OTHERWISE SPECIFIED

Disorders of eating that do not meet the criteria for a specific eating disorder. Examples include:

1. All of the criteria for anorexia nervosa are met except the individual has regular menses.
2. All of the criteria for anorexia nervosa are met except, despite significant weight loss, the individual's current weight is in the normal range.
3. All of the criteria for bulimia nervosa are met except binges occur at a frequency of less than twice a week or a duration of less than three months.
4. An individual of normal body weight regularly engages in inappropriate compensatory behavior after eating small amounts of food (e.g. self-induced vomiting after the consumption of two cookies).
5. An individual who repeatedly chews and spits out, but does not swallow, large amounts of food.

From the American Psychiatric Association (1987). *Diagnostic and Statistical Manual of Mental Disorders,* 3rd edn, revised. Washington, DC: APA. Reproduced by permission.

but do not regularly engage in purging. There is evidence that bulimic people who purge differ from binge eaters who do not purge in that the latter tend to have less body image disturbance and less anxiety concerning eating (Davis, Williamson and Strickler, 1986; Duchman, Williamson and Strickler, 1986). Bulimic people who do not purge tend to be obese. Bulimic patients have considerable concern about their body shape and weight. This is expressed in criterion D of bulimia nervosa (Wilson and Smith, 1989).

Based on their clinical work and a survey of the literature, Devlin et al (1992) came to the conclusion that a significant number of people had serious problems with binge eating but did not meet criteria for bulimia nervosa. People with this disorder lack the compensatory weight-control behaviors and the over-concern with weight and shape. Spitzer et al (1992) proposed criteria of this syndrome and termed it "binge eating disorder". Until field trials are conducted providing sufficient evidence that "binge eating disorder" be a specific diagnostic category, this disorder will be listed in the "not otherwise specified" category of the DSM-IV for eating disorders.

COMORBIDITY OF PSYCHIATRIC DIAGNOSES IN EATING DISORDERS

Anorexia Nervosa

Depressive and anxiety symptoms have been noted in anorexia nervosa for several decades (Kay and Leigh, 1954; Halmi, 1974). The Minnesota Experiment (Keys et al, 1950) showed that the psychological effects of starvation closely mimic depressive symptomatology. Not until the past decade were structured interviews designed for specific diagnostic criteria used to determine the presence of other psychiatric diagnoses in patients with anorexia nervosa. The study by Morgan and Russell in 1975 was one of the first to look at rates of depression. This was a follow-up study by 41 anorectics 4–10 years after the initial presentation. Personal interviews were used for data collection. At the time of the study 55% of the patients were eating normally, 20% remained fully anorectic and the remainder had some ongoing difficulties with anorectic symptoms. However, the rates of depression remained constant—42% at presentation and 45% at follow-up.

Cantwell et al (1977) followed up 26 adolescents 5 years after discharge and found 45% of them were depressed at follow-up. Only one of these adolescents had a continuing diagnoses of anorexia nervosa. Toner, Garfinkel and Garner (1988) in a 5–14 year follow-up study of 47 patients found that 40% of the anorectics had a lifetime history of major depression compared with only 12% of a control group. Neither the lifetime rate of major depression nor the occurrence of depression in the past year was correlated with the outcome of the eating disorder.

More recently Halmi et al (1991) found a lifetime history of depression in 68% of 62 anorectics in a 10-year follow-up study compared with 21% of the control population. At the time of follow-up 8% remained anorectic and 24% had no eating disorder at all. The lifetime prevalence of depression was not correlated with the outcome of anorexia. There was a trend for more major depression to occur in patients who binged at some time compared with pure restrictors. Also at the time of the 10-year follow-up, there was significantly more *current* major depression in the normal-weight bulimics compared with those who had recovered, those who had mild eating disorder symptomatology and those with continuing anorexia nervosa. The DIS structured interview was used in this study to determine diagnoses meeting DSM-III criteria. The lifetime prevalence of 68% for major depression in patients with anorexia nervosa is considerably higher in this study compared with the 36% in the study by Laessle et al (1987) using the same DIS structured interview. However, it should be noted that patients in the latter study were on the average 8 years younger than the patients presented at the time of the DIS interview in the Halmi et al (1991) study. The Toner et al (1988) study had a problem in that the 47 patients participating in their DIS interview represented only one-third of the original 139 patients that were traced, and therefore this study may represent a biased sample of the original group. The only other study with a similar prevalence of major depression was that of Gershon, Hamovit and Schreiber (1984). The Schedule for Affective Disorders and Schizophrenia lifetime interview was used in that study to establish the diagnosis of major affective disorder in 13 (54%) of anorectic patients. The mean age at the time of interview in that study was only 3 years less than the median interview age in the Halmi et al (1991) study. In this same study, first degree relatives were examined and major affective disorder was found to be the most prevalent psychiatric disorder in the families of anorectic patients. However, the presence of affective disorder in the anorectic proband was not predictive of affective illness in the relatives. The Halmi et al (1991) study supported these findings. Strober et al (1990) had contradictory results but the authors acknowledged that some of their young probands may carry a susceptibility to affective disorders that could become manifest in later years. The lack of finding an increased prevalence of eating disorders in the first degree relatives of probands with affective disorder in the Strober et al (1990) study indicates that anorexia nervosa is not merely a *forme fruste* of affective disorder.

Anxiety disorders include obsessive–compulsive disorder, a wide range of phobias, panic disorder and generalized anxiety disorder. Obsessional behavior and phobic anxiety were measured by Stonehill and Crisp (1977) in a large population of anorexia nervosa patients. They found the obsessional behaviors to remain rather stable over a 4–7 year follow-up and the phobic anxiety scores to increase over this period. The author stated this increase was due to higher scores on social phobia. In the Halmi et al (1991) study and the Toner et al (1988) study the lifetime prevalences for anxiety disorders in patients with anorexia nervosa were respectively 65% and 60%. The two most prevalent in both studies were social phobia and obsessive–compulsive disorder. In the Halmi et al (1991) study, 26% of the anorectic population had lifetime obsessive–compulsive disorder and 34% had a diagnosis of lifetime social phobia. In this latter study it is of interest to note that obsessive–compulsive disorder was significantly more prevalent in anorectic mothers compared with mothers of the control sample. In the Halmi et al (1991) study, comparison of lifetime psychiatric diagnoses of patients who at some time engaged in bingeing with those who never binged revealed that obsessive–compulsive disorder occurred more frequently in the patients who never binged compared with those who binged at some time.

Twenty-five years ago Crisp (1967) conceptualized anorexia nervosa as a phobic disorder when he suggested that it represented a phobic avoidance response to food resulting from the tensions arising in puberty. Brady and Rieger (1972) suggested that for anorectics, eating generates anxiety and the refusal to eat and purging are reinforced by anxiety reduction. There are very few adequate controlled studies with structured interviews assessing the presence of phobias in eating disorders. Both the Toner et al (1988) study and the Halmi et al (1991) study found the lifetime occurrence of social phobia was significantly higher in the anorectics (29% and 33% respectively) than in control samples. Recent data by Brewerton et al (1993) indicate that social phobia precedes the onset of anorexia nervosa in many patients and thus cannot be regarded as merely representing a symptom of anorexia nervosa.

It is probably reasonable to conclude from the uncontrolled and controlled studies that anxiety disorders are present in at least 40% of anorectic patients. In the Toner et al (1988) study, early-onset anxiety disorders which were present before onset of anorexia nervosa predicted a poor outcome with regard to the anorexia. This finding needs further study since it may indicate a group of anorectic patients that are particularly prone to treatment resistance.

Two decades ago a retrospective chart analysis showed an increased incidence of alcoholism in the parents of anorectic patients (Halmi and Loney, 1973). Szmukler and Tantam (1984) suggested that anorexia nervosa could be conceptualized as a dependency disorder. They noted that anorexia and problem drinking shared many features. Both generally start out alleviating anxiety and eventually lead to impaired self-control and increased self-destructiveness. In both disorders there is a compulsive need to engage in the behavior with considerable distress when the behavior is interrupted. Denial is the central mechanism used to perpetuate both disorders. Finally, they are both often characterized by a chronic course with frequent relapses. The only study with a large sample to systematically assess the presence of substance abuse in anorexia nervosa (Halmi et al, 1991) showed that only 8% of the patients had alcohol abuse and 12% had cannabis abuse, which was the most frequently abused drug. There was no significant difference in the prevalence of substance abuse in the anorectics compared with a control group. There also was no increased prevalence of alcoholism in the parents of anorectic patients compared with the anorectic subjects. However, when all the first degree relatives were considered, alcoholism occurred with a higher frequency in the relatives of the anorectic patients compared with the relatives of the controls.

Studies of the relationship between personality and eating disorders have yielded widely discrepant results. This could be due to the use of interviews and self-report questionnaires of questionable reliability and specificity, to the use of instruments which may be distorted by Axis I states, and to inconsistencies in psychiatric terminology between DSM-III and DSM-III-R definitions. However, in considering the three studies that have used DSM-III-R eating disorder criteria and examined the full range of personality disorders with established diagnostic interviews, the findings are still contradictory. Anorectic restrictors have been reported to have a personality disorder incidence of 80% (Wonderlich et al, 1990), 33% (Gartner et al, 1989) and 23% (Herzog et al, 1992). A more recent study (Braun, Sunday and Halmi, in press) found that anorectic restrictors were less likely to have any personality disorder diagnosis compared with other eating disorder subgroups. The anorectic restrictors had no personality disorder diagnoses in cluster B, the dramatic group of personality disorders. In this latter study 23% of the anorectic restrictors had a cluster C (anxious) diagnosis, with 12% having the diagnosis of avoidant personality disorder and 8% with a diagnosis of dependent or obsessive–compulsive personality disorder. The prevalence of cluster B personality disorders in the anorectic bulimics (38%) did not significantly differ from the prevalence in the normal weight bulimics. In this study all the interviews were conducted with the SCID-P.

Axis II personality disorders are less precisely defined and less specific than Axis I disorders. It is clear that patients with anorexia nervosa often have significant Axis II psychopathology. Many of these patients will require lengthy therapy after refeeding because of personality disorder problems. At this time it is unclear whether or not specific personality disorders are related to outcome of the eating disorder.

Bulimia Nervosa

In his first paper describing the syndrome of bulimia nervosa, Russell (1979) noted severe signs of depression in 43% of his group of 30 female bulimics. Russell stated that "next to the preoccupations directly concerned with eating and weight, depressive features were the most prominent feature of the patients' mental state". Later in studies with large sample sizes and using structured interviews with control groups, the lifetime rate of major depression in bulimia ranged from 36% to 70% with DSM-III criteria or RDC (Piran et al, 1985; Walsh et al, 1985; Laessle et al, 1987). These studies show that at the time of treatment for bulimia about one-third to one-half of bulimics will meet criteria for major depression and about one-half to two-thirds of bulimics will ultimately develop a major depression. Major depression can precede, occur simultaneously with, or follow the onset of bulimia (Herzog, 1984; Lee et al, 1985; Toner et al, 1988). This variability in the relative onset of these disorders strongly suggests that neither is a secondary phenomenon of the other.

In Russell's original group of 30 bulimics (Russell, 1979), 11 made at least one suicide attempt of which five were serious and one successful. Hatsukami et al (1984) reported suicide attempts in 16% of 108 bulimic females. In earlier studies Casper et al (1980) and Garfinkel et al (1980) found a higher prevalence of suicidal ideation in anorectics with bulimia compared with restricting anorectics. The family studies for psychiatric comorbidity of bulimic probands are so fraught with methodological flaws that no conclusion can be made about the familial incidence of psychopathology in bulimia nervosa.

The prevalence of alcohol or substance abuse has varied from 18% to 33% in bulimic patients and these rates of substance abuse were significantly higher in bulimic women compared with controls (Hatsukami et al, 1984a; Mitchell et al, 1985; Bulic, 1987). In a more recent study, Braun et al (in press) found significantly more substance abuse in all bulimia subgroups of eating disorders compared with the anorectic restrictors.

Problems in studies assessing Axis II personality disorder diagnoses in bulimia nervosa are the same as those mentioned for anorexia nervosa. The percentage of DSM-III-R bulimics who have at least one personality disorder in studies using established diagnostic interviews has been reported to be 77% (Powers et al, 1988), 69% (Wonderlich et al, 1990), 62% (Gartner, 1989), 61% (Schmidt and Telch, 1990), 33% (Amos-Franco et al, 1992) and 28% (Herzog et al, 1992). In a more recent study using the SCID-P interview, Braun et al (in press) found one-third of the bulimic subgroups to have a cluster B (dramatic) personality disorder diagnosis. Within that cluster the most frequently diagnosed personality disorder was that of borderline which was diagnosed in about one-third of the bulimics. The more surprising result was that the prevalence of cluster C (anxious) personality disorders was just as high in the bulimic subgroups of eating disorders as in the anorectic restrictors. Again, the prevalence of the cluster C personality disorders was present in about one-third of the bulimic population. This latter study has shown that bulimics have a mixture of impulsive, dramatic symptomatology (cluster B personality disorders) and the anxious personality disorders, mainly avoidant and obsessive–compulsive personality disorders. Those bulimics with no current or past history of anorexia nervosa had no obsessive–compulsive personality disorder.

In a study assessing the effect of comorbid psychopathology on eating disorder symptomatology, Sunday, Levey and Halmi (1993) found that affective disorder diagnoses (both current and lifetime) strongly influenced eating disorder symptomatology and general psychiatric symptoms. Borderline personality characteristics had little influence on eating disorder symptomatology. These findings underscore the importance of assessing affective disorder diagnoses in conjunction with borderline psychopathology in bulimic subjects. As the criteria and interviews for Axis II personality diagnoses continue to be refined, we will obtain a better idea of the influence of these personality disorders on outcome in bulimia nervosa.

A SYSTEMS CONCEPTUALIZATION OF EATING BEHAVIOR IN EATING DISORDERS

At the beginning of this chapter the model for conceptualizing eating disorders showed that they begin with dieting behavior. In trying to understand the development of eating disorders most investigators have focused on the so-called "core psychopathology" of anorexia nervosa and bulimia nervosa. Recently some thought has been given to the complexity of eating behavior in general and how disturbances in the complex phenomena of eating behavior may help explain the development and perpetuation of AN and BN. Booth (1981) developed the concepts of nutritional hedonic conditioning which states that the integration of sensory characteristics of foods (including nutritional functions), culturally derived attitudes and satiation cues (GI tract, peptide hormones, neurotransmitters) produces a nutritional hedonic conditioning. If one considers this hypothesis in terms of human eating behavior then it is possible to equate the sensory characteristics of food as a conceptual identity. This conceptual identity is present in persons as cognitive sets which include attitudes towards and the identity of nutritional content of food. These cognitive sets and the internal physiology affecting eating behavior are integrated through perceptions of hunger and satiety which in turn strongly influences eating behavior (Halmi, 1992). This means that nutritional hedonic conditioning can be investigated in human eating behavior by studying the integrating processes of hunger and satiety perceptions. Thus, eating is not an isolated event, but rather an interaction between an organism's physiological state and sensory input, including environmental condition (Blundell and Hill, 1986).

Blundell and Hill (1987) stated that the capacity to control nutrient intake to meet bodily needs requires specialized mechanisms to harmonize physiologic information in the internal milieu with nutritional information in the external environment. Two essential features are:

1. perceptual capacities to identify characteristics of food materials in the environment
2. mechanisms to link the biochemical consequences of ingested food with the consumed structural form.

Thus, a control over selection of foods must involve conditioned and unconditioned components.

The chronicity of disturbed eating behavior in both anorectic and bulimic patients, the high percentage of relapse in eating disorder patients who have been treated, and the resistance of maladaptive eating behavior to change (treatment) indicate dysfunctions in perceptual capacities, internal physiology, or integrating mechanisms regulating eating behavior.

Using an experimental meal paradigm, Halmi et al (1989) found marked disturbances in the hunger and satiety perceptions of both anorexia nervosa and bulimia nervosa patients compared with control subjects. In the control subjects the hunger and fullness curves were inversely proportional throughout the meal with one intersection during the meal. The anorectic patients were not at all hungry throughout the entire meal and were extremely full throughout the meal. The bulimic patients had an opposite profile of being hungry throughout the meal and not at all full or multiple intersections of hunger and fullness so that the patients could not really identify whether they were hungry or full. After treatment both restricting anorectic patients and bulimic anorectic patients had fewer "abnormal" hunger and fullness curve patterns. Patients who had a history of binge eating and purging had significantly higher palatability ratings after treatment compared with restricting anorectic patients and controls. These patients should be tested at least a year after maintaining a normal weight and after abstinence from bingeing and purging to determine whether these eating related characteristics such as perception of hunger and satiety represent a state or trait phenomena.

The post-meal cognitions were most interrelated for normal-weight bulimics. Urge to eat was positively correlated with monthly binge frequency in the bulimic patients, and the bulimic patients who binged the most were the most depressed (Halmi and Sunday, 1991).

Halmi and Sunday (1992) studied the responses of AN and BN patients to meals consisting of (a) high fat, low carbohydrate, (b) low fat, high carbohydrate, and (c) high fat, high carbohydrate macronutrient proportions. In this study the bulimics had a significant rebound of hunger after the end of the high fat meals. Most bulimics did not have this response after the high carbohydrate, low fat meals. This is some evidence showing bulimics may reduce their urge to binge by eating high carbohydrate, low fat meals.

SUMMARY

The multidimensional model presented earlier in this chapter represents most current thought in the pathogenesis of eating disorders. As better techniques for assessing neuroendocrine function develop it is likely that the influence of neuroendocrine function from the initiation to maintenance of disturbed eating behavior in anorexia and bulimia nervosa will be elucidated. In the next decade with prospective longitudinal studies, the influence of comorbid psychiatric disorders on the course and outcome of anorexia and bulimia nervosa will be clarified. Multicentered collaborative studies in both anorexia nervosa and bulimia nervosa will continue to define the effectiveness of various treatment modalities for these disorders.

REFERENCES

Amos-Frankel, J., Devlin, N.J., Walsh, B.T., et al (1992). Personality disorder diagnoses in patients with bulimia nervosa: clinical correlates and changes with treatment. *J. Clin. Psychiat.,* **53**, 90–96.

Anderson, A.E. (1985). *Practical Comprehensive Treatment of Anorexia Nervosa and Bulimia.* Baltimore: Johns Hopkins University Press.

Blundell, J.E. and Hill, A.J. (1986). Behavioral pharmacology with feeding: relevance of animal experiments for study in man. In: *Pharmacology of Eating Disorders* (ed. M. Carruba and J.E. Blundell), pp. 51–70. New York: Raven Press.

Blundell, J.E. and Hill, A.J. (1987). Nutrition, serotonin and appetite: case study and the evolution of a scientific idea. *Appetite,* **8**, 183–194.

Booth, D.A. (1981). How should questions about satiation be asked? *Appetite,* **2**, 237–244.

Brady, J.P. and Rieger, W. (1972). *Behavior Treatment of Anorexia Nervosa: Proceedings of the International Symposium on Behavior Modification,* p. 57. New York: Appleton-Century-Croft.

Braun, D.L., Sunday, S.R. and Halmi, K.A. (in press). Psychiatric comorbidity in patients with eating disorders. *Psychol. Med.*

Brewerton, T.D., Lydiard, R.B., Balenger, J.C. and Herzog, D.B. (1993). Eating disorders and social phobia. *Arch. Gen. Psychiat.,* **50**, 70.

Bulik, C. (1987). Drug and alcohol abuse by bulimic women and their families. *Am. J. Psychiat.,* **144**, 1604–1606.

Cantwell, D.P., et al. (1977). Anorexia nervosa: an affective disorder? *Arch. Gen. Psychiat.,* **34**, 1087–1093.

Casper, R., Eckert, E., Halmi, K.A., et al. (1980). Bulimia: its incidence and clinical importance in patients with anorexia nervosa. *Arch. Gen. Psychiat.,* **37**, 1030–1035.

Crisp, A.H. (1967). The possible significance of some behavioral correlates of weight and carbohydrate intake. *J. Psychosom. Res.,* **11**, 117–125.

Davis, C.G., Williamson, D.A. and Goreczny, T. (1986). Body image distortion in bulimia: an important distinction between binge purgers and binge eaters. Paper presented at the Annual Convention of the Association of the Advancement of Behavior Therapy, Chicago, Ill, March 1986.

Devlin, M.J., Walsh, B.T., Spitzer, R.L., et al. (1992). Is there another binge eating disorder? A review of the literature on overeating in the absence of bulimia nervosa. *Int. J. Eating Dis.,* **11**, 341–350.

Duchman, E.G., Williamson, D.A. and Strickler, P.M. (1986). Dietary restraint in bulimia. Paper presented at the Annual Convention of the Association of the Advancement of Behavior Therapy, Chicago, Ill, March 1986.

Eckert, E., Halmi, K.A., Marchi, P., et al. (1987). Comparison of bulimic and non-bulimic anorexia nervosa patients during treatment. *Psychol. Med.,* **17**, 891–898.

Fairburn, C.J. and Cooper, P.J. (1984). The clinical features of bulimia nervosa. *Br. J. Psychiat.,* **144**, 283–246.

Garfinkel, P.E., Moldofsky, H. and Garner, D.M. (1980). The heterogeneity of anorexia nervosa: bulimia as a distinct subgroup. *Arch. Gen. Psychiat.,* **37**, 1036–1040.

Gartner, A.F., Marcus, R.N., Halmi, K.A., et al. (1989). DSM-III-R personality disorders in patients with eating disorders. *Am. J. Psychiat.,* **146**, 1585–1591.

Gershon, E., Hamovit, J. and Schreiber, J., (1983). Anorexia nervosa and major affective disorders associated in families: a preliminary report. In: *Childhood psychopathology,* (eds. F.J. Earls and J.D. Barrett). New York: Raven Press.

Halmi, K.A. and Sunday, S.R. (1992). Macronutrient effects on eating behavior in anorexia and bulimia nervosa. Meeting of the Society for the Study of Ingestive Behavior, Princeton University, NJ, 24–28 June 1992.

Halmi, K.A., Eckert, E., Marchi, P.A., et al. (1991). Comorbidity of psychiatric diagnoses in anorexia nervosa. *Arch. Gen. Psychiat.,* **48**, 712–718.

Halmi, K.A. and Loney, J. (1973). Familial alcoholism in anorexia nervosa. *Br. J. Psychiat.,* **123**, 53–56.

Halmi, K.A. and Sunday, S.R. (1991). Temporal patterns of hunger and satiety ratings and related cognitions in anorexia and bulimia. *Appetite,* **16**, 219–237.

Halmi, K.A., Sunday, S.R., Puglisi, A., et al. (1989). Hunger and satiety in anorexia and bulimia nervosa. *Ann. NY Acad. Sci.,* **575**, 431–445.

Halmi, K.A. (1974). Anorexia nervosa: demographic and clinical features of 94 cases. *Psychom. Somat. Med.,* **36**, 18–24.

Halmi, K.A. (1992). Psychobiology of eating behavior. In: *Psychobiology and Treatment of Anorexia Nervosa and Bulimia Nervosa* (ed. K.A. Halmi), pp. 79–91. Washington, DC: Appl. Press.

Hatsukami, D.K., et al. (1984). Eating disorders: a variant of mood disorders?. *Psych. Clin. N. Amer.,* **7**, 349–365.

Hatsukami, D.K., et al. (1984a). Affective disorder and substance abuse in women with bulimia. *Psychol. Med.,* **14**, 701–704.

Herzog, D.B. (1984). Are anorexic and bulimic patients depressed? *Am. J. Psych.,* **141**, 1594–1597.

Herzog, D.B., Keller, M.B., Lavori, P.W., et al. (1992). The prevalence of personality disorders in 210 women with eating disorders. *J. Clin. Psychiat.,* **53**, 147–152.

Kay, D.W. and Leigh, D. (1954). The natural history, treatment, and prognosis of anorexia nervosa, based on a study of 38 patients. *J. Mental Sci.,* **100**, 411–431.

Kaye, W. and Weltzin, T.E. (1991). Serotonin activity in anorexia and bulimia nervosa: relationship to the modulation of feeding and mood, *J. Clin. Psychiat.,* **52**, 41–48.

Keys, A., et al. (1950). *The Biology of Human Starvation*, Vols. 1 and 2, pp. 68–81, 819–921. Minneapolis: University of Minnesota Press.

Laessle, R., Kittl, S., Fichter, M., et al. (1987). Major affective disorder in anorexic nervosa and bulimia. *Br. J. Psychiat.,* **151**, 785–789.

Lee, N.F., et al. (1985). Bulimia and depression. *J. Affect. Dis.,* **9**, 231–238.

Lindholm, L. and Wilson, G.T. (1988). Body image assessment in patients with bulimia nervosa and normal controls. *Int. J. Eating Dis.,* **7**, 527–539.

Lucas, A.R. (1981). Towards the understanding of anorexia nervosa as a disease entity, *Mayo Clin. Proc.,* **56**, 254–264.

Mitchell, J., Hatsukami, D., Eckert, E., et al. (1985). Characteristics of 275 patients with bulimia. *Am. J. Psychiat.,* **142**, 482–485.

Morgan, H.G. and Russell, G.F.M. (1975). The value of family background in clinical features as predictors of longterm outcome in anorexia nervosa: four year follow-up of 41 patients. *Psychol. Med.,* **5**, 355–371.

Nylander, I. (1971). The feeling of being fat and dieting in a school population: epidemiologic, interview investigation. *Acta Socio. Med., SAN,* **3**, 17–26.

Piran, et al. (1985). Affective disturbance in eating disorders. *J. Nerv. Mental Dis.,* **173**, 395–400.

Ploog, D. (1984). The importance of physiologic, metabolic and endocrine studies for the understanding of anorexia nervosa. In: *The Psychobiology of Anorexia Nervosa* (ed. K.M. Pirke and K. Ploog), pp. 1–4. Berlin: Springer.

Powers, P.S., Coovert, D.L., Brightwell, B.R., et al (1988). Other psychiatric disorders among bulimic patients. *Compr. Psychiat.,* **29**, 503–508.

Russell, G.F.M. (1979). Bulimia nervosa; an ominous variant of anorexia nervosa. *Psychol. Med.,* **9**, 492–448.

Russell, G.F.M. and Berdwood, C.J. (1970). Amennorhea in the feeding disorders: anorexia nervosa and obesity. *Psycho. Ther. Psycho. Som.,* **18**, 358–364.

Schmidt, M.B. and Telch, M.J. (1990). Prevalence of personality disorders among bulimics, non-bulimic binge eaters and normal controls. *J. Psychopath. Beh. Ess.,* **12**, 170–185.

Spitzer, R., Devlin, M.J., Walsh, B.T., et al. (1992). Binge eating disorder: multisite field trial of the diagnostic criteria. *Int. J. Eating Dis.,* **11**, 191–203.

Stonehill, E. and Crisp, A.H. (1977). Psychoneurotic characteristics of patients with bulimia nervosa before and after treatment and at a follow-up 4–7 years later. *J. Psychosom. Res.*, **21**, 187–193.

Strober, M., Lampert, C., Morrell, W., et al. (1990). A controlled family study of anorexia nervosa: evidence of familial aggregation and lack of shared transmition with affective disorders. *Int. J. Eating Dis.*, **9**, 239–254.

Strober, M., Salkin, B., Burroughs, J., et al. (1982). Validity of the bulimia-restrictor distinctions in anorexia nervosa: parental personality characteristics and familial psychiatric morbidity. *J. Nerv. Mental Dis.*, **170**, 345–351.

Sunday, S.R., Levey, C.M. and Halmi, K.A. (1993). Effects of depression and borderline personality traits on psychological states and eating disorder symptomatology. *Compr. Psychiatr.*, **34**, 70–74.

Szmukler, G.I. and Tantam, D. (1984). Anorexia nervosa: starvation dependence. *Br. J. Med. Psychol.*, **57**, 303–314.

Toner, B.B., Garfinkel, P. and Garner, D., (1988). Affective and anxiety disorders in the longterm follow-up of anorexia nervosa. *Int. J. Psychiat. Med.*, **18**, 357–364.

Walsh, B.T., et al. (1985). Bulimia and depression. *Psychosom. Med.*, **147**, 123–131.

Wilson, G.T. and Smith, D. (1989). Assessment of bulimia nervosa: an evaluation of the eating disorders examination. *Int. J. Eating Dis.*, **8**, 173–179.

Wonderlich, S.A., Swift, W.J., Slotnick, H.B., et al. (1990). DSM-III-R personality disorders in eating-disorder subtypes. *Int. J. Eating Dis.*, **9**, 607–616.

Yellowlees, A.J. (1985). Anorexia and bulimia in anorexia nervosa: a study of psychosocial functioning and associated psychiatric symptomatology. *Br. J. Psychiat.*, **146**, 648–652.

Part II

Aetiology

Introduction to Part II

In this section, the contributors were asked to address areas usually ascribed as defining fundamental causes. Significant hypotheses or models are examined with special attention to the evidence supporting them, and to the range and limitations of their explanatory power. We consider models at levels of abstraction from the genetic to the cultural. By putting these chapters together, side-by-side, we hoped we would emerge with a deeper, and broader, appreciation of the major current ideas.

Alfred North Whitehead once remarked that if we wish to discover the basic assumptions underlying our thinking, we ought to consider what is *not* said as well as what is said. Campbell's chapter on what an explanation of the eating disorders would look like tackles this issue. What is the nature of the observations we make, do psychological theories represent knowledge of a different kind from those of biology (Karl Jasper's *understanding* as opposed to *explanation*), what are the limitations of each, how do they relate to each other, what do we mean by "multifactorial causation"? In the hurly-burly of our everyday work, by failing to reflect on these issues, we may stray down paths that lead to conundrums and false oppositions rather than progress towards solutions. Campbell's chapter is rooted in the tradition of descriptive psychopathology, one which has been so formative in developing our notions of what anorexia nervosa is, but which tends nowadays to be neglected.

Treasure and Holland examine the genetics of anorexia nervosa and bulimia in an unusually comprehensive manner. A variety of methods comprise modern genetic investigation and most are now being applied to the eating disorders. The evidence for a significant genetic contribution to anorexia nervosa is strong, less so for bulimia nervosa. However, the nature of the inherited disposition is unclear. A number of propositions are examined in which dieting triggers mechanisms leading to clinical disorder.

Fichter and Pirke review our understanding of neuroendocrine disturbances, an area of extensive research in which hopes have been high that a fundamental cause would be discovered. Drawing on their investigations of both patients and volunteers engaged in rigorous dieting, they conclude that most, if not all, abnormalities are a consequence rather than a cause of the disorders. That major endocrinological disturbances may be seen in many subjects who restrict their dietary intake, even in the absence of major weight loss, is especially noteworthy in attempts to define an underlying "trait" or vulnerability marker.

Robinson and McHugh examine the proposal that disturbances in another major physiological system, the gastrointestinal, and especially gastric emptying, may lie near the heart of the eating disorders. Further, the relationship between these disturbances and the "gut hormone" cholecystokinin is evaluated. A primary role is difficult to sustain; a maintaining role in established disorder is more likely, even thought it is difficult to explain why a starving person should find it harder to eat. These authors, in an exemplary fashion, also unravel intriguing connections between biological and psychological events, between gastric function and not only perceptions of satiety and hunger, but also typical psychopathological manifestations of the eating disorders.

We then move on to two chapters reviewing psychological models of the eating disorders. Dare and Crowther consider psychodynamic observations and theories. They see the contribution of this discipline as the illumination of patients' experiences and the meanings of their symptoms, rather than the provision of explanations in the sense talked about in the previous chapters: "Psychodynamic psychology emphasises the place of infancy and subsequent experiences in shaping the person so that when that person meets up with the possibility of being anorexic, she clasps it to her emaciated breast and makes it her own". The historical perspective adopted by the authors supports their contention that the evolving understanding of patients with eating disorders deriving from the psychodynamic approach has proceeded independently of changing theories.

Da Silva examines behavioural and cognitive–behavioural explanations. Cogent models, some associated with effective treatments, are summarised by him. They have found an important place in our understanding of the eating disorders, particularly bulimia, but Da Silva concludes, as have so many of the previous contributors to this section, that they are strong in explaining their maintenance rather than their development. He also notes a paucity still of empirical evidence supporting the most influential models.

Broadening the domain of explanatory constructs, we move on to family and sociocultural influences. Eisler, in reviewing family factors, concludes that there is no "anorexigenic" family constellation that leads to the disorder. A careful consideration of the evidence concerning disturbances in family functioning in patients' families compared with control families suggests that differences are small, especially when community samples are studied. The family characteristics commonly described in the literature result from close scrutiny of subjects in specialist clinics, and may be associated with chronicity rather than the disorder itself. The possibility that observed family characteristics may be the result of the presence of the disorder and not its cause is difficult to exclude. The family approach stresses context; the disorder occurs within relationships and helps to construct and organise those relationships. From this perspective, the difference between causes and consequences becomes arbitrary.

Szmukler and Patton review the results of epidemiological research concerning the incidence, prevalence, and "risk factors" for eating disorders. Important changes have occurred in ideas about these disorders consequent on shifting attention to "cases" beyond the confines of the clinic, and especially outside western cultures. Epidemiological studies reveal a wider range of problems making up eating disorders in the population than in the clinic. Furthermore, questions about the relationship between these disorders and self-starvation states in other settings pose challenges to some of our institutionalised ideas about their core features. Is there a common element, constant across cultures? Comparing populations with different rates of disorder, variably defined, points to possible aetiological factors. The epidemiological findings point to dieting acting on vulnerable individuals as the major precipitant of eating disorders. In this respect, a full circle seems to have been reached in which the conclusions of these authors coincide with those of the authors examining genetic influences. The nature of the vulnerability remains largely unknown.

A multifactorial approach to causation is generally accepted. But, by pushing each single perspective to its limits a clearer picture of relative contributions emerges, as well as where and when in the process they act most strongly. Aetiological conclusions are modest. Most accounts seem almost silent on "necessary" causes, completely so on "necessary and sufficient" causes. Non-specific influences leading to dieting are reasonably well understood, as are some of the specific self-perpetuating consequences of eating disorders. In between, it is almost as if an accident in some subjects triggers a process which provides an arena for a range of influences obstructing recovery.

3

What Would a Causal Explanation of the Eating Disorders Look Like?

P.G. CAMPBELL
Royal Free Hospital, London, UK

INTRODUCTION

> "No clear-cut causes for anorexia nervosa have yet emerged, but data are being accumulated from more precise fields of enquiry—applied psychology, family studies, endocrinology, and nutritional physiology and chemistry". (Russell, 1970)

Gerald Russell's writings on anorexia nervosa and bulimia nervosa have not shirked the issue of causes, and the research he has vigorously fostered has explored many aspects, yet he has remained cautious and undogmatic in acknowledging how much is still unknown. His statement of 1970 (above) was updated and refined in a tentatively proposed flow-diagram of "circular interactions" (Russell, 1977; Figure 3.1), in which the thickness of the lines reflects the weight of evidence supporting each interaction.

Russell's pioneering description of bulimia nervosa (1979) emphasised the role of morbid concern about weight and anorexia-like psychopathology in its occurrence. More recently he has interpreted social factors as the reason why the presentation of anorexia nervosa has changed, particularly in terms of its psychopathology and the emergence of bulimia nervosa (Russell and Treasure, 1989). In Chapter 1 he emphasises the importance of maintaining a "flexible aetiological frame of

---

Handbook of Eating Disorders: Theory, Treatment and Research.
Edited by G. Szmukler, C. Dare and J. Treasure.

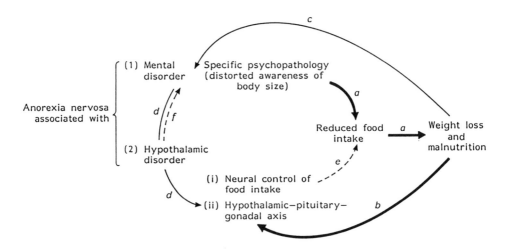

FIGURE 3.1 Russell's tentative flow-diagram of "circular interactions" (reproduced from Russell, 1977, by permission of Cambridge University Press).

reference", and the possible need now for a broader formulation of the psychopathology of anorexia nervosa to allow for recognition that food avoidance and weight loss may serve the attempted resolution of psychosocial conflicts which may vary over time and between different cultures.

Such illustrations serve to emphasise the virtue of humility in the attainment of wisdom. What emerges most clearly from his writings is Russell's persuasive argument that anorexia nervosa (and bulimia nervosa) has a clinical identity which is not to be subsumed under other designations or explained away by simplistic theorising: anorexia nervosa has "a firm place in classifications of psychiatric illness" (Russell, 1970). These disorders exist and are therefore to be explained, by discoveries which are yet to be made. But what sort of explanation are we seeking?

THE CAUSAL ENIGMA OF THE EATING DISORDERS

The eating disorders present a special kind of challenge to psychiatric approaches to theories of causality, particularly because they seem to implicate a strong degree of conscious choice, which may be actively hostile to medical or other therapeutic intervention. They may be difficult to demarcate sharply from variants of normal eating behaviour in a society beset with changing cultural preferences about diet and body shape (unless operational definitions, with their risk of conceptual vacuity, are applied), and they predominantly affect women in western culture at a time when the majority of doctors have been men. Medical causes have not been identified despite a profusion of research, and medical treatments have had limited success and have probably caused much suffering and even avoidable deaths.

Some of the many questions posed by the eating disorders can be stated, probably oversimply, in the form of polar alternatives. Is the sufferer a deliberate agent or an afflicted victim? Are we dealing with matters of individual human choice, which primarily reflect social processes such as early upbringing, family interactions, attitudes to sexual development, personality, body-size preferences, dietary habits and the roles of the sexes—or with morbid mental and physical processes which, though they may be provoked, precipitated and shaped by social factors and perhaps often initially by conscious choices, are ultimately explicable only when we can identify as necessary causes specific kinds of physical frailty and altered bodily function, the potential for which is perhaps intrinsic in varying degree to the human (and especially female) condition? Are we looking for one or more unitary mechanisms as necessary causal conditions, or must we be content to strive for some way of understanding in causal terms a multifactorial, interactive mass of disparate elements and systems which will encompass genetic predisposition, individual physiology, personality development, social stresses, family processes, cultural circumstances and prevailing fashions and *mores*?

GROUND RULES FOR THEORIES OF CAUSES

At a time when no widespread agreement exists about the aetiology of eating disorders or the language in which an aetiological account should be couched, workers in the field are free to choose the kind of explanatory model which they find appealing and useful, and their choice is likely to be influenced by their personal history, their training and probably also by the kind of patients they see. Illuminating and helpful as these personal models have been, they do not command the kind of scientific acceptance which transcends personal perspectives and which must be one of the requirements for any theory of aetiology which can presage a substantial advance in knowledge. Other basic requirements of such theories can be demanded as follows:

1. They must be couched in such a way as to be testable or refutable, or readily to generate testable hypotheses.
2. They should use explicit theoretical frameworks which embrace the central phenomena they attempt to explain.
3. They need to be consistent with established factual evidence.
4. They should be concerned not just with the pathogenesis of particular cases, but with the aetiology of the disorder.
5. They should identify whether the causal factors which are said to be implicated are to be regarded as necessary or sufficient factors, or whether they are contributory, or, to use Birnbaum's (1923) term, "pathoplastic".

Many authors, while acknowledging probable contributory causal or "risk" factors, such as cultural fashions in eating behaviour and body-shape ideals, genetics, personality structure, family environment, sexual experience etc., simply state that the causation is "unknown" or "multifactorial". The latter term, though widely popular in psychiatry, may seem to have little explanatory power, if any at all. It is usually not stated whether the implication is that the disorder may be the end-result of many different pathways or interacting systems, or whether specified factors, necessary or otherwise, which are thought to be involved are acting in some potentially predictable linear sequence or in one or more interactive systems. Many identified factors discussed as possibly contributing to the development of eating disorders seem to have little specificity to eating disorders.

Too complacent an acceptance of a "multifactorial" causation could direct attention away from the search for possibly identifiable singular and necessary causes. Or it may be that, lurking behind claims of such "multifactorial" causation, there is often an unexpressed hope that one day we will find a more unitary necessary causal element, as has been possible in many physical illnesses after the essential clinical features have been brought into clear focus. Such a process of illumination is described by Rosen (1968), who illustrates it by quoting Krafft-Ebing's (1877) account of the diverse aetiological factors contributing to a particular clinically defined syndrome; the factors included heredity, the menopause, trauma to the head, excessive heat and cold, fright, alcoholism, excessive venery, exhaustion as a result of earning a living and the smoking of from 10 to 20 Virginia cigars daily. Other observers of the time also thought social and psychological factors as potent aetiologically as physical ones. Rosen writes:

> The more frequent occurrence of the disease among former officers and soldiers of the Napoleonic armies was explained in terms of the privations experienced by these men, the terrors of war, their excessive drinking and the disappointment resulting from the defeat of Napoleon. Emotional causes such as violent love or profound jealousy seemed to be involved in some cases. In others, excessive intellectual activity, grief, sorrow, and similar factors predisposed to the disease.

There was much discussion at the time as to whether the disease was a modern phenomenon and whether the increase in its recognition represented a real or only an apparent rise in incidence. Syphilis was considered a possible aetiological factor, but was only one of several. The disease in question was syphilitic general paralysis, whose syphilitic causation (a necessary factor, if by no means a sufficient cause) could not be confirmed until the development of appropriate laboratory tests and finally, in 1913, the demonstration of the syphilitic organism in paretic brains. Are we hoping that new technology will one day reveal, if not the "anorexicoccus" and the "bulimichaete", at least one comparably definable physical entity or process which can do service as a necessary cause for the eating disorders?

DO WE NEED A CAUSAL ACCOUNT AT ALL?

In psychiatry today, the classification of "functional" disorders is intended to be free of adherence to any major theoretical system and to be virtually atheoretical, or at least, as Sartorius (1988) puts it, "theoretically unenterprising". Yet there are many present-day commentators, mostly outside psychiatry, who are critical of the theoretical assumptions which they see as implicit within the language of psychiatry, particularly in the adoption of the "medical model". The latter is commonly believed to depend upon assumptions of underlying physical disorder or "biochemical inferiority". Edlund (1986), for instance, states that "Psychiatric classificatory schemata presently used in research possess underlying assumptions regarding causality, and these assumptions need examination".

The very designation of "eating disorders" is not theoretically neutral, since it can be taken to suggest that there is a locus of morbid abnormality centred on the function and control of eating. The latter, however, is a necessary human and animal activity, subject to many internal and external influences and constraints, and implicated in many psychological, interpersonal and cultural processes and in many other disorders, such as depression. Why should these "eating disorders" not be seen, therefore, as variants in the form, perhaps, of variously motivated or variously meaningful under- or over-eating? We do not designate third-world starvation as an "eating disorder", nor observance of religious fasting, nor hunger-striking for a political cause, nor even do we usually designate obesity as an "eating disorder". We have to ask what it is about the "eating disorders" that makes us seek explanations in terms of diagnosis and causes, rather than in other kinds of explanation more directly meaningful in analysing and understanding the reasons why people act as they do.

The "medical model" can be taken to be many things, but its central assumption in psychiatry, I believe, is the essentially humanitarian hypothesis that in seeking an explanation for some dysfunctional behavioural phenomenon we take the view:

- that something has gone "wrong" within the functioning of a person and their relationship to the social environment, to the extent that they suffer distressing and/or disabling consequences for which they are less than fully responsible, and
- that other kinds of everyday explanation of human behaviour in terms of conscious motives and reasons, and of social pressures such as cultural fashions, will not suffice. Some other kind of language is needed.

Such a hypothesis also promotes beliefs that a therapeutic response is to be sought and that doctors and members of related clinical disciplines have a legitimate, but by no means exclusive, role to play in such an endeavour.

In searching for causes, we hope to identify both the "what" that has gone wrong and, if possible, the "why" and "how"; we also hope to find ways of putting it right or preventing it happening. And in this search, the medical researcher is not limited to physical processes reducible to an abnormality definable in static terms such as morbid anatomy, a particular numerical quantity of a physical substance or score on a test, or the presence or absence of a toxic agent. The methods of behavioural science and new technologies promise the possibility of being able to define abnormalities in more dynamic or systemic terms, such as defects of learning or information processing, weight regulation or control of satiety.

In the absence of such reproducible findings, the diagnoses of psychopathological syndromes themselves can assume causal significance, so that to state that somebody suffers from a defined eating disorder can be taken to offer a causal explanation, of a kind, for particular aspects of behaviour. In the case of anorexia nervosa, for instance, attribution of the syndrome allows prediction of more-than-averagely probable concomitants, such as interest in preparing food, stealing or the presence of lanugo hair growth. We should not overlook, therefore, the explanatory and predictive power which can be provided by the clear delineation of clinical syndromes, a task in which Russell's contribution stands pre-eminent.

In designating the "eating disorders" as qualitatively different from normal variants of human behaviour, we have to identify our reasons for choosing this approach in preference to other more "normalising" ones which have become popular, for instance, among some feminist writers and social historians. Epidemiological enquiries into the occurrence of milder in-between cases, or *formes frustes*, in different populations may be helpful here, but the presence of discontinuities in the occurrence of health-endangering behaviour is not, of course, enough to justify the application of the "medical model". People either do or do not go hang-gliding, for instance, but we do not often have to seek "medical" causes for the behaviour of those who do.

The crucial difference in kind between the motivation of such behaviour and some types of eating disorder may lie in our suspicion that in the latter something has gone wrong with, or has taken over, the normal freedoms of autonomous choice, to the extent that we see something qualitatively different *happening* to a person. This may perhaps be represented by a discontinuity in some aspect of functioning which cannot be represented simply as an extreme case, but the outstanding characteristic which makes us look for medical rather than purely psychosocial explanations may lie more in our sense of some fundamental change in the normally understandable relationship between a person's choice of actions and the intentional predispositions and strategies which we comprehend as part of their usual personality. The person appears to have moved, to at least a significantly disabling degree, away from the role of free agent towards that of physically and mentally afflicted victim. As evidence of this change in the mental realm, we see the form and quality of their beliefs and attitudes to have undergone a change, from the expression of preferences and choices towards obsessive preoccupation, with or without retention of insight, and sometimes even towards delusion. Intuitive understanding of their actions becomes less easily and less generally available (although still claimed by some) and we may recognise a need to move beyond the quest for empathic comprehension towards the need for scientific explanation, or in Jaspers' (1963) terms, from *verstehen* towards a need for *erklären*.

What makes this change of focus so exceptionally perplexing in some instances of eating disorders, and especially anorexia nervosa, may be the patient's apparent insistence on the freedom, autonomy and necessity of their actions, to an extent which may seem appallingly incongruous with realities perceived by other observers and with the lamentable effects of their behaviour on physical functioning and well-being. Something, indeed, seems to have gone mysteriously and devastatingly wrong—and many patients become able to tell us so, acknowledging their own sense of being in the grip of motivational forces and preoccupations which they cannot, or dare not, resist.

CAUSES FOR WHAT—AND FOR WHAT PURPOSE?

A causal explanation is required to answer questions of "why?" and "how?", and such an explanation can take many forms, according to the purpose it serves, which may range from scientific elucidation to the requirements for better public health policy. We are unlikely to be able to find answers to every such question and, of course, the more questions we answer, the more will be raised. What we seek here are explanatory models or theories which lead us from particular instances to more general laws, models or theories in a productive and meaningful way, allowing us to develop further testable hypotheses about, say, amelioration and the prediction of onset and course. In the case of the major functional psychoses, therapeutic success with medicinal agents has strongly encouraged physical theories of causation. Such questionable logic could not apply in the case of the eating disorders until recent claims of successful treatment of bulimia with antidepressant drugs.

What particular questions of "why?" and "how?" are we trying to answer? In the case of anorexia nervosa, as defined by Russell in 1970, we need causal explanations of three types of phenomenon and their concurrence, namely, a hormonal disturbance, a psychological disturbance, and behaviour limiting calorie-intake and leading to severe loss of weight. In the case of the bulimic disorders, classification may have crucial implications, since if we do not demand the occurrence (at some time) of associated features found in anorexia nervosa, we may be looking for explanations primarily of particular attitudes and behaviour patterns and their physiological consequences without the requirement, necessarily, of viewing physiological deviations from normal body function as primary determinants. It could be, for instance, that bulimics are, in a sense, "failed" or "spared" anorexics—people for whom the behaviour which in some constitutionally susceptible people triggers anorexia nervosa cannot, or can no longer, lead on to the development or maintenance of the anorexic syndrome of emaciation and hormonal impairment. Compared with anorexia nervosa, bulimic behaviour might be more a "normal" compensatory response to attempts at limitation of food intake which, in a more limited number of physically susceptible subjects, may progress to anorexia nervosa.

At first sight, a medical type of explanation, in the sense of identifying something that has gone "wrong" about the mental and physical functioning of a person, seems more likely to be appropriate and necessary in the syndrome of anorexia nervosa, with its prominent hormonal disorder (which provides the qualitatively abnormal occurrence of amenorrhoea and thereby simplifies classification), than in non-anorexic bulimic disorders. But even in anorexia nervosa a medical explanation, with its incorporation of a biological, physical strand in its approach to aetiology, may be regarded as unnecessary if we can reduce the three defining criteria to a primarily psychological or psychosocial focus which can be envisaged as a central organising determinant of the whole syndrome, such as Gull's (1874) "morbid mental state", or Lasègue's (1873) "perversion mentale", Bruch's (1974) characterisation of the essential elements of primary anorexia nervosa, Crisp's (1967) weight phobia or Minuchin et al's (1978) systemic model of the "psychosomatic" family. All such characterisations appear to relegate the hormonal disturbance to a secondary role.

This leads inevitably to the question of whether anorexia nervosa is "psychogenic" in origin. Familiar as such questions are in psychiatry, it is complicated, in the case of anorexia nervosa, by some unusual features of the disorder. On the one hand is the fact that diagnosis has always depended on there being, at some time, gross physical disorder in the form of emaciation, a hormonal disturbance (in postpubertal subjects) and perhaps other visible physical abnormalities such as bradycardia and lanugo hair growth. On the other is the fact that the sufferer may appear to be acting (albeit very strangely and at great physical risk) in a consciously deliberate and purposive way, perhaps without any complaint or admission of distress. Denial of illness, to the extent even of overt antagonism in response to enquiries about any reasons for the behaviour, may make it extremely difficult, at least initially, for an observer to understand the nature of the sufferer's subjective experience.

PSYCHOGENESIS

With regard to anorexia nervosa, Crisp (1965) explained what was to be understood by a "psychogenic" approach:

> Many workers have assumed that the disorder is psychogenically determined. That is, that the development of the disorder, together with much of the overtly abnormal behaviour, is primarily organised at the level of an abnormal psychological and conceptual attitude, probably acquired during development.

A fundamental difficulty in any theory of psychogenesis, as Sir Aubrey Lewis (1972) emphasised in his critical commentary on the concept, is the role played by individual susceptibility. Even if we relegate to second place genetic and other factors which may determine this susceptibility, and ignore for the moment the defining physical criteria of anorexia nervosa (as many authors, in their exploration of the mental origins of the syndrome, seem happy to do), we are left with grave difficulties in the case of the eating disorders because of uncertainties about the extent to which the abnormal mental attitude, inferred as the primary origin of the behaviour, is the cause of it rather than, say, a descriptive concept inferred from the behaviour it is intended to explain, or a mental concomitant or even consequence of the behaviour. We can seek parallels here with other types of habitual or compulsive behaviour, where we are likely to view the perpetrator's attitudes towards the need to continue the behaviour as largely consequent upon the behaviour itself (with or without the intermediacy of an addictive substance such as a psycho-active drug). Such a view has been cogently argued by Szmukler and Tantam (1984) in their discussion of anorexia nervosa as "starvation dependence", with many similarities to alcohol dependence. We are also familiar with circumstances in which we may, even without allegiance to psychoanalytic theories, regard the subject's attribution of conscious purpose to their behaviour as mere rationalisation; an example of this is provided by the explanation which a subject may give for carrying out an action suggested to them previously in a hypnotic trance. More generally, we are often ready to attribute to other people explanations for their behaviour in this form (e.g. X always sees things in psychoanalytic terms because he invested so much in undergoing psychoanalysis) even if we wholly repudiate such explanations for our own behaviour.

PHILOSOPHICAL ISSUES IN MENTAL CAUSATION

The issue of whether, and under what conditions, an attitude of mind can be said to be a cause of behaviour has been of interest to philosophers. Peters (1958) in his monograph *The Concept of Motivation* has suggested that what he calls "purposive rule-following behaviour" cannot be *sufficiently* explained in terms of causal mechanisms such as physiological changes, unconscious motives and the like. The latter may be *necessary* conditions for the behaviour to occur but can never be specified in adequate number to give a *sufficient* explanation. This sort of behaviour requires for its sufficient explanation answers to questions about the purpose the agent is pursuing. When the behaviour does not conform to accepted standards, it may still be possible to find a sufficient explanation in terms of the rule-following purposive model if the person manifesting the behaviour can be said to be acting rather than to be experiencing something happening to them. One then needs to ask why the "rules" the person is following are different from other peoples'. Purpose, Peters argues, is irreducible, and an explanation in terms of the rule-following purposive model represents a logical ceiling beyond which explanation cannot go. If, on the other hand, it seems that the person is not acting as a "true" agent (in the sense that they are not experiencing themselves as determining their actions) it may be appropriate to seek explanations of their rule-breaking behaviour in terms of causal mechanisms such as physiological disturbances, intervention of unconscious motives and so on.

A similar argument is developed further by Howard (1971) in a critical assessment of the deficiencies of behaviourist and psychodynamic models of explanation. Howard follows Davidson (1980) in proposing that the reason somebody gives for doing something may be regarded as the *cause* of his behaviour if he has a conscious predisposition to act in a particular way and if he has also a conscious belief that his particular action will fulfil a particular aim. By arguing that a person's reasons for actions constitute causes, and thereby defending an ancient and commonsense view against attack from other philosophers, Davidson (1980) does not suggest that these are the only kinds of causes for actions, but that they must be accepted as one particular kind of cause.

Applying this to anorexia nervosa, one would be able to say that a cause of a patient's not eating was her wish to get thin if (a) she said she *wanted* to get thin and *had the capacity to decide* to do this, and (b) she knew that by not eating she would get thin. If these conditions could be fulfilled, a sufficient explanation of her behaviour, at least initially, could only be given if her conscious purpose was specified and she knew what she was doing; all sorts of conditions might be necessary for her to have such an aim but they would not give *sufficient* cause of her behaviour. If one could not meet these conditions, the abnormal attitude inferred by a third party could not be regarded as a cause of her behaviour, but only as a description of it. If, on the other hand, the patient was able to verbalise her awareness of an abnormal attitude but did not regard herself as acting autonomously, then again the attitude could not be said to be the cause of her behaviour but only a subjective accompaniment of it.

It is, of course, possible and indeed likely that the degree of autonomy experienced by the eating-disordered patient may vary over time. She might well decide to lose weight or get thinner or stop eating high-calorific foods but not decide to develop anorexia nervosa or bulimia nervosa. The development of either of the latter syndromes might depend on other factors quite outside her conscious awareness or control, and it is possible that they could, in some circumstances, develop without a preceding period of deliberate dieting or avoidance of food intake. In the same way, in discussing the causes of why a person has been the victim of a car accident, we can distinguish, if the accident was not intended, the reasons why somebody was driving the car from the cause of the accident. The point, and the questions which may be begged about the voluntary or involuntary nature of food-avoidance, is strikingly illustrated in the reported instance of two female IRA hunger strikers (sisters) who developed anorexia nervosa while in prison and who were subsequently released on medical grounds. In such an instance, it might appear that avoidance of eating, which was initially motivated in both sisters by a primary desire to proclaim a political statement, progressed to anorexia nervosa.

These philosophical problems are not simply metaphysical ones inaccessible to empirical examination. Throughout the literature on anorexia nervosa, there is considerable ambivalence about the degree of autonomy attributed to the anorexic patient. Bruch (1974) has described the illness as analogous to hunger strikes in political detainees and defined it as "pursuit of thinness", a formulation which emphasises the purposiveness of the behaviour. Other authors, however, emphasise non-purposiveness, by envisaging the patient as a sufferer, for instance as a victim of a "weight phobia" (Crisp, 1967) rather than an agent, and other parts of Bruch's formulation, such as the hypothesis of a distorted body image, appear to take this stance. In hunger strikes, a sufficient explanation of the behaviour could most readily be obtained by asking the striker why he was doing it, although all sorts of other conditions besides his own conscious motives might be necessary conditions for his behaving in this way (such as family environment, genetic constitution etc.). But is this analogy valid? To what extent can the patient with anorexia nervosa or bulimia nervosa be said to be autonomously and deliberately pursuing a consciously perceived aim? While various experimental approaches have demonstrated the anorexic's ability to modify behaviour in response to consciously perceived cues about the calorific value of food, body size and weight (Russell et al, 1973), other observers have sought to identify perceptual distortions of so-called body image in an attempt to characterise something that has gone "wrong" about the way that the anorexic perceives herself or other people.

THE LIMITATIONS OF PSYCHOGENIC MODELS

A fundamental problem about accepting a primarily psychological model of causation in anorexia nervosa may lie in the possible occurrence of hormonal changes leading to amenorrhoea before significant weight loss, or the probability of occurrence of amenorrhoea at an earlier stage in the progression of the disorder than would be predicted from the effects of calorie-limitation alone. To some observers, such an occurrence is seen as no more than a response to "stress" and equated with the amenorrhoea observed in other responses to stressful situations. In this way it is envisaged as a process which, though possibly requiring an explanation in terms of individual susceptibility and physiology, is not seen as holding centre-stage in the development of anorexia nervosa itself. To others, it argues for a more necessary role for a disturbance of physical mechanisms in cerebral function. The latter possibility is also supported by accounts of physical lesions, such as hypothalamic tumours, being associated with the development of anorexia nervosa-like syndromes.

But are there any elements of mental attitude which can be elicited in all patients who will speak about their concerns, other than, stated most broadly, an overwhelming preoccupation with the ingestion of food, a remarkably determined "anti" attitude towards ingesting food and/or gaining weight and/or increasing physical bulk and, perhaps, a "pro" attitude towards limitation of calorie-intake and/or weight loss and/or slimness? More specifically, is it possible to distinguish patients with these disorders from other members of the population who show heightened concern about eating, weight and body bulk, solely on physiological or social criteria? Such concerns may be very susceptible to cultural influences which change over time (as Russell argues in this volume) and may not be the necessary causes we may hope to find, any more than, say (referring back to Rosen's example quoted earlier), being a soldier in the Napoleonic wars was a necessary cause of neurosyphilis.

Some patients conform closely to the illuminating descriptions provided by Bruch and Crisp; others seem to belong to the kind of dysfunctional families described by Minuchin—and so on, but there are some who do not. Some can verbalise extensively and at times with a wealth of affecting detail and insight about their inner conflicts, while others speak little or nothing about it or confront the problem with steadfast denial. Some seek medical help for associated physical complications but resolutely deny that their conscious decisions about eating are the cause. Some describe a heightened sense of self-worth and well-being when in control of their eating and/or weight and/or bodily size, but others describe no such satisfaction. Some protest at their affliction, possibly to the extent of suicidal intent, and some deny it. Some express unpleasant feelings of heightened satiety after eating small amounts, while others admit to ravenous hunger. Some protest they are too fat when they are clearly very underweight, while others appear perfectly aware of how thin they are. Some show markedly obsessional or depressive features, but others do not. These variations occur not only between patients but may also occur in the same patient over the course of time.

Many patients who undergo a refeeding programme appear to undergo very profound changes for the better in attitude and behaviour, as their weight returns to normal limits, sometimes to the extent that they express a rediscovered zest for eating, social and sexual activity, a relative lack of concern about their weight or size, and a sense of surprise at their previous folly. Some do not show such changes, and a few become increasingly distressed as their weight returns towards normal levels. Many or even the majority of those who improve in response to refeeding programmes sooner or later relapse. The changes towards improvement resulting from refeeding are sometimes attributed to purely psychological and social processes, such as the abandonment of responsibility to others, or, more crudely put, the effects of "brain-washing". But they are great enough to make one wonder how much of the mental anguish discernible in anorexic patients when they are unwell can be attributed to the consequences of the weight loss and the accompanying changes in physiology.

THE SEARCH FOR EXPLANATION THROUGH NOSOLOGICAL RECATEGORISATION

Attempts to subsume anorexia nervosa and, less often, bulimia nervosa under other diagnostic categories of disorder has been a continuing strand in the literature of the eating disorders over the past 40 years. The list includes depressive illness, schizophrenia, obsessional neurosis, hysteria, personality disorders, self injury, dysmorphophobia, addictive behaviour, malingering, and culture-bound syndromes. Similar in kind, perhaps, are attempts to deny any peculiarly "medical" status to the eating disorders and instead to categorise them as understandable responses to the pressures which bear on all women to achieve socially-desirable body size and weight. Such models are seldom fully developed in a way which can provide a secure basis for the proposed recategorisation. Szmukler and Tantam's (1984) discussion of anorexia nervosa's similarities to addictive behaviour or starvation dependence is a striking exception. The important question highlighted by their elegant analysis concerns the nature of the addictive agent in anorexia nervosa. If we could find a way of identifying and describing such an agent or process (in terms, they suggest, of endorphins and the like) we could have found a necessary cause. Other attempts at recategorisation of the syndrome have not yielded such clear-cut aetiological hypotheses.

EQUATING EFFECTS WITH CAUSES

Common to several psychologically or socially oriented descriptions of the origins of anorexia nervosa is the description of the eating-disordered behaviour as motivated to communicate or otherwise to influence the immediate family or wider culture in particular ways. Some models are expressed in simple linear terms, such as emphasis on the fact that avoidance of weight gain has the possibly rewarding effect of delaying sexual maturation, while other employ more complex and explicitly systemic and cybernetic terms, such as Minuchin et al's (1978) family model, or Garner et al's (1982) multidimensional and Martin's (1990) multi-system models. Such models, which have in common the priority of an observer's *interpretation* of events, pose difficult problems of refutability, since they can, by virtue of their equation of effects with causes, be adapted to explain any situation. It is likely that such theories, which tend, in Freud's terminology, to equate *secondary gain* with *primary gain*, will survive in full vigour only as long as there are no advances in knowledge which either point to necessary causal processes distinct from effects of the illness and its associated behaviour or which offer more effective alleviation. Without such knowledge, this type of approach can have powerful appeal for the therapist, whose hermeneutic potency is greatly enhanced by it. Patient and family may be in such desperate plight that they will grasp at theories which emphasise their own potency as controlling agents in the tragedy which embroils them, or they may repudiate them as false and cruelly wrong. If further knowledge of an aetiology of eating disorders emerges, it is likely that such theories of causation will recede in significance to the status of secondary, aggravating or maintaining factors, as are important in all illnesses and disability, rather than continuing to have primary status.

THE COGNITIVE APPROACH

The emergence of cognitive approaches to psychiatric disorders and their treatment during the past 25 years has brought a re-emergence of interest in communicable thought processes; the patient has recovered an aspect of mental life which had been all but banished by previously predominant psychodynamic and behaviourist models. Delineation of the cognitive processes of patients with eating disorders (e.g. Fairburn, 1985) and the extent to which the patient's behaviour can be understood as consistent with their cognitive structure is likely to be an interesting area for research. Any successful approach to treatment is likely to have to engage the cognitive processes of the patient, at the very least to try to gain their cooperation. The task for theories of aetiology and pathogenesis, however, needs to go further, to explore how and why these cognitive structures develop.

SO WHAT COULD A CAUSAL THEORY LOOK LIKE?

To attempt to answer the question this chapter poses, there is little to be gained from criticising the theories so far proposed to account for the phenomena of eating disorders, which will be discussed with much greater detail and clarity elsewhere in this volume. The short answer must be that we do not yet know, and there does not appear to be much agreement about what we are looking for. The literature offers little sense of a strategic approach towards developing explanatory models or of great progress. Much work appears fragmentary and lacking systematic examination of a developed theoretical model. What is discernible, however, is that the multiplicity of approaches to studying the eating disorders reflects the current variety within, and tensions between, the kinds of descriptive and would-be explanatory models currently popular in psychiatry and the wider mental health field, ranging from the predominantly physical to the predominantly social and psychological, with the prominence also of current preoccupations about the abused role of women within male-dominated western society. It is also likely that the eating disorders attract greater public interest at a time when concerns about diet and health (among other social and economic factors) lead to the selection and ingestion of food in the developed world being increasingly seen as a matter of conscious choice rather than a process of less self-aware and more automatic regulation by physiological processes or by economic necessity. One may be tempted to view the increasing recognition of eating disorders as being one of the morbid consequences of the freedom (or social pressure) to choose what and how much one eats.

Progress in epidemiology can offer important clues. I think we are likely to find growing confirmation that a variety of bulimic disorders are increasing in incidence and can be correlated with adoption of western cultural ideals about slimness but that anorexia nervosa is likely to be increasing in incidence less markedly.

Changes in the frequency and popularity of dieting behaviour provides a possible link between the occurrence of eating disorders and temporal and cultural patterns of incidence. We need to find answers to questions about why it is that dieting behaviour appears to have, in some susceptible individuals, such a catastrophic triggering effect in reversing or delaying the processes of puberty, together with profound effects on the control of eating and satiety and on the attitudes and emotions of the sufferer. In some people, the mechanisms of pubertal development and control of eating are perhaps so unstable, at least at particular times, that dieting is not a necessary preliminary to development of a syndrome of eating disorder. The nature of the genetic predisposition has still to be elucidated.

If we are to find necessary causal processes, it seems unlikely that an aetiological account will achieve general acceptance unless it can be specified in testable scientific terms. Many factors, including a wide range of the psychological, social and physical factors so far studied, are likely to contribute more to our understanding of probabilities as regards the predisposition to develop such disorders and the factors which favour or impede recovery, but no description has yet identified a necessary causal element which can give greater coherence to the multiple defining factors by which the eating disorders are operationally defined. While it may be possible to identify many pressures and reasons which make young women and other people want to control their food intake, weight and body shape to a degree which may adversely affect their health and survival, the syndrome of anorexia nervosa has about it a continuing mystery and unfathomability which defies understanding or explanation by present-day knowledge. The patients may, for the most part, start out as agents, exercising conscious choice in an attempt to resolve a personal source of distress, but they become terribly afflicted victims of an often-incurable illness whose causes still elude clarification.

A Personal Note

The professional persona of every psychiatrist is likely to be largely made up of introjected models from people who have acted as influential teachers and mentors. Gerald Russell has been such a model for many generations of students and trainees. The inspiration he gave, during the seven years I spent in his unit at the Maudsley and the Royal Free, has set a standard always to aspire to, as a great clinician and teacher, as a doggedly determined and clear-thinking researcher, as an inspiring and courageous leader, as a man who shows great kindness and endless forbearance to patients, and a generosity and loyalty to colleagues I have never seen surpassed.

It is now 13 years since I moved from the field of eating disorders to more general psychiatry, but the experience of working with Gerald Russell's unit and his severely afflicted patients left an indelible experience. The questions posed by the eating disorders, which Gerald Russell's work has done so much to clarify and delineate clinically, have stayed with me as enduring enigmas with a wide bearing on questions about the ways our profession approaches questions of aetiology and pathogenesis, and the way it relates to other disciplines in the mental health field, including the "anti-psychiatry" movement. More specifically, it has given me a continuing awareness of the occurrence of eating disorders in many settings, in forms often milder than the ones I saw in Gerald Russell's units, and previously undiagnosed. After working in a specialist anorexia nervosa unit, the world (and not least a performance of classical ballet) can never be seen through quite the same eyes again.

REFERENCES

Birnbaum, K. (1923). *Der Aufbau der Psychose*. Berlin: Springer. Pages 1–46 translated by H. Marshall in *Themes and Variations in European Psychiatry* (eds. S.R. Hirsch and M. Shepherd), 1974, pp. 199–238; Bristol: John Wright & Sons.

Bruch, H. (1974). *Eating Disorders: Obesity, Anorexia Nervosa, and the Person Within*. New York: Basic Books.

Crisp, A.H. (1965). Clinical and therapeutic aspects of anorexia nervosa: a study of 30 cases. *Journal of Psychosomatic Research*, **9**, 67.

Crisp, A.H. (1967). The possible significance of some behavioural correlates of weight and carbohydrate intake. *Journal of Psychosomatic Research*, **11**, 117–131.

Davidson, D. (1980). Actions, reasons and causes. Chap. 1 in *Essays on Actions and Events*. Oxford: Clarendon Press.

Edlund, M.J. (1986). Causal models in psychiatric research. *British Journal of Pscychiatry*, **148**, 713–717.

Fairburn, C.G. (1985). Cognitive–behavioural treatment for bulimia. In: *Handbook on Psychotherapy for Anorexia Nervosa and Bulimia* (eds. D.M. Garner and P.E. Garfinkel), pp. 160–192. New York: Guilford Press.

Garner, D., Garfinkel, P. and Bemis, K. (1982). A multidimensional psychotherapy for anorexia nervosa. *International Journal of Eating Disorders*, **1**, 1–46.

Gull, W.W. (1874). Anorexia nervosa (apepsia hysterica, anorexia hysterica). *Trans Clin. Soc. London*, **7**, 22–28.

Howard, C. (1971). A conceptual enquiry into dynamic and behaviouristic explanations in psychiatry. Dissertation for M. Phil. (Psychiatry), Institute of Psychiatry, University of London.

Jaspers, K. (1963). *General Psychopathology*, 7th edn., transl. J. Hoenig and M.W. Hamilton, 1963, p. 302. Manchester: Manchester University Press.

Krafft-Ebing, R. von (1877). Zur Kenntniss des paraltischen Irreseins beim weiblichen Geschlecht. *Archiv für Psychiatrie und Nervenkrankheiten*, **7**, 182–188.

Laségue, C. (1873). De l'anorexie hysterique. *Archives Générales de Médecine*, **21**, 385–403.

Lewis, A. (1972). "Psychogenic": a word and its mutations. *Psychological Medicine*, **2**, 209–215.

Martin, F.E. (1990). The relevance of a systemic model for the study and treatment of anorexia nervosa in adolescents. *Canadian Journal of Psychiatry,* **35**, 496–500.

Minuchin, S., Rosman, B.L. and Baker, L. (1978). *Psychosomatic Families: Anorexia Nervosa in Context.* Cambridge, Mass.: Harvard University Press.

Peters, R. (1958). *The Concept of Motivation.* London: Methuen Monographs.

Rosen, G. (1968). *Madness in Society: Chapters in the Historical Sociology of Mental Illness.* Chicago: University of Chicago Press.

Russell, G.F.M. (1970). Anorexia nervosa: its identity as an illness and its treatment. In: *Modern Trends in Psychological Medicine*, Vol. 2 (ed. J. Harding Price), pp. 131–164. London: Butterworth.

Russell, G.F.M. (1977). Editorial: the present status of anorexia nervosa. *Psychological Medicine,* **7**, 363–367.

Russell, G.F.M. (1979). Bulimia nervosa: an ominous variant of anorexia nervosa. *Psychological Medicine,* **9**, 429–448.

Russell, G.F.M., Campbell, P.G. and Slade, P.D. (1973). Awareness of body dimensions in anorexia nervosa: cross-sectional and longitudinal studies. *Psychoneuroendocrinology,* **1**, 45–56.

Russell, G.F.M. and Treasure, J. (1989). The modern history of anorexia nervosa: an interpretation of why the illness has changed. *Annals of the New York Academy of Sciences,* **575**, 13–30.

Sartorius, N. (1988). International perspectives of psychiatric classification. *British Journal of Psychiatry,* **152** (Suppl. 1), 9–14.

Szmukler, G.I. and Tantam, D. (1984). Anorexia nervosa: starvation dependence. *British Journal of Medical Psychology,* **57**, 303–310.

4

Genetic Factors in Eating Disorders

JANET TREASURE
Institute of Psychiatry, London, UK
AND
ANTHONY HOLLAND
University of Cambridge, UK

INTRODUCTION

There is nothing new in the idea that genetic factors are relevant in anorexia nervosa. Earlier clinicians made comments about the family of origin. Marce, in 1860, wrote that "hypochrondriacal delirium", a condition we now recognise as anorexia nervosa, occurred in young subjects who were "predisposed to insanity from hereditary antecedents" (quoted in Silverman, 1989). Sir William Gull (1873) later observed that there was often "something queer in the family history". Ryle, an English physician 50 years later reporting on his personal experience of 51 cases, also observed a higher incidence of nervousness in the immediate family (Ryle, 1936). Subsequently there have been many reports of eating disorders amongst family members with reports of approximately 6–7% of sisters also being affected (Theander, 1970; Crisp, Hall and Holland, 1985; Morgan and Russell, 1975).

Standard methods used to determine the genetic contribution to aetiology are to determine prevalence rates in family pedigrees, in adoptees and their families, concordance rates between MZ and DZ twins, and finally linkage analysis. In this chapter we will review all of these methods in the context of eating disorders.

Handbook of Eating Disorders: Theory, Treatment and Research.
Edited by G. Szmukler, C. Dare and J. Treasure.
© 1995 John Wiley & Sons Ltd.

THE FAMILIAL NATURE OF EATING DISORDERS

A history of anorexia nervosa within the family is occasionally seen in clinical practice. The family tree of one such subject who presented to our clinic is shown in Figure 4.1. In this case many of the male line were doctors which may have facilitated recognition and diagnosis of the condition. Although the diagnosis of anorexia nervosa was not made on the grandmother of another of our patients, the family recognised the similarities and brought in this photograph to prove their case (Figure 4.2).

Several systematic family genetic studies have been reported. The findings on probands with anorexia nervosa or the mixed diagnosis of anorexia nervosa and bulimia nervosa are shown on Table 4.1. Those from probands with bulimia nervosa are shown in Table 4.2. We have displayed the results from the two diagnostic groups separately, but as we discussed below this is subject to errors. Although the majority of these studies had a comparison group, only in Rastam's study was there an attempt to match the groups accurately.

The demographic features and the ascertainment of the samples have varied and this needs to be taken into account when the results are being compared. In some

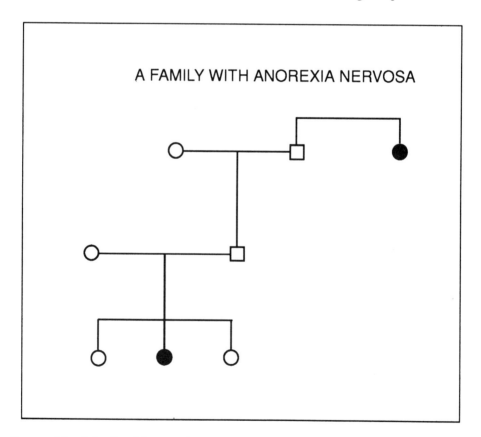

FIGURE 4.1   A family with anorexia nervosa.

FIGURE 4.2 Photograph taken in 1935 of the grandmother of a patient attending our clinic in 1990. The photograph was taken when the grandmother was aged 15 and her weight had fallen to 5st 12lb (37kg). The current patient's family recognised the similarities between the grandmother's teenage illness and her granddaughter's current symptoms.

samples such as those of Rastam (1990) and Strober et al (1985, 1990) a young sample was used, in the early stages of the course of their illness. It is uncertain how many, with time, would continue to be classified as anorexia nervosa. [This failure to account for the longitudinal course is a weakness of our current diagnostic criteria. Russell's criteria for bulimia nervosa included a prodromal phase of "cryptic anorexia nervosa" or anorexia nervosa but this is no longer included in ICD-10 or DSM-III-R criteria. The Swedish cohort, from a community survey, contains many cases detected before presentation to medical services. The course of the illness was prospectively followed and almost 60% of this young-onset sample developed bulimic symptoms within two years of developing anorexia. This proportion is much higher than in older series of anorexia nervosa where it lies between 7% and 40% (Herzog, Ratner and Vandereycken, 1992). Thus if a longitudinal perspective is taken this sample would include cases of both anorexia

TABLE 4.1   Eating disorders amongst relatives of probands with anorexia nervosa.

Author	Proband diagnosis:number Ascertainment	Diagnosis and rates in first degree relative (%) or other specified relation	Diagnosis and rates in relatives of controls (%)
Strober et al (1985)	AN:60 Clinic	AN:1.1 BN:1.5 Any ED:5.3	AN:0.2 BN:0.5 Any ED:0.7
Gershon et al (1984)*	AN + AN/BN:24 Clinic	AN:1.8† BN:4.0†	AN:0† BN:1.1†
Strober et al (1990)*	AN:97 Clinic	AN:4 BN:3	AN:0 BN:0.7 (comparison group relatives of probands with depression)
Halmi et al (1991)*	AN:57 Inpatients	BN:2 (mothers) EDNOS:1 (mothers)	BN:0 (mothers) EDNOS:0 (mothers)
Rastam (1990)	AN:51 Clinic and community sample	AN behaviour (mother):6 BN:0 Overweight:25 (mother)	AN behaviour (mother):2 BN behaviour:2 Overweight:12 (mother)
Treasure and Holland*	AN:58 Clinic and volunteers	AN:3 BN:4.3 EDNOS:7 Obesity:6.3	–

* Family study method.   † Age-corrected (%).
EDNOS = eating disorder not otherwise specified.

nervosa and bulimia nervosa. Therefore this study will not be as useful to distinguish between premorbid factors of relevance for anorexia nervosa rather than bulimia nervosa (Rastam, 1992). Also, young samples and their sisters have not passed the age of risk for the development of an eating disorder and so many potential cases are undetected]. All of these studies found an increased rate of eating disorders amongst the first degree relatives of probands with either anorexia nervosa or bulimia nervosa. There is a remarkable similarity in the rates of eating disorder within the families given the various sources of ascertainment of the cases and the wide confidence limits resulting from limited sample sizes.

Female relatives of probands with anorexia nervosa have a ten-fold greater risk of developing an eating disorder than the control population (Strober et al, 1990). Bulimia nervosa is more common in the families of bulimia nervosa probands and the opposite is true for anorexia nervosa, suggesting that there is a specificity in the familial liability.

TABLE 4.2   Eating disorder diagnosis amongst relatives of probands with bulimia nervosa.

Author	Proband diagnosis:number Ascertainment	Diagnosis and rates in first degree relative (%)	Diagnosis rates in relatives of controls (%)
Keck et al (1990)	EDNOS:50	AN:2.6 BN:2.6 EDNOS:4.3	0
Keck et al (1990)*	BN:66 Clinic	AN:0.8 BN:2.4 EDNOS:1.2	
Kassett et al (1989)*	BN:40 Inpatients	AN:2.2 BN:9.6 All ED:	AN:0 BN:3.5 All ED:
Treasure and Holland	BN:38 Clinic and volunteers	AN:3.2 BN:4.3 EDNOS:7 Obesity:6.3	

* Morbid risk.

Strober and colleagues (1985) also found that the risk of anorexia nervosa was increased amongst second degree relatives. We have collected data on families with multiple cases of anorexia nervosa. Ten families had more than two affected members and spanned several generations (in one case four). Of the first degree relatives, in 10 cases the mother was affected, in three cases the father and in seven cases it was a sibling (one brother). Of the families who had more distant relatives affected, 10 were from the maternal line and 12 from the paternal line. Several interesting conclusions can be drawn from this. Firstly, equal numbers of cases were found in second degree relatives from both sides of the family, suggesting that the genotype can be passed through maternal or paternal lines. Secondly, in the majority of cases the phenotype is not expressed; for example, cases were seen in second and third degree relatives in families where first degree relatives were unaffected. Thirdly, the expression of the phenotype occurs more commonly in women and also in the family members of the same generation, with sisters being the most commonly affected family member.

Clustering of an illness within families is necessary if a proposed trait is to be considered genetic, but it is not enough. Family studies do not discriminate between inherited factors and environmentally transmitted factors. Twin or adoption studies are needed to distinguish these hypotheses.

TWIN STUDIES

For a twin study to provide useful information many methodological problems have to be overcome. Zygosity must be determined with accuracy. The results must be sufficiently representative of the total population of twins and not subject to bias.

Problems arise when using twin methods for disorders as rare as anorexia nervosa. It is difficult for any centre to build up a large enough consecutive series of twins, free from selection bias. If twins are specifically recruited it tends to bias the sample in favour of monozygotic and concordant pairs. There are also problems if the phenotype is not fully expressed, as is the case in anorexia nervosa. Males are less likely to express the phenotype and so many twin studies have been restricted to samples of female twins. Ideally data should be collected and analysed after the period at risk for developing the illness has passed. This is not a major difficulty for patients with eating disorders as the peak of age of onset is in early adolescence.

Case reports of anorexia nervosa in twins have appeared (Garfinkel and Garner, 1982; Vandereycken and Pierloot, 1981; Askevold and Heiberg, 1979; Nowlin, 1983; Scott, 1986). Often the subjects are a mixture of twins seen by the authors and those reported in the literature. There is also a case report of monozygotic twins concordant for bulimia (Kaminer, Feingold and Lyons, 1988). It is difficult to draw conclusions from these idiographic studies and reviews because of possible reporting bias and unreliable methods of determining both zygosity and the co-twin's diagnosis.

Twin Studies in Anorexia Nervosa

In a study by the authors, collaboration between two regional centres with specialised eating disorder units meant that a large sample of twins were recruited without gross selection bias (Holland et al, 1984; Crisp et al, 1985). Thirty-four pairs of twins and a set of triplets were described. Of the 30 (female only) pairs, 9 out of 16 (55%) MZ pairs were concordant for anorexia nervosa whereas only one out of 14 (7%) DZ pairs was concordant. This significant difference in the concordance rate suggested that genetic factors contributed to anorexia nervosa. However, structured interviews to ascertain the form of the eating disorder were not used and only in 18 pairs were both sisters seen.

In a later study this sample was re-interviewed and further cases added. The concordance rates from this sample and from other reported series are shown on Table 4.3.

Significant differences between the proportions of MZ and DZ pairs concordant for anorexia nervosa can be attributed to genetic factors. The difference is greater when the diagnostic criteria are narrowed to restricting anorexia nervosa.

Twin Studies of Bulimia Nervosa

Concordance rates from published twin studies of bulimia nervosa and data from our own twin study are shown in Table 4.4. The ascertainment procedures used to obtain these samples varied. Even the large study of Kendler et al (1991) may be subject to some biases because, although the population was collected from a large population twin register, participation in the research was, of course, voluntary. All of the other studies came from clinic populations or were volunteers. There are also diagnostic differences between the studies. Three-quarters of our own sample

TABLE 4.3 Twin concordance rates for anorexia nervosa.

Sample	Diagnosis	Concordance rate		Difference* (SE) 95% CI
		MZ	DZ	
Vandereycken and Pierloot (1981) (Literature review)	Broad AN	0.30 (6/20)		
	Narrow AN	0.33 (3/9)		
Nowlin (1983) (Literature review)	AN	0.43 (9/21)	0.00 (0/2)	
Schepank (1992)	Core AN	0.57 (4/7)	0.00 (0/7)	
	Total AN	0.57 (8/14)	0.09 (1/11)	
Treasure and Holland		0.43 (16/37)	0.06 (2/31)	0.36(0.09) 0.18–0.56
	AN + BN			
	AN	0.45 (14/31)	0.07 (2/28)	0.37(0.1) 0.18–0.58
	Restricting AN	0.65 (11/17)	0.00 (0/12)	0.64(0.12) 0.42–0.87

* Difference between the proportion of concordant MZ and DZ pairs, and 95% confidence intervals (CI) of the difference.

fulfilled Russell's original criteria for bulimia nervosa as they had had a previous episode of anorexia nervosa. Only 10% of the study of Kendler et al (1991) fulfilled these criteria.

The differences between the proportions of MZ and DZ twins concordant for bulimia nervosa was less marked than was found in anorexia nervosa. Even in the best study in terms of size and unbiased ascertainment, that of Kendler et al (1991), the difference between the concordance rates of monozygotic and dizygotic samples did not reach significance. This rather crude analysis indicates that genetic factors are of less relevance than they are for anorexia nervosa. In our series we found that as the diagnosis was narrowed to that of Russell's original criteria, that is with a prior history of anorexia nervosa, then the differences in concordance rate increased.

The concordance rate for both twin types substantially exceeded the population risk, which indicates that familial factors are of relevance. Kendler and colleagues used more sophisticated model fitting procedures to analyse their data. A model which excluded any familial resemblance could be rejected. However a model which included additive genetic factors fitted the data better than one containing common environmental factors alone. The authors state:

> Model fitting results therefore need to be interpreted with caution. Although we do find evidence consistent with genetic influences on risk for bulimia, the evidence against an effect of familial-environmental factors is relatively weak.

72

TABLE 4.4 Twin concordance rates for bulimia nervosa.

Authors	Ascertainment (% co-twins seen)	Zygosity	Diagnosis	Concordance rate		Difference* (SE) 95% CI
				MZ	DZ	
Hsu et al (1990)	Clinic + volunteer (54%)	Questionnaire	Broad BN	0.33 (2/6)	0.00 (0/5)	0.33(0.19) (−0.04–0.71)
Fichter and Noegel (1990)	Clinic + volunteer (Self-report)	Physical similarity	Broad BN	1.00 (6/6)	0.33 (5/15)	0.67(0.12) (0.42–0.9)
			Narrow BN	0.83 (5/6)	0.26 (4/15)	0.56(0.19) (0.19–0.94)
Kendler et al (1991)	Register (91%)	Physical similarity	Broad BN	0.26 (18/69)†	0.16 (8/50)†	0.10(0.07) (−0.04–0.25)
			Narrow BN (9% PH AN)	0.23 (8/35)†	0.09 (2/23)†	0.14(0.08) (−0.04–0.25)
Treasure and Holland	Clinic (100%)	Blood group	Broad BN	0.35 (6/17)	0.26 (5/19)	0.09(0.15) (−0.2–0.39)
			Narrow BN	0.35 (5.14)	0.29 (5.17)	0.06(0.17) (−0.27–0.39)
			Russell's criteria (100% PH AN)	(6/12) 50%	(1/17) 6%	0.44(0.15) (0.14–0.74)

* Difference between the MZ and DZ concordance rates, and 95% confidence intervals (CI). † Probandwise concordance rate. PH AN = past history of anorexia nervosa.

From our own series we would argue that the larger discrepancy between the proportion of monozygotic as compared with the dizygotic pairs concordant for anorexia nervosa as opposed to bulimia nervosa suggests that genetic factors are of more relevance in the aetiology of anorexia nervosa than of bulimia nervosa. However, we acknowledge that the twin sample upon which these conclusions is drawn is small and subject to bias. It would take a study ten times the size of that of Kendler et al (1991) with 10–20 thousand twin pairs to obtain enough power to analyse the importance of genetic factors in a community sample of anorexia nervosa. There is an added difficulty: in all of the epidemiological studies to date, which have used two-stage screening procedures, cases of anorexia nervosa appear to actively avoid participation. This would mean that all of these individuals would have to be interviewed — a mammoth, if not impossible, task.

Twin Studies in Context

The form of analysis described above is merely the starting point in the use of twins in the investigation of a putative aetiological factor. Once it has been established that genetic factors are involved, then the discordant monozygotic twin model can be used to investigate aetiological factors more carefully. As monozygotic twins share the same genetic vulnerability and many external similarities, they can be used to focus on the specific environmental determinants which can lead to the development of the illness. Also, monozygotic twins who have not expressed the phenotype may exhibit markers of the underlying genetic vulnerability.

Out of the 66 female twin pairs interviewed in our study, 13/37 (35%) MZ twins and 22/31 (68%) DZ twins were discordant for anorexia nervosa; i.e. one twin had anorexia nervosa and the other twin had no form of eating disorder. The discordant MZ twins had a later age of onset than either the concordant MZ pairs or the discordant DZ pairs. The first question which we addressed with this model was whether the genetic predisposition to anorexia nervosa is specific or whether the inherited trait is merely a non-specific, neurotic vulnerability. For example, it has been argued that anorexia nervosa is a variant of an affective or obsessive–compulsive disorder (Cantwell, Struzenberger and Burroughs, 1977; Rothenberg 1986). We found that unaffected co-twins had less psychiatric morbidity in comparison with the probands with anorexia nervosa (non-AN 9/35 (26%) versus AN 28/35 (80%); Fisher's $p=0.001$). The probands with anorexia nervosa had depression, panic disorder and alcohol abuse significantly more frequently than their unaffected co-twin. The additional psychiatric symptoms seen in anorexia nervosa are more likely to be a secondary feature rather than an underlying neurotic vulnerability. No differences were found between the proportion of MZ co-twins (2/13; 15%) and DZ cotwins (7/22; 32%) with additional psychiatric illness. Any trend is towards the unaffected MZ twins having less rather than more morbidity.

Not only did the unaffected twins have little in the way of overt psychiatric symptoms, but they also were free of more non-specific symptoms such as those measured on the Hopkins Symptom Checklist and the General Health Questionnaire. Also their self-esteem and neuroticism scores (from Eysenck's personality questionnaire) were within normal limits. All of these findings reject the proposition that anorexia nervosa develops in the context of a non-specific neurotic personality.

A higher proportion of affected twins had experienced perinatal difficulties compared with the unaffected twins (AN 12/35 (34%) versus non-AN 5/35 (14%); Fisher's exact test $p<0.04$). There were no significant differences between the proportions of affected and unaffected twins who were second-born; smaller at birth; smaller during childhood; or experienced a physical or neurotic illness during childhood.

Age at menarche did not differ between affected and unaffected twins. Age at first coitus did differ significantly (log rank test, df $= 1$, $p = 0.026$) between the unaffected MZ and unaffected DZ co-twins. It was not possible to compare the age of marriage as too small a proportion of the twins were married when assessed. However, there was the suggestion that a similar pattern of a delay in this stage of psychosexual development was present in the MZ co-twins (at the age of 24, 90% of the unaffected DZ co-twins were married in comparison with 66% of the unaffected MZ co-twins and 40% of the twins with anorexia nervosa).

The affected twins had experienced more severe life events prior to onset than had occurred in the lives of unaffected twins (AN 11/35 (31%) versus non-AN 3/35 (9%); Fisher's exact test $p<0.03$). Six of the 13 MZ discordant twin pairs had severe health events affecting other family members or themselves prior to onset (including husband who developed epilepsy; father with multiple injuries from road traffic accident; death of husband from cancer; mother's death; stillbirth; mother developing leukaemia and elder sister Hodgkin's disease).

Slade (1982) produced a functional analysis of anorexia nervosa. In it, he suggests that anorexia develops, within the context of "setting conditions", dissatisfaction and perfectionism, following a stressful event. He devised the Setting Conditions for Anorexia Nervosa (SCANS: Slade and Dewey, 1980) questionnaire to measure these factors. We found that the unaffected twins (and their affected sister with anorexia nervosa) had high perfectionism scores. Twelve of the 13 (92%) unaffected MZ co-twins and 20/22 (91%) of the unaffected DZ co-twins scored above the cutoff point. This suggests that the family context in which anorexia nervosa develops is one which engenders perfectionism.

Bruch (1962) suggested that body image disturbance was pathognomonic of anorexia nervosa, but this has been the subject of controversy (Hsu and Sobkiewicz 1989). We, however, found that the discordant MZ twins but not the DZ twins had high levels of body dissatisfaction. This suggests that genetic factors contribute in some way to the dissatisfaction.

LINKAGE STUDIES

It is unlikely that linkage studies in eating disorders will be pursued with enthusiasm at the present time. There is no obvious chromosomal region of interest, and there are few families with multiple cases. Also, the phenotypic expression is low. There have, however, been studies which have investigated the association between eating disorders and other psychopathology. The premise upon which such

TABLE 4.5 Lifetime rates of affective disorder amongst first degree relatives of probands with eating disorders in comparison with controls.

Author	Ascertainment	Proband diagnosis: number	Rate in first degree relative (%)	Rates in relatives of controls (%)
Strober et al (1982)	Clinic	AN,AN/BN:70	8.8	0
Gershon et al (1984)*	Tertiary clinic	AN,AN/BN:24	3‡	5.8‡
Rivinus et al (1984)	Tertiary clinic	AN,AN/BN:40	6‡	4.7‡
Biederman et al (1985)	Clinic	AN:38	6.25	4.7‡
Strober et al (1990)*†	Clinic	Total AN:97 AN + depression:28 AN nondepression:69	Total = 9 AN + depression:18 AN nondepression:5	20
Keck et al (1990)	Volunteers	DSM3B:50§ BN:66	39‡ 25‡	9‡
Kassett et al (1989)*	Clinic/inpatients	BN:40	28‡	8.8‡
Halmi et al (1991)	Clinic/inpatients	AN:52	5	4.5
Rastam (1990)	Community/clinics	AN:51	16	9

* Family study method. † The controls are probands with affective disorder. ‡ Morbid risk.
§ DSM3B = DSM-III bulimia criteria (APA, 1980).
BN criteria for buliminia nervosa (APA, 1987).
AN criteria for anorexia nervosa (APA, 1987).

studies rests is that eating disorders are variants of other psychiatric illness (see above) and that a non-specific genetic liability could explain the familial clustering. Some evidence for this proposition has been found in Table 4.5.

Women with bulimia nervosa have a significantly (3–4 fold) higher prevalence of affective disorder amongst their first degree relatives. The situation in anorexia nervosa remains more controversial. Strober and colleagues (1990) separated patients with anorexia nervosa into two groups, depressed and non-depressed. (In order to remove the confounding effects of starvation upon mood, only subjects who remained depressed at normal weight were included in the depressed group.) The depressed AN subgroup had a prevalence of affective disorder in their family similar to that found in the relatives of probands with affective disorders. On the other hand, the non-depressed anorexia nervosa subgroup (three-quarters of the sample) had fewer family members with affective disorders. In a second study Strober reversed the argument and examined whether the risk of anorexia nervosa was higher in the relatives of affective disorder probands; the result was negative. Thus the thesis that there is a shared genetic liability between anorexia nervosa and affective disorder would appear to be disproved, whereas this argument does have some validity for bulimia nervosa.

TABLE 4.6   Rates of alcoholism in first degree relatives of probands with eating disorders.

Author	Ascertainment	Proband diagnosis: number	Rate in first degree relative (%)	Rate in relatives of controls (%)
Strober et al (1982)	Clinic	AN, AN/BN:70	9.9	0
Rivinus et al (1984)	Clinic	AN, AN/BN:40	11.9‡	6.9‡
Keck et al (1990)	Clinic	DSM3:B:50 DSM3R:BN:66	20‡† 12‡	6.5‡
Kassett et al (1989)*	Inpatients	BN:40	28‡†	14‡
Rastam (1990)	Community/clinic	AN:51	4	3
Halmi et al (1991)	Inpatients	AN:52	5.3†	0.6

* Family study method. † Significantly different from controls. ‡ Morbid risk.
DSM3B = DSM-III criteria for bulimia (APA, 1980).
BN criteria for bulimia nervosa (APA, 1987).
AN criteria for anorexia nervosa (APA, 1987).

The possibility of a similar association between eating disorders and substance abuse has also been made and the results are given in Table 4.6. An excess of alcoholism in the families of both forms of eating disorder has been found.

Other Familial Factors

Links with other conditions have not been so widely examined. Interestingly, two studies suggest that there may be links between obsessive–compulsive disorder and eating disorder. Rastam and Gilberg (1990) found a higher incidence of OCD personality amongst mothers of cases of eating disorders (4 versus 1 in the control group). Halmi and colleagues (1991) found a similar increase in obsessive–compulsive disorders in the mothers of patients with anorexia nervosa. Psychosexual difficulties were also more common than in the comparison group.

Obesity was also found more commonly in the families of the series of Rastam (1990) (22 versus 8 in the comparison group). We found in incidence of obesity of 6% of the female first degree relatives, which is no higher than in the general population. Other studies have failed to find an increased incidence of obesity in anorexia nervosa (Kalucy, Crisp and Harding, 1977; Halmi, Struss and Goldberg, 1978). It is possible that diagnostic differences account for this disparity as the Swedish series contained many cases which quickly evolved into bulimia nervosa. Therefore a genetic tendency to obesity may be of more relevance for bulimia nervosa than for anorexia nervosa.

One study reported a higher frequency of HLA-Bw16 among patients with anorexia nervosa as compared with controls (Biederman et al, 1985). This finding has not been replicated but whether this is because others have failed to reproduce the finding or have not been motivated to try remains unknown. Cases of anorexia nervosa have been reported in association with Turner's syndrome, but the balance of evidence again is that it is probably a chance association (Darby et al, 1981). A recent case controlled study found no chromosomal or sex chromatin abnormalities among 47 anorexics (Rastam and Gillberg, 1990).

WHERE DO THESE STUDIES LEAD US?

It appears that anorexia nervosa and bulimia nervosa *are* disorders which run in families. At least part of the explanation for this is that genetic factors play a role. Our own twin data suggest that *specific* genetic factors are more important for AN than for BN. In the case of bulimia nervosa a more *general* predisposition with links with substance abuse, affective disorder and obesity is seen. The next stage is to consider what these findings mean. We need to interpret them in the light of the clinical features of the conditions. Are there any premorbid features which are markers of the genetic trait? Given that non-genetic factors have relevance for both AN and BN, what are the relevant environmental components? Do they differ between the two conditions? Are there quantitative differences between the two conditions?

What Could the Genetic predisposition be?

Although the pathophysiology of eating disorders may reveal clues as to the genetic diathesis, it is difficult to disentangle primary abnormalities from secondary consequences of weight loss and chaotic eating. No one design can totally overcome this problem.

The discordant twin model offers the potential to delineate both genetic and environmental factors and can be used to compliment case control studies. Are there any parallels between the findings from our discordant twins and from the most impressive case control study of anorexia nervosa, that of Rastam (1990)? The most outstanding similarity is perfectionism. In the Swedish study, a major difference between anorexia nervosa cases and controls was a higher level of premorbid perfectionism, with compulsive personality traits. In the discordant twins model we found high levels of perfectionist traits in the sisters without anorexia nervosa. Also Halmi et al (1991) found obsessive–compulsive disorder to be more common amongst the mothers of patients with anorexia nervosa. These findings suggest that perfectionism could be a vulnerability trait, a view that was expressed earlier by Strober (1991):

> The symptoms of anorexia nervosa can take hold and endure so assiduously only in individuals in whom the heritable tendencies of harm avoidance and low novelty seeking are present to a greater degree . . . Individuals who shun harm and novelty will characteristically mitigate feelings of threat by maintaining fixed, highly patterned and compulsively ritualised actions.

In other areas, the discordant twin data and the case control data diverge. For example, Rastam and Gillberg (1990) found higher levels of obesity and a greater incidence of severe gastrointestinal problems in childhood. We would argue that a history of obesity may be of more relevance to bulimia nervosa, and that the Swedish study, because of its time frame in early adolescence, does not distinguish cases of anorexia nervosa from those of bulimia nervosa. Obesity, dieting and weight fluctuations are major risk factors for bulimia nervosa (Patton et al, 1990; Kendler et al, 1991).

CONCLUSIONS

Specific genetic factors appear to be important in the aetiology of anorexia nervosa. We are far from knowing what this genetic trait could be. Could it account for perfectionist compulsive personality, or is this an additional risk factor? Are the abnormalities in 5HT, noradrenaline and CRH function—seen in patients who have "recovered" from anorexia nervosa—markers of the underlying genetic vulnerability (Kaye et al, 1991)? One model which could draw together these threads is that articulated by Cloninger (1987), who suggests that low novelty seeking, high harm avoidance and high reward dependence could be related to high levels of 5HT.

It is unlikely that a unique biological abnormality will be present in bulimia nervosa. The clinical presentation and the familial context are both much more heterogeneous than for anorexia nervosa.

ACKNOWLEDGEMENTS

We are grateful to the Mental Health Foundation and the Society for Research into Anorexia Nervosa for their support. We are also grateful to all the centres in the United Kingdom who helped us to recruit patients. Special thanks are due to Professor Gerald Russell and Professor Arthur Crisp.

REFERENCES

American Psychiatric Association (1987). *Diagnostic and Statistical Manual of Mental Disorders: DSM-III-R* (third edition revised). Washington, DC: APA.

Askevold, F. and Heiberg, A. (1979). Anorexia nervosa—two cases in discordant MZ twins. *Psychother. Psychosom., 32*, 223–228.

Bassoe, H.H. (1990). Anorexia/bulimia nervosa. The development of anorexia nervosa and of mental symptoms: treatment and the outcome of the disease. *Acta. Psychiatr. Scand., 82* (Suppl. 361), 7–13.

Biederman, J., Rivinus, T., Kemper, K., Hamilton, D., MacFayden, J. and Harmatz, J. (1985). Depressive disorders in relatives of anorexia nervosa patients with and without a current episode of nonbipolar major depression. *Am. J. Psychiat., 142*, 1495–1497.

Bisdee, J.T., James, W.P.T. and Shaw, M.A. (1989). Changes in energy expenditure during the menstrual cycle. *Br. J. Nutr., 61*, 187–199.

Bruch, H. (1962). Perceptual and conceptual disturbances in anorexia nervosa. *Psychosom. Med.,* **24**, 187.

Cantwell, D.P., Struzenberger, S. and Burroughs, J. (1977). Anorexia nervosa: an affective disorder? *Arch. Gen. Psychiat.,* **34**, 1030–1035.

Casper, R.C. (1990). Personality features of women with good outcome from restricting anorexia nervosa. *Psychosom. Med.,* **52**, 156–179.

Cloninger, C.R. (1987). A systematic method for clinical description and classification of personality variants. *Arch. Gen. Psychiat.,* **44**, 573–588.

Crisp, A.H. (1980). *Anorexia Nervosa: Let Me Be.* London: Plenum.

Crisp, A.H., Hall, A. and Holland, A.J. (1985). Nature and nurture in anorexia nervosa: a study of 34 pairs of twins, one pair of triplets and an adoptive family. *Int. J. Eating Dis.,* **4**, 5–27.

Darby, P.L., Garfinkel, P.E., Vale, J.M., Kirwan, P.J. and Brown, G.M. (1981). Anorexia nervosa and "Turner syndrom"; cause or coincidence? *Psychol. Med.,* **11**, 141–145.

Dourish, C.T., Kennett, G.A. and Curzon, G. (1987). The 5HT 1A agonist 8-0H-DPAt, buspirone and ipsaprone attenuate stress-induced anorexia in rats. *J. Psychopharm.,* **11**, 22–30.

Fichter, M.M. and Noegel, R. (1990). Concordance for bulimia nervosa in twins. *Int. J. Eating Dis.,* **9**, 255–263.

Garfinkel, P.E. and Garner, D.M. (1982). *Anorexia Nervosa: A Multidimensional Perspective.* New York: Brunner Mazel.

Gershon, E.S., Schreiber, J.L., Hamovit, J.R., Dibble, E.D., Kaye, W., Nurnberger, J.I., Andersen, A.E. and Ebert, M. (1984). Clinical findings in patients with anorexia nervosa and affective illness in their relatives. *Am. J. Psychiat.,* **141**, 1419–1422.

Gull, W. (1873). Proceedings of the Clinical Society of London. *Br. Med. J.,* **1**, 527–529.

Haleem, D.J. (1988). Seronoinergic functions in rat brain: sex related differences and responses to stress. PhD Thesis. University of London.

Haleem, D.J., Kennett, G.A. and Curzon, G. (1988). Adaptation of female rats to stress: shift to male pattern by inhibition of corticosterone synthesis. *Brain Res.,* **458**, 339–347.

Halmi, K.A., Stuss, A. and Goldberg, S.C. (1978). An investigation of weights in the parents of anorexia nervosa patients. *J. Nerv. Mental Dis.,* **166**, 358–361.

Halmi, A.K., Eckert, E., Marchi, P., Sampugnaro, V., Apple, R. and Cohen, J. (1991). Comorbidity of psychiatric diagnoses in anorexia nervosa. *Arch. Gen. Psychiat.,* **48**, 712–718.

Herzog, W., Ratner, G. and Vandereycken, W. (1992). Long-term course of anorexia nervosa: a review of the literature. In: *The Course of Eating Disorders* (ed. W. Herzog, H.C. Deter and W. Vandereycken), pp. 15–29. Berlin: Springer.

Holland, A.J., Murray, R., Russell, G.F.M. and Crisp, A.H. (1984). Anorexia nervosa: a study of 34 pairs of twins and one set of triplets. *Br. J. Psychiat.,* **145**, 414–419.

Hsu, L.K.G. and Sobkiewicz, T.A. (1989). Bulimia nervosa: a four-to-six-year follow-up study. *Psychol. Med.,* **19**, 1035–1038.

Hsu, L.K.G., Chesler, B.E. and Santhouse, M.S.W. (1990). Bulimia nervosa in eleven sets of twins: a clinical report. *Int. Rev. Eating Dis.,* **9**, 275–282.

Kalucy, R.S., Crisp, A.H. and Harding, B. (1977). A study of 56 families with anorexia nervosa. *Br. J. Med. Psychol.,* **50**, 381–395.

Kaminer, Y., Feingold, M. and Lyons, K. (1988). Bulimia in a pair of monozygotic twins. *J. Nerv. Mental Dis.,* **176**, 246–248.

Kassett, J.A., Gershon, E.S., Maxwell, M.E., Guroff, J.J., Kazuba, D.M., Smith, A.L., Brandt, H.A., and Jimerson, D.C. (1989). Psychiatric disorders in the first-degree relatives of probands with bulimia nervosa. *Am. J. Psychiat.,* **146**, 1468–1471.

Kaye, W.H., Gwirstman, H.E., George, D.T. and Ebert, M.H. (1991). Altered serotonin activity in anorexia nervosa after long-term weight restoration. *Arch. Gen. Psychiat.,* **48**, 556–562.

Keck, P.E., Pope, H.G., Hudson, J.I., McElroy, S.I., Yurgelun-Todd, D. and Hundert, E.M. (1990). A controlled study of phenomenology and family history in outpatients with bulimia nervosa. *Compr. Psychiat.,* **31**, 275–283.

Kendler, K.S., MacLean, C., Neale, M., Kessler, R., Heath, A. and Eaves, L. (1991). The genetic epidemiology of bulimia nervosa. *Am. J. Psychiat.,* **148**, 1627–1637.

Kennett, G.A., Chaouloff, F., Marcou, M., Curzon, G. (1986). Female rats are more vulnerable than males in an animal model of depressions: the possible role of serotonin. *Brain Res.,* **382**, 416–421.

Lisner, L., Stevens, J., Levitsky, D.A., Rasmussen, K.M. and Strupp, B.J. (1988). Variation in energy intake during the menstrual cycle: implications for food-intake research. *Am. J. Clin. Nutr.,* **48**, 956–962.

Marce, L.A. (1860). On a form of hypochondriacal delirium occurring consecutive to dyspepsia and characterized by refusal of food. *J. Psychol. Med. Mental Pathol.,* **13**, 204–206.

Morgan, H.A. and Russell, G.F.M. (1975). Value of family background and clinical features as predictors of long-term outcome in anorexia nervosa: 4-year follow-up study of 41 patients. *Psychol. Med.,* **5**, 355–371.

Morton, R. (1694). *Phthisologica: Or a Treatise of Consumption.* London: S. Smith and B. Walford.

Mrosovsky, N. and Sherry, D. (1980). Animal anorexias. *Science,* **207**, 837–842.

Nowlin, N.S. (1983). Anorexia nervosa in twins: case report and review. *J. Clin. Psychiat.,* **44**, 101–105.

Nygaard, J.A. (1990). Anorexia nervosa: treatment and triggering factors. *Acta Psychiat. Scand.,* **82** (Suppl. 361), 44–49.

Nylander, J. (1971). The feeling of being fat and dieting in a school population. *Acta Sociomed. Scand.,* **3**, 17–26.

Patton, G.C., Johnson-Sabine, E., Wood, K., Mann, A.H. and Wakeling, A. (1990). Abnormal eating attitudes in London schoolgirls—a prospective epidemiological study: outcome at twelve-month follow-up. *Psychol. Med.,* **20**, 83–394.

Rastam, M. (1990). *Anorexia Nervosa in Swedish Urban Teenagers.* Gotenbörg.

Rastam, M. and Gillberg, G. (1991). The family background in anorexia nervosa: a population-based study. *J. Am. Acad. Child Adolesc. Psychiat.,* **30**(2), 283–289.

Rastam, M. (1992). Anorexia nervosa in 51 Swedish adolescents: premorbid problems and cormorbidity. *J. Am. Acad. Child Adolesc. Psychiat,* **31**, 819–219.

Rivinus, T.M., Biederman, J., Herzog, D.B., Kemper, K., Harper, G.P. Harmatz, J.S. and Houseworth, S. (1984). Anorexia nervosa and affective disorders: a controlled family history study. *Am. J. Psychiat.,* **141**, 1414–1418.

Rothenberg, A. (1986). Eating disorders as a modern obsessive compulsive syndrome. *Psychiatry,* **49**, 45–53.

Rowland, N.E. (1986). Effect of continuous infusions of defenfluramine on food intake, body weight and brain amines in rats. *Life Sci.,* **39**, 2581–2586.

Ryle, J.A. (1936). Anorexia nervosa. *Lancet,* **2**, 893–899.

Schepank, H. (1992). Genetic determinants of anorexia nervosa: results of studies in twins. In: *The Course of Eating Disorders* (eds. W. Herzog, H.C. Deter and W. Vandereycken, pp. 241-256.

Schmidt, U., Treasure, J., Tiller, J. and Blanchard, M. (1992). The role of life events and difficulties in the onset of eating disorders. *Neuroendocrin. Lett.,* **14**, 256.

Scott, D.W. (1986). Anorexia nervosa: a review of possible genetic factors. *Int. J. Eating Dis.,* **5**. 1–20.

Silverman, J.A. (1986). Anorexia nervosa in seventeenth century England as viewed by physician, philosopher and pedagogue: an essay. *Int. J. Eating Dis.,* **5**, 847–853.

Slade, P.D. (1982). Towards a functional analysis of anorexia nervosa and bulimia nervosa. *Br. J. Clin. Psychiat.,* **21**, 167–179.

Slade, P.D. and Dewey, M.E. (1986). Development and preliminary validation of SCANS: a screening instrument for identifying individuals at risk of developing anorexia and bulimia nervosa. *Int. J. Eating Dis.,* **5**, 517–538.

Strober, M., Salkin, B., Burroughs, J. and Morrell, W. (1982). Validity of the bulimia-restrictor distinction in anorexia nervosa. *J. Nerv. Mental Dis.,* **170**, 345–531.

Strober, M., Morrell, W., Burroughs, J., Salkin, B. and Jacobs, C. (1985). A controlled family study of anorexia nervosa: *J. Psychiat. Res.,* **19**, 239–246.

Strober, M., Lampert, C., Morrell, W., Burroughs, J. and Jacobs, C. (1990). A controlled family study of anorexia nervosa: evidence of familial aggregation and lack of shared transmission with affective disorders. *Int. J. Eating Dis.,* **9**, 239–253.

Strober, M. (1991). Disorders of the self in anoran orgasmic developmental paradigm. In: *Psychodynamic Treatment of Anorexia Nervosa and Bulimia* (ed. C.L. Johnson), pp. 354–373. New York: Guilford Press.

Theander, S. (1970). Anorexia nervosa: a psychiatric investigation of 94 female patints. *Acta Psychiatr. Scand.,* **214**, (Suppl.), 1–194.

Treasure, J.L. and Holland, A.J. (1989). Genetic vulnerability to eating disorders: evidence from twin and family studies. In: *Anorexia Nervosa* (eds H. Remschmidt and M.H. Schmidt), pp. 59–68. Toronto: Hogrefe & Huber.

Unvas-Moberg, K. (1989). Neuroendocrine regulation of hunger and satiety. In: *Obesity 1988: Proceedings of the 1st European Congress on Obesity* (eds. P. Bjomtorp and S. Rossner). London/Paris: John Libby.

Vandereycken, W. and Pierloot, R. (1981). Anorexia nervosa in twins. *Psychother. Psyhosom,* **35**, 55–63.

5

Starvation Models and Eating Disorders

M.M. FICHTER
Klinik Roseneck, University of Munich, Germany
AND
K.M. PIRKE
University of Trier, Trier, Germany

INTRODUCTION

The beginning of the scientific exploration of the effects of deliberate fasting and starvation can be traced to the end of the last century when the physician Tanner made a starvation experiment on himself (Keys et al, 1950). About 20 years later, the "Carnegie Nutrition Laboratory Fasting Experiment" was conducted by Benedict (1915) who studied healthy males under conditions of semistarvation. A milestone in the scientific exploration of starvation in humans was the "Minnesota Experiment" conducted by Keys et al (1950); they studied a group of male "semi-volunteers" (conscientious objectors to military service) under conditions of semistarvation over a period of 168 days. The "Minnesota Study" was the first to describe psychological changes such as tiredness, sensitivity to noise, irritability, apathy, loss of concentration, loss of libido, loss of vigilance, emotional instability, depression and decreased motor activity during semistarvation. Sophisticated neuroendocrine assessments were not possible at the time of the Minnesota Experiment.

Since the mid-70s our own research group has conducted a series of studies in patients with eating disorders and in healthy persons under conditions of (semi)-starvation, and the main results of these studies as well as the results of animal

Handbook of Eating Disorders: Theory, Treatment and Research.
Edited by G. Szmukler, C. Dare and J. Treasure.
© 1995 John Wiley & Sons Ltd.

studies are reported below. A large number of abnormalities of hormone regulation have been described for anorexia and bulimia nervosa. Two different hypotheses have been formulated to explain these abnormalities: one hypothesis assumes that hypothalamic abnormalities—especially neurotransmitter disturbances—are the primary cause of disturbed eating behaviour and neuroendocrine dysregulation in anorexia or bulimia nervosa. The second hypothesis assumes that the observed abnormalities of hormone and neurotransmitter regulation occur as a consequence of temporarily reduced caloric intake (starvation hypothesis). Much of the experimental evidence supporting the latter hypothesis has been obtained by our group and is summarised here. The evidence is overwhelming that most of the endocrine abnormalities in eating disorders are a consequence of temporarily reduced food intake (starvation).

ANIMAL MODELS

In animal models, mechanisms responsible for neuroendocrine disturbances can be studied in detail, since the underlying neurotransmitter changes can be measured directly in the brain. This, of course, is not possible in humans. One feature of anorexia nervosa patients besides fasting is motor hyperactivity (Falk, Halmi and Tyron, 1985; Kron et al, 1987). Therefore, rat studies on the effects of starvation have also addressed starvation-induced hyperactivity (Epling and Pierce, 1984; Richter, 1992; Routtenberg and Kuznesoff, 1967).

As in humans, starvation causes a rapid decrease of luteinising hormone (LH) in plasma of the rat (Pirke and Spyra, 1981). As a consequence gonadal hormone secretion is decreased. Stimulation of the gonads by HCG results in a rapid increase of gonadal hormones. The increase of gonadotropic hormones after GnRH is reduced but not abolished, indicating that starvation impairs the function of the hypothalamic–pituitary–gonadal axis at the hypothalamic level (Pirke and Spyra, 1981). The content of GnRH in the eminentia mediana of the starved rat is normal. *In vitro* superfusion experiments show that GnRH can be secreted into the median by depolarising stimuli (Warnhoff, Dorsch and Pirke, 1983). We therefore conclude that GnRH is available in sufficient concentration and in a releasable form. When studying the gonadal–pituitary feedback in starved rats by implanting gonadal hormone capsules of different size into gonadectomised rats, we observed that castration-induced LH increase is suppressed by much smaller testosterone plasma concentrations in starved than in control rats. This increased feedback sensitivity probably contributes to the reduced activity of the HPG axis as in the case in prepuberty. As with humans, rats increase activity of the adrenal gland during starvation (Pirke and Spyra, 1982). This hormonal alteration, which is centrally mediated, stimulates gluconeogenesis and thus is of major importance for survival during food deprivation. In order to evaluate the neurotransmitter changes responsible for the neuroendocrine changes mentioned above we have adopted two strategies:

1. Measurement of neurotransmitter turnover in the hypothalamus (norepinephrine, dopamine, serotonin).
2. Application of centrally active agonists and antagonists of neurotransmitters and neuromodulators.

Norepinephrine turnover was measured in the preoptic region, the medial basal hypothalamus, and the median eminence by two different techniques. In the alpha-methyl-paratyrosine technique, norepinephrine biosynthesis is blocked and the decrease of norepinephrine over 2 hours is measured (Pirke and Spyra, 1982). The other technique involves measurement of the norepinephrine metabolite MOPEG (3-methoxy-5-hydroxyphenylethylenglycol) (Schweiger, Warnhoff and Pirke, 1985a,b). Both methods revealed a starvation-induced reduction of central norepinephrine activity. These data indicate that norepinephrine turnover in starvation is reduced not only in peripheral tissue (Landsberg and Young, 1978) but also in the brain. We observed two mechanisms responsible for the impaired central sympathetic activity. Schweiger et al (1985a) found a close correlation between the influx of the norepinephrine precursor tyrosine into the brain and norepinephrine turnover. Philipp and Pirke (1987) described a reduction of the activity of the rate-limiting enzyme of norepinephrine biosynthesis, tyrosine hydroxylase. As judged from the measurement of dopamine and serotonin metabolites in the brain, starvation reduces dopaminergic activity and increases serotonin turnover (Broocks, Liu and Pirke, 1989). The mechanisms underlying these changes are unclear.

The second strategy involves neuropharmacological interventions to correct starvation-induced suppression of LH and the stimulation of corticosterone secretion. Norepinephrine neurons exert a stimulatory influence on the HPG axis and an inhibitory action on the HPA axis in the rat. Therefore the observed decrease of norepinephrine in the medial basal hypothalamus, and especially in the median eminence, might explain the neuroendocrine findings. In order to test this hypothesis we injected centrally active noradrenergic agonists and precursors in starved and control animals (Pirke and Spyra, 1982). L-Dopa abolished the starvation-induced corticosterone increase but did not stimulate the suppressed LH secretion. The data support the assumption that starvation-induced activity of the HPA axis may be caused by the reduced central norepinephrine turnover. It has been speculated that an increased endorphinergic activity might suppress LH secretion in anorexia nervosa and starvation. However, application of the endorphin antagonist naloxone was not able to reverse LH suppression in anorexia nervosa and in the starved rat (Küderling et al, 1984). In summarising the experiments described we can assume that starvation-induced reduction of noradrenergic activity stimulates the HPA axis. The mechanisms by which malnutrition suppresses the HPG axis remain unclear. An increased sensitivity of gonadal–pituitary feedback plays a role. The changes in neurotransmitter activity studied were not related to LH suppression. The possibility cannot be excluded that the GnRH neurons themselves might sense metabolic signs of malnutrition and reduce activity as a consequence.

Starvation-Induced Hyperactivity

Food restriction induces hyperactivity in rats and other rodents (Cornish and Mrosovky, 1965; Dourish, Hutson and Curzon, 1985; Finger, 1951; Hall and Hanford, 1954). Routtenberg and Kuznesoff (1967) restricted the availability of food to one hour per day and observed a rapid increase of running activity. This paradigm was studied in detail by Kanarek and Collier (1983) and by Epling and Pierce (1988) who systematically varied the time of food availability and access to the running wheel. Pirke et al. (1986) showed in a sophisticated experiment in which access to the running wheel had to be gained by lever pressing that female rats were much more eager to get into the running wheel than male rats. We modified the Routtenberg experiment by giving the rats a reduced amount of food so that their body weight decreased to 70% of its initial value (Broocks, Liu and Pirke, 1990a) and was then kept constant. Figure 5.1 shows a typical individual example of food intake, body weight, and running activity. It is remarkable that hyperactivity was maintained for up to 90 days when weight was kept constant at 70% of initial weight.

Endocrine Consequences of Starvation-Induced Hyperactivity

Broocks, Schweiger and Pirke (1990b) have measured the circadian pattern of plasma corticosterone, LH and testosterone in male rats after hyperactivity had been induced by reduced feeding for 10 days. Plasma corticosterone paralleled the circadian pattern of running activity. The average 24-hour concentrations were significantly greater in this group than in sedentary *ad lib.* fed rats and in *ad lib* fed rats having access to a running wheel. Starvation alone causes an increase in plasma corticosterone (Pirke and Spyra, 1982). When semistarved running rats and semi-

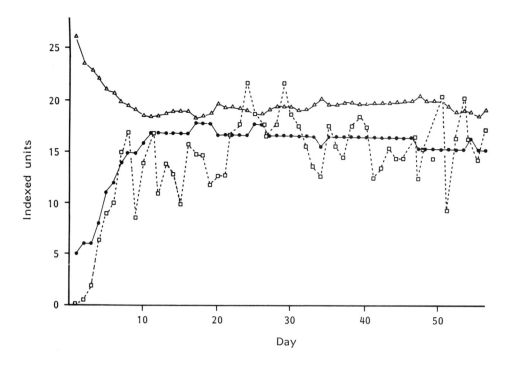

FIGURE 5.1   Body weight (Δ), food intake (●) and running activity (□) in semistarved rats.

starved sedentary rats were compared, a synergistic effect of starvation and hyperactivity on corticosterone was observed (Broocks et al, 1990b). Triidothyronine was also reduced by semistarvation and hyperactivity in a synergistic way. Increased activity of the adrenal gland and reduced production of T_3 can be considered as adaptations to the reduced caloric supply and the increased energy demand. The main role of corticosterone is the stimulation of gluconeogenesis while low T_3 probably has a protein-sparing effect. Reproductive function is impaired by starvation-induced hyperactivity in male and female rats. Marquard (1991) showed that menstrual cycles disappear much faster as a combined effect of semistarvation and hyperactivity. The faster the weight loss was the more rapidly the cycles disappeared.

Neurotransmitters in Semistarvation-Induced Hyperactivity

Central neurotransmitter changes in starvation-induced hyperactivity were studied by Broocks et al (1989, 1990a,b). Hyperactivity was again induced by reduced feeding after a 10-day period. Sedentary controls fed *ad lib*, *ad lib* fed rats with access to a running wheel, semistarved sedentary rats, and semistarved running rats were sacrificed at 4-hour intervals over a 24-hour period. The neurotransmitters norepinephrine, dopamine, serotonin and their metabolites methoxyhydroxyphenylglycol (MOPEG), dihydroxyphenylacetic acid (DOPAC) and hydroxy indol acetic acid (5-HIAA) were measured by HPLC including electrochemical detection in the medial basal hypothalmus (MBH) and in the preoptic area (POA). The *ad lib* fed rats run most during the dark hours. The semistarved rats show highest activity around the time of feeding.

Figure 5.2 shows the concentrations of MOPEG in the MBH. In the *ad lib* fed and in the semistarved rats, MOPEG concentrations parallel the running activity. Semistarvation alone reduces MOPEG concentrations in the MBH (Pirke and Spyra, 1982; Schweiger et al, 1985a,b). Hyperactivity reverses the effect of semistarvation on MOPEG. Serotonin turnover is stimulated by semistarvation. This effect is further enhanced by hyperactivity in the MBH.

The question arises whether the neurotransmitter changes observed can explain the endocrine findings. Semistarvation suppresses the activity of the HPG axis as discussed above. Many experiments in the rat have clearly demonstrated the stimulatory effect of NE on the HPG axis. We could therefore assume that reduced NE activity in semistarvation inpairs LH secretion. Activity reverses the effect of starvation on NE; it does not, however, reverse the effect on LH. If we assume that the effect of NE is inhibitory on the HPA axis we could explain high corticosterone values in semistarvation but not even higher values in semistarvation-induced hyperactivity. Our failure to explain neuroendocrine observations by changes in the neurotransmitter systems in the experimental paradigm discussed here probably has many reasons. The comparison of findings in the POA and in the MBH already shows that there may be major local differences in the effects of semistarvation and hyperactivity on neurotransmitters. Many more than the classical three neurotransmitters studied here are involved in the regulation of the HPG and the HPA axis.

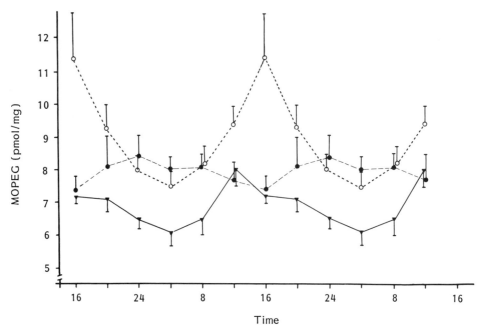

FIGURE 5.2   MOPEG in *ad lib* fed rats (●), semistarved rats (▼) and semistarved running rats (○).

Pharmacological Studies of the Noradrenergic System

Alpha$_2$ (but not alpha$_1$) agonists, beta-agonists and adrenoceptor antagonists suppress running activity. A dose–response curve for clonidine is plotted in Figure 5.3. This specific effect of the alpha$_2$-agonists was prevented by alpha$_2$-antagonists. There was no effect of prazozine, yomhibine and phentolamine on semistarvation-induced running (Wilckens, Schweiger and Pirke, 1992a). The assumption that clonidine suppresses running simply by lowering blood pressure must be rejected since neither prazozine nor phentolamine, which also reduce blood pressure, inhibited running activity. Semistarvation-induced hyperactivity has been shown to be accompanied by an increased NE-turnover (Broocks, Liu and Pirke, 1990a). Therefore one likely explanation for clonidine suppression of hyperlocomotion is that it reduces central NE-turnover, thus decreasing the stimulation of post-synaptic alpha-receptors. This would reduce the drive for feeding mediated via postsynaptic alpha$_2$-receptors (Leibowitz, 1984). Such an interpretation would be in line with reports of clonidine-induced sedation as a result of stimulation of somatodentric autoreceptors at ascending noradrenergic neurons (Scheinin and MacDonald, 1989).

Neuropharmacological Studies on the Serotonergic System

Wilckens, Schweiger and Pirke (1992b) studied the serotonergic system. In these experiments stable running was achieved for up to 6 weeks after an initial weight

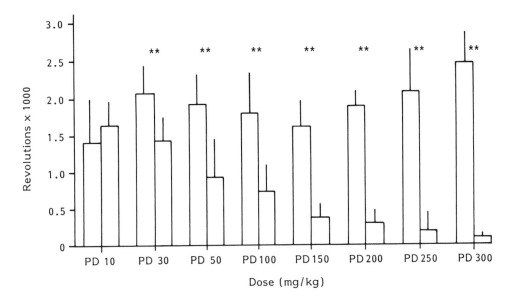

FIGURE 5.3   Dose–response curve of clonidine on starvation-induced hyperactivity. PD = activity on preceding day without drug.

loss of 20–30%. Serotonin agonists and antagonists were delivered by intra-peritoneal injection, in different doses either alone or in different combinations. Running activity was observed for 2 hours after injection. Different serotonin ago-nists were used in the study. None of these substances is totally specific for any one of the serotonin receptors (Bendotti and Samanin, 1987). Among these substances only m-trifluoromethyl-phenylpiperazine HCl (TFMPP), 1-(metachlorophenyl)-piperazine di HCl (mCPP), (±)-1-(2,5-dimethoxy-4-iodophenyl)-2-aminopropane HCl (DOI) and quipazine which share a relatively high affinity for the serotonin 1c receptor suppress running activity in a dose-dependent manner. Agonists which act only on peripheral 5-HT receptors did not suppress running activity. Figure 5.4 shows the dose–response curve of one of these substances (mCPP). Among the antagonists tested, only those substances which shared a high affinity for the serotonin 1c receptors (Van de Kar et al, 1989) blocked the effects of the agonists mentioned above on running activity. These data indicate that semistarvation-induced hyperactivity can be blocked by serotonin 1c agonists.

Can the neurotransmitter studies reported here explain the development of hy-peractivity in the rat? Although the most specific drugs available were used in our studies, the specificity for any given subtype of serotonin and norepinephrine recep-tors is limited. Thus any explanation must remain highly speculative. We could for instance conclude that semistarved rats learn to run faster and faster because the increased serotonergic activity thus achieved makes them feel less hungry. Similarly, the semistarved rat may learn to overcome starvation-induced reduction of norepinephrine turnover and thus "feel better". Although the first conclusion is supported by the fact that wheelrunning reduces food intake (Epling and Pierce,

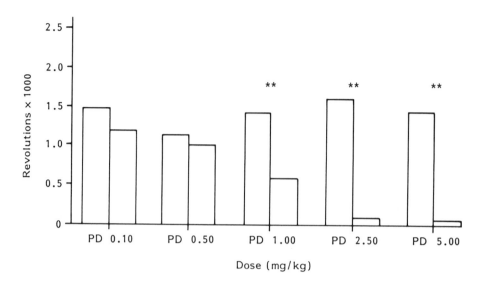

FIGURE 5.4   Dose–response curve of mCPP on starvation-induced hyperactivity. PD = activity on preceding day without drugs.

1984) it remains extremely speculative and has to be proven by further experiments which study the effect of running on food intake on a neurotransmitter basis. The second conclusion appears to be rather unlikely since we should assume that increasing the noradrenergic tone by giving alpha$_1$ and beta-agonists should be able to substitute for running as a measure to raise norepinephrine turnover. This however is not the case.

Relevance of the Animal Model for our Understanding of Hyperactivity in Anorexia Nervosa

Hyperactivity of patients with anorexia nervosa has been interpreted in different ways. Some argue that anorexia nervosa patients increase their activity on purpose to help burn more energy and get thin even faster. Other investigators believe that the permanent physical activity and the fidgeting could be "biological" in origin. Indeed, hyperactivity in some anorectic patients impresses the physician by its similarity to an addiction. Although we do not understand the nature of starvation-induced hyperactivity in the rat and other rodents, it is quite clear that all rats without exception develop hyperactivity when starved. There are reasons to assume that this mechanism is not relevant in humans. Not all patients with anorexia nervosa are hyperactive (Falk, Halmi and Tyron, 1985). The semistarved young men in the Minnesota Experiment did not develop signs of hyperactivity. Therefore we cannot expect an explanation for the hyperactivity of anorectic patients from the study of semistarved rodents and running wheels. However, the study of central neurotransmitter changes in the animal model can help us to generate hypotheses on neurotransmitter changes attributable to starvation and hyperactivity in the anorectic patient. As shown above, we have demonstrated that several drugs interfering with the noradrenergic and the serotonergic system can inhibit hyperactivity. Among these, serotonin 1c agonists appear to be the most promising. They could provide a pharmacological way of inhibiting hyperactivity without inhibiting eating behaviour. The suppression of hyperactivity in anorectic patients is clinically very important because many expend a huge amount of calories in this way. This behaviour makes it very difficult for the patient to gain weight.

Animal research can increase our understanding of neuroendocrine and neurotransmitter changes when these issues cannot, for practical or ethical reasons, be studied in humans. However, the results—especially when they exist only for certain species—are of limited generalisability to humans with anorexia or bulimia nervosa or healthy persons under conditions of starvation.

PROTEIN-CALORIE MALNUTRITION IN THIRD WORLD COUNTRIES

The unfortunate situation of famine in third-world countries provides opportunities for studying the effects of protein-calorie malnutrition in humans. Cooke et al (1964), Alleyne and Young (1967), and Smith, Bledsoe and Chhetri (1975) described increases in plasma cortisol concentrations, changes in the 24-hour plasma cortisol pattern, prolonged half-life of plasma cortisol (indicating a slower cortisol catabolism) and impaired suppression of cortisol secretion after application of dexamethasone in undernourished people in third-world countries and in patients suffering from malnutrition due to various other organic diseases. Schelp et al. (1976, 1977, 1978) showed decreased levels of albumin, prealbumin, transferrin, proteinase inhibitors, inter-alphatrypsin inhibitor, and $alpha_2$-macroglobulin in patients with protein-energy malnutrition with infection. The results provide evidence for the hypothesis that decreased proteinase inhibitors limit the synthesis of albumin, prealbumin and transferrin in protein-energy malnutrition with infection.

There is a problem, however, in generalising findings in protein-calorie malnutrition to patients with anorexia nervosa or bulimia nervosa who usually eat a high-protein, low-carbohydrate, low-fat diet.

ENDOCRINE CHANGES IN EATING DISORDERED HUMANS: ANOREXIA AND BULIMIA NERVOSA

A large number of changes in neuroendocrine and neurotransmitter functioning have been described for anorexia nervosa. Similar but less pronounced findings have been reported for bulimia nervosa with temporarily reduced food intake. Fichter and Pirke (1990b) and Pirke (1990a) have recently summarized these findings.

One strategy to find out if a certain abnormality, such as hypercortisolism, is a state or trait characteristic of an eating disorder is to study patients *longitudinally* from the acute stage of illness to the recovered stage. If, for example, a certain abnormality found in cachectic anorexia nervosa patients normalises with weight restoration it can be concluded that it is not a primary feature or cause of anorexia nervosa but rather a consequence of the state of starvation.

Following this rationale we have studied 16 patients with anorexia nervosa who were consecutive admissions for inpatient treatment. The study focused on the hypothalamic–pituitary–adrenal (HPA) axis and the hypothalamic–pituitary–gonadal (HPG) axis (Doerr et al, 1980; Ficther et al, 1982; Pirke et al, 1979). The patients' ages ranged between 13 and 29 years and their average weight was 63% of ideal body weight (Metropolitan Life Insurance, 1959). Patients were assessed longitudinally on admission, after 10% initial weight gain and before discharge.

With respect to the HPA-axis, anorexia nervosa patients in the study showed: hypercortisolism, with elevated 24-hour plasma cortisol levels especially at times when cortisol secretion normally is low; an impaired suppression of cortisol after administration of dexamethasone; an increased number of secretory spikes over 24 hours; and a reduced metabolisation of cortisol (in the liver). Our cross-sectional results in underweight anorectics were in accordance with those reported on a smaller patient sample by Boyar et al (1974, 1977). A major new finding of our study was that these abnormalities in the HPA-axis normalised after a relatively small (10%) increase in body weight in almost all cases. At discharge, when the patients had achieved normal weight, the HPA-axis was also functioning normally in (recovered) anorexia nervosa patients.

Concerning the HPG axis, severely underweight patients with anorexia nervosa on admission showed abnormalities in the secretion of luteinising hormone and follicle stimulating hormone (FSH). The secretion patterns of these pituitary hormones regressed in most cases to an infantile secretory pattern. All 16 patients with anorexia nervosa developed, with 10% weight increase or with normalisation of weight at discharge, either a pubertal or an adult secretory pattern of LH and FSH. On admission, 14 of the 16 anorexia nervosa patients had an infantile LH secretory pattern. The average 24-hour LH plasma level increased with an increase in body weight; however, this increase was less pronounced in older than in younger anorexics and in anorexics with a long history of the eating disorder. These results gave support to the hypothesis that abnormalities found in the acute state of anorexia nervosa were not trait characteristics and were not a cause of the illness. Rather, the results suggested that reduced caloric intake, low body weight or a state of starvation lead to these hormonal changes which disappeared with weight recovery.

In a few studies of anorexia nervosa patients by other research groups, some neuroendocrine abnormalities did not disappear completely with weight recovery. However, "recovery" has not been sufficiently defined. A normal body weight at the time of assessment does not preclude reduced caloric intake in the preceding days or weeks when the patient is fluctuating in weight. Therefore markers of temporarily reduced caloric intake, such as beta-hydroxybutyric acid and T_3, as well as a detailed history of body weight and food intake in the preceding days and weeks, must be obtained in order to be able to define "recovery".

In a later study (Fichter et al., 1990a) we assess 24 female patients with bulimia nervosa according to DSM-III criteria (American Psychiatric Association, 1980).

These patients showed a variety of neuroendocrine disturbances which, however, were not as pronounced as in low-weight anorexia nervosa patients. Neuroendocrine abnormalities in bulimia appeared to correlate with indices of temporarily reduced food intake in these normal-weight patients. Other studies by our group of bulimia nervosa patients (Fichter and Pirke, 1989; Pirke, Fichter and Schweiger, 1987) showed that normal-weight bulimic patients had significantly reduced LH and FSH plasma levels. Only 3 of 30 bulimic patients (10%) showed a normal pattern of secretion of LH, estradiol and progesterone over the complete menstrual cycle; 40% showed a luteal phase defect (LPD); and 50% had low estradiol and progesterone plasma levels and thus did not develop a dominant follicle. These findings are relevant for a better understanding not only of neuroendocrine secretion, but also of reproductive function and fertility, and the risk of developing osteoporosis. Young adult females with low body weight or weight cycling and consequent low levels of estradiol have an increased risk of developing osteoporosis of a relatively young age.

EFFECTS OF STARVATION ON HEALTHY HUMANS

The HPG Axis

The first well-controlled study of neuroendocrine functioning in healthy subjects under conditions of complete food abstinence using modern radioimmunoassay techniques for determining plasma hormone levels was the Munich Starvation Experiment (MUSE). The hypothesis was tested that temporarily reduced caloric intake will result in the same or similar endocrine changes as have been reported in anorexia nervosa in the acute stage. In this study we chose total food abstinence (and not semistarvation) in order to use a powerful intervention since at that time there was only limited knowledge and scientific evidence for an association between starvation and hormonal changes. In the MUSE, 5 healthy paid female volunteers were assessed over the following four phases of the experiment:

1. A baseline phase during which body weight was maintained at the starting (ideal) body weight.
2. A phase of fasting until each subject had lost 15% of the starting (ideal) body weight; this phase lasted on the average 3 weeks and weight loss amounted to an average of 8.0 kg.
3. A phase of restoration of body weight to the original (ideal) level.
4. A final phase during which the ideal body weight was maintained.

The results have been described by Fichter and Pirke (1986a,b; 1990b) and Fichter et al. (1986). Plasma concentrations of cortisol, LH. FSH, growth hormone (GH), thyroid-stimulating hormone (TSH), and prolactin were measured over 24 hours in 30-minute intervals before weight loss (end of phase 1), after weight loss (end of phase 2), and after weight restoration (end of phase 3). In addition, dexamethasone suppression tests (DSTs), thyrotropin-releasing hormone (TRH) tests, and

TABLE 5.1 Neuroendocrinological finding in starvation, anorexia nervosa and bulimia nervosa.

	Starvation		Anorexia nervosa		Bulimia nervosa	
	Literature	Complete food abstinence (MUSE)	Literature	Own observations*	Literature	Own observations*
Gonadotropins						
Decreased plasma gonadotropin (LH/FSH)	Pirke and Spyra, 1981†	Yes	Boyar, 1974	Yes	NI	Yes
Reduced response to LHRH	Pirke and Spyra, 1981†	NI	Halmi and Sherman, 1975	NI	NI	NI
Reduced response to clomiphene	NI	NI	Marshall, 1971	NI	NI	NI
Regression of the 24-hour plasma LH secretory pattern	NI	Yes	Boyar, 1974	Yes	NI	Yes
Anovulatory cycle or LPD	Schweiger et al, 1987 Pirke et al, 1989	Yes	(by definition amenorrhea)	Yes	NI	Yes (Fichter and Pirke, 1990)
Thyroid gland						
T_4 normal	Palmblad et al, 1977	Yes	Miya et al, 1975 Moshang et al, 1975	NI	NI	NI
T_3 decreased	Palmblad et al, 1977	Yes	Miyai et al, 1975 Moshang et al, 1975	NI	NI	Yes
Decreased basal metabolism	Brozek et al, 1977	NI	Warren and van de Wiele, 1973	NI	NI	NI
TSH normal to slightly decreased	Palmblad et al, 1977	Yes	Vigersky, 1976a	NI	NI	NI
TSH response to TRF reduced	NI	Yes	Vigersky, 1976b	Yes	NI	Yes

							Negative result
Adrenal gland							
Increased plasma cortisol	Alleyne and Young, 1967; Palmblad et al, 1977; Smith et al, 1975	Yes	Vigersky, 1976a; Walsh et al, 1978; Warren and van de Wiele, 1973; Boyar, 1977	Yes	Negative result Walsh et al, 1987	Yes	Negative result
Path. 24-hour plasma cortisol secretory pattern							
Insufficient suppression of dexamethasone test	Alleyne and Young, 1967; Smith et al, 1975	Yes	Walsh et al, 1978; Boyar, 1977; Walsh et al, 1978; Walsh et al, 1978	Yes	Walsh et al, 1987; Walsh et al, 1987	Yes	Yes
Retarded cortisol catabolism	Alleyne and Young, 1967; Smith et al, 1975	Yes	NI	Yes	NI	NI	Negative result
Increased cortisol production rate	Smith et al, 1975	Yes	Boyar, 1977; Walsh et al, 1978	Yes	Negative result Walsh et al, 1987	Yes	Negative result
Growth hormone							
Increased	Kling, 1978‡	Yes	Vigersky, 1976a	Yes	NI	NI	(Yes)
Reduced growth hormone release after stimulation with clonidine	NI	Yes	NI	NI	NI	NI	Yes
Prolactin (PRL)							
Decreased nocturnal prolactin secretion	NI	Yes	Brown et al, 1979	NI	NI	NI	(Yes)
Reduced PRL response to TRF	NI	NI	Brambilla et al, 1981; Waldhauser et al, 1984	NI	NI	NI	Yes

NI = not investigated; No = finding not confirmed; Yes = finding confirmed; (Yes) = finding mainly confirmed.
T_4 = thyroxine; T_3 = triiodothyronine; TSH = thyroid-stimulating hormone; TRF = thyrotropin-releasing hormone; LH = luteinising hormone; LHRH = luteinising hormone releasing hormone.
* Own observation in patients with anorexia nervosa, bulimia nervosa, or fasting test subjects. † Animal experiments. ‡ Observations in subjects with increased body weight.

clonidine tests were performed (see Fichter and Pirke, 1986a,b). This experiment constituted a fundamental analysis of neuroendocrine and neurotransmitter changes as a result of starvation. The design of the study excluded possible confounding factors which could have been of influence in a study of eating disordered patients (nutrition, possible primary biological alterations of the illness) or malnourished persons in the third-world countries (protein-calorie malnutrition, vitamin deficiencies). The MUSE can be seen as an "experimentum crucis" to analyse the effects of total food abstinence with supplementation of minerals and vitamins in healthy subjects. The study led to the following observations which confirm the hypothesis that reduced caloric intake (in this case total food abstinence) causes specific neuroendocrine and neurotransmitter changes:

1. A regression in the 24-hour secretion pattern of gonadotropic hormones (LH, FSH).
2. A diminished TSH response to stimulation with TRH (TSH levels were not reduced).
3. Hyperactivity of the HPA-axis (hypercortisolism) and impaired plasma cortisol suppression in the DST.
4. Increased basal growth hormone secretion after weight loss.
5. A blunted growth hormone response to stimulation with the alpha$_2$-adrenergic receptor agonist clonidine after subsequent weight gain.

Later studies of starvation and neuroendocrine and neurotransmitter functioning used a semistarvation paradigm (Schweiger et al., 1986, 1987; Pirke et al, 1986; Pirke et al, 1989; Mullen, Linsell and Parker, 1987). The results of the Mullen et al (1987) study are presented in the section on the HPA-axis.

Recently Gorozhanin and Lobkov (1990) exposed healthy volunteers to prolonged starvation of 14 days. This resulted in an increase in plasma and urinary epinephrine, ACTH, beta-endorphin, plasma cortisol, somatotropin, glucagon, cyclic adenosine monophosphate and acetylcholine. Other effects of starvation were decreases in plasma norepinephrine, T_3, T_4, prolactin, insulin, C-peptide, FSH, LH, testosterone, histamine, prostaglandins A and E, and a decrease in the pH level. The effects of a short (36-hour) fast were studied by Jung et al (1985) in six healthy men. This procedure resulted in a reduction of the serum T_3, a blunted TSH response to TRH, and an increased LH response to GnRH. The FSH response to GnRH and the basal serum prolactin level was unaffected by this short-term starvation.

Table 5.1 gives an overview of findings concerning neuroendocrine changes in anorexia nervosa, in bulimia nervosa and in healthy subjects under various conditions of starvation.

As reported above, patients with anorexia nervosa (Fichter et al, 1982) had an infantile plasma LH secretion pattern on admission to inpatient treatment. All developed a pubertal or adult secretion pattern either after 10% weight gain or by the time of discharge. Devlin et al (1989) confirmed our previous finding of fewer LH secretory spikes and lower mean 24-hour LH levels in both anorectic and bulimic patients; in addition, they reported a blunted LH response to stimulation with GnRH in anorexia nervosa and elevated LH responses to GnRH in bulimia nervosa. These authors concluded that HPG-axis abnormalities in eating disordered patients "cannot entirely be attributed to emaciation and that factors other than subnormal weight contribute to disturbed hypothalamic–pituitary function in these patients" (p. 11). However, our results with patients with anorexia nervosa and bulimia nervosa and with healthy fasting subjects make it likely that not body weight, but a temporary reduction of caloric intake, is primarily responsible for the observed changes.

As mentioned above, in patients with bulimia nervosa according to DSM-III criteria, we found significantly lowered LH and FSH plasma levels at night, compared with healthy controls (Fichter et al, 1990; Pirke et al, 1987). They were significantly lower in patients with lower body weight, reduced calorie intake, or a higher number of "fasting days" with calorie intake below 1000 kcal, as compared with levels in bulimic patients with non-reduced food intake.

In the MUSE, a most remarkable finding was that three of five *healthy female subjects* showed a total regression to an infantile plasma LH secretory pattern after only 21 days of fasting, and minor weight loss (8 kg) compared with anorexia nervosa patients. The remaining two subjects showed an adult plasma secretory pattern after fasting. Generally, these findings in humans are in accordance with animal data (see above).

Schweiger et al (1986) and Pirke et al (1986) studied 18 healthy normal-weight women under conditions of *semistarvation* (1000 kcal/day). Nine women received a "non-vegetarian (mixed) diet". Both groups on average lost 1 kg per week. The "vegetarian diet" (equal caloric content to the "non-vegetarian diet") had more impact on gonadotropin and gonadal hormone functioning than the "non-vegetarian diet". The "vegetarian diet" resulted in significant decrease of the average LH values during the mid-cycle and luteal phase. Also, estradiol and progesterone plasma levels were significantly lower during the luteal phase. The women receiving a "non-vegetarian (mixed)" 1000 kcal diet did not show significant reductions in LH, estradiol and progesterone levels during any part of the menstrual cycle. Most women in the "non-vegetarian" group (7 out of 9) maintained normal ovulatory cycles. On the other hand, mood during the last weeks of dieting was better in the "vegetarian" than in the "non-vegetarian (mixed)" diet group. An important finding was that there was a significant correlation between carbohydrate intake and mood—the lower the percentage of carbohydrates in the food the worse was the mood ($R = 0.74$; $p < 0.01$). The difference in carbohydrate content may have been the major factor contributing to the differences between the two dieting groups (Schweiger et al, 1986). The results of the study indicate that low caloric diets appear to have differential effects on hormonal regulations during the menstrual cycle (Pirke et al, 1986).

Schweiger et al (1987) compared menstrual cycles in 22 healthy normal-weight women under conditions of dieting (high-carbohydrate vegetarian 1000 kcal/day) and conditions of non-restricted food intake conditions. During dieting there were significantly more luteal phase defects (14 of 22 women) than in the unrestricted controls (5 of 22 women). No evidence of follicular phase disturbance was observed. Plasma concentrations of gonadotropins and gonadal hormones were lower in younger than in older women and in women with greater weight loss. In a study with a similar design using a 800 kcal "vegetarian" diet in 13 healthy normal-weight young women, Pirke et al (1989b) found normal cyclic gonadal function during the control cycle and disturbances of gonadal function in the diet cycle: only 2 women (15%) during the diet cycle had normal cyclic gonadal function; 4 (31%) showed impaired progesterone secretion with a normal follicular development, and 7 (54%) did not develop a dominant follicle. The average LH concentrations and the frequency of episodic LH secretions were significantly reduced during the follicular but not the luteal phase where FSH levels were not affected by this type of dieting.

The HPT Axis

Casper and Frohman (1982), Norris, O'Malley and Palmer (1985) and Kiyohara et al (1987) reported blunted and delayed TSH responses after injection of TRH for low-weight patients with anorexia nervosa. Tamai et al (1986) reported significantly lowered serum levels for T_4, free T_4, T_3, free T_3, TSH, and binding proteins such as the thyroxine-binding globulin; they also found a delayed (in 66%) or blunted (in 24%) TSH response to TRH in patients with anorexia nervosa. After weight gain the patients showed a significant increase in T_3, free T_3, T_4, TSH and binding proteins (thyroxine-binding globulin).

In our studies, bulimia nervosa patients also showed a blunted 30-minute TSH response to TRH. In order to analyse the effects of previous calorie intake, we split the bulimic group at the median with respect to variables indicating reduced calorie intake (low calorie intake, high betahydroxibutyric acid plasma levels and low T_3 plasma levels). Based on these calculations, we found a significantly decreased 30-minute TSH repsonse for bulimic patients with a low percentage of carbohydrate intake and a trend for a blunted TSH response to TRH for other variables indicating low calorie intake (Fichter et al, 1990a).

Healthy subjects in our starvation experiment (MUSE) showed a significantly reduced TSH response to TRH during the fasting phase as compared with the baseline phase. The TSH response in healthy women normalised when body weight was restored. A blunted TSH response to TRH has been claimed to be a "biological marker" for depression (Loosen and Prange, 1980). On the basis of these findings, blunted TSH responses to TRH in depression can be seen as a result of reduced appetite and consequent reduced calorie intake and weight loss, frequent symptoms in depression.

Reduced T_3 levels are apparently associated with a reduction in energy expenditure and conservation of protein during starvation. Thus, changes in thyroid hormone metabolism during starvation are of an adaptive nature. Substitution of these hormones, such as treatment with L-thyroxine to restore serum thyroid concentrations, therefore does not appear appropriate in anorexia nervosa or conditions of starvation (Tibaldi and Surks, 1985). Komaki et al (1986) assessed 21 non-obese euthyroid patients with psychosomatic diseases following a 5-day fast, reporting decreased free T_4, T_3 and TSH plasma levels and increases in reverse T_3. Serum angiotensin-converting enzyme as an index of thyroid hormone action decreased significantly as a result of fasting, showing a further decrease during 5 days of refeeding (Komaki et al, 1988). Decreases in angiotensin-converting enzyme activity (not mediated by T_3) as a result of fasting were also reported by Butkus, Burman and Smallridge (1987).

The HPA Axis

As already reported above, anorexia nervosa patients in our longitudinal study showed a significantly increased 24-hour plasma cortisol level on admission to inpatient therapy and all but one of the anorexic patients showed impaired cortisol suppression in the DST. These normalised with minimal weight increase. In a longitudinal study with anorexia nervosa patients, Estour et al (1990) confirmed earlier findings of impaired cortisol suppression in response to intravenous dexamethasone and reported that reinvestigating the patients after refeeding and weight gain resulted in normal cortisol suppression in the DST in 5 of 9 patients only. The authors concluded that cortisol escape in the DST "is not related to the degree of starvation" (p. 45). However, body weight may not necessarily correlate with nutritional intake in the preceding days. According to our results, nutritional intake (and not body weight) is critical for insufficient cortisol suppression in response to dexamethasone. Kaye et al (1989) reported starvation-related disturbances of peptides such as corticotropin-releasing hormone, beta-endorphin and neuropeptide Y measured in the cerebrospinal fluid of patients with anorexia nervosa. They concluded that changes in the activity of neuropeptides induced by starvation may contribute to neuroendocrine and behavioral alterations in anorexia nervosa such as hypercortisolism, amenorrhea and other symptoms such as physical hyperactivity, depression and abnormal feeding behavior.

For bulimia nervosa, conflicting results concerning the HPA axis have been reported. In our sample of 24 patients with bulimia nervosa (DSM-III criteria) we found no increased nocturnal plasma cortisol levels from 1.00a.m. to 6.30a.m. compared with healthy controls (Fichter et al, 1990). The same (negative) result was obtained by Walsh et al (1987). However, Kennedy et al (1989) did find elevated basal cortisol levels in patients with bulimia nervosa. Gwirtsman et al (1989) reported normal ACTH and cortisol levels in bulimic patients on hospital admission, but after the patients had abstained from binge–purging behavior, the cerebrospinal fluid ACTH levels showed a significant decrease. In our study we found some evidence for impaired cortisol suppression following ingestion of dexamethasone in bulimic patients, especially in patients with greater calorie restriction or with high beta-hydroxybutyric acid plasma levels indicating reduced food intake in the preceding days. Depression in bulimic patients was not associated with insufficient cortisol suppression in the DST.

In the MUSE with healthy subjects there was clear evidence for elevated 24-hour cortisol levels and increased plasma cortisol half-life at the end of the fasting phase. Restoration of body weight resulted—as in patients with anorexia nervosa—in a normalisation of the plasma cortisol level and plasma cortisol half-life. The DST sufficiently suppressed cortisol in all 11 tests performed in the five subjects during the initial baseline phase. Half of all DSTs (7/14) showed insufficient suppression of cortisol during the fasting phase. All 11 DSTs which were performed during the weight gain phase were sufficiently suppressed. Of the 18 cortisol probes at 4.00p.m. and at 9.00p.m., 17 were normally suppressed in the final baseline phase. Dexamethasone plasma levels were significantly lower during fasting, indicating reduced absorption and transport of dexamethasone from the gastrointestinal tract to the circulating blood.

In a later study using a semistarvation paradigm, Mullen, Linsell and Parker (1987) studied 14 healthy female subjects during a low-calorie diet (1000–1200 kcal/day). As in the MUSE, reduced cortisol suppression in response to dexamethasone was observed. Mullen and coworkers also reported shortened rapid-eye-movement (REM) latencies in the sleep EEG under conditions of reduced calorie intake. A reduced REM latency (Kupfer, 1984) as well as impaired suppression in the DST (Carroll, 1982) has been claimed to be a "biological marker" for depression. These and our results shed doubt on this notion and show that disturbances in the HPA axis in eating disorders are most likely a result of temporarily reduced calorie intake.

Noradrenergic Function

A reduced activity of the sympathetic nervous system in anorexia nervosa is reflected in symptoms such as low blood pressure, bradycardia and hypothermia. Pirke (1990b) has recently reviewed the literature about the noradrenergic system in anorexia and bulimia nervosa. Norepinephrine and its metabolites in plasma, urine and cerebrospinal fluid show low concentrations in anorexia nervosa. Baseline norepinephrine values may not reflect the actual activity of the sympathetic nervous system (Kopin, 1978). This is one reason why a variety of challenge tests are used. When the (reduced) sympathetic nervous system activity in anorexia nervosa is stimulated by an orthostatic challenge (Kaye et al, 1985; Heufelder, Warnhoff and Pirke, 1985) or by physical exercise (Nudel et al, 1984; Pirke et al, 1989a) the responses are blunted compared with healthy controls. Pirke et al (1992) showed that under-weight and, to a slightly lesser extent, "recovered" anorexia nervosa patients showed a blunted norepinephrine response to a challenge with a liquid test meal of 750 kcal. The finding that "weight recovered" anorexics still showed a blunted response may be due to the fact that they quite frequently still show signs of restrained eating, and subtle changes in food intake may still affect the sympathetic nervous system. Another explanation could be that it takes some time to normalise (for example when compared with the HPA axis).

Clonidine is an alpha$_2$-adrenergic receptor agonist that induces a temporary increase in growth hormone secretion in healthy subjects. Several studies have reported a blunted growth hormone response to clonidine in depression (Ansseau et al, 1988; Charney et al, 1982; Checkley, Slade and Shur, 1981). A blunted growth hormone response to clonidine has also been claimed as a biological marker for depression; our data with healthy starving subjects question this conclusion.

Clonidine challenge tests have so far not been performed in anorexia nervosa because of hypotensive side-effects. Cabranes et al (1988) reported increased basal plasma growth hormone levels in both pubertal and postpubertal patients with anorexia nervosa; somatomedin-C concentrations were lower in pubertal but not in postpubertal anorectic patients. In a study of patients with bulimia nervosa we found a significantly lower (blunted) growth hormone response in bulimic patients (excluding patients with basal growth hormone levels above 5 ng/ml) as compared with controls. The clonidine test is sensitive to the menstrual cycle. Blunting of the growth hormone response to clonidine was present only in bulimic patients and only during the luteal phase (Fichter and Pirke, 1990a,b). Heufelder et al (1985) reported an increased capacity and a decreased affinity of platelet alpha$_2$-receptors, and increased prostaglandin E$_1$ stimulatory and epinephrine inhibitory effects on cyclic adenosine monophosphate production in patients with anorexia nervosa or bulimia nervosa whose body weight was largely in the normal range.

In the MUSE with healthy subjects under conditions of starvation, we found elevated basal growth hormone levels over 24 hours at the end of the fasting phase. Growth hormone responses were normal during baseline and after fasting, but blunted after weight gain. A blunted growth hormone response to clonidine presumably reflects a reduction in postsynaptic alpha$_2$-adrenergic receptor sensitivity. According to our results and other evidence presented by Pirke (1990a,b), there appears to be a reduced sympathetic nervous system activity in patients with anorexia nervosa, in healthy starving subjects (with a time delay) and to a lesser extent in bulimic patients.

Episodic release of growth hormone in humans is infrequent and erratic; unlike GH release in the rat, release of growth hormone in humans apparently has no discernible ultradian periodicities. Ho et al (1988) showed that 5 days of fasting led to an enhancement of circadian and ultradian cycles of growth hormone release in humans. These changes in growth hormone release probably play a role in substrate homeostasis during starvation. Using epinephrine infusions in 11 normal-weight healthy subjects, Mansell, Fellows and MacDonald (1990) presented evidence for an enhancement of the chronotropic, lipolytic and thermogenic effects of infused epinephrine by prior starvation despite lower plasma epinephrine levels.

OPEN ISSUES

Food and Mood

Keys et al (1950) were the first to report depression-like symptoms during semistarvation. We have made similar observations in the MUSE. One of five women developed a depressive syndrome during complete food abstinence. There have also been several reports on "crash diet depression"—a depressive syndrome resulting from harsh dieting (Robinson and Winnek, 1973). Smoller, Wadden and Stunkard (1987) have reviewed issues concerning dieting and depression. From the study by Schweiger et al (1986) there is some evidence that dieting involving foods with low carbohydrate content is associated with negative mood. From these observations, it is possible to speculate that part of depressive symptoms in patients with eating disorders may be a result of nutrient selection. However, more research is needed to understand the interactions between food composition, neurotransmitters and mood.

Weight Cycling

In western societies "yo-yo" dieting is widely practised, especially by young women. Brownell et al (1986) reported significant increases in food efficiency (weight gain per kcal of food intake) in rats in a second food restriction phase and refeeding period compared with a first. In the second cycle of weight loss and gain, the loss of weight occurred at half the rate and weight gain at two times the rate compared with the first cycle in the same animals. There was a fourfold increase in food efficiency in weight cycled animals compared with control rats at the end of the experiment. If weight cycling or frequent dieting lead to increased food efficiency in humans as well, repeated dieting could increase the risk of gaining (!) weight rather than losing in the long term. Very few studies have been performed in humans. Findings concerning weight cycling in humans have recently been reviewed by Garner and Wooley (1991) and by Wing (1992). At present, the data are conflicting and more research is needed.

Defining (Weight) Recovery in Anorexia Nervosa

"Weight recovered" anorexia nervosa patients who appear to have normal body shape frequently still show marked disturbances in eating behavior. A group of weight recovered anorexia nervosa patients studied by us (Pirke et al, 1992) still had significantly elevated scores for restrained eating in the Three Factor Eating Questionnaire of Stunkard and Messink (1985). Restrained eating in recovered anorexics may explain why some biological variables do not normalise in all patients. It is not sufficient only to report body weight of recovered anorexia nervosa patients, but one must assess attitudes and eating behaviours in detail. The same applies to research on neuroendocrine and neurotransmitter abnormalities in depression since loss of appetite is a common symptom of depression. It has been shown that restrained eaters selected from a group of healthy controls had pathological values in biological variables such as (lowered) norepinephrine at all points of time after a standardised test meal (Pirke et al, 1990).

In conclusion, there are a large number of neuroendocrine and neurotransmitter changes in anorexia nervosa. Similar but less marked changes have been reported in bulimia nervosa as well. Data from a series of studies by our group and from others accord with the hypothesis that temporarily reduced reduction of caloric intake causes substantial neuroendocrine and neurotransmitter changes. The clearest evidence for this starvation hypothesis to explain neuroendocrine changes in anorexia nervosa and other eating disorders comes from recent starvation experiments with healthy subjects as well as from animal experiments. Thus, neurotransmitter and neuroendocrine changes in anorexia nervosa and related eating disorders appears to be an adaptation to the state of starvation.

REFERENCES

Alleyne, G.A.O. and Young, V.H. (1967). Adrenocortical function with severe protein calorie malnutrition. *Clin. Sci.*, **33**, 189.

American Psychiatric Association (1980). *Diagnostic and Statistical Manual of Mental Disorders*, 3rd edn. Washington, DC: APA.

Ansseau, M., Frenckell, R.V., Cerfontaine, J.L., et al (1988). Blunted response of growth hormone to clonidine and apomorphine in endogenous depression. *Br. J. Psychiat.*, **153**, 65–77.

Bendotti, C. and Samanin, R. (1987). The role of putative 5-HT$_{1A}$ and 5-HT$_{1B}$ receptors in the control of feeding in rats. *Life Sci.*, **41**, 635–642.

Benedict, F.G. (1915). A study of prolonged fasting. Washington, DC: Carnegie Institute Publication 203 (cited in Keys et al, 1950).

Boyar, R.M., Katz, J., Finkelstein, J.W., Kapen, S., Weitzman, E.D. and Hellman, L. (1974). Immaturity of the 24-hour luteinizing hormone secretory pattern. *New Engl. J. Med.*, **291**, 861–865.

Boyar, R.M., Hellmann, L.D., Roffwarg, H., Katz, J., Zumoff, B., O'Connor, J., Bradlow, L. and Fukushima, D.K. (1977). Cortisol secretion and metabolism in anorexia nervosa. *New Engl. J. Med.*, **296**, 190–193.

Broocks, A., Liu, J. and Pirke, K.M. (1989). Influence of hyperactivity on the metabolism of central monoaminergic neurotransmitters and reproductive function in the semistarved rat. In: K.M. Pirke, W. Wuttke and U. Schweiger (Eds), *The Menstrual Cycle and Its Disorder*, pp. 88–96. Berlin: Springer Verlag.

Broocks, A., Liu, J. and Pirke, K.M. (1900a). Semistarvation-induced hyperactivity compensates for decreased norepinephrine and dopamine turnover in the mediobasal hypothalamus of the rat. *J. Neural. Transm.*, **79**, 113–124.

Broocks, A., Schweiger, U. and Pirke, K.M. (1990b). Hyperactivity aggravates semistarvation-induced changes in corticosterone and triidothyronin concentrations in plasma but not luteinizing hormone and testosterone levels. *Physiol. Behav.*, **48**, 567–569.

Brownell, K.D., Greenwood, M.R.C., Stellar, E., et al. (1986). The effects of repeated cycles of weight loss and regain in rats. *Physiol. Behav.*, **38**, 459–464.

Butkus, N.E., Burman, K.D. and Smallridge, R.C. (1987). Angiotensin-converting enzyme activity decreases during fasting. *Horm. Metab. Res.*, **2**, 76–79.

Cabranes, J.A., Almoguera, I., Santos, I.L., et al (1988). Somatomedin-C and growth hormone levels in anorexia nervosa in relation to the pubertal or post pubertal stages. *Prog. Neuropsychopharmacol. Biol. Psychiat.*, **6**, 865–871.

Carroll, B.J. (1982). The dexamethasone suppression test for melancholia. *Br. J. Psychiat.*, **140**, 292–304.

Casper, R.C. and Frohman, D. (1982). Delayed TSH response in anorexia nervosa following injection of thyrotropin-releasing hormone (TRH). *Psychoneuroendocrinology*, **7**, 59–68.

Charney, D.S., Henninger, G.R., Sternberg, D.E., et al (1982). Adrenergic receptor sensitivity in depression: effects of clonidine in depressed patients and healthy subjects. *Arch. Gen. Psychiat.*, **39**, 290–294.

Checkley, S.A., Slade, A.P. and Shur, E. (1981). Growth hormone and other response to clonidine in patients with endogenous depression. *Br. J. Psychiat.*, **138**, 51–55.

Cooke, J.N.C., James, V.H.T., Landon, J., et al (1964). Adrenocortical function in chronic malnutrition. *Br. Med. J.*, **1**, 662–666.

Cornish, E.R. and Mrosovsky, N. (1965). Activity during food deprivation and satiation of six species of rodent. *Anim. Behav.*, **13**, 242–248.

Devlin, M.J., Walsh, B.T., Katz, J.L., et al (1989). Hypothalamic–pituitary–gonadal function in anorexia nervosa and bulimia. *Psychiat. Res.*, **1**, 11–24.

Doerr, P., Fichter, M.M., Pirke, K.M. and Lund, R. (1980). Relationship between weight gain and hypothalamic pituitary adrenal function in patients with anorexia nervosa. *J. Steroid. Biochem.*, **13**, 529–537.

Dourish, C.T., Hutson, P.H. and Curzon, G. (1985). Characteristics of feeding induced by the serotonin agonist 8-hydroxy-2-(di-n-propylamino) tertralin (8-OH-DPAT). *Brain Res. Bull.*, **15**, 377–384.

Epling, W.F. and Pierce, W.D. (1984). Activity-based anorexia in rats as a function of opportunity to run on an activity wheel. *Nutr. Behav.*, **2**, 37–49.

Epling, W.F. and Pierce, W.D. (1988). Activity-based anorexia: a biobehavioral perspective. *Int. J. Eating Dis.*, **7**, 475–485.

Estour, B., Pugeat, M., Lang, F., et al. (1990). Rapid escape for cortisol from suppression in response to i.v. dexamethasone in anorexia nervosa. *Clin. Endocrinol.*, **1**, 45–52.

Falk, J.R., Halmi, K.A. and Tyron, W.T. (1985). Activity measures in anorexia nervosa. *Arch. Gen. Psychiat.*, **42**, 811–814.

Fichter, M.M. and Pirke, K.M. (1986a). Effects of experimental and pathological weight loss upon the hypothalamo–pituitary–adrenal axis. *Psychoneuroendocrinology*, **11**, 295–305.

Fichter, M.M. and Pirke, K.M. (1986b). Effects of experimental starvation on thyroid axis disorder of eating behavior: a psychoneuroendocrine approach. In: E. Ferraria and F. Brambilla (Eds), *Advances in the Biosciences*. Oxford: Pergamon.

Fichter, M.M. and Pirke, K.M. (1989). Disturbances of reproductive function in eating disorders. In: K.M. Pirke, W. Wuttke and U. Schweiger (Eds), *The Menstrual Cycle and its Disorders*, pp. 179–188. Berlin: Springer.

Fichter, M.M. and Pirke, K.M. (1990a). Endocrine dysfunctions in bulimia (nervosa). In: M.M. Fichter (Ed.), *Bulimia Nervosa: Basic Research, Diagnosis and Therapy*, pp. 235–257. Chichester: John Wiley.

Fichter, M.M. and Pirke, K.M. (1990b). Psychobiology of human starvation in anorexia nervosa. In: H. Remschmidt and M.H. Schmidt (Eds), *Anorexia Nervosa*, pp. 15–29. Stuttgart: Hogrefe & Huber.

Fichter, M.M., Doerr, P., Pirke, K.M. and Lund, P. (1982). Behavior, attitude, nutrition and endocrinology in anorexia nervosa: a longitudinal study in 24 patients. *Acta Psychiat. Scand.*, **66**, 429–444.

Fichter, M.M., Pirke, K.M. and Holsboer, F. (1986). Weight loss causes neuroendocrine disturbances: experimental study in healthy starvation subjects. *Psychiat. Res.*, **17**, 61–72.

Fichter, M.M., Pirke, K.M., Pöllinger, J., Wolfram, G. and Brunner, E. (1990a). Disturbances in the hypothalamo–pituitary–adrenal and other neuroendocrine axes in bulimia. *Biol. Psychiat.*, **27**, 1021–1037.

Finger, F.W. (1951). The effect of food deprivation and subsequent satiation upon general activity in the rat. *J. Comp. Physiol. Psychol.*, **44**, 557–564.

Garner, D.M. and Wooley, S.C. (1991). Confronting the failure of behavioral and dietary treatment for obesity. *Clin. Psychol. Rev.*, **11**, 729–780.

Gorozhanin, V.S. and Lobkov, V.V. (1990). Hormonal and metabolic reactions in the human body during prolonged starvation. *Kosm. Biol. Aviskosm. Med.*, **3**, 47–50.

Gwirtsman, H.E., Kaye, W.H., George, D.T., et al (1989). Central and peripheral ACTH and cortisol levels in anorexia nervosa and bulimia. *Arch. Gen. Psychiat.*, **46**, 61–69.

Hall, J.F. and Hanford, P.V. (1954). Activity as a function of a restricted feeding schedule. *J. Comp. Physiol. Psychol.*, **47**, 362–363.

Heufelder, A., Warnhoff, M. and Pirke, K.M. (1985). Platelet alpha$_2$-adrenoceptor and adenylate cyclase in patients with anorexia nervosa and bulimia. *J. Clin. Endocrinol. Metab.*, **6**, 1053–1060.

Ho, K.Y., Veldhuis, J.D., Johnson, M.L., et al. (1988). Fasting enhances growth hormone secretion and amplifies the complex rhythms of growth hormone secretion in man. *J. Clin. Invest.*, **4**, 968–975.

Jung, R.T., Rosenstock, J., Wood, S.M., et al. (1985). Dopamine in the pituitary adaption to starvation in man. *Postgrad. Med. J.*, **717**, 571–574.

Kanarek, R.B. and Collier, G.H. (1983). Self-starvation: a problem of overriding the satiety signal? *Physiol. Behav.*, **30**, 307–311.

Kaye, W.H., Jimerson, D.C., Lake, C.R. and Ebert, M.H. (1985). Altered norepinephrine metabolism following long-term weight recovery in patients with anorexia nervosa. *Psychiat. Res.*, **14**, 333–342.

Kaye, W.H., Berrettini, W.H., Gwirtsman, H.E., et al. (1989). Contribution of CNS neuropeptide (NPY, CRH and beta-endorphin) alterations to psychophysiological abnormalities in anorexia nervosa. *Psychopharmacol. Bull.*, **3**, 433–438.

Kennedy, S.H., Garfinkel, P.E., Parienti, V., et al (1989). Changes in melatonin levels but not cortisol levels are associated with depression in patients with eating disorders. *Arch. Gen. Psychiat.*, **46**, 73–78.

Keys, A., Brozek, J., Henschel, A., et al (1950). *The Biology of Human Starvation.* Minneapolis, MN: University of Minneapolis Press.

Kiyohara, K., Tamai, H., Karibe, C., et al (1987). Serum thyrotropin (TSH) response to thyrotropin-releasing hormone (TRH) in patients with anorexia nervosa and bulimia: influence of changes in body weight and eating disorders. *Psychoneuroendocrinology*, **12**, 21–28.

Komaki, G., Tamai, H., Kiyohara, K., et al (1986). Changes in the hypothalamic–pituitary–thyroid axis during acute starvation in non-obese patients. *Endocrinol. Jpn.*, **3**, 303–308.

Komaki, G., Tamai, H., Mori, T., et al. (1988) Changes in serum angiotensin-converting enzyme in acutely starved non-obese patients: a possible dissociation between angiotensin-converting enzyme and the thyroid state. *Acta Endocrinol.*, **118**, 45–50.

Kopin, I.J. (1978). Plasma levels of norepinephrine. *Ann. Intern. Med.*, **88**, 671–680.

Kron, L., Katz, J.L., Gorzynski, G. and Weiner, H. (1987). Hyperactivity in anorexia nervosa: a fundamental clinical feature. *Compr. Psychiat.*, **19**, 433–440.

Küderling, I., Dorsch, G., Warnhoff, M. and Pirke, K.M. (1984). The actions of prostaglandin E2, naloxone and testosterone on starvation-induced suppression of luteinizing hormone-releasing hormone and luteinizing-hormone secretion. *Neuroendocrinology*, **39**, 530–537.

Kupfer, D.J. (1984). Neurophysiological "markers"—EEG sleep measures. *Psychiat. Res.*, **18**, 467–475.

Landsberg, L. and Young, J.B. (1978). Fasting, feeding and regulation of the sympathetic nervous system. *New Engl. J. Med.*, **298**, 1295–1301.

Leibowitz, S.F. (1984). Noradrenergic function in the medial hypothalamus: potential relation to anorexia nervosa and bulimia. In: K.M. Pirke and D. Ploog (Eds), *The Psychobiology of Anorexia Nervosa*, pp. 35–35. Berlin: Springer Verlag.

Loosen, P.T., Wilson, I. and Prange, A.J. (1980). Endocrine and behavioral changes in depression after TRH: alteration by pretreatment with thyroid hormone. *J. Affective Disord.*, **2**, 267–278.

Mansell, P.I., Fellows, I.W. and MacDonald, I.A. (1990). Enhanced thermogenic response to epinephrine after 48-h starvation in humans. *Am. J. Physiol.*, **258**, R87–93.

Marquard, R. (1991). Tiermodell zur Anorexia nervosa: Mangelernährungsbedingte Hyperaktivität bei der weiblichen und bei der männlichen Ratte. Doctoral thesis, University of Munich.

Metropolitan Life Insurance Company (1959). *Statistical Bulletin*, **40**, 1–9.

Miyai, K., Yamamoto, T., Azukizawa, M., et al (1975). Serum thyroid hormones and thyrotropin in anorexia nervosa. *J. Clin. Endocrinol. Metab.*, **40**, 334–338.

Mullen, P.E., Linsell, C.R. and Parker, D. (1987). Der Einfluß von Schlafentzug und Kalorienrestruktion auf biologische Merkmale der Depression. *Lancet* (German edition), **1**, 114–118.

Norris, P.D., O'Malley, B.P. and Palmer, R.L. (1985). The TRH-test in bulimia and anorexia nervosa: a controlled study. *J. Psychiat. Res.*, **19**, 215–229.

Nudel, D.B., Gootman, N., Nussbaum, M.P. and Shenker, I.R. (1984). Altered exercise performance and abnormal sympathetic responses to exercise in patients with anorexia nervosa. *J. Pediatr.*, **105**, 34–37.

Philipp, E. and Pirke, K.M. (1987). Effect of starvation on hypothalamic tyrosine hydroxylase activity in adult male rats. *Brain Res.*, **413**, 53–59.

Pirke, K.M., Trimborn, P., Platte, P. and Fichter, M. (1986). Average total energy expenditure in anorexia nervosa, bulimia nervosa, and healthy young women. *Biol. Psychiatr.*, **30**, 711–718.

Pirke, K.M. (1990a). Central neurotransmitter disturbances in bulimia (nervosa). In: M.M. Fichter (Ed.), *Bulimia Nervosa: Basic Research, Diagnosis and Therapy*, pp. 223–234. Chichester: John Wiley.

Pirke, K.M. (1990b). The noradrenergic system in anorexia and bulimia nervosa. In: H. Remschmidt and M.H. Schmidt (Eds), *Child and Youth Psychiatry*, pp. 30–44. Stuttgart: Hogrefe & Huber.

Pirke, K.M., Fichter, M.M., Lund, R. and Doerr, P. (1979). Twenty-four-hour sleep–wake pattern of plasma LH in patients with anorexia nervosa. *Acta Endocrinol.*, **92**, 193–204.

Pirke, K.M. and Spyra, B. (1981). Influence of starvation on testosterone-luteinizing hormone feedback in the rat. *Acta Endocrinol. (Copenh.)*, **96**, 413–421.

Pirke, K.M. and Spyra, B. (1982). Catecholamine turnover in the brain and the regulation of luteinizing hormone and corticosterone in starved male rats. *Acta Endocrinologica*, **100**, 168–176.

Pirke, K.M., Schweiger, U., Laessle, R., Dickhaut, B., Schweiger, M. and Waechtler, M. (1986). Dieting influences the menstrual cycle: vegetarian versus nonvegetarian diet. *Fertil. Steril.*, **46**, 1083–1088.

Pirke, K.M. Fichter, M.M. and Schweiger, U. (1987). Gonadotropin secretion pattern in bulimia nervosa. *Int. J. Eating Dis.*, **6**, 655–661.

Pirke, K.M., Dogs, M., Fichter, M.M. et al (1988). Gonadotropins, oestradiol and progesterone during the menstrual cycle in bulimia nervosa. *Clin. Endocrinol.*, **29**, 265–270.

Pirke, K.M., Eckert, M., Ofers, B., et al (1989a). Plasma norepinephrine response to exercise in bulimia, anorexia nervosa and in controls. *Biol. Psychiat.*, **25**, 799–802.

Pirke, K.M., Schweiger, U., Strowitzki, T., Tuschi, R.J., Laessle, R.G., Broocks, A., Huber, B. and Middendorf, R. (1989b). Dieting causes menstrual irregularities in normal-weight young women through impairment of episodic luteinizing hormone secretion. *Fertil. Steril.*, **51**, 263–268.

Pirke, K.M., Tuschl, R.J., Spyra, B., et al. (1990). Endocrine findings in restrained eaters. *Physiol. Behav.*, **47**, 903–906.

Pirke, K.M., Kellner, M., Philipp, E., Laessle, R., Krieg, J.C. and Fichter, M.M. (1992). Plasma norepinephrine after a standardized test meal in acute and remitted patients with anorexia nervosa and in healthy controls. *Biol. Psychiat.*, **31**, 1074–1077.

Richter, C.P.A. (1992). A behavioristic study of the activity of the rat. *Comp. Psychol. Monog.*, **4**, 1–55.

Robinson, S. and Winnek, H.Z. (1973). Severe psychotic disturbances following crash diet weight loss. *Arch. Gen. Psychiat.*, **29**, 559–562.

Routtenberg, A. and Kuznesoff, A.W. (1967). Self-starvation of rats living in activity wheels on a restricted feeding schedule. *J. Comp. Physiol. Psychol.*, **64**, 414–421.

Scheinin, M. and MacDonald, E. (1989). An introduction to the pharmacology of alpha$_2$-adrenoceptors in the central nervous system. *Acta Vet. Scand.*, **85**, 11–19.

Schelp, F.P., Migasena, P., Saovakontha, S., et al (1976). Serum protein fractions from children of differing nutritional status analysed by polyacrylamide gel electrophoresis and electroimmunoassay. *Br. J. Nutr.*, **35**, 211–222.

Schelp, F.P., Migasena, P., Pongpaew, P., et al (1977). Serum proteinase inhibitors and other serum proteins in protein-energy malnutrition. *Br. J. Nutr.*, **38**, 31–38.

Schelp, F.P., Migasena, P., Pongpaew, P., et al. (1978). Are protein inhibitors a factor for the derangement of homeostasis in protein-energy malnutrition. *Am. J. Clin. Nutr.*, **31**, 451–456.

Schweiger, U., Warnhoff, M. and Pirke, K.M. (1985a). Central noradrenergic turnover and corticosterone secretion in semistarvation. *Acta Endocrinologica*, **108**, 267.

Schweiger, U., Warnhoff, M. and Pirke, K.M. (1985b). Norepinephrine turnover in the hypothalamus of adult male rats: alteration of circadian patterns by semistarvation. *J. Neurochem.*, **45**, 706–709.

Schweiger, U., Laessle, R., Kittl, S., Dickhaut, B., Schweiger, M. and Pirke, K.M. (1986). Macronutrient intake, plasma large neutral amino acids and mood during weight-reducing diets. *J. Neural. Transm.,* **67**, 77–86.

Schweiger, U., Laessle, R., Pfister, H., Hoehl, C., Schwingenschloegel, M., Schweiger, M. and Pirke, K.M. (1987). Diet-induced menstrual irregularities: effects of age and weight loss. *Fertil. Steril.,* **48**, 746–751.

Smith, S.R., Bledsoe, T. and Chhetri, M.K. (1975). Cortisol metabolism and the pituitary–adrenal axis in adults with protein-calorie malnutrition. *J. Clin. Endocrinol. Metab.,* **40**, 43–52.

Smoller, J.W., Wadden, T.A. and Stunkard, A.J. (1987). Dieting and depression: a critical review. *J. Psychosom. Res.,* **31**, 429–440.

Stunkard, A.J. and Messink, S. (1985). The three factor eating questionnaire to measure dietary restraint, disinhibition and hunger. *J. Psychosom. Res.,* **29**, 71–81.

Tamai, H., Mori, K. Matsubayashi, S., et al (1986). Hypothalamic–pituitary–thyroidal dysfunctions in anorexia nervosa. *Psychother. Psychosom.,* **46**, 127–131.

Tibaldi, J.M. and Surks, M.I. (1985). Effects of nonthyroidal illness on thyroid function. *Med. Clin. North Am.,* **69**, 899–911.

Treasure, J.L. (1988). The ultrasonographic features in anorexia nervosa and bulimia nervosa: a simplified method of monitoring hormonal states during weight gain. *Psychosom. Res.,* **32**, 623–634.

Van der Kar, L.D., Carnes, M., Maslowski, J., Bonadonna, A.M., Rittenhouse, P.A., Kunimoto, K., Piechowski, R.A. and Bethea, C.L. (1989). Neuroendocrine evidence for denervation supersensitivity of serotonin receptors: effects of the 5-HT agonist RU 24969 on corticotropin, corticosterone, prolactin and renin secretion. *J. Pharamcol. Exp. Ther.,* **251**, 428–434.

Walsh, B.T., Lo, E.S., Cooper, T., et al (1987). The DST and plasma dexamethasone levels in bulimia. *Arch. Gen. Psychiat.,* **44**, 799–800.

Warnhoff, M., Dorsch, G. and Pirke, K.M. (1983). Effect of starvation on gonadotrophin secretion and on *in vitro* release of LRH from the isolated median emminence of the male rat. *Acta Endocrinologica,* **103**, 293–301.

Wilckens, T., Schweiger, U. and Pirke, K.M. (1992a). Activation of alpha$_2$-adrenoceptors suppresses excessive wheel running in the semistarvation-induced hyperactive rat. *Pharmacol. Biochem. Behav.,* **43**, 733–738.

Wilckens, T., Schweiger, U. and Pirke, K.M. (1992b). Activation of 5-HT$_{1C}$-receptors suppresses excessive wheel running induced by semi-starvation in the rat. *Psychopharmacology,* **109**, 77–84.

Wing, R.W. (1992). Weight cycling in humans: a review of the literature. *Ann. Behav. Med.,* **14**, 113–119.

6

A Physiology of Starvation that Sustains Eating Disorders

P.H. ROBINSON
Gordon Hospital, London, UK
AND
P.R. McHUGH
Johns Hopkins University Hospital, Baltimore, USA

INTRODUCTION

Anorexia nervosa and bulimia nervosa are behavioural disorders in which psychological and physiological manifestations are intriguingly combined. We will argue that some of the physiological features act to *sustain* the behaviour of fasting in these conditions even though these physiological features are the consequences of starvation and thus cannot be presumed to be *provocative* or *precipitating* causes of the disorders.

In this essay in honour of our colleague and friend, Professor Gerald Russell, who has pioneered the identification of both the psychological and the physiological features of these conditions, we shall propose a set of hypotheses about the role of gastric physiology—particularly changes in gastric emptying that could have survival value during "natural" starvation—in provoking a sensation of fullness or satiation that may encourage or sustain the anorexic behaviour in these disorders. We believe that gastric responses to starvation are just one of several "peripheral" physiological events that do not precipitate but sustain anorexic behaviour once

Handbook of Eating Disorders: Theory, Treatment and Research.
Edited by G. Szmukler, C. Dare and J. Treasure.
© 1995 John Wiley & Sons Ltd.

launched by rigorous dieting. However, information on gastric physiology both under "normal" conditions of feeding and under the "emergency" of starvation is sufficiently advanced to provide a basis for such proposals and further investigation.

In the study of basic mechanisms controlling food intake, much evidence has accumulated indicating that control of the rate of gastric emptying is an important physiological modulator of caloric intake. It has also been shown that patients with eating disorders have patterns of gastric emptying that vary from controls. Our hypothesis is that alterations in feeding patterns in eating disorders may be, at least in part, explained by variations in gastric emptying rate.

CCK (cholecystokinin) is a brain–gut peptide with established roles in the modulation of both food intake and gastric emptying. The peptide has also been the subject of some study in anorexia nervosa. Again, our hypothesis is that variation in cholecystokinin function may explain in part patterns of feeding and gastric emptying in eating disorders.

We will first consider our studies of food intake in eating disorders, and then relate them to the relevant studies of underlying physiological processes.

CONTROL OF FOOD INTAKE IN EATING DISORDERS: RESEARCH FINDINGS

Gastric Emptying

The study of gastric emptying covers a number of functions, including accumulation of solids and liquids within the stomach, trituration of solids, and controlled release of solids and liquids into the duodenum. It is the last function which has received most attention in the investigation of gastric function in relation to control of feeding behaviour.

In anorexia nervosa, gastric emptying has been studied several times using different techniques. The consensus, however, is that emptying of both solids and liquids is delayed to a variable extent in patients compared with controls (Robinson, Clarke and Barrett, 1988). It has also been reported (Dubois et al, 1977) that secretion of gastric fluids is reduced in anorexia nervosa. In two studies (Robinson, Clarke and Barrett, 1988; Szmukler et al, 1990) patients controlling their own diet were found to have significantly delayed emptying while patients eating a full diet on a refeeding regimen had normal gastric emptying. This suggests that delayed gastric emptying in anorexia nervosa is dependent on dietary intake. In Figure 6.1, a gastric scan of a patient two hours after ingestion of a meal of radiolabelled poached egg-white is compared with that of a patient with anorexia nervosa, demonstrating delayed gastric emptying in the patient.

In bulimia nervosa, agreement has been less complete. Delayed gastric emptying was found in some studies (Geliebter et al, 1992) but not in others (Robinson, Clarke and Barrett, 1988; Hutson and Wald, 1990). In one study (Robinson, Clarke and Barrett, 1988), delayed gastric emptying was found in patients with bulimia nervosa whose eating disorder was severe enough to cause major weight loss, sufficient to attract the diagnosis of anorexia nervosa. In some patients with bulimia

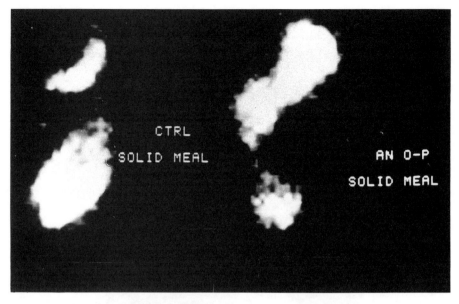

FIGURE 6.1   Technetium-labelled meals two hours after ingestion in a normal control (left) and in a patient with anorexia nervosa controlling her own diet (right). The meal (based on poached egg-white) has largely emptied into the small intestine in the control, but emptying is grossly delayed in the anorexic patients.

nervosa, gastro-oesophageal reflux has been observed, sometimes unnoticed by the patient (Figure 6.2).

CCK and Eating Disorders

In anorexia nervosa, CCK has received some attention. Blood levels were shown to be elevated in two studies (Harty et al, 1991, Phillipp et al, 1991) and normal in another (Geracioti et al, 1992), so the field is still open for study. In bulimia nervosa, one study reported a reduction in CCK levels compared with healthy controls and patients with hyperphagia associated with depression, and this reduced level improved with treatment (Geracioti et al, 1989).

Hunger and Satiety in Eating Disorders

The terms "hunger" and "satiety" are seldom defined or clearly distinguished. In man they can be measured by means of a score on a visual analogue scale (VAS). In other words, hunger is what subjects report they feel when they score "hungry" on the scale. Similarly, with satiety or "fullness". In studying a group of subjects, a shared language and culture is assumed and a subject may well give a different meaning and significance to words used in a scale compared with other subjects or the experimenter. Despite these problems, important information has come from studies of hunger and satiety reports.

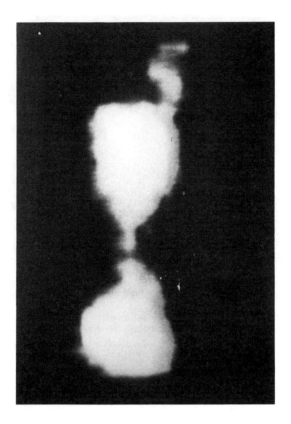

FIGURE 6.2   Technetium gastric scan in a patient with bulimia nervosa, demonstrating gastro-oesophageal reflux, which was unnoticed by the patient.

Patients with anorexia nervosa frequently complain of "bloating" or excessive fullness after eating, and results of gastric emptying studies suggest a possible biological basis for this symptom. Surprisingly, studies of hunger and satiety in eating disorders are rather few (Coddington and Bruch, 1970; Robinson et al, 1983; Robinson, 1989). It has, however, been demonstrated that patients with anorexia nervosa do report feeling fuller on VAS ratings than do matched controls both before and after eating. A typical series of ratings is shown in Figure 6.3. Data from gastric emptying would predict slow recovery of preprandial fullness ratings following a meal. What is observed, however, is elevated ratings at all points, before, immediately after and two hours after the meal. These results invite at least two possible explanations:

1. Preprandially, the stomach of a patient with anorexia nervosa still contains food from the previous day and the ratings reflect a real increase in gastric contents (physiological explanation).
2. Patients with anorexia nervosa have a tendency to rate highly on fullness in a way which may be analogous to the increased ratings of body size (psychological explanation).

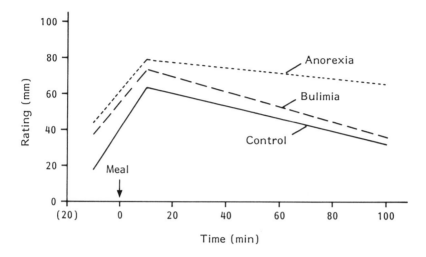

FIGURE 6.3   Ratings of fullness before and after a standard meal in controls and in patients with eating disorders. Ratings are elevated in the anorexic group of patients ($p < 0.001$) two hours after the meal, in spite of normal mean gastric emptying rate.

Studying a group of patients with anorexia nervosa who were being re-fed at an inpatient unit provided information bearing on this question. This group of patients had normal gastric emptying. However, their VAS results were indistinguishable from those of patients with slow gastric emptying. Both groups were significantly different from controls. The results indicate that patients with anorexia nervosa have satiety report patterns consistent with delayed gastric emptying, irrespective of current characteristics of gastric emptying. These findings suggest that the latter of the two explanations (i.e. the psychological) is the better.

The following question then arises: What is the origin of enhanced satiety in anorexia nervosa? Again, two answers suggest themselves:

1. Patients with anorexia nervosa have a tendency to exaggerate in relation to perceptions of nutritional state and body image, particularly when such exaggeration provides a rationale for undereating (i.e. "I am full, therefore I need not eat", and "I am fat, therefore I must not eat"). In other words, they have a predetermined cognitive set or antecedent condition in anorexia nervosa.
2. Patients with established anorexia nervosa have, when controlling their own diet, delayed gastric emptying. When the gastric emptying has been normalised, the learned association between eating and prolonged satiety persists, overrides the unaccustomed change in gastric function, and reported sensation accords with expectations rather than physiology. In other words, there is a learned cognitive distortion or a consequential condition in anorexia nervosa.

We do not have adequate data to distinguish these two hypotheses, but it is quite possible that both mechanisms may be active and interrelated especially in patients with anorexia and a significant degree of starvation.

VAS responses over the pre- to postprandial phase can be analysed by observing which ratings are related to gastric contents. This was done in the studies of one of the authors (PHR) by labelling gastric contents with 99ᵐ-technetium, measuring the counts in the area of the stomach at different times after a standard meal with a gamma camera, and obtaining analogue scale ratings of hunger, satiety and other constructs made at the same time. To quantify the association between gastric contents and analogue scale ratings, Spearman's rank correlation coefficients were calculated.

In normal control subjects and in normal-weight patients with bulimia nervosa, correlations of approximately ±0.6 were found between gastric contents and "hunger", "urge to eat" (negative correlation) and "fullness" (positive correlation). No other scale yielded significant correlations. "Hunger" and "fullness" were highly significantly correlated with each other. In anorexia nervosa patients, the mean correlation coefficient between gastric contents and fullness was about 0.5, not significantly different from controls. However, "hunger" and "urge to eat" were not significantly correlated with either gastric contents or with "fullness". These constructs ("hunger", "urge to eat") were, therefore, dissociated from gastric contents and a measure of satiety ("fullness") in anorexia nervosa patients.

In both bulimia nervosa and anorexia nervosa patients, high correlations were often observed between gastric contents and other scales, including "depression" and "fatness". This association, which was not observed in normal controls, was termed *paraceptivity*, indicating a distortion of gastric perception so that it is closely linked with scales measuring affective and affect-laden symptoms. It may be likened to the "conditioned emotional response" explored by Joseph Brady in the 1950s.

LABORATORY RESEARCH BEARING ON THE CLINICAL FINDINGS

Gastric Emptying

Much research has indicated that modulation of gastric emptying is an important factor in the normal control of food intake. Consumption of nutrients may be modified by a number of manipulations that act, at least in part, by inhibiting gastric emptying and enhancing satiety, including intraduodenal glucose (Brener, Hendrix and McHugh, 1983), fenfluramine treatment (Robinson, Moran and McHugh, 1986) and CCK infusions (Moran and McHugh, 1982). This evidence indicates, therefore, that delayed gastric emptying could be an important inhibitory factor on food intake in anorexia nervosa.

In order to test whether delayed gastric emptying actually does make a contribution to reduced food intake in anorexia nervosa, an experimental model of delayed gastric emptying has been developed in the rat. To date the model has been used to explore the role of diet in the genesis of delayed gastric emptying and this work will be summarised.

Twelve Sprague-Dawley rats were allowed to feed only between 9.00 a.m. and 11.00 a.m. Gastric emptying was measured at 5.00 p.m. by giving the rat, by gavage,

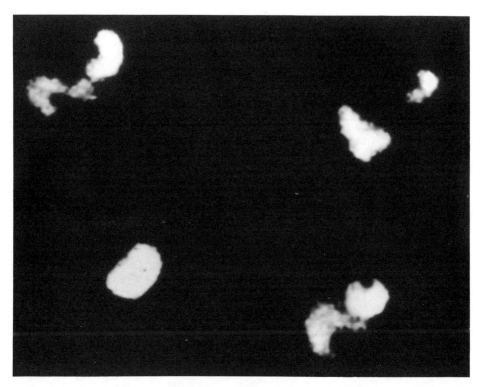

FIGURE 6.4   Abdominal scans of two rats after a meal of Tc-labelled egg, showing gastric and small-intestinal contents post-prandially (left) and after 120 min (right). The meal-time restricted rat is shown at the bottom, the control rat above. Food restriction markedly slows the rate of gastric emptying.

5 ml of cooked egg-white labelled with technetium and taking 5-second gastric images using a gamma camera every 30 minutes for 2 hours. Control animals were allowed free access to food over the whole 24 hours.

After 4 months of the time-restricted diet, gastric emptying was measured. Gastric emptying in the experimental animals was grossly delayed (Figure 6.4). In these animals, growth was also significantly curtailed. All animals were then given free access to food. Weight increased but did not, even after 3 months, catch up with controls. Gastric emptying after 3 months did return to normal control levels.

Gastric emptying can, therefore, be delayed by dietary manipulation. It is likely, though not certain, that the delayed gastric emptying of anorexia nervosa and that of the mealtime-restricted rat, share physiological mechanisms. A number of questions remain unanswered:

1. Is the delayed gastric emptying of the mealtime-restricted rat observed throughout the 24 hours?
2. What is the mechanism of the delayed gastric emptying?
3. What is the effect on food intake of having delayed gastric emptying in the mealtime-restricted rat?

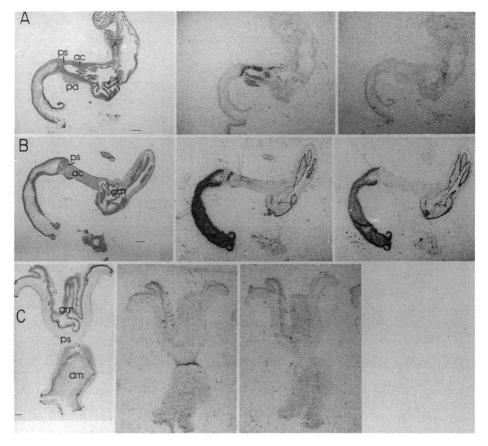

FIGURE 6.5   CCK receptors in a rat's upper gastrointestinal tract. (A) 10-day rat: histology (left), total CCK binding (centre), non-specific binding (right). Specific binding is observed in pyloric sphincter, antral circular muscle and pancreas. (B) 15-day rat: specific binding is confined to pyloric sphincter. (C) Adult rat: specific binding is confined to pyloric sphincter. Reproduced by permission from Robinson et al, 1987.

ps = pyloric sphincter; ac = antral circular muscle; pa = pancreas; gm = gastric mucosa; am = antral mucosa.

Cholecystokinin

CCK is a peptide of variable length (between 8 and 54 amino acids) with specific full activity residing in the 8 C-terminal amino acids, the last four of which it shares with gastrin, a closely related peptide. Its functions in the body are exceedingly complex and none has yet been shown unequivocally to be physiologically necessary. However, inhibition of food intake by CCK has been demonstrated after intravenous, intraperitoneal and intracerebral delivery, after paraventricular nucleus micro-injection as well as after injection at other central sites (e.g. Della-Fera and Baile, 1979). CCK is thought, in part, to reduce feeding by inhibiting gastric emptying. The proposal has been the subject of many experiments but none has proved that CCK does not act by this means. The hypothesis has proven of great heuristic value,

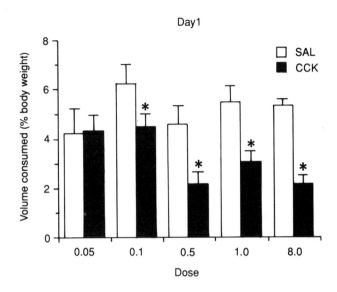

FIGURE 6.6   Volume of milk consumed by day-1 rats, ingesting independently in an incubator containing a milk-soaked towel, after different doses (µg/kg) of CCK-8 and vehicle. At 0.1 µg/kg and above ingestion is significantly (*) inhibited. Reproduced by permission from Robinson, Moran and McHugh, 1988.

as it has spawned a large number of research projects aimed at disproving it. The evidence in favour of the proposal is as follows:

1. CCK inhibits feeding.
2. It also inhibits gastric emptying.
3. The inhibition of feeding by CCK is augmented by placing a preload in the stomach (Moran and McHugh, 1982).
4. A receptor system exists which is highly specific for CCK and which appears to mediate inhibition of gastric emptying.

   CCK receptors in the stomach of the rat were first identified autoradiographically in 1984 (Smith et al, 1984) (Figure 6.5(c)). In the adult rat they form a tight band of receptors localised to the distal part of the pyloric sphincter. They have also been identified in humans in an analogous location (Robinson, McHugh, Moran and Stephenson, 1988). In the rat the receptors appear early in development (Figure 6.5(a) and (b)) and can be observed in the neonatal and even the foetal rat (Robinson et al, 1987). Moreover, inhibition of feeding (Figure 6.6) and gastric emptying by CCK can be demonstrated in the rat during the neonatal period (Robinson, Moran and McHugh, 1988) when brain CCK receptors are poorly developed. Moreover, at pyloric CCK receptors, CCK and gastrin are well distinguished in displacement experiments, while central CCK receptors, for the most part, possess a lower degree of specificity. The receptors of higher specificity have been termed type A (alimentary), while those of lower specificity, found mostly in the brain, have been termed type B (Moran et al, 1986).

Evidence obtained using CCK antagonists has suggested that CCK is an important physiological mediator of satiety in some circumstances and that it also plays a part in the physiological control of gastric emptying. In summary, there is much circumstantial evidence suggesting that induction of delayed gastric emptying contributes to the development of CCK satiety.

GASTRIC EMPTYING AND CONTROL OF FOOD INTAKE: SOME HYPOTHESES

The research findings reviewed above can be summarised as follows:

1. Gastric emptying is delayed in patients with anorexia nervosa who are restricting their diet.
2. CCK levels in plasma of patients with eating disorders are variably different from controls.
3. Ratings of satiety are elevated in anorexia nervosa, whether or not gastric emptying is prolonged.
4. Rats fed on a growth-inhibiting restricted time schedule developed delayed gastric emptying.
5. CCK affects both gastric emptying and feeding via a complex receptor system, the gastric segment of which appears early in development.

In this section the significance of these findings will be discussed and future research options considered.

Slow gastric emptying in anorexia nervosa appears to be a response to reduced gastric filling and starvation. In patients who were restricting their caloric intake, gastric emptying was abnormally slow. It was also abnormal in patients who overate and vomited, provided the calories absorbed were few enough to maintain a very low body weight. In these patients, plenty of calories reached the stomach, but they did not enter the duodenum. It appears, therefore, that in anorexia nervosa and bulimia nervosa, gastric emptying is delayed when calories entering the duodenum fall below a certain threshold level.

Two pieces of evidence suggest that, at least in mammals, delayed gastric emptying during starvation is a general phenomenon. It occurred in rats on a restricted feeding schedule and it was also observed in men subjected to a prolonged period of caloric deprivation (Keys et al, 1950). This suggests a biological function. When food is in short supply, gastric emptying slows. It might appear counter-intuitive that satiety should be enhanced under conditions of poor food supply, when survival might depend on the animal actively searching for food. There are other possible explanations with intriguing implications.

1. Enhanced satiety would prevent the animal from embarking on *fruitless* searches for food. This suggests that the stomach may entrain itself to the food supply. Thus, an animal with a continuous source of food—modern western man being one of the few examples—would have rapid gastric emptying, whereas an animal

in which food appeared rarely, as is the case in most carnivores, would have proportionately slower gastric emptying.

2. Slow gastric emptying might improve the efficiency of nutrient absorption. This could be tested experimentally.

3. The stomach acts as a reservoir for as yet unabsorbed food. If food supply is scarce, delayed gastric emptying would enhance the action of the stomach as the body's "larder" and delay absorption of nutrients, especially protein which cannot easily be stored. Moreover, expenditure of the energy required for digestion, absorption and storage would be delayed. Slowing of gastric emptying, with retarded absorption, may be one of the mechanisms that reduce metabolic rate during the "emergency" of starvation.

4. If the stomach does entrain its emptying rate to food supply, the mechanism whereby this "gastric learning" occurs is quite obscure, and may be mediated by central, peripheral, neural or chemical (e.g. peptide) processes.

The Role of Delayed Gastric Emptying in Anorexia Nervosa

The concept of one or more primary causes of anorexia nervosa seems difficult to sustain. In fact one of the original efforts in seeking a specific physiological cause for anorexia nervosa was for some primary hypothalamic dysregulatory event manifest in possible changes such as hypothermia, endocrine suppression or gonadal dysfunctioning. These efforts all seemed for naught when every one of the phenomena evident in an anorexic patient was demonstrated to be secondary to starvation and recovered with refeeding (see Chapter 5). It thus could not be considered a "predisposing" or "precipitating" condition. The efforts to find either a particular kind of hypothalamic dysfunction or some specific endocrine disorder as the primary aetiology of anorexia nervosa have all but been abandoned.

Eating disorders are, in fact, the results of dieting behaviour and this behaviour, provoked as it usually is psychosocially from aspects of family life or by some psychodynamic conflict, must be considered the precipitating cause—perhaps made more powerful in the context of the psychosocial factors mentioned. However, as most women diet at some time and only a few develop anorexia nervosa, some other influences which emerge subsequent to dieting must be proposed that shift common dieting into anorexia nervosa or bulimia nervosa. These factors—which might be termed "transforming" and "sustaining" factors subsequent to the "precipitating" factor of dieting—probably include some of the physiological responses to nutritional restriction that had previously been investigated as clues to a hypothalamic "primary" cause for eating disorders.

We thus propose a shift of emphasis in the study of the physiology of anorexia nervosa and bulimia nervosa away from a search for evidence of some central nervous system dysregulation that explains the onset and course of the disorder, towards a search through the several physiological changes provoked by starvation for those that might sustain the behaviour. These might turn out to be key "anorexigenic" processes not because they start a patient on a course of dieting or because they evoke anorexia *de novo*, but because they act—perhaps along with psychological stressors—to shift dieters into anorexics and then help to sustain the resolve to avoid nutrients. We see here a similar shift of emphasis as occurred in the study of food intake itself when a focus on "central" hypothalamic mechanisms for hunger and satiety was replaced by a study of "peripheral" physiological events tied to food intake that might provoke the sensations of hunger and satiety.

We chose to study gastric function only because the stomach is the first site affected by the profound diminution of food intake, leading eventually to cachexia. Other physiological systems might as well be surveyed for their potential for combining with psychological factors in sustaining fasting behaviour. Moreover, similar sustaining and exacerbating roles can be postulated for psychological and family processes, for example, engaging in destructive relationships in bulimia nervosa, and "high expressed emotion" patterns of family interaction. The eating disorder can be seen as the result of action and reaction between the patient and his or her environment at and between all levels of organisation, from molecular to cultural.

The development of delayed gastric emptying appears very likely to follow the onset of dieting and the resulting enhanced satiety could well aid the downward trend in weight. The determinants of the degree of delayed gastric emptying are unknown. It may be that, amongst youthful females with a particular genetic disposition, a very marked delay in gastric emptying occurs with the onset of dieting, and this interaction between genetic make-up, development and eating behaviour leads to increasing food restriction and frank anorexia nervosa.

It is likely that delayed emptying is responsible for prolonged satiety after meals. This continued feeling of gastric fullness persisted even when gastric emptying had returned to normal, suggesting an abnormality of interoception, perhaps analogous to that in exteroception (in body image) which has been well established. It would be of interest to study, in anorexia nervosa, perception of a physiological variable such as bladder contents or muscle power that did not clearly relate to body weight and shape.

The association of symptomatic scales with gastric contents (paraceptivity) is of interest, suggesting as it does the close association between distress and satiety in these patients. Thus, a patient who had just eaten might well feel more "sad" and this state would decline as stomach distention reduced. Equally, she or he might relate stomach fullness to feelings of fatness which decline as the stomach empties. This connectedness between psychological symptom and the physiological state of an organ may not be confined to eating disorders and could merit study in other disorders—for example, measures of cardiac and respiratory physiology in anxiety and panic disorders. The lack of association between either fullness or gastric contents and the term "hunger" represents a disconnection between hunger and satiety which, to our knowledge, had not previously been described when we reported it first in 1983. It suggests that the concept "hunger" is not used normally in patients with anorexia nervosa. Sometimes hunger was denied (very low scores) but in other patients it was chaotic and unrelated to eating or gastric emptying. It may be that a rating of *fullness* (which, although elevated in anorexia nervosa, did vary in the expected direction with gastric contents) is an expression merely of gastric state; *hunger* implies a readiness to eat.

Gastro-oesophageal reflux has not been studied systematically, but is often suspected clinically, when symptoms such as "heartburn" and regurgitation of gastric contents occurs. It appears to develop after the onset of self-induced vomiting, and it may become a sustaining factor by rendering vomiting more easy to perform. This important area, with implications for treatment, remains to be investigated.

Might Abnormal CCK Function be an Aetiological Factor in Anorexia Nervosa or Bulimia Nervosa?

Studies have, as yet, been too few to rule out a disturbance of CCK secretion or receptor sensitivity in eating disorders. Such studies have presented a number of problems. Assay of plasma levels of CCK has until recent years been uncertain because of the molecular heterogeneity of the peptide. A number of different forms circulate—some but not others are active; some are precursors; others are active end-products. Bioassay and specific radioimmunoassay have largely overcome these problems. CCK is secreted postprandially after nutrients have entered the duodenum. Hence, variations in gastric emptying rate will profoundly affect plasma levels of CCK after a meal. Simultaneous measurement of CCK levels and gastric emptying has not been reported. CCK levels could be unremarkable in eating disorders, but receptor sensitivity might be elevated or depressed. This could be investigated using receptor autoradiography in biopsy specimens or by observing the physical response (pancreatic, cholecystokinetic and gastric emptying) to different doses of exogenous CCK. Lastly, specific CCK receptor antagonists (e.g. devazepide, loxiglumide, and others) could be administered to patients with eating disorders to establish a measure of receptor sensitivity. They could also be administered to experimental animals (e.g. restricted-meal-schedule rats) to attempt antagonism of the delayed gastric emptying in that model. Preliminary work (Robinson and Stephenson, unpublished observations) suggests that the specific CCK-A antagonist devazepide does not reverse the delayed gastric emptying observed in meal-restricted rats.

At present there is little evidence to implicate abnormal CCK function in the aetiology of eating disorders. Abnormal gastric emptying with clear implications for contributing to the development of eating disorders is well established, and these and other findings suggest a range of further studies in both the clinical population and in laboratory animals to enhance understanding of eating disorders.

CONCLUSIONS

It is our contention that "peripheral" physiological events—of which altered gastric emptying is one—give to anorexia nervosa a pathophysiology that follows but sustains the psychosocially induced commitment to dieting. This pathophysiology provides "fullness" signals conducive to abnormal perceptions, to conditioned states and to conditioned emotional responses. That is to say: these sensations of fullness not only inhibit feeding itself, but as well (a) act as conditioned signals tied to body weight, suggesting that efforts at dieting must be redoubled, and (b) evoke fear and depression in these individuals committed to controlling their body weight.

Amongst the several advantages of demonstrating interrelationships between psychological and physiological aspects of anorexia is the obvious therapeutic implication. If physiological states produced by starvation can sustain anorexic behaviour, then renourishment is once again emphasised as a first step in treatment— as Gerald Russell proposed decades ago. Renourishment will not deal with the precipitating or sustaining psychosocial causes of anorexia nervosa, but will make an approach to them—in individual, group and family therapy—easier. Some beneficial effects of renutrition are:

1. Correcting the abnormal physiology of starvation.
2. Regularising the gastrointestinal, endocrine, and autonomic status of the body.
3. Placing the patient into an extinction mode as regards the abnormal conditioning states such as exaggerated responses to gastric filling and the conditioned emotional responses of "paraceptivity".

Rectifying physiological disturbances, perceptual distortions, as well as family and psychodynamic conflicts takes time, and intervention at physical, psychological, family and social levels of organisation. Only by paying due attention to all these areas can we hope to provide a systematic approach that considers both the psychological and the physiological aspects of these complex conditions.

REFERENCES

Brener, W., Hendrix, T.R. and McHugh, P.R. (1983). Regulation of the gastric emptying of glucose. *Gastroenterology*, **85**, 76–82.

Coddington, R.D. and Bruch, H. (1970). Gastric perceptivity in normal, obese and schizophrenic subjects. *Psychosomatics*, **11**, 571–579.

Della-Fera, M.A. and Baile, C.A. (1979). Cholecystokinin octapeptide: continuous picomole injections into the cerebral ventricles of sheep suppress feeding. *Science*, **206**, 471–473.

Dubois, A., Gross, H.A., Ebert, M.H. and Castell, D.O. (1979). Altered gastric emptying and secretion in primary anorexia nervosa. *Gastroenterology*, **77**, 319–323.

Geliebter, A., Melton, P.M., McCray, R.S., Gallagher, D.R., Gage, D. and Hashim, S.A. (1992). Gastric capacity, gastric emptying, and test-meal intake in normal and bulimic women. *American Journal of Clinical Nutrition*, **56**, 656–661.

Geracioti, T.D., Kling, M.A., Joseph, V., Kanayama, S., Rosenthal, N.E., Gold, P.W. and Liddle, R.A. (1989). Meal-related cholecystokinin secretion in eating and affective disorders. *Psychopharmacology Bulletin*, **25**, 444–449.

Geracioti, T.D., Liddle, R.A., Altemus, M., Demitrack, M.A. and Gold, P.W. (1992). Regulation of appetite and cholecystokinin secretion in anorexia nervosa. *American Journal of Psychiatry*, **149**, 958–961.

Harty, R.F., Pearson, P.H., Solomon, T.E. and McGuigan, J.E. (1991). Cholecystokinin, vasoactive intestinal peptide and peptide histidine methionine responses to feeding in anorexia nervosa. *Regulatory Peptides*, **36**, 141–150.

Hutson, W.R. and Wald, A. (1990). Gastric emptying in patients with bulimia nervosa and anorexia nervosa. *American Journal of Gastroenterology*, **85**, 41–46.

Keys, A., Brozek, J., Henschel, A., Michelson, O., Taylor, H. (1950). *The Biology of Human Starvation*. Minneapolis: University of Minnesota Press.

Moran, T.H. and McHugh, P.R. (1982). Cholecystokinin suppresses food intake by inhibiting gastric emptying. *American Journal of Physiology,* **242**, (*Regulatory Integrative Comp. Physiol.,* **11**): R491–497.

Moran, T.H., Robinson, P.H., Goldrich, M. and McHugh, P.R. (1986). Two brain CCK receptors: implications for behavioral actions. *Brain Research,* **362**, 175–179.

Phillipp, E., Pirke, K.M., Kellner, M.B. and Krieg, J.C. (1991). Distrubed cholecystokinin secretion in patients with eating disorders. *Life Science,* **48**, 2443–2450.

Robinson, P.H. (1989). Perceptivity and paraceptivity during measurement of gastric emptying in anorexia and bulimia nervosa. *British Journal of Psychiatry,* **154**, 400–405.

Robinson, P.H., Clarke, M. and Barrett, J. (1988). Determinants of gastric emptying in anorexia nervosa and bulimia nervosa. *Gut,* **29**, 458–464.

Robinson, P.H., McHugh, P.R., Moran, T.H. and Stephenson, J.D. (1988). Gastric Control of Food Intake. *Journal of Psychosomatic Research,* **32**, 593–606.

Robinson, P.H., Moran, T.H., Goldrich, M. and McHugh, P.R. (1987). Development of cholecystokinin receptors in rat upper gastrointestinal tract. *American Journal of Physiology,* **252** (*Gastrointest. Liver Physiol.* **15**), G529–534.

Robinson, P.H., Moran, T.H. and McHugh, P.R. (1986). Inhibition of gastric emptying and feeding by fenfluramine. *American Journal of Physiology,* **250** (*Regulatory Integrative Comp. Physiol.* **19**): R764–769.

Robinson, P.H., Moran, T.H. and McHugh, P.R. (1988). Cholecystokinin inhibits independent ingestion in neonatal rats. *American Journal of Physiology,* **255** (*Regulatory Integrative Comp. Physiol.* **24**): R14–20.

Robinson, R.G., Tortosa, M., Sullivan, J., Buchanan, E., Andersen, A.E. and Folstein, M.F. (1983). Quantitative assessment of psychologic state of patients with anorexia nervosa or bulimia: response to caloric stimulus. *Psychomatic Medicine,* **45**, 283–292.

Smith, G.T., Moran, T.H., Coyle, J.T., Kuhar, M.J., O'Donahue, T.L. and McHugh, P.R. (1984). Anatomic localization of cholecystokinin receptors to the pyloric sphincter. *American Journal of Physiology,* **246**, (*Regulatory Integrative Comp. Physiol.* **15**): R127–130.

Szmukler, G.I., Young, G.P., Lichtenstein, M. and Andrews, J.T. (1990). A serial study of gastric emptying in anorexia nervosa and bulimia. *Australian and New Zealand Journal of Medicine,* **20**, 220–225.

7

Psychodynamic Models of Eating Disorders

CHRISTOPHER DARE
AND
CATHERINE CROWTHER
Institute of Psychiatry, London, UK

INTRODUCTION

Eating disorder patients have monotonously repetitive fixations. The problem for the clinician is to have a sympathetic understanding of the patient's experience, neither rejecting the patient's views as alien and ridiculous, nor going overboard in sympathy for and acceptance of the patient's attitudes to weight, shape, life and future. The preoccupations are familiar: the patient obsessed with food, compulsively vomiting to avoid the weight increase felt to have immediately ensued from a "binge" of three slices of bread and two low-calorie yoghurts; enormous guilt about having eaten and having vomited; frantically wanting to exercise to shed imaginary fat-inducing calories; screaming with misery that the beam balance suggests a 100 gram weight gain; an appalling lack of inner resources of self-esteem; the fear of separation and of sexuality; the dread of loss of control and of control from the outside. This chapter presents ways of understanding the development of these symptoms by exploring their meaning for the whole person that is the patient.

For historical reasons it is important to maintain a strict distinction between psychodynamic psychopathology and the therapy derived from it. In the early years of psychoanalysis, the understanding of the patient, in psychodynamic terms, was postulated as a literal precursor of specific interventions. Later developments in

Handbook of Eating Disorders: Theory, Treatment and Research.
Edited by G. Szmukler, C. Dare and J. Treasure.
© 1995 John Wiley & Sons Ltd.

psychodynamic psychotherapy differentiate ever more sharply the interpretation of the patient in the therapist's mind (that is to say the therapist's understanding of the patient's dynamic psychopathology) and the interventions (the mobilisation of the understanding) needed to help the patient.

The subject matter of psychodynamic thinking is the *meaning* of the symptomatic state. By convention, in the psychoanalytic model, the *interpreted message* of the symptomatic behaviour is the *cause* of those thoughts and acts. That this is a convention must be emphasised for, of course, the patients' psychopathologies do not create the symptoms; the object relations, the infantile experiences do not predict the anorexia or the bulimia although they may characterise the development of the *experience* of the person with these problems. Psychodynamic psychology emphasises the place of infancy and subsequent experiences in shaping the person so that when that person meets up with the possibility of being anorexic she clasps it to her emaciated breast and makes it her own. The chance to embrace the symptom, its availability to the patient, is determined by social, cultural, familial, biological and cognitive processes. The *need* for, and a psychological *function* derived from embracing, the symptom may have meaning in terms of the developmentally understandable psychological qualities of the person. This chapter is more about a *hermeneutic* of the patient's experience of eating disorder rather than an explanatory aetiology (cf. Laplanche, 1992).

As has been suggested on many occasions (e.g. Sandler, Dare and Holder, 1972, 1973; Dare, 1981), there is not one model of psychodynamic psychology, but many. Because psychodynamic models are derived to contribute to the therapeutic conversations between a particular therapist and a particular patient, the explanations are not constructed with a view to the evolution of a coherent and integrated structure. Manifestly alternative models are often used side by side or one on top of the other in an apparently casual way. The situation is complicated by the bias within psychodynamic theory for fresh insights to be constructed into a new, would-be-all-embracing model which is then added to, rather than used to replace, those that came before. This confusing practice is implicit within the nature of psychodynamic models: they are not empirically derived by formal experimental techniques. Rather, they are built up as classes of "explanations" for patients' experiences. These factors complicate a consistent and extensive account of the psychopathology of eating disorder. In order to cope with these exigencies, this chapter follows, to some extent, the historical development of psychoanalysis, as a means whereby a range of psychodynamic interpretations of eating disorder can be sketched.

PSYCHODYNAMIC PSYCHOPATHOLOGY

Symptoms as Symbolically Meaningful

In attempting to find meaning in the symptoms of a patient, the earliest and a persisting model in psychoanalytic thinking has been the idea that the somatic state can be a symbolic picture of the trauma. Vomiting, for example, has been understood as though it were an attempt to eliminate the unwanted penis of an oral sexual trauma. Fear of fatness has been seen as a rejection of any possible pregnancy. A patient may have an open repulsion for the idea of becoming pregnant and this may be linked to specific thoughts of the mother's pregnancy. The thinness has a symbolic significance representing a theoretical or actual fear. Some patients with symptoms of bingeing and vomiting who have been orally sexually abused may make this connection quite explicit. The extreme emaciation may be an unconscious expression of an identification with a relative dead from an emaciated state.

Mental Mechamisms producing symptoms

Psychoanalytical models assume that the mind functions to manage intense affects. In early models these affects were considered always to have been generated by a psychological trauma. The mind was thought of as functioning to disconnect memories from feelings. This was thought to limit the impact of a painful, frightening or socially unacceptable memory trace. A memory can be conscious, but the affect 'displaced' to be attached to another memory as occurs in an anorexic with obsessional features. A patient may recall, without obvious feeling, real memories (e.g. her displacement at the birth of a much wanted and highly praised younger brother) whilst expressing huge anxiety about a harmless reality, such as the link between eating and gaining weight.

In anorexia or bulimia there may quite often be a history of a specific sexual trauma preceding the onset. Although there are always central problems in the acceptance of sexuality in restricting disorder, it is possible that, in these conditions, bereavement as much as unwanted sex is a more regular theme. This may be especially so in the pre-pubertal and young post-pubertal patient. Rastam and Gillberg (1991) have shown by using a case control method that there is indeed a higher rate of loss by death of first-degree relatives in their population of the families of an adolescent group of anorexic patients.

Rahman, Richardson and Ripley (1939) implied that the wish to starve and waste away was aimed at killing the "'gross' or the 'physical' in the patient". This was added to by Waller, Kaufman and Deutsch (1940) in conceptualising that: "The syndrome [of anorexia nervosa], schematically reconstructed, represents a symbolic wish to be impregnated. Eating is a denial of the wish and an acting out at an unconscious level of this fantasy." The impact of sexual feelings in puberty is clearly a dominant issue in the psychology of anorexic and bulimic patients and the symptoms can often be construed as a way to manage the affects associated with sexuality. Full repression of such affects is regularly observable in restricting eating disorder. This is facilitated by the physiological diminution of secondary sexual endocrine activity. If the symptoms have an onset, after the patient has had an abusive sexual experience, in the authors' patients, this sexual abuse has been extrafamilial. In adult onset or adult re-occurrence, anorexia nervosa may occur in the context of marriage, pregnancy or childbirth, when an overt wish to control sexuality may be a conscious thought.

The mental mechanisms whereby sexuality could be controlled were elaborated in Freud's description of the defence associated with phobic states (Freud, 1894). A memory could be eliminated by repression into unconscious parts of the mind, the affect being then attached to quite another topic. For example, in one of our cases a girl was witness to her parents' intercourse. To her, the mother seemed to be in a dangerous and exciting fight with the father ('The Primal Scene'). The memory was mostly repressed, and that part remaining in consciousness was without feeling. In adolescence, her sexual awakening enabled a reinterpretation of her memory. She became frightened of herself being in intercourse, the whole of the memory was repressed, but the fear of the excitement associated with it became attached to eating food (Waller, 1993; see also Chapter 9).

The idea of the mind as a sort of Leyden jar, filled with a static charge awaiting discharge (which is the implicit imagery of this model of the mind), is not one that can be taken literally. However, it stands as potentially meaningful and evocative. People can experience themselves as filled with emotions or memories that need expression: to be bursting with anger or to experience images from memory as flashbacks. The exploration of memories leading to a relief of the feelings associated with the remembrance is an aspect of a number of psychotherapeutic treatment techniques such as catharsis or forced mourning. The theory associated with the origin of the conceptualisation can be discarded whilst retaining aspects of the usefulness in making contact with and helping patients.

Developmental Aspects

In classical but now outdated psychoanalytic thinking, the disparate varieties of sexuality were conceived of as being differentiated by their endowment with specific sexual energies. This had structural as well as developmental implications. The topographical model was described as though the mind was formed to contain energies. The unconscious part of the mind was thought to hold mental contents strongly supplied with sexual energy. The preconscious and conscious parts of the mind functioned to control the release of sexual energies. This meant discharging sexual drives in a manner acceptable to society and to those aspects of the mind that represent the demands of the external world. An anorexic patient does regard her hunger and her sexuality as an unsocial, greedy force within herself, against which she has to fight for control. The subjective experience of the patient may well be captured using the imagery of drive energy and a topographically structured unconscious and conscious mental apparatus as described by Freud so long ago.

"Orality", "Anality" and Eating Disorder

The sensual interests of children were supposed to demonstrate a phasic quality, with different stages being characterised by distinctive drive energies. Anorexia nervosa was postulated, developmentally, within drive theory, as showing "oral fixation", with "anal" character qualities. The preoccupation with food, the preparation of meals, menues and cuisine, were seen as showing the qualities of a mind under the influence of the developmentally earliest, oral sexual energies. The personality characteristics of parsimony, perfectionism, rigidity and defiance were acquired in reaction to the anal sexual drives: anal pleasures and activities and interest and pride in faeces.

Once more it can be stressed that the original context and aetiological implications of this model need not be accepted. Patients do connect the demand for control of their excretion as parental insistence on giving up freedom and enjoyment in the potential sensuality of anal (and urethral) functions). It is true to say that anorexic patients struggle (as do many adolescents) with what seems to be a problem; that the site of sexual sensuality is adjacent to excretory sphincters and that the sensual pleasures of sexuality interact with sphincter function. Although the theory of part instinctual energies is no longer cogent, discussion of the power struggle between patient and the parent over feeding widens into discussion of the nature of autonomy for the developing person and may well be vividly evoked by metaphors of the contests surrounding the development of the control of sphincter function. Problems of control of impulses is of great and general importance in eating disorder patients. The loss of control that occurs in bingeing needs exploration in understanding bulimic patients and it may be necessary to make available the imagery of early excretory control and lack of control to complete the venture.

The psychodynamic propositions if taken literally may seem absurd. In the context of a dialogue between a therapist helping a patient express in detail her experience of herself, then they may be invaluable. The anorexic psychopathology is crazy unless the complexity and contradictions of the normal human mind are fully appreciated by the therapist. It is essential that therapists have accepted their own irrationality, their own absurdities, their own infantile origins, for a patient to feel accepted and understood. In bulimic patients, the messiness, the odd admixture of pride and disgust around vomiting may be encapsulated within fantasies with an excretory quality. Identifying and exploring such a fantasy can have a use in directing such a patient's thinking into alternative routes.

The "Phallic" Ingredients

After anality, Freud supposed that the sexual life of infants became focused upon their genitalia. He hypothesised that at this stage male and female development separated as children became aware of, and were influenced by, their realisation of the physical differences between the genders. The anorexic woman might be hypothesised, by this thinking, to have displaced her concern with physical lack of the penis towards a preoccupation with her body shape. She attempted to perfect herself physically and to lose the unacceptable (i.e. feminine) appearance. The secondary sexual body shape of a woman being abolished by the starvation represents, psychologically speaking, the young woman's rejection of femininity and her subservience to the fantasy that she could reach another, ideal state.

The particular focus of the preoccupation with appearance that occurs in normal, female adolescent development certainly represents a gender difference in western society, and it is certainly likely to be relevant in the analysis of the relationship between social and psychopathological factors in the ontogeny of anorexia. It is striking how often the beginnings of an anorexia is associated with a preadolescent young woman describing her peers' waxing interest in sexuality as "boring" or repugnant. Underneath, she is fascinated and frightened. The classical psychodynamic formulations of feminine body image as being dominated by feelings of castration and penis envy are not sustainable. There is, occasionally, a history and persistence of a feeling that the masculine state is to be preferred. For some patients, useful work can be done around the imagery of the anorexic woman's body as being damaged, disgusting, insufficient or incomplete. Such ideas need not be constructed into generalisations. They can be discovered in our patients and explored without in any way adhering to a disparaging view of women.

In multi-impulsive, bulimic patients, the cutting behaviour that may be part of the clinical picture is often accompanied by sadistic, mutilating fantasies. Particularly in survivors of sadistic sexual abuse, the cutting behaviour may be part of a fantasy of vengeful castration. There may even be a reluctance to change in therapy, if the enactment of revenge upon the self is felt to be the only available expression for such feelings. One patient with a history of bulimia, substance abuse and sexual endangering behaviour, enacted fully the fantasy to be male. She changed her name to that of a man and tried to persuade a surgeon to reassign her physical gender. For some patients the compulsive self-harming, skin-cutting, vomiting and so on, can become consciously sexualised and revealed by the patient to be close to masturbation in the associated excitement. There is, usually, an absence of any overt, genital pleasure either in intercourse or in masturbation. Such a state of affairs causes great shame and humiliation to patients. The topics are difficult to discuss for young adults and require that therapists are in touch with the diversity and complexity of their own sexuality so that the topics are handled openly and comfortably with patients.

The "Oedipal" Components

The oedipal phase is next in the Freudian developmental chronology. Freud (1905) picked upon a particular aspect of the Oedipus myth. He stressed the rivalrous, murderous wishes that a child might have for a father if the mother was desired as a sexual partner. Freud theorised from a masculine point of view. He evoked a society within which adult men were accorded great power over their children and partners, an inequitable societal arrangement properly challenged by the feminist movement. Society has altered, and in the contemporary world the father as the representative powerful male is not usually registered in the Victorian manner. Nonetheless, all children, in growing up, get to a time in their lives when they are confronted, more or less forcefully, with the problems of jealousy, rivalry and competition in three-person relationships and with the power differences between men and women. This is likely to involve one or more of their parents, but siblings are also likely to be implicated. The passionate aspects of a three-person relationship involves rivalry for love and intimate physical closeness. "Oedipal" problems can be used as an epithet to describe the nature of the relationship with the parents both within the patient's fantasies as well as in the external world. In contemporary thinking, the successful resolution of the oedipal conflicts leads to the capacity to manage rivalry and sharing in threesomes, whatever their constitution.

Nicolle (1938), in an early paper on the psychodynamics of eating disorder, emphasised the oedipal level of the disturbance. The sharing of friendships and relationships is often problematic for anorexic and bulimic patients, perhaps on account of the intense fear of greediness that these patients feel. However, the specific sense of the oedipus epithet can also be relevant. The anorexic patient has often experienced her family as one in which closeness to one parent is felt, by the other parent, to be a betrayal. (To the outside observer, this may or may not be visible.) There are certainly anorexic young women who have felt close to and of special importance to their father. At the same time, the mother is seen as an important although sometimes pitied person. If the patient has an idea that her father has a sexual interest in herself, she may fear that her own developing sexuality will be a danger to herself and to the integrity of the family. It will also put at risk her closeness to her mother. Under such a circumstance, a young woman may gain great relief from the discovery that slimming reduces both secondary sexual characteristics and her sexual interests. The physical state of her body may give her father a legitimate right to be interested in her body so that the anorexic state, whatever its origins, may solve a problem of an actual or a feared incestuous possibility with her father. Although such feelings may well surface in the work with a now adult and partially recovered anorexic patient, it is unusual to hear of this directly with an adolescent patient. More often it is a visible issue in family therapy with this age group. (An example of such a configuration was described in Pincus and Dare, 1978, pp. 70–76.)

Eating Disorder and the Psychopathology of Aggression

Although the sexual aspects of anorexia nervosa are obviously important, psychoanalytic theory also directs interest towards aggression. An *aggressive drive* is described as though it were an exact parallel of the putative sexual drive. At one stage, Freud proposed that the aggressive drive was a derivative, in turn, of a death wish (Freud, 1920). This construction need not be accepted in order to acknowledge that eating disordered patients are struggling with the expression of aggression. Anorexic patients, so controlled in so much of their life, can become screaming, scraggy bundles of fury in defence of their right to starve. Sometimes it appears that the anorexia has a psychological function of creating what from the patient's point of view, is a legitimate way to express aggression. Without this resource, the patient allows herself/himself no opportunity to be angry and to enact frustration and rage (whatever its original source). A bulimic patient with problems of impulse control can demonstrate anger more directly but may do so against herself/himself, in self injury or, sometimes, in the vomiting itself. In such patients there may be a complex relationship between being angry, being anxious and being sexually aroused.

A Changing Emphasis on the Nature of the "Preoedipal Phase"

Modifications appeared in the notion of the early phases of development being dominated by sexual drives even in the era of psychoanalysis dominated by the living Freud. Freud had thought of the child, before the oedipal phase, as being dominated by essentially autoerotic drives (Freud, 1905). It was realised by a number of early critics that the infant had a need for the mother and that experiences within that relationship were a major force in development. For a while, these notions were described in terms of a putative "preoedipal" phase. Hence Lorand (1943, p. 299), in describing an analysis of a case of anorexia nervosa, referred to many conflicts in the sexual sphere but there was also a: "deeper struggle going on within the patient—a struggle involving not only a fight and defense against sexual drives, but drives which were more diffuse and pertained to disturbances in the whole personality structure." These struggles represented not only oedipal, sexual conflicts but also "very early attachment to the mother". In keeping with the terminology of the time, Lorand emphasised the eating problem as relating to early oral desires for the breast.

Modern Object Relations Theory

The ultimate failure of instinctual drive theory led to the evolution of what is called "object relations theory". This is a curious phrase. Its origins are in a move away from preoccupation with the energies of a given drive towards the importance of the other person (or bit of a person) towards whom the drives are directed. As the *other person*, in the early days of psychoanalytic psychology, was the *object* of the drives, the phrase *the object* became the antonym of *the self*. The idea that the psychology of the person is dominated by the way that the self relates to the important other people in the life of the person, became known as *object relations theory*. At the same time, the paradigmatic condition for psychoanalytic psychology ceased to be conversion hysteria and moved towards severe personality disorder and the psychoses. In the contemporary psychoanalytic writings, eating disorders are understood in terms of disorder of personal relationships and the organisation of the self.

Nicolle (1938, in Kaufman and Heiman, 1964, pp. 227–244), in considering "prepsychotic anorexia", addressed the issue of what we would now term the "borderline personality character of the patient". For example, she specifically discussed the differentiation of anorexia nervosa and hysteria whilst also mentioning cases that developed schizophrenia. This can be seen as the beginning of the development of a psychodynamic view of anorexia nervosa as a severe, non-neurotic disturbance.

In the psychoanalytic theory of personality disorder, the mental mechanisms that distort relationships are central. It is suggested that in early life there are two crucial, related processes. The first is to do with the sense of differentiating the existence and separateness of other people and finding that separateness to be bearable. That which might render it unbearable is the extent to which the developing child might fear the consequences of separateness. There is a risk of painful envy and despair when it is realised that other people are sources of support, nurturance and comfort. This gives the other power over the self. To accept and welcome the separateness of the other person, he or she must be thought of as reliable. The second process that can be associated with problems of personality development are to do with the extent to which other people and the self can be seen and accepted as containing mixtures of good and bad aspects. The person who is unable to tolerate such admixtures is dominated by the psychological processes of splitting. It appears that patients with eating disorder tend to have a weak sense of being able to be in control of their own well-being, safety and their destiny. They feel that other people have a too dominating power over themselves and that they themselves have to strive to be perfectly good because, otherwise, they are perfectly bad. In these ways the personality problems of many eating disorder patients conform to that of people who in personality theory are designated as suffering from a "borderline personality" (cf. Swift and Wonderlich, 1988).

The Self in Eating Disorder

Eating disorder patients commonly display an intense and characteristic difficulty in believing in the integrity of their selves. The self has an experiential and a structural implication. The experienced self is to do with the strength or weakness as well as the "shape", the personal uniqueness, of "being me". The structured self ("self representation") is an analogue of the body schema. It is a psychological map. The gender determined qualities of the self are important. Traditional psychoanalysis has been criticised for manifesting ideas of feminine psychology that are scarcely disguised expressions of traditional male attitudes towards women. In working with eating disorder patients it is important to acknowledge these criticisms of psychoanalysis. In the following schematic account of the psychopathology of eating disorder, the verion of psychodynamic thinking employed has taken such considerations into account.

AN "INTEGRATED MODEL"

The beginnings of an eating disorder lie outside as well as inside the person. These external factors become incorporated, in some way, into the psychology of the individual. The starting point, for the person developing an eating disorder, includes the processes and contents of this internalisation.

The aetiological forces that generate eating disorders engender dramatic differences in the incidence of the disorders between men and women. Socially and historically determined attitudes towards food, body shape and the formation of gender identity are relevant here (cf. Shorter, 1984). The age-old concern of humankind to have sufficient food to survive (and to live a religious and moral life) has been complicated, in the contemporary, western industrial world, by the possibility that large sections of society can afford to eat excessively. He or she is born into a world that has rather specific, demanding expectations about body weight and shape. The excess of food has had gender differentiated effects. In societies where there was a relative lack of food, people tend to be small and wiry. The complementary ideal of feminine beauty was (or is) that of a body well covered with fat, distributed according to female secondary sexual characteristics. In contemporary, western, post-industrial society, men who eat well and engage in hard physical exercise can develop tall and strong bodies with broad shoulders, and outstanding muscles. This is the ideal towards which many male adolescents strive. The complementary ideal for a woman, is that her secondary sexual physique should begin to become perceptible, in puberty, and that this process should then be halted.

The representation of womanly shape upheld by fashion models, beauty (pageant) queens and by film stars is of a slender woman, small, firm breasted, slim in thigh and buttock and flat of belly. Such a woman appears to be scarcely out of childhood. The ideal for the man is less widespread, less oppressive and is more easily ignored by adolescent males than is the ideal established for women (cf. Leupnitz, 1988, p. 224). This difference derives from the societal pressures on women which emphasise that they should be concerned with social judgments about their appearance more than on their more general personal characteristics. The different pressures on men and women as to the nature and importance of ideals of adult shape become a part of the internal world. By some process operating from the beginnings of social life, personal psychology is shaped by these patriarchal structures along gender differentiated lines (cf. Benjamin, 1990; Luepnitz, 1988; Orbach, 1985). The process is internalised and becomes an aspect of the fundamental organisation of the identity of the person.

We can only speculate on the gender discriminating socially determined influences affecting the character structure of the smallest baby. People clearly treat a newborn baby girl or boy in subtly different ways (or not so subtly, viz: "blue for a boy, pink for a girl"). When the earliest identity begins to be perceptible (cf. Spitz and Cobliner, 1965) in the second half of the first year, gender differentiation may not be maximal; but one year later, distinctions become much more identifiable (cf. Roiphe and Galenson, 1981). It is also true that, in the second year of life (in the anal phase discussed already), the struggle for autonomy and differentiation is obvious. The self-denial and restrictiveness that goes with so-called anal traits may enable the person to lock on to anorexic ways of dealing with the developmental hazards occurring at the beginning of the eating disorder. In the second year of life, a struggle around toilet training that occurs in some cultures may be a special case of a more universal contest between adults and their offspring as to who is in charge of the activity and personality of the child. This can be expressed, cogently, by posing the question: Is the toddler in charge or is the parent? Do toddlers have the right to say who they are and choose their own direction, or is that only or mainly the business of adults? And for whom do the toddlers exist, themselves or for others? Whom do they serve, themselves or others? These struggles are represented in the internal world and come to the fore in the anorexic patients' concern to control and manage themselves, their bodies and their bodily needs, in their diet. The struggle is around whether or not to become the person that the mother wants or to be self-created. The circumstance is complicated by the child's fears that what she herself creates is bad if it is felt to be in defiance of the beloved parent.

Modern psychodynamic thinking, in seeking to understand these gender differences, would speculate that socially determined disparities between the ways boys and girls are treated in early childhood must be considered. A baby only survives because a number of people dedicate their life to the nurturance of the baby. In our society, the person or persons is overwhelmingly likely to be female (which is not to say that men cannot or should not care for babies). The person who becomes most familiar to a child is a woman (or women) who focuses on the baby in such a way as to put the needs of the baby (the 'object') before the needs of the self (the 'subject'). The baby comes to see the world in terms of that dedication but also learns, eventually and to a greater or lesser extent, that the mother has needs of her own, she exists in her own right. The baby that becomes a woman has, in one sense, an easier task than does a male: the girl can learn that she is a female and can become, like her, a primary carer, a woman. The little boy learns that he is not the same as his mother and is going to become like a much less omnipresent person, a man. On the other hand, the girl soon knows that the woman she is going to become will be strongly expected to put the needs of the other, the object of her interests and loves, especially if they are male, before the needs of her subject, her self. The boy who will become a man will realise that he is permitted, encouraged or perhaps forced, to put the needs of himself first, and that he can expect women to subjugate their needs to his own. The patient who *is* anorexic seems to *have been* a girl child who has been very sensitive to the psychological processing of these issues in herself and in the family. This aspect of self organisation, the placing of the self under the orders of the other, seems to be experienced by the person destined to develop an eating disorder in a particular way. She seems to have identified it as involving a forceful intrusiveness on the mother's part, an intrusiveness that the child has felt weak to resist. In consequence, or so it seems, all subsequent phases of development are in some way coloured by a problem of differentiating the self and its needs from the apparent demands of others. The girl who becomes an anorexic feels that she is not allowed to become the person that she wants to be, but must attend to the expectations and wishes of others (this aspect of the psychopathology of anorexia was demonstrated by Bruch (e.g. 1978). The anorexic symptom is at least twofold in its meaning. On the one hand, the intense concern over food intake expresses a message: "This is an area in which I am in control, which makes me feel I am being myself, by which I can defy the demands of others." On the other hand, and at the same time, the symptom appears to say: "I am only a little child, I cannot live by myself, I have to be looked after; I am not going to take up much space, I do not want to make demands on resources."

As described above, the patient-to-be is especially troubled by the fact that her eating, as it impinges on others, is likely to be identified as greediness, so that, more than most, the anorexic-to-be is frightened of her own hunger (cf. Sandler and Dare, 1970). Anorexic and bulimic patients believe themselves to be dangerously and disgustingly greedy. The sensuality of the mouth is experienced as bad. The appetite for food (and other sensual gratifications) is disgusting and repellent. This can be associated with behaviour that is really disgusting, such as vomiting and gross bingeing. Commonly, however, the sensitivity to the accusation of greediness is in excess of the actual food intake. Many patients have a fear of eating in the presence of others. This may represent an avoidance of exposure to the accusation of greed (a belief held with almost delusional intensity). In the patient's mind, eating may also seem to be a self-assertive activity ("I have a right to eat"). This may be subject to repression as are all other claims of a right to live according to self-derived needs. Ordinary pangs of hunger have curious effects upon an anorexic person. The hunger stimulates the wish to eat and take in the food. The fear of the overwhelming appetite means that this process has to be resisted at all costs. One way of achieving this is by seeing the hunger as existing outside the self. Often the hunger seems to be placed in the food itself so that the patient says: "I must not eat. Once I start to eat, I cannot stop. It is eating that makes me feel so greedy. It is fine whilst I am not eating." These are complicated recursive aspects of the symptomatology of eating disordered patients. The symptomatic self-starvation produces intense pangs of hunger. The longer the self-starvation goes on, the more chronically the patient is undernourished, the more the psychopathology of starvation itself makes an appearance. The young woman may not have had earlier, developmentally determined ambivalence about food and the expression of oral demands. However, once under way, the self-starvation engenders intense, inescapable food and eating preoccupations. This alone may convince the patient that she is disgustingly greedy. The food preoccupation is accompanied by a need to feed others. The compulsive insistence that her mother eats, at least as much as she, may be reparative, for the pain and distress imposed, or it may be in order to demonstrate innocence of greedy intentions. This process is facilitated by experiencing hunger as existing in others. This makes it possible to gain relief by feeding others, especially of the mother or siblings. In the first instance it gives what she feels to be a legitimate interest in food. It also seems to proclaim: "It is not me that is hungry and greedy, it is others. It is not me that is greedy, I feed others. I am immune from passionate needs. I do not take food from them."

There is a strong symbolic component in the anorexic attitude to food, a symbolism which is intensified by starvation and food preoccupation. Food is taken inside the self, and the strength of desire for food may give it a threatening power. Resisting eating can be felt to be a titanic struggle against an invincible, intrusive force. The food has to be seen as alien in order to bolster the resistance to its intrusive potency. The more the food is felt to be delicious and attractive, the more it is feared.

As such descriptions of a sensuality to be resisted or consummated are developed, it becomes clear why sexuality and food seem to be so confused in these patients' inner world. The sexual feelings that occur in normal adolescence carry with them the possibility of allowing another person's sexuality to attract and empower a relationship. This makes sexual consummation much more terrifying. The sense of being controlled by sexual feelings, the potential longing for intercourse, all have the quality of intrusion and overwhelmingly desirable but dangerous submission to the other, a loss of control.

There are complex internalisations of family attitudes into the personality of the patient. These include attitudes to food, as well as towards the definitions of femininity and body shape. Obviously, food is never a neutral topic in families and the choice of an eating-related symptom may not only be societally donated but may also have intense personal meaning for the individual in a particular family because of the personal and familial history. For some patients, a focus on eating and dieting are part of what can be called the subcultural givens of the family. These qualities are likely to be internalised and to affect the psychopathology of an eating disorder. In some individuals there is also a family experience of the death, in an emaciated state, of a significant person. The patient may possess an internalised representation of this person that, in some ways, functions as a model for herself in the creation of the anorexic symptomatology. The reason for this identification is likely to be idiosyncratic but a common feature is that it shows the patient's participation in and loyalty to her family. In at least two patients known to the authors, the father had died in a starving state of cancer. In another two patients the identification appeared to be with their mothers' withered arm. The patient in one way feels that she can assert her identity with the family, by sharing a common grief at a loss, and, at the same time, she may be proclaiming her especial loyalty and commitment to the dead (or injured) person by taking on some of the dead person's most dangerous qualities. In this way she is saying: "I am part of the family, but I am also special. I am me!" This assertion seems to be very important to the patient who, in some ways, feels herself to be unsure as to who she is and who feels that she can very easily be submerged by the demands of others to become the person whom they want her to be. There is a proclamation in being thin and starving. She asserts herself as being unlike the rest of the family. She is also showing her virtue, a contradiction of her fear that she is ineffective, unworthy and some sort of failure.

The anorexic young woman may well have experienced her father as a relatively distant figure, not in a close emotional contact with either his wife or his daughter. This has, in turn, made it more difficult for her to experience her own sexuality as likely to be accepted as part of an overall love relationship.

CONCLUSIONS

This chapter presents an overview of the psychodynamic psychological understanding of the aetiology of eating disorder. Psychodynamic thinking has much to say to inform us in understanding our patients and in facilitating the evolution of effective and humane treatments. Historically, psychoanalysis claimed an overarching theory of psychopathology which also aspired to be an aetiological theory. These assertions and aspirations have done a disservice to the contribution of psychodynamic thinking in the field of eating disorder. The understanding of patients is sufficient. The claim to constitute an ultimate, aetiological theory is an irrelevant burden. A major aspect of the multiple contributions to the development of an eating disorder is the social context with its special attitudes towards body shape and gender identity. This is incorporated into a psychodynamic formulation as in the feminist criticisms of the ideological biases of psychoanalysis. The theme song of the chapter is the attempt to make sense of the extraordinary capacity to live out an addiction to starvation, vomiting or laxatives as the preferred form of self-expression. The emphasis has been upon the work that we have done with adult patients and those with restricting disorder.

REFERENCES

Benjamin, J. (1990). *The Bonds of Love*. London: Virago.

Bruch, H. (1978). *The Golden Cage: The Enigma of Anorexia Nervosa*. Cambridge, Mass: Harvard University Press.

Dare, C. (1981). Psychoanalytic theories of the personality. In: F. Fransella (Ed.), *Personality: Theory, Measurement and Research*, pp. 204–215. London: Methuen.

Freud, S. (1894). The neuro-psychoses of defence. In: *The Standard Edition of the Complete Psychological Works of Sigmund Frued*, Vol. 3, pp. 43–61. London: Hogarth Press.

Freud, S. (1905). Three essays on sexuality. In: *The Standard Edition of the Complete Psychological Works of Sigmund Freud*, Vol 7, pp. 125–243. London: Hogarth Press.

Freud, S. (1920). Beyond the pleasure principle. In: *The Standard Edition of the Complete Psychological Works of Sigmund Freud*, Vol. 18, pp. 3–64. London: Hogarth Press.

Kaufman, M.R. and Heiman, M. (eds) (1964). *Evolution of Psychosomatic Concepts. Anorexia Nervosa: A Paradigm*. New York: International Universities Press.

Laplanche, J. (1992). Interpretation between determinism and hermeneutics: a restatement of the problem. *International Journal of Psycho-Analysis*, **73**, 429–445.

Lorand, S. (1943). Anorexia nervosa: a case report. Reprinted in: M.R. Kaufman and M. Heiman (Eds), *Evolution of Psychosomatic Concepts. Anorexia Nervosa: A Paradigm*, pp. 298–319. New York: International Universities Press.

Luepnitz, D.A. (1988). *The Family Interpreted: Psychoanalysis, Feminism and Family Therapy*. New York: Basic Books.

Nicolle, G. (1938). Prepsychotic anorexia. *Proceedings of the Royal Society of Medicine*, **32**, 153–161.

Orbach, S. (1985). Accepting the symptom: a feminist psychoanalytic treatment of anorexia nervosa. In: D. Garner and P. Garfinkel (Eds), *Handbook of Psychotherapy for Anorexia and Bulimia Nervosa*, pp. 83–106. New York: Guilford Press.

Pincus, L. and Dare, C. (1978). *Secrets in the Family*. Faber & Faber, London.

Rahman, L., Richardson, H.B. and Ripley, H.S. (1939). Anorexia nervosa with psychiatric observations. *Psychosomatic Medicine*, **1**, 335–365.

Rastam, M. and Gillberg, C. (1991). The family background in anorexia nervosa: a population-based study. *Journal of the American Academy of Child and Adolescent Psychiatry*, **30**, 283–289.

Roiphe, H. and Galenson, E. (1981). *Infantile Origins of Sexual Identity*. New York: International Universities Press.

Sandler, J. and Dare, C. (1970). The psychoanalytic concept of orality. *Journal of Psychosomatic Research*, **14**, 211–222.

Sandler, J., Dare, C. and Holder, A. (1972). Frames of reference in psychoanalytic psychology. I: Introduction. *British Journal of Medical Psychology*, **45**, 127.

Sandler, J., Dare, C. and Holder, A. (1973). *The Patient and the Analyst*. London: Allen & Unwin.

Shorter, E. (1984). *A History of Women's Bodies*. New York: Viking Books.

Spitz, R. and Cobliner, W.G. (1965). *The First Year of Life*. New York: International Universities Press.

Swift, W.J. and Wonderlich, S.A. (1988). Personality factors and diagnosis in eating disorders: traits, disorders and structures. In: D. Garner and P. Garfinkel (Eds), *Diagnostic Issues in Anorexia Nervosa and Bulimia Nervosa*. New York: Brunner/Mazel.

Waller, G. (1993). Sexual abuse and eating disorders: borderline personality disorder as a mediating factor. *British Journal of Psychiatry,* **162**, 771–775.

Waller, J.V., Kaufman, M.R. and Deutsch, F. (1940). Anorexia nervosa: psychosomatic entity. *Psychosomatic Medicine,* **2**, 3–16.

8

Cognitive–Behavioural Models of Eating Disorders

PADMAL DE SILVA
Institute of Psychiatry, London, UK

While the term "eating disorders" normally refers to a wide range of problems, the main focus in this chapter will be on the two main disorders: anorexia nervosa and bulimia nervosa. Both of these have been extensively written about, and many theoretical accounts have been proposed. The focus here will be on cognitive–behavioural models; other major psychologial models are dealt with in other chapters of this volume.

BEHAVIOURAL CONCEPTS AND MODELS

Behavioural models of disorders typically employ certain basic concepts derived from learning theory. When behaviourism entered psychology in the first decade of this century, much of the field was dominated by mentalistic concepts. Behaviourism, as propounded by its founder John Broadus Watson and other pioneers, rejected mentalistic concepts, and the introspective method that went with them, as unscientific and untenable, and proposed instead behavioural concepts and a strictly behavioural methodology (e.g. Watson, 1925). The stimulus–response analysis of behaviour which dominated psychology for a good part of this century was the direct result of this approach. *Stimuli* in the environment led to *responses* in the organism. The way

Handbook of Eating Disorders: Theory, Treatment and Research.
Edited by G. Szmukler, C. Dare and J. Treasure.
© 1995 John Wiley & Sons Ltd.

connections were established between stimuli and responses, and between stimuli and stimuli, was seen as systematic and predictable, through the laws of *learning*. Concepts in learning included *respondent* or *classical conditioning, operant* or *instrumental conditioning, stimulus generalisation, extinction, reinforcement* and *punishment*. These and other related concepts were seen as the basic building blocks of any behavioural model that was postulated to describe and explain a particular behaviour, including behavioural abnormalities. The work of Ullman and Krasner (1969) provides an excellent example of this approach applied to abnormal behaviour.

In more recent years, mainly due to the work of cognitive psychologists and cognitive therapists such as Albert Ellis and Aaron Beck, the role of cognitions (thoughts, images, ideas, attitudes, and so on) have come to be recognised as important variables that determine behaviour (e.g. Beck, 1976; Ellis, 1970). It is the recognition of the role of cognitions in behaviour that has led to cognitive models of behavioural problems. Pure cognitive models are rarely postulated nowadays as providing explanatory accounts of complex behaviours. What are commonly found, instead, are cognitive–behavioural models, where behavioural and cognitive concepts are both used as major elements. There have been detailed theoretical discussions of these issues (e.g. Brewin, 1988; Williams et al, 1988).

In the field of the eating disorders, both behavioural models and explicitly cognitive–behavioural models have been postulated and discussed. These will be selectively reviewed in the following sections.

MODELS OF ANOREXIA NERVOSA

In its most basic form, anorexia nervosa may be conceptualised as a learned behaviour, which is then maintained by positive reinforcement. The individual engages in excessive dieting to lose weight to achieve a slim figure. This is reinforced by the positive reaction of peers and others, and society in general. There is also negative reinforcement in that being overweight, or even just being of a full figure, is met with direct and indirect disapproval and sometimes even ridicule. The relief from, and avoidance of, this disapproval and ridicule, provide negative reinforcement for slimming and anorexic behaviour. Thus, in response to perceived social pressures, the individual engages in a certain set of behaviours (eating less, skipping meals etc.) which lead to reinforcement both by approval and by freedom from disapproval. The reinforcement is so powerful that the individual maintains this behaviour despite the obvious threats to health and well-being.

The above is essentially the basic behavioural model of anorexia nervosa. However, in this simple form, it leaves many questions unanswered. One of the most important ones is with regard to reinforcement. As social approval is a long-term and general event, remote from the actual eating situation, what does provide reinforcement immediately? Early behavioural writers offered fairly simple answers to this. For example, Allyon, Haughton and Osmond (1964) stated that "in conditioning terms, food rejecting behaviour is reinforced by the attention it produces" (p. 151). Bachrach, Erwin and Mohr (1965) provided an analysis of the positively reinforcing stimuli in the environment of a severely emaciated, hospitalised, anorexic female. They concluded that the positive reinforcers included the pleasantly decorated room and view, access to visitors, the consequent concern and attention, and the range of entertainment available through radio, television, books and records. Leitenberg, Agras and Thomson (1968) conceptualised anorexia nervosa as an avoidance behaviour, where dieting is maintained by avoidance of the anxiety associated with eating and weight gain. The mechanism postulated was, thus, negative reinforcement. These early behavioural analyses were clearly simplistic, although they highlighted some aspects of anorexic behaviour. The search for other explanations of how anorexic behaviour is reinforced has led to different models in more recent years.

It has been noted that starvation is a learned response that generates pleasure in many anorexics. Many workers have commented on the pleasure with which some anorexics refrain from eating. The feeling of having an empty stomach is pleasurable and may be said to provide immediate reinforcement for the non-eating, or eating-very-little, behaviour (Gilbert, 1986).

A similar but more sophisticated learning view of anorexia nervosa has been proposed by Szmukler and Tantam (1984). In this view, too, starvation itself may acquire reinforcement value for the anorexic. They suggest that anorexia nervosa may be a disorder of dependence, where the dependence is on starvation. The model also has a physiological dimension. It is assumed that the addiction is to an endogenously produced substance, arising from starvation. This starvation dependence is similar to the alcoholic's dependence on alcohol, or the drug addict's dependence on certain substances. Like the alcoholic, the anorexic denies that she has a problem. Starving behaviour becomes a major and salient factor in the individual's life and a high degree of tolerance to starvation develops—again like the case of the alcoholic who becomes increasingly tolerant of, and dependent on, alcohol. In this model, eating is seen as withdrawal, which leads to negative consequences, such as feelings of tension. The anorexic is afraid of, and avoids, this situation.

Another behavioural model is that of Wyrwicka (1984), who sees anorexia nervosa as a case of complex instrumental conditioning. According to Wyrwicka, non-eating is undertaken to avoid being overweight and perceived social failure, but this behaviour becomes reinforced in its own right by the feeling of satisfaction the individual feels about being in control.

These clearly behavioural models obviously have some value and validity. They are useful in accounting for the maintenance of anorexic behaviour. Where they are inadequate is with regard to the actual origins of the problem. This is essentially the case with the behavioural models of many disorders. For example, behavioural models of obsessive–compulsive disorder are excellent in accounting for its maintenance or persistence, but are much less convincing about its origins (de Silva, 1988). In the case of anorexia nervosa, it is now clear that the actual origins may be related to numerous antecedent conditions, including adolescent conflict, family problems, sense of failure and loss of control, in addition to the social pressure to achieve a slim figure. This is recognised by many of the authors on this subject (e.g. Garfinkel and Garner, 1983; Gilbert, 1986). Once the problem behaviour gets started, the way it is maintained appears to be explained well by the behavioural model. The role of reinforcement, both positive (being rewarded by social approval; feeling rewarded by one's sense of control etc.) and negative (avoidance of social disapproval or even ridicule; avoidance of feeling out of control; avoidance of feeling a failure etc.), has much relevance.

The need to consider the various antecedent and triggering factors is a crucial one in any explanation of anorexia nervosa. The literature has numerous ideas and investigations of this—as noted above, family dynamics, social and cultural factors, predisposing factors etc. Recognition of the relevance of these has led to different models of anorexia nervosa, which are discussed in some of the other chapters of this volume. Some of the antecedent and/or triggering factors, however, can be incorporated into a behavioural framework without too much difficulty, as in the model proposed by Slade in 1982. This is summarized below.

Slade (1982) stresses the need to take account of the antecedents of the problem behaviour, and proposes a sophisticated behavioural and functional analysis. In Slade's view, the adolescent conflicts that arise from problems in the family of an anorexic girl combine with interpersonal problems to contribute to a state of general dissatisfaction with life and with oneself. This includes difficulties in establishing independence and autonomy, interpersonal anxiety, and the experience of stressful events such as failure in examinations or personal relationships. This setting condition of dissatisfaction then combines with another predisposing factor, the perfectionistic tendencies that the girl has, and generates a need to control completely, and achieve total success in, some aspect of her life. Self or bodily control is the perfect candidate for this as it is, in the final analysis, independent of the behaviour of other people.

Under these conditions, triggers such as critical comments from peers may lead to the initiation of dieting behaviour. This is positively reinforced by the resultant feelings of success and satisfaction. There is also negative reinforcement through fear of weight gain and the avoidance of the stressors which preceded the onset of the disorder, and any other difficulties and problems. These reinforcements have the effect of intensifying the dieting behaviour, with the consequent downward spiralling of weight. Together with the endocrine disturbance, which may be a direct effect of stress or an indirect effect caused through weight loss, this eventually leads to the full-blown clinical state of anorexia nervosa.

There is much evidence for the antecedent factors and triggering events assumed by Slade. For example, there is evidence that many anorexics show perfectionistic or obsessional tendencies (e.g. Dally and Gomez, 1979). There is also evidence of a relationship between the onset of dieting and stressful events such as family difficulties and examinations (e.g. Beumont, George and Smart, 1976). Slade's model remains clearly the most versatile of all behavioural models of anorexia nervosa.

An area in which the behavioural models are seriously deficient is that of cognitions. Indeed, most behavioural models of abnormal behaviour have been criticised for not giving due place to cognitions. In the decades following the advent of behaviourism, psychologists shunned cognitions on the grounds that they were mentalistic constructs. When they *were* recognised, the tendency was to regard them as covert behavioural events. The recognition that in human behaviour cognitions do play a major part, including at times a causal one, has come to be accepted in modern psychology only in relatively recent times (Brewin, 1988).

With regard to anorexia nervosa, the role of cognitions has of course been implicitly recognised for a long time. The role of social pressures to be slim, for example, would be mediated by relevant cognitions. The anorexic girl's belief that she is overweight, when in fact she is not, is essentially a cognitive phenomenon. The implicit recognition of the role of cognitive variables was turned into a formal model, however, only in the last decade. Much of this development is due to the work of Garner and Bemis (1982, 1985). The writings of Fairburn and his colleagues on patients with bulimia nervosa (e.g. Fairburn, 1981; Fairburn, Cooper and Cooper, 1986) have also had a major influence in the recognition of cognitive factors in the eating disorders as a whole. Preceding these, historically, were the clinical observations of Hilde Bruch (e.g. Bruch, 1962, 1973) highlighting the importance of maladaptive thinking in the development of anorexia nervosa.

The major feature of cognitive–behavioural models of anorexia nervosa is the postulation that the main psychopathological disturbance in these patients is their distorted, or faulty, ideas about body weight and shape and about eating. It is held that much of the other clinical features can be understood in terms of this basic psychopathology. In their key paper, Garner and Bemis (1982; see also Garner and Bemis, 1985) propose a cognitive–behavioural model similar to that of Beck's on depression (e.g. Beck, 1976). Like the cognitive distortions of the depressed patient (e.g. "I am a worthless person"; "No one cares for me"), the patient with anorexia nervosa also has a set of dysfunctional cognitions which underlie and determine her behaviour. Some of these cognitive dysfunctions are given below, with examples:

- *Selective abstraction* (selecting out small parts of a situation while ignoring other evidence, and coming to conclusions on that basis). Examples:

  "I am very special if I am thin".
  "The only way I can be in control is through eating."

- *Dichotomous reasoning* (thinking in terms of extremes and absolutes). Examples:

  "If I am not in complete control, then I will lose all control."
  "If I put on one pound, I'll go on and put on enormous weight."

- *Overgeneralisation* (deriving a rule from one event and applying it to other situations or events). Examples:

  "I failed last night. So I am going to fail today as well."
  "I was unhappy when I was at normal weight. So I know that putting on weight is going to make me unhappy."

- *Magnification* (exaggerating the significance of events). Examples:

  "Gaining two pounds will push me over the brink."
  "I have gained a pound. So I won't be able to wear shorts again."

- *Superstitious thinking* (assuming causal relationships between unrelated things). Examples:

  "If I eat this, it will be converted into fat immediately."
  "If I enjoy anything, it will be taken away."

- *Personalisation* (interpreting events in a self-centred way). Examples:

  "They were laughing, I am sure they were laughing at me."
  "What will people think if they see me eating all this."

Dysfunctional thinking such as the above is said to characterise the anorexic patient's cognitive functioning with regard to matters that are important to her. In short, she is governed by faulty thoughts in relation to body shape, size, weight, eating, food, control, and so on. These are never critically or logically examined by her, and thus contribute to the persistence of her problem behaviours.

It is worth noting the way Garner and Bemis see how the role of dysfunctional cognition gets established in anorexia nervosa. In their view there are several sources of positive reinforcement for dieting. First, there is self-reinforcement for the successful experience of exercising control over weight and eating. Second, there is also social reinforcement for being slim. Later, as weight loss progresses, this social response may shift towards concern and attention, which are also reinforcing. By now, however, the idea that slimness is of paramount importance is firmly established; so, external reinforcement becomes less significant as the complex of anorexic beliefs and behaviours becomes functionally autonomous. As the disorder progresses, the individual becomes increasingly isolated and so increasingly exposed to her own dysfuncational thinking. This isolation is heightened by the cognitive and emotional sequelae of starvation, which include depression, anxiety and social withdrawal. The anorexic now clings to her anxiety and negative cognitions about gaining weight, as these are functional in maintaining the dieting behaviour.

The model proposed recently by Williamson et al (1990) also takes into account cognitive factors. According to them, distorted thoughts concerning body shape and weight produce high anxiety, and it is the desire to reduce this anxiety which motivates the extreme weight reduction methods used by the anorexic patient. While the main mechanism proposed is a behavioural one (anxiety and the need to reduce it), the model considers disturbance of body image, fear of weight gain, and overconcern with body size as the central characteristics of the disorder. Due recognition is given to cognitive factors (distorted cognitions) in the explanation offered.

In the cognitive–behavioural formulation, both the maladaptive cognitions themselves and the dysfunctional or distorted ways of thinking play crucial roles in determining the actual behaviour of the individual. It is not just that she thinks these thoughts in this way, she also acts accordingly. Her starvation is justified by her own logic. Any attempt to persuade her to eat more, or different, food is met with rejection, because her thinking shows her that these changes are disastrous.

The cognitive–behavioural model of anorexia nervosa clearly has face validity, and clinicians often find evidence of dysfunctional thinking in anorexic patients (e.g. Channon, 1988). There is also supporting evidence from empirical studies. The presence of dysfunctional attitudes towards weight, eating and body size in anorexia nervosa has been repeatedly documented (e.g. Bruch, 1973). Indeed, it constitutes one of the essential diagnostic criteria of the disorder (American Psychiatric Association, 1987; Russell, 1983). Indirect evidence also comes from the large body of evidence on body image distortion (e.g. Rosen, 1990).

MODELS OF BULIMIA NERVOSA

The literature on bulimia nervosa is more limited than that on anorexia, but there has been a rapid growth of interest since Russell (1979) published his definitive account of this disorder.

Many of the behavioural and cognitive–behavioural models of bulimia nervosa are clearly related to their counterparts with regard to anorexia. One major behavioural model of bulimic behaviour considers the role of vomiting/purging as essentially anxiety-reducing, like the compulsive act in obsessive–compulsive disorder (Rosen and Leitenberg, 1982). The anxiety-reduction is seen as maintaining the vomiting/purging. This clearly can claim to explain part of the behaviour in bulimia nervosa, but is not a comprehensive model. Some of the inadequacies of this model may be listed as follows: Firstly, it says little about the origins of the problem. Secondly, it does not accommodate psychosocial and cognitive factors which seem linked to the development of bulimia nervosa. Thirdly, the overall two-factor, anxiety-reduction model of Mower (1960), which provides the theoretical basis of the model, has been shown to be severely inadequate for a range of disorders (e.g. Rachman, 1976). A detailed critique of Rosen and Leitenberg (1982) is found in Wilson (1989).

The Rosen and Leitenberg anxiety-reduction model of bulimia has been extended by Williamson et al (1985). They postulated that other psychopathological states (e.g. depression), distorted body image, interpersonal problems and stress function as background factors that exacerbate the binge–purge cycle. Binge eating is attributed to a biological demand (food deprivation). Cognitive factors are not emphasised as major variables. Williamson et al (1990) have offered a revised version of this model more recently, where cognitive factors are given more prominence. Body image disturbance, fear of weight gain, and overconcern with body size are seen as central underlying determinants of the disorder. These writers also postulate that the individual develops rigid rules regarding food intake. These cognitions are often manifested in an all-or-none attitude about eating. This leads to high anxiety and related cognitions when the dieting rules are broken, and these lead to the purging behaviour.

Models of bulimia nervosa that do take cognitive factors into account as a major variable have been current for over a decade now, starting with the early writings of Fairburn and his colleagues (e.g. Fairburn, 1981, 1985).

Current cognitive–behavioural models of bulimia nervosa attempt to explain both the basic psychopathology, which is shared with anorexia nervosa, and the special features of the disorder. Like with those suffering from anorexia nervosa, bulimic patients also have dysfunctional cognitions and values. Evidence from several studies confirms that cognitive distortions exist in bulimics. For example, Freemouw and Heyneman (1983) found that overweight bulimics, when compared with non-bulimic controls, displayed a distinctive cognitive style. They evaluated themselves more negatively following a failure experience. They were also more dichotomous or extreme in their evaluative style. Ruderman (1985) found that female college students scoring high on a measure of bulimia were significantly more prone to distorted cognitions of a rigid, perfectionistic, and demanding type than those who scored lower.

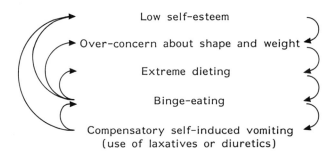

FIGURE 8.1   The cognitive–behavioural view of maintenance of bulimia nervosa presented by Fairburn, Cooper and Cooper (1986). Reproduced by permission.

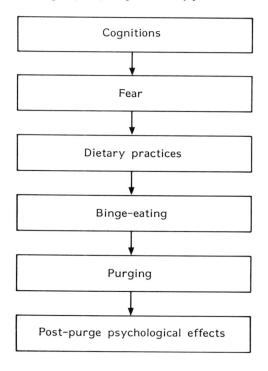

FIGURE 8.2   The essential sequential elements of Wilson's learning model of bulimia nervosa.

The widely known cognitive–behavioural model of bulimia of Fairburn and his colleagues (e.g. Fairburn, Cooper and Cooper, 1986) is presented graphically in Figure 8.1). This has been quite influential in shaping the understanding and treatment of bulimia in the last few years.

Perhaps the most comprehensive cognitive–behavioural model of bulimia nervosa is that proposed by Terence Wilson (1989), shown in Figure 8.2. In recognition of the social factors which are involved, he calls it a "cognitive–social learning model of bulimia nervosa". The sequential elements are as follows:

- *Cognitions.* These include dysfunctional attitudes, cognitions about body weight and shape, and emphasis on thinness.
- *Fear.* Fear of gaining weight and being fat.
- *Dieting practices.* Restrained eating pattern, consisting of stringent diet, diet pills or physical exercise.
- *Binge eating.* Binges, or episodes of overeating, following the violation of excessively rigid dietary standards. These are facilitated by negative affects, such as depression, anger and stress.
- *Purging.* This may take the form of self-induced vomiting, laxative abuse, stricter diet, or stricter periods of starvation.
- *Post-purge psychological effects.* First, there is anxiety reduction and physical relief. Second, guilt and depression; lower self-esteem; worry about psychological and physical consequences; promise never to do it again ("purification promise"); and increased dietary restraint.

It can be seen that a key variable here is the violation of the diet. Once this happens, presumably because the body craves for food after prolonged starvation (cf. Wardle, 1983), and/or because of negative affect, the individual loses control over the eating in that episode. The critical factor here may be cognitive (Polivy and Herman, 1985; see also Herman and Polivy, 1975). The cognitive meditation appears to be something like: "I have failed, so might as well go on eating", which is in keeping with the dysfunctional thinking in eating disorders postulated by Garner and Bemis (1982). This is also consistent with the model of Williamson et al. (1990), noted above.

Wilson's model is more comprehensive than other cognitive–behavioural models of bulimia nervosa, and provides a valuable framework for the understanding and assessment of bulimic problems. However, there are some limitations.

The main problem concerns the fact that not all restrained eaters develop bulimia nervosa. Both many normal-weight restrained eaters and many with anorexia nervosa do not develop bulimia nervosa or even bulimic episodes. It is obvious that many other variables play an overall role in determining whether someone develops bulimia nervosa or not. These may, as Wilson has stated, include genetic, family, personality and specific social-learning factors.

EVALUATION OF THE MODELS

As noted above, a full explanation of anorexia nervosa or of bulimia nervosa will need to take into account a complexity of factors that go beyond the scope of purely behavioural, or cognitive–behavioural, models. Simpler behavioural disorders, including less complex eating problems, can be adequately accounted for by basic behavioural and/or cognitive-behavioural models. For example, most human food aversions can be satisfactorily explained, in terms of both aetiology and maintenance, by a simple behavioural model based on classical conditioning. Where social and cultural factors are involved, the aversion can usually be fully explained within a cognitive–behavioural model (de Silva and Rachman, 1987). In contrast to such simple phenomena, both anorexia nervosa and bulimia nervosa are complex entities. As many authors have clearly demonstrated (e.g. Hsu, 1990; Garfinkel and Garner, 1983), these disorders are multidimensional and multifactorial in origin. Behavioural and cognitive–behavioural models are unable to provide full explanations of them.

Evaluation of models of these disorders should be on the basis of whether there is empirical evidence for the assumptions they make, and whether they have heuristic value for generating useful studies and suggesting effective therapeutic strategies.

The evidence for a purely behavioural model of either anorexia nervosa or bulimia nervosa is very limited. Apart from clinical observations and theoretical accounts, the literature is sparse on this, and certainly there is not much empirical evidence. Work carried out with bulimics on the basis of the Rosen and Leitenberg (1982) model, using exposure and response prevention as a treatment strategy, has been claimed as providing evidence for the model itself (cf. Smith and Medlik, 1983). Some of the work (e.g. Giles, Young and Young, 1985; Rosen and Leitenberg, 1982; Leitenberg et al, 1984; Wilson et al, 1986), but certainly not all, appears to show that the exposure and response prevention model, based on the established paradigm in the treatment of obsessive–compulsive patients (de Silva and Rachman, 1992; Rachman and Hodgson, 1980), does have therapeutic efficacy with bulimic patients. However, it is not at all clear that the mechanism of action is the extinction of a conditioned anxiety response. It is possible that the main action is through the changes in cognitions (Wilson, 1989) including the processes involved in Bandura's concept of self-efficacy (1977, 1982).

As for cognitive–behavioural models which, one may argue, have impressive face validity (e.g. Cooper and Cooper, 1988), there are several pieces of evidence which lend support to this type of formulation. For example, there are now limited but clear data which show that there is differential processing of information which has relevance to food and eating, in patients with these disorders. Using this Stroop Colour Naming paradigm, Channon (1988) was able to demonstrate this effect in anorexic patients. Wilson and his colleagues (Wilson, 1989) tested patients with bulimia nervosa using a similar paradigm, along with two other groups—non-bulimics high in eating restraint, and matched unrestrained eaters. The bulimics were significantly slower in the Stroop task (naming the colour of the target words—i.e. words which were relevant to their bulimic concerns). However, they were not significantly different from the group of restrained eaters. Both groups differed from the unrestrained eaters. This provides evidence for the importance of cognitive factors in bulimia nervosa, but it also highlights that weight-conscious normal women show similar processes.

All of these models, however, are particularly weak with regard to explaining the aetiology of the disorders in question. Behavioural and cognitive–behavioural models focus, by their very nature, on proximal causes and maintenance variables. They do not fully explain why some dieters develop an eating disorder while others do not, and why some end up with one disorder rather than the other. However, these models have a useful role in the domain to which they are limited; that is, in accounting for how proximal factors lead to certain behaviours, and how the latter are maintained and strengthened. It must be pointed out that they are not incompatible with some of the other models of aetiology and can effectively complement them. Indeed, the complex nature of these disorders clearly provides scope for different models complementing one another.

Finally, behavioural and cognitive–behavioural models are also useful in generating effective strategies of treatment, as the work of Fairburn (1981) and Wilson (1989) has shown.

REFERENCES

Ayllon, T., Haughton, E., and Osmond, H.P. (1964). Chronic anorexia: a behaviour problem. *Canadian Pshchiatric Association Journal,* **9**, 147–157.

American Psychiatric Association (1987). *Diagnostic and Statistical Manual of Mental Disorders*, 3rd revised edn. Washington, DC: APA.

Bachrach, A.J., Erwin, W.J., and Mohr, J.P. (1965). The control of eating behavior in an anorexic by operant conditioning techniques. In: L.P. Ullman and L. Krasner (Eds), *Case Studies in Behavior Modification*. New York: Holt, Rinehart & Winston.

Bandura, A. (1977). Self-efficacy: towards a unifying theory. *Psychological Review,* **84**, 191–215.

Bandura, A. (1982). Self-efficacy mechanisms in human agency. *American Psychologist,* **37**, 122–147.

Beck, A.T. (1976). *Cognitive Therapy and Emotional Disorders*. New York: International Universities Press.

Beumont, P.J.V., George, G.C.W. and Smart, D.E. (1976). 'Dieters and 'vomiters and purgers' in anorexia nervosa. *Psychological Medicine,* **6**, 617–622.

Brewin, C. (1988). *Cognitive Foundations of Clinical Psychology*. Hove, UK: Lawrence Erlbaum.

Burch, H. (1962). Perceptual and conceptual disturbances in anorexia nervosa. *Psychosomatic Medicine,* **24**, 187–194.

Bruch H. (1973). *Eating Disorders*. New York: Basic Books.

Channon, S. (1988). Anorexia nervosa: clinical and experimental studies. PhD dissertation, University of London.

Cooper, P.J. and Cooper, Z. (1988). Eating disordrs. In: E. Miller and P.J. Cooper (Eds), *Adult Abnormal Psychology*. Edinburgh: Churchill Livingstone.

Dally, P. and Gomez, J. (1979). *Anorexia Nervosa*. London: Heinemann.

de Silva, P. (1988). Obsessive–compulsive disorder. In: E. Miller and P.J. Cooper (Eds), *Adult Abnormal Psychology*. Edinburgh: Churchill Livingstone.

de Silva, P. and Rachman, S. (1987). Human food aversions: nature and acquisition. *Behaviour Research and Therapy,* **25**, 457–468.

de Silva, P. and Rachman, S. (1992). *Obsessive–Compulsive Disorder: The Facts*. Oxford: Oxford University Press.

Ellis, A. (1970). *The Essence of Rational Psychotherapy: A Comprehensive Approach to Treatment*. New York: Institute for Rational Living.

Fairburn, C. (1981). A cognitive–behavioural approach to the management of bulimia. *Psychological Medicine,* **11**, 697–706.

Fairburn, C. (1985). A cognitive–behavioural treatment of bulimia. In: D.M. Garner and P.E. Garfinkel (Eds), *Handbook of Psychotherapy for Anorexia Nervosa and Bulimia*. New York: Guilford.

Fairburn, C., Cooper, Z. and Cooper, P.J. (1986). The clinical features and maintenance of bulimia nervosa. In: K.D. Brownell and J. Foreyt (Eds), *Physiology, Psychology and Treatment of Eating Disorders*. New York: Basic Books.

Fremouw, W.J. and Heyneman, N.E. (1983). Cognitive styles in bulimia. *Behavior Therapist,* **6**, 143–144.

Garfinkel, P.E. and Garner, D.M. (1983). *Anorexia Nervosa: A Multi-dimensional Perspective*. New York: Brunner/Mazel.

Garner, D.M. and Bemis, K.M. (1982). A cognitive–behavioral approach to anorexia nervosa. *Cognitive Therapy and Research*, **6**, 123–150.

Garner, D.M. and Bemis, K.M. (1985). Cognitive therapy for anorexia nervosa. In: D.M. Garner and P.E. Garfinkel (Eds), *Handbook of Psychotherapy for Anorexia Nervosa and Bulimia*. New York: Guilford.

Gilbert, S. (1986). *Pathology of Eating*. London: Routledge & Kegan Paul.

Giles, T.R., Young, R.R. and Young, D.E. (1985). Behavioral treatment of severe bulimia. *Behavior Therapy*, **16**, 393–405.

Herman, C.P. and Polivy, J. (1975). Anxiety, restraint and eating behavior. *Journal of Abnormal Psychology*, **84**, 666–672.

Hsu, L.K.G. (1990). *Eating Disorders*. New York: Guilford.

Leitenberg, H., Agras, W.S. and Thomson, L.G. (1968). A sequential analysis of the effect of positive reinforcement in modifying anorexia nervosa. *Behaviour Research and Therapy*, **6**, 211–218.

Leitenberg, H., Gross, J., Peterson, J. and Rosen, J.C. (1984). Analysis of an anxiety model and the process of change during exposure plus response prevention treatment of bulimia nervosa. *Behavior Therapy*, **15**, 3–20.

Mowrer, O.H. (1960). *Learning Theroy and Behavior*. New York: John Wiley.

Polivy, J. and Herman, P. (1985). Dieting and binging: a causal analysis. *American Psychologist*, **40**, 193–201.

Rachman, S. (1976). The passing of the two-stage theory of fear and avoidance: fresh possibilities. *Behaviour Research and Therapy*, **14**, 125–131.

Rachman, S. and Hodgson, R. (1980). *Obsessions and Compulsions*. Englewood Cliffs, NJ: Prentice Hall.

Rosen, J.C. (1990). Body image disturbances in eating disorders. In: T.F. Cash and T. Pruzinsky (Eds), *Body Images: Development, Deviance and Change*. New York: Guilford.

Rosen, J.C. and Leitenberg, E. (1982). Bulimia nervosa: treatment with exposure and response prevention. *Behavior Therapy*, **13**, 117–124.

Ruderman, A. (1985). Dysphoric mood and overeating: a test of restraint theory's disinhibition hypothesis. *Journal of Abnormal Psychology*, **94**, 78–85.

Russell, G.F.M. (1979). Bulimia nervosa: an ominous variant of anorexia nervosa. *Psychological Medicine*, **9**, 429–448.

Russell, G.F.M. (1983). Anorexia nervosa and bulimia nervosa. In: G.F.M. Russell and L. Hersov (Eds), *The Neuroses and Personality Disorders*. Cambridge: Cambridge University Press.

Slade (1982). Towards a functional analysis of anorexia nervosa and bulimia nervosa. *British Journal of Clinical Psychology*, **21**, 167–179.

Smith, G.R. and Medlik, L. (1983). Modification of binge eating in anorexia nervosa: a single case report. *Behavioural Psychotherapy*, **11**, 249–256.

Szmukler, G.I. and Tantam, J. (1984). Anorexia nervosa: starvation dependence. *British Journal of Medical Psychology*, **57**, 303–310.

Ullman, L.P. and Krasner, L. (1969). *A Psychological Approach to Abnormal Behavior*, Englewood Cliffs, NJ: Prentice Hall.

Wardle, J. (1980). Dietary restraint and binge eating *Behaviour Analysis and Modification*, **4**, 201–209.

Watson, J.B. (1925). *Behaviorism*. New York: North.

Williams, J.M.G., Watts, F.N., MacLeod, C. and Mathews, A. (1988). *Cognitive Psychology and Emotional Disorders*. Chichester: John Wiley.

Williamson, D.A., Davis, C.J., Duchmann, G.G., McKenzie, S.J. and Watkins, P.C. (1990). *Assessment of Eating Disorders: Obesity, Anorexia and Bulimia Nervosa*. New York: Pergamon.

Williamson, D., Kelley, M.L., Davis, C.J., Ruggiero, L. and Vietia, M.C. (1985). The psychophysiology of bulimia. *Advances in Behaviour Research and Therapy*, **7**, 163–172.

Wilson, G.T. (1989). The treatment of bulimia nervosa: a cognitive–social learning analysis. In: A.J. Stunkard and A. Baum (Eds), *Perspectives in Behavioral Medicine: Eating, Sleeping and Sex.* Hillsdale, NJ: Lawrence Earlbaum.

Wilson, G.T., Rossiter, E., Kleifield, E. and Lindholm, L. (1986). Cognitive–behavioral treatment of bulimia nervosa: a controlled evaluation. *Behaviour Research and Therapy,* **24**, 277–288.

Wyrwicka, W. (1984). Anorexia nervosa as a case of complex instrumental conditioning. *Experimental Neurology,* **84**, 579–589.

9

Family Models of Eating Disorders

IVAN EISLER
Institute of Psychiatry, London, UK

INTRODUCTION

In spite of a growing number of empirical studies, most beliefs about families of eating disordered patients have their origin in clinical observations (Gull, 1874; Laseque, 1873; Bliss and Branch, 1960; Bruch, 1973; Morgan and Russell, 1975; Selvini-Palazzoli, 1974; Minuchin, Rosman and Baker, 1978; Crisp, 1980; Root, Fallon and Friedrich, 1986; Dare and Eisler, 1992). These provide a rich source of insight into the functioning of these families but can also give a one-sided, and at times misleading, picture. While different authors stress different aspects of family life in understanding anorexia nervosa, overall there appears a fair degree of agreement between them. The picture which emerges tends to be a negative one of an overclose, overinvolved family that has high expectations of its children and which is unable to provide the impetus and support for individuation and separation during adolescence. The negative account of families of anorexics can be traced back to Gull (1874) and Laseque (1873) both of whom saw the patients' families primarily as a hindrance to treatment. Many clinical accounts have continued to give the family a rather bad press. Take Bliss and Branch (1960) as an example:

> Some mothers were overprotecting and inhibited normal maturation; others were vacillating, weak, distant or neurotic. But the mother was not necessarily the sole or chief cause of personality malformation. There were fathers who were unfaithful,

Handbook of Eating Disorders: Theory, Treatment and Research.
Edited by G. Szmukler, C. Dare and J. Treasure.
© 1995 John Wiley & Sons Ltd.

sexually assaultive, alcoholic, or uninterested. Some familes appeared congenial, but in many cases there were intense parental disharmonies that created unhappy home environments. (p. 47)

And later:

One can only conclude that a large number of these patients were nurtured in family environments which tend to produce emotionally impaired individuals. (p. 48)

Although other authors, especially more recently, might express their views somewhat less stringently, the above view would not stand out as being particularly unusual. Many authors have cautioned against the dangers of equating observations of current family functioning with notions of a familial genesis of the illness. Such observations are usually made at a point where the eating disorder has already developed and often continued for many years. Inevitably, some of the features observed will have arisen as a response to the illness rather than being the cause. Although this is commonly recognised, it is striking how frequently observations of a particular pattern of family interaction are automatically assumed to be of aetiological significance.

The fact that our beliefs about eating disorder families are so strongly based on clinical accounts is an important reason for not drawing conclusions too readily. Clinical observations of family interaction can be made quite reliably (Eisler, Szmukler and Dare, 1985), but by their very nature they are likely to be idiosyncratic. They will highlight any unusual or striking aspects of family functioning, which may be prominent in a small number of families and only minimally or not at all present in others, but the account that will become part of the professional literature will be the one where these features are most prominent. Over the years such accounts become part of the "professional folklore" and their self-reinforcing nature gradually gives them the status of "fact".

The clinician is not a detached observer. In developing a therapeutic alliance with the patient, his view of the family will be strongly coloured by the patient's own perception of her relationships and by the relationship that the clinician himself develops with the patient and her family. Frustrated, because he finds his therapeutic efforts are not accepted by the family, he may feel the parents are overinvolved or overprotective. At other times he may feel sorry for the parents who have to put up with a difficult daughter but conclude they are ineffective and weak, or in empathising with the daughter's sense of ineffectiveness he may see the parents as domineering and controlling.

The empirical evidence for the role of family factors in the genesis of eating disorders will be reviewed under the following headings: (1) sociodemographic family features; (2) adverse events in the family; (3) parental personality and attitudes; (4) specific characteristics of the parent–child relationship; (5) the family as a social system.

SOCIODEMOGRAPHIC FACTORS

Factors such as social class, parental age, family composition and family size are often seen as possible aetiological factors, as they may influence child rearing or attitudes to food. Many authors have reported an association between these factors and eating disorders.

Social class has been a consistent descriptor of families of eating disordered patients. Many studies based on clinical samples have shown a disproportionate number of families in higher social classes (Crisp et al, 1980; Morgan and Russell, 1975; Garfinkel and Garner 1982; Johnson, Stuckey and Lewis, 1982). Studies of adolescent schoolgirls (Crisp, Palmer and Kalucy, 1976; Eisler and Szmukler, 1985) support these findings for anorexia nervosa though not for bulimia nervosa (Crowther, Post and Zaynor, 1985). Three recent community based studies, however, bring into question the universality of these findings (Dolan, Evans and Lacey, 1989; Rastam and Gillberg, 1991; Freeman and Gard, 1994). There are several possible interpretations of these recent findings. The findings based on clinical samples may be misleading, reflecting referral patterns in specialist centres. The social class distribution of bulimia nervosa may be different from that of anorexia nervosa. Finally, the nature of the pattern of distribution of eating disorders may have changed in recent years. Whichever interpretation(s) is correct, these studies illustrate the need for caution when interpreting even apparently consistent and robust findings.

Birth order, family composition and family size have all been suggested as possible contributing factors in the aetiology of anorexia nervosa. The evidence for these has not been very consistent (Theander, 1970; Kay, Schapira and Brandon, 1967; Hall, 1978; Johnson et al, 1984; Gowers, Kadambari and Crisp, 1985) and again the most recent empirical studies have not found any differences either for anorexics (Rastam and Gillberg, 1991) or for bulimics (Dolan, Evans and Lacey, 1989).

Parental age at the time of birth of the child has often been reported as higher than expected (Dally, 1969; Theander, 1970; Garfinkel et al, 1983; Hall, 1978; Dolan, Evans and Lacey, 1989), leading to speculation that this might reflect an ambivalence about sexual relationships (Dally, 1969) or about having children (Szmukler, 1993). The principal exception to the above studies is Rastam and Gillberg (1991), who did not find a difference between anorexics and controls although both groups were somewhat older than would be predicted from population norms.

In summary, while the sociodemographic features of the families of eating disordered patients show some differences from the normal population, these are probably smaller and less consistent than was thought previously.

ADVERSE EVENTS IN THE FAMILY

Significant adverse life events occurring in the context of the family will often emerge clinically. These include the death of a parent or other close relative, the break-up of the family due to divorce, the experience of physical or sexual abuse during childhood, or other significant life events such as migration, unemployment or illness. For the clinician such events, and the way that the family responds to them, are often important in gaining an understanding of a particular patient. The patient or her family may see such events as playing a significant role in the development of the illness, but even though their impact often seems self-evident, we cannot assume that they have a role in the aetiology of the illness in general.

Parental loss due to death or break-up of the family does not appear to be associated with the development of eating disorder (Rastam and Gillberg, 1991; Dolan et al, 1990; Kendler et al, 1992). Rastam and Gillberg (1991) also compared the frequency of all deaths in the immediate family (including those that happened many years prior to the onset of the illness) and found that this happened significantly more often in the lives of anorexics than controls. This finding is intriguing but difficult to interpret. The deaths happened mostly many years earlier, and several deaths were of siblings who had died before the birth of the anorexic herself. While it may be plausible to postulate that the deaths continued to remain unresolved for the family, the above study was of course not designed to test such an hypothesis and simply showed a statistical association between death amongst first-degree relatives and the occurrence of an eating disorder in the family.

Schmidt, Tiller and Treasure (1993), in a careful study of childhood antecedents of eating disorders, also investigated the role of parental loss as antecedents of eating disorders. The death of a parent was a rare occurrence in their sample (less than 5%). When different kinds of parental loss or separation were taken together (parental separation, death of a parent or being sent to boarding school), they found, however, that a relatively high proportion of bulimics had experienced such loss, though this was not true for the anorexics.

Child sexual abuse and its possible impact has received a considerable amount of attention recently. Oppenheimer and colleagues (Oppenheimer et al, 1985; Palmer et al, 1990) found that 31% of their anorexic patients reported child sexual abuse. Extending the definition of sexual abuse to "any unwanted, unpleasant or coercive sexual event" increased this figure to 57%. Root and Fallon (1988) found that a third of their sample of 172 bulimic patients reported being sexually abused as a child and two-thirds reported either sexual or physical abuse. Bulik, Sullivan and Rorty (1989) give a similar figure of 34% of mainly intrafamilial and repetitive sexual abuse.

Comparisons of different studies are difficult because of diverse definitions of abuse, methods (ranging from simple yes/no self-report measures, through detailed questionnaires to in-depth interviews) and the use of different samples. In an excellent review Connors and Morse (1993) conclude that, while the percentages quoted in various studies range from 6% to 66%, most cluster around 30%. This is somewhat higher than the rates of abuse of 15–30% that have been reported in the general population but the difference is relatively small (Bifulco, Brown and Adler, 1991; Russell, 1986). In a carefully designed case control study, Welch and Fairburn (1994) compared a group of bulimics from a community-based sample with psychiatric controls and a non-disturbed group and also a matched clinic-based sample of bulimics. They found that the bulimics in the community sample had experienced sexual abuse more frequently (1/4) than did the controls (1/10). The matched psychiatric controls (mainly depressed patients) recalled an experience of childhood sexual abuse as frequently as the bulimics.

There were no differences between the clinic-based and community-based groups of bulimic sufferers. Other studies of sexual abuse in psychiatric samples have tended to report rates of sexual abuse that are higher than the ones discussed above (Morrison, 1989; Beck and van der Kolk, 1987; Herman and Schatzow, 1987). There is conflicting evidence whether bulimic patients are more likely to have experienced sexual abuse than restricting anorexics (Steiger and Zanko, 1990; Palmer et al, 1990; Schmidt, Tiller and Treasure, 1993).

Physical abuse has been studied relatively infrequently in eating disorders although the experience of violence, at least amongst bulimic patients, is not uncommon. Piran et al (1988) reported that a third of the their bulimic subjects had been physically abused (compared with 17% of anorexics), and Schmidt, Tiller and Treasure (1993) in their study found that 29% of bulimics and 7% of anorexics had experienced violence against themselves. Nearly 30% of the bulimics also experienced violence directed at another family member.

Schmidt, Tiller and Treasure's (1993) study suggests that the difference between bulimics and anorexics in terms of abusive experiences is perhaps part of a broader picture, in which bulimics were more likely than anorexics to experience a variety of childhood adversity (including indifference, discord, abuse, inconsistency in care arrangements), though the extent to which these occur more frequently than in the population in general remains unclear.

PARENTAL PERSONALITY AND ATTITUDES

A belief that a particular type of parental personality and parental attitudes are associated with eating disorder is remarkably persistent, in spite of a dearth of supporting evidence. A common stereotype portrays the mothers as dominant, overinvolved and at the same time emotionally unavailable for their daughters, while the fathers are typically seen as distant, weak and marginal in the family. Apart from anecdotal support for these stereotypes (Bliss and Branch, 1960; Szyrynski, 1973), there is little real evidence for them. It is worth noting how similar these stereotypes are to earlier accounts of the parents of schizophrenics (Tietze, 1949), which have long been shown to lack discriminatory value between different clinical and non-clinical samples. There is some empirical evidence (Kalucy, Crisp and Harding, 1977; Crisp, Harding and McGuiness, 1974) that parents of eating disordered patients tend to have a history of weight problems or high preoccupation with food. In comparison with control subjects, however, while bulimics may differ in this respect from controls (Kent and Clopton, 1992), anorexics probably do not (Hall, 1978; Garfinkel et al, 1983).

The factors discussed so far have been general; even if found to be linked to eating disorder, they are unlikely to be specific. The following sections will consider family factors postulated as having a very clearly defined role in the development of the disorder. These are to do with specific qualities of the parent–child relationship and the transactional style of the family. For many authors these are necessary, if not sufficient, conditions for the development of an eating disorder.

SPECIFIC PATTERNS OF PARENT–CHILD RELATIONSHIPS

Bruch (1973) argued that at the heart of anorexia nervosa is a particular early mother–child relationship, in which there is a lack of appropriate responses from the mother to the child's needs. Instead, the mother acts on her own need to feel in control. The needs and impulses of the infant remain poorly differentiated and instead she tries to comply with what she believes are her mother's needs (Gordon, Beresin and Herzog, 1989). Even in adolescence her biological and psychological needs remain blurred and she is unable to cope with the developmental demands for individuation and separation. Bruch's theory is persuasive as it offers both an explanation of the more general psychological features observed in anorexia nervosa (e.g. the anorexic's lack of a sense of separateness and her pervasive sense of ineffectiveness), as well as an account of the development of a specific deficit in the processing of bodily cues underlying the body–image disturbance.

Bruch's writing has been influential, but her theories are difficult to evaluate empirically in the absence of prospective studies of parent–infant interaction (which are difficult to mount). Indirect evidence comes from retrospective studies of childhood care patterns and from studies of current family relationships of the eating disordered patient. Studies of childhood care patterns have found some differences between clinical samples and controls, though not necessarily in the predicted direction. Using the Parental Bonding Instrument (PBI), several studies have reported lowered scores on the parental care scale (Palmer, Oppenheimer and Marshall, 1988; Steiger et al, 1989; Calam et al, 1990), while scores on protectiveness were either the same as for controls or in one study raised for fathers but not mothers (Calam et al, 1990). Two recent studies using the PBI, with different samples from the earlier studies, are of interest. Russell et al (1992) compared adolescent anorexic patients with normal controls and an assorted group of psychiatric patients and found that the anorexics' reports of their childhood experiences were more like those of the control subjects than of the psychiatric controls. Kent and Clopton (1992) studied a group of female students amongst whom they identified a subgroup who suffered from bulimia nervosa. The bulimics did not differ from the controls on the PBI.

FAMILY SYSTEMS ACCOUNTS

The strongest advocates of family models of eating disorders have understandably come from the field of family therapy. Many family therapy accounts have drawn on the psychodynamically oriented writings of Bruch and others, but offer a different theoretical perspective. The family is viewed as a complex social system in which the various family features are seen as part of a complex matrix of interacting factors, in which the eating disorder is somehow embedded (Eisler, 1993). Causality is seen as a circular rather than a linear process. The family systems accounts make a distinction between the notion of the family (or particular aspects of the family) as a *cause* of the disorder (a linear concept) and the family as the *context* of the disorder. Because of the constant interaction between different components of the family system, cause and effect are impossible to distinguish. Take for example the lack of independence of the anorexic child and the overprotective behaviour of the parent. The anorexic youngster may feel that she has no independence in her life and that self-starvation provides her with one area where she has control. Her behaviour, however, makes her ever more dependent on her parents, reinforcing her childlike role. The parents' perception of her vulnerability reinforces their need to protect her, which in turn makes the adolescent feel that her individuality is being denied. The circle is a continuous one with no obvious starting or ending point.

The family systems accounts from different family therapists show considerable overlap, with different aspects being highlighted by different authors. Common to most is a description of an extremely close family, with blurred intergenerational boundaries, where conflict and disagreement are feared and avoided. Selvini-Palazzoli (1974) emphasises the family's need to have a compliant, perfect child, which the child incorporates in her own self-perception. Selvini-Palazzoli also stresses the rigidity of interactional patterns in the family and the upholding of traditional family roles. She suggests that anorexia nervosa is a manifestation of the family conflict of loyalty between the present-day family and the parents' or grandparents' family of origin.

Loyalty to the family, to the extent that the fulfilment of individual need is ignored (particularly in relation to adolescent individuation) is also emphasised by Stierlin and Weber (1989a,b), while Stern et al (1981) stress that both the anorexic youngster and her parent(s) are developmentally arrested in the area of individuation/separation and that the family becomes organised around the need to prevent separation from taking place.

The most comprehensive account of families of eating disordered patients comes from the work of Minuchin and his coworkers (Minuchin et al, 1975; 1978). They developed a model of the so-called "psychosomatic family", of which anorexia nervosa they thought was a prime example. This model has three factors:

> First, the child is physiologically vulnerable; . . . Second, the child's family has four transactional characteristics: enmeshment, overprotectiveness, rigidity and a lack of conflict resolution. Third, the sick child plays an important role in the family's pattern of conflict avoidance; and this role is an important source of reinforcement for his symptoms. (Minuchin et al, 1975, p. 1033)

Discussions of the "psychosomatic family" and any attempts at empirical verification generally focus on the four transactional features of the "psychosomatic family".

The family systems accounts by Selvini-Palazzoli, Minuchin, Stierlin and others are clinically persuasive and provide important insights into family dynamics, but the empirical evidence in support of these accounts is limited. Family therapists would argue that the only meaningful tests can come from observational studies and these are few and far between. The methodological problems of mounting observational studies that would provide reliable and clinically meaningful data are such that most researchers opt for the simpler approach of relying on self-report accounts of families by patients or other family members. These will be discussed first.

Three questionnaires have been used most often in studies of family functioning in eating disorder:

- *The Family Environment Scale (FES)* (Moos and Moos, 1981) measures three areas of family functioning: (a) *interpersonal relationships* (cohesion, expressiveness, conflict), (b) *personal growth* (independence, achievement orientation, intellectual–cultural orientation, active–recreational orientation, moral–religious emphasis) and (c) *basic organisational structure* (organisation and control).
- *The Family Assessment Device (FAD)*, based on the McMasters model of the family (Epstein et al, 1978, 1983) assesses six areas of family functioning: (a) task differentiation (roles), (b) concern and involvement between family members (affective involvement), (c) appropriate expression of emotions (affective responsiveness), (d) ability to resolve problems (problem solving), (e) clarity of communication (communication) and (f) clarity of "family rules" (behaviour control).
- *The Family Cohesion and Adaptability Scales (FACES)* were developed by Olson, Sprenkle and Russell (1979) as a measure of family functioning based on their Circumplex model of family functioning. This assesses families on two dimensions: (a) *cohesion*, or closeness of family members, and (b) *adaptability* of family organisation. Optimal family functioning is defined by midpoint values on both dimensions. FACES can be given in two forms ("as perceived" by the respondent—*perceived score*—and as the respondent "would like it to be"—*ideal score*). A comparison of the scores on the two forms provides an index of "family dissatisfaction".

The studies using the FES seem at first sight to provide a fairly clear picture. Several studies (Johnson and Flach, 1985; Stern et al, 1989; Shisslak, McKeon and Cragg, 1990), comparing eating disordered patients in a specialist unit with controls, found that bulimics (and to a lesser degree anorexics) perceived their families as less cohesive, less encouraging of independence, low on expressiveness of feeling, but reported higher levels of conflict and higher levels of achievement orientation than did the controls. Two further studies using the FES, however, spoil this rather clear picture. Kent and Clopton (1992), in a college-based study, compared three groups of subjects (BN, subclinical bulimia, controls) selected from a screen of 820 psychology students. With one exception the FES did not differentiate between bulimics and controls. The expressiveness scale, though not as low as for the bulimics in the Johnson and Flach (1985) study, was significantly lower than for the controls. The other study is by Blouin, Zuro and Blouin (1990) who replicated the Johnson and Flach (1985) study but found that when they controlled for depression the differences all but disappeared.

The studies that have used the FAD provide a similar story. When clinical groups are compared with normal controls (Waller, Calam and Slade, 1989; Steiger et al, 1991), families of eating disordered patients show poorer functioning particularly in terms of communication and affective responsiveness. College-based samples, however, provide a less clear picture. McNamara and Loveman (1990) screened 600 students and identified 31 normal-weight bulimics, 61 repeat-dieters and 59 non-dieters. The bulimic subjects reported poorer general functioning of their families and also communication, affective involvement and affective responsiveness and problem solving. The level of scores, however, was generally quite low, with the bulimics obtaining scores comparable to the controls in the Steiger et al (1991) and Waller et al (1989) studies. The two comparison groups scored significantly lower on all scales, but it is questionable whether they can be thought of as "normal controls" in the same sense as the control groups in the two previously mentioned studies. Rather than being a random sample of control subjects they were specifically selected on the basis of their attitude to weight and dieting ("non-dieters" had to be satisfied with their weight and had rarely if ever dieted). The 450 students who were excluded by the screening from the study itself were probably more likely to be comparable to "normal controls".

The FACES questionnaire is theoretically closest to the "psychosomatic family" model, though it has been criticised on conceptual grounds (Olivieri and Reiss, 1984; O'Sullivan, Berger and Foster, 1984). The two dimensions of the Circumplex model (Olsen, Sprenkle and Russell, 1979) appear closely related to two of the central aspects of the "psychosomatic family". Studies comparing clinical samples with controls show some consistent differences (though not necessarily in the predicted direction). Waller, Slade and Calam (1990a) found that anorexic and bulimic patients perceived their families to be both more rigid and disengaged than did controls. Humphrey (1986) on the basis of a factor analysis of FACES scores concluded that bulimic anorexics see their families as less close and more isolated than do controls. These results need to be contrasted with Rastam's study (Rastam, 1990; Rastam and Gillberg, 1991). In a population-based study she identified 51 cases of anorexia nervosa and compared them with a sample of 51 children of the same age and gender from the same school. The differences between anorexics and controls were generally small and statistically insignificant. Overall Rastam concludes that there is "very little to suggest that families of children with anorexia nervosa conform to the generally held stereotype". And further she concludes that "a small subgroup of families (less than one in five families) conform to the stereotype of enmeshment, rigidity and overprotectiveness, but so did a number of families without anorexia nervosa". This last point is important. Most studies simply present mean scores for subgroups of families, which masks the fact that there is a wide variation between families rather than there being a particular pattern to which they conform.

Our own study of 26 families with an adolescent suffering from anorexia nervosa ($N = 18$) or bulimia nervosa ($N = 8$) (LeGrange, 1989; Dare et al, 1994) illustrates this clearly. From the "psychosomatic family" model one would predict that anorexic families would generally have fairly extreme scores which would fall in the "rigidly enmeshed" part of the Circumplex grid (for description of FACES labels see Figure 9.1). Figure 9.1 shows that the scores of family members in our sample in fact have a wide scatter, with the majority falling in the mid-range or "balanced" section. Comparison of the mean FACES scores of the parents and children shows that mothers and fathers tend to share the view of their families as "balanced" ("flexibly

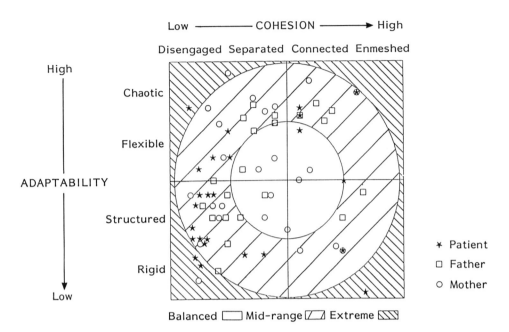

FIGURE 9.1   FACES perceived scores for family members (Reproduced by permission from
Dare et al., 1994.)

separated") and also express, as their "family ideal", a desire for greater cohesion
and greater flexibility. The children view their families as significantly less cohesive
than do the parents. The patients compared to parents also perceived their families as
more structured. The children's "ideal" scores, however, closely resemble the comparable scores of their parents. In other words, both the parents and the children
express a desire for greater closeness and greater flexibility in family functioning.

The one systematic finding that emerged was in a comparison of perceived and
ideal scores. Olson, Spenkle and Russell (1979) define "dissatisfaction" as the
absolute difference between "ideal" and "perceived" scores. A somewhat different
picture emerges if the direction of the dissatisfaction is taken into account. We can
then distinguish between dissatisfaction ensuing from the experience of too much
closeness ("smothering") and the sense of excessive distance ("isolation").
Similarly, a distinction can be made between dissatisfaction with a too rigid family
structure ("constrain") and the opposite feeling that the family provides insufficient
structure ("insecurity"). Figure 9.2 shows that when the difference between the
ideal and perceived scores on the two dimensions of the Circumplex model are
plotted in this way there is a remarkable consistency, with the overwhelming majority of family members expressing a sense of feeling isolated and constrained. Our
study did not have a comparison group and we do not know whether this finding is
in any way specific to our group of patients or whether a similar pattern would be
found in other groups.

There are obvious parallels between Olson et al's (1979) concept of cohesion (the
degree of bonding between family members) and Minuchin's delineation of en-

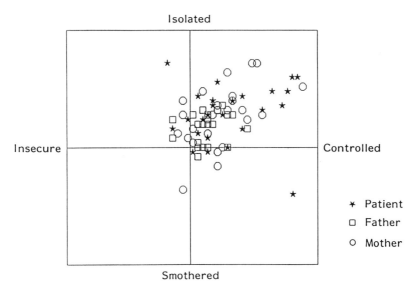

FIGURE 9.2   Difference between perceived and desired scores on FACES (Reproduced by permission from Dare et al., 1994.)

meshment. At first sight, the findings that families of eating disordered patients tend not to rate themselves as particularly cohesive seems to contradict Minuchin's model. Our study offers a possible alternative explanation. Minuchin et al (1978) view the psychosomatic family as one where closeness is highly valued and our finding that nearly all of the families in our study saw themselves as too "isolated" (regardless of the level of their "perceived" scores) is consistent with this. A family that values closeness highly may interact in a way that will make them appear to the external observer as very close, even though they themselves may feel that they are not achieving their desired level of closeness.

This highlights one of the inherent limitations of questionnaire-based family studies. Models of family functioning are mainly derived from observations of family interaction made by independent observers. However accurate such observations might be, the family members themselves may not necessarily see their family in this way, simply because of the different perspective from which their observations are made. The differences between the "internal" and "external" perspectives do not invalidate one another and can be equally valid. However, even where different families might seem quite similar to the outside observer, the families' own experiences of themselves might vary. The reason why the unidimensional discrepancy between perceived and ideal scores may be more robust, as our study indicates, is because fewer assumptions have to be made about the families' own concepts of closeness and adapatability.

The finding that the families see themselves as too constrained by family rules would appear to support Minuchin's model but such a conclusion is also problematic. Minuchin's description of rigidity has been described as "too narrow" and lacking in two important elements (Kog, Vandereycken and Vertommen, 1985a,b).

Firstly, it makes no reference to states where too much change is present, and unlike Olson's definition of "adaptability", it is therefore unidimensional. Secondly, it does not take into account two distinctive uses of the term: (1) a limited repertoire in the current, interactional processes of the family, and (2) an inability to change over time (Kog et al, 1985a,b). What both have in common, of course, is that the family responds in very limited ways to external cues and appears to function as if it was isolated from the outside world. The clinical assessment of rigidity is, in a sense, a negative one—it is based on an observation of a *lack* of change in transactional style where a change might be expected (e.g. in response to an intervention from the therapist). From a research point of view the assessment of rigidity is, therefore, problematic. A self-report instrument (such as FACES) makes the assumption that family members can make the relative judgements that are needed, but the more rigid the family, the less likely they are to be able to make use of the external referents that make such judgements possible.

Conclusions

The picture that emerges from the various questionnaire studies, while showing a considerable variation between different studies (and between families within each study), does allow some overall conclusions. Most studies report a perception of a lower level of closeness or at least a level of closeness that is less than the subject would ideally like. Communication in general, and affective expression in particular, is reported as restricted in many studies. Some studies report differences between families of anorexics and families of bulimics (e.g. higher levels of conflict) while other studies have not found this.

Relatively few studies have compared perceptions of different family members. Those that have suggest that parents perceive the family as more "normal" than do their offspring. It is misleading to conclude (as do Waller et al, 1990b) that this means that the sufferers have a more realistic perception of their families' interactional styles. Such a conclusion assumes that the families really are different from normal—a somewhat circular argument! It highlights, however, that questionnaires provide a limited and, usually, one-sided snapshot of the family.

A consistent finding with different questionnaire methods is that the differences that are found may apply only to highly selected clinical samples. Community-based samples or studies that have controlled for factors such as depression find little or no differences between the eating disordered groups and controls.

OBSERVATIONAL STUDIES

There have been relatively few studies based on actual observations of family interaction. Moreover, the existing studies tend to be fairly small and often raise questions (particularly about methodological issues) rather than provide substantive answers. The small number of studies and small samples mean that there is an insufficient body of empirical evidence to start piecing together a coherent overall picture.

Kog, Vandereycken and colleagues (Kog et al, 1985b, 1986, 1987; Kog and Vandereycken, 1989) attempted to operationalise Minuchin's constructs. In an initial
methodological study they used an ambitious design which included three different
interactional tasks and three types of operationalisations of variables (direct observation; comparisons of behavioural outcomes between family members; self-
report). The coding of the behavioural observations, however, turned out to have a
relatively low inter-rater reliability, and in their subsequent substantive study in
which anorexics and controls were compared these measures were abandoned. On
the remaining observational measure, they found lower levels of disagreement for
eating disordered patients (particularly among low-weight bulimics) than for controls (Kog and Vandereycken, 1989).

Røijen (1993) studied 18 families with an anorexic child. He used the Beavers
scales of family assessment (Lewis et al, 1976; Beavers, 1982) to rate interaction
during a family interview and during a family task. He found three distinct styles of
interaction: a close, enmeshed style ("centripetal families"), a disorganised style
("centrifugal families") and a mixed, well-functioning style. Only the first of these
three seems to conform to the traditional concept of the "psychosomatic family".
More importantly, when the families were rated in terms of how well they were
functioning, ony four were rated as moderately or severely dysfunctional and of
these, three were in the "centrifugal" group.

A number of studies have used the Express Emotion (EE) scales, a reliable
measure that has been shown to be of relevance in a large number of disorders
(Brown et al, 1962; Leff and Vaughn, 1985). EE consists of five subscales (critical
comments, hostility, emotional overinvolvement (EOI), warmth, positive remarks)
of which critical comments is the scale that has shown to be the most robust and
consistent measure. In eating disorder, EE has been shown to predict response to
treatment and the subsequent course of the illness (Szmukler et al, 1985; van Furth,
1991) and that levels of EE are reduced after successful family treatment
(LeGrange et al, 1992b). Several studies (Szmukler et al, 1985; van Furth, 1991;
LeGrange et al, 1992a) have shown that the scales discriminate between families of
anorexics and families of bulimics.

In families of anorexics, the levels of EE are generally quite low. Compared, for
instance, with schizophrenic patients, the number of critical comments is small and
hostility is rare. Perhaps more surprisingly, EOI is also low while warmth is rated as
moderate and relatively few positive remarks are made. The low levels of criticism
and hostility are consistent with the clinical accounts of these families as conflict
avoiding, but the overall EE findings suggest that this might be part of a broader
picture of subdued affective expression. Higher levels of criticism are associated
with bulimia but also with a more chronic illness.

The one EE finding that is difficult to fit into the commonly accepted clinical
picture is the low EOI found in all the above studies. EOI is defined by the EE
scales in terms of a parent showing exaggerated emotional behaviour in response to
the child's problems, or marked overprotective behaviour. The parent's inability to
distance him or herself from the child's problem could, in Minuchin's terms, be
understood as a manifestation of enmeshment (although enmeshment is a more
broadly defined construct), but more specifically EOI is closely related to

Minuchin's concept of overprotectiveness. The consistently low EOI scores suggest that at least overprotectiveness may not be such a common family feature as clinicians often claim.

A final point is worthy of note from our EE studies. We have compared cohorts from two consecutive studies from the same clinical setting. The first was from a pilot study of a clinical trial for adolescent anorexics (LeGrange et al, 1992b), the second was from the definitive study that followed the pilot study. The two studies were conducted in the same outpatient clinic and using the same selection criteria. The second study started approximately 2 years after the end of recruitment for the first study. The two cohorts were clinically very similar, being of comparable ages, duration, age of onset and severity of illness. The patients in the second cohort, however, had a larger number of previous treatments and, most significantly from the point of view of the current discussion, their parents were considerably more critical of the anorexic child. The raised level of criticism may be a reflection of a growing dissatisfaction on the part of the parents (though it is clearly not simply related to chronicity as the duration of illness was the same in both samples). However, we know that high EE families are more difficult to engage in treatment and our result may simply be a reflection of a selection process whereby a growing number of difficult to treat cases are seen in a tertiary centre. It may therefore be that factors that are found to characterise the families in our clinical samples have little or nothing to do with the genesis of the illness but rather with factors that have prevented the family from solving the problem.

A very different approach to observational studies of families is found in the work of Humphrey (Humphrey, 1987, 1989, 1992) who has used the Structural Analysis of Social Behaviour (SASB), a methodology developed by Benjamin (1974). The methodology exists both in a self-report version and as an observational coding scheme. The SASB observational coding scheme makes use of a demanding microanalytic assessment of family interaction in which verbatim transcripts are used, together with videotapes, to rate every speech unit (i.e. a simple sentence) both for content and process which includes the non-verbal and paralinguistic aspects of communication. Each speech is rated on two dimensions, affiliation and interdependence, and related to three levels of focus: (a) focus on self, (b) focus on other, and (c) intrapsychic focus.

The complexity of the SASB methodology makes it difficult to summarise the findings in a simple way. Humphrey (1992), in summarising the findings from her studies, concludes that:

> . . . the families of bulimic children are enmeshed in a hostile, rigid pattern combining issues of attachment and autonomy. Families of anorexics are not so overtly hostile, and instead communicate a mixed message of loving affection with control or negation of the daughters' needs to separate.

However, a careful examination of Humphrey's results (particularly Humphrey, 1989) shows that if instead of examining the *differences* between the clinical and control families we start by looking at the *similarities* between them, rather different conclusions emerge. Figure 9.3 presents a simplified diagram of one aspect of the SASB model, showing the clusters that define the interpersonal surface" of the model and reproduces a small part of Humphrey's data, showing the profile of the mother–daughter interactions (the profiles of father–daughter interactions have a very similar pattern) in three eating disordered groups and normal controls. The most striking aspect of the graph is the overall similarity of the profiles of all four groups. When viewed in this context the differences that we find are important but take on a somewhat different significance. Apart from the overall similarity certain differences stand out. The first comes from a comparison of the most commonly rated clusters (4 and 5) which are defined by the balance between affiliative and controlling behaviours. The control families show a preponderance of cluster 4 behaviours (which is characterised by a balance between affiliation and control) while the three eating disordered groups show a greater frequency of cluster 5 behaviours (where control is more prominent than affiliation). The second thing to note is that clusters 6, 7 and 8 (all three of which are in the direction of disaffiliation) are rated infrequently in all groups. Two exceptions stand out. Mothers of bulimics are more frequently rated, compared with the other groups, on cluster 6, and mothers (as well as fathers) of anorexics on cluster 8. The finding of a tendency to blame and belittle is consistent with the earlier mentioned findings of raised levels of criticism and hostility in bulimic families. The fact that parents of anorexics, compared with controls, are more likely to be rated as rejecting and neglecting (cluster 8) has to be compared with the much greater frequency of their affiliative behaviours.

This brief presentation obviously cannot do justice to the very complex SASB model. For instance, the above examines only the behaviour of the parents towards their daughters, whereas the behaviour of the anorexic and bulimic youngsters towards their parents differed much more systematically from the controls. Figure 9.3 is presented here primarily to illustrate the important point, that while the family interaction in eating disorder families may indeed differ from control families, such differences may in fact represent a relatively small shift from "normal" and should not in themselves be seen as pathological or for that matter as pathogenic.

CONCLUSIONS

The principal thrust of this chapter has been to argue against the notion that there are common family factors that lead to the development of an eating disorder. The notion that there is a *particular* type of family constellation or style of family functioning that is invariably associated with eating disorder is difficult to sustain. Families of both anorexics and bulimics vary considerably and do not conform to a single pattern. In comparison with non-clinical families there are some differences, but these are much less pronounced and less consistent than the clinical literature would lead us to believe.

Many of the observed differences are found only in clinical samples. In community-based samples the differences are smaller or disappear altogether. Some of the differences found, particularly on self-report measures, may be due to

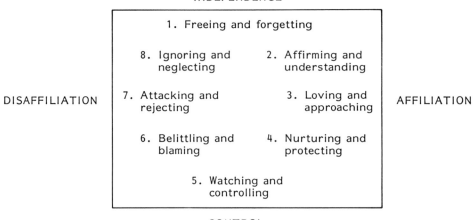

INDEPENDENCE

1. Freeing and forgetting

8. Ignoring and neglecting   2. Affirming and understanding

DISAFFILIATION   7. Attacking and rejecting   3. Loving and approaching   AFFILIATION

6. Belittling and blaming   4. Nurturing and protecting

5. Watching and controlling

CONTROL

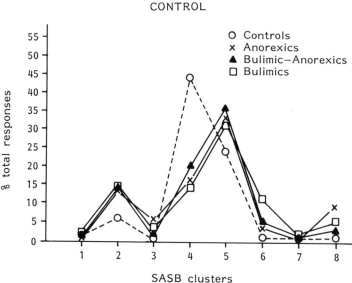

SASB clusters

FIGURE 9.3   At the top is shown one aspect of the SASB model. Underneath is shown a part of Humphrey's data—profiles of mother–daughter interactions in three eating disorder groups (adapted by permission from Humphrey, 1989).

other factors such as depression that have not been controlled for in the various studies. The simplest explanation of this would be that the observed differences are consequences rather than the antecedents of the illness. Such an explanation, however, would be just as misleading as the notion that the illness is caused by the family. Relationships and styles of family functioning are not statistic entities, but evolve in the constant interaction between family members. This is true even of the earliest parent–infant interaction. This will be shaped not just by the parents' personality, attitudes or needs, but equally strongly by the way the infant responds.

In any case, the fact that there is a range of family interactional styles in eating disorder, argues against the disorder having its origin in a specific type of experience in the family. The differences between the clinic-based and community-based samples suggest that much of what we regularly do identify in the families that we see may be factors that are associated with a more chronic course of the illness, either as a consequence of it or because they interfere with attempts at finding a solution to the problem.

Developing a family aetiological model of eating disorders requires us to ask two questions:

1. What are the common features of families of an eating disorder sufferer?
2. How are the families different from other families?

In doing this we often forget how misleading these two questions can be. Some of the similarities that we observe will not be specific to the disorder but might be characteristic of families struggling with any life-threatening or chronic illness in their midst (a reluctance to engage in open conflict or difficulties in adapting to change are good examples). Other similarities will be to do with the fact that the families are at a particular stage in the family life-cycle, when all families at this developmental stage have to struggle with specific issues, such as individuation/ separation issues or adaptation on the part of the parents to children leaving home. Clinicians, and families themselves, are often too quick to conclude that the difficulty that a family is experiencing is either a cause or a consequence of the eating disorder and ignore the fact that a large part of it is simply a normal developmental process.

An eating disorder develops in the *context* of a particular relationship(s) but this is not the same as saying that it is caused by it. However, it also becomes *part of the relationship* so that what we observe is a pattern of relationships that has evolved around the eating disorder and in which the eating disorder will have a very central role. While in theory we can distinguish what the family was like before the illness started and what it is like after the illness has been there for some time, in practice a distinction between antecedents and consequences is going to be fairly arbitrary. The differences will often be one of degree. Certain features which may have been present for a long time will become more prominent as the illness begins to dominate family life. Families, whose preferred style is non-conflictual, may respond to the increasing anxiety about their daughter's life by attempting to avoid conflict at all cost. Clinically, there is often an impression that the family is poised in a balancing act, where putting one foot wrong could bring everything crashing down. The family feels paralysed and restricts its transactional repertoire which gives the impression of a "frozen", rigid family, for whom time has virtually come to a standstill. Just as the anorexic youngster seems to remain stuck in her functioning in a pre-adult stage, so the family continues to function as a family of a younger child. The normal struggles and difficulties that all families face at this particular stage of their life-cycle seem to become magnified and distorted and if the illness continues for a long time will appear incongruent, given the actual age of the youngster (or by now adult).

Understanding this process is important, as it can help us tackle the question of what makes it difficult for the family to move on and find a solution to the problem in their midst. The assumption that observed differences in family functioning are indications of family pathology that have caused the illness are both misguided and unhelpful. Family studies in eating disorders have been hampered by the attempts to find the elusive "anorexogenic" family. Such a quest is probably futile and is probably best abandoned. This does not mean we should stop investigating how families function. The focus should, however, be on differences between families, to try to identify the strengths and weaknesses of different family transactional styles. Understanding how families cope with adversity will tell us more about how to help than trying to identify what is wrong with a family. Rather than asking the question of why an individual develops an eating problem in the context of a certain family or why the problem continues to be unresolved, we should be asking what makes it possible for some families to tackle the problem more effectively than others.

REFERENCES

Beavers, R.W. (1982). Healthy, midrange, and severely dysfunctional families. In: F. Walsh (Ed.), *Normal Family Processes*. New York: Guilford.

Beck, J. and van der Kolk, B. (1987). Reports of childhood incest and current behaviour of chronically hospitalised psychotic women. *Am. J. Psychiat.*, **144**, 1474–1476.

Benjamin, L.S. (1974). Structural analysis of social behaviour. *Psychol. Rev.*, **81**, 392–425.

Bifulco, A., Brown, G.W. and Adler, Z. (1991). Early sexual abuse and clinical depression in adult life. *Br. J. Psychiat.*, **159**, 115–122.

Bliss, E.L. and Branch, C.H. (1960). *Anorexia Nervosa: Its Psychology and Biology*. New York: Hoeber.

Blouin, A.G., Zuro, C. and Blouin, J.H. (1990). Family environment in bulimia nervosa: the role of depression. *Int. J. Eat. Dis.*, **9**, 649–658.

Brown, G.W., Monck, E.M., Carstair, G.M. and Wing, J.K. (1962). Influence of family life on the course of schizophrenic illness. *Br. J. Prev. Soc. Med.*, **16**, 55–68.

Bruch, H. (1973). *Eating Disorders: Obesity, Anorexia Nervosa, and the Person Within*. New York: Basic Books.

Bulik, C.M., Sullivan, P.F. and Rorty, R. (1989). Childhood sexual abuse in women with bulimia. *J. Clin. Psychiat.*, **50**, 460–551.

Calam, R., Waller, G., Slade, P. and Newton, T. (1990). Eating disorders and perceived relationships with parents. *Int. J. Eat. Dis.*, **9** 479–485.

Connors, M. and Morse, W. (1993). Sexual abuse and eating disorders: a review. *Int. J. Eat. Dis.*, **13**, 1–11.

Crisp, A.H. (1980). *Anorexia Nervosa: Let Me Be*. London: Academic Press.

Crisp, A.H., Harding, B. and McGuiness, B. (1974). Anorexia nervosa. Psychoneurotic characteristics of parents: relationship to prognosis. *J. Psychosom. Res.*, **18**, 167–173.

Crisp, A.H., Palmer, R.L. and Kalucy, R.S. (1976). How common is anorexia nervosa? A prevalence study. *Br. J. Psychiat.*, **128**, 549–554.

Crisp, A.H., Hsu, L.K.G., Harding, B. and Hartshorn, J. (1980). Clinical features of anorexia nervosa: a study of a consecutive series of 102 female patients. *J. Pychosom. Res.*, **24**, 179–191.

Crowther, J.H., Post, G. and Zaynor, L. (1985). The prevalence of bulimia and binge eating in adolescent girls. *Int. J. Eat. Dis.*, **4**, 29–42.

Dally, P. (1969). *Anorexia Nervosa*. New York: Grune & Stratton.

Dare, C. and Eisler, I. (1992). Family therapy for anorexia nervosa. In: P.J. Cooper and A. Stein (Eds), *Feeding Problems and Eating Disorders in Children and Adolescents*. Reading: Harwood.

Dare, C., Le Grange, D., Eisler, I. and Rutherford, J. (1994). Redefining the psychosomatic family: family process of 26 eating disorder families. *Int. J. Eat. Dis.* (in press).

Dolan, B.M., Evans, C. and Lacey, J.H. (1989). Family composition and social class in bulimia: a catchment area study of a clinical and a comparison group. *J. Nerv. Ment. Dis.*, **177**, 267–272.

Dolan, B.M., Lieberman, S., Evans, C. and Lacey, J.H. (1990). Family features associated with normal body weight bulimia. *Int. J. Eat. Dis.*, **9**, 639–647.

Eisler, I. (1993). Families, family therapy and psychosomatic illness. In: S. Moorey and M. Hodes (Eds), *Psychological Treatments in Human Disease and Illness*. London: Gaskill.

Eisler, I. and Szmukler, G.I. (1985). Social class as a confounding variable in the eating attitudes test. *J. Psychiat. Res.*, **19**, 171–176.

Eisler, I., Szmukler, G. and Dare, C. (1985). Systematic observation and clinical insight—are they compatible? *Psychol. Med.*, **15**, 173–188.

Epstein, N.B., Bishop, D.S. and Levin, S. (1978). The McMaster model of family functioning. *J. Mar. Fam. Coun.*, **40**, 19–31.

Epstein, N.B., Baldwin, L.M. and Bishop, D.S. (1983). The McMaster family assessment device. *J. Mar. Fam. Ther.*, **9**, 171–180.

Freeman, C.P. and Gard, M.C.E. (1994). Eating disorders in the homeless. Submitted.

Garfinkel, P.E. and Garner, D.M. (1982). *Anorexia Nervosa: a Multidimensional Perspective*. New York: Brunner & Mazel.

Garfinkel, P.E., Garner, D.M., Rose, J., Darby, P.L., Brandes, J.S., O'Hanlon, J. and Walsh, N. (1983). A comparison of characteristics in the families of patients with anorexia nervosa and normal controls. *Psychol. Med.*, **13**, 821–828.

Gordon, C., Beresin, E. and Herzog, D.B. (1989). The parents' relationship and the child's illness in anorexia nervosa. *J. Am. Acad. Psychoanal.*, **17**, 29–42.

Gowers, S., Kadambari, S.R. and Crisp, A.H. (1985). Family structure and birth order of patients with anorexia nervosa. *J. Psychiat. Res.*, **2/3**, 247–251.

Gull, W.W. (1874). Anorexia nervosa (apepsia hysterica, anorexia hysterica). *Trans. Clin. Soc. Lond.*, **7**, 222–228.

Hall, A. (1978). Family structure and relationships of 50 female anorexia nervosa patients. *Aust. NZ J. Psychiat.*, **12**, 263–268.

Herman, J. and Schatzow, E. (1987). Recovery and verification of memories of childhood sexual trauma. *Psychoanal. Psychol.*, **4**, 1–14.

Humphrey, L.L. (1986). Family relations in bulimic–anorexic and non-distressed families. *Int. J. Eat. Dis.*, **5**, 223–232.

Humphrey, L.L. (1987). Comparison of bulimic–anorexic and non-distressed families using structural analysis of social behavior. *J. Am. Acad. Child. Adoles. Psychiat.*, **26**, 248–255.

Humphrey, L.L. (1988). Relationships within subtypes of anorectic, bulimic, and normal families. *J. Am. Acad. Child. Adoles. Psychiat.*, **27**, 544–551.

Humphrey, L.L. (1989). Observed family interactions among subtypes of eating disorders using structural analysis of social behavior. *J. Cons. Clin. Psychol.*, **57**, 206–214.

Humphrey, L.L. (1992). Family relationships. In: K.Halmi (Ed.), *Psychobiology of Anorexia Nervosa*. Washington, DC: American Psychiatric Press.

Johnson, C.L., Stuckey, M. and Lewis, L.D. (1982). Bulimia: a descriptive survey of 316 cases. *Int. J. Eat. Dis.*, **2**, 3–18.

Johnson, C.L., Lewis, C., Love, S. and Stuckey, M. (1984). Incidence and correlates of bulimic behaviour in a female high school population. *J. Youth Adolesc.*, **13**, 6–10.

Johnson, C. and Flach, A. (1985). Family characteristics of 105 patients with bulimia. *Am. J. Psychiat.*, **142**, 1321–1324.

Kalucy, R.S., Crisp, A.H. and Harding, B. (1977). A study of 56 families with anorexia nervosa. *Br. J. Med. Psychol.*, **50**, 381–395.

Kay, D.W.K., Schapira, K. and Brandon, S. (1967). Early factors in anorexia nervosa compared with non-anorexic groups. *J. Psychosom. Res.*, **11**, 133–139.

Kendler, K.S., Neale, M.C., Kessler, R.C., Heath, A. C. and Eaves, L. J. (1992). Childhood parental loss and adult psychopathology in women. *Arch. Gen. Psych.*, **49**, 109–116.

Kent, I.S. and Clopton, J.R. (1992). Bulimic women's perceptions of their family relation-ships. *J. Clin. Psychol.,* **48,** 281–292.

Kog, E., Pierloot, R. and Vandereycken, W. (1983). Methodological considerations of family research in anorexia nervosa. *Int. J. Eat. Dis.,* **2,** 79–84.

Kog, E., Vandereycken, W. and Vertommen, H. (1985a). The psychosomatic family model: a critical analysis of family interaction concepts. *J. Fam. Ther.,* **7,** 31–44.

Kog, E., Vandereycken, W. and Vertommen, H. (1985b). Towards a verification of the psychosomatic family model: a pilot study of 10 families with an anorexia/bulimia nervosa patient. *Int. J. Eat. Dis.,* **4,** 525–538.

Kog, E., Vertommen, H. and Vandereycken, W. (1987). Minuchin's psychosomatic family model revised: a concept validation study using a multitrait-multimethod approach. *Fam. Proc.,* **26,** 235–253.

Kog, E. and Vandereycken, W. (1989). Family interaction in eating disordered patients and normal controls. *Int. J. Eat. Dis.,* **8,** 11–23.

Laseque, E.C. (1873). De L'anorexie hysterique. *Archives Generales De Medecine, 21,* 384–403. Reprinted in R.M. Kaufman and M. Heiman (Eds), *Evolution of Psychosomatic Concepts. Anorexia Nervosa: A Paradigm.* New York: International Universities Press, 1964.

Leff, J. and Vaughn, C.E. (1985). *Expressed Emotion in Families: Its Significance for Mental Illness.* New York: Guilford.

LeGrange, D. (1989). Anorexia nervosa and family therapy: a study of changes in the individual and the family during the process of weight restoration. PhD thesis, University of London.

LeGrange, D., Eisler, I., Dare, C. and Hodes, M. (1992a). Family criticism and self starvation: a study of expressed emotion. *J. Fam. Ther.,* **14,** 177–192.

LeGrange, D., Eisler, I., Dare, C. and Russell, G.F.M. (1992b). Evaluation of family treat-ments in adolescent anorexia nervosa: a pilot study. *Int. J. Eat. Dis.,* **12,** 347–357.

Lewis, M., Beavers, W.R., Gossett, J. and Phillips, V. (1976). *No Single Thread.* New York: Brunner/Mazel.

McNamara, K. and Loveman, C. (1990). Differences in family functioning among bulimics, repeat dieters, and non-dieters. *J. Clin. Psychol.,* **46,** 518–523.

Minuchin, S., Baker, L., Rosman, B.L., Liebman, R., Milman, L. and Todd, T.C. (1975). A conceptual model of psychosomatic illness in children. *Arch. Gen. Psychiat.,* **32,** 1031–1038.

Minuchin, S., Rosman, B.L. and Baker, L. (1978). *Psychosomatic Families: Anorexia Nervosa in Context.* Cambridge, Mass: Harvard University Press.

Moos, R. and Moos, B. (1981). *Manual for the Family Environment Scale.* Palo Alto, CA: Consulting Psychologists Press.

Morgan, H.G. and Russell, G.F.M. (1975) Value of family background and clinical features as predictors of long-term outcome in AN: a four year follow-up study of 41 patients. *Psychol. Med.,* **5,** 355–371.

Morrison, J. (1989). Childhood sexual histories in women with somatization disorder. *Am. J. Pschiat.,* **146,** 239–241.

O'Sullivan, S., Berger, M. and Foster, M. (1984). The validity of structural family therapy nomenclature: a pilot study. *J. Mar. Fam. Ther.,* **10,** 179–184.

Olivieri, M. and Reiss, D. (1984). Family concepts and their measurements: things are seldom what they seem. *Fam. Proc.,* **23,** 33–48.

Olson, D.H., Sprenkle, D.H. and Russell, C.S. (1979). Circumplex model of marital and family systems. I: Cohesion and adaptability dimensions, family types, and clinical applica-tions. *Fam. Proc.,* **18,** 3–28.

Oppenheimer, R., Howells, K., Palmer, R.L. and Chaloner, D. (1985). Adverse sexual experi-ence in childhood and clinical eating disorders: a preliminary description. *Br. J. Psychiat.,* **156,** 699–703.

Palmer, R.L., Oppenheimer, R. and Marshall, P.D. (1988). Eating disorder patients remem-ber their parents: a study using the parental-bonding instrument. *Int. J. Eat. Dis.,* **7,** 101–106.

Palmer, R.L., Oppenheimer, R., Dignon, A., Chaloner, D. and Howells, K. (1990). Child-hood sexual experiences with adults reported by women with eating disorders: an extended series. *Br. J. Psychiat.*, **156**, 699–703.

Piran, N., Lerner, P., Garfinkel, P.E., Kennedy, S.H., Brouilette, C. (1988). Personality disorders in adult patients. *Int. J. Eat. Dis.*, **7**, 589–599.

Rastam, M. (1990). Anorexia nervosa in Swedish urban teenagers. University of Göteborg.

Rastam, M. and Gillberg, C. (1991). The family background in anorexia nervosa: a population-based study. *J. Am. Acad. Child. Adoles. Psychiat.*, **30**, 283–289.

Rǿijen, S. (1993). Are anorexia nervosa families a homogeneous group? A descriptive inter-action study of 18 families. Paper presented at International Conference on Eating Disor-ders, April 1993, London.

Root, M.P.P., Fallon, P. and Friedrich, W.N. (1986). *Bulimia: A Systems Approach to Treat-ment*. New York: W.W. Norton.

Root, M.P.P. and Fallon, P. (1988). The incidence of victimisation experiences in a bulimic sample. *J. Interper. Viol.*, **3**, 161–163.

Russell, D. (1986). *The Secret Trauma: Incest in the Lives of Girls and Women*. New York: Basic Books.

Russell, J.D., Kopec-Schrader, E., Rey, J.M. and Beumont, P.J.V. (1992). The parental bonding instrument in adolescent patients with anorexia nervosa. *Acta. Psychiat. Scand.*, **86**, 236–239.

Schmidt, U., Tiller, J. and Treasure, J. (1993). Setting the scene for eating disorders: child-hood care, classification and course of illness. *Psychol. Med.* (in press).

Selvini-Palazzoli, M. (1974). *Self-Starvation: From the Intrapsychic to the Transpersonal Ap-proach*. London: Chaucer.

Shisslak, C.M., McKeon, R.T. and Cragg, M. (1990). Family dysfunction in normal weight bulimic and bulimic anorexic families. *J. Clin. Psychol.*, **46**, 185–189.

Steiger, H., Van der Feen, J., Goldstein, C. and Leichner, P. (1989). Defense styles and parental bonding in eating disordered women. *Int. J. Eat. Dis.*, **8**, 131–140.

Steiger, H. and Zanko, M. (1990). Sexual traumata among eating-disordered, psychiatric, and normal female groups. *J. Interper. Viol.*, **5**, 74–86.

Steiger, H., Liquornik, K., Chapman, J. and Hussain, N. (1991). Personality and family disturbances in eating-disorder patients: comparison of "restricters" and "bingers" to normal controls. *Int. J. Eat. Dis.*, **10**, 501–512.

Stern, S.L., Dixon, K.N., Jones, D., Lake, M., Nemzer, E. and Sansone, R. (1989). Family environment in anorexia nervosa and bulimia. *Int. J. Eat. Dis.*, **8**, 25–31.

Stern, S., Whitaker, C.A., Hagemann, N.J., Anderson, R.B. and Bargman, G.J. (1981). Anorexia nervosa: the hospitals role in family treatment. *Fam. Proc.*, **20**, 395–408.

Stierlin, H. and Weber, G. (1989a). Anorexia nervosa: lessons from a follow-up study. *Fam. Sys. Med.*, **7**, 225–234.

Stierlin, H. and Weber, G. (1989b). *Unlocking the Family Door: A Systemic Approach to the Understanding of Anorexia Nervosa*. New York: Brunner/Mazel.

Szmukler, G.I. (1993). Family aspects of eating disorders. In: S. Bloch, H. Hafner, S. Harari and G.I. Szmukler (Eds), *The Family in Psychiatric Practice*. Oxford: University Press.

Szmukler, G.I., Eisler, I., Russell, G.F.M. and Dare, C. (1985). Anorexia nervosa, parental "expressed emotion" and dropping out of treatment. *Br. J. Psychiat.*, **147**, 265–271.

Szyrynski, V. (1973). Anorexia nervosa and psychotherapy. *Am. J. Psychother.*, **27**, 492–505.

Theander, S. (1970). Anorexia nervosa: a psychiatric investigation of 94 female patients. *Acta Psychiat. Scand.* (Suppl.), **214**, 1–94.

Tietze, T. (1949). Study of mothers of schizophrenic patients. *Psychiatry*, **12**, 55–65.

van Furth, E.F. (1991). Parental expressed emotion and eating disorders. PhD thesis, Univer-sity of Utrecht.

Waller, G., Calam, R. and Slade, P. (1989). Eating disorders and family interaction. *Br. J. Clin. Psychol.*, **28**, 285–286.

Waller, G., Slade, P. and Calam, R. (1990a). Family adaptability and cohesion: relation to eating attitudes and disorders. *Int. J. Eat. Dis.*, **9**, 225–228.

Waller, G., Slade, P. and Calam, R. (1990b). Who knows best? Family interaction and eating disorders. *Br. J. Psychiat.,* **156**, 546–550.

Welch, S.A. and Fairburn, C.G. (1994). Sexual abuse and bulimia nervosa: three case control comparisons. *Am. J. Psychiat.*, **151**, 402–408.

10

Sociocultural Models of Eating Disorders

G.I. SZMUKLER
Bethlem Royal and Maudsley Hospitals, London, UK
AND
G. PATTON
University of Melbourne, Victoria, Australia

INTRODUCTION

Rarely has a notion of social processes as causes of psychiatric disorder received more attention than in anorexia nervosa. Over a century ago, Fenwick (1880) hinted at the role of social forces when he described anorexia nervosa as principally a disorder of the upper classes. However, only in the last twenty years have hypotheses about the social causation of eating disorders been more fully elaborated. Three decades ago Bliss and Branch (1960) speculated that the American preoccupation with slimness was a common initiating factor in anorexia nervosa. Bruch (1973) later suggested that the emphasis placed by fashion and the media on slimness provided the means for the dissemination of the societal ideals which underlay the eating disorders. Subsequently, sociocultural formulations of the eating disorders have continued to stress the pressures on young women to achieve a sylph-like appearance.

Although western society's preoccupation with female body ideals has attracted most comment, other social influences have been noted. Bruch (1978), for example, argued that societal changes allowing a greater range of opportunities for young women were significant, that for sexual experience being particularly important. Writers from a feminist perspective elaborated this view and suggested that the

Handbook of Eating Disorders: Theory, Treatment and Research.
Edited by G. Szmukler, C. Dare and J. Treasure.
© 1995 John Wiley & Sons Ltd.

complex and contradictory roles that women played in a modern, yet still patriarchal, society led to an insecurity which underlay the "anorexic" drive for perfection and autonomy (Palazzoli, 1974). Similarly, Boskind-Lodahl (1976) argued that susceptibility to eating disorders arose from women's acceptance of a culturally determined passive, accommodating role. She outlined two opposing themes, the need for self-validation from men and an inordinate fear of the power of men, as crucial social influences. As a result of this conflict, she argued, self-worth comes to be equated with a desirable slim appearance, with a resultant vulnerability to eating disorders.

Adoption of ascetic ideals has been viewed as a further predisposing factor in particular sociocultural settings. Bliss and Branch (1960) noted the prominence of ascetic practices in some cases of anorexia nervosa. Drawing parallels with the behaviour of Catherine of Sienna, Rampling (1985) suggested that ascetic ideals, similar to those apparent in religiously motivated self-imposed starvation in young women in the middle ages, may also be implicated in modern cases of anorexia nervosa. Other writers (Yates, 1991) have also observed the prominence of other culturally sanctioned ascetic practices such as obligatory running in subjects with eating disorders.

Several interweaving lines of epidemiological evidence lend support to sociocultural hypotheses of the origins of anorexia nervosa. From around 1960, an increase of cases alerted clinicians in many western countries to the possibility that societal changes might underpin the change (Theander, 1970). Later observations in other settings supported the role of societal pressure to be thin. Very few cases of anorexia presented to clinicians in non-western cultures where female ideals were not linked to thinness (DiNicola, 1990). In contrast, in some high-risk groups such as dancers, fashion models and athletes, thinness in young women was even more required than in society generally (Garner and Garfinkel, 1980). In the last decade, the pronounced change in the morphology of eating disorders manifest in the emergence of bulimia nervosa has brought speculation that societal forces influence not only rates of eating disorders, but also their syndromal form (Russell and Treasure, 1991).

The following sections draw together the lines of epidemiological work underpinning sociocultural hypotheses in the form of a series of key questions:

1. How common are eating disorders in western settings?
2. Have eating disorders become more common?
3. Who gets eating disorders and how?
4. Have eating disorders changed?
5. How "universal" are they?

HOW COMMON ARE EATING DISORDERS IN WESTERN SETTINGS?

Although a focus of much epidemiological work, establishing prevalence rates of eating disorders has not been easy. Notable discrepancies have arisen in reported estimates for both anorexia (Crisp, Palmer and Kalucy, 1976; Szmukler, 1985; Rastam, Gillberg and Garton, 1989) and bulimia nervosa (Halmi, Falk and Schwartz, 1981; Schotte and Stunkard, 1987; Fairburn and Beglin, 1990).

Anorexia nervosa has posed particular problems. It is rare, so that very large populations are needed to achieve reliable prevalence estimates. Relative rarity is compounded by other problems. Outside the clinic setting, the illness course is more transient, and thus point prevalence estimates may not accurately reflect the proportion of a population affected. Even more problematic has been the reluctance of subjects with anorexia nervosa to participate in population surveys, which may have contributed further to the fact that even large surveys have identified few cases (Szmukler, 1985; Johnson-Sabine et al, 1988; Whitaker et al, 1989).

One Swedish study satisfactorily negotiated many of these difficulties (Rastam, Gillberg and Garton, 1989). Growth charts recorded by school nurses were used to screen 15-year-old schoolchildren in Gotenborg for anorexia nervosa. Following a further interview assessment, accumulated prevalence rates for anorexia nervosa were calculated to be 0.7% for girls to the age of 16 years. This is a little lower than earlier rates, but arguably the most accurate estimation in a western population to date.

Incidence rate estimates have varied widely. Highest rates from case registers are 4 to 5 per 100 000 population per year in the early 1980s. A general practitioner continuous registration study in Holland found 6.3 per 100 000 (Hoek, 1991), while Lucas et al (1991), in a study involving all health services (described below), found an incidence of 14.2 per 100 000 per year for the period 1980–84 in Rochester, Minnesota (see Chapter 1).

Surveys of bulimia nervosa face similar problems. Bulimia frequently pursues a fluctuating course so that again point estimates may not adequately reflect its frequency (Bushnell et al, 1990). Self-report questionnaire surveys have tended to produce inflated estimates of the prevalence of "bulimic" symptoms. These deficiencies have been illustrated in surveys with a second, interview stage; prevalence estimates based on self-reports have subsequently shown substantial reduction (Schotte and Stunkard, 1987; Fairburn and Beglin, 1990).

Inconsistencies in case definition of bulimia nervosa pose difficulties in interpretation of earlier prevalence estimates. Bulimic symptoms exist on a spectrum, with individual symptoms being quite common in the general population (Patton, 1988; Whitaker et al, 1989). No clear points of discontinuity in the spectrum have as yet been established, different definitions thus being possible. How this can influence prevalence estimates was well demonstrated in a New Zealand survey where point estimates for bulimia in women 18–44 years ranged from 0% for Russell's definition to 0.5% using DSM-IIIR (Bushnell et al, 1990). Lifetime estimates were 1.6% for the DSM-IIIR definition.

Two-stage surveys—in which a population is initially screened with a self-report questionnaire, and then high-scoring subjects together with a sample of low-scoring subjects are selected for second-stage evaluation—have been usefully applied to the study of bulimia nervosa and more broadly defined eating disorders. The approach has been adopted in a number of settings: adolescent schoolgirls (Szmukler, 1985; Johnson-Sabine et al, 1988; Patton et al, 1990), university students (Button and

Whitehouse, 1981; Schotte and Stunkard, 1987) and general practice (King, 1986). Findings are in broad agreement that 3–5% of young western women suffer with significant symptoms of eating disorder. Defining bulimia nervosa as a syndrome in which both frequent binge eating and purging occur, around 1% of young western women fulfil this clinical definition at any one time, so that bulimia nervosa appears now to be the commonest clinical eating disorder.

Recent reported incidence estimates for bulimia nervosa include 9.9 per 100 000 population per year in general practice settings (Hoek, 1991), and 26.5 per 100 000 from Lucas' Rochester study (see Chapter 1).

HAVE EATING DISORDERS BECOME MORE COMMON?

Anorexia nervosa has often been characterised as a modern disorder. The widespread assumption that it has become more common derives in large part from clinical settings where an increase in referrals for anorexia nervosa was noted more than 30 years ago (Theander, 1970). Psychiatric case register data further substantiated clinician impressions, finding substantial increases in referred cases. In Monroe County, for example, annual incidence increased by 80% between the decades 1960–69 and 1970–78 (Jones et al, 1980). In North-East Scotland a 150% increase in incidence was observed between the periods 1966–69 and 1978–82 (Szmukler, et al, 1986). In Switzerland, a threefold increase in incidence of hospitalised cases of AN was found in the canton of Zurich between 1956–58 and 1973–75, data being gathered retrospectively from case histories on file at all medical, paediatric and psychiatric institutions (Willi and Grossmann, 1983). The size of these increases was taken by some as an indication of a modern "epidemic" of anorexia nervosa.

However, this consensus has not gone unchallenged as a "medical myth" (Williams and King, 1987). The deficiencies of psychiatric case register data for drawing conclusions about changing incidence are apparent. Case identification by psychiatric case registers is incomplete, with changing referral rates and patterns potentially accounting for observed changes. Willi et al (1989), for example, demonstrated a shift to primary psychiatric referral and away from paediatric, medical and gynaecological services between 1956 and 1973. Such changes would be reflected as an increase in new cases on a purely psychiatric register and might thus be misinterpreted as evidence of rising incidence. The register approach is also handicapped in case definition. This was demonstrated in North-East Scotland where only 23% of patients and a register diagnosis were found to fulfil standard criteria for anorexia nervosa given the information available in the case notes (Szmukler et al, 1986).

Williams and King (1987) used data from the Mental Health Inpatient Inquiry for England and Wales between 1972 and 1981 to suggest that two factors— demographic change and a rise in readmission rates—could have produced the apparent rise in incidence. A rise observed in first admissions paralleled a rise in the proportion of young women in the general population. In contrast, rates for readmission rose considerably more, which might explain clinical impressions of increasing prevalence. Some subsequent studies, based on local and national registers of admissions, have drawn similar conclusions about the stable incidence of anorexia nervosa in the past decade or two (Willi et al, 1990; Nielsen, 1990; Jorgensen, 1992). Over the same period, readmission rates have increased substantially (Nielsen, 1990). On the other hand, a study by Moller-Madsen and Nystrup (1992), using the Danish national register, has shown a significant increase in first admissions with anorexia nervosa between 1970 and 1989, not explained by changes in demography.

Satisfactory data concerning the changing incidence of anorexia nervosa derives for the most part from studies of the last two decades. One exception has been a retrospective study of 50 years of case records from Rochester, Minnesota (Lucas et al, 1991). In a painstaking study, all cases presenting to hospital services with a broad range of diagnoses with clinical similarities to anorexia nervosa were examined. This study did not reveal any overall significant trends in incidence rates for anorexia nervosa between 1935 and 1979. This study is particularly significant since, unlike other studies of incidence, it covers the period before 1960 when incidence rates were thought to be low, and it encompasses the whole range of medical services in which patients with anorexia nervosa, recognised or not, might be seen. Although a rise in newly presenting cases for girls (15–19 years in the 5-year period (1980–84) was later found, more than most studies it probably has undermined the concept of anorexia nervosa as being a modern disorder.

We remain uncertain about whether there has been a real increase in the incidence of anorexia nervosa in western societies. The methodological obstacles to be overcome are formidable, as shown in Lucas' Rochester Study. Even then, the relatively small number of cases detected in a year makes reliable conclusions about change difficult. This is the strongest study, and its results are the best we have. Changes in incidence of anorexia nervosa over the past 50 years have often been subject to exaggerated claims. An increase over the past 30 years for young females in their late teens seems likely.

Although anorexia nervosa's status as a modern disorder remains to be resolved, there is little doubt about bulimia nervosa. From its initial description as an uncommon sequela of anorexia nervosa, bulimia nervosa came a few years later to be recognised as the commonest clinical presentation. Retrospective data from earlier birth cohorts clearly suggest that bulimia was rare before the 1970s (Kendler et al, 1991).

WHO GETS EATING DISORDERS AND HOW?

Eating disorders are overwhelmingly disorders of young women. General population studies have confirmed gender ratios observed in clinical settings. Rastam's study of adolescents in Gotenborg indicated a gender ratio of 9.1:1 for anorexia nervosa. Clinical and register-based studies suggest that these disorders reach a peak age of onset in mid to late adolescence (Szmukler et al, 1986).

Although the relationship with age and gender is clear-cut, few other demographic associations have emerged consistently to point to the aetiology of eating disorders. Contrary to longstanding clinical impressions, little evidence has emerged outside patient groups seen in specialist units in support of an association with higher social class. One psychiatric case register reported a significant relationship but was based on a small number of patients with anorexia nervosa (Kendell, 1973). In a much larger study, there was no clear relationship (Szmukler et al, 1986).

The influence of the thin aesthetic ideal has been the focus of considerable research. Garner et al (1980), for example, demonstrated a 20-year trend to thinner ideals for young women. More recently, dieting, which is the tangible manifestation of this ideal, has attracted study. Survey data over three decades indicate that point prevalence rates for dieting in this group range from 30% to 40%, with period prevalences being considerably higher (Huenemann et al, 1966; Nylander, 1971; Johnson-Sabine et al, 1988).

On the basis of retrospective reports, clinicians have long suspected that adolescent dieting puts an individual at risk of developing an eating disorder (Bliss and Branch, 1960; Bruch, 1978). A recent prospective study of a representative group of mid-adolescent schoolgirls has indeed supported this link in finding that dieters had an eight-fold increase in the incidence of broadly defined eating disorder 12 months on (Patton et al 1991). It was also clear that for most dieters the outcome in the short-term was unproblematic, with the largest group ceasing dieting, a result consistent with findings of earlier studies (Huenemann et al, 1966; Schleimer, 1984).

That dieting precedes the development of disorder lends support to a putative causal role. However, the association may result from shared antecedents, or dieting may represent a common "prodromal" state preceding the development of disorder without being causally related. Even so, dieters remain a particularly high-risk group. In a teenage cohort, using the measure of "aetiological fraction", Patton (1990) suggested that over 60% of cases of eating disorder, broadly defined, potentially arose from recent dieting. As diets are often short-lived in adolescent girls, some antecedent diets will not have been measured in this study. Thus the actual contribution of dieting may have been even higher.

As yet it is not clear what factors cause some dieters to progress to eating problems. The links between obesity, obsessionality, social stress, and dissatisfaction with bodyweight, on the one hand, with dieting, rather than eating disorders, on the other, suggest that many individual and psychosocial risk factors have a non-specific role in the development of disorder. But by predisposing to dieting these factors may increase an individual's risk of disorder.

One clue perhaps lies in the greater psychiatric symptomatology found in dieters who progress to disordered eating (Patton, 1990). Similar findings were reported in Rastam and Gillberg's (1992) case control study, where depression and recent severe life events were among the commonest identifiable antecedents of anorexia nervosa. Given the links between depression and current life stress it is possible that affective disturbances might determine the transition from dieting to disorder. In this situation an individual may adopt increasingly pathological weight control strategies in an attempt to maintain a threatened self-concept. A popular alternative explanation is that individuals vary in their cognitive and physiological responses to dietary restraint and the extent or peculiar nature of these responses may determine the development of disorder (Goodwin, Fairburn and Cowan, 1987; Tuschl, 1990; Blundell, 1990).

The links between dieting and eating disorder are clearly consistent with a sociocultural framework of causation which stresses the role of a slim female ideal. Other sociocultural models (e.g. ascetic and feminist) have attracted less study. Obsessionality and perfectionism are constructs which overlap with the rigorous self-discipline and austerity of the ascetic. These characteristics have also sometimes been linked to anorexia nervosa (Dally, 1969). Using a case-control methodology, Rastam and Gillberg (1992) reported that obsessional traits were particularly common antecedents of anorexia nervosa. Though usually interpreted as a personality characteristic there is still a possibility that these traits result from the adoption of ascetic behaviours.

High-risk groups potentially provide insights into the environmental causes of eating disorder. Dancers have attracted particular attention, but athletes, models and racing jockeys have also been studied. Prevalence rates for eating disorders in dancers have been up to 32% with rates for anorexia nervosa ranging from 7% to 11% (Hamilton, Brooks-Gunn and Warren, 1985; Szmukler et al, 1985). The usual conclusion has been that the particular emphasis on slimness causes the high rates of eating disorder. Garner and Garfinkel (1980) reported that higher rates of anorexia nervosa and preoccupation with weight occurred in the more competitive dance settings and speculated that competition pressure was a further modulating factor. However, no direct measure of competition pressure was made and it is unclear whether the finding issues from a specific additional contribution or whether the pressure to achieve and maintain a slim figure were more intense in this group.

HAVE EATING DISORDERS CHANGED?

The major interest here has been in anorexia nervosa. The answer to the question "has it changed" depends on how we define "it". If "it" refers to a state of self-starvation, apparently deliberately pursued by the sufferer, then it appears that it has changed. Such states have a long history as described by, for example, Bell (1985) and Brumberg (1988). In the late medieval period, self-starvation occurred in the service of a heightened spirituality, sexual purity, asceticism, or religious goals. In the seventeenth and eighteenth centuries these goals were less prominent, but the phenomenon of "fasting girls" persisted. Religious or miraculous ideas were still invoked to account for these cases, but the sufferers appear to have been less articulate about their personal motivations. The attention aroused in others, including a commercial interest in some cases, was notable. With the descriptions of Gull and Lasegue, the reasons given by the sufferer for her failure to eat are rarely mentioned. They seem usually to have been expressed in physical terms, food for some reason making the young woman uncomfortable or distressed. Charcot in 1885 described a patient who wore a rose-coloured ribbon around her waist to help her judge whether she was getting fatter, and who stated that this was to be avoided because she would "prefer dying of hunger to becoming big as mamma". Habermas (1989; 1992) has drawn our attention to other nineteenth century case reports alluding to fears of becoming fat, most of them French and by authors related to the

Salpetriere where Charcot was influential. However, Janet in 1903 remained quite unconvinced by this observation and attributed his cases of self-starvation to an *idée fixe* related to "pudicity", or body shame. Self-starvation as a defence against sexuality was a prominent theme in the early twentieth century, vying with its conception as an enodcrine disease. It was not until the 1960s that a fear of fatness, now a major *identifying* characteristic of anorexia nervosa, became the dominant motive given by patients for their failure to eat.

We agree with Brumberg that these conditions are best viewed as related within an important historical continuity. Like anorexia nervosa today, they predominantly affected young females, and they were positively valued by the sufferer (and sometimes by those around her) who denied the need to change and deliberately sought to maintain her state. Thus the same biological state appears to have assumed different meanings during different epochs. These meanings are grounded in contemporary cultural values (for example, religious at one time, secular at another), and are usually concerned with contemporary notions of femaleness, at least in certain sectors of the population (for example, asceticism and the primacy of the spiritual over the carnal at one time, slimness at another). As we shall argue later, the *incidence* of the disorder is also significantly determined by cultural factors.

As noted above, the emergence of bulimia nervosa appears more clearly a relatively recent phenomenon (Russell and Treasure, 1989; Habermas, 1989; 1992; Russell in Chapter 1 of this volume). Its relationship to anorexia nervosa has been stressed by Russell and Treasure (1989) on the basis that both share a morbid dread of weight gain, and that patients may move from one condition to the other. We shall return to this relationship later.

HOW "UNIVERSAL" ARE THEY?

In this section we address two related questions: does anorexia nervosa occur in all societies, and is it similar in form in all of them? At the outset we note that the evidence bearing on these issues is meagre. This has been reviewed by DiNicola (1990). The major findings to date are as follows.

Eating Disorders in Ethnic Groups in Western Countries

Convincing cases of anorexia nervosa and bulimia nervosa have been reported in black populations in both the USA and the UK, in Asian populations in those countries, in an Arab group in the UK, and in recently arrived South-East Asian refugees in the USA. However, there are no convincing data suggesting that eating disorders are more or less common in these groups than in the indigenous western populations. Population studies using questionnaire reports of abnormal eating attitudes (e.g. Pumariega, Edwards and Mitchell, 1984) are not satisfactory. Cases can only be adequately ascertained on the basis of an interview. Usually, it is not clear in these studies that questionnaires are being interpreted in similar ways across the comparison groups.

Three studies have used a two-stage design, first screening by questionnaire for subjects who might have an eating disorder, and second, interviewing possible cases. Fichter et al (1988) compared samples of Greek girls aged 13–19 years in the Greek towns of Veria (2700) and Ioannina (569) with Greek girls in Munich, Germany (867). Using a broad definition of anorexia nervosa, the percentages of girls with this diagnosis were 0.42%, 0.35% and 1.10% respectively. Interestingly, although anorexia nervosa occurred more often in the Munich sample, this population scored lower than the Greek samples on many questionnaire items related to anorexic attitudes and behaviours. Nasser (1986) compared 50 Arab female undergraduate students in London with 60 in Cairo. All were from "upper and middle class" backgrounds. The scores on the Eating Attitudes Test (EAT) were high, and 6 cases of bulimia nervosa were found in London, none in Cairo. There were no cases of anorexia nervosa. The third study (Mumford and Whitehouse, 1988; Mumford, Whitehouse and Platt, 1991) in Bradford, England, compared 204 schoolgirls aged 14–16 of Asian origin with an indigenous group of 355. One case of anorexia nervosa was found in the Asian group, none in the other. The figures for bulimia nervosa were 3.4% versus 0.6%.

The conclusion drawn by the first two groups of investigators was that eating disorders become more common in subjects who have moved from a country in which eating disorders are uncommon to one in which they are more common. The stress of acculturation may contribute to this, as may the adoption of the host society's "idioms" for the expression of distress. Mumford and colleagues used a similar explanation for their finding, adding that eating disorders may be even more common in the acculturating group than in the established population. These findings are not convincing. The samples studied have been too small to instill real confidence in differences between populations when the disorders are so uncommon. The much higher "positive predictive values" of the screening instruments in each study in the immigrant groups than in the comparison groups are surprising and may indicate that interpretations of questions by respondents are not equivalent to those in the comparison groups. In the Nasser and Bradford studies, the excess was of bulimia nervosa, not anorexia nervosa. We wonder how the cases identified compare with bulimia nervosa in western societies, and whether there might be significant differences in behaviours, their meanings, and cultural responses to them which cast doubt on their status. Unfortunately, no descriptions are offered of the cases found, a major omission.

DiNicola's conclusion that eating disorders can be regarded as a "Culture Change Syndrome" (CCS) emerging under conditions of rapid economic and sociocultural change is far from proven. Besides the inconclusiveness of the best studies to date, as described above, DiNicola is vague about the meaning of CCS. He seems to imply that any culture change will increase the risk of anorexia nervosa or bulimia nervosa. But surely the change must be to a culture in which thinness is valued; it seems unlikely that an American moving to Botswana would be at increased risk. A demonstration of a relationship between acculturation stresses, assessed independently, and the development of an eating disorder is also necessary before such a hypothesis can be accepted.

Eating Disorders in Non-Western Countries

Most of the data here are anecdotal, yet consistent. The impression of psychiatrists and other health workers in non-western non-industrialised countries is that anorexia nervosa and bulimia nervosa are rare, and when they are found, occur in westernised segments of the population. These reports have come, for example, from India, Africa, Malaysia, China and New Guinea (see DiNicola, 1990, for further details).

Some recent reports warrant close examination. Lee, Chiu and Chen (1989) stated that fewer than 10 cases of anorexia nervosa had been treated in a psychiatric unit of a general hospital serving a population of 500 000 over 5 years. Also cited is an unpublished epidemiological survey using standardised instruments of 3786 female subjects aged 18–64 in Shatin where only one possible case of anorexia nervosa was found, and she had a concomitant major depression. Lee (1991) later described Chinese patients with anorexia nervosa treated in psychiatric units in Hong Kong between 1985 and 1990. These patients engaged in strict dieting, but noteworthy was the absence of a fear of fatness, or only a mild expression of it, in 13 of the 16 patients. They typically admitted to their emaciation and gave a desired weight very close to their premorbid weight. The patients' most consistent complaint was of abdominal discomfort after eating a small amount of food. As Lee points out, thinness is undesirable in Chinese cultures, probably explaining why these patients fail to give a fear of fatness as a reason for their self-starvation. One is struck by the similarity between these cases and those described by Gull and Lasegue in the nineteenth century; the patients' explanation for their state is given in terms of physical discomfort associated with eating. Yet there were signs that the "weight loss appeared ego-syntonic, and a varying amount of resistance to weight gain was almost always present", features which we see as according well with the positive evaluation of the state of self-starvation evident in our brief historical review of such conditions.

Mumford and colleagues, following their study in Bradford, went on the examine population samples of schoolgirls in Lahore and Mirpur, Pakistan, the regions from which the families of their Asian girls in England originated (Mumford, Whitehouse and Choudry, 1992; Choudry and Mumford, 1992). In both surveys they used the same methods of case detection as in Bradford, but paid special attention to ensuring that the questionnaires were linguistically and conceptually equivalent. Factor analyses of the EAT showed similarities with the results found in Bradford for the middle-class English-speaking Lahore group. This was not the case for the Urdu-speaking rural girls in Mirpur despite careful translation procedures. Some items were not valid across the two cultures. Nevertheless, following interviews with possible cases, the prevalence of DSM-IIIR bulimia nervosa was 0.4% (of 369 girls) in Lahore and 0.4% (of 271 girls) in Mirpur. No cases of anorexia nervosa were detected. There were, however, more atypical cases of eating disorder and dieters in Lahore than in Mirpur (1.4% versus 0%, and 11% versus 2%, respectively).

Reservations concerning the Bradford study, particularly those of small sample sizes and the absence of case descriptions, also apply here.

At this point we need to comment further on the comparability of cases with eating disorders across cultures. There are two points. The first concerns *the scope to be adopted in defining a "case"*, and the second, the need for a *description of cases together with their context*. It is entirely reasonable to look for DSM-IIIR cases of eating disorders across cultures. However, it is far from enough. Cross-cultural comparisons of other disorders, such as depression, indicate that nosological categories developed in one culture do not necessarily fit in others (Littlewood, 1989). Some features may be reported in one culture but not another, or they may be given a different expression missed by questionnaires or interviews designed elsewhere. We suggest, based on the history of self-starvation states, that at this stage cross-cultural studies should adopt a broader definition of caseness, one which includes for further consideration, *subjects who became emaciated through restricting their dietary intake for whatever reason, this restriction is deliberate, and the resulting state is positively valued by the subject.* The motivation for the self-starvation may have no connection with the pursuit of thinness, yet it may be informative for our understanding of anorexia nervosa.

The second point is related to the first. When such cases are detected, a detailed description is necessary of the context in which the behaviour occurs. This includes reasons given by the subject and others (family, friends, society) for the behaviour, other associated beliefs and behaviours, what others believe should be done about it and why, and ways in which the self-starvation state reflects significant cultural values. In other words, account must be taken of the *meanings* of the behaviour. Given this information, a determination of the extent to which such conditions are similar to eating disorders as we know them in the west can proceed on a sounder footing than hitherto. We have seen how Lee's description of cases of anorexia nervosa in Hong Kong has been helpful in discerning such commonalities and differences.

When self-starvation is explained in physical terms, mental health services are unlikely to see cases so other "agencies" must be studied. It remains possible that in many cultures there are persons who display some of the features of anorexia nervosa as we know it, but who are not regarded by their fellows as being "sick". Those who fast for what may be regarded as ascetic reasons are an example. A report of instances of "holy anorexia" in the Alto Minho region of Portugal today is an example (Bynum, 1988). Such people will not be detected by health services at all. As we have noted earlier, meanings given to similar states may vary greatly from one society to another, yet continuities can be traced. Whether some of these cases might be termed "anorexia nervosa" or not may well depend on where we set the boundaries; definitions may prove less important than the insights to be gained into some underlying processes—cultural, psychological, and biological.

CONCLUSIONS

Sociocultural studies, in providing data on both the rates and the spectrum of eating disorder, have significantly deepened our understanding. We now have some data on the incidence and prevalence of anorexia nervosa and bulimia nervosa in western societies, but equally important is the recognition that anorexia nervosa and bulimia nervosa as seen in the specialist clinic are not representative of eating disorders in the community. This has challenged and broadened our concepts. Although not conclusive, the evidence suggests that there has been an increase in anorexia nervosa and bulimia nervosa over recent decades, at least in younger females, consistent with the operation of social forces. Some major non-specific risk factors have also been defined, dieting looming especially large. Cross-cultural studies (which in a sense include the historical) pose many methodological difficulties which have not yet been adequately met. Even so, substantial progress has occurred. Again, recent studies have challenged our conventional notions of the eating disorders, their institutionalised classifications, and what lies at their "core". Anorexia nervosa as defined in the west is probably rare in developing countries, but seems to become more common as western ideals of slimness are adopted. However, self-starvation states may occur in other contexts with other meanings in other societies, and their study promises to tell us much about eating disorders in our own. We have made some suggestions concerning further studies.

We now offer what seems the most parsimonious explanation for the eating disorders in accordance with the epidemiological data. The evidence reviewed is consistent with the basic idea that dietary restriction, from whatever motivation (losing weight, asceticism, aversion to certain food types), is the major cause of anorexia nervosa (or self-perpetuating self-starvation states). In those populations where dieting is more common, anorexia nervosa is more common. Not everyone who diets develops the disorder, but the number increases as more people diet. Clearly, a small number of subjects have a special vulnerability to developing anorexia nervosa. Young females are particularly at risk. This may be because they diet more often than males, perhaps because food and the body have always been near the heart of cultural notions of femaleness (see also Chapters 7 and 12). On the other hand, the female preponderance may be due to biological factors. Cultural influences may determine the *frequency* of the disorder, through the extent to which dieting is encouraged, and influence its *expression*, through the meanings it is given. Its *persistence* in an individual may also be culturally influenced since it may be valued by the subject or others, and thus reinforced, to varying degrees in different societies.

What constitutes the special *vulnerability* to anorexia nervosa? Two kinds of models receive support. In the first, self-starvation and weight loss assume a special psychological significance and compulsion through solving an underlying psychological problem. This is discussed in detail in Chapters 7 and 12 in this volume. In the second, dieting triggers a set of abnormal physiological responses which assume a "life of their own" leading to continued self-starvation. A model of "starvation dependence" proposed by one of the authors (Szmukler and Tantam, 1984) straddles both, and was initially prompted by a resemblance, epidemiologically, to alcohol dependence. In both cases a behaviour (drinking, dieting), normally practised in moderation in the general population, assumes an overwhelming salience in an occasional subject, and despite the obvious harmful effects and the subject's loss of control over the behaviour, a problem with it is denied. This self-affecting behaviour alters the subject's psychological and physical state and is initially perceived as pleasant. When dependence is established, the behaviour becomes stereo-typed, and is accompanied by a compulsion to continue. The development of toler-ance requires increasing "doses" of starvation, and withdrawal symptoms (marked distress when eating) follow attempts to stop. The behaviour is maintained in part by the need to prevent such symptoms from emerging. Also striking is the rapid reinstatement of self-starvation following "withdrawal" by refeeding, the subject attempting just a "little bit" of dieting, but rapidly relapsing into the old pattern of self-starvation. The meaning of this behaviour arises from the sociocultural context in which it occurs.

We have seen that cross-cultural studies have found "bulimia nervosa-like" syn-dromes in a variety of cultures. A range of conditions could be subsumed under this comparatively non-specific rubric, some perhaps having little in common with bulimia nervosa as we understand it in the west. We have noted the common view that bulimia nervosa is related to anorexia nervosa through the dread of fatness evident in both conditions. However, taking a broader view of anorexia nervosa, one where the fear of fatness may not always be apparent, this argument loses force. Comparing psychopathologies also presents a problem on logical grounds. Because bulimia nervosa patients are not emaciated like those with anorexia ner-vosa, their attitudes to their weight cannot be tested in the same way—they do not have to account for emaciation, nor are they in a position to deny its severity. Bulimic episodes in our clinical practice seem to arise when desperate attempts at self-starvation aimed at weight loss are unsuccessful. Possibly, such episodes may occur in quite different contexts in other cultures; for example, Nasser (1986) notes that binge eating may be unremarkable in some circumstances in Arab cultures. If this is so, and a "morbid fear of fatness" is culturally shaped, then the scope of cognitive–behavioural models of eating disorders which centre on this (for both anorexia nervosa and bulimia nervosa) will prove restricted.

Whether or not our conclusions are supported by further work, it should be apparent how the study of eating disorders from an epidemiological–cultural perspective has changed our understanding. This approach provides us with one of our most fertile sources of explanatory hypotheses. Furthermore, we seem to have moved from a circumscribed view of sociocultural influences to a broader one, from a study of rates of disorders, narrowly defined, to one where common assumptions and definitions lying at their very heart have been challenged. Indeed, placed as they are almost at one pole of sociocultural "malleability", the eating disorders are important in illuminating fundamental issues in the cross-cultural study of other psychiatric disorders.

REFERENCES

Bell, R. (1985). *Holy Anorexia*. Chicago: University Press.
Bliss, E.L. and Branch, C.H. (1960). *Anorexia Nervosa: Its History, Psychology and Biology*. New York: Hoeber.
Boskind-Lodahl, M. (1976). Cinderella's stepsisters: a feminist perspective on anorexia ner-vosa and bulimia. *Journal of Women in Culture and Society*, **2**, 342–356.
Bruch, H. (1973). *Eating Disorders*. New York: Basic Books.

Bruch, H. (1978). *The Golden Cage: The Enigma of Anorexia Nervosa*. England: Open Books.

Brumberg, J.J. (1988). *Fasting Girls*. Harvard: University Press.

Bushnell, J.A., Wells, J.E., Hornblow, A.R., Oakley-Browne, M.A. and Joyce, P. (1990). Prevalence of three bulimia syndromes in the general population. *Psychological Medicine,* **20**, 671–680.

Button, E.J. and Whitehouse, A. (1981). Subclinical anorexia nervosa. *Psychological Medicine,* **11**, 509–516.

Bynum, C.W. (1988). Holy anorexia nervosa in modern Portugal. *Cult. Med. Psychiatry,* **12**, 239–248.

Choudry, I.Y., Mumford, D.B. (1992). A pilot study of eating disorders in Mirpur (Pakistan) using an Urdu version of the Eating Attitudes Test. *International Journal of Eating Disorders*, **11**, 243–251.

Crisp, A.H., Palmer, R.L. and Kalucy, R.L. (1976). How common is anorexia nervosa? A prevalence study. *British Journal of Psychiatry,* **128**, 549–554.

Dally, P. and Gomez, J. (1969). *Anorexia nervosa*. London: Heinemann.

DiNicola, V.F. (1990). Anorexia multiforme: self-starvation in historical and cultural context. II: Anorexia nervosa as a culture-reactive syndrome. *Transcultural Psychiatric Research Review*, **27**, 245–286.

Fairburn, C.G. and Beglin, S.J. (1990). Studies of the epidemiology of bulimia nervosa. *American Journal of Psychiatry,* **147**, 401–408.

Fenwick, S. (1880). *On the Atrophy of the Stomach and on the Nervous Affections of the Digestive Organs*. London: Churchill.

Fichter, M., Elton, M., Sourdi, L., Weyerer, S., et al (1988). Anorexia nervosa in Greek and Turkish adolescents. *European Archives of Psychiatry and Neurological Sciences*, **237**, 200–208.

Garner, D.M., Garfinkel, P.E., Schwartz, D. and Thompson, M. (1980). Cultural expectations of thinness in women. *Psychological Reports,* **47**, 483–491.

Garner, D.M. and Garfinkel, P.E. (1980). Socio-cultural factors in the development of anorexia nervosa. *Psychological Medicine,* **10**, 647–656.

Goodwin, G.M., Fairburn, C.G. and Cowen, P.J. (1987). Dieting changes serotonergic function in women, not men: implications for the aetiology of anorexia nervosa? *Psychological Medicine,* **17**, 839–842.

Habermas, T. (1989). The psychiatric history of anorexia nervosa and bulimia nervosa. *International Journal of Eating disorders,* **8**, 259–273.

Habermas, T. (1992). Further evidence on early case descriptions of anorexia nervosa and bulimia nervosa. *International Journal of Eating Disorders,* **11**, 351–359.

Halmi, K.A., Falk, J.R., Schwartz, (1981). Binge eating and vomiting: a survey of a college population. *Psychological Medicine,* **11**, 697–706.

Hoek, H.W. (1991). The incidence and prevalence of anorexia nervosa and bulimia nervosa in primary care. *Psychological Medicine,* **21**, 455–460.

Huenemann, R.L., Shapiro, L.R., Hampton, M.C. and Mitchell, B.W. (1966). A longitudinal study of gross body conformation and the association with food and activity in a teenage population. *American Journal of Clinical Nutrition,* **18**, 325–338.

Janet, P. (1929). *The Major Symptoms of Hysteria*. New York: Macmillan.

Jørgensen, J. (1992). The epidemiology of eating disorders in Fyn County, Denmark, 1977–86. *Acta Psychiatrica Scandinavica,* **85**, 30–34.

Johnson-Sabine, E., Wood, K., Patton, G., Mann, A. and Wakeling, A. (1988). Abnormal eating attitudes in London schoolgirls. *Psychological Medicine,* **18**, 615–622.

Jones, D.J., Fox, M.M., Babigian, H.M. and Hutton, H.E. (1980). Epidemiology of anorexia nervosa in Monroe County, New York: 1960–76. *Psychosomatic Medicine,* **42**, 551–558.

Hamilton, L.H., Brooks-Gunn, J. and Warren, M.P. (1985). Sociocultural influences on eating disorders in professional female ballet dancers. *International Journal of Eating Disorders,* **4**, 465–477.

Kendell, R.E., Hall, D.J., Hailey, A. and Babig, H.M. (1973). The epidemiology of anorexia nervosa. *Psychological Medicine*, **3**, 200–203.

Kendler, K.S., Maclean, C., Neale, M.C., Kessler, R.C., Heath, A.C. and Eaves, L. (1991). The genetic epidemiology of bulimia nervosa. *American Journal of Psychiatry*, **148**, 1627–1637.

King, M.B. (1986). Eating disorders in general practice. *British Medical Journal*, **293**, 1412–1414.

Lee, S. (1991). Anorexia nervosa in Hong Kong: a Chinese perspective. *Psychological Medicine*, **21**, 703–712.

Lee, S., Chiu, H.F. and Chen, C. (1989). Anorexia nervosa in Hong Kong: why not more Chinese? *British Journal of Psychiatry*, **154**, 683–688.

Littlewood, R. (1990). From categories to contexts: a decade of the "New cross-cultural psychiatry". *British Journal of Psychiatry*, **156**, 308–327.

Lucas, A.R., Beard, C., O'Fallon, W. and Kurland, L.T. (1991). 50-year trends in the incidence of anorexia nervosa in Rochester, Minn: a population-based study. *American Journal of Psychiatry*, **148**, 917–922.

Moller-Madsen, S., Nystrup, J. (1992). Incidence of anorexia nervosa in Denmark. *Acta Psychiatrica Scandinavica*, **86**, 197–200.

Mumford, D.B. and Whitehouse, A.M. (1988). Increased prevalence of bulimia nervosa among Asian schoolgirls. *British Medical Journal*, **297**, 718–719.

Mumford, D.B., Whitehouse, A.M. and Platts, M. (1991). Sociocultural correlates of eating disorders among Asian schoolgirls in Bradford. *British Journal of Psychiatry*, **158**, 222–228.

Mumford, D.B., Whitehouse, A.M., Choudry, I.Y. (1992). Survey of eating disorders in English-medium schools in Lahore, Pakistan. *International Journal of Eating Disorders*, **11**, 173–184.

Nasser, M. (1986). Comparative study of the prevalence of abnormal eating attitudes among Arab female students of both London and Cairo universities. *Psychological Medicine*, **16**, 621–625.

Nielsen, S. (1990). The epidemiology of anorexia nervosa in Denmark from 1973 to 1987: a nationwide register study of psychiatric admission. *Acta Psychiatrica Scandinavica*, **81**, 507–514.

Nylander, I. (1971). The feeling of being fat and dieting in a school population. An epidemiologic interview investigation. *Acta Socio-Medica Scandinavica*, **3**, 17–26.

Palazzoli, M. (1974). *Self-Starvation: From Individual to Family Therapy in the Treatment of Anorexia Nervosa*. London: Chaucer.

Patton, G.C. (1988). The spectrum of eating disorder in adolescence. *Journal of Psychosomatic Research*, **32**, 579–584.

Patton, G.C., Johnson-Sabine, E., Wood, K., Mann, A.H. and Wakeling, A. (1990). Abnormal eating attitudes in London schoolgirls—a prospective epidemiological study: Outcome at twelve month follow-up. *Psychological Medicine*, **20**, 383–394.

Pumariega, A.J., Edwards, P. and Mitchell, C.B. (1984). Anorexia nervosa in black adolescents. *Journal of the American Academy of Child Psychiatry*, **23**, 111–114.

Rampling, D. (1985). Ascetic ideals and anorexia nervosa. *Journal of Psychiatric Research*, **19**, 89–94.

Rastam, M., Gillberg, C. and Garton, M. (1989). Anorexia nervosa in a Swedish urban region: a population-based study. *British Journal of Psychiatry*, **155**, 642–646.

Rastam, M. and Gillberg, G. (1992). Background factors in anorexia nervosa. *European Child and Adolescent Psychiatry*, **1**, 54–65.

Russell, G.F. and Treasure, J. (1989). The modern history of anorexia nervosa: an interpretation of why the illness has changed. *Annals of New York Academy of Sciences*, **575**, 13–27.

Schleimer, C. (1984). Dieting in teenage girls. *Acta Paediatrica Scandinavica Supplement*, **312**.

Schotte, D.E. and Stunkard, A.J. (1987). Bulimia *vs* bulimic behaviors on a college campus. *Journal of the American Medical Association*, **258**, 1213–1215.

Szmukler, G.I. (1985). The epidemiology of anorexia nervosa and bulimia. *Journal of Psychiatric Research,* **19**, 143–153.

Szmukler, G.I. and Tantam, D. (1984). Anorexia nervosa: starvation dependence. *British Journal of the Medical Psychology,* **57**, 303–310.

Szmukler, G., McCance, C., McCrone, L. and Hunter, D. (1986). Anorexia nervosa: a psychiatric case register study from Aberdeen. *Psychological Medicine,* **16**, 49–58.

Szmukler, G.I., Eisler, I., Gillies, C., Hayward, M. (1985). The implications of anorexia nervosa in a ballet school. *Journal of Psychiatric Research,* **19**, 177–181.

Theander, S. (1970). Anorexia nervosa: a psychiatric investigation of 94 female patients. *Acta Psychiatrica Scandinavica,* **214** (supplementum), 1–194.

Tuschl, R.J. (1990). From dietary restraint to binge eating: some theoretical considerations. *Appetite,* **14**, 105–109.

Whitaker, W.A., Davies, M., Shaffer, D., Johnson, J., Abrams, S., Walsh, B.T. and Kalikow, K. (1989). The struggle to be thin: a survey of anorexic and bulimic symptoms in a non-referred adolescent population. *Psychological Medicine,* **19**, 143–163.

Willi, J. and Grossmann, S. (1983). Epidemiology of anorexia nervosa in a defined region of Switzerland. *American Journal of Psychiatry,* **140**, 564–567.

Willi, J., Giacometti, G. and Limacher, B. (1990). Update on the epidemiology of anorexia nervosa in a defined region of Switzerland. *American Journal of Psychiatry,* **147**, 1514–1517.

Willi, J., Limacher, B., Grossmann, S. and Giacometti, G. (1989). Langzeitstudie zur Inzidenz der Anorexia nervosa (Longitudinal study on the incidence of anorexia nervosa). *Nervenarzt,* **60**, 349–354.

Williams, P. and King, M. (1987). The "epidemic" of anorexia nervosa: another medical myth? *Lancet,* **1**, 205–207.

Yates, A. (1991). *Compulsive Running and the Eating Disorders: Towards an Integrated Theory of Activity.* New York: Brunner/Maze.

Part III

Consequences and Maintaining Factors

Introduction to Part III

In this section contributors were asked to consider the consequences of suffering from an eating disorder. Also examined are maintaining factors arising from the illness, either within the individual or in relationship to family, friends, or society at large.

In considering biological consequences of eating disorders, Treasure and Szmukler focus on a number of areas which are currently the subject of major concern—disruptions of growth and development, osteoporosis, effects on fertility and pregnancy, and central nervous system abnormalities. The full delineation of these complications requires long-term studies, some of which are now beginning to emerge. Questions remain concerning the completeness of their reversibility, even with later weight recovery. A variety of mechanisms are identified in which biological consequences of the disorder can be linked to key features of the psychopathology, serving to perpetuate it. Significant implications for treatment are noted.

Professor Beumont and his Sydney colleagues, by largely disregarding the suggestions of the editors as proclaimed in their introduction, manifest an Australian flair for anti-authoritarianism, boldness, and originality. Psychological aspects of eating disorders are considered from some unusual perspectives. In attempting to answer the question "Why is there such a gender discrepancy in the eating disorders?", a powerful "feminist" perspective is presented portraying the contrived and impossible demands in which women are trapped, and the consequences. A study of media influences on patients is consistent with the argument and suggests a possible role in maintaining the condition. The authors also examine the disquieting possibility that the "labelling" and characteristation of disturbed behaviours associated with weight concerns as "illness" may have acted iatrogenically, accounting to an unknown extent for their increased incidence.

Colahan and Senior present a rich tapestry in which the eating disorders may be woven. A "fit" is described between the sufferer's experience, described in terms of "object relations" theory, and the organisation of the family such as to sustain the disorder. The patient's symptoms, the structure of her inner world, her relationships to food, and the family's response are seen as influencing each other in mutual, recursive patterns. While the major conflict is acted out between mother and patient, others, including siblings, are induced to play the "roles of bit players in the patient's inner world", often cast to fulfil the "soothing role of the transitional objects of childhood". The inner psychic conflicts of these others and particular patterns of family interaction may suit them to accept the identifications in question. The patient and family thus become "stuck" in sets of relationships, conceived at several, interconnected levels. Implications for treatment are derived.

Schmidt, Tiller and Morgan discuss the social consequences for subjects suffering from an eating disorder. Noting that research in this area has reached dramatically different conclusions, especially for bulimia nervosa, they aim to clarify the issues and to identify the mechanisms associated with variable outcomes. Social functioning in a number of spheres is examined—family, sexual, child-rearing, friends, and forensic. The effects of starvation, of bulimic symptoms (for example, their frequency), premorbid personality features, concurrent psychopathology, poor social support, and the responses to the condition by others may all make significant contributions to the eventual level of adjustment achieved by the patient. The relationship in bulimia nervosa between symptom severity and social adjustment may not be a close one. Quality of life studies in anorexia nervosa and bulimia nervosa show a broad range of impairments. A caution is entered that some difficult behaviours may adversely influence the judgement of health professionals to the patient's further detriment.

11

Medical Complications of Chronic Anorexia Nervosa

JANET TREASURE
AND
GEORGE SZMUKLER
Institute of Psychiatry, London, UK

INTRODUCTION

The physical consequences of the eating disorders loom large in the clinical presentation and seriously threaten the health of the patient. In this review we shall not provide a comprehensive account of all complications; we list most in tables together with references for the interested reader. We shall focus on those which have been the subject of recent interest and which are of clinical significance: disruptions of growth and development, osteoporosis, effects on fertility and pregnancy, central nervous system abnormalities, and detrimental effects of weight cycling. We also examine the reversibility of physical changes in anorexia nervosa following full weight recovery. Finally, we explore possible mechanisms whereby the physical consequences of the eating disorders may serve to perpetuate the disorder itself.

By physical consequences or complications, we mean changes which are observable at the clinical level or by employing standard investigations. Information which is pertinent to the routine management of patients is our prime concern. "Complications", as used here, does not imply irreversibility.

Handbook of Eating Disorders: Theory, Treatment and Research.
Edited by G. Szmukler, C. Dare and J. Treasure.
© 1995 John Wiley & Sons Ltd.

The Size of the Problem

The mortality rate for anorexia nervosa is approximately 0.5–1% per year of observation (Herzog et al, 1992). The standardised mortality rate of anorexia nervosa is six times that of the control population. The mortality rate is higher amongst those who have the most severe degree of weight loss (15-fold greater if weight <35 kg) (Patton, 1988) but the trend is for it to be lower in those who are given specialised treatment (Crisp et al, 1992). Suicide has been the commonest cause of death reported in all series. The standardised mortality rate for all cases of anorexia nervosa (both outpatients and inpatients) is similar to that found for other psychiatric conditions, schizophrenia, affective disorder and personality disorder 5 years after a period of inpatient treatment (Zilber, Schufman and Lerner, 1989), but is not as high as for psychiatric conditions complicated by alcohol abuse and substance abuse.

Mortality represents the severe end of the level of morbidity. The majority of the physical complications are weight-related and so predominate in the half whose illness runs a chronic course. Some consequences may be irreversible, such as those on the skeleton, teeth and reproductive function. This physical ill-health contributes to the impaired quality of life reported in both anorexia nervosa and bulimia nervosa (Figure 11.1) and functional disability (Figure 11.2) (Keilen et al, 1994). Anorexia nervosa therefore poses a large burden of ill-health upon the community as it is the third commonest chronic condition in adolescence (Lucas et al, 1991).

A Summary of the Problem

Many of the medical consequences of eating disorders are described in case reports and it can be difficult to obtain an overall perspective of the problem. Large-scale follow-up studies provide an invaluable overview. An example of such work is that undertaken by Herzog and his team (Herzog et al, 1992). The medical morbidity of

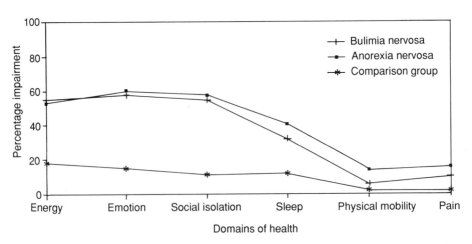

FIGURE 11.1   Assessments of ill-health in eating disordered patients at the Maudsley Hospital.

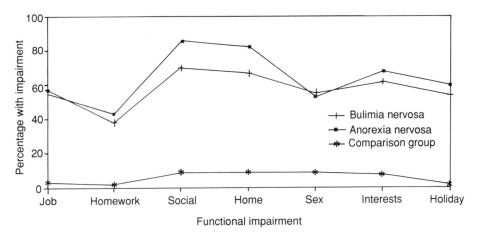

FIGURE 11.2 Assessments of functional impairments in eating disordered patients at the Maudsley Hospital.

a series of 103 patients over 12 years was described in detail. Fifteen per cent died. The causes of death fell within four areas: suicide, infection, gastrointestinal complications and severe emaciation. Thirty-five per cent of the survivors had an associated medical disorder. Osteoporosis with multiple fractures and terminal renal deficiency accounted for the most severe disability. Infections were common. A smaller-scale follow-up study of 50 young adolescent girls found gastrointestinal complications; two perforated a duodenal ulcer and several were left with irritable bowel syndrome (Kreipe, Churchill and Strauss, 1989).

THE SKELETON AND TEETH

The Skeleton

Puberty and adolescence are a critical time for skeletal development when 15% of adult height and 58% of skeletal mass are attained (Benson et al, 1985; Bonjour et al, 1990). Weight and hormonal levels are critical for bone development (Dhuper et al, 1990). Malnutrition leads to poor bone growth (Himes, 1978) and reduced bone turnover (Branca et al, 1992), and delayed puberty is associated with decreased bone density (Finkelstein et al, 1992). It is uncertain whether bone proliferation can occur once the critical early phase of pubertal development has passed (Stanhope, 1992). In men with idiopathic hypogonadism, even 1–3 years of hormonal replacement failed to restore bone mass to the normal range and low-turnover osteoporosis persisted (Finkelstein et al, 1992). Thus anorexia nervosa which occurs early in puberty might be expected to lead to stunting and irreversible osteoporosis, whereas the osteoporosis of later onset anorexia nervosa may have the potential for recovery or prevention.

Stunting of growth in cases of anorexia nervosa with primary amenorrhoea has been reported (Russell, 1985). Only 2 of a series of 20 such patients were above the 50th percentile for height and 7 were below the 2nd percentile. Bone density is reduced in anorexia nervosa (Rigotti et al, 1984; Szmukler et al, 1985; Treasure et al, 1987; Rigotti et al, 1991; Kiriike et al, 1992; Seeman et al, 1992) particularly in cases with a long duration and profound weight loss (Hay et al, 1992; Davies et al, 1990). This osteopenia is of clinical significance and leads to the development of pathological fractures. The annual incidence of non-spine fracture of 0.05 per person-year, found in anorexia nervosa, is seven-fold higher than the rate reported for a community sample of women aged 15–34 (Rigotti et al, 1991).

It is uncertain whether failure of peak bone development or bone loss accounts for the osteoporosis as it is difficult to separate the relevant factors, particularly in small studies. For example, although Seeman et al (1992) found the lowest bone densities in the subgroup with primary amenorrhoea, this group also had a lower body mass index and longer duration of illness. This question is of therapeutic relevance given the findings of irreversible osteopenia in men with delayed puberty discussed above.

Evidence from cross-sectional studies supports the idea that bone density is recoverable as the subgroup who have gained weight have bone densities within the normal range (Treasure et al, 1987; Bachrach et al, 1991; Hay et al, 1989; Herzog et al, 1992). However, these studies cannot rule out the possibility that the recovered group had clinical features which independently predicted a higher bone mass (such as a milder or briefer illness).

An additional question which has not been satisfactorily answered is whether oestrogens, such as those in the contraceptive pill, are prophylactic. The results so far are in conflict—Seeman et al (1992) found that bone density was higher in those on the pill whereas Hay et al (1989) and Davies et al (1990) did not. Anecdotal accounts do not suggest that oestrogen (Rigotti et al, 1991; Kreipe et al, 1992) or calcium (Salisbury and Mitchell, 1991) can restore bone density. Clearly there is a need for a prospective study to investigate the value of oestrogen.

Weight gain alone may be sufficient to restore bone density. In a pilot project we found that acute (2–3 month) nutritional rehabilitation led to a 2% increase in vertebral bone density and total body density in 13 out of 16 patients. Other prospective studies have found that patients who have gained weight increase their bone density (Bachrach et al, 1991; Rigotti et al, 1991).

Dental Consequences

The stages of dental destruction seen in patients with eating disorders are shown in Table 11.1. The most common stigma of persistent vomiting is erosion of dental enamel which occurs in the majority of patients who have vomited three times a week for a minimum of 4 years (Simmons et al, 1986). Enamel is lost from the lingual and palatal surfaces of the anterior teeth. Eventually dentine is exposed and the teeth become sensitive and vulnerable to caries. Finally vertical height is lost. The erosion is probably exacerbated if the teeth are brushed after vomiting. Bicarbonate or fluoride rinses are good prophylactic measures. Dietary acids such as those in fruit and carbonated drinks also contribute to the tooth destruction.

Vomiting and nutritional changes in mouth pH lead to a change in mouth flora. This may be useful as an objective measure of symptoms (Bretz et al, 1993).

TABLE 11.1   Stages of dental damage in eating disorder patients.

Tooth surface becomes smooth and dull
Yellowing as dentine becomes exposed
Blunting of cusps of molars and premolars
Amalgam fillings protrude
Loss of vertical height
Pulp necrosis
Abscesses form

REPRODUCTIVE FUNCTION

Eating disorders have marked effects on reproductive function. Many of these are merely the consequences of starvation, but some (for example, the effect on mothering) are more specific for the eating disorder itself. Even short-term diets in normal women can have a marked effect on the amplitude and frequency of LH release and upon follicular development and luteal function (Schweiger et al, 1987; Pirke et al, 1989; see also Chapter 5). Therefore much of the menstrual dysfunction in eating disorders can be explained by dieting alone.

Fertility is also compromised by low weight (Bates et al, 1982) with ovulation failure resulting from follicular phase defects, and luteal phase defects. Low progesterone levels arising from luteal deficits are associated with repeated abortions (Horta et al, 1977). Once conception has occurred, poor maternal nutrition adversely effects fetal outcome. Low maternal weight at conception and inadequate weight gain during pregnancy result in poor fetal growth (Abrams and Laros, 1986; Van der Spuy, 1988; Doyle et al, 1991). In these cross-sectional studies there may be additional confounding effects. However, in a small prospective study, birthweight fell in normal-weight mothers who were advised to lose weight (Greive, Campbell-Brown and Johnston, 1979). Low birthweight is associated with neonatal and childhood morbidity such as cerebral palsy (Torfs et al, 1990). These findings suggest that reproductive function in anorexia nervosa will be severely compromised.

Anorexia Nervosa and Menstrual Function

The amenorrhoea of anorexia nervosa is a consequence of impaired gonadal hormone secretion caused by hypothalamic dysfunction. The hypothalamic–pituitary axis in these patients resembles that of a prepubertal girl with diminished pulsatile release of LH (Boyar et al, 1974; Pirke et al, 1989), reduced pituitary gland output to gonadotrophin releasing hormone stimulation (Beumont et al, 1976), loss of positive feedback to oestrogen (Wakeling et al, 1977) and multifollicular changes in the ovaries (Treasure et al, 1985; Treasure, 1988). (For further details see Chapter 5).

The spectrum of menstrual irregularities in bulimia nervosa parallels the varying degrees of under-nutrition seen in this population. The abnormalities span from amenorrhoea in 30–50%, absent follicular development in 20%, and luteal phase dysfunction with impaired inadequate progesterone secretion in a further group.

Reductions in the amplitude of LH and FSH secretion underpin these changes in ovarian function (Pirke et al, 1988).

In addition to these nutritional changes, polycystic ovarian syndrome has been found to be associated with abnormal eating attitudes. This questionnaire survey did not detail the clinical presentation. Although obesity is a feature of polycystic ovarian syndrome, these women did not have a higher body mass index than the comparison group (McCluskey et al, 1991). It is possible, therefore, that the abnormal eating attitudes represent no more than these women's successful dieting strategies.

Fertility and Eating Behaviour

Women attending infertility clinics may have hidden eating disorders. Of 69 women attending an infertility clinic (Stewart et al, 1990), 11 cases (16%) of eating disorder emerged. A questionnaire screening method was used, but there were three false negatives; two were having treatment for an eating disorder and one was said to have an eating disorder by her family. Many of these women harboured fears that their eating disorders had caused the infertility but had been unable to discuss this with their doctors. This guilt and secretiveness may explain why one of the three women who refused to participate in the initial screening procedure later admitted to having bulimia nervosa. It suggests that the presence of eating disorders may be underestimated in obstetric and gynaecological practice.

Although it is unusual for pregnancy to occur in anorexia nervosa, there have been reports from specialist centres of patients with the chronic illness who have gained sufficient weight to become pregnant or who have received treatment to induce fertility. Pregnant women with eating disorders are torn between two fears: loss of control over their own weight and concern that poor nutrition might harm the baby. Problems which could be ascribed to nutritional deficiency do arise and pregnancies in this group should be categorised as "high risk". However, women with eating disorders are reluctant to disclose their problem to their obstetrician and use half-truths (for example, ascribing their symptoms to hyperemesis gravidarum) to indicate their concern (Lembert and Phillips, 1989).

Women with eating problems have been entered into GnRH treatment programmes for infertility but this practice has been questioned. Of a series of 14 described by Abraham and colleagues (1990), 12 became pregnant and 4 babies were small-for-dates; one baby died in the neonatal period.

One of the largest studies of the reproductive effects of anorexia nervosa reports from a series of 140 patients of whom 50 had had children at the time of follow-up 10–12 years later (Brinch et al, 1988). Ten per cent of the total sample had infertility problems. Twenty per cent became pregnant whilst still anorexic. The rate of prematurity was twice the expected rate and perinatal mortality was increased sixfold. Out of a total of 86 children born, 79 were alive at the time of follow-up. Seven deaths occurred within the first week (5 because of prematurity, one stillbirth and one hydrocephalus). Fourteen per cent as compared with 6.8% of the normal population had babies weighing less than 2500 g.

TABLE 11.2   The outcome of pregnancy in patients with eating disorders.

	AN in remission (7 mothers; 13 children)	Active RAN (4 mothers; 7 children)	ANBN (3 mothers; 3 children)
Weight gain in pregnancy (kg)	12.7	7.2	2.6
Birthweight (kg)	3.6	2.7	2.4
Apgar score	8.8	7.5	4.0
Infant health		Intrauterine death Spontaneous abortion	Respiratory distress Jaundice Poor weight gain/ prematurity
Maternal post partum health	2 relapsed	Continuation or worsening of symptoms	

The foregoing study is of interest because of its large size, but it did not analyse the outcomes according to the mothers' clinical state at conception. Table 11.2 displays the findings from a retrospective review of 15 mothers (23 pregnancies) from a cohort of 74 women with eating disorders (Stewart et al, 1987). It is clear from this study that mothers who have active symptoms at the time of conception have difficulty gaining weight during pregnancy and have smaller babies with additional problems.

In a prospective study of 7 pregnancies in 5 women with active anorexia nervosa at the time of conception, we found that, despite intensive supervision, weight gain during pregnancy was poor (8 kg, compared with 11 kg, the recommended weight gain) (Russell and Treasure, 1988). Intrauterine growth during the third trimester was impaired in 5 of the women who were monitored, and the abdominal circumference of all 7 babies was below the third centile. All of the babies were small at birth but there was evidence of catch-up growth in infancy.

Children's Health

Risks are not limited to the perinatal period. In the Danish study referred to above (Brinch et al, 1988), one premature child was visually handicapped. Seventeen per cent had poor growth in the first year of life. One child developed anorexia nervosa herself at the age of 13 and died of it aged 15. One boy was overweight with emotional and social problems and a 5-year-old had tritichollomania.

There have been additional reports of poor nutrition and stunting of growth in the children of mothers with anorexia nervosa (O'Donoghue et al, 1991). Van Wezel-Meijer and Wit (1989) reported on seven children from three families. It is salutary to note that two of these pregnancies were artificially induced. One alarming case report described a child of a mother with anorexia nervosa which died as a result of starvation and neglect (Smith and Hanson, 1972).

Pregnancy in Bulimia Nervosa

It is much more common for women with bulimia nervosa either to have children or to become pregnant during the course of their illness. A miscarriage rate twice as high as that in the control population was found in a case controlled survey of 20 actively bulimic women (Willis and Rand, 1988), but weight gain, duration of gestation and birthweight were normal. Lacey and Smith (1987) suggested that birth complications were more common in bulimia nervosa. Out of a series of 20 mothers, one baby had a cleft palate, another a cleft lip, and one, whose mother abused alcohol and soft drugs, was born prematurely and died shortly after birth. A larger series is needed to see whether this complication rate is more generally found.

The mothers controlled their eating disorder symptoms during pregnancy as they feared damage to the unborn child, but many relapsed post partum. The continuing disorder can lead to additional problems. Stein and Fairburn (1989) interviewed 5 mothers who all acknowledged that their disturbed eating habits interfered with their role as mothers as it led to inattention, irritability, poor care and variable levels of control. All had difficulties breast feeding and 3 of the 6 children had feeding difficulties. Three of the mothers had unwarranted concerns about the weight and shape of the children. Fahy and Treasure (1989) also reported on 5 bulimic mothers who had feeding and parenting difficulties.

THE CARDIOVASCULAR SYSTEM

Sudden deaths account for a proportion of the mortality in anorexia nervosa and cardiac events have been implicated. Prolongation of the QT interval may account for these acute dysrhythmias (Isner et al, 1985; Schocken et al, 1989; Cooke et al, 1993). Similar prolongation of the QT interval has been found in healthy volunteers (Simonson et al, 1948) undergoing experimental starvation or following surgery for morbid obesity. The prolonged QT interval in anorexia nervosa shortens with refeeding and is not merely a consequence of an electrolyte abnormality (low calcium or magnesium).

Although reports have suggested that mitral valve prolapse is found more commonly in patients with anorexia nervosa than in the normal population (Johnson et al, 1986) we have been unable to confirm this finding.

CENTRAL NERVOUS SYSTEM CHANGES

Brain structural changes have been consistently found in anorexia nervosa, and more recently in bulimia nervosa. Computerised tomographic (CT) brain scan studies have usually demonstrated widening of sulcal spaces and cerebroventricular enlargement in anorexia nervosa (Enzman and Lane, 1977; Datloff et al, 1986; Kreig et al, 1988; Dolan et al, 1988; Palazidou et al, 1990) and "normal weight" bulimia (Kreig et al, 1989). Magnetic resonance imaging (MRI) studies have confirmed these findings and further have shown reductions in pituitary size as well as of midbrain area (Doraiswamy et al, 1990; Husain et al, 1992).

Structural changes are at least to some degree reversible with weight gain, although they may persist even after weight restoration for as long as one year (Kreig et al, 1988; Dolan et al, 1988). The finding of enlarged spaces in bulimia nervosa suggests that weight loss is not the only influence. However, "normal weight" bulimia patients may still be substantially below their premorbid weight, and may have highly abnormal eating patterns. It has not been established whether structural abnormalities are simply the consequence of the eating disorder or whether some might have pre-existed, being indeed associated with a vulnerability to its development.

Consistent relationships between brain structural changes and clinical features such as age of onset of the disorder or its duration have not emerged so far. However, Kreig et al (1988) and one of the authors in a recently completed, yet unpublished, study involving 46 patients with anorexia nervosa found a significant inverse relationship between ventricular enlargement and body mass index. Kreig et al (1986) also found ventricular enlargement to be inversely associated with lowered triiodothyronine levels.

A few functional imaging studies have been performed on small numbers of patients with AN and BN. Patients with AN may have increased metabolism in the cortex and caudate nucleus (Herholz et al, 1987; Kreig et al, 1991), while bulimic patients may have abnormalities in the balance between left and right hemisphere activity (Wu et al, 1990).

Neuropsychological functions have also been studied in AN. An early study was consistent with attentional deficits which improved with weight gain (Hamsher et al, 1981). These deficits were also predictive of a poorer weight outcome one year later. Early studies were uncontrolled, but three recently have been. Unfortunately the use of different tests, different samples of patients, and methodological problems limit the conclusions that can be drawn. Deficits in attention, particularly in the focusing/execution aspect, are the most convincing (Jones et al, 1991; Szmukler et al, 1992). Memory and visuospatial analysis are probably also impaired (Jones et al, 1991; Szmukler et al, 1992). New learning may be less affected, but some individuals stand out with poor performance. Each of these findings has been replicated in a larger current controlled study by one of the authors. The magnitude of the deficits is small compared with that seen in brain-damaged subjects. However, they may still be large enough to significantly affect judgement and problem-solving in daily life, or the ability to use psychotherapy in treatment. Weight restoration results in an improvement of neuropsychological functioning. This is most rapid and complete for attention, less so for impairments in memory, visuospatial functions, and learning (Szmukler et al, 1992).

Few attempts have been made to relate structural CNS changes to neuropsychological deficits (Laessle et al, 1988; Palazidou et al, 1990). Correlations have not been evident, but patient numbers have been small and statistical power weak. The current study of Szmukler and colleagues involving 46 patients with AN has found only weak relationships between ventricular enlargement and some cognitive deficits.

The question of whether self-starvation in adolescence and early adulthood has irreversibly damaging effects on the developing brain remains open. We know that structural brain development normally continues into the early 20s. To date, no study has succeeded in following up and retesting a group of patients to full and stable weight recovery.

THE HEALTH CONSEQUENCES OF WEIGHT CYCLING

Several large-scale studies have found that weight cycling is associated with an increased mortality (Pamuk et al, 1992; Lee and Paffenbarger, 1992; Lissner et al, 1991). The relevance of these large epidemiological surveys to health in eating disorders is uncertain. Weight cycling is a common consequence of eating disorders (Garner and Wooley, 1991) and may produce adverse metabolic consequences (Dulloo and Girardier, 1990; Lissner et al, 1991) with a rebound in lipids and insulin levels (Ernsberger and Haskew, 1987).

GENERAL MANAGEMENT ISSUES

It is impossible to review all of the medical consequences of eating disorders in one chapter. We have therefore prepared a table which details many of the abnormalities (see the Appendix to this chapter). The complications that arise during refeeding are highlighted in italics and are discussed in further detail in Chapter 5. Further information can be obtained from other sources (e.g. Bhanji and Mattingly, 1988; Kaplan and Garfinkel, 1993; Sharpe and Freeman, 1993).

RECOMMENDED INVESTIGATIONS

It is difficult to know how detailed any investigation into the medical implications of anorexia needs to be. About any test will be abnormal but probably of no relevance in clinical management. The most appropriate management of the majority of the complications is refeeding. In Table 11.3 we list the investigations which have been included in recent reviews. These lists may have medical rather than clinical implications.

PHYSICAL COMPLICATIONS AS PERPETUATING FACTORS

In thinking about causal factors, it is useful to divide these temporally into those which predispose to the disorder, those which precipitate it, and those which maintain an already present illness. Physical complications may play a role in the third phase of causation.

TABLE 11.3   Recommended investigations.

Initial assessment
1. Full blood count
2. Urea and electrolytes, including magnesium, calcium and phosphate
3. Liver function test and protein
4. Electrocardiogram
5. Bone density (duration > 1 year)

During refeeding
1. Full blood count
2. Urea and electrolytes, including phosphate
3. Creating clearance (rarely)
4. Amylase (rarely)
5. Abdominal or chest X-ray (rarely)

In severe chronic anorexia nervosa
1. Full blood count (3/12)
2. Urea and electrolytes (3/12)
3. Liver function (3/12)
4. Glucose (3/12)
5. Thyroid function (6/12)
6. Creatinine clearance (annual)
7. Bone density (annual)
8. Body composition (annual)

Weight Loss. Other contributions to this volume have discussed evidence that weight loss may precipitate anorexia nervosa in vulnerable subjects. Whatever the mechanisms involved, it thus seems likely that preservation of the state of emaciation, the most obvious physical complication of AN, will abet its continuation. This may explain why the other symptoms, including psychological ones, usually improve strikingly with refeeding, and why treatment in the absence of weight gain as a cause of the illness, as well as a consequence of it, makes the dissection of its contribution difficult; however, the good response to weight gain argues for a significant causal, or at least maintaining, role.

The burden of disease or debility. The physical complications of anorexia nervosa (for example, weakness associated with emaciation or metabolic disturbances) may heighten the patient's sense of vulnerability or personal inadequacy, especially so when illness is denied. Impairments may be construed as further evidence of "personal weakness' requiring intensified efforts at achieving self-control, and for the patient with AN this usually means more rigorous dieting. Thus, a self-defeating viscious cycle is reinforced.

Emaciation-induced emotional disturbances. Physical processes associated with emaciation may lead to emotional disturbances directly, in contrast with the non-specific burden of debility described above. For example, central nervous or endo crine system changes may lead to a depressed mood, a common feature in AN. Again, the patient may attempt to deal with these "unacceptable" aspects of herself by escalating her "anorexic" behaviours.

Direct CNS and cognitive effects of starvation. CNS complications and neuropsychological impairments have already been described. Direct effects of self-starvation, or an associated depressed mood, on concentration, attention, memory, learning, problem-solving, and possibly perception have been noted. These may contribute to poor judgement about the effects of the illness, the need for treatment, and ways of solving life's problems in general. Finding solutions which do not involve being anorexic may be hampered; options become restricted. In this way, persistence of the disorder is favoured. Furthermore, the ability to use psychological treatments requiring, as they do, new learning and flexibility in thinking may be curtailed, reducing further the chances of recovery.

Of interest is the finding that recovery in some cognitive domains following weight gain may be slow, lagging behind the physical improvements and possibly predisposing to relapse.

Discomfort associated with eating a meal. Surprisingly little studied have been the effects of eating a meal. All patients with AN describe the meal as a highly distressing experience. Abnormal temperature changes, sometimes associated with sweating, have been documented (Luck and Wakeling, 1980), and these may contribute to the unpleasantness of eating. Separation of these experiences from the somatic accompaniments of anxiety about weight gain is difficult, but the pattern of autonomic response described in the study above is not typical of anxiety.

The other group of physical phenomena which may result in distress when the AN patient is pressed to eat more than a small amount relate to the induction of premature satiety. The common complaint of "bloating" or rapid fullness may be due in part to the delay in gastric emptying (see Chapter 6). Humoral agents may play a role, possibly involving an enhanced secretion in the starved state of "gut" hormones such as CCK or pancreatic polypeptide. It seems odd that an emaciated person should be physiologically handicapped in eating more. If this does occur in AN, perhaps these mechanisms are aberrantly induced by dietary restriction in subjects vulnerable to the disorder. If so, this would represent a vulnerability factor only revealed by dieting and some degree of weight loss.

Endocrine abnormalities. Reduction in secretion of sex hormones results in physical and psychological changes which may be welcomed. Regression of secondary sexual characteristics together with the infantilising effect on the fiture resulting from emaciation may provide relief from sexual demands. The associated loss of libido and of sexual thoughts may be a further relief, while the cessation of menstrual periods means that even this fundamental reminder of womanhood disappears. The rewarding nature of these abnormalities is evident for an adolescent or young woman ill-prepared to face the challenges of sexual maturity.

Complications Associated with Refeeding and Weight Gain

Dread of fatness may be exacerbated by unfortunate complications of refeeding. Fluid retention occurs particularly in the first few weeks and may be associated with oedema. The sensation of bloating and swelling which may occur can act to vindicate the patient's fantasies about what an increase in food consumption will do to her. The pattern of fat distribution during weight gain may cause further disquiet. A tendency to central adiposity, perhaps related to hormonal factors, may become the focus of many of the patient's thoughts about the "disastrous" effects of food on her body.

Good evidence now exists that, following weight restoration, patients with AN require greater than normal calories to maintain their recently achieved weight. Increased energy requirements may persist for some months. The risk of relapse may be increased as the patient's guilt about eating "too much" is exacerbated by her need to eat even more than others.

Co-existing Diseases

A number of diseases result in weight loss, and these may facilitate the symptoms of AN. Possibly, a wasting disease such as diabetes mellitus, inflammatory bowel disease, or thyrotoxicosis, may precipitate anorexia nervosa. Certianly, such diseases may perpetuate the disorder and presage a poorer outcome. Non-compliance with recommended treatment for the wasting disorder (for example, insulin, steroids) may be an important pointer to a synergism between the two conditions.

There is often a morbid interaction between eating disorders and additional medical illness (see Table 11.4). Peripheral neuropathy and retinopathy occur frequently in young diabetics with eating disorders (Steele et al, 1987). The management of Crohn's disease associated with an eating disorder may be difficult (Meadows and Treasure, 1989).

CLINICAL IMPLICATIONS

The patient's knowledge that she has a serious and severe physical complication may have a significant effect on her motivation to struggle for recovery. In our

TABLE 11.4 Some morbid interactions in eating disorders.

Diabetes mellitus	Prevalence possibly increased (Fairburn, 1992) Management difficult (Szmukler, 1984) Side-effects increased (Steele et al, 1989)
Crohn's disease	Treatment difficult (Meadows and Treasure, 1989)
Thyroid disease	Prevalence possibly increased (Tiller et al, 1994) Management difficulties (Kuboki et al, 1987; Krahn et al, 1990; Fonseca et al, 1990; Schmidt and O'Donoghue, 1992)

experience, the effects of such information appear unpredictable. Some patients, rattled by the knowledge, make intensified efforts to get well, while others see the future now as even more hopeless. Care must be exercised in the manner and timing of the presentation of such bad news.

Physical complications must be taken into account in the management of patients with eating disorders. They require attention not only in their own right, but also because they may contribute to underlying processes perpetuating the disorder. Discussions with patients need to be informative and educational, and to point out ways in which the physical consequences may be misconstrued by her as behavioural weaknesses. The ways in which these physical impairments interfere with the process of recovery can be highlighted, and attempts to function normally without attending to them can be likened to swimming with one arm tied behind one's back. Reversal of the emaciation is the key to reversal of most complications, freeing the patient to resume the struggle to get on with her life. Serious complications should be broached sensitively, without hope being destroyed. Sometimes their presence may act as a spur to renewed motivation to recover, but fine clinical judgement may be necessary to inject it in the right way, at the right time.

APPENDIX: PHYSICAL ABNORMALITIES ASSOCIATED WITH EATING DISORDERS

Fluid and electrolyte abnormalities

Dehydration	When severe can lead to circulatory failure (low blood pressure, increased heart rate) and pre-renal failure Secondary aldosterone (increased urea, urate and creatinine)
Rebound peripheral oedema	Rebound dehydration of laxatives, diuretics and vomiting Mechanism refeeding oedema unknown Dramatic increase in weight 5–20 kg (Mitchell et al, 1988)
Low sodium	5% (Mitchell et al, 1983) If acute leads to lethargy and weakness; < 120 mM/l, coma, seizures and death
Low potassium	14% skeletal and smooth muscle weakness/tetany Decreased gastrointestinal motility Cardiac conduction defects Renal tubular dysfunction
Low chloride	24%, reciprocal with increase in bicarbonate
Metabolic alkalosis	27% due to loss of stomach acid and $NaHCO_3$ reabsorption in kidney
Metabolic acidosis	8% due to laxatives and loss of alkaline bowel fluid (Mitchell et al, 1987)
Low magnesium	Diminished concentration, confusion Muscle weakness and cramps Cardiac arrhythmias (Hall et al, 1988)

Low phosphate	Refeeding complication, risk increased with intravenous feeding (Weinsier et al, 1981) Cellular hypoxia, muscle weakness, cardiac arrhythmias, CNS symptoms

Gastrointestinal complications

Taste	Reduced perception in bulimia nervosa (Rodin et al, 1990)
Paratid enlargement	"Nutritional mumps" (Batsakis and McWhirter, 1972; Hasler, 1982) in 25% of BN (Riad et al, 1991) Salivary amylase increased (Mitchell et al, 1983; Kaplan, 1987)
Oesophageal trauma/ dysfunction	Oesophagitis, tears, bleeding Reflex regurgitation (Palla and Litt, 1988)
Delayed gastric emptying	Bloating, postprandial discomfort (Robinson et al, 1988) Resolves with nutrition (Szmukler, et al, 1990)
Peptic ulcers	16% of anorexia nervosa (Hall et al, 1989)
Gastric dilatation	Acute nausea and vomiting with abdominal pain and dilatation Necrosis and perforation can occur (Abdu et al, 1987; Saul et al, 1981)
Superior mesenteric artery syndrome	Symptoms of upper gastrointestinal obstruction (Sours and Vorhaus, 1981)
Malabsorption	Steatorrheoa, protein losing enteropathy (Mitchell and Boutacoff, 1986)
Ileus	50%: duodenal dilation (Scobie, 1972) Jejunal dilation (Cuellar and Van Thiel, 1986) Cause of mortality (Herzog et al, 1992)
Constipation	Damage to mysenteric plexus with laxatives (Oster et al, 1980)
Pancreatitis	Caused by binge-eating (Gavish et al, 1987) or refeeding (Gryboski et al, 1980)
Liver	Nutritional hepatitis, 30% (Hall et al, 1989)

Cardiovascular complications

Low heart rate	< 40 beats per minute can occur (Palla and Litt, 1988)
ECG	QRS amplitude decreases ST and T wave changes Prolonged/sudden death (Isner et al, 1985) Cardiac arrhythmias particularly if hypokalaemic and hypomagnesaemia "U" wave (Schocken et al, 1989)
Cardiomyopathy	Ipecac (Palmer and Guay, 1986)
Mitral valve prolapse	Positive association (Meyers et al, 1986; Johnson et al, 1986)
Hypotension	Warren and Van de Weile (1973)
Heart failure	Refeeding (Hall and Beresford, 1989; Schocken et al, 1989)

Metabolic rate decreased

Glucose	Low glucose Impaired glucose tolerance in anorexia nervosa (Casper et al, 1977) In bulimia nervosa, decreased insulin secretion and clearance (Goldbloom et al, 1989)
Cholesterol	Increased in 50% (Mira et al, 1987; Crisp, 1985; Mattingly and Bhanji, 1982
Fat	Beta-hydroxybutyric acid increased (Pirke et al, 1985)
Protein	Deficiency is rare, but associated with poor prognosis
Carotene	Increased in 72% (Gupta et al, 1987; Curran-Celentano et al, 1985; Schwabe et al, 1981)
Zinc	Little evidence of deficiency Symptoms include fatigue, mood disturbance, sexual dysfunction (Casper et al, 1980; Katz et al, 1987)
Temperature	Impaired temperature regulation (Mecklenburg et al, 1974)
Sleep	Less deep, more disrupted (Lacey et al, 1975)

Skeletomuscular complications

Proximal myopathy	Alloway et al (1985)
Skin and bone collagen loss	Savvas et al (1989)
Skin	Downy hair—thin/dry Vitamin deficiency rare Purpura (platelet deficiency/scurvy)

Renal function

Pre-renal failure (dehydration)	Boag et al (1985)
Impaired concentration	Dyscontrol of ADH secretion (Gold et al, 1983)
Hypokalaemic nephropathy	Mesangial hyalinisation and sclerosis and interstitial renal fibrosis develop when these electolyte disturbances are prolonged (Riemenschneider and Bohle, 1988)
Renal stones	Dehydration and possible high oxalate (Silber and Kass, 1984; Brotman et al, 1986)

Endocrine function

Hypothalamic–pituitary–gonad axis	LH FSH decreased Loss of positive feedback to oestradiol LHRH test reduced Multifollicular ovaries
Hypothalamic–pituitary–thyroid axis	rT3 increased, T4 and T3 decreased (Schwabe et al, 1981) TSH normal TRH test normal/delayed
Hypothalamic–pituitary–adrenal axis	Cortisol increased (Gold et al, 1986) Non-suppression of dexamethasone Blunt response to CRH (Gwirstman et al, 1989)

Growth hormone	Increased Challenge increased or normal (Kaplan et al, 1989)
Prolactin	Normal (Pirke et al, 1987; Casper, 1977)
Vasopressin	Impaired release (Gold et al, 1983)
Haematological problems	
Anaemia	30% (Rieger et al, 1978)
Leukopenia	30% (Bowers and Eckert, 1978)
Thrombocytopenia	Shur et al (1988)
Leukaemia	Increased (Nishizono-Maher at al, 1993; but Howard, 1993, disagrees)

REFERENCES

Abdu, R.A., Garritano, D. and Culver, O. (1987). Acute gastric necrosis in anorexia nervosa and bulimia. *Arch. Surg.,* **122**, 830–832.

Abraham, S., Mira, M. and Llewellyn-Jones, D. (1990). Should ovulation be induced in women recovering from an eating disorder or who are compulsive exercisers? *Fertil. Steril.,* **53**, 566–568.

Abrams, and Laros (1986). Prepregnancy weight, weight gain and birth weight. *Am. J. Obstet. Gynecol.,* **154**, 503–509.

Alloway, R., Reynolds, E.H., Spargo, E. and Russell, G.F.M. (1985). Neuropathy and myopathy in two patients with anorexia and bulimia nervosa. *J. Neurol. Neurosurg. Psychiat.,* **48**, 1015–1020.

Bachrach, L.K., Katzman, D.K., Litt, I.F., Guido, D. and Marcus, R. (1991). Recovery from osteopenia in adolescent girls with anorexia nervosa. *J. Clin. Endocrin. Metab.,* **72**, 602–606.

Bates, G.W., Bates, S.R. and Whitworth, N.S. (1982). Reproductive failure in women who practice weight control. *Fertil. Steril.,* **37**, 373–378.

Batsakis, J.G. and McWhirter, J.D. (1982). Non-neoplastic diseases of salivary glands. *Am. J. Gastroenter.,* **57**, 226–247.

Benson, J., Gillien, D.M., Boudet, K. and Looslie, A.R. (1985). Inadequate nutrition and chronic calorie restrictions in adolescent ballerinas. *Phys. Sports Med.,* **137**, 79–90.

Ben-Tovim, D.I. and Walker, M.K. (1991). Further evidence for the Stroop test as a quantitative measure of psychopathology in eating disorders. *Int. J. Eat. Dis.,* **10**, 609–613.

Beumont, P.J.V., Russell, J.D. and Touz, S.W. (1993). Treatment of anorexia nervosa. *Lancet,* **341**, 1635–1640.

Beumont, P.J.V., George, G.C.W., Pimstone, B.L., et al. (1976). Body weight and the pituitary response to hypothalamic releasing hormones in patients with anorexia nervosa. *J. Clin. Endocrin. Metab,* **43**, 487–496.

Bhanji, S. and Mattingly, D. (1988). *Medical Aspects of Anorexia Nervosa.* London: Wright.

Biller, B.M.K. et al. (1989). Mechanism of osteoporosis in adult and adolescent women with anorexia nervosa. *J. Clin. Endocrin. Metab.,* **68**, 548–554.

Boag, F., Weerakon, J., Ginsberg, J., Havard, C.W.H. and Dandona, P. (1985). Diminished creatinine clearance in anorexia nervosa: reversal with weight gain. *J. Clin. Pathol.,* **38**, 60–63.

Bonjour, J.P., Theintz, G., Buchs, B., Slosman, D. and Rizzoli, R. (1991). Clinical years and stages of puberty for spinal and femoral mass accumulation during adolescence. *J. Clin. Endocrin. Metab.,* **73**, 555–563.

Bouchard, C. (1991). Is weight fluctuation a risk factor? *New Engl. J. Med.,* **324**, 1887–1888.

Bowers, T.K. and Eckert, E. (1978). Leukopenia in anorexia nervosa. Lack of increased risk of infection. *Arch. Inter. Med.,* **138**, 1520–1523.

Boyar, R.M., Katz, J., Finkelstein, J.W., Kapen, S., Weiner, H., Weitzman, E.D., and Hellman, L. (1974). Anorexia nervosa: immaturity of the 24-hour luteinizing hormone secretory pattern. *New Engl. J. Med.,* **291**, 861–865.

Branca, F., Robins, S.P. and Ferro-Luzzi Golden, M.H.N. (1992). Bone turnover in malnourished children. *Lancet,* **340**, 1493–1496.

Bretz, W.A., Krahn, D.D., Drury, M., Schork, N. and Loessche, W.J. (1993). Effects of fluoxetine on the oral environment of bulimics. *Oral Microbiol. Immunol.,* **8**, 62–64.

Brinch, M., Isager, T. and Tolstroop, K. (1988). Anorexia nervosa and motherhood: reproduction pattern and mothering behavior of 50 women. *Acta Psychiat., Scand,* **77**, 98–104.

Brotman, A.W., Stren, T.A. and Brotman, D.L. (1986). Renal disease and dysfunction in two patients with anorexia nervosa. *J. Clin. Psychiat.,* **47**, 433–434.

Casper, R.C., Davis, J.M. and Pandey, G.N. (1977). The effects of nutritional status and weight changes on hypothalamic function tests in anorexia nervosa. In: R.A. Vigersky (Ed), *Anorexia Nervosa*, pp. 137–147. New York: Raven Press.

Casper, R.C., Kirschner, B., Sandstead, H.H., Jacob, R.A. and Davis, J.M. (1980). An evaluation of trace metals, vitamins and taste function in anorexia nervosa. *Am. J. Clin. Nutr.,* **33**, 1801–1808.

Channon, S., Hemsley, D. and de Silva, P. (1988). Selective processing of food words in anorexia nervosa. *Br. J. Clin. Psychol.,* **27**, 259–260.

Cooke, R.A., Chambers, J.B., Singh, R., Todd, J., Smeeton, N.C., Treasure, J.L. and Treasure, T. (1994). The QT interval in anorexia nervosa. *Br. Heart J.,* **72**, 69–73.

Crisp, A.H. (1965). Some aspects of the evolution, presentation and follow-up of anorexia nervosa. *Proc. Roy. Soc. Med.,* **58**, 814–820.

Crisp, A.H., Callender, J.S., Halek, C. and Hsu, L.K.G. (1992). Long-term mortality in anorexia nervosa: a 20-year follow-up of the St George's and Aberdeen Cohorts, *Br. Med. J.,* **161**, 104–107.

Cuellar, R.E. and Van Theil, D.H. (1986). Gastro-intestinal consequences of the eating disorders: anorexia and bulimia. *Am. J. Gastroenter.,* **81**, 1113–1124.

Curran-Celentano, J., Erdman, J.W., Nelson, R.A. and Grater, S.J.E. (1985). Alterations in vitamin A and thyroid hormone status in anorexia nervosa and related disorders. *Am. J. Clin. Nutr.,* **42**, 1183–1191.

Datloff, S., Coleman, P.D., Forbes, G.B. and Kreipe, R.E. (1986). Ventricular dilatation on CAT scans of patients with anorexia nervosa. *Am. J. Psych.,* **143**, 96–98.

Davies, K.M., Pearson, P.H., Huseman, C.A., Greger, N.G., Kimmel, D.K. and Recker, R.R. (1989). Reduced bone mineral in patients with eating disorders. *Bone,* **11**, 143–147.

Davies, M.C., et al. (1990). Bone mineral loss in young women with amenorrhoea. *Br. Med. J.,* **301**, 790–793.

Dupher, S., Warren, Brooks Gun J. and Fox, R. (1990). Effects of hormonal status on bone density in adolescent girls. *J. Clin. Endocrin. Metab.,* **71**, 1083–1088.

Dolan, R.J., Mitchell, J. and Wakeling, A. (1988). Structural brain changes in patients with anorexia nervosa. *Psychol. Med.,* **18**, 349–353.

Doraiswamy, P.M., Krishnan, K.R.R., Figiel, G.S., Husain, M.N.M., Byoko, O.B., Rockwell, W.J.K. and Ellinwood, E.H. (1990). A brain magnetic resonance imaging study of pituitary gland morphology in anorexia nervosa and bulimia. *Biol. Psych.,* **28**, 110–116.

Duloo, A.G. and Girardier, L. (1990). Adaptive changes in energy expenditure during refeeding following low-calorie intake: evidence for specific metabolic component favoring fat storage. *Am. J. Clin. Nutr.,* **52**, 415–420.

Doyle, W., Wynn, A., Wynn, S. and Crawford (1991). Low birth weight and maternal diet. *Midwife Health Vis. Commun. Nurse,* **27**, 44–45.

Ernsberger–Haskew (1987). Health implications of obesity: an alternative view. *J. Obes. Weight Reg.,* **6**, 58–137.

Enzman, D.R. and Lane, B. (1977). Cranial computed tomography findings in anorexia nervosa. *J. Comput. Assist. Tomogr.,* **1**, 410–414.

Fahy, T. and Treasure, J.L. (1989). Children of mothers with bulimia nervosa. *Br. Med. J.,* **299**, 1031.

Fahy, T.A. and O'Donoghue, G. (1991). Eating disorders in pregnancy. *Psychol. Med.,* **21**, 577–580.

Fairburn, C.G., Peveler, R.C., Davies, B., Mann, J.I. and Mayou, R.A. (1992). Eating disorders in young adults with insulin dependent diabetes mellitus: a controlled study. *Br. Med. J.,* **303**, 17–20.

Ferland, M., Despres, J.P., Nadeau, A., Moorjani, S., Tremblay, A., Lupien, P.J. and Theriault Bouchard, C. (1991). Contribution of glucose tolerance and plasma insulin levels to the relationship between body fat distribution and plasma lipoprotein levels in women. *Int. J. Obesity,* **15**, 677–688.

Finkelstein, J.S., Neer, R.M., Biller, B.M.K., Crawford, J.D. and Klibanski, A. (1992). Osteopenia in men with a history of delayed puberty. *New Engl. J. Med.,* **326**, 600–604.

Fonseca, V., D'Souza, F., Houlder, S. (1988). Vitamin D deficiency and low osteocalcin concentrations in anorexia nervosa. *J. Clin. Pathol.,* **41**, 195–197.

Fonseca, V., Wakeling, A. and Harvard, C.W.H. (1990). Hyperthyroidism and eating disorders. *Br. Med. J.,* **301**, 322–323.

Garner, D.M. and Wooley, S.C. (1991). Confronting the failure of behavioural and deitary treatments for obesity. *Clin. Psychol. Rev.,* **11**, 729–780.

Gavish, D., Eisenerg, S., Berry, E.M., Kleinman, Y., Wiztum, E., Norman, J. and Leitersdorf, E. (1987). Bulimia: an underlying behavioral disorder in hyperlipidaemic pancreatitis: a prospective multidisciplinary approach. *Arch. Inter. Med.,* **147**, 705–708.

Gold, P.W., Kaye, W., Robertson, G.L. and Ebert, M. (1983). Abnormalities in plasma and cerebrospinal fluid arginine vasopressin in patients with anorexia nervosa. *New Engl. J. Med.,* **308**, 1117–1123.

Gold, P.W., Riemenschneider, P.W., Gwirtsman, H., Avgerinos, P.C. et al (1986). Abnormal hypothalamic–pituitary–adrenal function in anorexia nervosa. *New Engl. J. Med.,* **314**, 1335–1342.

Goldbloom, D., Zinman, B. and Hicks, L. (1989). The baseline metabolic state in bulimia nervosa: abnormality and adaptation. *Psychosom. Med.,* **51**, 246.

Goldman, L. and Tosteson, A. (1991). Uncertainty about postmenopausal oestrogen: time for action not debate. *New Engl. J. Med.,* **325**, 800–802.

Greive, J.F.K., Campbell-Brown, M. and Johnston, F.D. (1979). Dieting in pregnancy: a study of the effect of a high-protein low-carbohydrate diet on birthweight of an obstetric population. In M.V. Sutherland and J. Stowers (Eds) *Carbohydrate Metabolism in Pregnancy and the New Born.* Berlin: Springer-Verlag, pp. 518–533.

Gryboski, J., Hillemeier, C., Kocoshis, S., Anyan, W. and Seashore, J.S. (1980). Refeeding pancreatitis in malnourished children. *J. Paediat.,* **97**, 441–443.

Gupta, M.A., Gupta, A.K. and Haberman, H.F. (1987). Dermatologic signs in anorexia nervosa and bulimia nervosa. *Arch. Dermatol.,* **123**, 1386–1390.

Gwirstman, H.E., Kaye, W.H., George, D.T., Jimerson, D.C., Ebert, M.H. and Gold, P.W. (1989). Central and peripheral ACTH and cortisol levels in anorexia and bulimia. *Arch. Gen. Psychiat.,* **46**, 61–69.

Haleem, D.J., Kennet, G.A. and Curzon, G. (1988). Adaptation of female rats to stress: shift to male pattern by inhibition of corticosterone synthesis. *Brain. Res.,* **454**, 339–347.

Hall, R.C.W., Hoffman, R.S., Beresford, T.P., Wooley, B., Tice, L. and Hall, A.K. (1988). Hypomagnesemia in patients with eating disorders. *Psychosomatics,* **29**, 264–272.

Hall, R.C.W., Hoffman, R.S., Beresford, T.P., et al. (1989). Physical illnesses encountered in patients with eating disorders. *Psychosomatics,* **30**, 174–191.

Hamsher, K., Halmi, K.A. and Benton, A.L. (1981). Prediction of outcome in anorexia nervosa from neuropsychological status. *Psychiat. Res.,* **4**, 79–88.

Hasler, J.F. (1982). Parotid enlargement: a presenting sign in anorexia nervosa. *Oral Surg.,* **52**, 567–573.

Hay, P.J., Hall, A., Delabunt, J.W., et al (1989). Investigation of osteopaenia in anorexia nervosa. *Aust. NZ J. Psychiat.,* **23**, 261–268.

Hay, P.J., Delahunt, J.W., Hall, A., Mitchell, A.W., Harper, G. and Salmond, C. (1992). Predictors of osteopenia in premenopausal women with anorexia nervosa. *Calcif. Tiss. Int.,* **50**, 498–501.

Heaney, R., Gallagher, J. and Johnson, C. (1986). Calcium nutrition and bone health in the elderly. *Am. J. Clin. Nutr.,* **36**, 986–1013.

Hersholz, K., Kreig, J., Emrich, H.M, Pawlik, G., Beil, G., Pirke, K.M., Pahl, J.J., Wagner, K., Wienhard, K., Ploog, D. and Heiss, W-D. (1987). Regional cerebral glucose metabolism in anorexia nervosa, measured by positron emission tomography. *Bio. Psych.,* **22**, 43–51.

Herzog, W., Deter, H.C., Schellberg, D., Seilkopf, S., Sarembe, E., Kroger, F., Minne, H., Mayer, H. and Petzold, (1992). Somatic findings at 12-year follow-up of 103 anorexia nervosa patients: results of the Heidelberg–Mannheim follow-up. In: W. Herzog et al (eds), Berlin: Springer-Verlag.

Himes, J.H. (1978). Bone growth and development in protein calorie malnutrition. *World Rev. Nutr. Diet.,* **28**, 143–187.

Horta, J.L.H., Fernandez, J.G., Soto de Leon, B., Cortes-Gallegos (1977). Direct evidence of luteal insufficiency in women with habitual abortion. *Obstet. Gynaecol.,* **49**, 705–708.

Howard, M.R. (1993). Letter: Increased risk of leukaemia in eating disorders likely to be small. *Br. Med. J.,* **306**, 1131.

Husain, M.M., Black, K.J., Doraiswamy, P.M., Shah, S.A., Rockwell, W.J.K., Ellinwood, E.H. and Krishnan, R.R. (1992). Subcortical brain anatomy in anorexia and bulimia. *Biol. Psych.,* **31**, 735–738.

Isaksson, O.G.P., Lindahl, A., Nilsson, A., Isgaard, J. (1987). Mechanisms of the stimulatory effect of growth hormone on longitudinal bone growth. *Endocrin. Rev.,* **8**, 426–438.

Isner, J.M., Roberts, W.C., Heymsfield, S.B. and Yager, J. (1985). Anorexia nervosa and sudden death. *Ann. Inter. Med.,* **102**, 49–52.

Johnson, G.L., Humphries, L.L., Shirley, P.B., Mazzoleni, A. and Noonan, J.A. (1986). Mitral valve prolapse in patients with anorexia nervosa and bulimia. *Arch. Inter. Med.,* **146**, 1525–1529.

Jones, B.P., Duncan, C.C., Brouwers, P. and Mirsky, A.F. (1991). Cognition in eating disorders, *J. Clin. Exper. Neuropsychol.,* **13**, 711–728.

Kaplan, A.S. (1987). Hyperamylasemia and bulimia: a clinical review. *Int. J. Eat. Dis.,* **6**, 537–543.

Kaplan, A.S., Garfinkel, P.E., Warsh, J.J. and Brown, G.M. (1989). Clonidine challenge test in bulimia nervosa. *Int. J. Eat. Dis.,* **8**, 425–435.

Kaplan, A.S. and Garfinkel, P.E. (1993). Medical Issues and the Eating Disorders: The Interface. New York: Brunner/Mazel.

Katz, R.L., Keen, C.L., Litt, I.F., Hurley, L.S., Kellam-Harrison, K.M. and Glader, L.J. (1987). Zinc deficiency in anorexia nervosa. *J. Adoles. Health Care,* **8**, 400–406.

Keilen, M., Treasure, T., Schmidt, U. and Treasure, J. (1994). Quality of life measurements in eating disorders, angina, and transplant candidates: are they comparable? *J. Royal Soc. Med.,* **87**, 441–444.

Kiriiki, N., Iketani, T., Nakanishi, S., Nagata, T., Inoue, K., Okune, M., Ochi, H., Kawakta, Y. (1992). Reduced bone density and major hormones regulating calcium metabolism in anorexia nervosa. *Acta Psychiat. Scand.,* **86**, 358–363.

Krahn, D.D., Gosnell, B.A. and Majchrzak, M.J. (1990). The anorectic effects of CRH and restraint stress decrease with repeated exposures. *Biol. Psychiat.,* **27**, 1094–1102.

Kreig, K.C., Backmund, H. and Pirke, K.M. (1986). Endocrine, metabolic and brain morphological abnormalities in patients with eating disorders. *Int. J. Eat. Dis.,* **5**, 999–1005.

Kreig, J.C., Pirke, K.M., Lauer, C. and Backmund, H. (1988). Endocrine, metabolic and carnial computed tomography findings in anorexia nervosa. *Biol. Psychiat.,* **23**, 377–387.

Kreig, J.C., Lauer, C., Pirke, K.M. (1989). Structural brain abnormalities in patients with bulimia nervosa. *Psychiat. Res.,* **27**, 39–48.

Kreig, J.C., Holthoff, V., Schreiber, W., Pirke, K.A. and Herholz, K. (1991). Glucose metabolism in the caudate nuclei of patients with eating disorders, measured by PET. *Eur. Arch. Psychiat. Clin. Neurosci.,* **240**(6), 331–333.

Kreip, R.E., Churchill, B.H. and Strauss, J. (1989). Long-term outcome of adolescents with anorexia nervosa. *AUDC*, **143**, 1322–1327.

Kuboki, T., Suematsu, H., Ogata, E., Yamamoto, M. and Shizume, K. (1987). Two cases of anorexia nervosa associated with Grave's disease. *Endocrinol. Japonica*, **34**, 9–12.

Lacey, H. and Smith (1987). Bulimia nervosa. The impact of pregnancy on mother and baby. *Br. J. Psych.*, **150**, 777–781.

Lacey, J.H., Crisp, A.H., Kalucy, R.S., et al. (1975). Weight gain and the sleeping electroencephalogram: a study of 10 patients with anorexia nervosa. *Br. Med. J.*, **ii**, 556–558.

Laessle, R.G., Kittle, S., Fichter, M.M. and Pirke, K.M. (1988). Cognitive correlates of depression in patients with eating disorders. *Int. J. Eat. Dis.*, **7**, 681–686.

Laessle, R.G., Kreig, J.C., Fichter, M.M. and Pirke, K.M. (1989). Cerebral atrophy and vigilance performance in patients with anorexia nervosa and bulimia nervosa. *Neuropsychobiology*, **21**, 187–191.

Larsson, B., Seidell, J., Svardsudd, K., Welin Tibblin, G.L., Wilhelsen, L. and Bjorntorp, P. (1984). Obesity, adipose tissue distribution and health in men: the study of men born in 1913. *Appetite*, **13**, 37–44.

Larsson, B., Svardsudd, K., Welin, L., Wilhelsen, L., Bjorntorp, P. and Tibb (1989). Abdominal adipose tissue distribution, obesity, and risk of cardiovascular disease and death: a thirteen-year follow-up of participants in the study of men born in 1913. *Br. Med. J.*, **288**, 1401–1404.

Lee, L.M. and Paffenbarger, R.S. (1992). Change in body weight and longevity. *JAMA*, **268**(15), 2045–2049.

Lembert, R. and Phillips, J. (1989). The impact of pregnancy on anorexia nervosa and bulimia. *Int. J. Eat. Dis.*, **8**, 285–295.

Lind, T. (1984). Nutrition—the changing scene: would more calories per day keep low birthweight at bay? *Lancet*, **i**, 501–502.

Lissner, L., Odell, P.M., D'Agosino, R.B., Stokes, J., Kreger, B.E., Belanger, A.J. and Brownell, K.D. (1991). Variability of body weight and health outcomes in the Framingham population. *New Engl. J. Med.*, **324**, 1839–1844.

Lucas, A.R., Beard, C.M., Fallon, W.M. and Kurland, L.T. (1991). 50-year trends in the incidence of anorexia nervosa in Rochester: a population-based study. *Am. J. Psychiat.*, **148**, 917–922.

Luck, P.E. and Wakeling, A. (1980). Altered thresholds for thermoregulatory sweating and vasodilation in with clomiphene citrate. *Br. Med. J.*, **4**, 590–592.

Mattingly, D. and Bhanji, S. (1982). The diagnosis of anorexia nervosa. *J. Roy. Coll. Phys. Lond.*, **16**, 191–194.

McCluskey, S., Evans, C., Lacey, J.H., Pearce, M.J. and Jacobs, H. (1991). Polycystic ovary syndrome and bulimia. *Fertil. Steril.*, **55**, 287–291.

Meadows, G. and Treasure, J. (1989). Bulimia nervosa and Crohn's disease: two case reports. *Acta Psychiat. Scand.*, **79**, 413–414.

Mecklenburg, R.S., Loriaux, D.L., Thompson, R.H., et al. (1974). Hypothalamic dysfunction in patients with anorexia nervosa. *Medicine*, **53**, 273–278.

Meyers, D.G., Starke, H., Pearson, P.H. and Wilken, M.K. (1986). Mitral valve prolapse in patients with anorexia nervosa. *Ann. Inter. Med.*, **105**, 384–385.

Mira, M., Stewart, P.M., Vizzard, J. and Abraham, S. (1987). Biochemical abnormalities in anorexia nervosa and bulimia nervosa. *Ann. Clin. Biochem.*, **24**, 29–35.

Mitchell, J.E. and Boutacoff, L.I. (1986). Laxative abuse complicating bulimia, medical and treatment implications. *Int. J. Eat. Dis.*, **5**, 325–334.

Mitchell, J.E., Pyle, R.L., Eckert, E.D., Hatsukami, D. and Lentz, R. (1983). Electrolyte and other physiological abnormalities in patients with bulimia. *Psychol. Med.*, **13**, 273–278.

Mitchell, J.E., Hatsukami, D., Pyle, R.L., Ekert, E.D. and Boutacoff, L.I. (1987). Metabolic acidosis as a marker for laxative abuse in patients with bulimia. *Int. J. Eat. Dis.*, **6**, 557–560.

Mitchell, J.E., Pomeroy, C., Seppala, M. and Huber, M. (1988). Pseudo-Barrters syndrome, diuretic abuse, idiopathic oedema and eating disorders. *Int. J. Eat. Dis.*, **6**, 557–560.

Newman, M.M. and Halmi, K.A. (1988). The endocrinology of anorexia nervosa and bulimia nervosa. *Endocrin. Metab. Clin. North Am.*, **17**, 195–212.

Nishizono-Maher, A., Sakamaki, H., Mizukami, H., Kuraki, T., Minakawa, K. and Masuda, Y. (1993). Leukaemia linked to eating disorders. *Br. Med. J.*, **306**, 830–831.

O'Donoghue, G., Treasure, J.L. and Russell, G.F.M. (1991). Eating disorders and motherhood. *Signpost* (newsletter for the Eating Disorders Association), April, 1–5.

Oster, J.R., Materson, B.J. and Rogers, A.I. (1980). Laxative abuse syndrome. *Am. J. Gastroenter.*, **74**, 451–458.

Ott, S.M. (1991). Bone density in adolescents. *New Engl. J. Med.*, **325**, 1646–1647.

Palazidou, E., Robinson, P. and Lishman, W.A. (1990). Neuroradiological and neuropsychological assessment in anorexia nervosa. *Psychol. Med.*, **20**, 521–527.

Palla, B. and Litt, I.F. (1988). Medical complications of eating disorders in adolescents. *Paediatrics*, **81**, 613–623.

Palmer, E.P. and Guay, A.T. (1986). Reversible myopathy secondary to the use of ipecac in patients with eating disorders. *New Engl. J. Med.*, **313**, 457–459.

Pamuk, R.E., Williamson, D.F., Madans, J., Serdula, M.K., Kleinman, J.C. and Byers, T. (1992). Weight loss and mortality in a national cohort of adults, 1971–1987. *Am. J. Epidemiol.*, **136**, 686–697.

Patton, G.C. (1988). Mortality in eating disorders. *Psychol. Med.*, **18**, 947–951.

Pirke, K.M., Fichter, M.M., Chloud, C. and Doerr, P. (1987). Disturbances of the menstrual cycle in bulimia nervosa. *Clin. Endocrin.*, **27**, 245–251.

Pirke, K.M., Dogs, M., Fichter, M.M. and Tuschl, J. (1988). Gonadotrophins, oestradiol and progesterone during the menstrual cycle in bulimia nervosa. *Clin. Endocrin.*, **29**, 265–270.

Pirke, K.M., Schweiger, U., Strowitzki, T., Tuschl, R.J., Laessle, R.G., Brooks, A., Huber, B. and Middendorf, R. (1989). Dieting causes menstrual irregularities in normal-weight young women through impairment of episodic luteininizing hormone secretion. *Fertil. Steril.*, **51**, 263–268.

Rebuffe-Scrive, M., Eldh J. Hafstrom, L.O. and Bjorntrop, P. (1986). Metabolism of mammaty abdominal and femoral adipocytes in women before and after the menopause. *Metabolism*, **35**, 792–797.

Riad, M., Barton, J.R. and Wilson, J.A. (1991). Paratoid salivary secretion pattern in bulimia nervosa. *Acta Otolaryngol.*, **111**, 392–395.

Rieger, W., Brady, J.P. and Weisberg, E. (1978). Hematologic changes in anorexia nervosa. *Am. J. Psychiat.*, **135**, 984–985.

Riemenschneider, Th. and Bohle, A. (1988). Morphologic aspects of low-potassium and low-sodium nephropathy. *Clin. Nephrol.*, **19**, 271–279.

Rigotti, N.A., et al (1984). Osteoporosis in women with anorexia nervosa. *New Engl. J. Med.*, **311**, 1601–1606.

Rigotti, N.A., Neer, R.M., Skates, S.J., Herzog, D.B. and Nussbaum, S.R. (1991). The clinical course of osteoporosis in anorexia nervosa. *JAMA*, **265**, 1133–1137.

Rodin, J., Bartoshuk, L., Peterson, C. and Schank, D. (1990). Bulimia and taste: possible interactions. *J. Abnorm. Psychol.*, **99**, 32–39.

Robinson, P.H., Clarke, M. and Barrett, J. (1988). Determinants of delayed gastric emptying in anorexia nervosa and bulimia nervosa. *Gut*, **29**, 458–464.

Rothenberger, A., Blanz, B. and Lahmkuhl, G. (1991). What happens to electrical brain activity when anorexic adolescents gain weight? *Eur. Arch. Psych. Clin. Neurosci.*, **240**, 144–147.

Russell, G.F.M. (1985). Premenarchal anorexia nervosa and its sequelae. *J. Psychiat. Res.*, **19**, 363–369.

Russell, G.F.M. and Treasure, J.L. (1988). Intrauterine growth and neonatal weight gain in anorexia nervosa. *Br. Med. J.*, **296**, 1038.

Salisbury, J.J. and Mitchell (1991). Bone mineral density and anorexia nervosa in women. *Am. J. Psychiat.*, **148**, 768–774.

Saul, S.H., Dekker, A. and Watson, C.G. (1981). Acute gastric dilatation with infarction and perforation. *Gut*, **22**, 978–983.

Savvas, M., Treasure, J.L. and Studd, J. (1989). The effect of anorexia nervosa on skin thickness, skin collagen and bone density. *Br. J. Obstet. Gynaecol.*, **96**, 1392–1394.

Schmidt, U. and O'Donoghue, G. (1992). Bulimia nervosa and thyroid disorder. *Int. J. Eat. Dis.*, **12**, 93–96.

Scobie, B.A. (1973). Acute gastric dilatation and duodenal ileus in anorexia nervosa. *Med. J. Aust.*, **2**, 335.

Schwabe, A.D., Lippe, B.M. and Chang, R.J. (1981). Anorexia nervosa. *Ann. Int. Med.*, **94**, 371–381.

Schocken, D.D., Holloway, J.D. and Powers, P.S. (1989). Weight loss and the heart. *Arch. Inter. Med.*, **149**, 877.

Schweiger, U., Laessle, R., Pfister, H., Hoehl, C., Schwingen-Scholoegel, M., Schweiger, M.M. and Pirke, K.M. (1987). Diet induced menstrual irregularities: effects of age and weight loss. *Fertil. and Steril.*, **48**, 746–751.

Seeman, E., Szmukler, G.I., Formica, C., Tsalamandris, C. and Mestrovic, R. (1992). Osteoporosis in anorexia nervosa: the influence of peak bone density, bone loss, oral contraceptive use and exercise. *J. Bone Min. Res.*, **7**, 1467–1474.

Sharpe, C.W. and Freeman, C.P.L. (1993). The medical complications of anorexia nervosa. *Br. J. Psychiat.*, **162**, 452–462.

Shur, E., Alloway, R., Obrecht, R., et al. (1988). Physiological complications in anorexia nervosa: haematological and neuromuscular changes in 12 patients. *Br. J. Psychiat.*, **153**, 72–75.

Silber, T.J. and Kass, E.J. (1984). Anorexia nervosa and nephrolitiasis. *J. Adolesc. Health Care*, **5**, 50–52.

Simmons, M.S., Grayden, S.K. and Mitchell, J.E. (1986). The need for psychiatric-dental liaison in the treatment of bulimia. *Am. J. Psychiat.*, **143**, 783–784.

Simonson, E., Henschel, A. and Keys, A. (1948). The Electrocardiogram of man in semistarvation and subsequent rehabilitation. *Am. Heart J.*, **35**, 584–602.

Smith, S.M. and Hanson, R. (1972). Failure to thrive and anorexia nervosa. *Postgrad. Med. J.*, **48**, 382–384.

Sours, J. and Vorhaus, L. (1981). Superior mesenteric artery syndrome in anorexia nervosa: a case report. *Am. J. Psychiat.*, **138**, 519–520.

Stanhope, R., Albanese, A. and Shalet, S. (1992). Delayed Puberty. *Br. Med. J.*, **305**, 790.

Steele, J.M., Young, R.J., Lloyd, G.G. and Clarke, B.F. (1987). Clinically apparent eating disorders in young diabetic women: associations with painful neuropathy and other complications. *Br. Med. J.*, **294**, 859–862.

Steele, J.M., Young, R.J., Lloyd, G.G. and MacIntyre, C.C.A. (1989). Abnormal eating attitudes in young insulin-dependent diabetics. *Br. J. Psychiat.*, **155**, 515–521.

Stein, A. and Fairburn, C.G. (1989). Children of mothers with bulimia nervosa. *Br. Med. J.*, **299**, 777–778.

Stewart, D.E., Raskin, J., Garfinkel, P.E., MacDonald, O.L. and Robinson, G.G. (1987). Anorexia nervosa, bulimia and pregnancy. *Am. J. Obstet. Gynaecol.*, **157**, 1194–1198.

Stewart, D.E., Robinson, G.E., Goldblook, D.S. and Wright, C. (1990). Infertility and eating disorders. *Am. J. Obstet. Gynaecol.*, **163**, 1196–1199.

Szmukler, G.I. and Tantam, D. (1984). Anorexia nervosa: starvation dependence. *Br. J. Med. Psychol.*, **57**, 303–310.

Szmukler, G.I., et al (1985). A premature loss of bone in chronic anorexia nervosa. *Br. Med. J.*, **290**, 26–27.

Szmukler, G.I., Andrewes, D., Kingstoh, K., Chen, L., Stargatt, R. and Stanley, R. (1992). Neuropsychological impairment in anorexia nervosa before and after refeeding. *J. Clin. Exper. Neuropsychol.*, **14**, 347–352.

Szmukler, G.I., Young, G.P., Lichtenstein, M. and Andrews, J.T. (1990). A serial study of gastric emptying in anorexia nervosa and bulimia nervosa. *Aus. NZ J. Med.*, **20**, 220–225.

Tarui, S., Tokiunaga, K., Fujioke, S. and Matsuzawa, Y. (1991). Visceral fat obesity: anthropological and pathophysiological aspects. *Int. J. Obesity*, **15**, 1–8.

Tiller, J., Macrae, A., Schmidt, U., Bloom, S. and Treasure, J. (1994). The prevalence of eating disorders in thyroid disease: a pilot study. *J. Psychosom. Dis.*, **38**, 609–616.

Torfs, C.P., Van den Berg, B., Oechsli, I.W. and Cummins, S. (1990). Prenatal and perinatal factors in the aetiology of cerebral palsy. *J. Paediatr.*, **116**, 615–619.

Treasure, J.L. (1988). The ultrasonographic features in anorexia nervosa and bulimia nervosa: a simplified method of monitoring hormonal states during weight gain. *Crin. Endocrinol.*, **29**, 607–616.

Treasure, J.L., Gordon, P.A.L., King, E.A., et al. (1985). Cystic ovaries: a phase of anorexia nervosa. *Lancet*, **ii**, 1379–1382.

Treasure, J.L., Fogelman, I., Russell, G.F.M. and Murby, B. (1987). Reversible bone loss in anorexia nervosa. *Br. Med. J.*, **295**, 474–475.

Van der Spuy, A.M., Steer, P.J., MacCusker, M., Steele, S.J. and Jacobs, H.S. (1988). Outcome of pregnancy in underweight women after spontaneous and induced ovulation. *Br. Med. J.*, **296**, 962–965.

Van Wezel-Meijer, G. and Wit, J.M. (1989). The offspring of mothers with anorexia nervosa: a high-risk group for under nutrition and stunting? *Eur. J. Pediatr.*, **149**, 130–135.

Wakeling, A., De Souza, V.F.A. and Beardwood, C.J. (1977). Assessment of the negative and positive feedback effects of administered oestrogen on gonadotrophin release in patients with anorexia nervosa. *Psychol. Med.*, **7**, 397–405.

Warren, and Van de Weile (1973). Clinical and metabolic features of anorexic nervosa. *Am. J. Obstet. Gynecol.*, **117**, 435–449.

Weinsier, R.L., Krumdieck, P.H. and Krumdieck, C.L. (1981). Death resulting from overzealous total parenteral nutrition: the refeeding syndrome revisited. *Am. J. Clin. Nutr.*, **34**, 393–399.

Willis and Rand (1988). Pregnancy in bulimic women. *Obstet. Gynecol.*, **71**, 708.

Wu, J.C., Hagman, J., Buchsbaum, M.S., Blinder, B., Derrflet, M., Win Ye Tai, B.S., Hazlett, B.S. and Sicotte, N. (1990). Greater left cerebral hemispheric metabolism in bulimia assessed by positron emission tomography. *Am. J. Psych.*, **147**, 309–312.

Zilber, N., Schufman, N. and Lerner, Y. (1989). Mortality among psychiatric patients: the groups at risk. *Acta Psychiat. Scand.*, **79**, 248–256.

12

Psychological Concerns in the Maintenance of Dieting Disorders

P.J.V. BEUMONT
J.D. RUSSELL
University of Sydney, NSW, Australia
AND
S.W. TOUYZ
Westmead Hospital, NSW, Australia

INTRODUCTION

In their invitation to us, the editors suggested that we consider issues such as the inhibiting effects of starvation on cognitive performances, psychological growth, and the patient's ability to form relationships and eventually assume the role of an adult and parent. These are admirable suggestions as each has been the object of important studies in the literature. For instance, Keys and his colleagues (1950), in their classic monograph, graphically described the psychological effects of starvation; Crisp (1980) in his numerous publications has emphasised the retardation of normal psychosexual development; and Hilda Bruch's writings (1974) remain the standard source for understanding the anorexic patient's problems in relationships with self and others.

We have decided to write on none of these topics. They all relate to things patients do badly. Our patients are excessively critical of their own performance, and we are tired of hearing from them and from others about their deficiencies. We

Handbook of Eating Disorders: Theory, Treatment and Research.
Edited by G. Szmukler, C. Dare and J. Treasure.
© 1995 John Wiley & Sons Ltd.

would like our contribution to Gerald Russell's *Festschrift* to be more positive than that. Rather than look at deficits in the objective manifestations of mental life which may establish vicious circles of dysfunction, we would prefer to explore our patients' novel attempts at adaptation and survival. These are things our patients do well, albeit with variable consequences for their health. They arise in the context of the patients' perceptions of themselves, their illnesses and their place in the world. There are five such issues we wish to consider:

- First is the matter of gender. These disorders are far more prevalent in females than in males (Lucas et al, 1991). Has this to do with the experience of being a woman in our society? How can our patients escape from the tyranny of their gender?
- Media influences on girls and young women are alleged to play a role in the causation and maintenance of dieting disorders (Garfinkel and Garner, 1982). How do our patients and their peers perceive these influences? Do they eventually outgrow them?
- Then there is the importance of a label. The reported prevalence of anorexia nervosa increased markedly in the years of Hilda Bruch's seminal writings about the illness (Brumberg, 1990), while bulimia nervosa changed from being a rare to an extremely common condition at around the time of Russell's classic article in 1979. To what extent were these changes dependent on the popular interest that had been aroused by the description of the illness in the medical literature? Once a label of anorexia or bulimia nervosa is acquired, how difficult is it to shed?
- A distorted body image was once considered integral to the diagnosis of anorexia nervosa (Bruch, 1962). Are there really peculiarities in the way our patients see themselves? Do they persist?
- Of all functional psychiatric illnesses, anorexia nervosa has the highest mortality rate (Theander, 1985). Some observers consider the patient's anorexic behaviour as a suicide equivalent. Paradoxically it might be seen as a unique form of survival. Are anorexia nervosa patients preoccupied with death?

A brief comment is necessary about terminology. This volume is about eating disorders, but we are not capable of covering that extensive field. We know little about the psychology of obesity, of pica, of rumination disorder, or of the many other forms of disturbed eating. Our special knowledge is restricted to anorexia and bulimia nervosa and *formes frustes* of these conditions. In Sydney, we have coined the term "dieting disorders" for these illnesses, and it is about them that we write.

DIETING DISORDERS AND THE EXPERIENCE OF BEING FEMALE

It is an indubitable fact that dieting disorders are far more prevalent among girls and young women than they are among boys and men (Beumont, Beardwood and Russell, 1972; Touyz, Kopec-Schrader and Beumont, 1993). Is this biased distribution a matter of sex or of gender? By sex we mean the biological differences between males and females: differences in anatomy and physiology. Gender, however, is concerned with culture, and its manifestations vary from one society to another.

There are reasons to believe that sex does play a role in determining the occurrence of dieting disorders. The proportion of fat in the body composition of women is higher than it is in men, and the difference relates to the hormonal milieux characteristic of the sexes (Mitchell and Truswell, 1987). The dissonance becomes apparent after puberty, at the time when dieting disorders develop. As boys go through puberty, their gonads produce testosterone which enhances muscular development. The average 18-year-old youth consumes 25% more calories than the 12-year-old boy (Burke et al, 1959), yet the proportion of fat in his body composition is hardly altered. On the other hand, menarche in girls does does not result in any significant increase in muscle bulk. The post-pubertal girl eats less than she did as a 12-year-old child, but the proportion of fat in her body composition has increased because energy is no longer needed for purposes of growth.

If adequate food is available one would expect most young women to be plumper than young men. This indeed appears to have been appreciated in many human societies since Cro-Magnon man carved the celebrated Venus of Willendorf 30 000 years ago. The ready acceptance of this biological difference, and the esteem accorded to the beauty of well-rounded young women in some cultures, is perhaps the main reason why dieting disorders are rare among people such as the Bantu speakers of Africa. Rubens' adored Hélène Fourment is an example from the western tradition (Figure 12.1). But women are created by the societies in which they live, and as societies differ so do their women. In our modern western societies, women's gender role is in conflict with the dictates of biology: young women are praised for being slender, dieting is the norm and dieting disorders are common.

Why is this cultural influence so strong? To answer the question it is necessary to think more deeply about the process of acculturalisation into the feminine role. Paradoxically, some of the evidence about this process comes from the study of women who themselves have suffered from a dieting disorder, and it is interesting to consider why this should be so.

Most people leave no personal account of their lives. A few women write diaries or hand down their letters, and an occasional woman is interviewed by an oral historian. But most official biographies are of the powerful and famous, and in earlier times this almost always meant of men. To female anonymity, however, there have been three important exceptions. One is the detailed descriptions preserved by the Roman Catholic Church of the lives of women recognised as saints, blessèds, venerables or servants of God. These records have been surveyed comprehensively by authors such as Bell (1985), Bynum (1987), Van Deth and Vandereycken (1988). Another source of information about the lives of women is that portrayed in novels. Not only have many of the most outstanding novelists been women writing about the concerns of women (Jane Austen, Virginia Woolf, Margaret Drabble), but some male writers too appear to have had a genuine interest in the experience of women, as exemplified by Gustav Flaubert's Madame Bovary and James Joyce's Mrs Bloom. A third source of detailed descriptions of women's lives, and one particularly relevant to our topic, is hospital case records, particularly those

FIGURE 12.1 Portrait by Rubens of his second wife Hélène Fourment, whom he married when she was 16. Although overweight by today's standards, she was considered one of the most beautiful women of her time. Portrait reproduced by permission of the Kunsthistorisches Museum, Vienna.

of psychiatric institutions (Matthews, 1984). Psychiatric case notes are written to give comprehensive biographies of the patients concerned, recorded in the hope that in the family and personal history clues will be found to the cause of the illness.

To these sources, a new dimension of interpretation has been added in recent decades: the dimension of feminism. Feminism takes the experiences of women as its central theme and attacks the masculine domination of society. It focuses on the irrationality of the rigid polarisation between male and female, and especially on the unfairness of society's impositions on women. Its rhetoric has been perceived as shrill, yet its message is still not fully appreciated.

Feminist writers have used all three of the sources listed above to support their arguments, and from them a common theme emerges. The ideal of femininity in our society is unattainable!

> The process of becoming a woman is . . . the attempt to live up to the various standards of her society, the struggle to behave . . . according to her own and her society's standards. Because femininity is an idealised and illusory quality, and because it is composed of inconsistent and contradictory parts, its pursuit is doomed to failure. She cannot please all the people all the time. To be a woman is thus necessarily to carry a sense of failure. (Matthews, 1984).

The self-esteem of prepubertal and adolescent girls is an important factor in their vulnerability to dieting disorders (Shisslak and Crago, 1987). A low self-esteem in girls is fostered in all sorts of ways. Gender inequality in education is one. Girls are conditioned in the classroom to believe that they are intellectually inferior to boys, and their expectations of their performance in those subjects which determine university entry and competitive career options reflect their conditioning.

Girls and women are seldom encouraged to assess themselves for what they do, are seldom free to be genuinely assertive (Steinem, 1992). Society is organised for the convenience of men, and women are demoted to a second-class citizenship, inappropriately confined to the limitations of their biological destiny by rigid cultural stereotyping. They are taught that their value is in passivity rather than activity, in how they look rather than what they are or what they do. Slenderness has become the most valued component of this image in our society (Wolf, 1991). Hence Susie Orbach is right in claiming that "Fat is a Feminist Issue" (1978). Women waste their lives in quest of an ideal body image (Wolf, 1991).

It has been suggested that the promotion of a thin prepubertal male body as the ideal for females represents a neurotic rejection of mature womanhood by our society (Chernin, 1987). In Australia, however, the recent popularity of the model Elle promotes an ideal woman who is extremely slender, but of mature male height and with astonishingly large breasts. This "ideal" would be achievable for the normal woman only through a combination of sustained dietary restraint, dedicated exercising and plastic surgery, not to mention unusual genetics. The image appears to have been contrived so as to remain unattainable for most of those at whom it is aimed.

This perverted situation has arisen in affluent westernised societies where food and leisure are plentiful and where the average body weight of females is increasing (Garner et al, 1987). Slenderness must be sought through a variety of means which are all costly to the woman in terms of money, time and energy, preventing her from investing in things which are more worthwhile. To ensure that women continue to feel inadequate and continue to assuage these feelings by supporting the dieting, fashion and beautification industries, the task is made even more challenging by regular and frequent changes to the image. For instance, Elle is now in danger of being superseded by a waif-like and seriously emaciated model, Kate Moss, who was chosen by the designer Calvin Klein to promote his androgynous underwear.

A masterpiece of painting or sculpture in earlier times usually depicted a beautiful woman and served to demonstrate the power and prestige of its male owner (Berger, 1972). As exemplified by the advertisements for Calvin Klein's underpants, this has been now replaced by a photograph which celebrates the elongated and tapering female body. The owner now is a corporate collective which exploits women by the implicit and explicit advertising to which the image is attached. The messages are twofold: "This is how you should look in order to be chosen (by men who matter)"; and "You too can look like this if you buy our product". Thus are women persuaded to deplete both their finances and their bodies while the notion is reinforced that they are valued only for how they look, not what they do. Action remains a male preserve.

The dissatisfaction born of societal constraint, lack of real control, passivity and an inevitable sense of failure is expressed in bodily disparagement and played out in attempts to control body weight and shape. All females are vulnerable but none more so than the adolescent and pre-teen girl whose identity is in the making, and who is already being shaped by her mother's and sisters' experience. But even adult women are not spared. Remaining slender is promoted as the antidote to ageing— fat and age have become twin bogeys in our society. From the subtle state of debilitation and demoralisation resulting from continued engagement in weight-losing behaviour, one of two possible self-perpetuating scenarios may evolve— anorexia or bulimia nervosa.

The challenge is to attempt both primary and secondary prevention. The media and the advertising industry have been held responsible for this "relentless pursuit of thinness", driven by the billion dollar concerns of the beautification and weight loss industries (Shisslak and Crago, 1987). Their immense profitability ensures their survival, but perhaps their message to women can be modified. For instance, health might be promoted rather than appearance, achievement recognised without automatic reference to age or weight. Bold initiatives have been suggested (Collins, 1988; Shisslak and Crago, 1987), such as using plump actresses, average sized rather than scrawny models, realistic-looking mothers in television commercials, jeans which are sized to fit normal females, even magazines for the female market with topics other than diets, weight, shape and looks. The list is endless but unlikely to become reality because of fears that products promoted by the current system would no longer sell. If the collective self-esteem of women were better and perhaps if they were not so worn down from their battles with their own bodies (Wolf, 1991), they might be able to achieve a healthy degree of social subversion and with it the prospect of mobilising change to this, the most insidious and pervasive of sexist influences. Not only might some women thus be protected from developing a dieting disorder, but many so afflicted might better be able to escape from the tyranny of their illness (Russell and Beumont, 1994).

THE PERCEPTION OF CULTURAL PRESSURES BY PATIENTS AND THEIR PEERS

The feminist approach to the problem of dieting disorders is stimulating and thought-provoking, but is there direct evidence to support its conclusions? Feminist writing is not impartial, but rather it is deeply partisan. Beyond feminism or even its more moderate "second stage" (Frieden, 1983), there is still a need for a careful examination of the hypotheses that it endorses. While most modern authors accept the feminist viewpoint, at least tacitly, and acknowledge that sociocultural factors in our society contribute to the occurrence of dieting disorders, there has been little empirical research on this topic. A recent study in our department has attempted an objective exploration of the role of sociocultural factors in the causation and maintenance of anorexia and bulimia nervosa (Murray, 1991).

One of the aims of the study was to examine the subjects' awareness of cultural ideals about weight and shape, the influence these ideals exerted, and the subject's criticisms of these pressures. Fifty female anorexic and 30 female bulimic patients were studied, as well as a sample of 82 female and 69 male controls. An open-ended interview was used, together with a number of questionnaires, so as to obtain qualitative as well as quantitative data.

Eighty-five per cent of all subjects reported that some types of female figures are unacceptable in society, namely those which were "overweight" or "very overweight". Almost all subjects (98%) believed that the media promote a certain image of women, and 75% stated this image is one of slimness. While previous studies have documented the emphasis placed on women's thinness in current western culture, we believe that this is the first report of the extent to which subjects are aware of these pressures. What was striking was that all groups were equally aware. There was nothing to suggest that the dieting disordered patients were particularly perspicacious in this respect.

The great majority of subjects commented only on society's demand for thinness:

- "They like a girl to starve herself." (Female control aged 23)
- "Bones . . . everywhere you look you see skinny people in magazines." (Female control aged 21)

but a few suggested that the message was really ambivalent:

- "There are two things. You look in a magazine and see some skinny 12-year-old kid done up as if she were 19 and 20. There is no hope that a real 19- or 20-year-old can look as thin as that. Then you open *Playboy* and see this very buxom doll. You've got to choose which way you go because the two images don't fit." (Female control aged 19)

It may be that the societal ideal body shape for women incorporates both thinness and large breasts. Davies and Furnham (1986) support this suggestion, finding that 90% of 16-year-old girls considered themselves overweight generally but were happy with the size of their breasts.

While 70% of respondents believed there is also a body shape ideal for men, this ideal is to be muscular rather than thin. Further, they believed the societal ideal is less strongly endorsed for men than for women:

- "It's OK for a man to be fat but if you're a girl, forget it." (Female control aged 23)
- "Men are allowed to get away with a lot more. You wouldn't see Prince Andrew being pulled to shreds because he had put on half a stone! Poor Fergie!" (Bulimia patient aged 24)

Almost all subjects were extremely interested in issues concerning cultural pressures on body shape, and appeared to have given some prior thought to these matters. They were also aware of the effects these pressures exert on their own and on others' lives:

- "Many men [on TV shows] don't have a great body but the girls on the show with them always do. I think that filters down to the audience. The guys can relate to the man. I watch the programme and think 'My body is no better or worse than his'. But if I am sitting with a girl, she would be thinking, 'Gee, she's got a good figure . . . I'm fatter than her, what are the guys going to think of me?'." (Male control aged 26)

Males were significantly less likely than female controls to report that they were influenced by the media to attempt to alter their body shape. Men emphasised the health and fitness aspects of media messages, whereas women were more concerned with weight and appearance. Of course, this difference may have been due to actual differences in the messages presented by the media. Interestingly, men were also less likely to report their ideas about what constituted a "good" figure for either sex came from the media.

Males were far less influenced than females by the comments of acquaintances of their own gender, but they were almost as likely to be affected by comments from the opposite sex. Even here, however, there were important qualitative differences. Men reported that compliments about their looks made them feel good, while women were more likely to state that criticisms of their bodies had upset them. Many of the criticisms reported by the female controls were cruel and unfair:

- "My husband used to say that he'd divorce me if I got fat. Now he says our sex life will be null and void."
- My ex-boyfriend said I was fat. I'd get upset and angry because I knew I wasn't overeating and I was doing exercise."

Although both groups were equally affected by members of the opposite sex, and there were no differences in the types of effects reported, patients were more likely than female controls to say that other women influenced them.

Although a good deal of research has established that women are the primary object of social pressures concerning weight and shape, the extent to which these pressures actually affect men and women has not previously been documented. Of even greater interest, moreover, are the differences that have emerged between dieting disordered patients and female controls in this study (Murray, 1991). Many authors have suggested that patients with dieting disorders are particularly vulnerable to the influence of external standards such as those portrayed in the media, especially in regard to appearance (Bruch, 1974; Crisp, 1980; Garfinkel and Garner, 1982; Gordon, 1990). Murray (1991) found that dieting disordered patients were significantly more likely than female controls to report that they were influenced by the media, usually so that they wished to look like the ideals shown:

- "It's become a total obsession: wanting to look like the models in the magazines, looking at the diets they put in magazines. And trying to look like them, become like them." (Bulimic patient aged 19).

Some patients stated directly that they felt they were more influenced by social pressures than were their peers:

- "I am tremendously affected [by magazines]. They've portrayed the way we should eat and look, and I've sort of followed blindly along behind." (Bulimic patient aged 21)

Many patients regarded these influences in a negative way, as undermining their independence: others merely acknowledged their existence. It is of interest that some patients endorsed the popular impression that dieting disordered patients were more vulnerable to external pressures because of a poorly developed sense of self and a feeling of personal ineffectiveness:

- "Other people are affected by the media, but I think the ones that are influenced have the same problems as I have—low self-esteem and so on. I can't imagine anyone who is confident about themselves being the least bit interested in what's being presented by the media." (Anorexia patient aged 32)

It is unclear whether a heightened susceptibility to social pressures is a predisposing factor for the development of a dieting disorder, or whether the effect of these social pressures is increased as a result of having the illness. Nevertheless, the study did indicate that the social pressures reported by the patients play a role in the maintenance of their disturbance.

The extent to which women were critical of the influence of social pressures was determined by asking directly about this issue. Subjects were classified as "uncritical" if they endorsed current ideals concerning body shape and slimness or expressed the view that such ideals are reasonable or desirable. Subjects who were "partially critical" believed that current ideals were overemphasised or too stringent, but did not object to the notion of a body shape ideal *per se*. "Critical" subjects were opposed to the existence of any body shape ideal.

While most women in all categories expressed some criticisms of the cultural ideal, the control and patient groups showed some interesting variations. The majority of control subjects were partially critical of the current ideal. Patients, on the other hand, were usually either strongly critical of the current ideal, or not at all so. Age did not exert any effect on their criticism status, but duration of illness did. The great majority of patients who had been ill for less than 2 years were uncritical, while most of those who had been ill for longer periods were very critical of the current ideal.

Some tentative conclusions may be drawn from these findings. Being critical towards the cultural ideal does not enable patients to become less aware of or less influenced by such pressures, nor to overcome their illnesses. Thus the development of a critical stance may not promote recovery from a dieting disorder. On the other hand, the finding that control subjects are more critical than are patients in the early phase of illness suggests that a healthy degree of criticism may play a role in preventing some women from developing a dieting disorder. These findings echo Steiner-Adair's (1986) comments equating resistance to dieting disorders with the ability to recognise and reject those societal values which prejudice developmental needs.

THE IMPORTANCE OF THE LABEL

If the patients' awareness of the societal ideal for body shape is relevant to the development of dieting disorder, what of their awareness of the diagnoses of anorexia and bulimia nervosa themselves? This question has received insufficient attention from the many recent publications addressing the history of these illnesses. Joan Brumberg's book provides an example (Brumberg, 1988).

Like some other feminist authors (Wolf, 1991), Brumberg deals with anorexia nervosa as if it were almost an exclusively American phenomenon. She pays scant attention to the earlier European literature, although as late as 1931 a British commentator had noted that the most illuminating accounts of the illness were in French (Crookshank, 1931). Her book appears to contain errors of detail as to historical facts and clinical matters. Despite these faults, Brumberg's account of anorexia nervosa in the bourgeois families of the nineteenth century is fascinating, and her ideas about the current wave of the disorder in our society strike a cautionary note. She has suggested that the increase in anorexia nervosa in the United States in the 1960s and 70s might be attributed at least in part to Bruch's eloquent writings about the illness (Brumberg, 1990). Perhaps a similar iatrogenic influence has operated in respect to bulimia nervosa.

Brumberg attempts to integrate biological, psychological and cultural factors in the genesis of the illness, and proposes a two-phase model. In the first phase of "recruitment", cultural factors attract a wide range of persons to the risk behaviour of dieting. In the second phase of "illness career", individual psychological and biological characteristics determine which persons engaging in the risk behaviour become entrapped in the illness. As Habermas (1991) points out, there are serious problems with this model. The influence of cultural factors on the individual are seen as important only in that they cause the risk behaviour. And the model takes no account of the impact of the diagnostic label, both in acquiring the illness and in its perpetuation.

Habermas (1990) argues that the history of anorexia and particularly of bulimia nervosa offers a unique opportunity to examine the differential effects of *various types* of sociocultural factors on illness. These disturbances of behaviour existed long before they were classified as diagnostic entities, and even then cultural factors were important in their presentations. Thus the religious ascetics and the celebrated fasting girls of previous centuries also need to be understood in their cultural context (Van Deth and Vandereycken, 1988). Bulimia may be seen as a response to an otherwise insoluble predicament (Beumont, 1988). But once these conditions were assigned diagnostic labels, additional cultural influences became important, compounding the earlier factors. In analysing such interactions specifically in respect of bulimia nervosa, Habermas utilises a model proposed by Devereux (1970) for culture-bound syndromes. It encompasses the influence of cultural factors on unconscious conflicts which lead to the formation of symptoms, and also deals with the effects of labelling.

Habermas (1992) suggests that the conflicts aroused in adolescent girls in respect to the development of gender-identity and the changes in their anatomy, combined with the abuse of culturally condoned techniques such as dieting, led some individuals to "invent" bulimia nervosa. As Beumont (1988) had commented, their behaviour may best be considered simply as a response to the predicament of overconcern with body weight and shape. However, once it was established that impulsive binge-eating, self-induced vomiting and an exaggerated concern about body weight constitutes a syndrome and merits a medical diagnosis (Russell, 1979), it might be predicted that a series of effects would ensue:

1. Bulimic women who previously had regarded their disturbed behaviour as a unique perversion of which they were ashamed, came to realise that it was an experience they shared with many others.
2. Consequently, they could feel free to seek professional help for their disorder rather than hide it from their medical and other attendants.
3. The attribution of the label of illness rather than that of deviant behaviour diminished their sense of responsibility and reduced the feelings of shame and guilt associated with the disturbance.
4. Some patients actually came to imitate bulimic behaviour, to assume its characteristics merely for the secondary gain accorded to the diagnosis.
5. Hence, even the motivation for bulimic behaviour changed. In the days when bulimia nervosa patients concealed their behaviour, it was their emotional needs for intimacy and dependency which were displaced to eating and purging. Women tried to solve conflicts concerning autonomy by the pseudo-autonomy of their disordered eating behaviour. As bulimia has become a matter of public concern, the disturbed behaviour has assumed a new meaning. By not hiding their symptoms, patients have access to secondary gain from their illness. The status of being a bulimia patient confers on the sufferer a sense of identity through membership of an exclusive group. This phenomenon is not dissimilar to that operating for the "me too anorexic" described by Bruch (1987).

A net result of these processes is that bulimia nervosa has rapidly changed from being a rare condition to a common one. It took Russell (1979) six and a half years to collect the 30 patients he described in his pioneering publication from the Maudsley Hospital, one of London's main dieting disorders units. Hoek (1991) now reports an annual incidence of 9.9 per 100 000 in the Netherlands. Furthermore, as the illness has acquired status, it has become something to which patients may cling as a means of avoiding the traumata of everyday life. The assumption of an invalid role is as important in dieting disorders as it is in other illnesses.

While Habermas's thesis is provocative, his historical reconstruction must be assessed carefully against the evidence of the literature. Many of the characteristics he sees as the end-result of the process of labelling were described in earlier accounts of the syndrome. For instance, Abraham and Beumont (1982) reported that some patients used their behaviour in a manipulative way against parents or husband, as if to say "now look what you have made me do". The label itself was not necessary to invoke guilt and care. It is yet to be shown that this sort of reaction is more common in the mid-1990s than it was in the early 1980s.

PATIENTS' PERCEPTIONS OF THEIR BODY SHAPE

Do dieting disordered patients have a distorted perception of their body shape? Lasegue (1873) first suggested they might:

> The patient, when told she cannot live upon an amount of food that would not support an infant, replies that it furnishes her sufficient nourishment, and adds she is neither changed nor thinner.

Bruch (1962) attached great importance to statements like these. She believed they did not signify simply a denial of illness, but rather that they indicated an important psychopathological feature characteristic of the illness. She believed that normalisation of body image was a precondition for recovery.

Every clinician who deals with anorexia nervosa will recall patients who deny their emaciation, sometimes with good insight:

- "I realise you are right when you say I am too thin, but I just can't see it myself."

Others will argue differently, holding untenable assumptions:

- "I know I'm fat because the tops of my legs touch each other and my stomach sticks out. I should be able to put a ruler across my hip bones without it touching my stomach."

Slade and Russell (1973) undertook the first empirical studies into body shape perception in anorexia nervosa patients, stimulating other groups, such as Garner and Garfinkel in Toronto and Vandereycken and Meerman in Europe, to follow their lead. A "distorted body image" was included as one of the five necessary criteria for the diagnosis of anorexia nervosa in DSM-III (APA, 1980), and the concept persisted, albeit more tentatively, in DSM-III-R (APA, 1987); thus: "[there is] a disturbance in the way in which one's body weight, size or shape is experienced." However, both Garner and Garfinkel (1981) and Hsu (1982) have pointed out the inconsistency of reports in the literature. Not all patients with anorexia nervosa have a distorted perception of themselves and, on the other hand, the phenomenon is not confined to anorexia patients—it occurs in other subjects as well, particularly during adolescence.

There have been several detailed surveys of the area, notably by Garfinkel and Garner (1982), Slade (1985), Meerman, Vandereycken and Napierski (1986) and Touyz and Beumont (1987), as well as a special issue of the *British Journal of Psychiatry* in 1988 which was devoted to body image perception. It is not our intention to present yet another review, but rather to summarise some of our own studies which may be relevant to the persistence of illness in dieting disordered patients.

We used a camera with a distorting lens which could be manipulated so as to alter the horizontal dimension of the subject's image projected through a video monitor. Test–retest reliability was comparable to that reported by Garfinkel and colleagues (1978, 1979) using a similar technique. In our first study (Touyz et al, 1984b) we compared 15 female anorexia nervosa patients with age- and sex-matched healthy controls. The mean responses of our patient and control groups were similar and accurate when asked to gauge their current silhouette, although responses in the patient group varied more widely in either direction. Furthermore, although they were clearly underweight (mean BMI=17.2), the anorexic subjects indicated that they wished to be 20% thinner than they already were.

The latter responses instigated an attempt, inspired by a report of Crisp and Kalucy (1974), to distinguish between the subjects' actual perception of their body shapes, and how they "felt" themselves to be. Differing sets of instructions were devised for various tasks, leading to the identification of four different responses:

1. A cognitive response, or how the subject actually knew she looked objectively.
2. An affective response based on how she felt she looked.
3. An optative response which represented how she would have liked to look.
4. An "average physique" response, or how the subject considered a normal person would look. For this, the subject's picture on the screen was replaced by a picture of a young woman of average weight for height, and the instruction given to adjust the dial so that the image represented what the subject considered "average".

Using these parameters, we studied 33 anorexia nervosa patients, 13 bulimia nervosa patients and 15 healthy controls (Touyz et al, 1985). All subjects were female, and none had previous experiences of body-shape perception experiments.

Control subjects were able to estimate their current shape accurately, both in response to the cognitive and the affective instruction. Bulimia patients overestimated on the cognitive response, and both anorexia and bulimia patients overestimated on the affective response, "feeling" themselves much larger than they actually were. Bulimia patients and normal subjects chose an ideal shape significantly thinner than their present silhouette, but the anorexia patients were content with their present cachetic appearances. This last finding was at variance with the responses of anorexics in the first study, who had been partially re-fed and were at higher weights.

A third (and as yet unpublished) study was devised to examine the effects of treatment on these estimations. A large group (N=73) of hospitalised anorexia nervosa patients (and a smaller group N=16) of bulimia nervosa patients were assessed during 4 weeks' of treatment. In this time the anorexia nervosa patients had gained weight at a rate of 1.5 kg per week while the bulimia nervosa patients maintained their normal weights. Our findings (labelled Tests 1–4) are illustrated in Figure 12.2. There were no significant differences between the anorexia and bulimia nervosa patients on the cognitive, affective or "average physique" tasks over the 4-week period. However, their optative responses were significantly different at both the first and second assessment (p = 0.05). The anorexia nervosa patients initially acknowledged that they were too thin and wished to be larger, whilst the normal-weight bulimia nervosa patients wished to be 80% of their current size. This difference was no longer apparent after 4 weeks. Like their bulimic counterparts, the anorexia nervosa patients, who had gained weight, now wished to be smaller. This pattern of findings is consistent with the clinical observation that anorexia nervosa patients will often agree to gain some weight initially only to become anxious after a few kilogrammes that they will become or have already become too fat.

PREOCCUPATION WITH DEATH IN PATIENTS WITH DIETING DISORDERS

Unfortunately, one of the things anorexia nervosa patients do well is to bring about their own premature demise. Long-term follow-up studies in anorexia nervosa (Theander, 1985; Tolstrup, et al, 1985; Crisp et al, 1992; Ratnasuriya et al, 1991) suggest that 20% die within 20 years, with the chronicity rates approaching mortality rates over this time. This is unacceptably high when the youth and premorbid health of the sufferers is considered. Patients at greatest risk are those with clinical features of emaciation and persistent purging behaviours leading to metabolic derangement. During severe emaciation, it is hard to argue that death is far away, figuratively or realistically. The appearance of the patient attests to this fact and despite initial denial, many will recount death-related dream imagery, concerns and preoccupations if enquiry is made in a suitably open-ended and impersonal manner (Jackson et al, 1993).

The following vignette describes a 16-year-old girl who participated in a study in which anorexic patients were compared with normal adolescent school pupils using the Concepts of Death Questionnaire (Russell, Halasz and Beumont, 1991). Her drawings, shown in Figure 12.3, demonstrate what was occupying her thoughts at a time when her weight was only 35 kg. She drew her own "gift-wrapped coffin" with the family standing in line above it and later her smiling face in a transparent coffin preceded by a crying skeleton and an obese, hirsute adolescent—her perception of herself before she started dieting. She also drew a thin and forlorn Paddington Bear

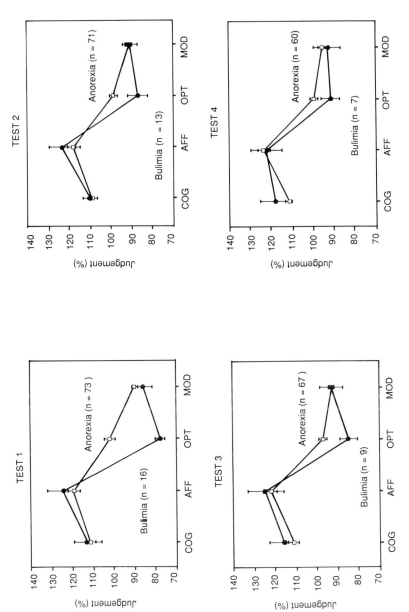

FIGURE 12.2   Cognitive, affective, optative and model (average) scores for patients with anorexia and bulimia nervosa.

Figure 12.3 Drawings by a 16-year-old anorexia nervosa patient who was preoccupied with themes of death.

with a label attached which beseeched the reader to "please take care of this bear". This was at a time when her parents could not bring themselves to insist that she accept medical treatment.

Case History Nerida was the older child of middle-aged parents. She became moderately obese after a precocious puberty, and began to diet 2–3 years later on the advice of her dancing teacher. One year prior to presentation, her maternal grandmother had become terminally ill with carcinoma of the ovary and had "wasted away" by the time of her death 5 months later. Nerida and her mother went on an overseas trip soon after the funeral (the trip being recalled in her drawings of the Tower of London and some forbidden food items). From this point on, weight loss due to restriction and vomiting was severe, the patient described mood swings (depicted as crying and smiling faces) and declared her determination to starve even if it resulted in her death. Hospitalisation was recommended but Nerida refused, supported by her father who said later, by way of justification, that his daughter had threatened to "die" if she were admitted to hospital. Nevertheless, in response to repeated threats of enforced hospitalisation, and with supervision from a nutritionist, she gained weight as an outpatient, stabilising at a healthy level and resuming menstruation nine months after presentation. During her therapy sessions, she spoke of her feelings occasioned by the death of her grandmother and expressed angry feelings towards her parents for what she saw as their tendency to infantilise and overprotect her. She also stated her determination to "show them" (and her pessimistic therapist) that she could recover without hospitalisation.

This girl made a full recovery and has remained well for more than 4 years at the time of writing. When last seen she chatted excitedly about the dress she would wear at her school ball and the young man who would escort her. The death-defying preoccupations of the illness were relegated to the past and seemingly forgotten.

It has been suggested by Goodsitt (1985) that the patient's "concentration camp" appearance is an unconscious expression of protest at her parents for unwittingly thwarting the emergence of self. Knowing the fragile self-esteems of our patients' parents, their rigidity, their well-meaning intrusiveness and their unhappiness to which their "perfect child" has been the antidote, we can see how this might come about with the advent of adolescence. We can also understand the painful dilemma posed by the normative tasks of this developmental period. Anorexia nervosa then represents both the solution and a mode of survival of the self. When asked to rate the parenting they had received, anorexic adolescents idealised it, reporting their parents to be more affectionate and less overprotective than did matched controls or unselected adolescent psychiatric patients (Russell, Kopec-Schrader, Beumont and Kay, 1992). Perhaps this finding was to be expected, as our patients find it hard to deal constructively with anger, which they internalise in self-destructive, guilt-ridden, death-related behaviours.

Of course, these phenomena are relevant to the patients' treatment. Validating the emergence of the healthy self is the prime objective of psychotherapy and must occur *pari passu* with the restoration of the body. Essentially, the approach should be eclectic lest slavish adherence to any particular method or school leads the therapist to behave unwittingly in ways which might be experienced as persecutory (Meares and Hobson, 1977). Therapeutic pitfalls which must be avoided include failing to listen to what the patient is saying (or more often not saying), invasively insisting on disclosure of a "pathogenic secret", being beguiled by articulation of psychological jargon or colluding with placatory elements to foster the emergence of a "false self". The defensive purpose of the latter is to forestall intrusion, and hence avoid therapeutic engagement leading to change.

In the early part of treatment, engaging the patient is the primary objective. This can be achieved by being "real", demonstrating respect for and non-intrusive interest in the patient's likes, dislikes, beliefs and feelings so as to generate the sense of secure acceptance and self-worth necessary for the tentative experiment of being oneself. The therapist must then assist the patient in becoming more aware of and responsive to her own physical and emotional states. The ultimate goal of treatment is to obviate the necessity for the anorexic "defence".

The need for privacy and secrecy which underlies the deviant behaviour should be understood as an expression of difficulty with boundaries and identity. Similarly the preoccupation with death and its message of desperation must be appreciated even if it cannot be verbalised. Fear of change, growing-up, separation, retribution, existential loneliness, unforeseen loss—even death itself are aspects of this. Anorexia nervosa may afford the sufferer a spurious sense of control. Recovery is attended by the reassertion of "healthy" denial (Russell, Halasz and Beumont, 1991), the return of a sense of humour, and involvement in age-appropriate activities such as dating . . . and fighting with parents!

The development of a trusting relationship with someone outside the often idealised and overenmeshed family not only signifies psychological separation, but may permit expression of disavowed affects leading to disclosure of a "pathogenic secret". Whilst this must never be pursued too assiduously, it is important not to ignore the shame and self-loathing associated with abusive experiences, be these physical, sexual or emotional. Validation can lead to mastery and empowerment, but regressive self-destructive behaviours and dissociative symptoms often obfuscate the process, as may the power differential between therapist and patient.

Treatment should be made as user-friendly as possible so that patients are not deterred from seeking help. Initiatives here include lenient, ambulant, hospital nutritional rehabilitation programmes (Touyz et al, 1984a), incorporating exercise rewards (Beumont et al, 1994), using leave and outings as incentives for weight gain and compliance. As hospitalisation itself can lead to invalidism and de-skill patients for life in the real world, it is important that attention be directed towards using outpatient treatment whenever possible, minimising interruption of education. Work experience or part-time employment should also be encouraged provided that they do not compromise treatment goals, which must include not only work with the patient's family but ongoing education in respect to nutrition and to appropriate social interactions. As the patient moves back to the world and concerns of her peers, the threat of death recedes into the background of an active and healthy life.

CONCLUSIONS

There are many factors that contribute to the maintenance of illness in anorexia and bulimia nervosa patients. Self-starvation and the consequent undernutrition set up a vicious circle of emotional upset and behavioural disturbance. This pattern of illness must be interrupted and the patient returned to normal eating and a normal weight if therapy is to have a chance of success (Touyz and Beumont, 1989). But besides that, other psychological processes must be addressed. We have suggested some of the concerns of our patients that inhibit recovery from their illness: their low self-esteem, fostered by sexist community atittudes; their susceptibility to influence by the media; the advantages offered by an invalid role; their disturbed perception of what is a normal body shape; and even their deliberate courting of death by their risk taking behaviours.

We must learn the virtue of patience for it often takes years to complete the therapeutic process in these illnesses (Hsu, Crisp and Harding, 1979). Then, freed from the shackles of anorexia or bulimia nervosa, our patients can do well at something which has hitherto evaded them—namely, being their own valuable and unique selves, at which point we as therapists should quietly withdraw and leave them to it.

ACKNOWLEDGEMENT

We wish to thank Dr S. Murray for permission to quote from her unpublished doctoral thesis at the University of Sydney.

REFERENCES

Abraham, S.E. and Beumont, P.J.V. (1982). How patients describe bulimia or binge-eating. *Psychological Medicine*, **12**, 625–635.

American Psychiatric Association (1980). *Diagnostic and Statistical Manual of Mental Disorders*, 3rd edn. Washington, DC: APA.

American Psychiatric Association (1987). *Diagnostic and Statistical Manual of Mental Disorders*, 3rd revised edn. Washington, DC: APA.

Bell, R.M. (1985). *Holy Anorexia*. Chicago: University Press.

Berger, J. (1972). *Ways of Seeing*. London: BBC and Penguin Books.

Beumont, P.J.V. (1988). Bulimia: is it an illness entity? *International Journal of Eating Disorders*, **7**, 167–176.

Beumont, P.J.V., Arthur, B., Russell, J.D. and Touyz, S.W. (1994). Excessive physical activity in dieting disordered patients: theoretical aspects and treatment implications. *International Journal of Eating Disorders*, **15**, 21–36.

Beumont, P.J.V., Beardwood, C.J. and Russell, G.F.M. (1972). The occurrence of the syndrome of anorexia nervosa in male subjects. *Psychological Medicine*, **2**, 216–231.

Bruch, H. (1962). Perceptual and conceptual disturbances in anorexia nervosa. *Psychological Medicine*, **14**, 187–194.

Bruch, H. (1974). *Eating Disorders: Obesity Anorexia Nervosa and the Person Within*. London: Routledge & Kegan Paul.

Bruch, H. (1987). Four decades of anorexia nervosa. In: D. Garner and P. Garfinkel (Eds), *Handbook of Psychotherapy in Anorexia Nervosa and Bulimia Nervosa*. New York: Guilford Press.

Brumberg, J.J. (1988). *Fasting Girls: The Emergence of Anorexia Nervosa as a Modern Disease*. Cambridge, Mass.: Harvard University Press.

Brumberg, J.J. (1990). Invited address to the Fourth International Conference on Eating Disorders, New York.

Burke, B.S., Reed, R.B., Van der Berg, A.S. and Stuart, H.C. (1959). Caloric and protein intakes of children between 1 and 18 years of age. *Paediatrics*, **24** (Suppl. 93), 922–940.

Bynum, C.W. (1987). *Holy Feast and Holy Fast*. Berkley: University of California Press.

Chernin, K. (1987). *Womansize: The Tyranny of Slenderness*. Allen & Unwin, Sydney.

Collins, E.M. (1988). Education for healthy body weight: helping adolescents balance the cultural pressure for thinness. *Journal of School Health*, **58**, 227–231.

Crisp, A.H. (1980). *Anorexia Nervosa: Let Me Be*. London: Academic Press.

Crisp, A.H., Calender, J.S., Halek, C. and Hsu, L.K.G. (1992). Long term mortality in anorexia nervosa. *British Journal of Psychiatry*, **161**, 104–107.

Crisp, A.H. and Kalucy, R.S. (1974). Aspects of the perceptual disorder in anorexia nervosa. *British Journal of Medical Psychology*, **47**, 349–361.

Crookshank, F.G. (1931). Quoted by Habermas, T. (1991): The role of psychiatric and medical traditions in the discovery and description of anorexia nervosa in France, Germany and Italy, 1873–1918. *Journal of Mental Disease*, **179**, 360–365.

Davies, E. and Furnham, A. (1986). The dieting and body shape concerns of adolescent families. *Journal of Child Psychology and Psychiatry*, **27**, 417–428.

Devereux, G. (1970). Normal and abnormal. Reprinted in: G. Devereaux (Ed.), *Basic Problems of Ethnopsychiatry*. Chicago: University Press, 1980.

Frieden, B. (1983). *The Second Stage*. London: Abacus.

Galdston, R. (1974). Mind over matter: observations of 50 patients hospitalised with anorexia nervosa. *American Academy of Child Psychiatry*, **13**, 246–263.

Garfinkel, P.E. and Garner, D.M. (1982). *Anorexia Nervosa: A Multidimensional Perspective*. New York: Brunner/Mazel.

Garfinkel, P.E., Moldofsky, H., Garner, D.M. (1979). The stability of perceptual disturbances in anorexia nervosa. *Psychological Medicine*, **9**, 703–708.

Garfinkel, P.E., Moldofsky, H., Garner, D.M., Stancer, H.C. and Coscina, D.V. (1978). Body awareness in anorexia nervosa: disturbances in "body image" and "satiety". *Psychosomatic Medicine*, **40**, 487–498.

Garner, D.M. and Garfinkel, P.E. (1981). Body image in anorexia nervosa: measurement, theory and clinical implications. *International Journal of Psychiatry in Medicine*, **11**, 263–284.

Garner, D.M., Garfinkel, P.E., Rockert, W. and Olmsted, M.P. (1987). A prospective study of eating disturbances in the ballet. *Psychotherapy and Psychosomatics*, **48**, 170–175.

Goodsitt, A. (1985). Self psychology and the treatment of anorexia nervosa. In: D. Garner and P. Garfinkel (Eds), *Handbook of Psychotherapy in Anorexia Nervosa and Bulimia Nervosa*. New York: Guilford Press.

Gordon, R.A. (1990). *Anorexia and Bulimia: Anatomy of a Social Epidemic*. Cambridge, Mass.: Basil Blackwell.

Habermas, T. (1990). *Heisshunger: Historische Bedingungen der Bulimia Nervosa*. Frankfurt: Fisher, Taschenbuch Verlag.

Habermas, T. (1991). The role of psychiatric and medical traditions in the discovery and descriptions of anorexia nervosa in France, Germany and Italy, 1873–1918. *Journal of Mental Diseases*, **179**, 360–365.

Habermas, T. (1992). Possible effects of the popular and medical recognition of bulimia nervosa. *British Journal of Medical Psychology*, **65**(1), 59–66.

Hoek, H.W. (1991). The incidence and prevalence of anorexia nervosa and bulimia nervosa in primary care. *Psychological Medicine*, **2**, 45–60.

Hsu, L.K.G. (1982). Is there a disturbance in body image in anorexia nervosa. *Journal of Nervous and Mental Disease*, **170**(5), 305–307.

Hsu, L.K.G., Crisp, A.H. and Harding, B. (1979). Outcome of anorexia nervosa. *Lancet*, **i**, 62–55.

Jackson, C., Tabin, J., Russell, J. and Touyz, S.W. (1993). Themes of death: Helmut Thomas' Anorexia Nervosa (1967). A Research note. *International Journal of Eating Disorders*, **14**(4), 433–437.

Keys, A., Brozek, J., Henschel, A., Mickelsen, O. and Taylor, H.L. (1950). *The Biology of Human Starvation*. Minneapolis: University of Minnesota Press.

Lasegue, E.C. (1873). Translated as "On anorexia", in: M.R. Kaufman and M. Heiman (Eds), *Evolution of Psychosomatic Concepts: A Paradigm*. New York: International Universities Press, 1964, p. 148.

Lucas, A.R., Beard, C.M., O'Fallon, W.M. and Kurland, L.T. (1991). Fifty year trends in the incidence of anorexia nervosa in Rochester, Minn: a population-based study. *American Journal of Psychiatry*, **148**, 917–922.

Matthews, J.J. (1984). *Good and Mad Women: The Historical Constitution of Femininity in Twentieth Century Australia*. Syndey: George Allen & Unwin.

Meares, R. and Hobson, R. (1977). The persecutory therapist. *British Journal of Medical Psychology*, **50**, 349–359.

Meerman, R., Vandereycken, W. and Napierski, C. (1986). Methodological problems of body image research in anorexia nervosa patients. *Acta Psychiatrica Belgica*, **86**, 42–51.

Mitchell, P.B. and Truswell, A.S. (1987). Body composition in anorexia nervosa and starvation. In: P.J.V. Beumont, G.D. Burrows and R.C. Casper (Eds), *Handbook of Eating Disorders. Part 1: Anorexia and Bulimia Nervosa*. Amsterdam: Elsevier, pp. 45–72.

Murray, S.H. (1991). Sociocultural factors in eating disorders. Unpublished doctoral thesis, University of Sydney.

Orbach, S. (1978). *Fat is a Feminist Issue*. New York: Paddington Press.

Ratnasurya, R.H., Eisler, I., Szmukler, G.I. and Russell, G.F.M. (1991). Anorexia nervosa: outcome and prognostic factors after 20 years. *British Journal of Psychiatry,* **158**, 495–502.

Russell, G.F.M. (1979). Bulimia nervosa: an ominous variant in anorexia nervosa. *Psychological Medicine, 9,* 429–448.

Russell, J. and Beumont, P.J.V. (in press). Risk and prevention in eating disorders. In: G. Burrows and B. Raphael (Eds) *Handbook of Preventative Psychiatry*. Amsterdam: Elsevier.

Russell, J., Halasz, G. and Beumont, P.J.V. (1991). Death related themes in anorexia nervosa. *Journal of Adolescence, 13,* 311–326.

Russell, J.D., Kopec-Schrader, E., Beumont, P.J.V. and Rey, J. (1992). The PBI in adolescent patients with anorexia nervosa. *Acta Psychiatrica, 86,* 236–239.

Shisslak, C.M. and Crago, M. (1987). Primary prevention of eating disorders. *Journal of Consulting and Clinical Psychology, 55,* 660–667.

Slade, P.D. (1985). A review of body-image studies in anorexia nervosa and bulimia nervosa. *Journal of Psychiatric Research, 19,* 255–265.

Slade, P.D. and Russell, G.F.M. (1973). Awareness of body dimensions in anorexia nervosa: cross-sectional and longitudinal studies. *Psychological Medicine, 3,* 188–199.

Steinem, G. (1992). *Revolution from within—a Book of Self-esteem*. Boston: Little Brown.

Steiner-Adair, C. (1986). The body politic: normal female adolescent development and the development of eating disorders. *Journal of the American Academy of Psychoanalysis, 14,* 95–114.

Theander, S. (1985). Outcome and prognosis in anorexia nervosa and bulimia: some results of previous investigations, compared with those of a Swedish long-term study. *Journal of Psychiatric Research, 19,* 493–508.

Tolstrup, K., Brinch, M., Isagen, T., Severin, B. and Olesson, N. (1985). Long-term outcome of 151 cases of anorexia nervosa. *Acta Psychiatrica Scandinavica, 71,* 380–387.

Touyz, S.W., Beumont, P.J.V., Glaun, D., Philips, T. and Cowie, I. (1984a). Comparison of lenient and strict operant conditioning programmes in refeeding patients with anorexia nervosa. *British Journal of Psychiatry, 144,* 512–520.

Touyz, S.W., Beumont, P.J.V., Collins, J.K., McCabe, M. and Jupp, J. (1984b). Body shape perception and its disturbance in anorexia nervosa. *British Journal of Psychiatry, 144,* 167–171.

Touyz, S.W., Beumont, P.J.V., Collins, J.K. and Cowie, I. (1985). Body shape perception in bulimia and anorexia nervosa. *International Journal of Eating Disorders, 4,* 259–265.

Touyz, S.W. and Beumont, P.J.V. (1987). Body image distortion. In: P.J.V. Beumont, G.D. Burrows and R. Casper (Eds), *Handbook of Eating Disorders. Part 1: Anorexia Nervosa and Bulimia.* Amsterdam: Elsevier, pp. 173–189.

Touyz, S.W. and Beumont, P.J.V. (1989). Anorexia and bulimia nervosa. In: P.J.V. Beumont and R. Hampshire (Eds) *Textbook of Psychiatry*, Melbourne: Blackwells Australia.

Touyz, S.W., Kopec-Schrader, E.M. and Beumont, P.J.V. (1993). Anorexia nervosa in males. *Australian and New Zealand Journal of Psychiatry, 27,* 512–517.

Vandereycken, W. and Meerman, R. (1988). Body image disturbances in eating disorders from the viewpoint of experimental research. In: K. Pirke, W. Vandereycken and D. Ploog (Eds), *The Psychobiology of Anorexia Nervosa.* Berlin: Springer Verlag.

Van Deth, R. and Vandereycken, W. (1988). *Van Vastenwonder Tot Magersucht.* Amsterdam: Boon Heppel.

Wolf, N. (1991). *The Beauty Myth: How Images of Beauty Are Used Against Women.* London: Vintage.

13

Family Patterns in Eating Disorders: Going Round in Circles, Getting Nowhere Fasting

MIREILLE COLAHAN
AND
ROB SENIOR
Institute of Psychiatry, London, UK

For many years researchers and therapists have considered the involvement of families in the development and maintenance of eating disorders. Gull (1874) and Charcot (1889) both felt that the anorexic needed to be removed from the family environment. Selvini-Palazzoli (1974) saw the family's involvement in terms of secret coalitions, transgenerational loyalties and covert marital disharmony. Bruch (1974) felt that the problem lay in the patient's difficulty in gaining a sense of independence from her mother. Minuchin et al (1978) considered that the "anorexic family" has a particular structure, with problems concerning enmeshment, overprotectiveness, rigidity, and lack of conflict resolution. Stern et al (1981) located the problem around issues of separation and individuation at adolescence. Szmukler et al (1985) have considered the contribution of expressed emotion (EE) in families to the outcome of therapy. Others have thought in terms of intergenerational influences, hierarchical control systems, myths and loyalties, loss and grieving, and sexual abuse.

All of these ideas have greatly influenced clinicians, and many of these concepts and theories have been used and adapted in their clinical work with adolescent and adult patients with eating disorders and their families. Current evidence supports a

Handbook of Eating Disorders: Theory, Treatment and Research.
Edited by G. Szmukler, C. Dare and J. Treasure.
© 1995 John Wiley & Sons Ltd.

multidetermined aetiology (Garfinkel and Garner, 1982), in which families can play an important but unpredictable part. However, within a systemic model, the search for a family aetiology becomes less relevant. Not only has research failed to find any consistent family characteristics to account for the appearance of eating disorders (see Chapter 9), but theories of family causation have also had the effect of blaming families, which only increases the paralysing guilt experienced by many families and hinders therapeutic endeavours to find solutions.

The separation of "aetiology" and "treatment" represents, in family systems thinking, a linear chronological view which, while helping us to think about the natural history of the condition, runs the risk of keeping professionals "stuck" in their search for family aetiology and pathology. Therapists struggle to make sense of the situation in which the patient, her family and the professionals find themselves. The process of exploring the different beliefs that people hold, and the contrasting meanings which they ascribe to the same behaviour or event, is central to our view of therapy. The descriptions of family dynamics which appear later in this chapter have been gained from our explorations with families. They cannot sensibly be separated from therapy or treatment because the process of exploration is so much a part of therapy. Thus the therapist tries to uncover what is maintaining the situation, what are the beliefs that go on informing the family's behaviour, that lead them to become entrenched in a repetitive pattern of interaction that maintains the symptom in a potentially fatal family paralysis.

Viewing the family as a system, the anorexic "symptom" and the family's response influence each other in a mutual, recursive manner in which cause and blame have little place. One thing leads to another, and is then influenced in return. Thus, when (in the first vignette) we describe Hannah and her mother united in their criticism of a father who resorts to tyrannical outbursts before disappearing to the pub, leading to further collusion between mother and daughter, we are describing a state of affairs, a predictable repetitive cycle for which no single individual can be held responsible and to which all contribute. While avoiding blame, such a view is not without problems. Feminist writers have pointed out that in the face of sexual abuse and violence, where power in relationships is abused almost exclusively by men in relation to women and children, then systemic descriptions which give equal weight to the contributions of all participants are dangerous, and can appear to condone inexcusable behaviour and blame the victims of abuse rather than the perpetrators (Goldner et al, 1990). We are aware of this dilemma, particularly in writing about a condition that primarily affects women and which represents, in view of some authors (e.g. Orbach, 1986), a struggle for power and control.

Throughout this chapter we will take "family" to mean not simply biological family but those closely involved or living with the anorexic. The examples we give are all of female sufferers. The infant's primary caregiver will be referred to as "mother", although it is our belief that this relationship can take many forms and is not necessarily provided by the biological mother; it can be shared between women or men in heterosexual or homosexual couples; it is often provided by grandparents or other members of the extended family. The clinical situations we describe will be of individuals suffering from anorexia nervosa usually of the restricting type

(Garner and Garfinkel, 1988). Some also have bulimic symptoms and many of our observations are equally relevant to bulimia nervosa. We use the term "anorexic" as shorthand, while accepting that to describe individuals in this way has implications for the way in which they are seen.

When an individual develops an unshakeable conviction that it is a vital necessity that she should starve and lose weight, this conviction, and her subsequent behaviour, cannot avoid having a considerable impact on other members of the family. The families whom we see in therapy have not been able to find a way out of this dilemma in which they feel that everything they do to help seems only to provoke more pain and distress, and in which the harder they try to solve the problem, the more entrenched they get. Their ability to create an effective solution has become suppressed, and the chosen solution serves only to perpetuate the problem.

Faced with young people close to death, we must often take a strong, clear and directive position about the desired outcome of the therapy—namely that a way must be found for the patient to eat. A major current school of family therapy, the "co-constructivists" (Hoffman, 1990), disagree with this position. We cannot remain neutral to the outcome of the therapy; we are, however, much concerned with stories and narratives, and in the importance of helping families to construct alternative accounts of their situation in order to empower them to act in different ways.

Working with the families of adult and adolescent anorexics, we have observed that, whereas life-cycle issues may be different, the problems encountered have much in common. Our clinical experience has led us to wonder about separation/individuation issues, as we observe strong links between the onset of the symptom and life-cycle stages which revive separation anxieties, such as entrance into secondary school, puberty, leaving home, marriage, divorce, birth and death. Speculation about the prototype of all separation experiences (i.e. birth and the weaning process) has shown us that, where it has been possible to access information regarding this period of our patients' lives, they have experienced traumatic loss or disruption. It is our view that some of the most painful separation traumas influence the elaboration of the infant's early relationships, and are relevant to her subsequent relationship to food.

Adolescents with eating disorders present as youngsters whose lives appear to have been put on "hold": they are no longer children, but neither can they achieve adulthood. Adults who develop eating disorders demonstrate a similar difficulty in dealing flexibly with the process of development and moving on. Whilst appearing to lead more or less normal lives in certain areas, the focus and variety diminishes. Major issues of separation, control and independence are at stake and they appear to fear that any kind of closeness or intimacy will reduce their autonomy. In order to be their own being they have to find a way of differentiating from the family. By chance they find that they are good at slimming, at something which is different from the family and which does not involve relationships with others: this becomes an obsessive hobby, and gradually an autonomous condition which rules their lives.

As we try to make sense of the anorexic individual's behaviour and her family's response to it, we describe a "fit" or compatibility between the anorexic's inner world and the family's behaviour. In outlining our view of the inner world of the anorexic we draw on psychodynamic constructs, whilst descriptions of the family's response are based on our clinical observations. These descriptions would conventionally be seen as formulations—psychodynamic in the case of the inner world, systemic in terms of family dynamics—but are best used as maps and guides for the understanding of therapists and of the patients and families who seek their help. Their relevance and utility change from patient to patient, and from family to family.

Our understanding of the anorexic's inner world is based on a psychodynamic view of the mechanisms and processes involved in the very early stages of the elaboration of the infant's object relations (see Chapter 7). This portrays the origins of a "bind" between mother and daughter which leads to their mutual stuckness when the anorexia develops.

In utero and for the first months of life, the infant is in a state of symbiotic fusion with the mother. She can only represent her own body and her mother's body as an indivisible unit. For her to develop into a separate and autonomous individual, two processes have to take place: she must break free from her mother, and she must establish a distinct and different identity for herself (Mahler, 1961). Klein (1977) describes the fundamental importance of the newborn's first relationship with her mother. The mother is felt to be the source of nourishment and of life itself, but, due to complex and primitive processes of projection and introjection, she is also experienced as threatening and persecutory. In this way the infant has a relationship to both a gratifying and nourishing mother, and a devouring and persecutory one, and the balance between good and bad objects is in a constant state of fluctuation, both in the infant's inner world and in its external world.

However, external circumstances play a vital role in the elaboration of this relationship: if adaptation to the external world is disturbed, the relationship to the mother starts at a great disadvantage. In this case the infant will find it harder to experience gratification, and as a result will not retain a good enough experience of her mother.

The infant's desire to maintain this close "symbiotic" relationship with her mother, whilst also desperately striving to separate, is clearly observable and is re-enacted before our eyes by the adolescent anorexic; but we also see it in both the adolescent's and the adult's relationship to food—how they simultaneously have to surround themselves with it, but fight to avoid it.

In our attempts to understand the anorexic's relationship to people and to food, we have also found Winnicott's (1951) view of the evolution of the infant's earliest relationships very useful. He describes the use she makes of the "transitional object", which bridges the gap between a state of undifferentiation with the mother, and a state in which the infant has achieved a sufficiently good internalised mother with whom to identify, leading to a sense of having been well cared for. He considers the transitional object as a "permitted object of addiction" created by the infant as a soothing transition between the external and the internal mother.

Our observations of adolescent and adult anorexics suggest to us that there appear to have been difficulties both in absorbing a sense that they have been looked after well, but also in renouncing the initial "symbiotic" state with the mother. The anorexic's desire to maintain this very close bond can indeed bind her in a compulsive relationship, where the mother is experienced as being the only one able to feed her, yet unable to feed her anything but poison. There is a constant seeking for that close nurturing relationship, which is simultaneously feared as engulfing and dangerous, just as the craved nourishment itself is felt to be persecutory and poisonous. The mother can experience this as an endorsement of herself, but also feel very persecuted: she is reminded of the pleasure and tyranny of caring for a small baby.

However, whatever the reality of the nature and quality of the early mother/infant relationship, the manner in which the anorexic has experienced it does not make it easy for her to make good and permanent use of it. She is left with little or no internal resource on which to rely and with which to process painful and conflictual feelings. She appears to be constantly trying to replace the good nourishing mother of infancy, seeking repeatedly outside of herself symbolic substitutes that will replenish her and make her feel better. She makes use of "pathological transitory objects of addiction" (McDougall, 1989), which only appease her temporarily. She behaves like an addict, for whom the object of addiction is felt to be excessively desirable, even vital, yet when absorbed, becomes poisonous. Similarly, the mother finds herself compelled to fill the space inside her daughter even though what she offers is rejected as so dangerous.

We see the anorexic's need for closeness with her mother, and her desperate attempts to free herself; and how she surrounds herself compulsively with food, but is terrified of consuming it. So whilst convinced that she has control over food, and that this control will free her, her relationship with food binds her in a more restricting, demanding, intimate relationship than any personal alliance could ever do. She becomes taken over by this behaviour, which becomes of vital necessity to her, to which she is virtually addicted (Szmukler and Tantam, 1984): an addiction which is a state of enslavement very similar to the extremely dependent relationship of the infant to its mother.

In the anorexic "addictive play" (McDougall, 1989), other members of the family can be recruited into the dance. They are induced to play the roles of bit players existing in the patient's inner word, although of course their own psychic conflicts must suit them to the identifications in question. Once recruited, they are expected to fulfil the soothing role of the transitional objects of childhood, to maintain the anorexic's narcissistic homeostasis, to make everything better. However, they can only offer temporary relief, and she is bound to be frustrated and disappointed.

The father will often experience himself, and be experienced, as an unwelcome and threatening intruder, a "troublesome rival" (Freud, 1931), who gets in the space between the mother and the infant and disrupts the illusion of oneness. He is sometimes experienced as a disgusting and repulsive person, to be avoided at all costs, and from whom mother must be protected. If both parents collude with their adolescent's infantile fantasy, we observe an enmeshed mother/daughter dyad, and a peripheral father. This requires a father who is prepared to go along with the situation, allowing the intense enmeshed relationship with the mother to continue, maintaining his peripheral position and the image of a father who is seen as ineffectual and impotent in most respects.

The lack of an established and repeated father image diminishes the importance of the marriage, putting it in second place to the mother/child dyad; the daughter often fears that the father will become sexual with her, and this inhibits the father and the family from giving him a positive role in countering the anorexic behaviour. By remaining a "little girl", triumph over mother is avoided and sexuality in relation to father is kept in abeyance. Some fathers share the hope that if they do not interfere with the relationship between mother and daughter then everything will be all right. Other fathers respond to this situation in a variety of ways. Some appear bewildered, others indifferent. Yet others respond to the powerlessness and exclusion by becoming critical or rejecting of mother, daughter or both. This frequently leads to speculations concerning both physical and sexual abuse (see Chapter 9).

We are also aware that many men, fathers and spouses, respond to their powerlessness and frustration with violence and anger which borders on abuse. In addition, as described above, fathers may be experienced as dangerous or intrusive whatever they do. As a result they, like the mother, may become paralysed. For them, the prohibiting force is their fear that they will be seen as an abuser if they take a strong position against colluding with the anorexia.

Where the relationship between the parents already contains rejection or violence, the anorexic and her symptoms become drawn into the battlefield. She may take on the task of protecting her mother by placing herself and her symptoms between the parents, exposing herself in the process to real risks of violence, but in the name of anorexia. The quarrel between the parents that ensues further incapacitates them from functioning effectively to extract their daughter from her symptoms. This process is also evident in couples where the eating disorder can appear to be an acceptable alternative to hatred. Rejecting, cruel, even murderous feelings can be expressed, apparently rationally, as resentment of the anorexia. Alternatively, in adolescents particularly, the symptoms of the eating disorder may have the effect of bringing together parents in danger of separating, or of distracting from other parental crises—life-threatening illness, alcohol abuse, bereavement or other loss such as children leaving home. Under these circumstances an apparent need may perpetuate the symptom, reducing motivation to change.

Our own clinical observations and those of others suggest that in families with an anorexic member, siblings may appear relatively free to follow a path, familiar in British culture, of adolescent rebellion and self-discovery or, as in the vignettes below, the family preserves the belief in the "perfect" unaffected child. In either case the "freedom" is often illusory. Splitting off all badness and misery into the anorexic and all goodness and health into the siblings does not fully recognise either.

Roberto (1988) talks of the well sibling having forged their identity by a process of de-identification from their sick sister at great cost to both, and it would seem likely that the apparent freedom of the well sibling is at the expense of considerable loss of an appropriate sibling relationship and of parental attention. The perceived freedom of the well sibling needs to be challenged, as their choices may in fact be very limited, and that which is seen as healthy or unaffected may in a different sense be restricted or oppressive. The well siblings, from our observations, often experience themselves as needing to conform to particular family beliefs or to collude with the denial of their own distress. The parents may be keen to protect the well siblings from being damaged or contaminated by the therapy. On the other hand, the unaffected sibling may join with the parents in trying to get their sister to eat, thus further distorting the normal sibling relationship. These sibling-related processes also serve the pressure not to change, enhancing maintenance of the symptom.

The following vignettes illustrate some of the connections, as we have constructed them, between people's inner worlds, their experience of themselves and the responses of others. As we discussed earlier, there are alternative accounts that could be written from different perspectives, but these stories and the process of creating them has guided our therapy. A "good enough fit" between our ideas and those of the family would seem to be an important prerequisite of effective therapy. The therapeutic initiatives that resulted have not been included except where they clarify the ideas. (Chapter 18 discusses family approaches to treatment.)

VIGNETTE 1

Hannah is a 16-year-old girl who has been alternately starving and bingeing for 18 months, although she has had problems of self-esteem and concern over her body image since she was 13. She is quite socially isolated, and has not attended school regularly for the last three years. She has taken one overdose, although she says it was not a serious suicide attempt.

Hannah has a 19½-year-old brother, Nat, who is seen as the "blue eyed golden haired boy" by the rest of the family. He says that he copes well with his sister's disorder, by "ignoring it and putting it out of his mind". He has just started at university, and has a girlfriend; consequently he is not often at home.

Hannah's mother is in a caring profession. She is a sensitive, thoughtful, patient woman, who looks worried and worn and is very close to her daughter. Hannah's father works with computers. He says that he is "not good at emotional problems",

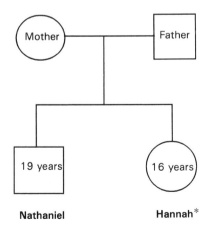

FIGURE 13.1   Vignette 1.

and feels everyone is better off if he does not get involved, leaving that to his wife.

Hannah is a plump, attractive but awkward young girl. All the family sees her as the "patient", and she herself is well informed about her condition. She is disgusted and horrified by her "overweight" body, and starves to reduce it. However, when her level of distress (which she describes as a form of psychic emptiness) becomes intolerable, she feels compelled to binge. This provides temporary relief, which eventually turns into despair and disgust. When she is prevented from bingeing she lashes out, usually harming herself, and sometimes the house and those around her. She does not vomit, therefore her bingeing results in weight gain, even though she exercises excessively. She is trapped in the vicious circle of bingeing–starving–bingeing, and is obsessed with thoughts of food to the exclusion of all else: food is her "whole life".

When Hannah gets distressed and feels the compulsive need to fill herself with food, the family responds: father tries to prevent her forcibly from doing so, Hannah fights back, he becomes enraged and breakages occur. If he does manage to prevent her from bingeing, she breaks the window, cuts herself, or hits her head against the wall until her agony subsides. Father is consumed with guilt at feeling he has harmed her, enraged that she has pushed him to such desperate measures and ends up feeling impotent and frustrated.

Meanwhile, Hannah calms down, phones her mother at work and tells her what her father has done. Mother returns from work, in a panic, furious with father, and berates him for being a useless violent brute, incapable of supporting her adequately; father in shame and despair goes to the pub; Hannah and mother console each other for having to put up with such a creature, Nat sleeps over at his girlfriend's house. Finally Hannah, exhausted, sleeps. Father returns, and a sexual reconciliation takes place between the parents. In the morning Hannah is outraged to find her father reinstated, she refuses to speak to him or to stay in the same room as him. Father feels driven out of the house by the hostility and disgust of his daughter, goes to work and straight to the pub afterwards. Mother's resentment at his lack of support increases, and the link between mother and daughter grows stronger. They form a tight couple, they confide in each other, there is a feeling of exclusion and self-sufficiency in this relationship, in which there is little place for anyone else. Mother's response to Hannah's bingeing is to attempt to "talk her out of it", which involves hours of close intimate talks. There is no place for father or brother in this dyad: mother and daughter unite in their criticism of father, his inability to be a sensitive and caring person. He returns to the pub, and Nat continues getting on with his own life.

The closeness of the mother/daughter dyad thus acts as a distance regulator between husband and wife, taking the pressure off the marital relationship; the illusion that this is a "happy family", and that mother and father are "good parents", is maintained by the "perfect child" Nat.

However, mother, whilst responding to Hannah's needs and joining her in unity against father when he is out of favour, has adult needs of her own which require her to make choices in favour of her husband. Hannah's impossible desire for a symbiotic relationship with her mother is thus repeatedly frustrated, and the vicious cycle continues.

Hannah was born prematurely by emergency Ceasarean section, and spent the first weeks of her life in an incubator. Her mother was unable to feed her baby as she had her first child. Father found his wife's emotional reaction to the event difficult to cope with and put his energy into caring for Nat. Hannah became very unhappy about her body at puberty, and the eating disorder started around the time Nat was leaving home for university. Hannah's initial experience of separation might well have been reactivated at puberty and when her brother left home.

We could hypothesise that Hannah's very early object relationship did not get off to a very auspicious start, and her subsequent behaviour bears this out. She does not appear to have a good enough object inside her to support her, and needs to draw constantly on the outside world in order to maintain any kind of a sense of well-being. Her present feeling of "psychic emptiness" creates a constantly recurring need to fill herself up, but her fix of food or violence gives only temporary relief. Her addiction requires constant refuelling (Colahan, 1991). The perfect vessel for keeping her in a state of permanent fullness is mother, who becomes source of all good, whilst the hostility and hatred is split off and located in father, who becomes the all-bad object.

Mother's response to this is partly activated by her feelings of guilt: she feels compelled to try to satisfy Hannah. She is also identifying with Hannah's projection: she is the good nourishing object, while father identifies and becomes the bad object. These projections are very powerful and compelling. They are compounded by the family dynamics relating to Nat and the marital relationship already described, and by beliefs handed down over generations relating to "perfect" parenting, and the idealisation of boys.

Thus we see how Hannah's primitive infantile need is matched by mother's guilt, how projective identification and splitting bind the family together, how the marital conflict is diverted, and the myth of the "blue eyed boy" is maintained, through the dynamics of the symptom in this family. Each individual is trying their best to improve matters, and paradoxically participating in the maintenance of the condition. Mother, by trying to make things better by spending all her time with her daughter, reinforces Hannah's need for outside sustenance. Father, by alternately forcibly preventing her from bingeing, or opting out, reinforces the strength of the mother/daughter dyad, and the process of splitting that Hannah operates between the parents. The marital couple, as they divert their conflict through the symptom, are not able to present a mature, adult parental unit for Hannah to identify with and eventually break free from. Nat, by "keeping out", reinforces the family split.

VIGNETTE 2

Sara is 12 years old. She appears self-possessed and shows no concern over her extremely emaciated state. She lost her two major female caretakers tragically before she was 5 years old, her mother and Nanny both dying prematurely of cancer.

When eventually her father, a busy barrister, remarried, the family, including the stepmother, a concert pianist, dealt openly with the difficult task of becoming a

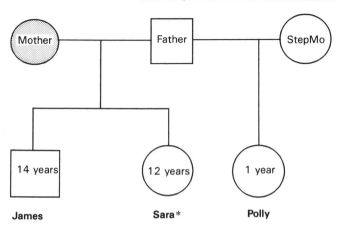

FIGURE 13.2   Vignette 2.

step-family, without denying the importance of Sara's original mother. Indeed, Sara was believed by the family to resemble her mother increasingly in temperament and appearance as she grew older. She and her elder brother, James, got on well with their stepmother, and difficulties only began to surface for Sara with the birth of a half-sister, Polly, when she was eleven.

The parents noticed that Sara was uninterested in her new sibling and seemed to be avoiding any contact with her. She became withdrawn, but the family, absorbed in the needs of the new baby, thought this unremarkable. Sara was a highly intelligent girl of whom great things were expected academically. There had been discussions about the possibility of her going to boarding school, and when this issue was raised at this time, Sara (who was given the choice) decided to go.

However, within two months of starting the new school, Sara had lost 15 kg and returned home. Throughout this period Sara consistently denied any distress. Her denial was mirrored by her parents' inability to recognise her underlying unhappiness.

At Polly's birth, stepmother was overjoyed. Father, remembering the repercussions of birth for his first wife, steeled himself yet more against painful memories. Sara protected herself similarly, but also cut herself off bodily from Polly, the concrete reminder of her losses. James appeared to take the whole situation in his stride. One could speculate that Sara was the receptacle for her family's grief. Her departure to boarding school, however, tipped the balance, and she was no longer able to contain the confusion and misery of what she experienced as the final rejection, and she stopped feeding herself.

On her return home, the family were able to see that sending her away had not been a good idea. However, stepmother was engrossed in her new baby, James was getting on with his own adolescent life, and angry at his sister for the disruption he felt she was causing, and father was torn between feelings of guilt and loyalty towards his two families.

Sara's behaviour is incomprehensible to everyone. She surrounds herself compulsively with food, but she will not eat it. Stepmother, a sensible, kind woman, cannot understand Sara's crazy obsession with food, and what she sees as her stubborn refusal to eat. When Sara cooks a delicious meal, stepmother is delighted, but when Sara is unable to eat the meal, stepmother cajoles, then, preoccupied with her own child, exasperatedly hands Sara over to her father, and Sara feels yet again abandoned.

Father, torn by contradictory loyalties, also reacts unpredictably. He has a warm, close relationship with Sara: they enjoy fishing together (an activity which he and his first wife shared). However, when she refuses to eat he is bewildered, pleads with her, and when she tearfully does not respond he becomes resentful, angry and rejecting towards Sara. Meanwhile, James, furious at the disruption, storms out of the house.

It would not be unreasonable to suppose that Sara's early life was experienced by her as traumatic, and her subsequent behaviour bears out this supposition. Her mother developed cancer shortly after the baby's birth, and died very rapidly; it is hard to imagine that her preoccupation with her own death would not have considerably affected her attitude to the new-born Sara. Her father dealt with his grief by denying it, and it is likely that the rest of the family colluded with his inability to tolerate his grief.

The rivalrous feelings provoked by the arrival of the new sibling and the feelings of yet more loss—of her father, who was creating a new family, and her stepmother who was preoccupied by her first baby—were all conveniently solved by Sara leaving the family. We can speculate that the experience of loss in early adolescence rekindled the early losses which had been only partially worked through. Perhaps the fact that Sara resembled her mother, in her father's eyes at least, increased the difficulty that he experienced at a time when he was celebrating the arrival of a new child. Denying Sara's feelings allowed him to deny in turn his own reawakened sense of loss, and his fears about the connection between birth and death.

Sara has the experience of an unpredictable and unreliable world, and we might assume that her internal world is equally insecure, and that she has few internal or external resources on which to draw. She wants so much to depend, to be close and be loved, but she cannot take the risk, she will be abandoned yet again. Her solution is to turn to food, but she cannot eat it: it would destroy her as she has been destroyed by her human objects. If her food is removed, she goes mad: she has to have it, it is her comfort, her drug, the only thing in her life over which she feels she has any control, and yet in her addiction it is she who is totally controlled by the food.

Sara's experience is that people she gets close to end up abandoning her, and this experience is constantly being acted out in her family. Stepmother, who feels guilty that she would really rather not have to deal with this "difficult " child, makes great efforts to get close and be a "good" stepmother; however, her preoccupation with her own child leads to her repeatedly and exasperatedly abandoning Sara in favour of Polly.

Father, who has not wholly worked through his own grief for his first wife (whose memory is kept alive by Sara), is not able to tolerate what he feels as Sara's rejection of him, and despite himself, in his turn, has to reject her. James' anger may also represent his own difficulty in dealing with his mother's death, and the fact that

Sara's condition does not allow this new family to move forward and leave the past behind.

Sara's experience of loss is thus constantly being re-enacted, reinforcing her erroneous belief that a relationship to food is the only safe one.

VIGNETTE 3

Carol is a 44-year-old severely emaciated housewife with advanced osteoporosis which has led to pseudofractures in her hips and pelvis. She is both child-like and has the appearance of an old woman.

Carol started dieting 18 years ago after the birth of her first child, Emily. Her husband, John, was out of the country at the time, and she felt unsupported and let down. The birth had been traumatic, and was followed by a period of depression, resulting in a growing vigilance about her body. When her son Kevin was born two years later by Caesarean section, she again suffered from depression, and countered her feelings of despair by imposing a strict regime of self-control over her weight and diet. Her husband was at first encouraging about her apparent commitment to healthy living. He himself had a back complaint for which he was encouraged to lose weight, and his own father had died of a heart attack in his fifties, and so the whole family willingly adopted a low-fat high-fibre diet.

Over time, however, his support turned to dismay and then to despair as Carol's weight fell. He presented himself as desperate for help in the face of his wife's intransigence. The more he tried to persuade her that she should eat more, that she needed help, the more she denied that there was any problem, and the more he felt

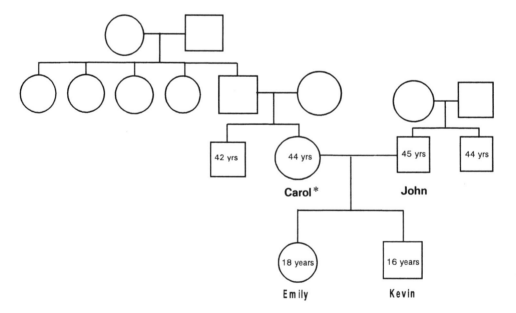

FIGURE 13.3   Vignette 3.

the need to redouble his efforts at persuasion. Each blamed the other for the near total lack of intimacy in their relationship, which had become a battleground for their competing points of view. The frustration and rejection which John felt turned into a sadistic attack, which served only to redouble Carol's efforts to deny that any problems existed apart from her husband's insensitivity and callousness, for which she maintained an open contempt. They were both caught in a cruel dance in a relationship starved of affection which they could neither leave nor nourish.

Carol's belief that the children were unaffected by the situation was challenged by John, who revealed conversations with their daughter which supported his view that the children also felt worried and powerless. Despite the father's wish to recruit them to the battle, both children publicly went along with the parents' other wish that they should get on with their own lives by being independent and mature beyond their years. For the daughter in particular, colluding with the denial was safer than forming an alliance with her father about her mother's condition, and risking replacing her mother as her father's partner.

Thus we can see how the family becomes paralysed by a combination of collusion and denial. By denying her self-destructive starvation, Carol maintains the illusion of a healthy life. Similarly, the others struggle to maintain the outward appearance of a happy, successful family.

Carol's mother was hospitalised for depression after the births of both her children. Her father was severe and prudish, dominated by his four "bossy" sisters who looked after Carol when her mother was in hospital. Carol, deprived of her mother at a crucial stage, and caught between her coldly detached father and her intrusive aunts, had a precarious sense of herself and her own worth. She describes her childhood as unremarkable, but in terms that sound lonely and depriving: as with her anorexia, there seems to be no fit between her feelings and the events which she describes. It is as though she is cut off from all pleasure and pain. We can speculate that the unhappiness was denied in order to preserve both the fragile family unity and the security of her inner world.

John is the younger of two brothers born within 15 months of each other. John's father's work took him regularly away from home: he was abroad at the time of John's birth, and didn't see his second son until he was over a year old. His mother, coping on her own with two small children, describes John as an "awful" baby, as difficult as his brother was delightful. The rivalry between the brothers persisted: John his father's favourite, his brother the apple of their mother's eye. John grew up in the shadow of his brother, anticipating disapproval from his mother and seeking the approval of his absent father. When Carol attacks him now, it is curiously safe and predictable. He seems to invite it, and then soak it up, full of resentful helplessness. She looks after him as a dutiful wife, while despising him for not being a strong enough man, or as good and successful as his brother. She is loyal to her family's rule about the role of women, both in supporting men and in the price they pay in terms of their own mental health. He has never felt "man enough" in relation to his own mother, and has always lost out in relation to his brother. Carol's taunts both cut him and paralyse him. She longs for containment and safety, but experiences his attempts as either pathetic or abusive. He is as unable to leave this hopeless and barren relationship as she is to give up her anorexia: they fit together so perfectly that neither can risk changing even in the face of such misery and possible death.

CONCLUSIONS

Our clinical experience is with individuals with chronic eating disorders who almost certainly make up a particular sub-group of eating disorders generally. The existence of the eating disorder over a long period of time in these families seems to lead to fixed patterns of interaction around it. Just as the eating disorder becomes a baffling and impenetrable autonomous condition within the individual, so also the organisation of the family around the individual and her behaviour has a life of its own.

The effects on families such as those in the vignettes above can be devastating. It appears, at least among the families that we see, that the parents, spouses and siblings remain involved despite their ambivalence or resentment. Unlike in psychotic breakdown, where there is a trend towards social isolation and separation (Wing, 1978), it seems that eating disorders generally weave a web from which it is difficult for family members to extricate themselves. This generalisation may be challenged by increasing knowledge about sub-groups such as socially deprived women with bulimia (Freeman and Gard, 1993). The situations described in the vignettes above are typical of our experience.

Eating disorders exist within cultures that support their existence; where food is freely available and the pursuit of thinness in women is encouraged and linked with acceptability and self-esteem. They therefore exist in relationship to others; both to society in general and in the relationships between individuals in families. Our experience is that eating disorders can be best understood when construed in terms of relationships with others; both in the "inner world" of the sufferer and in the "real world" of family relationships.

Biological explanations of physiology and genetic predisposition, as explained elsewhere in this volume, obviously have an important, perhaps a necessary, part to play in the production of eating disorders. However, whatever the predispositions may be, the eating disorders that we see appear to require relationships to maintain them. We have argued in this chapter that attempting to understand the meaning of the eating disorder in the context of these relationships is likely to lead to more effective therapy. This means allowing ourselves to become curious about how everyone in the family responds to the situation and how they understand their own and other people's behaviour. We have found that attempting to understand the sufferer's experience in terms of object relations has enriched our understanding of the apparent fit between the individual's predicament and other people's behaviour.

We have only our clinical impressions of the impact on family functioning of the eating disorder and conversely the impact of the families' beliefs or activities on the outcome of the condition. We can only speculate that when families can be freed to act differently in relation to the eating disorder, then the prognosis improves. We would argue that in order to act differently people need to think differently. The model we have offered in this chapter represents one way of doing that.

We need to understand more about the characteristics of the families that respond effectively to treatment methods including the family, in order to make more informed decisions about how to intervene and with whom. However, whether or not other family members are included in the treatment, their importance, both in relationships in the real world and as internal objects for the sufferer, should not be ignored.

REFERENCES

Bruch, H. (1974). *Eating Disorders, Obesity, Anorexia Nervosa and the Person Within.* New York: Basic Books.

Charcot, J.M. (1889). *Diseases of the Nervous System.* London: New Sydenham Society.

Colahan, M. (1991). L'anoréxie en tant qu'addiction: stratégie thérapeutique ou modèle théorique? Unpublished paper presented at third Congrès Internationale Ancre-Psy, Paris: Hospital St Anne.

Freeman, C.P. and Gard, M.C.E. (1993). Eating disorders in the homeless. Submitted.

Freud, S. (1931). Female sexuality. In: S. Freud, *On Sexuality.* Harmondsworth: Penguin Books, 1977.

Garfinkel, P.E. and Garner, D.M. (1982). *Anorexia Nervosa: A Multidimensional Perspective.* New York: Brunner/Mazel.

Garner, D.M. and Garfinkel, P.E. (Eds) (1988). *Diagnostic Issues in Anorexia Nervosa & Bulimia Nervosa,* Brunner Mazel, Eating Disorder Monograph Series.

Goldner, V., Penn, P., Sheinberg, M. and Walker, G. (1990). Love and violence: gender paradoxes in volatile attachments. *Family Process, 29,* 343–364.

Gull, W.W. (1874). Anorexia nervosa (apepsia hysterica, anorexia hysterica). *Transactions of the Clinical Society of London,* **7,** 22–28.

Hoffman, L. (1990). Constructing realities; an art of lenses. *Family Process, 29,* 1–12.

Klein, M. (1977). *Envy and Gratitude & Other Works 1946–1963.* New York: Delta Books.

Mahler, M. (1961). On sadness and grief in infancy and childhood. *Psychoanalytic Study of the Child,* **16,** 332–351.

McDougall, J. (1989). *Theatres of the Mind: Illusion and Truth on the Psychoanalytic Stage.* London: Free Association Books.

Minuchin, S., Rosman, B.L. and Baker, L. (1978). *Psychosomatic Families: Anorexia Nervosa in Context.* Harvard: University Press.

Orbach, S. (1986). *Hunger Strike.* London: Faber & Faber.

Roberto, G. (1988). The vortex: siblings in the eating disordered family. In: K.G. Lewis and M.D. Kahn (Eds), *Siblings in Therapy.* New York: W.W. Norton.

Selvini-Palazzoli, M. (1974). *Self-starvation: From the Intrapsychic to the Transpersonal Approach to Anorexia Nervosa.* Hayward's Heath, Sussex: Human Context Books, Chaucer Publishing Company.

Stern, S., Whitaker, C.A., Hagerman, N.J. and Bargman, G.J. (1981). Anorexia nervosa: the hospital's role in family treatment. *Family Process, 20,* 395–408.

Szmukler, G.I., Eisler, I., Russell, G.F.M. and Dare, C. (1985). Anorexia, parental expressed emotion and dropping out of treatment. *British Journal of Psychiatry,* **147,** 265–271.

Szmukler, G.I. and Tantam, D. (1984). Anorexia nervosa: starvation dependence. *British Journal of Medical Psychology,* **57,** 303–310.

Wing, J.K. (1978). Social influences on the course of schizophrenia. In: L.C. Wynne, R.L. Cromwell and S.S.E. Matthysse (Eds), *The Nature of Schizophrenia.* New York: Wyllie.

Winnicott, D. (1951). Transitional objects and transitional phenomena. In: D. Winnicott, *Collected Papers.* New York: Basic Books.

14

The Social Consequences of Eating Disorders

ULRIKE SCHMIDT
St Mary's Hospital, London, UK
JANE TILLER
Maudsley Hospital, London, UK
AND
H. GETHIN MORGAN
University of Bristol, Brisol, UK

Research into the social consequences of eating disorders has reached dramatically conflicting conclusions. Whilst Turnbull et al (1989) described their bulimic sample of consisting of "in the main, apparently well-adjusted young single women of education", another study found bulimic women to be less well adjusted than alcoholic or even schizophrenic women (Norman and Herzog, 1984). The situation in anorexia nervosa is similar, leading Steinhausen, Rauss-Mason and Seidel (1991) in a review of follow-up studies of anorexia nervosa to conclude that "psychosocial adaptation seems to be the most diverse and elusive outcome parameter to study".

The task of this review is (1) to put these conflicting views into perspective, and (2) to identify the mechanisms involved in the various social sequelae of eating disorders.

Handbook of Eating Disorders: Theory, Treatment and Research.
Edited by G. Szmukler, C. Dare and J. Treasure.
© 1995 John Wiley & Sons Ltd.

HOW DO EATING DISORDERS AFFECT SOCIAL RELATIONSHIPS?

Social Consequences of Starvation

The social consequences of starvation were described movingly in a classical study on 36 healthy male conscientious objectors who underwent a starvation phase of several months followed by a period of rehabilitation (Keys, Broze and Henschel, 1950). Apathy and social withdrawal were common amongst the men. One participant said: "Social graces, interests, spontaneous activity and responsibility take second place to concerns of food. I lick my plate unashamedly at each meal even when guests are present. I don't like to sit near guests, for then it is necessary to entertain and talk with them. That takes too much energy and destroys some of the enjoyment that comes from my food."

There was widespread reduction in sexual desire and activity. One of the men said: "I have no more sexual feeling than a sick oyster". The number of dates dropped drastically as starvation progressed. Those who continued to date women found their relationship strained. One participant said: "I am one of about three or four who still go out with girls. I fell in love with a girl during the control period but I see her only occasionally now. It's almost too much trouble to see her even if she visits me at the Lab. It requires effort to hold her hand. Entertainment must be tame. If we see a show, the most interesting part of it is contained in scenes where people are eating. I couldn't laugh at the funniest picture in the world, and love scenes are completely dull." This diminished interest in sexuality was not accompanied by abnormal attitudes or an aversion to sexual matters (Schiele and Brozek, 1948).

The men's capacity to do physical work decreased rapidly, and even after the rehabilitation phase took time to recover. One man said about his cognitive abilities: "I can talk intellectually; my mental ability has not decreased, but my will to use the ability has."

It is to be expected that those social sequelae of eating disorders which are the direct result of starvation are likely to fade upon reinstitution of a healthy weight and normal eating.

Effects of Bulimic Symptoms

There is evidence that bulimic symptoms, too, create difficulties in interpersonal relationships, interfering with the individual's time and involvement with others (Johnson and Larson, 1981). In addition to the direct effects of bulimic symptoms on social adjustment, bulimic symptoms may also indirectly lead to poor adjustment owing to their negative effect on self-esteem (Fairburn et al, 1987), problem-solving (Striegel-Moore, Silberstein and Rodin, 1986) and coping (Soukoup, Beiler and Terrell, 1990) and their association with depression (Cooper and Fairburn, 1986).

Johnson and Love (1985) attempted to identify which symptomatic features of the bulimic syndrome are associated with life impairment in a survey sample consisting of approximately 800 women volunteers with bulimia. An index of impairment was derived from a self-rating scale which asked respondents to note the degree to which binge-eating and other symptoms had interfered with their thoughts, feelings about themselves, work, daily activities, and interpersonal relationships, and they were also given the Hopkins Symptom Checklist. In a stepwise regression analysis, factors which best predicted life impairment were "feeling out of control" during binge-eating, frequency of bingeing and laxative abuse, feelings of guilt, early onset of eating problems and previous low weight. Together these factors explained 27% of the variance.

Social Consequences of Weight Abnormalities

Societal idealisation of thinness is almost a *sine qua non* for the development of anorexia nervosa. Recent press coverage has tended to glamorise eating disorders with its focus upon famous and beautiful victims of the illness. But even the families and friends of people with established anorexia—although often concerned about the patient's peculiar eating and exercise habits—may still be admiring of the patient's appearance and use words like "slender", "neat", "well-groomed" and "fashionable" to describe the patient rather than "skinny", "emaciated" or "haggard", and envy the patient's self-discipline and self-control (Branch and Eurman, 1980). This kind of positive feedback is likely to fuel the sufferer's desire for further weight loss.

Obesity, on the other hand, is one of the most stigmatised physical attributes in western society today leading to discrimination in a wide range of settings (Rothblum et al, 1990; Garner, 1993). Prepubertal children uniformly dislike obese body shapes (Feldman, Feldman and Goodman, 1988). Some college students would be willing to consider an embezzler, shoplifter, ex-mental patient or cocaine abuser as a spouse before choosing an obese person as a marriage partner (Venes, Krupka and Gerard, 1982). The proposed DSM-IV "binge eating disorder" is often associated with obesity. The stigma attached to being overweight is likely to maintain the disorder by pushing sufferers into continuing their often extremely punishing dietary routines (Schmidt et al, 1993).

Other Mechanisms

Certain social sequelae of eating disorders may be the result of premorbid personality characteristics of the sufferer which become accentuated by the eating disorder. For example, patients with a borderline personality disorder before onset of their eating disorder may become much more chaotic in their social interactions during the active phase of their eating disorder. These problems would be likely to persist beyond recovery, although probably in a milder form.

Personality traits may manifest as the anorexic patient's notorious denial of her illness, her obstinacy, and her deviousness. These create mistrust, hostility, frustration and outrage in those close to the sufferer, including those people working with her therapeutically (Morgan, 1977; Vandereycken, 1993). For example, young doctors were found to respond to anorexia nervosa patients with much more anger, stress and helplessness than to other physically ill patients (Brotman, Stern and Herzog, 1984).

Likewise, inadequate coping skills and poor general problem-solving contribute indirectly to the impaired social functioning seen in eating disordered patients. This has been discussed in relation to bulimic symptoms but is also of relevance in anorexia nervosa (Soukup, Beiler and Terrell, 1990). Eating disordered patients have been found to use more immature defences than non-eating disordered subjects (Steiger and Houle, 1991; Steiger et al, 1989; Steiger et al, 1990; Steiner, 1990) and these are associated with poor adult adjustment (Vaillant, Bond and Vaillant, 1986).

Some of the social consequences of eating disorders may be related to psychiatric comorbidity, most notably depression or obsessive–compulsive disorders. The abuse of alcohol or drugs (often for their appetite suppressing properites) is likely to lead to progressive disturbance in social functioning. Social adjustment would be expected to improve following the appropriate treatment of these conditions.

STUDIES OF SOCIAL ADJUSTMENT

A number of studies have assessed social adjustment in eating disorders using the Social Adjustment Scale—Self Report (SAS-SR; Weissman and Rothwell, 1976). This is a 42-item questionnaire measuring role performance in six areas of social functioning, including work (as a worker, housewife or student), social and leisure activities, relationships with extended family, and roles as a spouse, parent and member of a family unit. Each question is rated on a five-point scale with a higher score indicating greater impairment. Subjects receive a separate score for each area of functioning evaluated, as well as an overall total score.

Studies of bulimic subjects using the SAS-SR tend to agree that they are less well adjusted than normal controls (Johnson and Berndt, 1983; Norman and Herzog, 1984; Herzog et al, 1985, 1986, 1987; Bohle et al, 1991). In one study, 68% of bulimics scored within the clinically impaired range on at least one of the subscales compared with 13% of controls (Herzog et al, 1987). A clinical sample of 40 DSM-III bulimics had poorer social adjustment than normal women, alcoholic women, and schizophrenic women both at the time of evaluation and at one-year follow-up (Norman and Herzog, 1984). At one-year follow-up, those who had received treatment for their eating disorder showed a decrease in disturbed eating attitudes, depression and somatic concerns; however, social maladjustment persisted (Norman, Herzog and Chauncey, 1986). At three-year follow-up (Norman and Herzog, 1986), whilst eating and other symptomatology had improved considerably, social adjustment on the SAS-SR did not improve, with the exception of the work scale. Similarly, a 20-month follow-up study of 628 women volunteers with bulimic anorexia nervosa, normal-weight bulimia and subdiagnostic eating disorder found that, despite clinical improvement, on a psychosocial impact scale bulimic anorexics and normal-weight bulimics were impaired in the domains of work, non-work activities and personal relationships and did not improve at follow-up (Yager, Landsverk and Edelstein, 1987). In contrast, Swift et al (1987), in a follow-up study of 30 hospitalised bulimics, found them to be similar to normal females in their psychosocial outcome. However, only the "work" and "social leisure" subscales of the SAS-SR were examined.

Only one study has compared anorexia nervosa patients with normal controls and DSM-III bulimics on the SAS-SR, reporting the anorexia nervosa patients and bulimia patients to be significantly more impaired than the controls (Bohle et al, 1991). In follow-up studies of anorexia nervosa, in contrast to other outcome criteria of anorexia nervosa, the assessment of social adaptation is marred by "lack of explicit criteria, standardised interview schedules and rating scales" (Steinhausen, Rauss-Mason and Seidel, 1991).

QUALITY OF LIFE

The assessment of quality of life encompasses the assessment of physical, psychological and social functioning. Treasure, Schmidt and Keilen (1992) measured self-reported quality of life, using the Nottingham Health Profile (Hunt, 1980) in 52 patients with anorexia nervosa, 74 with bulimia nervosa, and a reference population of 91 college students. The Nottingham Health Profile consists of 38 statements in six dimensions: energy, pain, sleep, mobility, emotional reaction, social isolation. The second part of the instrument measures function in terms of job, home life, sex life, family life, social life and looking after the home and holidays.

Both patient groups showed significantly more impairment than controls in the health domains of the Nottingham Health Profile. The highest level of impairment was perceived in the psychosocial domains (emotional reaction and social isolation) with additional disturbance in energy and sleep. In addition to health difficulties the patient group also had functional difficulties in daily living. The anorexia nervosa group reported more problems with their home life and social life than did the bulimia nervosa patients, with the majority of patients in both groups having difficulties with their closest relationships. In contrast to other studies (Lehman, 1983), quality of life was not simply a measure of depression. Although 32% of the patients with anorexia nervosa and 36% of the patients with bulimia nervosa had a SCID (Structured Clinical Interview for DSM-III-R; Spitzer et al, 1989) diagnosis of depression at assessment, there were no significant differences in the summary scales of quality of life between the depressed and non-depressed groups. However, as would be expected the depressed patients had higher levels of impairment in the emotional and social isolation domains. The quality of life profile in the eating disordered sample differs from that seen in other patient groups evaluated with this method. Men who require coronary artery surgery have more pain, but emotional reaction, social isolation and sleep are less impaired (mobility and energy levels are similar) (Caine et al, 1991a); patients with cystic fibrosis awaiting a heart–lung transplant have a greater impairment of mobility, whereas emotional reaction, social isolation and sleep disturbance are less impaired than in the eating disordered group (Caine et al, 1991b).

SPECIFIC ASPECTS OF SOCIAL FUNCTIONING

Relationship with Parents

Much has been written about the contribution of family relationships to the origins of eating disorders, with most studies using cross-sectional questionnaire or observational data (see this volume; also e.g. Wonderlich, 1992; Schmidt et al, 1993). A "restricter/binger dichotomy" has been postulated, but is by no means uncontroversial. Family characteristics seen as typical for restricter families include over-involvement, rigidity and enmeshment (Minuchin, Rosman and Baker, 1987), whereas families of bulimics have been said to have high levels of discord and criticism (Szmukler et al, 1985). These family characteristics may to some extent be a consequence of the disorders rather than causal and may reflect the family's desperate attempts to cope with a difficult and frightening situation.

Sexual Adjustment

Anorexia nervosa has sometimes been conceptualised as the result of a fear of maturation and adult sexuality (Crisp, 1980; Bruch, 1981). Leon et al (1985) compared anorexics with normal controls and found them to be more negative regarding sexual and feminine appearance of their own body, evaluation of sexual feelings and sexual interest or arousal. There were no differences on the morality scale. Earlier studies (e.g. Russell, 1979; Garfinkel and Garner, 1982) stated that anorexics are less sexually active and experienced than bulimics. However, Rothschild et al (1991) found little difference between inpatients with anorexia nervosa or bulimia or both. All patients gave evidence of being sexually dissatisfied and restricted. Morgan and Russell (1975) found half of their anorectics to have had heterosexual contacts ranging from a boyfriend to an engagement before the onset of the disorder. At a 4-year follow-up, only 23% still had abnormal sexual adjustment. Steinhausen, Rauss-Mason and Seidel (1991) in a review of follow-up studies on anorexia nerova noted that "the reported number of former patients engaging in active sexual behaviour varied greatly from study to study".

Dating/Marital/Partner Relationships

Twenty-one per cent of 246 consecutive female anorexics seen at a specialist clinic were married. Two-thirds of these had a pre-marital onset and one-third a post-marital onset (Heavey et al 1989). The marital partners of anorexics have been described as immature, weak and neurotic (Dally, 1969; Crisp, 1980; Van den Broucke and Vandereycken, 1989), but systematic research in samples of reasonable size is lacking.

In bulimia, two studies failed to find problems with intimate relationships. Bulimic and non-bulimic students were similar in self-ratings of popularity, reported number of intimate relationships (Weiss and Ebert, 1983) and on a measure of social competency in dating situations (Katzman and Wolchik, 1984). However, these studies concentrated on relatively superficial or short-term aspects of relationships and tell us little about the quality of long-term partner relationships.

In contrast, another study of a student population found strong negative correlations between eating symptomatology and ratings of interpersonal relationships with men (Thelen et al, 1990). Married bulimics were similar to women seeking marital therapy in reporting greater marital dissatisfaction than normal women, use of fewer problem-solving skills, withdrawal from conflict and the belief that their partners could not change (Van Buren and Williamson, 1988).

In a catchment-area-based cohort of bulimics, two-thirds had a current sexual partner (Lacey, 1992). Patients were less likely to be married (21%) than their sisters (42%) or similarly aged women in the same district (51%). One-quarter of all partners had a weight or eating problem. Nearly 40% abused alcohol, raising the possibility of assortative mating between heavy drinking partners and multi-impulse bulimics. One-quarter of partners had a first-degree relative with a psychiatric disorder. Two main types of pathological relationships were found. Nearly 30% of patients chose a "safe" man, someone for whom she had few serious feelings, possibly to avoid being hurt (as in earlier relationships). More than one in ten described their relationship as abusive. The author concluded that "bulimics no less than the rest of the population demonstrate assortative mating".

Relationship with Children

A long-term follow-up study of 151 Danish patients with anorexia nervosa found reduced fertility, increased rates of prematurity and increased perinatal mortality (Brinch, Sager and Tolstrop, 1988). However, feeding difficulties and problems with the children's mental development did not differ from the rates found in the population at large. This contrasts with case reports of anorexic mothers who starve their children with serious effects on the children's physical and emotional development (Treasure et al, 1992). Similarly case series of mothers with bulimia noted ignoring, irritability and inability to cope with children during episodes of bingeing (Stein and Fairburn, 1989; Fahy and Treasure, 1989).

Social Support

Few studies have evaluated social support in eating disorders. One, using a student sample, did not find bulimic and non-bulimic women to differ in reported levels of social support (Jacobson and Robins, 1989). In another study, however, bulimics reported less perceived social support from friends and family, more negative interactions and conflict and less social competence compared with 21 control subjects (Grisset and Norvell, 1992). Tiller et al (in preparation) studied social support in a cohort of anorexic and bulimic patients who were compared with college students, using the Significant Others scale (Power, Champion and Aris, 1988). Patients had smaller social newtworks and they reported lower levels of emotional and practical support than did the comparison group. Bulimics were more dissatisfied with the support they received than AN patients and the comparison group. They showed greater discrepancies between their ideals of support and the level of support they perceived themselves as receiving.

Forensic Problems

High prevalences of stealing, most commonly of food or of money to obtain food, have been reported in several studies of patients with eating disorders. All note that the frequency of stealing is greater in the bulimic subgroup (Crisp, Hsu and Harding, 1980; Norton, Crisp and Bhat, 1985; for a review see Krahn et al, 1991). A study of 275 bulimic outpatients found that 22% had stolen before onset, whereas after onset this figure rose to 51.5% (Mitchell et al, 1986). Bulimic anorexics who stole differed from their non-stealing counterparts in older age at presentation and in terms of greater sexual activity (Norton, Crisp and Bhat, 1985).

Krahn et al (1991) compared stealers and non-stealers. Those with a history of stealing reported significantly more depression, interpersonal sensitivity, obsessive–compulsive behaviour and hostility. Crisp, Hsu and Harding (1980) thought that stealing in eating disordered patients either stemmed from premorbid impulsivity or was the direct result of starvation (with its behavioural accompaniments of grasping and hoarding). Gerlinghoff and Backmund (1987) noted that in their patients, in addition to being short of money, other reasons for stealing included: that it may serve as a form of revenge or a substitute for love and affection, or that it may be used by patients to make them feel alive, increase self-esteem, be a substitute for bingeing, or serve as an achievement.

SUMMARY AND CONCLUSIONS

The findings of the studies summarised in this chapter suggest that the different social sequelae of eating disorders are shaped by the effects of starvation, bulimic symptoms and weight abnormality as well as by the indirect effects of concurrent psychopathology and personality characteristics. The relative contributions of different mechanisms to the social sequelae of eating disorders remain uncertain. Studies of global social functioning or particular aspects of it, of the quality of life and of the social support of eating disordered patients have considerable methodological shortcomings as they all rely on self-report measures and are therefore vulnerable to distortion. Different personality characteristics of patients with anorexia nervosa and bulimia nervosa may lead to over- or under-reporting of social consequences. Patients with anorexia nervosa are shy and avoidant (Piran et al, 1988), whereas a subgroup of bulimics may dramatise and exaggerate their difficulties (Levin and Hyler, 1986). Depressed patients may have a more negative view of their social functioning compared with others.

Disturbed social functioning may act to maintain the eating disorder. The amount and quality of social support has been found to be one of the factors predicting outcome (Davis, Olmstead and Rocket, 1992; Keller et al, 1992). Thus for some patients, the social consequences of their eating disorder may serve to perpetuate the condition. Social functioning thus ought to be addressed directly in treatment. Cognitive behavioural treatment, interpersonal therapy and analytically based therapies such as cognitive–analytical therapy allow dysfunctional coping mechanisms and disturbed social interactions to be explored. Problem-solving is a recognised component of cognitive–behavioural therapy packages (Fairburn, 1981).

We too take part in social exchanges with our patients and our responses play a role in moulding the course of the illness. It is salutary to reflect that it is little over a hundred years since the parents of Sarah Jacobs "the Welsh fasting girl", were sent to prison for manslaughter after she had been allowed to starve to death, under medical supervision, in the pursuit of science and national honour (Morgan, 1977). Given the widespread disturbance in social adjustment seen in eating disordered patients, it may be illuminating to consider which of our reactions to these patients continue to be a consequence of disturbed social functioning and our own emotive response to it rather than objective decision-making.

REFERENCES

Bohle, A., von Wietersheim, J., Wilke, E. and Feiereis, H. (1991). Social integration of patients with anorexia nervosa and bulimia. *Zeitung für Psychosomatische Medizin und Psychoanalyse*, **37**, 282–291.

Branch, C.H. and Eurman, L.J. (1980). Social attitudes toward patients with anorexia nervosa. *American Journal of Psychiatry*, **137**, 631–632.

Brinch, M., Sager, T. and Tolstrup, K. (1988). Anorexia nervosa and motherhood: reproduction patterns and mothering behavior of 50 women. *Acta Psychiatrica Scandinavica*, **77**, 611–617.

Brotman, A.W., Stern, T.A. and Herzog, D.B. (1984). Emotional reactions of house officers to patients with anorexia nervosa, diabetes and obesity. *International Journal of Eating Disorders*, **3**, 71–77.

Bruch, H. (1981). Developmental consideration of anorexia nervosa and obesity. *Canadian Journal of Psychiatry*, **26**, 212–217.

Caine, N., Harrison, S.C.W., Sharples, L.D. and Wallwork, J. (1991a). Prospective study of quality of life before and after coronary artery bypass grafting. *British Medical Journal*, **302**, 511–516.

Caine, N., Sharples, L.D., Smyth, R., Scott, J., Hathaway, T., Higgenbottam, T.W. and Wallwork, J. (1991b). Survival and quality of life of cystic fibrosis patients, before and after heart–lung transplantation. *Transplantation Proceedings*, **23**, 1203–1204.

Cooper, P.J. and Fairburn, C.G. (1986). The depressive symptoms of bulimia nervosa. *British Journal of Psychiatry*, **148**, 268–274.

Crisp, A.H. (1980). *Anorexia Nervosa: Let Me Be*. London: Acacemic Press/Grune & Stratton.

Crisp, A.H., Hsu, L.K.G. and Harding, B. (1980). The starving hoarder and voracious spender: stealing in anorexia nervosa. *Journal of Psychosomatic Research*, **24**, 225–231.

Dally, P. (1984). Anorexia tardive—late-onset marital anorexia nervosa. *Journal of Psychosomatic Research*, **28**, 423–428.

Davis, R., Olmstead, M.P. and Rockert, W. (1992). Brief group psychoeducation for bulimia nervosa. II: Prediction of clinical outcome. *International Journal of Eating Disorders*, **11**, 205–211.

Fairburn, C.G. (1981). A cognitive–behavioural approach to the management of bulimia. *Psychological Medicine*, **11**, 707–711.

Fairburn, C.G., Kirk, J., O'Connor, M., Anastasiades, P. and Cooper, P.J. (1987). Prognostic factors in bulimia nervosa. *British Journal of Clinical Psychology*, **26**, 223–224.

Fahy, T. and Treasure, J. (1989). Children of mothers with bulimia nervosa. *British Medical Journal*, **299**, 1031.

Feldman, W., Feldman, E. and Goodman, J.T. (1988). Culture versus biology: children's attitudes toward thinness and fatness. *Pediatrics*, **81**, 190–194.

Garfinkel, P.E. and Garner, D.M. (1982). *Anorexia Nervosa: A Multidimensional Perspective*. New York: Brunner/Mazel.

Garner, D. (1993). Eating disorders and what to do about obesity? *International Review of Psychiatry*, **5**, 9–12.

Gerlinghoff, M. and Backmund, H. (1987). Stehlen bei Anorexia Nervosa and Bulimia Nervosa. *Fortschritte der Neurologie und Psychiatrie*, **55**, 343–346.

Grissett, N.J. and Norvell, N.K. (1992). Perceived social support, social skills, and quality of relationships in bulimic women. *Journal of Consulting and Clinical Psychology*, **60**, 293–299.

Heavey, A., Parker, Y., Bhat, A.V., Crisp, A.H. and Gowers, G.G. (1989). Anorexia nervosa and marriage. *International Journal of Eating Disorders*, **8**, 275–284.

Herzog, D.B., Keller, M.B., Lavori, P.W. and Ott, L.L. (1987). Social impairment in bulimia. *International Journal of Eating Disorders*, **6**, 741–747.

Herzog, D.B., Norman, D.K., Rigotti, N.A. and Pepose, M. (1986). Frequency of bulimic behaviors and associated social maladjustment in female graduate students. *Journal of Psychiatry Research*, **20**, 355–361.

Herzog, D.B., Pepose, M., Norman, D.K. and Rigotti, N.A. (1985). Eating disorders and social maladjustment in female medical students. *Journal of Nervous and Mental Disease*, **173**, 734–737.

Hunt, S.M., McKenna, S.P. and McEwen, J. (1980). A quantitative approach to perceived health status: a validation study. *Journal of Epidemiology and Community Health*, **34**, 281–286.

Jacobson, R. and Robins, C.J. (1989). Social dependency and social support in bulimic and nonbulimic women. *International Journal of Eating Disorders*, **8**, 665–670.

Johnson, C.L. and Larson, R. (1981). Bulimia: an analysis of moods and behaviour. *Psychosomatic Medicine*, **44**, 341–353.

Johnson, C.L. and Love, S.Q. (1985). Bulimia: multivariate predictors of life impairment. *Journal of Psychiatric Research*, **2/3**, 343–347.

Johnson, C.L. and Berndt, D.J. (1983). Preliminary investigation of bulimia and life adjustment. *American Journal of Pychiatry*, **140**, 774–777.

Katzman, M.A. and Wolchik, S.A. (1984). Bulimia and binge eating in college women: a comparison of personality and behavioral characteristics. *Journal of Consulting and Clinical Psychology*, **52**, 423–428.

Keller, M.B., Herzog, D.B., Lavori, P.W., Bradburn, I.S. and Mahoney, E.M. (1992). The naturalistic history of bulimia nervosa: extraordinary high rates of chronicity, relapse, recurrence, and psychosocial morbidity. *International Journal of Eating Disorders*, **12**, 1–9.

Keys, A., Broze, J. and Henschel, A. (1950). *The Biology of Human Starvation*, Vol. 2, Minneapolis, Minn: Minnesota University Press.

Krahn, D.D., Nairn, K., Gosnell, B.A. and Drewnowski, A. (1991). Stealing in eating disordered patients. *Journal of Clinical Psychiatry*, **52**, 112–115.

Lacey, J.H. (1992). Homogamy: the relationships and sexual partners of normal-weight bulimic women. *British Journal of Psychiatry*, **161**, 638–642.

Lehman, A.F. (1983). The effects of psychiatric symptoms on quality of life assessments among the chronic mentally ill. *Evaluation and Program Planning*, **6**, 143–151.

Leon, G.R., Lucas, A.R., Colligcan, R.C., Ferdinande, R.J. and Kamp, J. (1985). Sexual, body-image, and personality attitudes in anorexia nervosa. *Journal of Abnormal Child Psychology*, **13**, 245–258.

Levin, A.P. and Hyler, S.E. (1986). DSM-III personality diagnosis in bulimia. *Comprehensive Psychiatry*, **27**, 47–53.

Minuchin, S., Rosman, B.L. and Baker, L. (1978). *Psychosomatic Families*. Cambridge, Mass: Harvard University Press.

Mitchell, J.E., Hatsukami, D., Pyle, R.L. and Eckert, E.D. (1986). The bulimia syndrome: course of the illness and associated problems. *Comprehensive Psychiatry*, **27**, 165–170.

Mitchell, J.E., Fletcher, L., Gibean, L., Pyle, R.L. and Eckert, E. (1992). Shoplifting in bulimia nervosa. *Comprehensive Psychiatry*, **33**, 342–345.

Morgan, H.G. and Russell, G.F.M. (1975). Value of family background and clinical features as predictors of long-term outcome in anorexia nervosa: four-year follow-up study of 41 patients. *Psychological Medicine*, **5**, 355–371.

Morgan, H.G. (1977). Fasting girls and our attitudes to them. *British Medical Journal*, **2**, 1652–1655.

Norman, D.K. and Herzog, D.B. (1984). Persistent social maladjustment in bulimia: a one-year follow-up. *American Journal of Psychiatry*, **141**, 444–446.

Norman, D.K. and Herzog, D.B. (1986). A three-year outcome study in normal-weight bulimia: assessment of psychosocial functioning and eating attitudes. *Psychiatric Research*, **19**, 199–205.

Norman, D.K., Herzog, D.B. and Chauncey, S. (1986). A one-year outcome study of bulimia: psychological and eating symptom changes in a treatment and nontreatment group. *International Journal of Eating Disorders*, **5**, 47–58.

Norton, K.R.W., Crisp, A.H. and Bhat, A.V. (1985). Why do some anorexics steal? Personal, social and illness factors. *Journal of Psychiatric Research*, **19**, 385–390.

Piran, N., Lerner, P., Garfinkel, P.E., Kennedy, S.H. and Brouilette, C. (1988). Personality disorders in anorexic patients. *International Journal of Eating Disorders*, **7**, 589–599.

Power, M.J., Champion, L.A. and Aris, S.J. (1988). The development of a measure of social support: the Significant Others scale. *British Journal of Clinical Psychology*, **27**, 349–358.

Rothblum, E.D., Brand, P.A., Miller, C.T. and Oetjen, H.A. (1990). The relationship between obesity, employment discrimination and employment-related victimization. *Journal of Vocational Behavior*, **37**, 251–266.

Rothschild, B.S., Fagan, P.J., Woodall, C. and Andersen, A.E. (1991). Sexual functioning of female eating-disordered patients. *International Journal of Eating Disorders*, **10**, 389–394.

Russell, G. (1979). Bulimia nervosa: An ominous variant of anorexia nervosa. *Psychological Medicine*, **9**, 429–448.

Schiele, B. and Brozek, J. (1948). Experimental neurosis resulting from self-starvation in man. *Psychosomatic Medicine*, **10**, 31–50.

Schmidt, U., Tiller, J. and Treasure, J. (1993). Psychosocial factors in the origins of bulimia nervosa. *International Review of Psychiatry*, **5**, 51–60.

Schmidt, U., Keilen, M., Tiller, J. and Treasure, J. (1993). Clinical symptomatology and etiological factors in obese and normal-weight bulimic patients: a retrospective case-control study. *Journal of Nervous and Mental Disease*, **181**, 200–202.

Soukup, V.M., Beiler, M.E. and Terrell, F. (1990). Stress, coping style and problem solving ability among eating disordered inpatients. *Journal of Clinical Psychology*, **46**, 592–599.

Spitzer, R.L., Develin, M., Walsh, B.T., Hasin, D., Wing, R., Marcus, M., Stunkard, A., Wadden, T., Yanovski, S., Agras, S., Mitchell, J. and Nonas, C. (1992). Binge eating disorder: a multisite field trial of the diagnostic criteria. *International Journal of Eating Disorders*, **11**, 191–203.

Spitzer, R.L., Williams, J.B.W., Gibbon, M. and First, M.B. (1989). *Structured Clinical Interview for DSM-III-R: Patient Edition* (SCID-P, 9/1/89 version), Biometrics Research Department, New York State Psychiatric Institute.

Steiger, H, Van der Feen, J., Goldstein, C. and Leichner, P. (1989). Defense styles and parental bonding in eating-disordered women. *International Journal of Eating Disorders*, **9**, 141–151.

Steiger, H. and Houle, I. (1991). Defense style and object relations disturbances amongst university women displaying varying degrees of "symptomatic" eating. *International Journal of Eating Disorders*, **10**, 145–153.

Steiger, H., Goldstein, C., Mongraine, M. and Van der Feen, J. (1990). Description of eating disordered, psychiatric and normal women along cognitive and psychodynamic dimensions. *International Journal of Eating Disorders*, **2**, 129–140.

Stein, A. and Fairburn, C.G. (1989). Children of mothers with bulimia nervosa. *British Medical Journal*, **299**, 777–778.

Steiner, H. (1990). Defense style in eating disorders. *International Journal of Eating Disorders*, **9**, 141–151.

Steinhausen, H.Ch., Rauss-Mason, C. and Seidel, R. (1991). Follow-up studies of anorexia nervosa: a review of four decades of outcome research. *Psychological Medicine*, **21**, 447–454.

Striegel-Moore, R.H., Silberstein, L.R. and Rodin, J. (1986). Toward an understanding of risk factors for bulimia. *American Psychologist*, **41**, 246–263.

Swift, W.J., Ritholz, M., Kalin, N.H. and Kaslow, N. (1987). A follow-up study of thirty hospitalized bulimics. *Psychosomatic Medicine*, **49**, 45–55.

Szmukler, G.I., Eisler, I., Russell, G.F.M. and Dare, C. (1985). Anorexia nervosa, parental "expressed emotion" and dropping out of treatment. *British Journal of Psychiatry*, **147**, 265–271.

Thelen, M.H., Farmer, J., McLaughlin Mann, L. and Pruitt, J. (1990). Bulimia and interpersonal relationships: a longitudinal study. *Journal of Counselling Psychology*, **37**, 85–90.

Tiller, J., Slone, G., Schmidt, U., Troop, N., Powers, M. and Treasure, J. (1994). Social support and self-esteem in eating disorders. (Submitted).

Turnbull, I., Freeman, C.P.L., Barry, F. and Henderson, A. (1989). The clinical characteristics of bulimic women. *International Journal of Eating Disorders*, **8**, 399–409.

Treasure, J., Schmidt, U. and Keilen, M. (1992). "How do eating disorders affect the quality of life? A comparison between eating disorder sufferers and controls". Poster presented at the annual meeting of the Royal College of Psychiatrists, Dublin.

Treasure, J., Schmidt, U., Tiller, J., O'Donohue, G., Todd, G. and Malmberg, A. (1992). Children of mothers with eating disorders: a high risk group? Paper presented at the annual meeting of the Royal College of Psychiatrists, Dublin.

Vaillant, G.E., Bond, M. and Vaillant, C.O. (1986). An empirically validated hierarchy of defense mechanisms. *Archives of General Psychiatry*, **43**, 786–794.

Van Buren, D.J. and Williamson, D.A. (1988). Marital relationships and conflict resolution skills of bulimics. *International Journal of Eating Disorders*, **7**, 735–741.

Van den Broucke, S. and Vandereycken, W. (1989). The marital relationship of patients with an eating disorder: a questionnaire study. *International Journal of Eating Disorders*, **8**, 541–556.

Vandereycken, W. (1993). Naughty girls and angry doctors: eating disorder patients and their therapists. *International Review of Psychiatry*, **5**, 13–18.

Venes, A.M., Krupka, L.R. and Gerard, R.J. (1982). Overweight/obese patients: an overview. *The Practitioner*, **226**, 1102–1109.

Weiss, S.R. and Ebert, M.H. (1983). Psychological and behavioral characteristics of normal-weight bulimics and normal-weight controls. *Psychosomatic Medicine*, **45**, 293–303.

Weissman, M. and Rothwell, S. (1976). Assessment of social adjustment by self-report. *Archives of General Psychiatry*, **33**, 1111–1115.

Wonderlich, S. (1992). Relationship of family and personality factors in bulimia. In: Crowther, J.H., Tennenbaum, D.L., Hobfoll, S.E. and Stephens, M.A.P. (Eds), *The Etiology of Bulimia Nervosa: The Individual and Family Context*. Washington: Hemisphere Publishing Corporation.

Yager, J., Landsverk, J. and Edelstein, C.K. (1987). A 20-month follow-up study of 628 women with eating disorders. I: Course and severity. *American Journal of Psychiatry*, **144**, 1172–1177.

Part IV

Treatments

Introduction to Part IV

The volume provides ample evidence for a convergence of thinking in the contemporary approach to eating disorders: no one model can explain the phenomena of the disorders. All chapters in the section on aetiology refrain from claiming a unique power to explain the origin of the disorders; biological, psychological and social factors are called upon by all in attempts to understand origins. Likewise, in addressing the interesting question of maintaining factors, a range of interacting components are called upon to describe the manner whereby the symptoms, once in place, become established in the continuing biological, psychological, familial and social life of the person.

It is no surprise, therefore, that in this section on treatment no chapter is claiming central place in the therapeutic effort. No longer is it possible for psychoanalysts, family therapists, behavioural therapists, pharmacologists or ward managers to assert that their treatment is the one and only modality for all patients.

The different chapters reveal the problems that exist for the scientific assay of therapeutic practice in the field of serious, life-threatening psychological disorders. Some chapters (such as the one on family therapy and physical treatments) give considerable attention to the empirical evidence for the treatments being considered. Others (for example that on inpatient treatment and psychodynamic psychotherapies) are unable to draw upon any substantial body of evidence that defines the place of such treatments and that proves their efficacy. However, few clinicians doubt that there is a substantial place for inpatient treatment for the most "at-risk" patients, or that psychodynamic understanding is an enriching component in informing the treatment and management of all patients.

In the chapter on *inpatient and day-patient* treatments, Treasure and her colleagues point out that behavioural management, psychotherapeutic sensitivity, group interventions and medication all have a part to play. Refeeding has to occur, but there are no rigid guidelines as to the best means of achieving this. Morgan and Russell's follow-up studies long ago showed the uncertainty of claiming one or other element of the treatment as the decisive intervention, a viewpoint that Treasure and colleagues show is supported by The St George's studies led by Professor Crisp. Treasure and colleagues address the complicated question of involuntary treatment in both an ethical and practical way. The possibility of the spread of day-treatment facilities is alluded to, although there are even fewer scientific evaluations of day hospital than there are for inpatient programmes.

Individual psychodynamic psychotherapies have, until recently, been advocated in a partisan manner by psychoanalytic psychiatrists and other therapists as the only treatment that addresses the "fundamental" problems that give rise to eating disorders. This volume, and in particular this section, takes a different view, seeing the role of psychodynamic thinking as offering a way of identifying the experience and psychological process of suffering from an eating disorder, and suggesting that such a point of view complements and enriches other treatments. A considerable number of eating disordered patients are referred for psychodynamic psychotherapy, perhaps especially when the debilitating symptoms have lessened but existential distress continues. The chapter proposes a method of psychotherapy that enables the development of a subtle and detailed account of the psychological life of these patients, in interaction with the psychotherapist.

Freeman's chapter on *individual cognitive–behavioural therapies* is a detailed account of how to do such therapies with bulimic patients and gives ample evidence from controlled studies for the value of the approach. Space made it impossible to include an equally detailed description of work with anorexic patients for whom there is, as yet, much less evidence of benefit.

The chapter on *family therapy* concentrates on the series of treatment studies inspired by the last decade of Professor Russell's work at the Institute of Psychiatry and Bethlem Royal and Maudsley Hospital. These studies have gone some way towards defining the place of family treatment in restricting eating disorders. The chapter presents the evidence and describes the range of family treatment methods offered.

Physical treatments are discussed, and their place in the range of disturbances defined in Wakeling's elegant chapter. The problem of the difficult-to-treat and chronic case has long been a preoccupation of that author.

Finally, Andersen offers a wise summary integrating many treatment modalities in his discussion of *sequencing treatment decisions*, emphasising the central theme of the book as to the need in both theoretical modelling and treatment for a truly multifactorial and multidisciplinary approach.

15

The Inpatient Treatment of Anorexia Nervosa

JANET TREASURE
GILL TODD
AND
GEORGE SZMUKLER
Institute of Psychiatry, London, UK

EARLY TREATMENTS OF ANOREXIA NERVOSA

The consensus view of the treatment of anorexia in the last century was to remove the patient from her family and home surroundings. Thus:

> The hypochondriacal delirium, then, cannot be advantageously encountered so long as the subjects remain in the midst of their own family and their habitual circle: the obstinate resistance that they offer, the sufferings of the stomach, which they enumerate with incessant lamentation, produce too vivid an emotion to admit to the physician acting with full liberty and obtaining the necessary moral ascendancy. It is therefore indispensable to change the habitation and the surrounding circumstances and to entrust the patients to the care of strangers. (Marce, 1860)

> The inclination of the patient must in no way be consulted . . . patients should be fed at regular intervals and surrounded by persons who would have moral control over them: relatives and friends being generally the worst attendants. (Gull, 1874)

Later, not only was the patient separated from her family but she was also nursed in isolation (Charcot, 1889; Mitchell and Weir, 1907).

Handbook of Eating Disorders: Theory, Treatment and Research.
Edited by G. Szmukler, C. Dare and J. Treasure.
© 1995 John Wiley & Sons Ltd.

Physical treatments to supplement this model of nursing care were also tried. In the early half of this century, hormonal extracts such as thyroid hormone (Berkman, 1930) and ovarian or anterior pituitary extracts (Reifenstein, 1946) were given in an attempt to correct the widespread endocrine deficit. Insulin, used either alone or in combination with chlorpromazine, is still in use in some parts of the UK (Dally and Sargant, 1960; Bhanji and Mattingly, 1988). In Hamburg a "strict regimen" is used which consists of bedrest, tube feeding and phenothiazines (Engel and Meyer, 1982). Electroconvulsant therapy (ECT) and even prefrontal leucotomy have been tried (Laboucarie and Barres, 1954; Sargant, 1951).

THE CURRENT POSITION

Weight gain remains a critical component of treatment. However, the development of more specific, effective forms of psychotherapy has led to a move away from the position held by Russell in 1981: "Experience teaches that the patient is unlikely to respond to psychological methods of treatment until her loss of weight has been corrected."

In the UK and the USA, consensus treatment recommendations have been made (Royal College of Psychiatrists, 1992; American Psychiatric Association, 1993). In these reports a graded approach to treatment is advocated. Rather than forcibly separating the patient from the family, the family can be used as an ally in treatment (Minuchin, Rosman and Baker, 1978; Russell et al, 1987), particularly in the early stages of illness. Day-patient treatment offers an interesting alternative and has been developed in Toronto and Edinburgh (Piran and Kaplan, 1990; Freeman, 1992)—see below for further details. However, there remains widespread clinical opinion that inpatient treatment is necessary for some as a means of increasing weight reliably.

How Effective is Inpatient Treatment?

Inpatient treatment can lead to substantial weight gain, particularly if specialised nursing is available. In a series at the Maudsley Hospital, the average weight gain was 12.7 kg whereas the same patients' earlier admission to non-specialised units resulted in a weight gain of only 5.9 kg (Royal College of Psychiatrists, 1992).

Despite the short-term effectiveness of inpatient treatment, dissenting voices have been raised. The Bristol group state (Morgan, Purgold and Welbourne, 1983):

> Whilst admission to hospital might make the situation safe for a while, especially when weight is very low or there is a suicidal risk, it can also involve considerable disruption in the patient's management: it may represent counterproductive retreat from confrontation with certain life difficulties and signify confirmation of the sick role in the eyes of relatives who then dissociate themselves from active participation in therapy. It is not always a major therapeutic step forward to admit a patient to a hospital ward, and our findings suggest that criteria for hospital admission in anorexia nervosa should always be scrutinised carefully.

Anorexia nervosa often runs a prolonged course and relapse after inpatient treatment is common. A salutary reminder of this comes from a recent 5-year follow-up survey of 112 patients in New Zealand after their first hospital admission with anorexia nervosa (McKenzie and Joyce, 1990): 48% were readmitted on more than one occasion. A surprising finding was that patients under the age of 16 years were more likely to be readmitted. The cumulative length of stay in hospital was exceeded only by patients with schizophrenia or organic disorders.

What is the Current Place of Inpatient Treatment?

It is difficult to evaluate treatments of anorexia nervosa because the therapy needs to continue over the long term and emergencies may confound the planned interventions. Therefore the recent study by Crisp's group is to be commended (Crisp et al, 1991). It is unique in that it was designed to compare outpatient with inpatient treatments. Patients were randomly allocated to one of four programmes: admission to hospital; combined individual and family therapy as an outpatient; group therapy; or a control condition which consisted of one outpatient assessment. The methodological difficulties encountered and surmounted in this work were discussed in an earlier paper (Gowers et al, 1988). The constraints of the design led to a need to be selective about which patients could be involved in the study. For example, the patients had to have had a duration of illness of less than 10 years, had to live near the hospital and not have had prior treatment within the department. These conditions led to low recruitment (21/68=31% in 1986) (Gowers et al, 1988). This means that the results cannot, perhaps, be generalised to all patients.

The remarkable finding from this study was that, in terms of global measures of improvement on the Morgan & Russell scale, there were no differences between groups. On individual subscales there were a few differences; for example the nutritional outcome in the subset who had complied with their allocation to inpatient treatment was better than for the "no treatment" group. No other differences between the group allocated to inpatient treatment and the group given "no treatment" were found.

A major difficulty in interpreting these results was the poor adherence to the allocated treatment (Table 15.1). Only 60% allocated to inpatient treatment accepted this option, and all but 6 of those allocated to "no treatment" sought

TABLE 15.1 Compliance with treatment allocations (Crisp et al, 1991).

	Inpatient treatment	Group therapy	Individual family therapy	No treatment
Number	30	20	20	20
Take-up	18	18*	17	6
Mean duration treatment	20 weeks	9 sessions	5 sessions	–

* One death occurred before treatment began.

treatment elsewhere (6 inpatient treatment; 5 outpatient hospital treatment; 3 received regular support from general practitioners). Also, a large number of those allocated to outpatient treatment "dropped out" before their treatment was completed.

The results of this study are somewhat surprising given the huge differences in resources allocated to each treatment condition. A cynical interpretation would be that specialist treatment is unnecessary. Crisp's team argue that all subjects were given a specialist's assessment and reformulation which of itself may have a therapeutic impact. Also, because of the vagaries in compliance, all groups received treatment.

Further data to refute the cynics' interpretation were given by a study which compared the outcomes for patients seen at a specialised unit and for patients in an area without specialised services. The standardised mortality from the specialised unit was 136 compared with a standardised mortality of 471 in the area without specialised services (Crisp et al, 1992). The authors conclude: "Medical treatment may reduce early mortality while comprehensive medical and psychotherapeutic treatment may reduce late mortality."

Indications for Admission

The proportion of patients treated as inpatients has gradually decreased over the last decade as more patients are treated as outpatients and as the proportion of patients with bulimia nervosa increases. In the majority of cases the main reason for admission is for refeeding and weight restoration. Another reason is for a diagnostic assessment. Medical or psychiatric co-morbidity such as diabetes, self-harm, depression, obsessional symptoms or severe purging behaviour may make an admission necessary. Finally, inpatient treatment is necessary if outpatient treatment has failed.

Emergency Admissions

Immediate treatment is required if the patient's physical or mental state is dangerous or if there are contraindications to outpatient treatment. Some of the medical and psychiatric complications which signal the need for urgent treatment are listed in Table 15.2.

NURSING THE PATIENT WITH ANOREXIA NERVOSA

Inpatient treatment should not be conceptualised as a cure for anorexia nervosa, but as a means of alleviating the physical and psychological distress that starvation produces. The core of work undertaken during treatment is the work of the nurses, the main goals of which are: (1) forming a therapeutic alliance; and (2) weight restoration.

TABLE 15.2   Clinical and psychiatric grounds for admission.

Medical indications
1. Body mass index below 13.5 kg/m² (or a rapid rate of fall > 20% decrease in 6 months)
2. Syncope
3. Proximal myopathy
4. Hypoglycaemia
5. Electrolyte imbalance (e.g. K⁺ < 2.5)
6. Petechial rash and platelet suppression

Psychiatric indications
1. Risk of suicide
2. Intolerable family situation
3. Extreme social isolation
4. Failure of outpatient treatment

Forming a Therapeutic Alliance

Ambivalence about treatment in anorexia nervosa is usual and is what sets it apart from many other conditions. Thus there is a challenge to develop a therapeutic alliance, particularly in the context of inpatient treatment. As Bruch (1985) has put it: "On principle, these patients resist treatment: they feel that in their extreme thinness they have found the perfect solution to their deep-seated unhappiness."

The patient with anorexia nervosa has an overwhelming desire to lose weight despite the unpleasant thoughts, emotions and physical symptoms that are associated with it. The deceits which are used to maintain control over weight are to be expected as part of the illness and should not be interpreted as an attack upon treatment. The therapeutic relationship should be collaborative, with a kind, firm and consistent approach used to tackle the anorexic behaviour. The issues of power, control and trust within the therapeutic relationship need to be recognised as they can lead to coercion, frustration or collusion.

The forming of a therapeutic alliance begins with persuading the reluctant patient to accept admission. The best way to achieve this is to show her around the ward before admission. Discussion can then be held about meals, target weights, whether or not weight is to be talked about, visitors, groups, the personnel of the multidisciplinary team, and general ward routine. It is extremely helpful at this stage (or on the day of admission) to spend time talking to the accompanying person(s), in the presence of the patient.

Each aspect of a patient's behaviour should be questioned respectfully. Examples are: "I have noticed that you buy children's clothes—can you tell me why that is?" and "I understand that you are thinking of food and weight all the time—can you imagine what it might be like not to?".

Weight Restoration

The correction of life-threatening malnutrition requires regular mealtimes, an initial diet of small meals and snacks, and a controlled environment. Meals should be taken at a table, with others, and with discussion about every aspect of the problems of eating and the feelings this provokes. The free, uncontrolled availability of food may increase the risk of patients developing bulimia nervosa as they aim to eat their way out of hospital. Nursing interventions are crucial at this stage.

The following extract from Jenefer Shute's novel *Lifesize* (1992) portrays the subjective experience of a meal for a patient with anorexia nervosa:

> There is a big paper napkin on the tray, so I scrape exactly half the salad out of the bowl and into the napkin, along with half the roll. I bundle this mess up and start looking for a place to hide it: not easy in this cell. . . . Then I cut the lettuce, tomato, and pepper into tiny pieces, deciding I won't even pretend to eat the onion because lots of people don't like raw onion: it's legitimate, it's "normal". I cut the half roll into four sections and decide I will eat only one. Of the ice cream, I will eat exactly two spoonfuls, and the apple I will save for another time. So I put it away in my nightstand drawer along with the piece of roll I picked off the lunch tray: just in case.
>
> Now that these decisions have been made, now that the bad stuff has been removed, now that the food is separated, with white space showing on the plate, now I can start eating: one piece at a time, and at least three minutes (timed on a second hand) between mouthfuls, with the fork laid down precisely in the centre of the plate after each bite.

A common approach in specialised inpatient units is for the nurses to take control of eating away from the patient at first. Food portions are gradually increased to obtain a steady rate of weight gain, with snacks and drinks between meals. The daily calorie content of meals starts at about 1000 and gradually increases to 3000. Often the amount of choice offered to the patient is limited as patients will not be able to maintain their restrictions on the amount of fat, protein and fibre needed to achieve the appropriate amount of calories.

The nursing care delivered during and around mealtimes varies between units. One model is to have a nurse present during the meals, which are shared with other patients with anorexia nervosa. This offers an excellent opportunity to reintroduce the social aspects of eating and to model normal eating behaviour. It is important that the nurse sees her role as a therapist rather than as a prison guard. The expectation of the group process is that all of the food will be consumed and that it is the group's task to ensure this is done. The nurse aims to faciliate mutual support amongst the group. This may involve a patient nearing the end of treatment reassuring and empathising with a new patient. Abnormal eating habits can be highlighted as other group members notice and understand their difficulties. Typical anorexic eating rituals such as cutting food into tiny pieces or counting should be tackled. Similarly, behaviour techniques to combat excessive slowness can be used. In some units mealtimes have been videotaped and played back to the patient so that abnormal behaviours, such as rumination, can be recognised and targeted.

On other occasions the aim will be to remove the focus on food. Mealtimes are often prolonged. The countertransference can be intense and the nurse should be sensitive to this and use it; for example: "I am sitting here feeling frustrated and angry. I wonder if that is what some of you are also feeling?"

It is necessary to continue supervision after meals to prevent habitual vomiting.

Target Weight

Patients with anorexia nervosa will feel panic at the prospect of weight gain. They feel they are forfeiting their sole, tenuous, coping device and source of pleasure. In the short term, change leads to an increase in distress. Anxiety and despair are common, and the struggle to accept weight gain and to continue to increase nutrition becomes harder. With support this can sometimes become easier, but can change again to panic as discharge approaches. It is helpful to forewarn the patient and relatives that "anorexic attitudes" about weight, shape and eating may persist for several years even after the apparent recovery of weight and menstrual function. Benefits are in the long term.

Valued ideas about weight, shape and eating are impossible to shift by logical discussion. It is probably more reassuring for the patients to hear that the nurse understands but remains firm in her resolve to help the patients gain weight.

A weight gain of 1–2 kg per week leads to an average admission of 12–14 weeks. This is a reasonable compromise between the need to avoid institutionalisation, the loss of a social network, and the metabolic and psychic instability caused by too rapid a gain in weight. A target weight range (which can span over 5 kg) should be set. This normally encompasses the premorbid weight, defined as the weight that was comfortably held in late adolescence before the onset of the illness, after the start of periods. If the illness began before a mature weight was attained it may be necessary to set a target according to the body mass index (BMI) of 20–22 kg/m^2. for those who were obese (BMI >26) premorbidly a body mass index in the range 22–44 kg/m^2 is more appropriate. A study undertaken by Treasure et al (1988) suggested that pelvic ultrasonography is probably the best indicator for the weight which is required for full endocrine recovery. The study showed a positive association between functioning ovaries and premorbid weight.

It is necessary to establish a regular routine for weighing. The frequency of weighing, daily or three times a week, does not appear to effect the rate of weight gain (Touyz et al, 1990). One advantage of more frequent weighing is that fluctuations resulting from either medical complications or weight control methods (vomiting, laxatives) can be more clearly seen. There is no empirical evidence for the therapeutic value of sharing or not sharing the information with the patient, and the practice varies between units and over time. The argument for sharing the weight is to build an active collaboration and trust. The argument for keeping the weight secret is that it becomes a source of anxiety for all and leads to an unhealthy focus and preoccupation upon weight.

It is necessary to guard against the use of other methods of weight control, such as laxative abuse and furtive overexercising.

Alternative Goals

Shorter admissions may be offered for crisis intervention, as a life-saving manoeuvre so that treatment can begin. Another alternative is the development of a therapeutic alliance—a short admission of about one month can establish a set of rules about eating and diet in preparation for outpatient work (Kalucy et al, 1985).

MODELS OF NURSING TREATMENT

The models of nursing care used in the management of anorexia nervosa have often been written from a doctor's perspective (Pierloot et al, 1982; Hsu, 1986; Garfinkel and Garner, 1982; Crisp, 1985; Vandereyken, 1985). There are a few exceptions. Biley and Savage (1988) describe nursing practice in terms of Roper's "activities of daily living" model. Potts (1984) describes a dynamic involvement with the focus on feelings about weight gain, issues of control and body image.

Another inpatient treatment model is to have a split in staff functions, with one team attending to the nutrition aspects and a psychotherapist concentrating on the emotional aspects (Horne and Gallen, 1987).

Research has led to a move away from coercive methods of treatment. Strict behavioral regimes in which all privileges are taken away and total bedrest pre-scribed were found to be no more effective in terms of weight gain than lenient regimes, where the patients were more accessible for psychotherapy (Eckert et al, 1979); Touyz et al, 1984).

The nurse needs to maintain a balance between setting clear limits for behaviour and developing the patient's autonomy. The ideal goal (Bruch, 1985) is for "a patient to become an active participant in the treatment process, so that she can reach the point of differentiating herself from others . . . to grow beyond the helpless passivity, hateful submissiveness and indiscriminate negativism". Nurses working with patients with eating disorders have to work as a team, anticipate splitting, set limits without excessive coercion and cope with intense coun-tertransference. Such nursing skills are more effective than any drug treatment so far tried; but they can lead to exhaustion, so the medical staff and senior nursing staff need to provide a lot of support through regular supervision.

Psychotherapeutic treatment is directed at the developmental psychopathology (Crisp et al, 1992), and specialist inpatient treatment will mirror the patient's expe-rience of a controlling or non-controlling family. Inpatient treatment will be a balance between control taken by the staff over the patient's eating, and personal freedom to come and go, have visitors, make telephone calls, go to the toilet—patients taking responsibility for their own behaviour. As the patient is helped to progress developmentally, physically and psychologically, she will feel less con-trolled and more in control. Many inpatient programmes delineate the steps in a way which allows little variation between individuals. These can be contrasted with programmes which are more flexible, with little restriction, knowledge of weight gain and collaborative goals. A flexible programme puts more pressure on the staff, who will find that they need to justify why they treat one patient in one way and one in another way. There is no evidence at present to suggest an improved outcome either way in the longer term.

Some of the management problems encountered with these patients are outlined in Table 15.3.

TABLE 15.3   Nursing management problems and solutions.

Problem	Management solutions
Refusal to eat	Mobilise group support Set firm expectations After 1 hour, nurse individually If no food eaten on more than 3 occasions or if fluid intake refused, then assisted feeding should be considered
Slowness	As above Record the duration of each part of the meal Set goals with key nurse to reduce duration
Cutting/counting rituals	As above Modelling appropriate behaviour
Hiding food	Limit tissues from the table Be suspicious of clothes with pockets and long sleeves Check under and around tables and windows
Excess use of condiments	Set limits
Doubt over food consumption	Find underlying reason Is there "cheating" in some form?
Vomiting	Limit use of toilets 1 hour after meal Offer support from group or nurse Patient helps clear up if necessary Compensate by milkshake
Weight gain too rapid	Limit fluid consumption Is oedema present? Check clothes for weights
Weight gain too slow	?Inadequate intake ?Vomiting (check HCO_3, and K^+) ?Laxatives, diuretics (urine screen) Inform patient of need to search belongings
Exercise	Set limits on exercise Gradual group activities
Staff splitting	Avoid talk about other staff Interpret transference issues Have clearly established roles and responsibilites Good supervision and communication between staff
Countertransference; anger/hopelessness in staff	Supervision Support group/particularly with students and inexperienced staff

THE MULTIDISCIPLINARY TEAM

Professionals other than nurses and doctors can contribute to the management of patients with eating disorders. The occupational therapist can facilitate self-expression and self-awareness. The use of non-verbal therapies such as projective art can be of particular benefit to patients who tend to over-intellectualise their problems (Harries, 1992).

The patient's family should be involved in inpatient care so that they are aware of the treatment goals, the rationale for each treatment measure, and the potential difficulties of the post-discharge phase.

MEDICAL PROBLEMS ASSOCIATED WITH REFEEDING

The medical problems occurring most commonly with refeeding are:

- acute gastric dilatation
- low plasma phosphate level
- refeeding oedema.

Acute gastric dilatation is a rare but potentially lethal complication, so it is the practice of many units to gradually build up the quantities of food prescribed. The condition presents with vomiting, abdominal pain and distension. On examination a succussion splash can be heard, but other bowel sounds are absent. Risk factors include hypokalaemia and a rapid increase in food intake. If it is recognised early it responds to nasogastric aspiration and intravenous feeding. It can, however, be complicated by stomach rupture which has a high mortality.

Hypophosphataemia may become apparent on refeeding anorexic patients when the increased metabolic demands outstrip reserves. It has been called the "nutritional recovery syndrome". It may not lead to symptoms (Van Dissel, Gerritsen and Meinders, 1992). However, delirium, status epilepticus, cardiac abnormalities and suppression of the haematological system and respiratory failure can occur (Gustavsson and Eriksson, 1989; Cumming, Farquar and Bouchier, 1987; Beumont and Large, 1991). Regular monitoring of plasma phosphate levels is recommended during the initial phase of refeeding. Risk factors include severity of emaciation, intravenous feeding and alcoholism.

Refeeding oedema can be marked, particularly if laxatives have been used. It is not uncommon to see a weight gain of 1 kg per day. Measures such as avoidance of extra salt with meals and elevation of the limbs are usually sufficient, and diuretics are rarely indicated.

If intravenous fluids are being used with patients with anorexia nervosa, then regular monitoring of sodium, potassium, calcium, magnesium and phosphate levels are needed. The ECG may also need to be monitored as prolongation of the QT interval is common and increases the risk of a serious arrhythmia developing.

Patients with anorexia nervosa commonly assert that they never suffer from infections until they start to gain weight. Recent research provides theoretical support for this: superoxide formation in polymorphonuclear cells, which is thought to be important in microcidal and cytocidal actions, was normal when subjects were undernourished but decreased upon refeeding (Vaisman et al, 1992).

OTHER DIFFICULTIES IN MANAGEMENT

Eating disorders may lead to dangerous psychological complications. Depression usually arises as a consequence of the illness and may require active management. Depression increases in severity once the illness becomes established and the social repercussions, such as a contracted social life, loss of career (Tiller, Schmidt and Treasure, 1993; Keilen et al, 1992) and the general "starving" of life take their toll. This depression is difficult to treat. Antidepressants are ineffective at such profound degrees of weight loss (see Chapter 1), and there is no evidence that ECT is effective. Hopelessness and pessimism mean that there is little energy or will to struggle with the anorexic conditions. Death therefore can result from increasing malnutrition due to neglect or active suicide. All of the follow-up studies have found that half of the mortality of anorexia nervosa is a result of suicide (Treasure, 1991).

INVOLUNTARY TREATMENT

Occasionally a patient will lose insight into the dangerousness of her condition and a treatment order under the Mental Health Act or other mental health legislation needs to be implemented to ensure that her health and safety are safeguarded. Involuntary treatment for anorexia nervosa may also be necessary to allow normal maturation of secondary sexual features, growth and skeletal development.

This measure should be used only after there have been several interviews with the patient and her family. Parents are concerned that if they take this action their daughter will never forgive them. In contrast it is our experience that patients usually come to recognise the need for this step and are grateful that their life has been saved.

Why is the Compulsory Treatment of Anorexia Nervosa Controversial?

Although most expert opinion holds that the Mental Health Act is appropriate in the management of anorexia nervosa (e.g. Sims, 1992; Welbourne and Cockett, 1992), those who are less intimately involved are more uncertain. Such cases appear to hold fascination for the media. The question posed by Dyer (1992) in an article in *The Guardian* was: "Should a 16-year-old anorexic girl who is capable of making her own decisions be allowed to starve herself or can the court force her to have treatment?"

Anorexia nervosa, more than many forms of mental illness, is conceptualised as a conscious choice. This view prevails amongst the medical profession (Fleming and Szmukler, 1992). Psychological explanatory models perhaps fuel these beliefs. These range from the idea that anorexia nervosa is a political statement, a hunger strike (Orbach, 1986); a coping role within the family (Palazzoli, 1978); through to the extreme view that patients are overpriviledged manipulators, liars and cheats who abuse medical attention (Naish, 1979) or that they are undertaking a passive form of suicide.

A recent interpretation of the law in the UK by the Court of Appeal stated that there is a failure of insight in anorexia nervosa and so it is appropriate to overrule a patient's decision to refuse treatment in certain severe cases: "[anorexia] sometimes destroyed the ability of a sufferer to make a rational decision and Lord Justice Nolan said that the court had an inescapable responsibility to overrule J's wishes" (Roberts, 1992). It creates a compulsion to refuse treatment or to accept only treatment which is likely to be ineffective. That attitude *is part of the illness* and the more advanced the illness the more compelling it may become.

The other issue which arouses controversy is the form taken by involuntary treatment. Why does forced treatment with food cause more repugnance and anxiety in the public mind than does treatment with drugs? There is a popular misconception that involuntary treatment is synonymous with coercive practices. It is as if images of suffragettes or Strasbourg geese spring to mind. There have been recent debates within the Canadian medical community over whether there is any merit in prolonging the life of a seemingly treatment-resistant patient (Herbert and Weingarten, 1991; Kluge, 1991; Goldner, McKenzie and Kline, 1991).

Over the last decade we have seen a gradual increase in the number of involuntary patients at the Maudsley Hospital. We have never had to use tube-feeding as our nurses have the skills and confidence to deal with these problems.

Possible Adverse Effects

Apart from the idea that compulsory treatment for anorexia nervosa is cruel, others have argued without evidence that such treatment increases the risk of bulimia nervosa developing (Selvini-Palazzoli, 1974). Bulimia nervosa does develop in approximately a third of cases of anorexia nervosa (Treasure, 1990), but there is no evidence that this occurs more in those treated as inpatients rather than those treated as outpatients. Weight loss and dieting clearly increase the risk of developing bulimia nervosa, and this was also seen as a reaction of otherwise normal men to starvation (Keys, Brozek and Henschel, 1950).

Crisp (1980) has argued that involuntary treatment may precipitate depression and suicide, particularly in chronic patients. However, such patients have a high mortality from inanition and suicide (Theander, 1985). In our experience involuntary treatment does not preclude the development of a good therapeutic alliance.

Medication

There are two basic reasons for adopting a pharmacological approach in the management of eating disorders. The first is that a drug may correct the basic biochemical deficit underlying the condition. The second is that a drug may produce symptomatic benefit. There is little evidence that medication can improve upon the weight gain achieved by skilled nursing management.

Feeding Challenges

On rare occasions we have had to resort to assisted feeding on our unit. We prefer this approach as it has far fewer complications than tube or intravenous feeding. It does require skilled, sympathetic nursing.

The procedure is outlined to the patient. Two nurses are needed for this procedure: one nurse spoon-feeds whilst the other gently restrains and comforts the patient. It is sometimes necessary to have a third nurse in order to restrain a frightened patient. The nurses should explain that they have to take over control as the anorexia is putting the patient's life at grave risk. They explain that they have an ethical duty to safeguard the patient's life as her own judgement has become so clouded by her illness that she fails to recognise the danger she is in: "We will not let you die." It is usual for the patient to eat normally when she has experienced the firm resolution of the staff. In adult patients there is time for this graduated nursing strategy, but in children who have less reserves more acute measures such as nasogastric feeding may be necessary.

If nasogastric feeding is to be used it should be time-limited and needs to be carefully supervised. The goals should be set beforehand and normal meals offered. Only if these are not completely eaten is the tube used to deliver supplementary feeds. Hypophosphataemia or mechanical (aspiration) complications can occur with tube-feeding and so careful monitoring is necessary. Some patients prefer this approach and these extreme feelings need to be explored.

Intravenous feeding may be required particularly if there is a life-threatening medical emergency. The nursing in this case should be provided on a medical ward.

INPATIENT TREATMENT FOR BULIMIA NERVOSA

Patients who have severe symptoms and co-morbidity may require brief periods of hospitalisation at a time of crisis or for treatment of associated conditions such as diabetes, depression or alcohol abuse. Such admissions may serve as a break in the pathological eating pattern, but improvements are unlikely to generalise to the outside environment without additional treatment. Patients with severe electrolyte disturbance or physical illness may benefit from more intensive care. Day-patient treatment is probably the treatment of first choice (Piran and Kaplan, 1990) allowing the patient to remain in contact with the everyday situations that precipitate binge-eating whilst having intensive therapeutic contact.

The goals of inpatient treatment for bulimia nervosa are similar to those used in its outpatient management. Regular meals are given. Behavioural techniques to decrease vomiting should be employed. It may be preferred to cease laxatives abruptly within hospital, rather than gradually decreasing the number used.

Difficulties with relationships and personality characteristics which underlie the eating difficulties may become easier to define in these circumstances. These are the factors which often militate against effective outpatient treatment. Psychotherapeutic approaches such as interpersonal therapy or cognitive–analytic therapy may be helpful.

It is important to warn the patient that change will be uncomfortable. Physical discomforts include rebound oedema and impaired gastrointestinal function with bloating and constipation. Loss of the "habit" of bulimia which is often used as a coping strategy for distressing emotions and for idle time and loneliness will reveal the need to develop more adaptive strategies.

DAY-PATIENT TREATMENTS

Several specialist centres within the UK now offer day-patient treatment for anorexia nervosa. This can offer a greater degree of personal autonomy than an inpatient unit. The programmes that have been devised use a multidisciplinary team approach and use many of the components outlined above. At least one or perhaps two meals are supervised and patients usually attend 5 days a week for 2–4 months.

Peer support given by fellow patients and skilled nursing remain the main care provision. Relatives and friends are encouraged to learn, from the nurses, ways in which they can help the patient cope with their eating, and family meetings are regarded as an important component of therapy. Participation in ward groups (e.g. projective art, relaxation, assertiveness training and psychodrama) is required and an occupational therapy programme is tailored to the needs of each individual. Body-orientated exercises can help patients address the interoceptive disturbances which are characteristic of the illness. Patients have sessions with the dietician to evaluate their nutritional knowledge and to prevent the development of a limited repertoire of safe foods. Peer group support encourages patients to be more realistic in their self-appraisal and group discussions enable them to consider their attitudes to shape and weight in light of societal pressures. Medication if considered appropriate can safely be taken under supervision, and physical complications monitored.

Most of the patients with anorexia nervosa gain weight and are able to maintain this over a subsequent 6 months. The interested reader can find a detailed account of this treatment in Piran and Kaplan (1990).

POST-DISCHARGE TREATMENT

Inpatient treatment should be regarded as a preliminary step rather than the cure. It is important that outpatient treatment is given over the following months other-wise the chances of relapse are high. A randomised controlled trial which compared family therapy with individual treatment indicated that family therapy was more effective at preventing relapse in the subgroup whose illness had begun before the age of 18 and was of short duration (Russell et al, 1987). Individual therapy was more effective than family therapy in older patients.

CONCLUSIONS

Over the last hundred years the management of anorexia nervosa has changed. Treatment has shifted from medical wards, through to psychiatric wards and now, following the trends in all of medicine, towards community care. What is unclear is whether these changes reflect changes in the fashion of medical care or whether they result from the development of new skills and psychotherapeutic techniques.

Scientific enquiry poses difficulties (e.g. Gowers et al, 1988), but several groups have taken up the challenge with interesting results. Some issues, such as the place of inpatient treatment in the management of anorexia nervosa, remain to be resolved. The strides in our understanding of the treatment principles required for bulimia nervosa have overtaken those for anorexia nervosa.

Randomised studies, with minimal selection bias, are required to establish good clinical practice in the management of anorexia nervosa. So many questions remain unanswered. Is it necessary to aim for normal weight with inpatient treatment? What happens if the target weight gain is set for 5 kg? Are there adverse consequences of treatment? Will outpatient treatment lead to suboptimal weight gain and partial recovery? Does rapid weight gain lead to instability in the control of weight? Can we prevent the so-called "ominous variant" of anorexia nervosa developing? Do modern treatment methods improve the long-term recovery? Is the treatment of a patient with chronic anorexia nervosa (duration >15 years) really impossible?

REFERENCES

American Psychiatric Association (1992). Practice guidelines for eating disorders. *Am. J. Psychiat.,* **150**, 208–228.

Andersen, A.E. (1985). *Practical Comprehensive Treatment of Anorexia Nervosa and Bulimia.* London: Edward Arnold.

Bhanji, S. and Mattingly, D. (1988). *Medical Aspects of Anorexia Nervosa.* London: Wright.

Berkman, J.M. (1930). Anorexia nervosa, anorexia, inanition and low metabolic rate. *Am. J. Med. Sci.,* **180**, 411.

Beumont, P.J.V. and Large, M. (1991). Hypophosphataemia, delerium and cardiac arrhythmia in anorexia nervosa. *Med. J. Aust.,* **155**, 519–522.

Biley, F. and Savage, S. (1988). The role of the nurse in eating disorders. In: D. Scott (Ed.), *Anorexia and Bulimia Nervosa: Practical Approaches.* London: Croom Helm.

Bruch (1985). Four decades of eating disorders. In: P.E. Garfinkel (Ed.), *Handbook of Psychotherapy for Eating Disorders.* New York: Guilford Press.

Burgoyne, G. (1990). The CPN and eating disorders. *Nursing,* **4**(2).

Charcot, J.M. (1889). *Diseases of the Nervous System.* London: New Sydenham Society.

Crisp, A.H. (1980). *Anorexia Nervosa: "Let me be".* London: Academic Press.

Crisp, A.H., Callender, J.S., Halek, C., Hsu, L.K.G. (1992). Long-term mortality in anorexia nervosa: a twenty-year follow-up of the St George's and Aberdeen cohorts. *Br. J. Psychiat.,* **161**, 104–107.

Crisp, A.H., Norton, K.R.W., Jurczak, S., Bowyer, C. and Duncan, S. (1985). A treatment approach to anorexia nervosa—25 years on. *J. Psychiat. Res.,* **19**, 399–404.

Crisp, A.H., Norton, K.R.W., Gower, S., Halek, C. Bowyer, C., Yeldham, D., Levett, G. and Bhat, A. (1991). A controlled study of the effect of therapies aimed at adolescent and family psychopathology in anorexia nervosa. *Br. J. Psychiat.,* **159**, 325–333.

Cumming, A.D., Farquar, J.R. and Bouchier, I.A.D. (1987). Refeeding hypophosphataemia in anorexia nervosa and alcoholism. *Br. Med. J.,* **259**, 490–491.

Dally, P.J. and Sargant, W. (1960). Treatment and outcome of anorexia nervosa. *Br. Med. J.,* **2**, 793.

Dyer, C. (1992). Can J starve herself? *The Guardian,* 24 June.

Eckert, E.D., Goldberg, S.C., Halmi, K.A., Casper, R.C. and Davis, J.M. (1979). Behaviour therapy in anorexia nervosa. *Br. J. Psychiat.*, **134**, 55–59.

Engel, K. and Meyer, A.E. (1982). Theorie und Empirie einer mehrfaktoriellen stationaren Anorexie-therapie fur schwer erkrante Patientinnen. *Medsche Welt*, **33**, 1812–1816.

Fleming, J. and Szmukler, G.I. (1992). Attitudes of medical professionals towards patients with eating disorders. *Aust. NZ J. Psychiat.*, **26**, 436–443.

Freeman, C. (1992). Day-patient treatment for anorexia nervosa. *Br. Rev. Bulim. Anor. Nerv.*, **6**, 2–8.

Garfinkel, P.E. and Garner, D.M. (1982). *Anorexia Nervosa: A Multidimensional Perspective*. New York: Brunner/Mazel.

Goldner, E.M., McKenzie, J.M. and Kline, S.A. (1991). The ethics of forced feeding in anorexia nervosa. *Can. Med. Ass. J.*, **14**, 1205–1206.

Gowers, S., Norton, K., Yeldham, D., Bowyer, C., Levett, G., Heavey, A., Bhat, A. and Crisp, A. (1988). The St George's prospective treatment study of anorexia nervosa: a discussion of methodological problems. *Int. J. Eat. Disord.*, **8**, 445–454.

Gull, W.W. (1874). Anorexia nervosa (apepsia hysterica, anorexia hysterica). *Trans. Clin. Soc. Lond.* **7**, 22.

Gustavsson, C.G. and Eriksson, L. (1989). Case report: Acute respiratory failure in anorexia nervosa with hypophospharaemia. *J. Intern. Med.*, **225**, 63–64.

Harries, P. (1992). Facilitating change in anorexia nervosa: the role of occupational therapy. *Br. J. Occup. Ther.*, **55**, 334–339.

Herbert, P.C. and Weingarten (1991). The ethics of forced feeding in anorexia nervosa. *Can. Med. Ass. J.*, **144**, 141–144.

Horne, M. and Gallen, M. (1987). Anorexia nervosa: an objects relation approach to primary treatment. *Br. J. Psychiat.*, **151**, 192–194.

Hsu, L.K.G. (1986). The treatment of anorexia nervosa. *Am. J. Psychiat.*, **143**, 573–581.

Kalucy, R.S., Gilchrist, P.N., McFarlane, C.M. and McFarlane, A.C. (1985). The evolution of a multitherapy orientation. In: P.E. Garfinkel (Ed.), *Handbook of Psychotherapy for Eating Disorders*. New York: Guilford Press.

Keilen, M., Treasure, T., Schmidt, U. and Treasure, J.L. (1992). Quality of life measurements in eating disorders, angina, and transplant candidates: are they comparable? (Submitted.)

Keys, A., Brozek, J. and Henschel, A. (1950). *The Biology of Human Starvation*, Vol. 1. Minneapolis: Minnesota University Press.

Kluge, E.H. (1991). The ethics of forced feeding in anorexia nervosa: a response to Herbert and Weingarten. *Can. Med. Ass. J.*, **144**, 1121–1124.

Laboucarie, J. and Barres, J. (1954). Les aspects cliniques, pathogeniques et therapeutiques de l'anorexia mentale. *L'Evolution Psychiatrique*, **1**, 118–119.

Marce, L.A. (1860). On a form of hypochondriacal delirium occurring consecutive to dyspepsia and characterized by refusal of food. *J. Psychol. Med. Mental Pathol.*, **13**, 204–206.

McKenzie, J.M. and Joyce, P.R. (1992). Hospitalization for anorexia nervosa. *Int. J. Eat. Dis.*, **11**, 235–241.

Minuchin, S., Rosman, B.L. and Baker, L. (1978). *Psychosomatic Families: Anorexia Nervosa in Context*. Cambridge, Mass: Harvard University Press.

Mitchell, S. and Weir (1907). *Fat and Blood*. Philadelphia: J.B. Lippincott.

Morgan, H.G., Purgold, J. and Welbourne, J. (1983). Management and outcome in anorexia nervosa: a standardised prognostic study. *Br. J. Psychiat.*, **143**, 282–287.

Naish, J.M. (1979). Problems of deception in medical practice. *Lancet*, **ii**, 139–142.

Orbach, S. (1986). *Hunger Strike: The Anorectic's Struggle as a Metaphor for Our Age*. London: Faber & Faber.

Palazzoli, M. (1978). *Self Starvation: From Individual to Family Therapy in the Treatment of Anorexia Nervosa*. New York: Jason Aronson.

Patton, G.C., Johnson-Sabine, E., Wood, K., Mann, A.H. and Wakeling (1990). Abnormal eating attitudes in London schoolgirls: a prospective epidemiological study—outcome at twelve-month follow-up. *Psych. Med.*, **20**, 383–394.

Pierloot, R., Vandereycken, W. and Verhaest, S. (1982). An in-patient treatment programme for anorexia nervosa patients. *Acta Psychiat. Scand., 66*, 1–8.

Piran, N. and Kaplan, A.S. (Eds) (1990). *A Day Hospital Group Treatment Program for Anorexia Nervosa and Bulimia Nervosa.* New York: Brunner/Mazel.

Potts, N. (1984). Eating disorders: the secret pattern of binge/purge. *Am. J. Nursing, 84*, 32–35.

Reifenstein, E.C. (1946). Psychogenic or "hypothalamic" Amenorrhea. *Med. Clin. N. Amer., 30*, 1103.

Roberts, A. (1992). Judges explain why anorexia must be treated. *The Times*, 11 July.

Royal College of Psychiatrists (1992). *Eating Disorders.* Council Report CR14, London.

Russell, G.F.M. (1981). Comment: The current treatment of anorexia nervosa. *Br. J. Psychiat., 138*, 164–166.

Russell, G.F.M., Szmukler, G.I., Dare, C. and Eisler, I. (1987). An evaluation of family therapy in anorexia nervosa and bulimia nervosa. *Arch. Gen. Psychiat., 44*, 1047–1056.

Sargant, W. (1951). Leucotomy in psychosomatic disorders. *Lancet, 2*, 87.

Selvini-Palazzoli, M. (1974). *Self Starvation: From Individual to Family Therapy in the Treatment of Anorexia Nervosa* (A. Pomerans, trans). New York: Jason Aronson.

Shute, J. (1992). *Lifesize.* London: Secker & Warburg.

Sims, A. (1992). Letter: The law and anorexia. *The Times*, 11 September.

Theander, S. (1985). Outcome and prognosis in anorexia nervosa and bulimia: some results of previous investigations compared with those of a Swedish long-term study. *J. Psychiat. Res., 19*, 493–508.

Tiller, J., Schmidt, U. and Treasure, J. (1993). Compulsory treatment of anorexia nervosa: compassion or coercion? *Br. J. Psychiat., 162*, 679–680.

Touyz, S.W., Beumont, P.J.V., Glaun, D., Phillips, T. and Cowie, I. (1984). A comparison of lenient and strict operant conditioning programmes in refeeding patients with anorexia nervosa. *Br. J. Psychiat., 144*, 517–520.

Touyz, S.W., Lennerts, R., Freeman, R.J. and Beumont, P.J.V. (1990). To weigh or not to weigh? *Br. J. Psychiat., 157*, 752–754.

Treasure, J.L. (1991). Long-term management of eating disorders. *Int. Rev. Psychiatr., 3*, 43–58.

Treasure, J.L. and Mynors-Wallis, L. (1990). Anorexia nervosa. In: J.J. Studd (Ed.), *Progress in Obstetrics and Gynaecology*, Vol. 8. Edinburgh: Churchill Livingstone.

Treasure, J.L., Wheeler, E.A., King, P.A.L., Gordon and Russell, G.F.M. (1988). Weight gain and reproductive function: ultrasonographic and endocrine features in anorexia nervosa. *Clin. Endocrin., 29*, 607–616.

Vaisman, N., Tabachnik, E., Hahn, T., Voet, H., Guy, N. (1992). Superoxide production during refeeding in patients with anorexia nervosa. *Metabolism, 41*, 1097–1099.

Vandereycken, W. (1985). Inpatient treatment of anorexia nervosa: some research-guided changes. *J. Psychiat. Res., 19*, 413–422.

Van Dissel, J.T., Gerritsen, H.J. and Meinders, A.E. (1992). Severe hypophosphataemia in a patient with anorexia nervosa during oral feeding. *Miner. Electrolyte Metab., 18*, 365–369.

Welbourne, G. and Cockett, A. (1992). To treat or not to treat? *Br. Rev. Bulim. Anor. Nerv., 6*, 51–52.

16

Living Dangerously: Psychoanalytic Psycotherapy of Anorexia Nervosa

CHRISTOPHER DARE
AND
CATHERINE CROWTHER
Institute of Psychiatry, London, UK

INTRODUCTION

The psychodynamic psychopathology of eating disorders is described in Chapter 7. The patients described in this chapter are adults with anorexia nervosa, some of whom have bulimic symptoms, who were the definitive treatment group in two formal control trials of a one-year long psychoanalytic psychotherapy. Because the trials are still in progress there are no specific results. We describe the manner in which a strict transference focused psychotherapeutic technique can be applied in a research project in a general psychiatric setting with patients unselected for suitability for interpretative psychotherapy.

We have come to understand that patients with eating disorders fear that their own needs, and the people who might supply provision of those needs, cannot be controlled by themselves. They therefore fear the vulnerability of closeness. The anorexic symptoms are used to gain a spurious sense of control and as a substitute for a wide range of feelings. The understanding and management of the fears and the block to feelings is the technical problem of the psychotherapy and the life task of the patients. We describe the use of a focal hypothesis to guide the time-limited treatment.

Handbook of Eating Disorders: Theory, Treatment and Research.
Edited by G. Szmukler, C. Dare and J. Treasure.
© 1995 John Wiley & Sons Ltd.

There is a long history of attempts to explain and treat anorexia nervosa using psychoanalysis or psychoanalytic psychotherapy (Kaufman and Heiman, 1964). Depth psychologies not only provide perceptive and convincing accounts of the experiences and inner worlds of eating disordered patients, but also enable an understanding of the emotional effects upon the therapists who treat them (Thomä, 1967; Bruch, 1973, 1978; Orbach, 1985). To be involved in the therapy of such problems, especially when they have become chronic, is compelling. This is so, despite it being emotionally taxing and even frightening.

What distinguishes our treatment from other psychoanalytic accounts is that our patients were in no way selected for their sustainability for psychoanalytic psychotherapy, and that our once-a-week treatment, time-limited to one year, is unlike the more frequent, open-ended, long-term exploration that psychoanalytic pyschotherapy customarily offers. The setting in which the therapy took place fell far short of the basic requirements of freedom from interruption or impingements.

An aspect of the work which has been important to us as psychotherapists is that we have learned by combining our psychoanalytic insights with knowledge gained from the results of empirical investigation. We have also been eager to learn how far we can apply the theories and techniques of psychoanalysis within the constraints of an NHS psychiatric hospital.

People who are losing weight may give a strong impression of not being available for psychoanalytic psychotherapy. The anorexic patient has a great capacity to "glaze over" and cease to relate or listen at points when emotional contact might have been made. Even more strikingly, the patient may react actively, even violently, to a moment of real contact between herself and the therapist. Such defensiveness has a painful effect on the therapist. There is a great deal of frustration and fear in response to a patient losing weight. A belief that it is not possible to carry on doing therapy with a severely emaciated patient may become self-fulfilling, but may also be used as a protection for the therapist. In the therapies presented here, the therapist is compelled by the research protocol to attempt to complete the one-year treatments. This pressure has in some cases challenged our therapeutic presuppositions and led us to recognise that genuine psychotherapeutic work can be done with this unselected group of anorexic patients.

It is important to emphasise that for a psychotherapeutic approach such as this to be employed with patients who may become dangerously ill, a supportive clinical back-up and the opportunity for regular supervisory consultation are essential.

DEVELOPMENT OF THE MAUDSLEY RESEARCH TRIALS OF THERAPIES FOR ANOREXIA NERVOSA

Our investigation of the psychoanalytic approach to anorexia nervosa was reached by a somewhat curious route.

In an earlier research project at the Maudsley Hospital we compared family therapy with individual supportive (non-psychoanalytic) psychotherapy, for severe eating disorders (Russell et al, 1987; Dare et al, 1990). We showed that the adolescent patients had been well helped by the family therapy. Results for young adult patients were much less clear-cut, but seemed to indicate that the individual supportive therapy had had more benefit than family therapy. We undertook a detailed examination of the successes and failures of the individual therapy, seeking to uncover the effective ingredients in this therapy.

One factor alone emerged: the nature of the patient/therapist relationship. In this relationship, the crucial ingredient was the mutual accpetance of the nature of their joint work, the therapeutic alliance (see Sandler, Dare and Holder, 1992). An unsuccessful treatment was characterised by a long continued mismatch between the patient and the therapist as to their perceptions of the aim of treatment: the patient defined her primary need as keeping thin, perhaps to lose more weight. Her secondary aim was certainly to get away from painful preoccupation with food and to solve the other problems of life—work, leisure interests and relationship difficulties. But to the therapist, it seemed the patient wanted to make acceptance of help conditional upon being allowed to keep her problem. Unsuccessful therapies were dominated by this contradiction. The patient often experienced the therapist as an unhelpful, perhaps cruel and unsympathetic opponent. It was not possible to feel that therapist and patient were "on the same side".

In the successful therapies of the first trial, either from the beginning, or in the course of treatment, a major difference in the therapeutic alliance was experienced: the patient accepted or came to accept that sooner or later she had to give up her aim to be thin and to diet, and seek alternative ways of coping with her obsession. This required, eventually, an admission of a distorted view of the world and also that the therapist was not an opponent but a trustworthy ally struggling against a demon. This change of perception could come about even when the patient was still thin, miserable and living a severely restricted life, full of anorexic preoccupations. It was by no means a state of "being cured".

To investigate what had produced beneficial, as opposed to unhelpful, treatment relationships, we developed two further treatment trials. We used as the target treatment the only therapy that specifically concentrates upon the patient/therapist relationship: psychoanalytic psychotherapy. We drew upon Malan's (1976, 1979) focal psychoanalytic psychotherapy. This model had the additional advantage of brevity, for a non-time-limited psychotherapy would have been extremely difficult to confine within a research format.

In the second trial, we investigated the treatment of another group of chronic adult anorexic patients in the risky period after they have been discharged from the eating disorders ward at the Maudsley Hospital. After discharge, they were randomly allocated to one of three treatment modalities, psychoanalytic psychotherapy, supportive individual therapy or family therapy, for one year of treatment. Many patients had previously had frequent admissions elsewhere. Their severe condition is demonstrated by the fact that the average length of their illness is six and a half years, nearly a fifth had been ill for more than ten years and only a quarter for less than three. Some also had bulimic symptoms.

Hoping to prevent admission to hospital, a third research trial is comparing one year's psychoanalytic psychotherapy and family therapy for another group of adult anorexic patients who have had no previous contact with the Maudsley. They are treated from the start as outpatients. Some have had hospitalisations elsewhere. For others it is their first acknowledgement that they need help.

PSYCHOANALYTIC PSYCHOTHERAPY IN THE RESEARCH SETTING

In this paper we describe the psychoanalytic psychotherapy that has been adapted to working with these patients in a hospital setting. It is important to note that the patients are not assessed for psychotherapy in the usual manner. Their initial motivation is not identified, as it is not part of the criteria for admission to the treatment trials. Moreover, the patients may not have been motivated to enter the ward phase of the treatment and sometimes admission may have been compelled under a section of the Mental Health Act. The patients are likely to be naive about psychotherapy and their capacity for insight has not been tested. The therapist, likewise, has no choice over which patients to take on, nor to what type of treatment the patients will be randomly allocated. Despite these factors, the therapists have—remarkably—been able to engage 75% of the patients in the psychoanalytic psychotherapy.

The rooms allocated for the outpatient treatments are part of the general psychiatric clinics and are not therefore arranged to protect the inviolability of the time of the patient with the therapist. The therapists struggle to impose consistency, order and privacy for their work in the clinics, but this is only partially successful. The telephone may interrupt, people may knock on the door and the room may even be unexpectedly occupied by another clinician. We are stressing that the manner of selecting patients and the nature of the setting are quite different from the accepted minimum standards for the practice of psychoanalytic psychotherapy.

In the first outpatient session, the therapist tries to differentiate the nature of this encounter from what usually goes on in the outpatient clinic. The one-year duration of the treatment is highlighted, as it will be in many subsequent sessions. With those patients who have just left the ward, there is a deliberate attempt to move them from the phase of necessary submission to a ward regimen of weight gain into a new attitude of personal responsibility in the struggle to keep eating. Leaving hospital has been consciously longed for, but the therapist knows that the period following discharge from hospital is usually tense and bewildering for the patient. The recognition of the pain of the post-discharge time is commonly an early point of contact. Often the patient feels surprised and relieved that the therapist is not expecting her to be entirely capable of handling her eating problem without stress. Some part of the patient may be unrealistically expecting it of herself.

It is equally important with the patients who have had no previous contact with the Maudsley, that the nature of this psychotherapy is made distinct from the sort of professional response to their anorexia that they may have come to expect—a commonsense or educational approach, reproaches and injunctions, medical and dietary advice, or physical intervention.

Considerations of physical health are by no means ignored, but dealt with in a different way. In the first session the therapist will tell the patient that she must be weighed by the clinic nurse, on each attendance, and bring the nurse's written record of the weight to the therapy room, to be charted together, week by week. The therapist acknowledges that the patient may wish to keep her weight a secret and may dislike the weight chart despite its importance for the patient's own information as well as the therapist's. This introduces an important theme that regularly develops. The therapist comes to be seen as the persecuting, intrusive parent of an infantilised, resentful but ostensibly compliant, "good" little daughter/patient. We will discuss in detail the clinical importance of such transference processes later in the chapter.

In this early stage, the patient often asks what she should say. The therapist emphasises that the time is the patient's and she should decide what seems significant for her, but might prompt the patient by asking if she has any ideas about where her troubles come from. Usually the patient begins to describe her important relationships. The therapist reacts by trying to make sense of what is said and by linking what the patient says about her life outside the therapy room to what she may *not* be saying, overtly, about the therapist in the room. For example, one patient, in the first session, said that she was troubled by her inability to keep friends: "They start off being friendly and helpful and just when I am beginning to trust them, to rely on them, they just don't want to know about my troubles! Everything's all right for them! They're only interested in what they can get out of me!" The therapist said: "You may be thinking I will be the same. I'm only a professional interested in you as a case. I will be leaving you, letting you down, regardless, at the end of the year. Just when you are relying upon me."

At this stage the therapist has a twofold task. The first is *to establish the working relationship* appropriate for this style of therapy. The second is *to formulate the focal hypothesis*.

ESTABLISHMENT OF THE WORKING RELATIONSHIP

The style and aim of the first session is that the patient should come to realise that there is a special opportunity being offered to her. The therapist is there to facilitate the development of an understanding of the meaning of the patient's communications, her symptoms and her emotional life. The patient is invited, herself, to look into her mind for an understanding of her unconscious difficulties in living. The aim is that she might come to see her fear of eating as not just "having" anorexia nervosa but also as something that she is "doing". The aim is for her to see her *behaviour* as making sense in terms of her hidden and usually unexpressed feelings, her fears and wishes and her own history.

In general, the therapist's task is to identify the thoughts and feelings that are not those openly expressed but are guessed to be somewhere in the patient's mind. Often the patient's unacknowledged feelings will be conjectured from the apparently incompatible manner in which she is speaking; for example, a detached and cool verbal appraisal of an incident of severe hurt or rejection in the past; laughing self-deprecatingly about something that angers her. Above all, the therapist attempts to identify, within the flow of the patient's thoughts, the unexpressed attitudes, feelings,

hopes and fears about the therapy, and especially the therapist ("initial trans-
ferences"; Freud, 1912). The therapist's comments are intended to help the patient
express such preconscious ideas openly. The psychodynamic assumption is that the
patient's use of the therapy relationship will resemble her relationships outside the
therapy room. She will "transfer" onto the therapist all her conscious and unconscious preconceptions derived from past experiences of relationships, and come to
the therapy in a manner consistent with these deeply ingrained memories. The therapist also tries to detect the patient's unspoken feelings by being able to identify,
ponder, and make some relevant sense of, those feelings in himself or herself, arising
during the therapeutic session (countertransferences).

The therapist shows a particular interest in thoughts and feelings about people.
Inevitably, some of the people in the patient's life will be important witnesses,
helpers, critics or victims of the patient's starvation, secrets around food, vomiting
and so on. The therapist has an especial concern to identify the way that such
behaviour establishes a pattern of relationships. For example, a patient may complain bitterly of her parents' controlling nosiness in relation to the anorexia. The
therapist will try to show her how her behaviour belies her expressed wishes. While
she may consciously repudiate any wish for her parents' care and sympathetic
involvement, unconsciously her behaviour and appearance are making the opposite
appeal, and sending a much stronger, contradictory, message. Starving, bingeing
and vomiting compel parental interest.

DEVELOPMENT OF THE FOCAL HYPOTHESIS

The overall model that maintains the therapist's orientation amidst all the information is the *focal hypothesis*. The hypothesis links:

1. The patient's internalised representations of the significant people in her past,
    and her relationships with them, these being, for the most part, family members
    ("object relations").
2. The evolving patterns of feelings between the patient and therapist which are
    coloured by those object relationships ("transference/countertransference").
3. The use the patient makes of the symptoms in current personal relations ("the
    function of the symptom").
    (derived from Malan, 1976)

Object Relations

The concept of "objects" is important in psychodynamic theory (see Chapter 7). In
patients with eating disorders, the inner world of object relationships generates
fears for the consequences of getting close to others. A specific and intense fear of
relationships, and an accompanying abstract longing for an ideal relationship,
seems fundamental within the psychopathology of anorexia.

In going over the material of a therapy, the therapist usually will see that there is a quality that in one sense gives a "date label" to the most pivotal object relationships. Patterns of preoccupations are evoked suggesting a dominance of conflicts from major transitions in developmental processes during infancy and childhood, especially around the evolution of relationships.

> For example the psychotherapy of a 20-year-old anorexic patient was filled with her sense of never being able to ask for and get enough for herself, and of always feeling an unloved outsider. This ingrained feeling state seemed to derive from the time when she was 15 months old and her mother had twins. The therapist surmised that the developmental demands naturally required by weaning for relatively more self-management and independence, were enormously increased, beyond her capacity to tolerate, by the presence of her new siblings. This complex of emotions had come to symbolise in great intensity the patient's experience of herself with other people throughout her life. She had developed an exaggerated self-sufficiency as a protective shell to ward off any further disillusionment at her dimly remembered apparent loss of love. She often wore an air of outrage and suspicion which meant that she was unable to develop close relationships, a situation which she took as evidence to confirm her perception of people's rejection of her, and which became a self-fulfilling prophecy. The only explanation she could construct was that there must be something innately bad about herself to have caused all the rejections. The therapist wondered aloud if when the twins arrived, she suddenly had to learn to conceal her feelings of anger, envy and hurt about their arrival. In adult life, it seemed that starving herself was in part a slef-imposed punishment for her unexpressed anger, her "wrong" self, who had such uncharitable feelings towards her younger siblings.

We do not believe that these "date labels" necessarily represent a true chronological location for the development and quality of the patient's problems, but they often have great cogency for the patient, making sense of her experience and her own knowledge of her history. Nor do we believe that these apparently crucial conflictual experiences are *the cause* of the patient's problems. They represent for the patient the way that her problems are registered and given content and which in turn can provide her with a perceptual leverage, to gain a distance from and control of herself.

Transference/Countertransference

Like all other relationships, that with the therapist becomes drawn into the repetition of the internal object relationship processes. This relationship has a special quality, from the beginning. This is, in part, because the crisis of the illness and the need for help evoke the possibility of dependence. It also becomes special because the therapist observes and comments upon the evolution of the patient's feelings, attitudes and fantasies as they are revealed in the room. A therapist who is relatively "opaque", revealing little of him or herself to the patient, can attract a wide range of attributions from the patient. Many of these cluster to suggest that the patient is experiencing the therapist as one of her internal figures in a characteristic and emotionally important stance towards her. Over the course of the first few sessions a rather consistent transference configuration emerges, around which the therapy is likely to revolve, as the therapist gradually relates it to the patient's history and current relations.

What we have found to be characteristic of an anorexic patient's way of relating to a therapist is for the therapist's proffered helplessness or closeness to be treated with fear and suspicion. For the patient, lonely aloofness, though painful, is preferable to the acknowledgement of any need of another person, because neediness has been distorted in the patient's internal world into representing an invasion of her personal boundaries, a complete capitulation of her self-control and the annihilation of her self by the overwhelming power of another, who threatens almost to gobble her up. The oral image is particularly pertinent here. A *need* for food (one of the infant's earliest needs of a parent) feels like one's actual self being gobbled up and swallowed down by the food if it is allowed inside the body. It is hard to convey the delusional concreteness with which this belief is held by many eating disorderd patients, even when they know it is literally not so.

Anorexic patients evoke familiar responses from the therapists. These responses include countertransferences, which are processes whereby the therapist *as a person* becomes drawn into the treatment. The common caricature of a "cold", uninvolved therapist, quite unmoved and abstracted from the treatment, gives a false picture. In fact, at all stages, the therapist has complex, conflictual, painful layers of feelings. Some are easily acknowledged within oneself, while others are quite outside awareness and conscious control. The self-starvation of the anorexic patient is hard for the therapist to bear and it becomes even harder as the therapist realises that the "good and helpful" comments that are made, with the intent of showing care and understanding, are rejected as fiercely as if they were dreaded food. The struggle to become aware of their own feelings is an important discipline for psychotherapists for two reasons. The first is that some of the reactions may interfere with the proper professional activity of the psychotherapist. The second is that such responses can give additional information about the patient and of the sorts of unconscious tangles she gets into with people.

The therapist's countertransference feeling of utter hopelessness about being able to give anything to the anorexic patient is common. Even when the patient is physically out of danger, the therapist is assailed by the awareness that the patient so often feels hopeless about herself and her capacity to recover or to take in anything good. Sometimes, it is necessary to face the desolation head on, in order to stop the hopelessness interfering with the therapist's willingness to persevere.

A therapist described his experience with one patient as a famine relief worker in an Ethiopian camp without supplies. He felt tempted to get out on the next truck. Managing his despair by neither giving up nor denying it, seemed to coincide with the development of real therapeutic change in the patient who had evoked this powerful feeling. She may have needed to witness his struggle with a despair that was convincingly genuine in order to trust that hers too might be understood, endured and overcome eventually.

The existence of a supervision group is always extremely useful in holding the therapist on course with the hopelessness. It offers a perspective on the very strong emotional reactions evoked in the therapist in response to the inner world of the patient. On his own the therapist might have succumbed to the desire to leave the field of famine.

The Function of the Symptom

The symptoms of self-starvation, the absorption in food, the fanatical preoccupation with weight and body shape, and the emaciation produced, become an overwhelmingly powerful aspect of the patient. Other people cannot but be intensely affected. It becomes difficult to see the patient as a person: she is an anorexic. The minute body blocks the view of the woman. The symptoms control and modulate the pattern of current interactions with people. Although the patient often hates this, it also becomes familiar and reassuring, and avoids certain feared risks, especially those of being adult and sexual. Any concerns voiced by others about her health are contorted by an assumption that they wish the patient to be fat and independent. Often there is a fear that to eat more substantially will bring with it an expectation of coping in the world and that any emotional problems no longer exist. Often the anorexic person believes that the symptom is the only legitimate passport to attention and consideration, at the same time as rejecting this very idea. The symptom, if rigorously pursued, transforms the patient into a dependent, needy person of whom normal demands and expectations can scarcely be made. Often, these patients have been successful in achieving at school or work. They sometimes pursue success with a punishing internalised perfectionism. The success, however, is often felt to be as a result of conforming to the expectations of others. Success becomes a source of fear of the impossible demand, and of rage at the price to be paid. In this context, the anorexic symptom is felt by contrast to be a success of the patient's own creation and wards off the conventional demands of others.

Repeatedly, we observe anorexia being used as a way to avoid interpersonal feelings. The body and its state constitute a communication, and for many anorexic patients who are blocked from experiencing their feelings directly and have split it off into a bodily sensation, it is easier to transmit information by that means than by open speech. It is important for the therapist to be aware of these communications and to find a way of putting the presumed feelings into words.

Getting better may include having to face the pain of having feelings in her mind rather than simply as a degradation of her body.

One patient often became desperate after sessions at finding herself in possession of strong feelings. She would habitually seek to "work her feelings out" by vigorous activity. One day she did this by playing hockey. She did it carelessly and injured her ribs. Obviously, an aim of therapy in such instances, is to facilitate non-dangerous expressions of emotion.

This patient well demonstrated the belief that the experience of emotion is tantamount to a loss of control: "If you are not in control, you are a failure, if you have feelings at all, you're out of control and therefore you're a failure." To feel nothing is a state of perfection: 'I never want to go through that emotional business again." (On the ward she had wept for the first time for many years.) "At the moment I am working nine to nine and I am not giving myself time to think. An hour for lunch and an hour for supper. That's the only way to cope with it."

Symptoms, whatever their biological or social origins, become incorporated into the repertoire of unconscious mechanisms for controlling as well as shaping personal attachments to people in the wider world and to the therapist. The role of the symptom is conceptualised as being to "manage" painful affects generated within the internal object world, to protect the self from "danger". Any experience of an intense longing—for example, for sex, food, a hug—seems to be invariably accompanied by the idea that the person who might provide the gratification of the wishes will overwhelm the anorexic's own sense of individuality and threaten the very survival of the self as a separate person.

It is common to hear anorexic patients speak as if they do not have an idea of themselves as whole, separate individuals. They often describe an inner conflict, for and against an anorexic impulse, as if two distinct persons are warring inside one mind. They feel that the anorexic "voice" is a bullying, cruel tyrant, holding sway over a victim-like, suffering side of the personality who is too weak to fight against the tyrant. It is as if "anorexia" is an external entity in itself, often spoken about in this way by patients wishing to disown their contradictory feelings. The therapeutic task is to help the patient recognise that both tyrant and victim are equally her own. Whereas she can identify with the suffering victim of the anorexia, she disowns the punitive tyrant side of the self which maintains the anorexia's grip. Her miserable state unconsciously disguises how much her cruel self attack is also aimed at the people close around her, her family, the doctors, and of course the therapist, who as it were, go down to failure with her. The symptoms seem to demonstrate how non-responsible she is for whatever cruelty exists in the situation. But a contradictory belief is often also present—that the cruel punishment of anorexia is deserved because she is a thoroughly bad person, responsible for all the ills of the family. The secret, imagined wickedness of which patients accuse themselves is usually selfishness and voraciously greedy desire. Normal bodily satisfactions are treated as though they are gross self-indulgence, a loss of self-determination. The pursuit of asceticism in the anorexic state enables the patient to believe that the structure of her internal world is "right", is safe. There is a terrified need to control desire, and the power of the provider is felt to be wholly malign.

Asceticism may have another meaning in the patient's internal world and identification with a dead or ill person is often important in the multiple meanings of the symptom.

A patient developed anorexia nervosa after her father had died of an emaciating illness. By her anorexic self-starvation she came to believe that, in relation to her father, her imitative emaciation made her a more faithfully loving daughter than her mother was a heartbroken widow. It was as though the patient could believe herself to be under the approving gaze of her dead father.

At very low weights the physiological effects of starvation may put the patient beyond contact. She often seems to be in a "toxic" state, unavailable for understanding as with a drugged or drunk person. On the other hand, it seems that at these lowest weights, truths about the patient and especially the relationship between the patient and crucial others are revealed and sometimes starkly enacted as never before. At the point that the patient seems most unavailable, that which is of most avail is exposed.

A patient's weight had dropped dangerously low and the therapist had had to inform the managing psychiatrist. Although the patient knew readmission was almost inevitable, she expressed intense betrayal. She began to cheat on her written weight slip that she brought each week from the nurse to the therapist. She altered the record of her weight, upwards, using a different pen to the nurse, and so making the forge very evident. Perversely, she spent some of the session saying how much more open she was being in talking with her father and with the therapist of her difficulties.

The problem was discussed at the supervision group. The flagrancy of the deceit was noted. The fact that she herself was drawing attention to her illness by being so visibly thin had caused her employer to phone the hospital. It was the patient, not the therapist, who was making her serious state known, just as she was "showing" the therapist that she was cheating. By that means she was inducing the therapist to get angry; forcing her to become the angry, persecuting source of her difficulties. In the patient's mind, this in turn justified her own anger with the therapist for betraying her into having to see the doctor. She could believe it was the therapist, not herself, who was causing the alarm bells to sound.

The outside life of the patient in her family seemed to illuminate the transference further. Her mother had recently been hospitalised with a serious depression on top of her terminal carcinomatosis. The patient had returned to living at home, caring for her father. She regarded herself as a much better companion for her father than her mother. The relationship between the daughter and father reached a new level of mutual dependency and warmth, which the patient secretly believed has always before been impeded by the mother's presence. Her anorexic symptoms gave an illusion of dealing with her intense oedipal conflict. The possibility that she might take over full-time management of her father's household was counteracted by her self-starving and consequent weakness. She needed to show both that she was not her mother's usurper and that she had a continuing need to be cared for as a child, rather than as a sexual adult.

The supervision discussion led to a further formulation of the current transference: through the noticeable alteration on the weight slip, the patient was showing the therapist that she was cheating. Similarly she had shown her mother that she wanted to be close to father in a "cheating" way, possible only in her mother's absence. She felt compelled to make sure her mother/therapist would notice her miscreance. In the patient's mind the mother's rage is righteous and punishment should follow. The anorexia functions as her own self-imposed punishment. At the same time, and in contradiction, she had a belief funtioning at another, defensive level: if she could make the therapist angry with her, the patient could believe that she was being unfairly persecuted so that she could have some righteous anger to rebuff her mother's.

The anger with the patient which arose in the therapist and in the supervision group, is a piece of "countertransference information". Because she seemed, by the above formulation, to be driven to provoke the therapist to be angry, it was ob-viously important not to be angry, nor simply denying of it. A differernt way was needed of acknowledging the anger and making the transference work for, rather than against, the therapy. Over time, the therapist found a way of talking about the severe conflicts, rivalries and "cheating" in her oedipal situation which were being re-enacted in the quasi-oedipal triangle of patient, therapist and doctor.

This example shows how the whole range of material from a session is used, together with the "group countertransference" that evolved within the supervision discussion. This is characteristic of the dynamic reverberation of the symptom through the patient, therapist and supportive clinical team.

USE OF THE FOCAL HYPOTHESES IN THE MIDDLE PHASE OF TREATMENT

A focal hypothesis can be made very early on, in skeletal outline, from the account of the patient and the first impressions. Over the course of the therapy it undergoes a slow transformation as the therapist and patient learn more about the many layers of meaning that can be attached to their interaction. Most of the things that are seen, heard and felt in the therapy are likely to cause an initial puzzlement and curiosity in the therapist. For example, sometimes the therapist cannot concentrate and feels too lazy to make sense of what is happening. This may be due solely to factors within the therapist but may also be *information*, a product of an induced atmosphere, part of the picture of the patient. The apparent sleepiness may turn out to be a reflection of the prohibition that the patient seems to put upon the experi-ence of any disturbing emotion.

Another common example is that the therapist goes through a phase of being beguiled by the wish to indulge the anorexic patient. Sometimes the visible effects of the starvation are not so extreme and the patient appears as a pretty, vulnerable young woman. The therapist may be consumed by the thought that protectiveness should be offered rather than facing her up to harsh reality. On subsequent reflec-tion, perhaps within the supervision group, the therapist realises that the dispropor-tionate sense of loving protectiveness treats the patient as if she were a dear little girl. This countertransference "information" leads to the more detailed con-struction of the focal hypothesis. The therapist's impulse is seen as an enactment, an attempt to achieve a longed for experience for the patient, that of being with her parent in a sweet, enveloping cocoon. This attempted enactment may represent a repetition of an actual childhood time, which had been interrupted too soon for the child. The search for such a blissful union is expressed, albeit in a very risky way, by the anorexic symptoms. The therapist can verbalise the origins and legitimacy of the longings whilst demonstrating the dangers of the chosen vehicle. The therapist can also point to the powerful compulsion to put such feelings into concrete enact-ments, as words seem so weak to the patient.

The longing to be close and in union with the child's wishes prohibits conflict and disagreement: a pleasurable trap, for the parent in the past and the therapist in the present. It limits the natural development of growth and independence and tends to perpetuate the anorexic symptoms because they are such a powerful means of gaining care. Contradictorily the anorexia is also, paradoxically, a means to acquire a spurious separateness, and gives a sense of unique identity.

Part of the long, repetitive work of the middle phase may be towards finding less destructive ways of being angry with parents—i.e. not having to be anorexic. The domination of a phase of the patient's relationship with her mother or father is now influencing the therapeutic relationship and current expectations of life.

> After six months of therapy, the therapist realised how a "good" session, in which the patient and therapist had come to see something that they both felt was important, had a particular effect. The therapist would come to the next session, looking forward to the meeting and expecting the patient to be in a cooperative and optimistic state of mind. In fact, she would come complaining that the therapy was useless and that she was getting nowhere. One day this transformation occurred within a session and the therapist realised that the "useful" work was being taken by the patient to mean that she and the therapist were becoming too intimate. It seemed the patient had to stop any further intimacy developing even though she also knew that she wanted to continue therapy. She was a very adored and loved child of a couple who became estranged, leaving her father miserable and hurt, wanting to turn to his daughter for compensatory comfort. Just as her father's love came to feel dangerous in her adolescence, so the therapist's understanding and interest felt intrusive and risky.

The focal hypothesis is refuted and embellished, furthering the development of a new version. This is the essence of the *conscious* work of the therapist in focal psychoanalytic psychotherapy. Alongside of this deliberate activity, another process can be observed and is of equal importance. It is the creation of a unique and special relationship on a personal, empathic and involved level: unwilled and unguided in any conscious sense. The evolving trust which we work to facilitate may eventually allow the patient the confidence and freedom to contribute as a coworker or partner in the therapeutic task, in the moment by moment exploration of the meaning of what is happening between the two. The achievement of such a quality in the working relationship often seems to initiate a new and more hopeful phase in the treatment of these patients.

Throughout this middle phase the weight chart is kept present in the therapy room to remind the patient and therapist of an aspect of reality that can otherwise be lost as both become absorbed in their relationship. We have observed that the shape and direction of the weight graph often reveals a psychological truth. Changes in direction, halting weight loss or a turn to weight gain, mark a change in the transference. The supervision group is sometimes also needed for this purpose, to highlight imperceptible shifts and progressions in the therapy.

THE ENDING

The time constraint required by the research design constitutes an extremely important characteristic of the therapy, and, in this respect, marks it out as unlike most psychoanalytic psychotherapies. This affects the therapists' subjective orientation to their work, for example by adding pressure "to get something done" in what never feels to be a long enough time. On the other hand, it may also engender a sense of relief that the therapy has a definite end. Few sessions will go by without the ending being mentioned by the therapist. For some patients the knowledge that there is a set ending, and that the psychotherapy is "compulsory", allows them to take the risk to become involved. For others, the ending simply confirms that no-one is reliable or cares enough to stick with the patient. For most patients, a year initially seems a long and even generous time, but within a few months is felt to be stingy.

Many of the feelings for which the therapist probes can be denied by the patient, but the specific meaning of feelings about the ending is worked upon in the transference with a potency that derives from the reality of separating. Emotions generated about the ending are central material of the treatment: anger at the abandonment, sorrow at the loss, shame at the need, panic at the separateness and fear for the future. Such feelings concerning other attachment figures have been long shielded by the anorexic symptoms and hence from direct experience. But now she has, hopefully, a changed attitude towards her symptoms. They have previously been a familiar and even comforting resource to protect her. This is now less acceptable as her former defences are less available; the crisis of the ending is painfully augmented. The psychotherapist works with the patient to make their separating more mutually felt, and so less destructive than those with which she has struggled unproductively before.

For some patients, the therapist's repeated reference to the end of the therapy is felt as proof that the therapist *wants* to finish. Of course, the therapist may feel such wishes but, more usually, the patient's assumption that the therapist is eager for termination is a repetition of the patient's longstanding conviction that her attachment is resented and that she is not desirable or acceptable. This is especially poignant if, at the same time, the patient says that the therapist is the first person to whom she has ever really talked. It is quite common for a patient to try to avoid the pain of ending by setting her own time to leave, before that of the therapist. The therapist may be obliged to accept such a pre-emptive move, but will always point out to the patient her wish to control the feelings for herself and to minimise her sense of being a powerless, dependent, frustrated child.

Working on the ending is akin to the process of helping someone mourn; sympathising with the pain and loss, identifying hidden feelings, especially anger and fear for the future, facilitating the expression of bitterness, disappointment, betrayal and blame, as well as appreciation, shared pride in modest achievements, and maybe affection. Some contradictory responses arouse shame: a sense of triumph at ending uncured, a relief from the burden of the therapy relationship, a gratitude for the help that has been denied so often.

Most patients ask about arrangements for their future professional care. The therapist usually advises against making immediate arrangements, suggesting the patient take time to "digest" the psychotherapy and register the loss of an important relationship. Of course, where a patient is physically at risk the therapist will refer her for medical follow-up. Even when the therapy has, apparently, had no symptomatic benefit, and where the language of psychotherapy has been misused and derided, there can be surprising positive gains at the end. Psychotherapy can open the door on a particular way of thinking, can provide a new view of oneself in the world, and as an understanding of relationships can be a resource that the patient carries away into the future. Several patients have subsequently asked for help in finding further appropriate psychotherapy.

CONCLUSION

Trials of psychoanalytic psychotherapy are hard to fund, elaborate to execute and contradict some of the firmly held principles of the usual psychodynamic techniques. For this reason such trials are rarely undertaken, although currently most cases of anorexia nervosa are likely to require some form of psychotherapy (Russell, 1985). This chapter has explored the experience of conducting psychoanalytic psychotherapy with a group of patients with severe anorexia nervosa, some of whom will probably turn out to have benefited a lot, some a little and some not at all. The follow-up study will elucidate the exact outcome. At this stage, it is clear that the therapy engaged a good number of the patients, despite the absence of selection of suitability for the treatment. The psychotherapists were able to conduct the therapy despite the ethical unease and clinical doubts that the random case selection and control trial conditions imposed. A great deal has been learned about the nature of the anorexic experience and about the demand that is put upon the psychotherapist.

REFERENCES

Bruch, H. (1973). *Eating Disorders: Obesity, Anorexia and the Person Within*. New York: Basic Books.

Bruch, H. (1978). *The Golden Cage: The Enigma of Anorexia Nervosa*. Cambridge, Mass.: Harvard University Press.

Dare, C., Eisler, I., Russell, G. and Szmukler, G. (1990). Family therapy for anorexia nervosa: implications from the results of a controlled trial of family and individual therapy. *Journal of Marital and Family Therapy,* **16**, 39–57.

Freud, S. (1912). The dynamics of transference. In: S. Freud, *Standard Edition,* Vol. 12, pp. 98–108. London: Hogarth Press, 1958.

Kaufman, M.R. and Heiman, M. (Eds) (1964). *Evolution of Psychosomatic Concepts. Anorexia Nervosa: A Paradigm*. New York: International Universities press.

Malan, D.H. (1976). *Toward the Validation of Dynamic Psychotherapy*. New York: Plenum Medical.

Malan, D.H. (1979). *Individual Psychotherapy and the Science of Psychodynamics*. London: Butterworth.

Orbach, S. (1985). Accepting the symptom: a feminist psychoanalytic treatment of anorexia nervosa. In: D.M. Garner and P.E. Garfinkel (Eds), *Handbook of Psychotherapy for Anorexia Nervosa and Bulimia*, pp. 83–106. New York: Guilford Press.

Russell, G.F.M. (1985). Anorexia and bulimia nervosa. In: M. Rutter and L. Hersov (Eds), *Child and Adolescent Psychiatry: Modern Approaches*. Oxford: Blackwell Scientific.

Russell, G.F.M., Szmukler, G., Dare, C. and Eisler, I. (1987). An evaluation of family therapy in anorexia nervosa and bulimia nervosa. *Archives of General Psychiatry,* **44**, 1047–1056.
Sandler, J., Dare, C., Holder, A. (1992). *The Patient and the Analyst.* London: Karnac.
Thomä, H. (1967). *Anorexia Nervosa.* New York: International Universities Press.

17

Cognitive Therapy

CHRIS FREEMAN
Royal Edinburgh Hospital, Edinburgh, UK

INTRODUCTION

This chapter describes the application of cognitive behavioural psychotherapy (CBT) to the treatment of anorexia and bulimia nervosa. It is not possible in a single chapter to describe particular treatment techniques in detail. This chapter will concentrate on how the basic CBT model needs to be modified for the treatment of eating disorders, what specific techniques need to be used, and the outcome studies that have been carried out. Brief mention will be made of the training requirements for CBT.

Cognitive techniques have been widely used in the treatment of obesity but obesity is not covered here. I realised that by omitting it I am contributing to the unfortunate tendency for obesity to be marginalised in so-called eating disorder texts and conferences, and I apologise for that. Treatment of obesity would require a chapter on its own, particularly in regard to which overweight patients actually require psychological treatment.

THE BASIC MODEL OF COGNITIVE THERAPY

Aaron Beck, the father-figure of cognitive therapy, coined the term "collaborative empiricism" to describe the nature of the therapeutic enterprise where a patient,

Handbook of Eating Disorders: Theory, Treatment and Research.
Edited by G. Szmukler, C. Dare and J. Treasure.
© 1995 John Wiley & Sons Ltd.

closely assisted by a therapist, investigates the basis in reality for a personal hypotheses concerning the world. It is not about arguing with or haranguing the patient or confronting the patient with how absurd some of their beliefs may be; it is much more to do with encouraging the patient to collect evidence which may support or refute their beliefs and then to re-evaluate their beliefs in the light of that "hard evidence".

Garner and Bemis (1985) described what he felt were the five core features of cognitive therapy:

1. Reliance on conscious and pre-conscious experience rather than unconscious motivation.
2. Explicit emphasis on meaning and cognitions as mediating variables accounting for maladaptive feelings or emotions.
3. The use of questioning as a major therapeutic device.
4. Active and direct involvement on the part of the therapist.
5. Methodological adherence to behavioural and scientific psychology in which theory is shaped by empirical findings; this involves a commitment to the specification of treatment methods and objective assessment of target behaviours.

Table 17.1 shows the main characteristics of standard cognitive therapy. However, recent work on conditions such as post-traumatic stress disorder, obsessive–compulsive disorder and personality disorder have modified this standard approach, particularly in regard to the time that treatment takes and its non-historical nature.

It is unnecessary to make only minor adaptations to the cognitive model for the treatment of uncomplicated bulimia nervosa, but major changes have to be made for the treatment of severe anorexia nervosa.

CBT FOR BULIMIA NERVOSA

Introduction and Rationale

Over the past ten years CBT has become the treatment of choice for bulimia nervosa for many therapists. This has happened for a number of reasons. In the 1980s there was great enthusiasm for cognitive–behaviour therapy for all sorts of disorders, CBT being promoted vigorously by "experts" as the treatment for bulimia nervosa. In fact, the model as described for depression and anxiety does translate easily into a treatment approach for BN.

In many ways the cognitive model is even more overt for BN than for depression. The view that it is the dysfunctional thoughts about self-esteem, body shape and size which drive the bulimic cycle is a very persuasive one. Whereas in depression and anxiety it is often difficult to be clear whether the depressed mood comes first and the depressing thoughts follow, in BN it is usually clear that the thoughts and cognitive distortions come first and then lead to dieting, and then the bulimic cycle begins. An additional characteristic of CBT is that it appears to have high face

TABLE 17.1   Main characteristics of standard cognitive therapy.

Time-limit	15–22 sessions over 3–4 months
Structure	Each session lasts 1 hour
Agenda	Each session is structured by the use of an agenda to optimise the use of time
Problem-oriented	Therapist and patient focus on defining and solving the presenting problems
Not historical	It deals with the here and now without recourse to the distant past history of the patient
Learning model	It does not use psychodynamic hypothetical constructs to explain the patient's behaviour. Rather, dysfunctional behaviour is attributed to maladaptive learning. Relearning more functional behaviour is the goal
Scientific method	An experimental method is adopted: therapy involving collecting data (problems, thoughts, attitudes), formulating hypotheses, setting up experiments and evaluating results
Homework	The patient is given assignments for data collecting, verification of hypotheses and practice of cognitive skills
Collaboration	Patient and therapist work together to solve problems
Active and directive	The therapist adopts an active and directive role throughout treatment. He can be didactic sometimes but his main role is to facilitate the definition and resolution of problems
Socratic questioning	The principal therapeutic method is Socratic questioning, which is to ask a series of questions aimed at bringing the patient to identify his underlying thought, to perceive alternative solutions or to modify his opinions
Openness	The therapeutic process is not clouded in mystique. Rather, it is explicit and open, therapist and patient sharing a common understanding of what is going on in therapy

validity. It tackles both the cognitive and behavioural aspects of the disorder, the assumption being that simply helping the individual interrupt the behaviour is not sufficient (see Figure 17.1). There is usually also an attempt to help the individual alter the basic assumptions which lie behind the body disparagement and need to diet. Many different cognitive–behavioural treatment programmes have been described, but the best known and best evaluated is that of Fairburn et al (1986). The treatment programme I will describe here (see Table 17.2) has been developed in our unit and has been used in both individual and group settings (Freeman et al, 1988; Cullen Centre Manual, 1993).

Assessment (Stage 1)

The general assessment of patients with bulimia nervosa is dealt with in detail elsewhere in this book and does not need to be repeated here. There is no need to

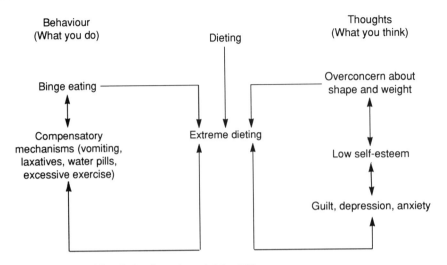

FIGURE 17.1   Cognitive–behavioural model for BN.

TABLE 17.2   Schedule for individual CBT for bulimia nervosa.*

Stage 1	Assessment	1–2 session	See text
Stage 2	Education, behavioural techniques, introduction of cognitive model	3–6 sessions	Keep monitoring (diary) going throught
Stage 3	Cognitive techniques become main focus but behavioural techniques continue	7–12 sessions	Add cognitive techniques without ignoring behavioural
Stage 4	Techniques for low self-esteem, body disparagement, whilst behavioural and cognitive techniques continue	13–15 sessions	Watch for depressed mood worsening as BN "given up". Decide if basic assumptions need to be tackled
Stage 5	Relapse prevention	16–18 sessions	See text
Stage 6	Follow-up, top-up sessions (usually single appointments)	1 month 3 months 6 months 12 months	Follow-up could be individual or group

* Be flexible, there are no hard and fast rules.

modify this for individual CBT. A full history, measurement of severity using rating scales, and relevant physical investigations should all be carried out in the first one or two sessions. Assessment for group CBT may need to be different. If the treatment is "group only" with no individual sessions, it may be important to negotiate with the patient's GP about relevant physical investigations such as monitoring of potassium levels. This should be made explicit to the patient before starting the group.

Much is often made of specific assessments for CBT. These usually involve some assessment of psychological mindedness, an ability to understand and accept the cognitive model of the disorder being treated, and may go as far as setting the patient some cognitive challenge or experiment in the first one or two sessions and monitoring how they respond to this. In my experience these techniques have no predictive value. Some patients readily adopt the cognitive model, seem very enthusiastic and motivated and yet appear to change hardly at all. With others it may take many sessions to get them to begin monitoring their behaviour and their thoughts, and yet after ten to twelve sessions these patients do begin to change and may end up doing very well. In my view, when it is delivered on an individual basis, there are no absolute contraindications to CBT except those that may preclude outpatient treatment altogether (e.g. marked suicidal intent or severe physical illness). What is important is to have a flexible treatment model of which individual CBT may be only one part. The treatment is time-consuming and intensive and in most busy clinics it is simply not possible to offer it to all sufferers. Simpler and less costly approaches may be suitable for some patients (see Figure 17.2).

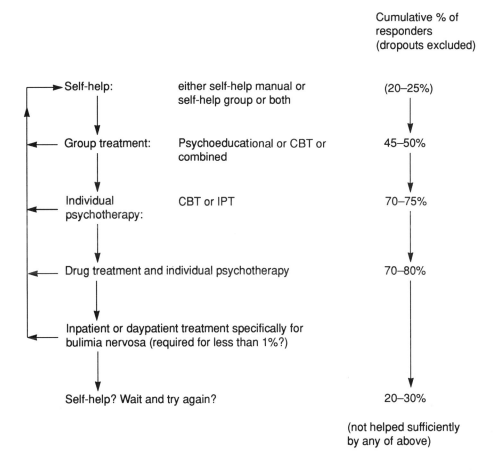

FIGURE 17.2 A tiered approach to treatment, showing how CBT can fit into a comprehensive treatment regime for BN.

Other factors may determine the type of treatment offered. The patient may refuse group treatment, express a desire for a less structured type of therapy, express a desire to ventilate feelings about sexual abuse or family problems early in treatment, or express a desire for drug treatment because they do no want to commit themselves to time-consuming psychotherapy. All these issues should be discussed openly in the assessment period. The therapist should be flexible enough to incorporate most of these wishes into a treatment programme. It is quite possible to use cognitive–behaviour therapy to deal with relationship and family difficulties and sexual abuse, and to begin treatment dealing with these before gradually moving back to the agenda set out in Table 17.2.

Introducing the Cognitive Model (Stage 2A)

Whilst running workshops on CBT, one of the things that constantly surprises me is how bad therapists are (even quite experienced ones) at explaining things simply and clearly to patients. In general, explanations tend to be too long, too complicated and often quite patronising in the way they are delivered. Getting the therapeutic style right early in treatment is important. This usually requires repeated practice, role play with colleagues and constant feedback from patients. The elements of any explanation should include:

- the link between thoughts and feelings
- the collaborative nature of the treatment
- the concept of experiment and the patient as scientist
- the importance of self-monitoring (diary keeping)
- the importance of regular measurement
- the idea of an agenda for each session which both patient and therapist can help to set
- the idea that treatment is about learning a set of skills which will help the patient regain their own control rather than coming to "an expert" to be made better
- the idea of regular feedback: both during and after sessions

Introduce the idea that feedback is a two-way process and that you as therapist need feedback about how you are performing as well as vice versa ("How could I have explained that better?").

It is good practice at this stage to introduce the idea that both the therapist and patient have a clipboard and that important things should be written down, diagrams frequently drawn etc. In general, complex diagrams such as Figure 17.1 are not useful. They may help the therapist conceptualise what is going on, but simpler diagrams such as Figure 17.3 may be more useful. These can then be elaborated with time.

Preparing the therapist for CBT. It is easy when beginning CBT to be overwhelmed with the numerous bits of paper: information booklets, diaries, handouts, automatic

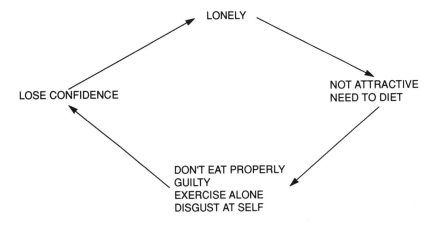

CHOICES 1. Continue above cycle: lose more weight, begin to feel ill, feel even more guilty, lose all confidence, become a recluse.

2. Try and break above cycle: I've tried stopping dieting, I've tried reducing exercise time and time again, it just doesn't work; perhaps I could go out more.

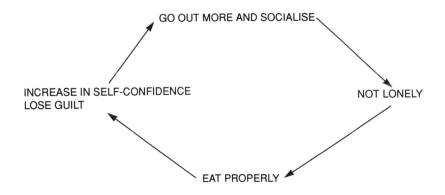

FIGURE 17.3 Breaking the cycle: examples of diagrams produced jointly in therapy.

thought sheets, rating scales etc. A useful technique is to have all these filed in a loose-leaf folder with several copies of each, so you don't have to go fumbling around at the beginning of each session looking for the relevant papers you need. It is also very important not to let the handouts and rating scales dominate the treatment. The core of this remains your interaction with the patient and other techniques are supposed to be in support of that rather than replacing it.

Introducing Behavioural Techniques (Stage 2B)

At this stage three main areas are discussed: breaking the cycle, principles of normal eating, and diary keeping.

Breaking the cycle. Discussion should be around the following themes, but the therapy should not become a lecture. Deal with issues as appropriate, while keeping to the principles of agenda setting and feedback.

- One of the first things to understand when overcoming bulimia nervosa is the vicious cycle that arises by dieting then bingeing.
- Obviously, there are many other factors involved in this pattern. Let's look at particular psychological triggers that may cause you to binge.
- In order for you to recover, this physiological cycle must be broken. Research has shown that strict dieting and starvation leads to preoccupation with food, carbohydrate cravings and a *strong drive to binge.*
- You do not have to be underweight to experience the starvation state.
- While you remain in this cycle of bingeing and dieting you will be continually *vulnerable* to strong biological urges to binge.
- By eating more regularly and more frequently, your urge to binge will reduce and thus become *more controllable.*
- A major fear you may have is that by ceasing dieting you will continue to gain more and more weight. Although it may be hard to imagine, by eating more regularly and more frequently, you will in time reduce the urge to binge.
- The consequence of a regular healthy eating pattern is that your body reverts to its normal point which is maintained despite moderate fluctuations in the calorie intake of your diet.

Methods of weight control that perpetuate the cycle of bulimia:

Self-induced vomiting
- Vomiting can very rapidly become a habit and leads to a decreased tolerance of food inside your stomach.
- Vomiting plays a major role in perpetuating the vicious cycle in bulimia nervosa. Some people "allow themselves to binge" because they know that they can vomit afterwards. The result of this is that the motivation to cease bingeing is less.
- Self-induced vomiting has many serious physical effects on the body that cause significant health risks. These include disturbances in the body's electrolyte balance, a sore bleeding throat, swollen glands (making the face look fat) and stomach complications.

Laxative abuse
- Using laxatives will not help you lose weight. Laxatives reduce the absorption of water in the lower gut but do not alter the absorption of food. Laxatives may make you "feel empty" but in reality all you are losing is water.
- Abuse of laxatives leads to dehydration and its associated complications. Persistent use of laxatives results in the digestive system becoming "lazy" and ineffi-

cient. When you try to cut down or stop taking them altogether you may become bloated because of water retention and constipated because the large intestine has become unused to working by itself. These symptoms will disappear with time when your body has been given a chance to function normally again. This may take many weeks.

Use of diuretics
- As with laxatives, the effect of diuretics is purely loss of water and the same problems arise with their abuse. Diuretics don't cause permanent weight loss but they do cause dehydration and may cause kidney damage if used over a prolonged period.

It is important to remember that:

- Recovery from bulimia nervosa requires restoration of *control* and this involves normal eating. You learn to control your eating rather than your eating controlling you.
- Recovery involves *risk taking*. You must be prepared to accept the risk of making changes in order to progress.
- Once you have regained control over your eating, you are in a much stronger position to make sensible reductions in your intake if you still desire to lose weight.
- The principles of normal eating are *steps* towards normal controlled eating that should be tested out slowly and at a pace that suits *you*.
- You are advised to *aim* at eating three meals and two snacks per day and strongly encouraged to cease "dieting" for the duration of the group.

Principles of normal eating. We use a list of 16 principles. The general aim is to help the patients gradually move towards a regular eating pattern. It is usually unrealistic to expect them to stop dieting immediately but the aim should be to steadily move towards this. Simple techniques like trying to eat in company, planning meals, introducing small meals earlier in the day, restricting food stocks in the house, identifying times of the day and of the month when bingeing is more likely, planning alternative activities, reducing weighing, using exercise and distraction, can be introduced at this stage.

Introduction of diary keeping. The use of self-monitoring is very important. A diary can be provided or the patient can keep her own notebook. The diary should have instructions about recording all food that is taken, which food is taken as a meal and which as a binge, when meals are social and when they are taken alone. There should be a column for recording vomiting, laxative use and other purging behaviours. It is also useful to have simple 10 cm line rating scales of mood and degree of control and a space for other comments. The diary should be brought to each session and should be one of the items reviewed at the beginning of each week. This should continue throughout treatment even when bingeing and vomiting have stopped. The diary can then be used to record the introduction of "forbidden" foods and to monitor periods of restraint.

Cognitive Restructuring Techniques (Stages 3 and 4)

By now the patient may have begun to diet less severely, and may have had some success in avoiding an occasional binge or decreased the size of her binges. The cognitive model will have been introduced several sessions ago and should have been referred to throughout. The style of treatment in Stages 1 and 2 adheres to the model but does not attempt cognitive restructuring. This should now begin. The stages involved are:

- explaining the nature of automatic thoughts and basic assumptions
- helping the patient learn to catch her automatic thoughts and then record them using a variety of cognitive techniques to help her challenge those thoughts and replace them by more helpful ones
- looking for evidence of basic assumptions or schemata
- helping the patient to challenge such schemata.

The steps of cognitive restructuring. First it is necessary to explain the nature of automatic thoughts. In BN it is usually not difficult to find examples (e.g. the thoughts before or after a binge, the thoughts around being weighed, buying new clothes, looking at oneself in a mirror can all be explored). I find it useful to give a personal example of a string of automatic thoughts showing that such thinking is universal, normal and can occur in many different situations.

It is important to agree a term for these thoughts. Beck originally used "negative" and "positive" automatic thoughts but these are not useful terms. For some patients they conjure up connotations of "the power of positive thinking" which is not what CBT is about. "Negative" does not really describe many thoughts that BN patients have. Other terms which could be discussed with the patient would be "reasonable" versus "unreasonable", "functional" versus "dysfunctional", "helpful" versus "unhelpful or problematic" thoughts.

An explanation of automatic thoughts should include the following:

Characteristics of truly automatic thoughts:

- They are automatic—they are not actually arrived at on the basis of reason or logic, they just seem to happen. It can help to think of them as part of the running commentary on life that goes on almost constantly inside our heads while we are awake. The analogy of popping up like toast from a toaster may be helpful.
- They are our own *interpretations* of what is going on around us rather than *facts*. They depend on all sorts of factors, such as our level of self-confidence and how things are going in our lives generally. If we feel confident and happy then the automatic thoughts we have are likely to reflect this by being positive and optimistic. If, however, we feel unhappy and low in confidence, the automatic thoughts are likely to be negative and pessimistic.
- The automatic thoughts are often *unreasonable* and serve no useful purpose. They are based on the individual's view of herself, and often do not coincide with reality. Even if they are not actually irrational they make you feel worse.

They can prevent you from getting better by persuading you that there is no point in trying to change before you have even tried to do so. They may allow you to justify putting things off (procrastinating for long periods of time). "There is no point in me going to treatment, I'll be wasting everybody's time because I've had bulimia for such a long time, I must be a hopeless case" or "I'll try to stop bingeing again tomorrow as everything is spoiled for today anyway because I've binged and vomited already".

- Even though these thoughts may be unreasonable and/or unhelpful to you, they probably seem to be very *believable* at the time when you actually think them, and because they are automatic it is very unlikely to occur to you to stand back from them and evaluate or question them. You tend to accept them as easily as an ordinary thought such as "the doorbell is ringing—I should answer it."

In summary, automatic thoughts:

are automatic
are frequent
are believable to you
alter your mood
alter your behaviour

Recording of automatic thoughts. The patient can do this in her diary or on a specially organised automatic thought sheet. Some patients find this easy and produce copious sheets of their thoughts; on these occasions one or two should be picked from the previous week's experience and dealt with in detail. Other patients find it extremely difficult. Sometimes this is because they are very embarassed about putting their thoughts on paper, sometimes because their general behaviour is so chaotic they cannot get themselves organised to do it, and sometimes because their reading and writing skills are so poor that they are unable to do it. In these cases it is useful to record thoughts during sessions and, using your clipboard, write these down for the patient.

The following are examples of thinking errors:

- *All-or-nothing thinking.* This is where things are seen only as black or white and there are no shades of grey. One mistake leads to total failure.
  "Because I cannot keep to my diet, I am a complete failure."
- *Overgeneralisation.* Here, one unfortunate event leads to the assumption that this will happen every time, but remember, there is no justification for seeing one instance as proving the rule.
  "The last few months have been a complete disaster because overall I have gained weight rather than lost any."
- *Mental filter.* This is where you pick out and dwell exclusively on the negative or worrying details.
  "I shouldn't have said that, I ruined the whole evening for everyone."
- *Disqualifying the positive.* Positive experiences do not count, for some reason. Successes are a "fluke". No pleasure is taken from positive events.
  "I've only managed to control my vomiting once in the past 24 hours."

- *Jumping to conclusions.* You assume the worst when there is no reason to (e.g. expecting failure before having tried).
  "People will laugh at me openly if I venture outside because I have put on so much weight."
- *Catastrophising.* Here, you exaggerate your own imperfections (e.g. "I made a mistake, how awful, I can never show myself here again."). Common misfortunes become disasters. Do you think about other people's mistakes in the same way?
  "I've binged again now, the whole weekend will be a write-off."
- *Emotional reasoning.* This means taking your feelings as facts (e.g. because you feel so afraid there must be really some danger).
  "I feel fat, I know I must be fat."
- *"Should" statements.* Thinking you *should* be able to stay calm all the time or you *should never* get angry. Rigid statements like this are overdemanding and unreasonable and cause unnecessary pressure.
  "I should never lose my temper, it shows how weak I am."
- *Labelling and mislabelling.* You label yourself as a "useless person" on the basis of one mistake. It makes as much sense as labelling yourself as a joiner because you put up a shelf.
  "I can't even control my food intake: I'm a complete failure."
- *Personalisation.* Everything that goes wrong you attribute to yourself, which causes guilty feelings.
  "People stare at me wherever I go because I am so grotesquely fat."
  "I don't want to go out because I am sure that just seeing me must ruin a person's day."

Sometimes a thought will fit into more than one category, so a patient should not worry about fitting her thoughts into exactly the right category. Nevertheless, she will probably find that there are certain patterns of errors she keeps on making.

Challenging automatic thoughts. One of the main therapeutic techniques in CBT is Socratic questioning. Examples of the types of questions are given in Table 17.3. Such questions should be used frequently during therapy sessions to help the patient generate alternative responses. The patient will, it is hoped, learn to use these questions herself to challenge her thoughts in between sessions. At this stage of treatment, role-play is very useful so that situations around meals times and other encounters can be relived in the therapy session (see Figure 17.4). It is very useful to use role reversal, going through a particular incident firstly with the patient playing herself and you playing the significant other and then with you playing the patient. If you are successful in generating alternatives, make sure that the patient writes these down so that they can be examined later when both of you are out of role.

Automatic images. It is useful to remember that many people do much of their thinking in pictures and that images of food, the patient's body or previous very painful experiences can be just as distressing as the thoughts. Full discussion of

TABLE 17.3   Socratic questioning: looking for rational answers.

What is the evidence?
What evidence do you have to support your thoughts?
What evidence do you have against them?

What alternative views are there?
How would someone else view this situation?
How would you have viewed it before you got depressed?
What evidence do you have to back these alternatives?

What is the effect of thinking the way you do?
Does it help you, or hinder you from getting what you want? How?
What would be the effect of looking at things less negatively?

What thinking error are you making?
Are you thinking in all-or-nothing terms?
Are you condemning yourself totally as a person on the basis of a single event?
Are you concentrating on your weaknesses and forgetting your strengths?
Are you blaming yourself for something which is not your fault?
Are you taking something personally which has little or nothing to do with you?
Are you expecting yourself to be perfect?
Are you using a double standard? How would you view someone else in your situation?
Are you paying attention only to the negative side of things?
Are you overestimating the chance of disaster?
Are you exaggerating the importance of events?
Are you fretting about the way things ought to be instead of accepting and dealing with them as they come?
Are you assuming you can do nothing to change your situation?
Are you predicting the future instead of experimenting with it?
Are you overlooking solutions to problems on the assumption they won't work?

What action can you take?
What can you do to change your situation?
What can you do to test out the validity of your rational answers?
Can you use "I want", "I need" and "I wish" instead of "I must", "I should" and "I ought"?

therapy with imagery is outwith the scope of this chapter, but there are certainly patients that I have treated where image work has been the main mode of treatment with little attention to automatic thoughts at all. Helping people control images, alter them, switch them on and off are all useful techniques. We should remember that because of our education, our professional training and our work practice, we as therapists are highly attuned to verbal methods of expression. We should not make this assumption for our patients.

Introducing the concept of basic assumptions. Once the patient has become practised at the idea of capturing, recording and challenging automatic thoughts, the concept of other levels of thinking should be introduced. A useful analogy is to describe the layers of skin on an onion, indicating that automatic thoughts represent the outer surface layer. Many terms are used for these deeper layers of thinking, including "basic assumptions", "underlying assumptions", "schema", "problematic attitudes" or "basic beliefs".

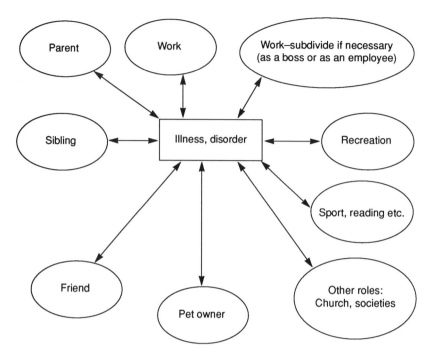

1.   How do you function in each of these roles?

2.   What causes you to function the way you do in these roles?

3.   Let us identify "islands" where you do have some self-worth.

      [Evaluate how much of low self-esteem is related to their disorder, their past
      experience, them as an individual or their core self.]

FIGURE 17.4   Role map for self-esteem.

In eating disorders these tend to cluster around certain themes such as control, perfectionism, self-indulgence, weakness and guilt. Many of the techniques used to perfectionism, self-indulgence, weakness and guilt. Many of the techniques used to elicit automatic thoughts can be used to get at basic assumptions. These should be described to the patient in terms of general psychologial rules that govern the individual's thoughts and behaviour. It is best to make the uncovering of these explicit: "Let's see if together we can discover three or four basic rules that may underlie all the automatic thoughts we have identified". Testing out basic assumptions is best done by experiment or role-play in the session: "Let's just assume for this part of the session that these rules are true to you, how would that effect the way you think and behave?" Sometimes after such role-plays basic assumptions are modified or discounted; but in general it is remarkable how often patients simply

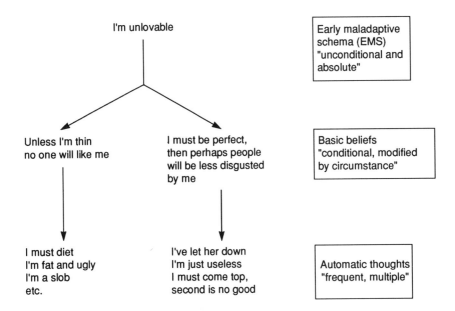

FIGURE 17.5   Cognitive processes in severe eating disorder.

role-play themselves and then realise how much a rule has dominated their lives. In general, basic assumptions are more difficult to challenge and to change than automatic thoughts, and in short-term CBT one may get no further than identifying these, helping the patient be aware of them and using simple techniques such as self-coping statements to avoid their impact. Basic assumptions tend to be conditional; because x is true, y will happen.

More deeply buried schemata are sometimes referred to as "early maladaptive schemata" (EMS) (see Figures 17.5 and 17.6). These are usually unconditional (e.g. I am bad, I am unlovable, I contaminate people, I am a failure etc.). They are laid down in childhood and adolescence, they tend to be rigid, actively defended and very difficult to change. Usually, longer-term CBT is required.

Relapse Prevention (Stage 5)

Although the last two sessions concentrate on this, the principles may well have been discussed earlier in treatment. The fluctuating nature of BN almost certainly means that relapsed will have occurred during treatment, and therefore some of the points outlined in Table 17.4 will already have been introduced. One of the themes of treatment is that CBT for bulimia nervosa is not a cure but "is a set of skills that you will learn during therapy and which you should continue to apply when active therapy is over". The table shows a list of points which should be addressed. This is modified from Fairburn's (1985) excellent handout. It should be used both as a handout at the end of treatment and as a guide for the therapist during the last two sessions.

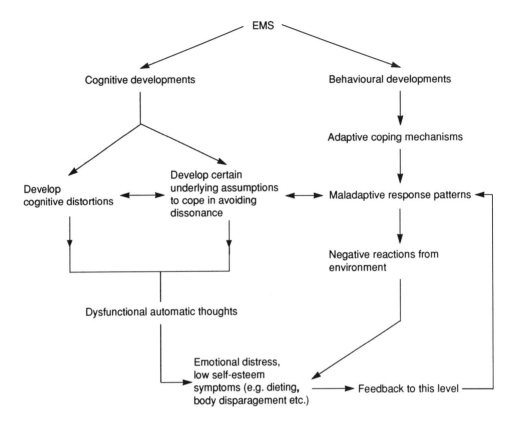

FIGURE 17.6   Early maladaptive (distorted) shemata (EMSs).

Another theme of prevention should be that relapse can be expected. In fact, the first relapse will be the best test of how effective treatment has been. The first relapse should be planned for and coping strategies worked out with the patient.

Follow-up (Stage 6)

Follow-up is an essential part of the treatment package. Different regimes may be organised according to local needs. In general, individual therapy is best followed by individual follow-up, though in some centres group sessions are used. Reasonable intervals would be one, three, six and twelve months. These sessions should incorporate a revision of the CBT model and measurements of severity. Rather than spend the whole session simply reviewing the past months, it is often more productive to take one or two particular problems that have occurred and tackle these using CBT techniques. In our unit we offer further follow-up at 18 months and two years, but in general numbers attending at these stages are very low.

Continuing Self-help (Stage 7)

We have found it useful in both individual and group therapy to emphasise the importance of self-help throughout treatment. In our group CBT treatments, members of one of the associated self-help groups come along to Session 5 or 6 to introduce themselves and the way they work and then are available at the end of the acute phase of treatment for people who wish to join. We have access to a variety of self-help groups, some run by the Eating Disorders Association (EDA), some set up independently by treated patients, and some as part of Overeaters Anonymous or Women's Therapy Centres.

SCIENTIFIC EVALUATION OF CBT FOR BULIMIA NERVOSA

There is little doubt that CBT is the best evaluated treatment for BN. Surprisingly there have been relatively few studies of individual CBT, although this is often claimed to be the treatment of choice. The studies that had been carried out are summarised in Tables 17.5 and 17.6. There are good recent reviews by Mitchell et al (1993) and Agras (1991). The problem with many of these studies is that it is often difficult to see how they would translate into ordinary clinical practice. They have all been carried out in specialised centres by highly skilled practitioners often with an understandable bias towards one of the psychotherapies they are evaluating. These comments of course apply to most, if not all, psychotherapy research. What we badly need to support these "scientific studies" are more pragmatic ones which audit the outcome of bulimia nervosa treated in ordinary clinics.

Nevertheless we can still draw some important and clinically relevant conclusions from the studies so far carried out. It is clear from several studies that it is the combination of cognitive and behavioural techniques which seems to be important. Wilson et al (1986) showed that cognitive restructuring was less effective than CBT. It has also been shown that behaviour therapy alone produces less change than behaviour therapy plus cognitive techniques, though interestingly another study (Freeman et al, 1988) showed little difference between the results with CBT and BT.

There seems to be a slight advantage for individual CBT over group treatment unless the group treatments are very intensive, such as in Mitchell's 1990 study. Mitchell et al (1993) have also demonstrated that the intensity of the treatment in the first few weeks, in terms of the frequency of sessions and the amount of therapeutic effort that is directed towards abstinence and reducing restraint, appears to be important.

When CBT is compared with drug treatment, psychotherapy is clearly superior. There seems to be little added effect of drugs plus psychotherapy, though in Mitchell's intensive group study (1990) the CBT group had already done so well that there was little scope for further improvement with the addition of imipramine. Where studies have compared CBT and drugs, the drugs used have been tricyclics such as desipramine or imipramine. As yet there are no comparative studies with

TABLE 17.4   A maintenance plan for bulimia.

HOW TO HELP YOURSELF IN FUTURE

Eating problems may **recur** at times of **stress**. You should regard your eating problems as an Achilles heel: it is the way you may react at times of difficulty.

You discovered during treatment that certain strategies helped you regain control over eating. The strategies you found most helpful are listed below. These should be re-established under two sets of circumstances:

- if you sense you are at risk of relapse, or
- if your eating problem has deteriorated

At such times there will often be some unsolved difficulty, underlying your relapse or fear of relapse. You must therefore examine what is happening in your life and look for any events or difficulties that might be of relevance. Once these have been identified, you should then consider all possible solutions to these problems and construct an appropriate plan of action. In addition, you should use one or more of the following strategies to regain control over eating:

1. Set some time aside so that you can reflect on your current difficulties. You need to devise a plan of action. Reckon on formally re-evaluating your progress every day or so. Some strategies may have worked; some may not.
2. Recommence monitoring everything you eat, when you eat it. (Use the diary we provided).
3. Try to eat in company, not alone.
4. Restrict your eating to three or four planned meals each day, plus one or two planned snacks. Try to have these meals and snacks at predetermined times.
5. Plan your days ahead. Avoid both long periods of unstructured time and overbooking. If you are feeling at risk of losing control, plan your meals in detail so that you know exactly what and when you will be eating. In general, you should try to keep "one step ahead" of the problem.
6. Restrict your food stocks. If you feel you are at risk of buying too much food, carry as little money as possible.
7. Identify the times at which you are most likely to overeat (from recent experience and the evidence provided by your diary), and plan alternative activies that are compatible with eating, such as meeting friends, exercising, or taking a bath.
8. Whenever possible, avoid areas where stocks of food are kept. Try to keep out of the kitchen between meals.
9. If you are thinking too much about your weight, make sure you are weighing no more than once a week. *If necessary, stop weighing altogether*. If you want to reduce weight, do so by cutting down the quantity you eat at each meal rather than by skipping meals. Remember, you should accept a weight *range*, and gradual changes in weight are best.
10. If you are thinking too much about your shape, this may be because you are anxious or depressed. You tend to feel fat when things are not going well. You should try problem-solving in order to see whether you can identify any current problems and do something positive to solve or at least minimise them.
11. Try not to be "phobic" about your body. Do not avoid looking in mirrors or using communal changing rooms.
12. If possible, confide in someone. Explain your present predicament. A trouble shared is a trouble halved. Remember, you would not mind any friend of yours sharing his or her problems with you.
13. Use exercise. Regular exercise increases metabolic rate and helps suppress appetite, particularly carbohydrate craving.
14. Take particular care in days leading up to your period. For many women, food cravings increase at this time.

15. Set yourself limited, realistic goals. Work from "hour to hour" rather than "day to day". One "failure" does not justify a succession of failures. Note your successes, however modest, in your diary.

Before seeking professional help, try to use the strategies listed above. **Remember, you have used them with benefit in the past.**

TABLE 17.5   Studies of individual CBT.

Reference	Treatments given	Subjects at start	Subjects completed	Reduction of bingeing	Abstinent at end of treatment
Fairburn et al	CBT	12	92%	87%	27%
(1986)	Short-term focal	12	92%	82%	36%
Freeman et al	CBT	32	66%	79%	40%
(1988)	BT	30	83%	87%	36%
Fairburn et al	CBT	25	84%	97%	47%
(1991)	IPT	25	88%	89%	37%
	BT	25	86%	91%	63%
Agras et al	CBT	23	96%	71%	55%
(1992)	CBT+desipramine*	16	83%	57%	64%
	CBT+desipramine†	24	83%	89%	70%
	Desipramine	16	83%	43%	33%
	Desipramine	24	83%	44%	42%
Garner et al	CBT	30	83%	69%	12%
(1993)	Psychodynamic	30	83%	73%	36%
Fairburn et al	CBT	25	80%	95%	36%
(1993) (12-month	IPT	25	68%	95%	44%
follow-up of 1991	BT	25	52%	–	20%
study)					

IPT = Interpersonal psychotherapy.
* 16 weeks of desipramine. † 24 weeks of desipramine.

specific serotonin reuptake inhibitors (SSRIs). However the general conclusion has to be that the anti-bulimic effect of drug treatment is very modest, relapse after drug treatment is extremely high, and drugs only have a limited place in the long-term management of bulimia nervosa.

When CBT is compared with other types of psychotherapy, on an individual or group basis, the results are much less clear-cut. Although there are tendencies in several studies for CBT to do better than other psychotherapies in the short term, only one study (Fairburn et al, 1993) has addressed even medium-term follow-up. When CBT and interpersonal psychotherapy (IPT) were compared at one year, there were no differences between the two treatments. CBT had been doing better at the end of treatment and early in the follow-up treatment in terms of bingeing and purging behaviour and, most importantly, in terms of attitude change. However, these results completely disappeared at 12-month follow-up. This study

TABLE 17.6   Studies of group CBT.

Reference	Treatments given	Subjects at start	Subjects completed	Reduction of bingeing	Abstinent at end of treatment
Yates and	CBT + BT	24	67%	–	13%
Sambrailo (1984)	CBT	24	67%	–	0
Kirkley et al	CBT	14	93%	97%	–
(1985)	Non-directive	14	64%	64%	–
Lee and Rush	CBT	15	73%	70%	29%
(1986)	Waiting list	15	–	–	–
Wilson et al	CR + ERP	9	85%	82%	71%
(1986)	CR alone	8	67%	51%	33%
Leitenburg et al	CBT + ERP	26	88%	70%	39%
(1988)	CBT	12	100%	40%	8%
Freeman et al	CBT	30	63%	87%	22%
(1988)					
Agras et al	Self-monitoring	19	86%	63%	24%
(1989)	CBT	22	77%	75%	56%
	CBT + ERP	17	94%	52%	31%
	Waiting list				
Mitchell et al	CBT + placebo	34	85%	89%	45%
(1990)	CBT + impramine	52	75%	92%	56%
	Imipramine	54	67%	49%	16%
Mitchell et al	Intensive CBT + HA	33	88%	77%	70%
(1993)	Regular CBT + HA	41	88%	80%	71%
	Intensive CBT + LA	35	86%	88%	76%
	Regular CBT + LA	34	82%	62%	30%

CR = cognitive restructuring; ERP = exposure, response prevention; HA = high abstinence; LA = low abstinence.

therefore indicates that a treatment such as IPT which does not address directly the behavioural–cognitive aspects of BN can be just as effective.

CBT FOR ANOREXIA NERVOSA

The standard model of CBT needs considerable modification for use with anorexic patients. For moderate and severely ill anorexics the treatment is difficult, often repetitive and much more prolonged than for the treatment of depression, anxiety and bulimic disorders. It is important before even contemplating CBT for anorexia nervosa that a therapist has considerable experience in the use of shorter-term CBT so as to feel confident in the basic model, its structure, pacing and collaborative method.

As to the scientific basis for CBT for anorexia nervosa, there is very little to be said. Controlled outcome studies of anorexia nervosa are rare and none have compared CBT with other treatments in a randomised controlled trial. It is unlikely that such a trial will ever be carried out in acutely ill very underweight anorexics. It will be almost impossible to distill out the role that CBT had played from all the other aspects of the programme. In our own study (Freeman et al, 1993), 32 consecutively referred women with severe anorexia nervosa (BMI 14 and under) were randomly allocated to conventional intensive inpatient treatment or to a day-patient programme using CBT. None of the day-patients were admitted, and at 18 months follow-up both groups were doing equally well. At 3-year follow-up, those treated in the day-patient programme had had fewer relapses, fewer readmissions and had more stable weight. Their social functioning was also markedly better. It cannot, however, be claimed that this study is a success for CBT. So many other factors were involved in the treatment packages that formal CBT may have been irrelevant. Nevertheless, the study does show that a more open, collaborative, trusting style of therapy using cognitive and behavioural experiments rather than rules can lead to as much, if not more, improvement than conventional inpatient treatment and refeeding.

There are a number of studies under way in which CBT is being compared with other forms of therapy for weight-restored anorexics and for those in the mild-to-moderate severity groups who would normally be treated on an outpatient basis.

CBT has been modified in recent years by Beck (1990), Young (1991) and Linnehan (1993) for use in the treatment of personality disorder. These more extended techniques will need to be evaluated in the longer-term treatment of anorexia nervosa.

TRAINING FOR COGNITIVE BEHAVIOUR THERAPY

Training involves more than simply attending a couple of one-day workshops on the general principles of CBT. The minimum requirement should be an intensive training course of one or two weeks followed by the taking on of individual patients under supervision. Supervision should involve video or audiotape monitoring and rating on the cognitive therapy competency scale. In my view, therapists should have at least a year of supervision of basic CBT for depressive and anxiety disorders and should have treated 10–15 cases before beginning CBT for eating disorders. Treating patients with anorexia nervosa will require experience and supervision of techniques used in longer-term CBT.

CONCLUSIONS

CBT is the best evaluated treatment for bulimia nervosa. It is clear that it is not the only effective treatment and that at medium-term follow-up other non-cognitive therapies do just as well. CBT is well tolerated by patients, has high face validity but is expensive and time-consuming to deliver on an individual basis. In our experience, simpler and less intensive treatments are appropriate for first-line interventions and CBT should be reserved for patients who do not respond to these interventions. These considerations certainly apply in a National Health Service setting and will increasingly do so in private medicine. CBT for anorexia nervosa is unevaluated and at present has no more than the status of a therapeutic style that an individual therapist adopts rather than a complete treatment for anorexia nervosa.

REFERENCES

Agras, W.S. (1991). Nonpharmacologic treatments of bulimia nervosa. *J. Clin. Psychiat.,* **52L** (Suppl.), 29–33.

Agras, W.S., Rossiter, E.M., Arnow, B., et al (1992). Pharmacologic and cognitive–behavioral treatment for bulimia nervosa: a controlled comparison. *Am. J. Psychiatr.,* **149**, 82–87.

Agras, W.S. , Schneider, J.A., Arnow, B., Raeburn, S.D. and Telch, C.F. (1989). *Cognitive–behavioural and response–prevention treatment of bulimia nervosa. J. Consult. Clin. Psychol.,* **57**, 215–221.

Baell, W.K. and Wertheim, E.H. (1992). Predictors of outcome in the treatment of bulimia nervosa. *Br. J. Clin. Psychol.,* **31**, 33–332.

Beck, A.T., Freeman, A. et al (1991). *Cognitive Therapy for Personality Disorders.* New York: Guilford Press.

Cullen Centre Manual (1993). Group treatment package for Bulimia Nervosa. Dept. of Psychotherapy, Royal Edinburgh Hospital, Scotland.

Fairburn, C. (1981). A cognitive behavioural approach to the treatment of bulimia. *Psychol. Med.,* **11**, 707–711.

Fairburn, C.G. (1985). Cognitive-behavioural treatment for bulimia. In D.M. Garner and P.E. Garfinkel (Eds) *Handbook of Psychotherapy for Anorexia Nervosa and Bulimia,* Chapter 8, pp. 160–192. New York: Guilford.

Fairburn, C.G., Jones, R., Peveler, R. et al (1991). Three psychological treatments for bulimia nervosa. *Arch. Gen. Psychiat.,* **48**, 463–469.

Fairburn, C.G., Jones, R., Peveler, R.C., Hope, R.A. and O'Connor, M. (1993). Psychotherapy and bulimia nervosa: longer-term effects of interpersonal psychotherapy behavior therapy, and cognitive behavior therapy. *Arch. Gen. Psychiat.,* **50**, 419–428.

Fairburn, C.G., Kirk, J., O'Connor, M. and Cooper, P.J. (1986). A comparison of two psychological treatments for bulimia nervosa. *Behav. Res. Ther.,* **24**, 629–643.

Freeman, C.P.F. and Newton, J.R. (1992). Anorexia nervosa: what treatments are most effective? In: K. Hawton and P. Cowan (Eds), *Practical Problems in Clinical Psychiatry.* Oxford: University Press.

Freeman, C.P.L., Barry, F., Dunkeld-Turnbull and Henderson, A. (1988). Controlled trial of psychotherapy for bulimia nervosa. *Br. Med. J.,* **296**, 521–525.

Garner, D.M. and Bemis, K.M. (1985). Cognitive therapy for Anorexia. In D.M. Garner and P.E. Garfinkel (Eds) *Handbook of Psychotherapy for Anorexia Nervosa and Bulimia,* Chapter 6, pp. 107–146. New York: Guilford.

Garner, D.M., Rockert, W., Davis, R. et al (1993). Comparison of cognitive–behavioral and supportive–expressive therapy for bulimia nervosa. *Am. J. Psychiat.,* **150**, 37–46.

Hartmann, A., Herzog, T. and Drinkmann, A. (1992). Psychotherapy of bulimia nervosa: what is effective? A meta-analysis. *J. Psychosom. Res.,* **36**, 159–167.

Herzog, D.B., Keller, M.B., Strober, M., Yeh, C. and Pai, S.Y. (1992). The current status of treatment for anorexia nervosa and bulimia nervosa. *Int. J. Eat. Dis.,* **12**, 215–220.

Hsu, L.K.G. (1991). Four treatments of bulimia nervosa. Paper presented at Seattle Symposium on Eating Disorders.

Kirkley, G.B., Schneider, J.A., Agras, W.S. and Bachman, J. (1985). Comparison of two group treatments for bulimia. *J. Consult. Clin. Psychol,* **5**, 43–48.

Lee, N.F. and Rush, A.J. (1986). Cognitive–behavioural group therapy for bulimia. *Int. J. Eat. Dis.,* **5**, 599–615.

Leitenberg, H., Rosen, J.C., Gross, J., Nudelman, S. and Varal, S. (2988). Exposure plus response-prevention treatment of bulimia nervosa. *J. Consult. Clin. Psychol.,* **56**, 535–541.

Linnehan, M. (1993). *Cognitive-behavioural Treatment of Borderline Personalities Disorder.* New York: Guilford.

Mitchell, J.E., Pyle, R.L., Eckert, E.D. et al. (1990). A comparison study of antidepressants and structured intensive group psychotherapy in the treatment of bulimia nervosa. *Arch. Gen. Psychiat.,* **47**, 149–157.

Mitchell, J.E., Pyle, R.L., Pomeroy, et al. (1993). Logistical variables. *Int. J. Eat. Dis.* (in press).

Tiller, J., Schmidt, U. and Treasure, J. (1993). Treatment of bulimia nervosa. *Int. Rev. Psychiat.,* **5**, 75–86.

Wilson, G.T., Rossiter, E., Kleifield, E.I. and Lindholm, L. (1986). Cognitive–behavioural treatment of bulimia nervosa: a controlled evaluation. *Behav. Res. Ther.,* **24**, 277–288.

Wolf, E.M. and Crowther, J.H. (1992). An evaluation of behavioral and cognitive–behavior group interventions for the treatment of bulimia nervosa in women. *Int. J. Eat. Dis.,* **11**, 3–15.

Yates, A.J. and Sambrailo, F. (1984). Bulimia nervosa: a descriptive and therapeutic study. *Behav. Res. Ther.,* **5**, 503–517.

Young, J.E. (1991). *Cognitive Therapy for Personality Disorders: A Schemata-focussed Approach.* Sarasota, Florida: Professional Resource Exchange Inc.

Zotter, D.L. and Crowther, J.H. (1991). The role of cognitions in bulimia nervosa. *Cogn. Ther. Res.,* **15**, 413–426.

18

Family Therapy

CHRISTOPHER DARE
AND
IVAN EISLER
Institute of Psychiatry, London, UK

INTRODUCTION

Treatments often have an association with a disorder which is paradigmatic for the treatment. For example, hysteria was the paradigm for psychoanalysis, while the treatment of phobias were the model for the development of behaviour therapy. Similarly, anorexia nervosa has been a paradigm, in some way, for family therapy. Two of the founding figures in the family therapy field, Selvini-Palazzoli and Minuchin, developed major aspects of their contributions to family therapy through the treatment of eating disorder (Selvini-Palazzoli, 1974; Selvini-Palazzoli et al, 1989; Minuchin et al, 1975, 1978). Other important figures such as Whitaker (Stern et al, 1981), White (1986), Wynne (1980) and Madanes (1981) have all described treatments of eating disordered patients to exemplify their contribution to the field. A characteristic of these contributions is that there has been an attempt to integrate the theory of the family, the origins of eating disorders and the role of family therapy. It has been easy to assume that successful treatments of cases of eating disorder by family therapy suggest a family aetiology for the eating disorder.

It appears to be logical to believe that effective treatment and aetiology are closely linked, even though such logic is not always born out by empirical evidence

Handbook of Eating Disorders: Theory, Treatment and Research.
Edited by G. Szmukler, C. Dare and J. Treasure.
© 1995 John Wiley & Sons Ltd.

(cf. Dare, 1993a). There are firmly held beliefs proposing and opposing a "family" aetiology for eating disorders. Parents must always have concerns to feed their children and infants, while eating together is a major ritual expressing family tradition and offering the possibility of a family to feel united. Having a member suffering from an eating disorder will often engender feelings of guilt and a sense of failure on the part of the parents and will be felt as an affront to the sense of well-being of the family as a whole. For the individual sufferer these considerations can seem irrelevant. The patient may have a strong sense of dissatisfaction with parents, but the family's sense of guilt and responsibility for the presence of the disorder is rarely reflected in the patient's attitudes. Unlike the parents, the patient believes that the eating problem is a personal issue, a matter of self-control for the individual and of private destiny. The research evidence (outlined in Chapter 9) supports the patient's views: there is little to confirm the clinical suspicion that the families of eating disordered patients are particularly unusual; certainly nothing to identify the family as a cause of the problem. While the eating disorder will frequently dominate family life to the point where relationships among family members will seem inseparable from interactions around food and eating, the family or the patient will rarely ask for family treatment, and when this is offered may, in fact, be extremely reluctant to accept the participation in the treatment of parents, let alone of siblings, and will expect an individually orientated therapy.

The disorders have profound consequences for the psychological development of the individual and may be understood, psychologically, as expressing crucial, developmental issues. Once established, whatever their origins, eating disorders have the features of intensely enduring, compulsively perpetuated habits. Yet family intervention is currently the only form of treatment for anorexia nervosa shown to be effective in the long term by controlled trials. The evidence of a series of clinical treatment trials conducted at the Maudsley Hospital are the subject matter of this chapter. The absence of an intuitive fit between some of the findings and the perceptions of the different family members as to the nature of the problem is central to understanding the resistance of patients and families to the use of family therapy. The clinician's warm acknowledgement of this resistance in the clinical setting, sympathetic acceptance of the natural dislike of family therapy by patients and families, are essential if family therapy is to be used in the treatment of anorexia nervosa.

THE MAUDSLEY STUDIES OF FAMILY THERAPY AND EATING DISORDER

The chapter will refer to the following four large controlled treatment trials, described as Maudsley Studies I–IV (see Figure 18.1):

- *I—A comparison of family therapy and individual supportive therapy.* The 1-year outpatient treatment followed an inpatient refeeding programme. This study included patients of all ages and covered 80 consecutive admissions to our inpatient unit. A 5-year follow-up of this study is reported briefly.

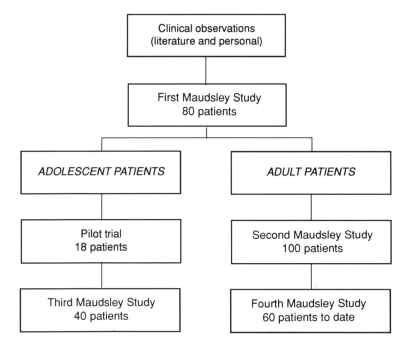

FIGURE 18.1   Development of the Maudsley trials.

- *II—A comparison of family therapy, individual focal (psychodynamic) psycho-therapy and individual supportive therapy in adult patients.* In this study, 100 consecutive admissions to the inpatient unit were included. After the first study, routine admission of adolescent patients was no longer considered appropriate and the second study included only adult patients (over 18 years of age). The detailed results of this study have not yet been published; preliminary results are reported here.
- *III—A comparison of family therapy and family counselling in adolescent patients.* This study compared two different family treatments conducted on an outpatient basis. The results of a pilot study of 18 patients are reported as well as the preliminary results of the definitive study in which 40 patients were enrolled.
- *IV*—In this ongoing study, adult patients who have not been admitted to the inpatient regime are being randomly allocated to family therapy, individual focal psychotherapy or standard outpatient treatment. In a linked study, cognitive analytic therapy is also being compared with the standard outpatient treatment.

Figure 18.1 shows the sequence of the treatment trials of family therapy conducted over the last dozen or so years, at the Maudsley Hospital and Institute of Psychiatry. At the top, the box shows the observations inspiring the first trial. These include the studies of Morgan and Russell (1975) that showed that family factors influenced the outcome of eating disorders and the retrospective studies of

Minuchin and his colleagues (Minuchin et al, 1975; 1978) illustrating the apparent efficacy of family therapy for anorexia nervosa. Methodologically, the pattern of the Maudsley studies have followed a specific pattern involving the following consistent features:

1. Patients are selected on diagnostic criteria for an eating disorder, not for the aptitude of the patient or the family for psychotherapy. Clinical and research assessments are conducted by workers independent of the treatment team.
2. The design of each study takes into account the known factors that affect the patients' prognosis so that, at random allocation to treatment category, the different treatment groups contain equal proportions of patients with a likelihood of relatively good or poor outcome.
3. In order to partial out the contribution of therapists with different capabilities ("therapist variables"), all participating psychotherapists undertake therapies in all the different modalities and will see a balanced number of patients in each treatment.
4. The treatments are given for one year with an intensity predetermined by the research protocol.
5. Consistent supervision is provided for the different treatments by highly qualified therapists who are independent of the assessment process and of the parallel treatments being studied. The supervision takes place in a group setting devised to ensure that the treatments are provided in a way that confirms to the research protocol.

Most of the results reported in this chapter are end-of-treatment results, giving the status of the patients one year after admission to the psychological treatment programme. At follow-up assessment, the research investigators repeat the battery of investigations including a psychiatric interview standardised for the study of eating disorders (Morgan and Russell, 1975). The results given in this chapter refer mostly to assignment of the patients to one of three outcome categories:

• "good" outcome (identified as G in the figures) in which weight and menstrual function are normal and there is an absence of bulimic symptoms
• an "intermediate" (I) group with adequate nutrition but a persisting disturbance of sexual physiology (menstrual irregularity, lack of libido), and an absence (or only sporadic appearance) of bulimic symptoms
• a "poor" (P) outcome in which weight is more than 15% below the mean of a matched population sample, and/or bulimic symptoms persist or have developed and occur once a week or more.

These classification criteria are based purely on the patient's symptoms but there is good evidence that they bear a close relationship to outcome on a range of other variables including personal relationships, social and psychosexual adjustment and in the modulation of self-esteem and affective state (Russell et al, 1987; Eisler et al, 1994).

Study I

This study (Russell et al, 1987; Dare et al, 1990) followed the course of 80 patients who had, during an inpatient refeeding programme, been stratified into one of four clinically distinguishable groups according to pre-established prognostic criteria. One group, those with Early Onset (before 19 years of age) and Short History (less than 3 years) (EOSH) anorexia nervosa fared very much better, at one year after discharge from hospital, if they had received family therapy as opposed to individual supportive psychotherapy. Another group, those with Late Onset (after 18 years) anorexia nervosa, showed some indications of improved weight maintenance in the individual supportive therapy as opposed to the family therapy treatment programme. Two further groups, patients with Early Onset (before 19 years) and Long History (more than 3 years) (EOLH) and patients with bulimia nervosa (BN, as defined by Russell, 1979) showed no between-treatment differences. This study established that family therapy has a powerful effect on the course of anorexia nervosa in a group of adolescent anorexic patients. There was no obvious indication for specific benefits of family therapy in the other groups of eating disordered patients.

The principal findings of this study have been confirmed in a 5-year follow-up study (Russell et al 1992; Eisler et al, 1994). The difference in general outcome for the EOSH group remained clear. Nine of ten of those patient's who had received family therapy in the year following discharge from hospital were at 5 years allocated to a good-outcome category. Of those who had received individual supportive therapy, five were still in the poor-outcome category, four had a good outcome and two were classed as intermediate in outcome (p 0.02; Fisher test—for G versus I + P). The difference in outcome between the two treatments in the LO group (in this case in favour of individual supportive therapy) is less clear-cut but nevertheless has again persisted over 5 years.

Study II

Figure 18.2 shows the structure of the, as yet unpublished, study involving a cohort of 100 severely ill adult patients with anorexia nervosa and low-weight bulimia nervosa. The mean age of the patients at assessment was 26.2 years (range 18–60 years). The mean age of onset of illness was 18.8 years (11–50 years) and the mean duration was 7.1 years (0.5–29 years). The severity of illness of this patient group is highlighted by the fact that nearly a third had been ill for 10 years or more.

The results of this trial are still being evaluated, but at this stage the overall findings suggest an extension of the role of family therapy in eating disorders. We can present the end-of-treatment data for those patients who accepted the outpatient treatment, stayed in treatment for at least 3 months, and were reassessed at the end of one year; that is a total of 74 patients out of an original 100 patients.

Overall, of the patients evaluated so far, of those who had received one of the two individual therapies approximately two-thirds had a poor outcome at one year, whereas for those in family therapy nearly two-thirds had either a good or

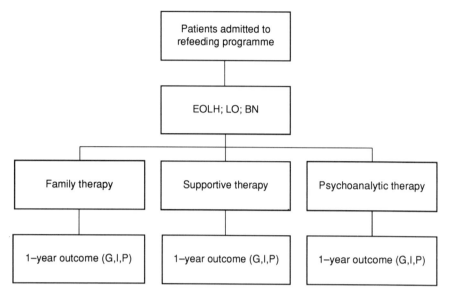

FIGURE 18.2   The second Maudsley trial.

intermediate outcome (χ^2 = 6.53; p = 0.04). One further surprise was provided in examining the patients with bulimia nervosa. In individual therapy, these patients did badly (2 out of 10 only having a "good" or "intermediate" outcome) whilst 5 of 6 in family therapy were so placed (p = 0.02, Fisher test). As the numbers are small and the data are still incomplete, the results must be viewed with great caution. Nevertheless, they may be a pointer to an extension of the role of family therapy in eating disorders.

Study III

The principal finding of the first Maudsley study was the suggestion that we were able to mobilise a form of family therapy that had the potential of offering long-term benefit for young anorexic patients. Our subsequent 5-year follow-up seemed to justify this view. However, we also thought that we should explore the specifications of our family therapy. To continue our studies, we gave much thought to what would constitute a family-based intervention that would be an appropriate control treatment for family therapy. We believed that the most parsimonious conclusion of the results of the first trial was that, in adolescent patients, the family had to be involved, in some way, in the outpatient treatment programme. We analysed the content of the family therapy and concluded that there were two main components which could be defined as (1) a "problem solving" component and (2) a "family systems" component:

1.   Interventions that were specifically focused on the eating disorder: giving information and advice about the nature of the condition; helping the parents be

more confident and direct in their handling of the self-starvation; discussion of general issues about the role of parents in relationship to the adolescence of their children.

2. Family systems interventions: instructions, interpretations, the facilitation of negotiations between the father and mother (or step or adoptive parents) and between the parents and children, all designed to change aspects of overall family functioning. These interventions are considered to be best conducted as an outcome of direct observation of the interactional processes within a family. The family systems interventions are aimed at: the clarification of roles, and of communication, the establishment of age-appropriate hierarchical organisations and boundaries within the family; the encouragement of a clear alliance between the adults of the family for the sake of effective parenting; the exploration of the history of the family in order to identify the specific traditions, attitudes and expectations of family life within the family.

The first component defines the parts of the family therapy that could, in principle, be conducted solely by seeing the parents. The second component defines aspects of treatment aimed at the family as a unit that are best tackled in whole-family interviews. These considerations led us to set up a comparison family intervention (which we call "family counselling") in which the therapist would see the parents as a couple to help them carry out the "problem solving" tasks. The same therapist would also see the patient on her own, in order to offer her counselling about the nature of her illness and to support her as the parents began to alter their management of her eating problem. We conducted a pilot trial (cf. Le Grange et al, 1992a) to test the feasibility of a comparison of family therapy with family counselling.

The family therapy followed our customary practice of one-hour meetings with all members of the patient's household. In family counselling the therapist saw the parent or parents together for 45 minutes and then saw the patient for the same length of time. In both treatments the therapist took responsibility for weighing the patient and keeping a weight chart which was shown to both parents and children. In both treatments, the therapist initiated detailed discussions as to the nature of anorexia nervosa, of the inability of the patient, voluntarily, to alter her dietary pattern, and of the need for supportive but forceful parental activity to ensure the restoration of a healthy feeding pattern and a healthy weight. In both treatments, as soon as the diet and nutrition of the patient showed solid improvement, the rapid return of the patient to a normal style of living was discussed and encouraged. The customary changes of parenting and parental attitude that came about during adolescence also became a significant subject matter.

In family therapy only, the therapist would set out to identify patterns of interactions which typified the manner in which the parents functioned as a couple and in relationship to all the children of the family. This included identification of the place that the illness of the patient had come to play in the pattern of family life. In the light of such observations, the therapist would try to help the family modify those patterns that seemed to diminish the capacity of the parents to be effective in challenging and restructuring their daughter's eating habits and that tended to perpetuate the patient in a sick role, different from the position of siblings. (For a description of the style of family therapy with adolescent patients with anorexia nervosa, see Dare (1988, 1993b) and Dare and Szmukler (1991).

Figure 18.3 shows the design of the main study. Forty patients were seen and treated. Their mean age was 15.5 years (standard deviation 1.6 years); the mean duration of the illness was 12.9 months (SD = 9.4 months); and the mean weight when first seen was 74.3% of matched population weight. In examining the characteristics of the sample population, an interesting fact emerged when we compared the group with the sample enrolled for the earlier pilot study. In spite of the fact that the selection criteria had remained unchanged and that there were no obvious changes in the sources of referral, several important differences emerged between the two groups. In terms of their ages, duration of illness and weight loss the patients in the definitive study were very similar to the cases seen in the pilot trial. In three respects, however, the patients in the second study were different. Firstly, the patients had significantly higher levels of eating disorder pathology as measured on the Eating Attitude Test. Secondly, the number of previous attempts at treatment was higher. The third difference is of particular interest in the context of the current discussion as it relates to an important family measure, namely the level of expressed criticism as measured by the Expressed Emotion (EE) scales (Leff and Vaughn, 1985; Le Grange et al, 1992b). While half of the pilot cases came from families where the parents made no criticism of the patient, in the definitive study this was true of only one-third of the families. The levels of criticism of the parents towards their anorexic offspring in the definitive study was in many cases surprisingly high. In the main trial, nearly 50% of the families had one or two parents who showed a score of four or more critical comments and 35% with five or more. In the pilot study, less than 12% scored five critical comments.

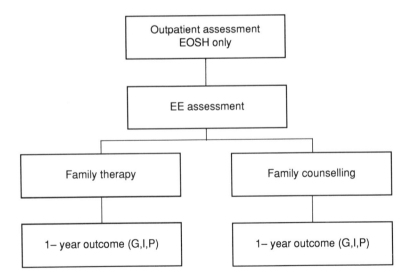

FIGURE 18.3   The third Maudsley trial.

The most obvious explanation of this finding is that as a tertiary referral centre the Maudsley Hospital gradually attracts an increasingly larger proportion of cases that are difficult to treat. Our previous work has shown (Szmukler et al, 1985; Le Grange, 1992b) that high levels of EE can make engagement of the family in effective treatment difficult. The changing nature of the referral population highlights the caution that is needed in drawing conclusions on the basis of studies in specialist centres.

The results of the comparison of family therapy and family counselling also proved a little surprising. Our expectation was that, at least in some cases, the rather simpler family counselling approach would be at a disadvantage. In the conjoint family sessions the therapist has the opportunity to observe directly the way the family interacts and can intervene in such a way so as to reinforce those patterns of interaction that are most likely to enhance parental effectiveness. In the family counselling setting this form of intervention is not available. While the therapist can talk with the parents about the ways in which they might be able to tackle the problem, there is no opportunity to intervene directly, breaking particular sequences of interaction and reinforcing specific parental responses. Our clinical experience suggests that such interventions can be highly effective and we assumed therefore that, for instance in families that might be "resistant" to change, the family counselling approach would be at a disadvantage.

The progress in terms of weight of the patients in the two treament groups demonstrates that there were comparable gains from family therapy and family counselling. Overall, those in family counselling in fact put on more weight than those in family therapy but the difference was not statistically significant. As these are only end-of-treatment results, clearly a degree of caution is needed before any conclusions are drawn about the relative benefits of the two treatments; the long-term benefits may of course be different. The pilot study (Le Grange et al, 1992a) suggested that there may be an interaction between type of treatment and levels of Expressed Emotion. The preliminary analysis of the definitive study confirms this finding, showing that families who expressed a high level of criticism to their ill daughter benefited more from family counselling than from conjoint family therapy. A 2-year follow-up of the pilot study (Squire-Dehouk, 1993) suggests that this is because in this group of families feelings of guilt and self-blame are particularly high and the therapists were less able to address such feelings in the conjoint family therapy setting.

Family Therapy in Bulimia Nervosa

Family therapy as a treatment for bulimia nervosa has received relatively little attention. The first two Maudsley studies included bulimic patients but in both cases these were generally very severely ill patients who had required an admission to an inpatient unit (mostly because of low weight), and comparisons with results of the many other published treatment studies (mostly of normal-weight bulimics seen in an outpatient setting) are therefore problematic. The outcome of these bulimic patients was generally quite poor regardless of the type of follow-up treatment. The small differences that were found were inconsistent. The 5-year follow-up of the first study showed that the bulimic patients who received individual supportive therapy had a better overall outcome than those who had received family therapy (Eisler et al, 1994). The second study, however, is showing an opposite result, with the preliminary analysis suggesting a better outcome for family therapy in comparison with individual supportive therapy or focal psychodynamic therapy.

There is a growing literature on the use of family therapy with a wide range of adult bulimic patients (Wynne, 1980; Madanes, 1981; Schwartz, Barrett and Saba, 1985; Roberto, 1986; Root, Fallon and Friedrich, 1986) but its empirical substantiation is weak. Fairburn et al (1993) have recently reported that the long-term benefits of "interpersonal therapy" are comparable to those achieved with the well-tried cognitive behaviour therapy. This is an intriguing finding because the descriptions of the interpersonal therapy resemble accounts by family therapists of "systemic therapy with an individual" (Jenkins and Asen, 1992).

We ourselves have conducted a preliminary study, evaluating the usefulness of family therapy in bulimia nervosa in adolescence (Dodge et al, 1994). This is a form of eating disorder that is rarely discussed in the literature. Patients with bulimia reported in the literature are usually young adults, but the cases seen as young adults regularly report that their symptoms, including bingeing, purging and vomiting, began before the age of 19 years. We gathered a series of eight patients with well established bulimia presenting at a mean age of 16.5 years (standard deviation 1.2 years), with a mean age of onset of 14.4 years (SD = 1.6 years) and a mean duration of 2.1 years (SD = 1.3 years). This was a small, open treatment study and did not include a comparison treatment. An indirect measure of the efficacy of the treatment is provided by comparing the results of the bulimic patients with a similar group of adolescent anorexic patients for whom we have established that family therapy is a highly effective treatment. The bulimic cases seen in the study were compared with a group of eight restricting, eating disordered patients (matched for age of onset and duration of illness), from the third Maudsley study. The end-of-treatment status of the bulimic patients reveals that a similar rate of recovery was obtained as with anorexic patients. The results suggest that family therapy with this age-group can be an effective treatment, though obviously a systematic comparison with other treatments is needed before any firm conclusions can be drawn.

IMPLICATIONS OF THE MAUDSLEY TREATMENT TRIALS

The first Maudsley study attempted to address the general question of the efficacy of family therapy, particularly as a way of preventing relapse after a successful inpatient treatment. The results of this study and the subsequent trials have helped to refine the questions being asked and have provided points for the direction for future research. The second and third studies are currently being evaluated in greater detail and therefore the conclusions that can be drawn at this stage have to be only tentative. Over the course of the years our approach to family therapy has evolved in a number of ways and we are now in a much better position to specify what form of family intervention to use with a particular patient or particular family. In the research context different treatments are compared as distinctive and alternative approaches. In practice there is a great deal of cross fertilisation of ideas that leads to treatments that can draw on aspects of a variety of approaches. A comparison of the results from the first and second studies indicates an apparently markedly improved capacity to use family therapy effectively with EOLH anorexia nervosa and with patients with bulimia nervosa. While there is undoubtedly a cumulative effect on the skills of the research therapist that increases the efficacy of the treatments, particularly those that have been practised longest, the incorporation of ideas from our other treatments has clearly also been an important factor in the development of the therapies.

For example, in Study II, the three family therapists involved in the study had had very long experience in the family therapy of eating disorders. They were also well qualified as individual, psychoanalytic psychotherapists and were in some ways more committed to careers in that area, although this form of therapy had not been used in any consistent way with severely ill, unselected eating disordered patients. The experience of conducting individual therapy with extremely ill eating disordered patients, whose motivation for change is often low, has altered our practice of family therapy. Over the years, a major change in our family therapy has been an increasing interest in the making of a more sympathetic and personal focus on the experience of the patient. The therapeutic teams have absorbed the knowledge about the feedback process between the adaptation of the patient and the psychological and physiological self-perpetuation on the symptom. An understanding of the extent to which the patient has an "addictive" relationship with the symptomatic behaviour is used much more extensively in the work with the families. In Study II, the way that family therapy was conducted was, therefore, altered in a particular respect: the patients were occasionally (no more than one in four sessions) seen on their own. Paradoxically, therefore, one effect of our now prolonged experience of family therapy in severe eating disorder is a more consistent focus upon the individual.

This greater focus on the individual in the context of seeing the family applies not only to adult patients but also to adolescents. The comparison of two forms of family intervention with adolescent patients in the third Maudsley trial has led to a more individually focused style of family therapy. Two factors were the main influence here. In the family counselling model of treatment the therapists were required to work individually even with severely emaciated anorexic youngsters. The received wisdom that the young person in a state of starvation is so preoccupied with thoughts of food and weight as to be unable to engage in a meaningful therapeutic relationship was shown to be wrong, and allowed the therapist to be both sympathetic and understanding of the youngsters's plight as well as being forceful in helping the parents to make a determined stand in insisting that they make sure that their daughter ends her starvation.

The finding that families in which there is open criticism of, or even hostility towards, the daughter are easier to engage in family counselling has also helped us to gain a better understanding of the parents' fears and uncertainties. There is the opportunity to combine the very forceful message about the need for the parents to take firm control with a clear expression that the therapist is aware and understands how awful this is for the parents.

CLINICAL PRACTICE

The simplest interpretation of the results of research is that the families that can best help the patients are those that are getting on reasonably well at the time they first meet the therapist. These families generally have a good level of satisfaction with family life and are not, or have not become, critical of the family member with the eating problem. The patients most likely to be extricated from their disorder with the help of their families, under the influence of the family therapist's interventions, are likely to have an adolescent onset for their eating disorder. Our evidence for this is substantial in restricting patients, but is limited in those with bulimic symptoms. How are these family therapies conducted?

There is a view amongst clinical scientists that in an ideal world all aspects of practice would be organised by empirical evidence. The broad sweep of the treatment strategy may well be informed by research, but few of the moment-to-moment therapeutic activities can be supported by empirical studies. For much of the time the work of a psychotherapist can be thought of as a form of well taught and trained intuition. There is a danger in that prejudice can blind the therapist to the errors of his or her ways. However, there is also an economy in basing therapy on clinically determined judgements in so far as the therapist can function smoothly and naturalistically and has the capacity to engage warmly with the family. The following account has to be seen as provisional even when informed by the results of controlled studies.

Assessment and Engagement

Special practice procedures have to be established to facilitate the incorporation of a family into the treatment process of an adolescent or adult with an eating disorder. We have alluded to two sources of problems involved. The first is that of the reluctance of the patient to have his or her family involved in therapy. The second are the, often intense, feelings of guilt and self-blame. Patients believe that the eating problem is their own. Patients do not usually believe that their parents are the source of their specific weight preoccupations and commitment to dieting. They therefore do not link any anger that they feel towards their parents to their disorder. Some patients express pleasure that their parents are discomfited by their symptoms and believe that they should suffer alongside themselves, but this is unusual. More often patients express regret for their parents' lives being so disrupted by the symptoms. Patients are often well aware of their apparent, characteristic and high level of dependence on their parents but it is not the case that they see this as connected to their symptoms (nor indeed is the link scientifically elucidated). They are more likely to be angered by their parents' wish to be part of the assessment and treatment. The parents, on the other hand, have an investment of care and love and a longing for freedom from the terror of their son's or daughter's illness. They wish to be involved in the assessment, but harbour a fear that they will be found to be the cause of the problem. A prescription of "family therapy" can easily be experienced as "proof" of the professional's belief that parents are the cause of the eating disorder. If family involvement is looked for in the treatment process, then the assessment strategy must find a compromise between a complete investigation of the individual, which leads to expectation of individual therapy, and a family focus that alienates the patient and arouses fears in the parents that they are the aetiology of the disorder. In addition, in very ill, hypokalaemic, emaciated and dehydrated patients, there is no time for a detailed, painstaking and sensitive assessment, nurturing patient and family into a treatment collaboration. Admission may be essential, but it is not the best way to begin a family-orientated therapy—for admission to an in-patient unit can also carry the message that specialist professional staff have unusual skills in helping eating disordered people which "ordinary", "lay" people cannot be expected to possess. Working with the family during the inpatient treatment programme can counteract such a message, and family therapy can be used effectively as a continuation of treatment after a successful hospital weight restoration programme; but it is often the case that there is a period after admission in which the patient begins to lose weight and the family's morale wanes.

With the adolescent, admission to hospital can generally be avoided. The most effective way to begin family therapy is for the parents themselves to be helped to find a way, rather quickly, to alter the patient's feeding pattern, to take control of the calorie intake and of the bulimic symptoms. In this age-group it often happens that, despite previous discouraging attempts, parents will devise a feeding regime that compels the patient to eat more than her disorder would dictate or whose bingeing, vomiting and laxative abuse are limited or even controlled by the family. With this adolescent age-group, therefore, assessment of the patient and engagement of the patient and family must proceed together. This is easiest done by the main assessments being conducted as whole-family interviews. A family meeting is compatible with a mental state evaluation and an investigation of the patient's feelings and attitudes towards food, weight and diet. Their sexual orientation, identity and attitudes are much less likely to be properly assessed in the family meeting. The family engagement need not be hindered by the interposition of one or two individual sessions to make such enquiries and to initiate an individual therapeutic alliance. It is much harder to move from a series of purely individual meetings to a family commitment to treatment. These considerations determine the setting up of the evaluation of a seriously ill, adolescent patient.

With patients older 18 years, we do not think that parents can be expected to find a way of directly influencing the symptomatic behaviours. We therefore advocate a higher proportion of individual to family interviews in the first and subsequent phases of therapy with adult patients. These factors will make it clear that with adult patients, it is even more true to say that admission will convey to the parents that they cannot expect of themselves to be much of a force for good in their offspring. With this age-group, the first steps must be even more taken up with showing approval and positive regard for the patient and family and with identifying the nature and sources of painful and handicapping feelings that diminish hope and expectation of change. The individual meetings with the patient will have to focus on establishing the possibility that the patient will eventually find a way to manage the symptoms, to control vomiting or to eat more and tolerate increasing weight and, at the same time, to heighten the patient's awareness of the unsatisfactory nature of a relationship with parents when food, eating, vomiting, weight and psychological dependence are so dominant. All these patients must be addressed as people who have fragile self-esteem, who feel that their symptoms are the only way they have to control what are otherwise overwhelming affects of fear, shame, humiliation and hopelessness and who expect a therapist to see them as stupid and useless. The patients fear that the therapist will want to sweep the symptoms impatiently away without regard for the extent to which they have become a major resource, a security for the patient. The more the therapist can acknowledge this range of feelings, both in individual and family meetings, the more the patient and family may come to feel that the therapist has the measure of the problem. This is enhanced if the therapist shows familiarity with both the pathophysiology and the psychopathology of the eating disorder. Engagement and a counter to family criticism can be achieved, we believe, by a mixture of intensely focused sympathy, specific knowledge of the eating disorders and a powerful, sustained insistence that somehow, something must change for the better.

Addressing the Symptoms

The family therapist, whether seeing the parents alone or in meetings with the whole family, asserts that, eventually, the symptoms must be diminished and eliminated, not simply as a consequence of emotional change but also as a necessary condition for emotional recovery. This requires that the therapist accepts, fully, the proposition that there may be underlying, even causative psychological processes sustaining and perhaps creating the eating problem. At the same time the therapist insists that continued starvation, low weight and/or a pattern of bingeing, vomiting, compulsive exercise and so on, are themselves to some extent addictive and self-perpetuating. Emotional problems, says the family therapist, are much more readily faced in a physically well state when access is denied to the powerful stimulants provided by the symptoms. The therapist must use all possible persuasion to sustain this assertion. The therapist should refer over and over to the dangers to life and health of the symptoms as well as to the possibility of the illness becoming chronic and capable of depriving the patient of many normal, desirable possibilities for life.

Parents will perhaps know much of this already, but long-term follow-up studies have shown how the therapist's forceful use of these ideas has been seen, retrospectively, as especially helpful. Much of this work can be as easily conducted in meetings in which the parents are seen alone. This is the pattern in the control treatment in the adolescent study we have described as "family counselling" and which has been shown to be as effective as formal family therapy. In family counselling, as in family therapy, the therapist pays great attention to the parents' fear that they have somehow caused the illness. The patient's assertion, in the presence of the parents, that she does not hold them responsible is often ineffectual, even when reinforced by the therapist. Indeed, we do not possess reliable methods whereby parental self-blame can be diminished. We think that it is important, in highly critical families, to use elements of the family counselling technique, in which we learned the benefits of a more gentle approach, inviting rather than compelling the parents to explore their own resources to take control of the symptoms. From the family counselling too, we gained considerable experience in counselling patients whose parents were changing their relationship to the symptoms, something that the patients may at first find to be frightening and alarming, especially if it is felt to be taking control away from them.

These principles are also applied in work with the families of older patients, especially those with an onset in adolescence.

Later Stages of Treatment

From these discussions, many parents who have a reasonably mutually supportive relationship with each other will, with adolescent patients, gradually find ways of opposing the abnormal eating patterns. They will be helped to do this by pointing out that, firstly, nurses in hospital use only their personal psychological pressure to change symptoms; and second, if admission were to occur, the problem would come back: the parents would once more be faced with the same crisis. With older patients, the aim is not that the parents find techniques to oppose the symptoms, but that the relationships between parents, siblings and patient be altered, to become much less dominated by the eating problems and less intense and overpowering. Movements towards greater independence of the patient from the family is sought, for example by actively encouraging both patient and parents to pursue their out-of-home ambitions. Pursuit of such change also occurs in the younger patients, if the parents find a means to diminish the disordered eating. If a transformation in the place of the symptoms can begin, the therapist uses great efforts to announce the change and to encourage patient and parents immediately to take advantage of the position to find new interests and involvements. In the course of treatment the family and the patient may come to relate in a way less dominated by the symptomatology, and new topics appear and are discussed. These matters are to do with the life of the individual in and outside the family, some of which will have been distorted, prevented, interrupted or held in abeyance by the illness. In the course of losing the anorexic symptoms, it is common for the patient to go through a period of depression, a sense of loss and bewilderment as though a new direction for life has to be achieved. This can puzzle and alarm the parents. Even more they are likely to be hurt if the patient becomes angry and rejecting of them. This seems especially common in those cases where a father has been able to be close to his daughter during her illness but feels lost as she finds more independent interests, including, perhaps, those revealing a gender identity and sexual motivation.

ACKNOWLEDGEMENT

Maudsley Studies I–III were funded by the Medical Research Council of Great Britain. The two linked programmes in Study IV are funded by the Leverhulme Trust and the Mental Health Foundation.

REFERENCES

Dare, C. (1988). Psychoanalytic family therapy. In: E. Street and W. Dryden (Eds), *Family Therapy in Britain*. Milton Keynes: Open University Press.

Dare, c. (1993a). Aetiological models and the psychotherapy of psychosomatic disorders. In: M. Hodes and S. Moorey (Eds), *Psychotherapy and Psychosomatic States*. London: Gaskell and the Society for Psychosomatic Research.

Dare, C. (1993b). The starving and the greedy: inner and outer objects in anorexia nervosa. *Journal of Child Psychotherapy* (in press).

Dare, C., Eisler, I., Russell, G.F.M. and Szmukler, G. (1990). Family therapy for anorexia nervosa: implications from the results of a controlled trial of family and individual therapy. *Journal of Marital and Family Therapy*, **16**, 39–57.

Dare, C. and Szmukler, G. (1991). The family therapy of early-onset, short-history anorexia nervosa. In: D.B. Woodside and L. Shekter-Wolfson (Eds), *Family Approaches to Eating Disorders*. Washington, DC: American Psychiatric Press.

Dodge, E., Hodes, M., Eisler, I. and Dare, C. (1994). Evaluation of family therapy for bulimia nervosa in adolescents. *Journal of Family Therapy* (in press).

Eisler, I., Dare, C., Russell, G.F.M., Szmukler, G. and Le Grange, D. (1993). A 5-year follow-up of a controlled trial of family therapy in severe eating disorder. (submitted).

Fairburn, C.G., Jones, R., Peveler, R.C., et al (1993). Psychotherapy and bulimia nervosa: the longer term effects of interpersonal psychotherapy, behaviour therapy and cognitive behaviour therapy. *Archives of General Psychiatry*, **50**, 419–428.

Jenkins, H. and Asen, K. (1992). Family therapy without the family: a framework for systemic practice. *Journal of Family Therapy*, **14**, 1–14.

Leff, J. and Vaughn, C.E. (1985). *Expressed Emotion in Families: Its Significance for Mental Illness*. New York: Guildford.

Le Grange, D., Eisler, I., Dare, C. and Russell, G.F.M. (1992a). Evaluation of family therapy in anorexia nervosa: a pilot study. *International Journal of Eating Disorders*, **12**, 347–357.

Le Grange, D., Eisler, I., Dare, C. and Hodes, M. (1992b). Family criticism and self starvation: a study of expressed emotion. *Journal of Family Therapy*, **14**, 177–192.

Minuchin, S., Baker, L., Rosman, B.L., Liebman, R., Milman, L. and Todd, T.C. (1975). A conceptual model of psychosomatic illness in children. *Archives of General Psychiatry*, **32**, 1031–1038.

Minuchin, S., Rosman, B.L. and Baker, L. (1978). *Psychosomatic Families: Anorexia Nervosa in Context*. Harvard: University Press.

Madanes, C. (1981). *Strategic Family Therapy*. San Francisco: Jossey-Bass.

Morgan, H.G. and Russell, G.F.M. (1975). Value of family background and clinical features as predictors of long term outcome in anorexia nervosa: a four-year follow-up study of 41 patients. *Psychological Medicine*, **5**, 355–371.

Roberto, L.G. (1986). Bulimia: the transgenerational view. *Journal of Marital and Family Therapy*, **12**, 231–240.

Root, M.P.P., Fallon, P. and Friedrich, W.N. (1986). *Bulimia: A Systems Approach to Treatment*. New York: W.W. Norton.

Russell, G.F.M. (1979). Bulimia nervosa: an ominous variant of anorexia nervosa. *Psychological Medicine*, **9**, 429–448.

Russell, G.F.M., Szmukler, G., Dare, C. and Eisler, I. (1987). An evaluation of family therapy in anorexia nervosa and bulimia nervosa. *Archives of General Psychiatry*, **44**, 1047–1056.

Russell, G.F.M., Dare, C., Eisler, I. and Le Grange, P.D.F. (1992). Controlled trials of family treatments in anorexia nervosa. In: K.A. Halmi (Ed.), *Psychobiology and Treatment of Anorexia Nervosa and Bulimia Nervosa*. Washington, D.C.: American Psychiatric Press.

Schwartz, R., Barrett, M.J. and Saba, G. (1985). Family therapy for bulimia. In: D. Garner and P. Garfinkel (Eds), *Handbook of Psychotherapy for Anorexia and Bulimia*. New York: Guildford.

Selvini-Palazzoli, M. (1974). *Self Starvation: From the Intrapsychic to the Transpersonal Approach*. London: Chaucer.

Selvini-Palazzoli, M., Civillo, S. and Selvini, M. (1989). *Family Games: General Models of Psychotic Processes in the Family*. London: Karnac.

Squire-Dehouk, B. (1993). Evaluation of conjoint family therapy *vs* family counselling in adolescent anorexia nervosa patients: a two-year follow-up study. Dissertation submitted in partial fulfilment for the Statement of Equivalence for the Masters of Science in Clinical Psychology, Institute of Psychiatry and University of Surrey.

Stern, S., Whitaker, C.A., Hagemann, N.J., Anderson, R.B. and Bargman, G.J. (1981). Anorexia nervosa: the hospital's role in family treatment. *Family Process, 20*, 255–273.

Szmukler, G. and Dare, C. (1991). The Maudsley hospital study of family therapy in anorexia nervosa and bulimia nervosa. In: D.B. Woodside and L. Shekter-Wolfson (Eds), *Family Approaches to Eating Disorders*. Washington, D.C.: American Psychiatric Press.

Szmukler, G., Eisler, I., Russell, G.F.M. and Dare, C. (1985). Anorexia nervosa, parental "expressed emotion" and dropping out of treatment. *British Journal of Psychiatry, 147*, 265–271.

Wynne, L.C. (1980). Paradoxical interventions: leverage for change in individual and family systems. In: M. Strauss, T. Bowers, S. Wayne Downey, et al (Eds), *The Psychotherapy of Schizophrenia*. New York: Plenum.

White, M. (1986). Anorexia nervosa: a cybernetic perspective. In: J. Elka-Harkaway (Ed.), *Eating Disorders and Family Therapy*. New York: Aspen.

19

Physical Treatments

A. WAKELING
Royal Free Hospital, London, UK

INTRODUCTION

The rigid separation of physical from psychological and social approaches in the treatment of most psychiatric disorders is, of course, artificial. This is particularly so in the case of eating disorders where in the course of the illness, physical, psychological and social factors so obviously coexist. Nevertheless, physical treatments have a relatively small role to play in current treatment programmes for eating disorders. They are seldom used as the single or even primary mode of treatment but may be used as one component of a treatment programme.

Treatment programmes should be based rationally on a knowledge of aetiology. But in eating disorders, as in most psychiatric disorders, such knowledge is generally lacking, and treatment is essentially empirical and pragmatic. Current aetiological speculations postulate a wide variety of possible factors operating to predispose an individual to the development of an eating disorder. Thereafter, a range of intrinsic and extrinsic factors are hypothesised to initiate the disorder in suitably predisposed individuals. Then a wide range of social, psychological and physical factors may operate to perpetuate the disorder. The aetiology therefore, will be multifactorial; a number of causal factors each contributing to varying degree to the genesis of the disorder. On this model, it would be anticipated that different factors operate in different strengths in different individuals. The pathways to the disorder

Handbook of Eating Disorders: Theory, Treatment and Research.
Edited by G. Szmukler, C. Dare and J. Treasure.
© 1995 John Wiley & Sons Ltd.

are multiple. This suggests that in eating disorders there can be no single or specific treatment but that treatment plans need to be adapted flexibly to the particular patient. Treatment may be limited to one approach although, of course, the emphasis will vary from individual to individual.

Nevertheless, within this general framework, there is a current consensus on certain basic principles underlying most treatment programmes, although research support for this consensus if weak. Firstly, treatment is multidimensional and staged, with emphasis on different aspects of treatment at different stages of the illness. Secondly, there is general agreement that where malnutrition or a starvation state exists, priority should be given to correcting this. Starvation, being recognised to have profound effects on psychological as well as physical functioning, seriously hinders the application of all types of treatment. Thirdly, some form of psychological treatment is deemed essential to address the personal, interpersonal and social factors hypothesised to underly and maintain the disorder.

There is much less consensus on the role of physical treatments. These are used in two main ways. Firstly, and much the least contentious, is the use of physical treatments directed at the obvious medical consequences of the disorder. These are, of course, important and may be life-threatening (see Sharp and Freeman, 1993, for a review). Secondly, physical treatments have been used on the grounds of treating the disorder as such and not specifically its conseqences. This is more contentious and this chapter focuses in the main on these aspects.

Many of these approaches to treatment have been based on very simplistic notions of aetiology, often betraying lack of awareness of the fundamental psychopathological aspects of the disorder. Such approaches have frequently failed to differentiate between the basic psychopathology of the disorder, the behaviours emanating from this, and the physical and psychological consequences of these behaviours. Thus, many treatments supposedly used to treat the disorder are in essence targeted at consequences rather than causes.

The use of physical treatments in anorexia nervosa has a long history, but from 1960 onwards, following the onset and development of modern psychopharmacology, these approaches have focused increasingly on psychoactive drugs. Phenothiazines and other major tranquillisers, antidepressants, minor tranquillisers and other groups of drugs, have been used in anorexia nervosa and more recently, with greater emphasis, in bulimia nervosa. They have been used typically without research evidence for their efficacy or even safety in these conditions and often on the most dubious and clinically uninformed theoretical notions. In psychiatry the advent of any new class of psychoactive drug is generally followed by its widespread and often inappropriate use. With subsequent experience, more specific and narrower criteria for its use are discerned.

Psychoactive drugs have been used in three overlapping ways in eating disorders:

1. They have been used as non-specific treatment methods to increase compliance to other more specific treatments.
2. They have been used to treat specific symptoms or symptom clusters appearing as part of the eating disorder.

3. They have been used in supposedly more specific ways to treat the causes of the disorder based upon particular views or hypotheses about the nature of the disorder.

TREATMENTS FOR ANOREXIA NERVOSA

Chlorpromazine and Other Neuroleptics

Shortly after its introduction for the treatment of schizophrenia in the 1950s, chlorpromazine was used in the treatment of anorexia nervosa. Dally and Sargant (1960) reported that this drug, given in doses up to 1000 mg/day with 40/80 units of insulin to stimulate appetite, to patients confined to bed and receiving a high-calorie diet, induced a more rapid weight gain than in a relevant control group of patients. These authors later reported that chlorpromazine was as effective without the use of insulin (Dally and Sargant, 1966). In their view, the beneficial effects resulted from a diminution in the panic and fear associated with eating which enhanced the impact of the strict refeeding programme. They suggested starting with a small dose of 150 mg/day increasing to 1.5 g/day if necessary. Crisp (1965) advocated a smaller dose of 400–600 mg/day, within the context, however, of a psychologically based treatment programme.

The use of chlorpromazine and other phenothiazines in the treatment of anorexia nervosa spread to Europe and America (Vandereycken, 1987). Although the vogue for this form of treatment rapidly subsided in Britain, Vandereycken reported that it was still widely used in Germany in the 1980s. The decline of this form of treatment stemmed in part from the recognition that rapid weight gain under rigidly controlled conditions was a very inappropriate and simplistic measure of improvement and outcome in anorexia nervosa (Russell, 1977). Moreover, it became clearly apparent that weight gain and nutritional rehabilitation could be achieved in most patients through general nursing care informed by appropriate psychological approaches without recourse to psychotropic medication (Russell, 1977; Vandereycken and Meermann, 1984; Crisp, 1984). In addition there was an increasing awareness of the adverse effects of these psychoactive drugs, particularly in malnourished subjects. Adverse effects include orthostatic hypotension, hypothermia, reduction of the convulsive threshold, blood dyscrasias and impairment of liver function. Such effects may be produced by starvation alone and may thus be exacerbated by phenothiazines. These drugs may also induce dyskinetic reactions and drug sensitivities and produce hyperprolactinaemia, which can delay the return of menstrual function even after weight gain.

In 1976, Barry and Klawans hypothesised that the major symptoms of anorexia nervosa might be accounted for by increased dopaminergic activity. This lead them to suggest a different and more specific rationale for the use of neuroleptics. They speculated that a specific dopamine blocking agent like pimozide might be used as a primary treatment. However, in controlled trials, this drug has been shown to be without therapeutic effect but with the capacity to produce unwanted physical effects (Vandereycken and Pierloot, 1983; Weizman et al, 1985). In a similar vein,

Vandereycken (1984) demonstrated that sulpiride, a substituted benzamide drug and another selective dopamine antagonist, was also without clinical value.

Given the recognised dangers of major tranquillisers, particularly in malnourished subjects, it is surprising that such drugs are used at all in anorexia nervosa. There is also a complete absence of any research evidence for their efficacy in terms of outcome. Nevertheless, these drugs may have a small and limited role in treatment used in a pragmatic way. Use is generally confined to those patients who continue to show marked anxiety and agitation and inability to eat in a general and supportive treatment setting. In addition they are sometimes worth trying in older patients with chronic and seemingly intractable illnesses who continue to resist refeeding. When prescribed, chlorpromazine should be given in doses not exceeding 300 mg/day and for short periods only. Thioridazine in small doses of up to 50 mg three times a day is an appropriate alternative.

Minor Tranquillisers

Anderson (1987) has described the selective use of anti-anxiety agents (minor tranquillisers) as a treatment adjunct in an integrated treatment programme at Johns Hopkins Hospital, Baltimore. The theoretical rationale is that anxiety plays a major role in the genesis and maintenance of eating disorders. Lorazepam 0.25–0.5 mg is given one hour befor meals two or three times a day to reduce anticipatory anxiety concerning eating. It is suggested that this can be helpful in certain patients for the first 2–3 weeks of the refeeding phase of an inpatient treatment programme. In addition, minor tranquillisers may occasionally be helpful during the maintenance phase of treatment when patients for the first time are exposed to situations that in the past regularly produced disabling anxiety and anorexic symptoms.

It is clear that in this programme these drugs are used with full awareness of the potential for dependence and misuse. However, this adjunctive approach to treatment has not found widespread use and there is an increasing reluctance to prescribe drugs of this sort. Non-pharmacological methods of anxiety reduction are obviously preferred wherever possible.

Antidepressants

Antidepressants are the most commonly prescribed psychotropic drugs for eating disorders. There has been continuing debate and controversy about their efficacy. The use of these preparations stems from three main lines of observation. Firstly, patients with eating disorders frequently have concurrent depressive symptoms to a degree that might fulfil diagnostic criteria for depressive disorder. Secondly, such patients may have higher than expected rates of previous episodes of depression. Thirdly, an enhanced risk of affective disorders in the relatives of patients with an eating disorder has been reported. Such observations have given rise to theoretical speculations about some possible relationship between eating disorders and affective disorders. The evidence overall is weak and the theoretical speculations simplistic. The category error of translating relationship or association to causal connection, so common in psychiatry, is apparent in much of this debate.

It is obvious that many patients with severe anorexia nervosa are demoralised, have low self-esteem and a wide range of depressive symptoms. Such a picture is not uncommon in many physical disorders and psychiatric disorders other than the depressive syndrome. Moreover, it is now well recognised that starvation *per se* can lead to a similar clinical state. The clinical assessment of depressive symptoms in acute anorexia nervosa is therefore a complicated one. Altschuler and Weiner (1985) have pointed out that criteria for diagnosis of anorexia nervosa and for affective disorder overlap considerably. Furthermore, although a wide range of depressive symptoms may occur in the acute presentation of anorexia nervosa, the psychopathology rarely resembles that seen in severe depressive illness. It is also a matter of clinical observation that many of the depressive symptoms and associated physical symptoms resolve with improvement in the patient's nutritional state.

The use of antidepressant drugs in anorexia nervosa is not buttressed by any research findings. What evidence there is points to their lack of efficacy. A few uncontrolled studies in the 1970s (Moore, 1977; White and Schnaultz, 1977; Needleman and Waber, 1977) reported successful short-term treatment with tricyclic antidepressants. The reported success was based upon short-term weight gain and some diminution in depressive symptoms. However, three controlled studies failed to demonstrate any real clinical relevance for such substances (Lacey and Crisp, 1980; Biederman et al, 1985; Halmi et al, 1986). There have as yet been no appropriate controlled trials of the newer antidepressants in anorexia nervosa. Such studies are called for following the report by Kaye et al (1991) of an open trial using the 5HT re-uptake inhibitor, fluoxetine. This drug was given to 31 patients after inpatient treatment for weight restoration and resulted in unusually good weight maintenance over a mean period of 11 months.

Overall, antidepressants have a very limited role in the treatment of anorexia nervosa. Clearly, it is entirely inappropriate to prescribe these drugs outside the setting of a treatment programme addressing in addition the core psychological aspects of the illness. Antidepressants alone would not be expected to affect the morbid attitudes, beliefs and associated behaviours which constitute the central features of the illness. If antidepressants are prescribed there should be full recognition that patients in the malnourished state are more prone to develop unwanted effects, particularly with the older tricyclics like amitriptyline, perhaps still the most widely prescribed of these preparations in anorexia nervosa. In addition such drugs can precipitate weight gain and carbohydrate craving (Paykel, Mueller and De Laveryne, 1973) which may induce panic and fear in the patient not supported in a therapeutic alliance. Many patients with anorexia nervosa have marked preoccupations with issues of control, autonomy and concerns about bodily function, which makes them particularly resistant to taking medication of any kind.

For most patients in an appropriate treatment alliance, depressive symptoms will remit over time with improvement in the general nutritional state. Antidepressants may be helpful in those patients with severe depressive symptoms that persist with or without weight gain. Anorexia nervosa may develop through a variety of aetiological pathways of which a depressive illness may be one (Szmukler, 1987).

An eating disorder developing in this way may perpetuate the depressive illness which will require appropriate treatment. Nevertheless, it is apparent that even here the eating disorder will need treating in its own right as well. It is possible that antidepressants have some role to play in the treatment programme of sub-groups of patients that have specific association with affective disorder, but further research is required to test this.

When antidepressants are prescribed, a careful physical appraisal is essential beforehand with attention to possible electrolyte imbalance, hypotension, cardiac and renal compromise. Medication should be started in a low dose with gradual increase to therapeutic levels over 3–4 weeks. Once initiated, the question as to how long the drug should be continued is raised. If improvement is obtained in terms of diminution in depressive symptoms and some weight gain, it should be possible to engage the patient more fully in a therapeutic programme addressing the core elements of the disorder. The exclusive use of antidepressants as a treatment is inappropriate and simplistic.

Other Drugs

Other drug treatments have been variously reported in anorexia nervosa. Such treatment approaches have rested on dubious theoretical speculations in relation to aetiology.

Cyproheptadine, a serotonin and histamine antagonist relatively free from serious side-effects, has had a limited trial as a possible treatment for anorexia nervosa. Clinical observations during the 1960s in non-eating-disorder subjects suggested that this drug had a beneficial effect on the promotion of weight gain in underweight patients. This was, of course, prior to the subsequent interest in the possible role of central serotonin pathways in feeding behaviour. Vigersky and Loriaux (1977) reported the first double-blind trial of cyproheptadine in anorexia nervosa. This study, albeit with limitations, showed no benefit for the drug in respect of weight gain over a brief 8-week period. Since then, Halmi and her group have published reports on the use of this compound in various sub-groups of anorexic patients (Goldberg, Halmi and Eckert, 1979; Goldberg et al, 1980; Halmi et al, 1986). The most detailed study was a controlled comparison of cyproheptadine with amitriptyline or placebo in 72 inpatients. Both drugs had only marginal effects over placebo on general measures of short-term weight gain within a general inpatient treatment programme. Interestingly, it was reported that cyproheptadine increased treatment efficacy in the non-bulimic and impaired efficacy in the bulimic sub-group of patients. Overall, however, the clinical effects of the drug were marginal and no other major group have reported on the use of this drug.

The suggestion from animal studies that endogenous opioids play some role in the regulation of appetite has prompted isolated attempts to use opioid antagonists such as naloxone and naltrexone in the treatment of anorexia nervosa (Moore and Mills, 1981; Luby, Marrazi and Kinzie, 1987). There is no evidence of any clinical benefit and there are clearly dangers in the administration and prolonged use of such substances.

Lithium has been used as an adjunct to treatment on the basis that it might improve mood and help to promote weight gain. No clinically meaningful effects have been demonstrated (Gross et al, 1981).

Finally, there is no theoretical or clinical case for the use of anticonvulsants as a specific treatment for anorexia nervosa.

TREATMENTS FOR BULIMIA NERVOSA

In contrast to anorexia nervosa, physical treatments in bulimia nervosa have been more vigorously pursued and researched. This is surprising in view of the well-documented efficacy of psychological interventions in this disorder (Freeman et al, 1988; Fairburn et al, 1991). These physical treatments have in the main been confined to the prescription of various types of antidepressant drugs. The rationale for this approach to treatment stems from three main factors:

1. There is an apparent frequency of mood-related symptoms and mood disorder in both subjects with bulimia nervosa and their families.
2. There is a body of experimental findings suggesting that central monoamine pathways, particularly 5HT-related pathways, are implicated in the control of feeding behaviour and satiety mechanisms. Antidepressants putatively exert their therapeutic action through effects on these pathways.
3. The use of antidepressants is presumed to be simpler and more cost-effective than labour-intensive and lengthy psychological interventions.

The Older Antidepressants

Several controlled trials of antidepressants have demonstrated some therapeutic effects in reducing bulimic symptoms such as bingeing and vomiting, and some improvement of mood-related symptoms in a proportion of patients varying between one-third to two-thirds. This has been demonstrated for imipramine (Pope et al, 1983; Agras et al, 1987; Mitchell et al, 1990); desipramine (Hughes et al, 1986; Barlow et al, 1988; Walsh et al, 1991), phenelzine (Walsh et al, 1988). These studies generally reported mean percentage reductions for groups of patients of bulimic symptoms such as bingeing and vomiting, and most were short-term studies of effects of drug administration over 8–12 weeks. However, treatment that may be helpful in the short term may have little bearing on the long-term outcome of the disorder. Moreover, there was little in these studies to suggest that in the short term dysfunctional attitudes at the core of the disorder had been affected. Such studies, of course, immediately raise the question of how long the medication should be continued and whether any treatment gain is sustained after cessation of medication.

Longer-term efficacy has been assessed in two controlled studies. Walsh et al (1991) used a three-phase treatment design to test the longer-term efficacy of desipramine. Eighty patients entered an 8-week double-blind trial of desipramine against placebo. Patients who responded satisfactorily to desipramine then entered a 16-week maintenance phase. Patients who continued to remain well were then randomly allocated to either desipramine or placebo for 6 additional months. In the initial phase, desipramine was superior to placebo and there was a mean reduction in binge frequency of 47% over 8 weeks with a remission rate of 11%. However, fewer than half the patients treated with desipramine met the criteria of a reduction of 50% or more in binge frequency for entry to the maintenance phase of the trial. Patients who completed the full 16 weeks of the maintenance phase did not show statistically significant improvement during this phase and 29% of patients relapsed. There were so few patients entering the final phase that no conclusion could be drawn from this aspect of the trial. Similar findings were reported by Pyle et al (1990). In this study patients who had improved on initial treatment with imipramine were maintained on this drug for a further 4 months.

The data from these studies, although incomplete, suggest serious problems with using antidepressants as a sole or main treatment method. They indicate that the relapse rate may be significant both during continued treatment after initial improvement and after cessation of treatment. Moreover, all the studies using antidepressants point to major problems of compliance with treatment of this kind, for two main reasons. Firstly, many patients are reluctant to take medication for a disorder they conceptualise as having predominantly behavioural or psychological origins. Secondly, serious problems arise with unwanted effects or side-effects. Sedative, anticholinergic and hypotensive effects are all reported in studies using tricyclic antidepressants. With phenelzine, hypotensive effects and insomnia are particularly troublesome. Problems of weight gain occur with some antidepressants. The drop-out rate in treatment trials using antidepressants may be as high as 40%.

The Newer Antidepressants

Despite difficulties with compliance and relative lack of efficacy, interest in this form of treatment continues. Recent attention has focused on the use of fluoxetine, a specific 5HT re-uptake inhibitor. This drug appears to have fewer unwanted (particularly anticholinergic) effects than tricyclic antidepressants, and thus may be more acceptable as a long-term treatment. In addition, it has been shown to produce weight loss in depressed patients (Cohn and Wilcox, 1985). Furthermore, there is some tentative experimental evidence to suggest that 5HT has some inhibitory effect on feeding behaviour (Leibowitz and Shor-Posner, 1986) and that decreased 5HT function may be implicated in the abnormal eating patterns in bulimia nervosa (Goldbloom and Garfinkel, 1990).

A recent multicentre American trial reported on the use of fluoxetine over an 8-week period in the largest group of bulimic patients yet studied (Fluoxetine Bulimia Nervosa Collaborative Study Group, 1992). 387 women received either 20 mg or 60 mg of fluoxetine daily or placebo. After 8 weeks of treatment, fluoxetine at 60 mg/day was found to be significantly superior to placebo, and 20 mg/day fluoxetine was modestly but not always significantly superior to placebo on measures of changes in frequency of binge-eating and vomiting. Interestingly, associated features of bulimia nervosa—including depression, carbohydrate craving and pathological eating attitudes—improved significantly, with the 60 mg dosage having more effect than the 20 mg dose. The proportion of so-called "responders" (those with 50% or greater improvement) in the 60 mg/day fluoxetine, 20 mg/day fluoxetine and placebo treatment groups were 63%, 49% and 43% respectively for binge-eating episodes per week and 57%, 45% and 26% respectively for vomiting episodes per week. The numbers of patients in remission at the end of the treatment period are not given. These figures are similar to those reported in short-term treatment trials of other antidepressants. However, incidence of side-effects was modest, albeit greater with the 60 mg/day dose, and the drug appeared to be relatively well tolerated. Disappointingly, even with this large group of patients, no predictors of drug response could be identified. Interestingly, the severity of depression at baseline was not specifically associated with response. No longer-term data are available for this group of patients.

Drug Treatment Versus Psychotherapy

These studies with antidepressants suggest that these drugs will suppress or modify bulimic behaviours such as vomiting and binge-eating, and will improve mood in some patients with bulimia nervosa, at least in the short term. The mood-elevating effects and the effects on bulimic behaviours appear to be unrelated, although this requires further clarification.

Many other serious questions remain unanswered. In particular, there is no adequate long-term data on such treatments. In addition these studies are all somewhat artificial as in the clinical situation drug treatment as a single treatment mode would be naive and inappropriate in most cases. The question then arises as to how drug treatments compare with psychological treatments and, perhaps more importantly, whether their effects are enhanced by combination with particular forms of psychological therapy.

To date only two studies have addressed this issue. Mitchell et al (1990) compared four different treatments over a 12-week period. 254 patients were evaluated and 171 were randomised to four treatment groups: (1) imipramine hydrochloride alone (300 mg/day maximum); (2) placebo treatment; (3) imipramine treatment combined with intensive group cognitive psychotherapy; and (4) placebo treatment combined with intensive group cognitive psychotherapy. All three active treatments resulted in significant reduction in target eating behaviours and in significant improvement in mood relative to placebo treatment. Imipramine alone had a modest effect, reducing the rate of bingeing by 64% and with a remission rate of 16% at the end of treatment. However, the amount of improvement achieved with group cognitive psychotherapy was superior to that for imipramine. With this treatment, rates of binge-eating dropped by 90%, with 51% of the subjects free of bulimic symptoms at the end of the treatment period. The addition of imipramine to the group psychotherapy programme produced no greater benefit than group therapy alone but did result in more improvement in the symptoms of depression and anxiety. The dropout rate in subjects treated with imipramine was high, approximately 40%, as a result of side-effects.

Agras et al (1992) examined the relative effectiveness of desipramine given for either 16 or 24 weeks against cognitive behaviour therapy and the combination of desiprimine and behaviour therapy. Subjects were assessed at 16, 24 and 32 weeks. At 16 weeks, both the combined treatment and cognitive behavioural treatment alone were superior to medication given for 16 weeks in reducing binge-eating and purging. However, at 32 weeks only the 24-week combined condition was superior to 16 weeks of medication. The results of this study suggest that the desipramine given for 24 weeks and combined with cognitive behaviour therapy produced the broadest therapeutic effects. This study also suggested that cognitive behaviour therapy may help prevent relapse after withdrawal of medication. The improvements noted in this study were similar to those reported by Mitchell and coworkers, but the numbers of patients involved were smaller.

To date, therefore, what evidence there is suggests that antidepressants alone are less effective than cognitive–behaviour therapy at least in the short term. In addition there is little evidence to suggest that a combination of antidepressants and cognitive–behaviour therapy is superior to cognitive–behaviour therapy alone. The question as to whether any specific sub-group of patients might be particularly responsive to antidepressants remains to be answered.

Conclusions

Drug treatment for bulimia nervosa (essentially antidepressant drug therapy) clearly has some limited beneficial effects, at least in the short term. However, many unanswered questions remain related to the acceptability of this form of treatment, the unwanted effects of drugs and the longer-term efficacy. At the present level of knowledge, drug treatment should not be used as a sole treatment approach but only within an overall treatment programme. The components of the overall programme will be decided by the severity of the condition and the specific personal and social circumstances in which it presents. Drug treatment should in general be confined to those patients who have failed to respond to psychotherapy. However, it may be appropriate to consider combined therapy in those subjects with marked symptoms of anxiety or depression. Antidepressant treatment may also be appropriate for those individuals with very severe and chaotic bingeing and vomiting behaviour who may be difficult to engage in any form of meaningful psychotherapy.

Fluoxetine is perhaps the drug of choice. It should be given at a dose of 60 mg/day and continued for at least 8 weeks. It is, of course, important that wherever possible the drug should be taken outside the main binge/vomiting period. If patients do respond, then treatment should be continued for 6 months but with the emphasis in treatment changing to a psychological mode. In severely ill patients, failure with one antidepressant should be followed by a trial of treatment with one or more different antidepressants.

REFERENCES

Agras, W.S., Dorian, B., Kirkley, B.G., Arnow, B. and Bachman, J. (1987). Imipramine in the treatment of bulimia: a double-blind controlled study. *International Journal of Eating Disorders,* **6**, 29–38.

Agras, W.S., Rossiter, E.M., Arnow, B., Schneider, J.A., Telch, C.F., Raeburn, S.D., Bruce, B., Perl, M. and Koran, L.M. (1992). Pharmacologic and cognitive–behavioural treatment for bulimia nervosa: a controlled comparison. *American Journal of Psychiatry,* **149**, 82–87.

Altschuler, K.Z. and Weiner, M.F. (1985). Anorexia nervosa and depression: a dissenting view. *American Journal of Psychiatry,* **142**, 328–332.

Anderson, A.E. (1987). Uses and potential misuses of anti-anxiety agents in the treatment of anorexia nervosa and bulimia nervosa. In: P.E. Garfinkel and D.M. Garner (Eds), *The Role of Drug Treatments for Eating Disorders.* New York: Bruner/Mazel.

Barlow, J., Blouin, J., Blouin, A. and Perez, E. (1988). Treatment of bulimia with desipramine: a double-blind crossover study. *Canadian Journal of Psychiatry,* **33**, 129–133.

Barry, V.C. and Klawans, M.L. (1976). On the role of dopamine in the pathophysiology of anorexia nervosa. *Journal of Neural Transmission,* **38**, 107–122.

Biederman, J., Herzog, D.B., Rivinus, T.N., Harper, G.P., Ferber, R.A., Rosenbaum, J.F., Harmatz, J.S., Tondorf, R., Orgulak, P. and Schildkraut, J.J. (1985). Amitriptyline in the treatment of anorexia nervosa. *Journal of Clinical Psychopharmacology,* **49**, 7–9.

Cohn, J.B. and Wilcox, C.A. (1985). A comparison of fluoxetine, imipramine and placebo in patients with major depressive disorder. *Journal of Clinical Psychiatry,* **46**, 26–31.

Crisp, A.H. (1965). Clinical and therapeutic aspects of anorexia nervosa. *Journal of Psychosomatic Research,* **9**, 67–78.

Crisp, A.H. (1984). Treatment of anorexia nervosa: what can be the role of psychopharmacological agents? In: K.M. Pirke and D. Ploog (Eds), *The Psychobiology of Anorexia Nervosa.* New York: Springer-Verlag.

Dally, P.J. and Sargant, W. (1960). A new treatment of anorexia nervosa. *British Medical Journal,* **1**, 1770–1773.

Dally, P.J. and Sargant, W. (1966). Treatment and outcome of anorexia nervosa. *British Medical Journal,* **2**, 793–795.

Fairburn, C.G., Jones, R., Peveler, R.C., Carr, S.J., Soloman, R.A., O'Connor, M.E., Burton, J. and Hope, R.A. (1991). Three psychological treatments for bulimia nervosa: a comparative trial. *Archives of General Psychiatry,* **48**, 463–469.

Freeman, C.P., Barry, F., Dunkeld-Turnbull, J. and Henderson, A. (1988). A controlled trial of psychotherapy for bulimia nervosa. *British Medical Journal,* **296**, 521–525.

Fluoxetine Bulimia Nervosa Collaborative Study Group (1992). Fluoxetine in the treatment of bulimia nervosa: a multicentre, placebo-controlled, double-blind trial. *Archives of General Psychiatry,* **49**, 139–147.

Goldberg, S.C., Halmi, K.A., Eckert, E.D., Casper, R.C. and Davis, J.M. (1979). Cyproheptadine in anorexia nervosa. *British Journal of Psychiatry,* **134**, 167-170.

Goldberg, S.C., Eckert, E.D., Halmi, K.A., Davis, J.M. and Roper, M. (1980). Effects of cyproheptadine on symptoms and attitudes in anorexia nervosa. *Archives of General Psychiatry,* **37**, 1083.

Goldbloom, D.S. and Garfinkel, F.E. (1990). The serotonic hypothesis of bulimia nervosa. *Canadian Journal of Psychiatry,* **35**, 741–744.

Gross, M.A., Ebert, M.M., Faden, U.B., Goldberg, S.C., Lee, L.E. and Kaye, W.H. (1981). A double-blind controlled trial of lithium carbonate in primary anorexia nervosa. *Journal of Clinical Psychopharmacology,* **1**, 376–381.

Halmi, K.A., Eckert, E.D., La Du, T.J. and Cohen, J. (1986). Anorexia nervosa treatment efficacy of cyproheptadine and amitriptyline. *Archives of General Psychiatry,* **43**(2), 177–181.

Hughes, P.L., Wells, L.A., Cunningham, C.J. and Ilstrup, D.M. (1986). Treating bulimia with desipramine: a double-blind placebo controlled study. *Archives of General Psychiatry,* **3**, 182–186.

Kaye, W.H., Weltzin, T.E., Hsu, L.K.G. and Bulik, C.M. (1991). An open trial of fluoxetine in patients with anorexia nervosa. *Journal of Clinical Psychiatry,* **52**, 464–471.

Lacey, J.H. and Crisp, A.H. (1980). Hunger, food intake and weight: The impact of clomipramine on a refeeding anorexia nervosa population. *Postgraduate Medical Journal,* **56**, 79–85.

Leibowitz, G.F. and Shor-Posner, G. (1986). Brain serotonin and eating behaviour. *Appetite,* **7**, S1–14.

Luby, F.D., Marrazi, M.A. and Kinzie, J. (1987). Treatment of chronic anorexia nervosa with opiate blockage. *Journal of Clinical Psychopharmacology,* **7**, 52–53.

Mitchell, J.E., Pyle, R.L., Eckert, E.D., Hatsukami, D., Pomeroy, C. and Zimmerman, R. (1990). A comparison study of antidepressants and structured intensive group psychotherapy in the treatment of bulimia nervosa. *Archives of General Psychiatry,* **47**, 149–157.

Moore, D.C. (1977). Amitriptyline therapy in anorexia nervosa. *American Journal of Psychiatry,* **134**, 1303–1304.

Moore, R. and Mills, I.H. (1981). Naloxone in the treatment of anorexia nervosa: effect on weight gain and lipolysis. *Journal of the Royal Society of Medicine,* **74**, 129–131.

Needleman, H.L. and Waber, D. (1977). The use of amitriptyline in anorexia nervosa. In: R.A. Vigersky (Ed.), *Anorexia Nervosa.* New York: Raven Press.

Paykel, E.S., Mueller, P.S. and De Laveryne, P.M. (1973). Amitriptyline weight gain in carbohydrate craving: a side effect. *British Journal of Psychiatry,* **123**, 501–507.

Pope, H.G., Hudson, J.I., Jonas, J.M. and Yurgelun-Todd, D. (1983). Treatment of bulimia with imipramine: a double-blind placebo controlled study. *American Journal of Psychiatry,* **14**, 554–558.

Pyle, R.L., Mitchell, J.E., Eckert, E.D., Hatsukami, D., Pomeroy, C. and Zimmerman, R. (1990). Maintenance treatment and 6-month outcome for bulimia patients who responded to initial treatment. *American Journal of Psychiatry,* **147**, 871–875.

Russell, G.F.M. (1977). General management of anorexia nervosa and difficulties in assessing the efficacy of treatment. In: R. Viergsky (Ed.), *Anorexia Nervosa.* New York: Raven Press.

Sharp, C.W. and Freeman, C.P. (1993). The medical complications of anorexia nervosa. *British Journal of Psychiatry,* **162**, 452–462.

Szmukler, G.I. (1987). Some comments on the link between anorexia nervosa and affective disorders. *The International Journal of Eating Disorders,* **6**, 181–189.

Vandereycken, W. (1984). Neuroleptics in the short-term treatment of anorexia nervosa: a double-blind placebo-controlled study with sulpiride. *British Journal of Psychiatry,* **144**, 288–292.

Vandereycken, W. (1987). The use of neuroleptics in the treatement of anorexia nervosa patients. In: P.E. Garfinkel and D.M. Garner (Eds), *The Role of Drug Treatments for Eating Disorders.* New York: Brunner/Mazel.

Vandereycken, W. and Meermann, R. (1984). *A Clinician's Guide to Treatment.* New York: Walter de Gruyter.

Vandereycken, W. and Pierloot, R. (1983). Combining drugs and behaviour therapy: a double-blind placebo/pimozide study. In: P.L. Darby et al (Eds), *Anorexia Nervosa: Recent Developments in Research.* New York: Alan R. Liss.

Vigersky, R.A. and Loriaux, D.L. (1977). The effect of cyproheptadine in anorexia nervosa: a double -blind trial. In: R.A. Vigersky (Ed.), *Anorexia Nervosa.* New York: Raven Press.

Walsh, B.T., Gladis, M., Roose, S.P., Stewart, J.W., Stetner, F. and Glassman, A.H. (1988). Phenelzine versus placebo in 50 patients with bulimia. *Archives of General Psychiatry,* **45**, 471–475.

Walsh, B.T., Hadigan, C.M., Devlin, M.J., Gladis, M. and Roose, S.P. (1991). Long-term outcome of antidepressant treatment for bulimia nervosa. *American Journal of psychiatry,* **148**, 1206–1212.

Weizman, R., Tyano, S., Wijsenbeek, H. and Ben David, M. (1985). Behvavior therapy, pimozide treatment and prolactin secretion in anorexia nervosa. *Psychotherapy and Psychosomatics,* **43**, 136–140.

White, J.H. and Schnaultz, N.L. (1977). Successful treatment of anorexia nervosa with imipramine. *Diseases of the Nervous System,* **38**, 967–968.

20

Sequencing Treatment Decisions: Cooperation or Conflict Between Therapist and Patient

ARNOLD E. ANDERSEN
University of Iowa, Iowa City, USA

INTRODUCTION

Eating disorders fall within the broad category of disorders of motivated behavior, a term used to describe human survival behaviors, centered in the limbic system, which attempt to meet the body's inner needs with the available environmental resources. Other motivated behaviors include thirst, sexual behavior, and some acquired behaviors such as alcohol or other drug seeking. The paradigm for understanding disorders of motivated behavior is fundamentally different from the infectious disease model which guided much of the last century of progress in general medicine, with great success, but at the cost of promoting reductionist thinking and attempts to find single etiologies and treatments for complex diseases.

Eating disorders, and other disorders of motivated behavior, require a more probabilistic and multifactorial conceptual approach whereby the final common dominator of the clinical eating disorder syndromes may be better understood as deriving from a variety of interacting factors (Andersen, 1990). Eating disorders represent, in many ways, the capturing, imprisonment and entrainment of a normal essential behavior to serve as a pseudo-solution to complex issues in development,

Handbook of Eating Disorders: Theory, Treatment and Research.
Edited by G. Szmukler, C. Dare and J. Treasure.
© 1995 John Wiley & Sons Ltd.

family functioning, mood stabilization and personality vulnerabilities, all interacting with changing, but relentlessly thinness-endorsing, sociocultural norms.

An understanding of the entrainment of normal eating behavior in the matrix of developmental and sociocultural forces may help not only in the treatment of eating disorders, but also in the broader application to chronic medical illness in our society. The major chronic *medical* problems facing industrialized societies now (chronic cardiovascular disease, cancer, drug abuse, and sexually transmitted diseases) are in large part consequences of *behavioral* problems. In contrast, the so-called major mental disorders such as mood disorders and schizophrenia have relatively small behavioral contributions to their onset or maintenance, and are primarily neurobiological in origin.

The principles taught by Professor Russell and illustrated in his clinical rounds almost two decades ago have always proved adequate throughout changing conceptual fads. During the 1950s, anorexia nervosa was, of course, a subtle form of schizophrenia. During the 1960s, it began to be seen as an anxiety disorder related to defenses against sexual impulses. During the 1970s, it was obviously a *forme fruste* of affective disorder. Overlapping in rapid sequence, anorexia nervosa was next a certain manifestation of family dysfunction, of borderline personality disorder, and more recently, an absolutely incontrovertible example of (take your choice) obsessive–compulsive disorder or multiple-personality disorder. Anorexia nervosa, in fact, is not reducible to a subset of another disorder.

RECOGNITION OF EATING DISORDERS: THE GREAT PRETENDERS

In the nineteenth century, two of the "great pretenders" were tuberculosis and syphilis, presenting to a variety of medical specialists as afflictions of different organ systems.

There are a number of reasons why eating disorders constitute twentieth century medical "pretenders". First, they are usually private disorders and not often brought voluntarily to the attention of health professionals. The symptomatology of slimming may be so normal in our society that recognition of its adverse consequences is easily ignored. Symptoms of binge-eating, private ruminations about the pleasures of small morsels of food, or the terrors of overestimating the size of hips or abdomen, are all inner and highly personal, emotionally charged, mental experiences not readily revealed to health professionals unless their empathy is obvious.

Eating disorders are also frequently overlooked because of the rudimentary state of knowledge about them. They are syndromes rather than more fundamentally understood disorders. The too common approach to diagnosis of eating disorders for several decades, and unfortunately still present to some degree, has been to "rule out" every conceivable medical cause for weight loss or vomiting before considering the eating disorders. Our experience at the National Institutes of Health between 1970 and 1975, with more than 40 cases of anorexia nervosa, found that where the central psychopathological features of self-induced starvation and a morbid fear of fatness, described by Professor Russell, were present, not a single case was later found to have a "medical" or "organic" cause for the symptomatology (Mecklenburg et al, 1974). Lack of training in psychiatric diagnosis plus fear of missing a medical causation have led practitioners to delay definitive diagnosis of an eating disorder, and additionally to produce iatrogenic morbidity through unneeded medical diagnostic investigations.

Another reason for the "pretender" status of eating disorder is the fact that they may present to clinicians only as occult symptoms that are not yet widely recognized as being "tip-offs" for the correct diagnosis. These may include loss of dental enamel, Russell's sign (scars on the knuckles of the hand where teeth meet the hand in inducing vomiting), persistent hypokalemia without obvious cause, or melanosis coli.

The clinician, as with appendicitis, must first think of a disorder as a diagnostic possibility before it can be recognized. Three patient groups that may be commonly overlooked who do develop eating disorders, even though less frequently than the prototypic adolescent female, are *matrons*, *males* and *minorities*. Physicians will be aided in their diagnostic efforts by knowing which demographic subpopulations are associated with a high probability of experiencing an eating disorder such as ballet dancers, models and wrestlers. Bulimic symptomatology tends to be even more private because of its association with normal weight.

In summary, eating disorders, while often presenting in disguised form, and frequently concealed because of their ego-syntonic and/or shame-producing symptoms, can be confidently recognized if Professor Russell's teachings are followed: search for the central shared psychopathological motif of a morbid fear of fatness in anorexia and bulimia, not delaying diagnosis or treatment because of fear of missing medical causation.

SEQUENCE OF TREATMENT DECISIONS

The remainder of the chapter attempts to describe the sequence of decisions involved in the treatment of eating disorders as an ongoing dialogue between therapist and patient. Treatment of eating disorders can rarely be accomplished by an expert's intervention in a passive patient who simply acquiesces to a variety of technical procedures. Successful treatment of eating disorders requires a collaborative effort, because eating disordered patients are, at least initially, primarily persuaded rather than stricken individuals. This interaction may be cooperative, conflicted, or a mixture. The cooperative interaction of patient and therapist is not only more pleasant for both, but will more often lead to a more successful outcome. There is virtually no aspect of eating disorders that cannot be substantially improved. There is no aspect of eating disorders that will invariably improve, however, without a good working doctor–patient relationship. The following principles summarize a relatively logical and experienced, but inevitably personal, and certainly not definitive, description of the treatment process.

MAKING A RECOMMENDATION FOR TREATMENT: ACCEPTANCE OR REJECTION

Recommendations for treatment may be sources of either conflict or cooperation. Not only are patients often reluctant to seek help, but simultaneously, western society remains in conflict about who, if anyone, should take responsibility for health care recommendations.

One of the benefits of media interest, partly counterbalancing its relentless endorsement of slimming, is the now widespread publication of the signs and symptoms of eating disorders. In a survey of more than 50 teachers attending an eating disorders conference, we found that the single most frequently asked question was: "How do we approach someone whom we think has an eating disorder and what do we say?" An empathetic but straightforward approach works best, suggesting that the person concerned may be suffering from an eating disorder and asking them to seek evaluation. When weight loss is precipitous, or when treatment is refused despite signs of serious medical or psychological dysfunction, then more urgent, legally sanctioned, involuntary intervention may be necessary. Families, while concerned, may simultaneously be hesitant to endorse treatment because of fear that family secrets will be revealed, or they will be blamed. Regarding timing, sooner appears to be better than later. There is a good bit of evidence to support the contention that eating disorders evolve over time to become increasingly refractory and autonomous, so that early, timely interventions may be crucial to full recovery.

Cooperation is higher when the individual is approached as a developing human being for whom the disorder represents a solution, albeit a pseudo-solution, to some important personal issue rather than a form of rebellion, bad behavior, or is seen as a source of failure or blame. Professor Russell has always insisted that neither the patient nor the family be blamed, scolded or criticized for the development of an eating disorder, but instead approached firmly, sympathetically and intelligently.

INPATIENT VERSUS OUTPATIENT TREATMENT: BENEFITS AND RISKS

Treatments in medicine, including psychiatry, are in many ways based on probabilities rather than certainties, weighing the benefits versus the risks for a given recommendation. In our experience, and as taught by Professor Russell, most classic anorexia nervosa patients are best treated in a structured inpatient hospital setting with an experienced multidisciplinary team. The loss of 20–30% of body weight diminishes the patient's ability to work effectively as an outpatient. Substantial weight loss, serious medical complications, significant comorbid psychiatric disorders, lack of response to, or unavailability of, outpatient treatment, are the most common, but not the exclusive, indications for inpatient care of anorexia nervosa.

In contrast, bulimia nervosa is often best treated as an outpatient, preferably through a combination of intensive group and individual treatments, emphasizing cognitive–behavioral or interpersonal techniques, rather than strictly behavioral or pharmacological methods. Exceptions which require inpatient care of bulimia nervosa are individuals with serious medical or psychiatric comorbid conditions, or outpatient treatment non-responders.

The ability to refer cases for needed inpatient care is not always guided by medical/psychiatric necessity, but is complicated, especially in the USA, by the present chaotic health care financing structure.

A strong pre-admission programme of psychoeducation for patient and family combined with a frank discussion of benefits versus risks of inpatient/outpatient care, and support for the family or individual decision-making process, will often lead to cooperation rather than conflict in the choice of treatment setting. Clinicians and parents may be worried, for example, that inpatient treatment on a ward for eating disordered patients will lead to the adoption of new symptoms or habits. The benefits of treatment significantly exceed the risks of treatment on an experienced inpatient unit. The death of the singer Karen Carpenter more than a decade ago has continued to produce a flurry of concerns and questions about whether weight restoration is in fact dangerous. Pre-admission psychoeducation is often necessary and helpful.

SETTING GOALS FOR TREATMENT: FEARS AND FANTASIES

Patients are often caught between the fears that treatment will result in excessive weight gain or loss of ability to cope without the eating disorder, versus the fantasy that treatment is guaranteed to cure or that the treatment is like a vacation. The goals for treatment will generally reflect the therapist's basic beliefs of the nature of the disorder. Where the disorder is viewed as a simple operant behavioral response to sociocultural norms promoting slimming, then weight gain by behavioral methods alone will be recommended. The other adventurous extreme goal, a clinician's fantasy, advocates nothing short of the reconstruction of the entire personality, the normalization of development, and resolution of all dynamic and all comorbid conditions.

A good beginning point for goal setting of treatment is to ask the patient what she/he would most like out of treatment. While doctors may be concerned about body weight, cardiac status, and comorbid depressive illness, the patient often has goals that sound quite different, such as how to feel good on the beach, how to make friends, how to feel in control of growing-up. The best treatment goals usually blend those of the clinician with those of the patient and family.

A balance between fears and fantasies regarding treatment may be assisted by a pretreatment tour of a treatment unit and a frank discussion of goals and methods. Families may be under the fantasy that they can "drop off" their child for treatment and pick them up cured and without any significant family involvement. Goals for treatment are generally defined within the first week of treatment and divided into the biomedical, the psychological, the behavioral, the social and the family goals. In a study by Hedblom, Hubbard and Andersen (1981), approximately 73% of specifically identified family goals were achieved during an average 10-week inpatient hospitalization.

In summary, setting goals for treatment begins before treatment commences and involves a combination of what the therapist, patient and family all value. Optimistic, but realistic, achievable, well defined, specific treatment goals attempt a middle ground between simple medical weight restoration and interruption of binge/purge behavior versus the other extreme of a total reconstruction of personality and psychodynamic functioning. A helpful method for documenting pretreatment status and for assessing progress toward achievement of goals is to complete eating disorders tests such as the validated Eating Attitudes Test (EAT) and Eating Disorders Inventory (EDI), and a general psychological profile, such as the HSCL-90, categorical and dimensional tests of personality features, and sometimes the WAIS or WISC. These patients, while often bright, may be under family pressures to function as "standard bearers" for the family out of proportion to their abilities. The American Psychiatric Association has just released its first guidelines for treatment of a specific psychiatric disorder, authored by Yager et al (1993), based on a consensus of experienced therapists. This document may guide goal setting for eating disordered patients in the near future.

DIAGNOSTIC ASSESSMENT: DSM-X?

Professor Russell has consistently taught that the essentials for diagnosis of anorexia nervosa are self-induced starvation, the presence of a psychopathological morbid fear of becoming fat that is out of proportion to reality, and an abnormality of reproductive hormone functioning. Bulimia nervosa requires the presence of binge-eating along with the shared central psychopathology of a morbid fear of fatness. Various sequential committees, in contrast, have devised diagnostic criteria for eating disorders that change without compelling logic or new data. There is no rational reason why 25% of weight loss was required for DSM-III in 1980, but only 15% in 1987, for example. These committee-based diagnostic criteria, unfortunately, also remain gender-based by not specifying analogous requirements for endocrine change in males as well as females.

The DSM method also remains excessively non-specific for the diagnostic classification of the large group of atypical eating disorders (eating disorders, not otherwise specified) whose classification is currently too reductionistic, being funnelled into a single residual category.

Some helpful advances in diagnostic sub-classification have been made in the last decade, some of which are included in the new DSM-IV (APA, 1994). These include dividing anorexia nervosa patients into predominantly food restrictors and those who experience binge/purge behavior at anorexic weights. The differentiation of Binge Eating Disorder separate from Russell's bulimia nervosa may also be helpful. The ongoing diagnostic problem for classification of any disorder whose symptoms are dimensionally arranged rather than categorically distinguished is shared between medicine and psychiatry. The lumping versus splitting approaches each have merits and advocates.

MEDICAL STABILIZATION: FIRST THINGS FIRST

If one had to be severely starved in the healthiest way possible, most anorexia nervosa patients are, unfortunately, good examples. Because they usually choose an adequate intake of protein, and frequently consume multivitamins, they avoid many of the third world starvation syndromes such as kwashiorkor or marasmus. The appearance of a skeletal figure barely clad in parchment-like skin striding vigorously down the ward, arguing articulately with staff about a morsel of food, provides a jarring mental contrast between the simultaneous pictures of vigor and debilitation.

Rapid assessment of a patient's vital signs and electrolytes, and assessment of the general physical status, combined with a history of the abnormal eating and purging behaviors, will usually allow the physician to prescribe the necessary, but minimal, acute medical interventions. When starvation has been slowly achieved, restoration does not need to be unphysiologically precipitous. Iatrogenic morbidity is often more of a risk than prudent measured intervention. Sir William Gull, more than a century ago, advised us to keep patients warm and feed them frequent meals (1874). Generally the signs and symptoms which need acute treatment are those not typical of the course of chronic starvation, meaning that clinicians do best who are thoroughly familiar with the natural history of starvation. Keep a close watch on medical specialists unacquainted with eating disorders who wish to perform biopsies, bone marrows, invasive radiological contrast procedures, or insert tubes in veins or stomachs without good reason. In contrast, warmly cultivate a relationship with medical specialists who will provide consistent, long-term, prudent, knowledgeable medical support for the eating disordered patient. More than 600 inpatients were treated successfully at the John's Hopkins Hospital on an eating disorders unit within a general psychiatric ward, without significant morbidity and no mortality (Andersen, 1992).

NUTRITIONAL RELEARNING: ENERGY IN, ENERGY OUT

Professor Russell has advocated for many years that we work with skilled nurses in the nutritional rehabilitation of patients with eating disorders. Most eating disordered patients have a superficially sophisticated knowledge of nutrition, but in fact, it is a selective and distorted nutritional knowledge. Skilled nurses best provide supervision at meals, psychological support before and after meals, instruction throughout the refeeding process, guidance in the resocialization process, and hopefully, as role-models for normal eating.

Caloric energy balance is unfortunately more complicated than the physical analogy of water in and out of a bathtub. The body's metabolism handles energy intake quite differently at starved weights, or in the presence of binge/purge behavior, than at normal or at higher weights. Nonetheless, patients are helpfully taught that, while not an entirely simple process, weight gain or loss represents the net difference between energy in and energy out. We often use the term "energy input" for food because food is, in fact, a form of stored energy. This cognitive relabelling may decrease the mental association between food and fatness, while increasing the mental connection between food as a source of energy.

Professor Russell has argued the need for the restoration of a fully healthy target weight, rather than a compromise of 80–90% as is often practised. The average pre-dieting weight of 600 patients in a 15-year series at the Johns Hopkins Hospital was 8–12% above an "ideal" body weight prior to the onset of dieting. Restoration to even the seemingly adequate target of 95–100% of "normal" weight of an insurance company scale, may, in fact, constitute a mildly inadequate weight for many individual patients.

Weight *restoration*, rather than weight *gain*, we believe, is the better term to use with patients. "Gaining weight" in virtually all western countries means becoming fat. Usually, restoration of weight with minimal physical symptoms is accomplished by first introducing simple foods several times a day, prescribing an initial total energy intake of 1200–1500 calories a day at the beginning of treatment and increasing 500 calories every three to five days until 3500–4500 calories per day are ingested. We were able to increase weight restoration from 2.2 to 3 pounds (1.0 to 1.4 kg) a week on the average without significant medical symptomatology by increasing the vigor of nutritional rehabilitation.

Finally, tubes and central venous lines are almost never necessary. There may be, of course, occasional exceptions, but in more than 600 inpatients we have never found them to be necessary. The use of feeding tubes usually represents an act of frustration or anger by staff and, we believe, a failure to persuade the patient that normal food eaten normally is essential.

Cooperation in refeeding, rather than conflict, is heightened when patients are prepared with information regarding the process of energy balance, transient medical symptomatology, and much reassurance. Group support to decrease the anxiety generated by distorted body perception, and relaxation exercises after meals are helpful. Occasionally, short-term anti-anxiety agents before meals are useful. The majority of medical symptomatology from refeeding can be avoided or minimized. A recent study found that, as a rule, no specific pro-kinetic agents or other GI interventions are routinely necessary. Conflict is generally heightened when there exists the perception that the weaker patient is being made to eat by the stronger staff, when the process of refeeding symptomatology is unexplained, when tubes and lines are introduced unnecessarily, or when weight restoration is a mechanical, operant, procedure.

A number of recent studies have suggested that the brain is vulnerable to starvation and may shrink by as much as 10–20%. This nutritionally caused shrinkage may affect the patient's reasoning ability, and therefore some more intensive psychotherapeutic work may best be postponed until body weight is more than 90% of normal.

BEHAVIORAL RELEARNING: B.F. SKINNER'S PROMISE AND HILDE BRUCH'S WARNING

The science of behavioral psychology was significantly contributed to, temporarily dominated by, and in some ways imprisoned by, Skinner's seminal work on operant behavioral conditioning. His now classical studies, revolutionary at the time, led to unwarranted extensions to a world view that all human behavior was the result of operant conditioning.

Hilde Bruch warned in an editorial of the danger of tricking patients into "eating their way out of hospital" (1979). Strict behavioral paradigms for treatment of anorexia nervosa lead to minimizing of important issues in psychological functioning. Seligman, Bandura and others were initially greeted with skepticism when they questioned operant behavioral dogma, and instead emphasized the importance of the meaning of an event to the individual rather than its strict operant antecedents and consequences. Their work has now been sufficiently validated to provide scientific support for Hilde Bruch's warning. Patients who are operantly re-fed with no attention paid to their central psychopathology, or to the central psychodynamic aspects of their eating disorder, generally learn to leave hospital by behavioral tricks and often promptly relapse.

While there are significant overlaps between eating disorders and alcohol abuse and other forms of drug abuse, neither the addiction model nor the 12-step programmes, when applied by themselves, are adequate to comprehensively treat eating disordered patients.

PSYCHOTHERAPY: THE ART OF PERSUASION

The achievement of a healthy body weight and the interruption of binge/purge behavior represent readiness to engage in the essential core of treatment—learning to think differently about body weight and shape, to "trade in and trade up" regarding their symptomatology, to find the human goals behind the eating disorder and to achieve them in healthier, more adaptive ways, to learn to live sanely in a weight-preoccupied society.

Even at very starved weights, initial psychoeducation and support are helpful for patients. The process requires much repetition, consistently assuring anorexic patients that they will not be allowed to gain too much weight. Psychoeducation gradually shifts to validated cognitive–behavioral techniques. For bulimia nervosa especially, cognitive behavioral, and more recently interpersonal psychotherapy methods are the "gold standards" against which other treatments are matched (Fairburn et al, 1991a). For some bulimic patients, cognitive–behavioral therapy (CBT) may by itself suffice. In anorexia nervosa, CBT is usually best combined with, or followed by, psychodynamic psychotherapy. The final aspect of psychotherapeutic treatment, existential psychotherapy, involves grappling with the issues of the meaning and purpose, using principles from Frankl and Yallom.

A final note regarding psychological treatment involves the assertion of Anna Freud (1966) that interpretation of transference is the center of the psychotherapeutic process. The eating disorders unit can, in fact, become a source of 24-hour interpretation of transference. A patient, very typically, will reproduce prototypic behaviors towards staff that reflect abiding patterns formed among members of the family around them during their developmental years. The overtly compliant patient, the limit-testing patient, the staff-splitting patient, the manipulative patient, all can be recognized.

By making psychotherapy a cooperative effort between patient and staff, by prescribing a sequence of psychotherapeutic methods appropriate to the stage of illness and the psychological skills of the patient, by practising psychotherapy as an ongoing effort by all staff 24 hours a day, and by using innovative and experiential techniques, for example, in the very young patient, a cooperative rather than conflicted psychotherapeutic milieu can be achieved.

TREATING PSYCHIATRIC COMORBIDITY: NO "LONE RANGERS"

We have hypothesized that eating disorders are generally accompanied by a variety of comorbid psychiatric conditions from Axis I and Axis II, but not with any single specific ones. If one uses, instead, a multifactorial model of etiology whereby origin is related to the number and severity of comorbid conditions, then overall treatment will be enhanced. We found in a series of 20 patients that the average restricting anorexic patient met criteria for two additional diagnosable psychiatric comorbid conditions; the bulimic subgroup of anorexia nervosa had almost four additional comorbid conditions; patients with bulimia nervosa at normal weight met criteria for three (Margolis et al, 1994). The most common accompanying comorbid psychiatric diagnoses are affective disorders, followed in quick succession by personality disorders, substance abuse disorders, anxiety states, and OCD, but seldom schizophrenia.

The exact relationship between these comorbid conditions and the onset and maintenance of eating disorders has not yet been fully elucidated. Here again, there is perhaps unnecessary conflict between those advocating the companion disorders as predisposing features and those seeing them as consequences. Russell and colleagues have shown clearly that, without any separate treatment, restoration of a healthy weight in an anorexic patient, by itself, often produces a decrease in depressive and obsessive symptomatology. Comorbid conditions, while they need to be initially and thoroughly assessed at the time of diagnostic evaluation, sometimes are best deferred in their treatment until weight has been fully restored and binge/purge behavior interrupted. Then, if these comorbid disorders remain present, and are not merely epiphonemena of weight loss/binge–purge behavior, they can be treated appropriately.

The most medically and psychiatrically afflicted subtype of eating disordered patients are the anorexic patients with bulimic features (Mickalide and Andersen, 1985). They have neither the ego-syntonic weight loss of the restricting anorexia patients, nor the seeming physical normality of bulimia nervosa patients, but suffer from both starvation, and being out of control in their binge behavior.

The implication of these data is that treatment of eating disorders is usually the treatment of a package, or cluster, of psychiatric disorders.

PSYCHOPHARMACOLOGY: PILLS, POTIONS AND POWDERS

While we look with amusement at the suggested treatments of several centuries ago, when tincture of newt and eye of toad were applied, there continues to be an unreflected belief that medications are helpful and necessary in the treatment of eating disorders. No psychopharmacological treatment for anorexia nervosa has ever proved satisfactory. The role of antidepressants in the treatment of bulimia nervosa continues to be evaluated by a multicenter study (see also Chapter 19). At the present time, the available data are best summarized by saying that psychotropic medications are often unnecessary, but may be sometimes helpful in the treatment of comorbid conditions or binge behavior, but have virtually no effect of the central psychopathology of the eating disorders.

TREATING CHRONIC MEDICAL COMORBIDITY: SYMPTOMATIC AND OCCULT

Eating disorders are accompanied by a variety of chronic medical disorders. An unsettled controversy exists whether endocrine disorders precede or perhaps initiate eating disorders, or whether they are non-specific, weight-related consequences. Most endocrine changes are part of an adaptive response to decreased energy intake and to the lowered body weight. The early loss of periods may reflect a non-specific endocrine response to weight loss in that group of individuals who only function normally at the upper part of a normally distributed weight range.

Chronic medical symptoms are generally best appreciated by a thorough physical examination and a selective group of laboratory tests. In many ways, the opportunity of a clinician to treat the psychological symptoms of patients depends on his/her ability to deal with complaints of GI distress; for example, being bloated, distended and overly full. Waldholtz and Andersen (1990) found that 100% of a series of 16 consecutive anorexia nervosa patients had significant gastrointestinal complaints, 80% of which were severe. All of these improved with a prudent programme of nutritional rehabilitation and psychotherapy without pro-kinetic or H2 blocking agents.

In contrast, a disorder that is often occult, asymptomatic and manifested only when severe is osteoporosis. In a study of 106 patients, we found that a significant number of eating disordered patients are as severely lowered in bone mineral density as elderly osteoporotic patients (Andersen and LaFrance, 1990). Forty per cent of patients with the bulimic subtype of anorexia nervosa were below the critical threshold of 0.965 gm/cm^2 of bone mineral density, while 30% of restricting anorexics were similarly abnormal. Interestingly, even when weight was restored to normal, patients continued to manifest a lowering of bone mineral density as if they had current anorexia nervosa, an ominous sign for their bone "retirement" beginning at above age 35.

The initial anecdotal reports that insulin-dependent diabetes mellitus was associated with a higher than expected incidence of eating disorders has been disproven in a careful study by Fairburn et al (1991b). What does seem to be true instead is that when insulin-dependent diabetics develop eating disorders they may be more medically ill and refractory, because of the misuse of insulin.

Treatment-produced medical symptoms may be divided into (1) those that are intrinsic to the refeeding process, such as occasional peripheral edema, but predictable and controllable through prudent management, and (2) others that are unpredictable, such as gastric dilatation, or that may be life-threatening.

LEAVING HOSPITAL

Leaving a structured hospital programme after intensive multidisciplinary care for an eating disorder may either be akin to falling off a curb or ambulating comfortably down a ramp. Successful short-term responses to comprehensive care may all be undone through precipitous discharge without adequate time to practise and internalize a new behavioral repertoire and an altered psychology, or if discharge takes place to an inadequate treatment facility. Many repeated admissions to inpatient care could be avoided and discharges might take place more promptly if a day hospital programme and 24-hour structured community living situation were available.

The Family's Role

Tolstoy said that happy families are all alike, while each unhappy family is unhappy in its own way. Vandereycken, Kog and Vanderlinden (1989) have asked the essential question: are families architects or victims of the eating disorders? Families function as semi-permeable membranes between society and the individual. Families may enhance, diminish or pass on unchanged the ambient sociocultural norms. The most persuasive initial theory of family functioning in anorexia nervosa was formulated by Minuchin, Rosman and Baker (1978) who suggested that anorexic families were "enmeshed". These families do not allow individuals to grow and develop, but instead "live in each other's pockets". A study by Hedblom, Hubbard and Andersen (1981) examined 73 consecutive eating disordered families and found that about two-thirds did, in fact, meet the Minuchin model, but 20% were disengaged and not at all enmeshed, while 15% were "apple pie normal" with no signs of imbalance, lack of appropriate boundaries, or unhealthy functioning in any significant way.

   While the exact contribution of the family to the onset and maintenance of the eating disorders may still be incompletely understood, family issues must be addressed through comprehensive evaluation and treatment. After relieving the family of the burdens of guilt, self blame, anger and exhaustion, the therapist will attempt to engage the family in the overall treatment process through education, support and identification of specific family and couples issues that may warrant treatment.

   Russell et al (1992) have demonstrated that for patients under 18 years of age, treatment of the family as a unit after discharge is superior to individual follow-up treatment in maintaining benefits from inpatient care.

Follow-up

Follow-up planning begins on the day of admission to hospital or before. It generally requires from one to several years of aftercare to assure that a patient will make a transition from a severe chronic eating disorder to a stable pattern of healthy medical, psychological and social functioning, and have a reasonable chance for success in everyday life. The natural history of treatment has been found to include a distressingly high rate of earlier than expected death, approximately 19% as documented by Theander. On the positive side, eventual improvement occurs in 90% of those who do not succumb. The improvement may take place over years or decades as documented by Professor Russell. Andersen (1990) has suggested a sequence of stages by which eating disorders evolve from culturally normative behaviors, to diagnosable psychopathological states, to entrenched chronic disorders stabilized by their biomedical mechanisms and identity-giving capacity (see Table 20.1).

Eating disorders are best seen as improved after treatment, rather than cured. There is no reason, however, why a patient may not eventually be "cured". Follow-up includes pre-discharge discussion of and preparation for some degree of relapse, but with the goal of a gradual transmutation of the energy behind the eating

TABLE 20.1 Proposed stages of illness of eating disorders.

	Anorexia nervosa	Bulimia nervosa	Hypothesized mechanisms
Predisposing stages	Sociocultural norms promoting thinness lead to dieting behavior, body image distortion, and low self-esteem	(a) Sociocultural norms promoting thinness lead to dieting behavior, body image distortion, and low self-esteem (b) Onset of binge-eating in response to hunger	Operant type II conditioning
↓ ↓ ↓ **Precipitating factors** ↓ ↓ ↓			
Defining and maintaining stage	Fear of fatness, pursuit of thinness, self-induced starvation, reproductive hormone abnormality, dysmorphophobia are present	(a) Fear of fatness, pursuit of thinness, at normal body weight (b) Relief of dysphoria predominates in perpetuating binge behavior	Operant type II conditioning plus defining psychopathology
Chronic illness stage	(a) Autonomous phase, illness-driven behavior (b) Anorexia nervosa consolidates as a professional identity and "friend"	(a) Autonomous phase, illness-driven behavior (b) Bulimia nervosa consolidates as a professional identity and "friend"	Biomedical–neuroendocrine plus existential mechanisms

disordered symptomatology into more healthy, age-appropriate, adaptive coping mechanisms. Follow-up is not a guarantee that there will be no falling down, but lack of follow-up is almost certainly a prescription for relapse.

Coming to Terms with Sociocultural Norms

How to learn to live in a society preoccupied with the belief that slimming and shape change are means of happiness and success remains a major challenge. Many patients, either by temperament or training, appear to be excessively influenced by an "external locus of control" mode of functioning whereby the opinions and attitudes of those around them count for more than their own. To send a medically improved, but psychologically untreated, and behaviorally unprepared, individual back into a slimness-orientated world is almost to guarantee a return to the chaos of an eating disorder.

Prior to discharge and throughout follow-up, experiential techniques such as role playing, food preparation, shopping for clothes with sympathetic trained nurses, and refuting irrational thoughts all help prepare patients for real-life interaction with society without absorption into the culture of dietary madness.

CAMUS AND FRANKL: THE INVINCIBLE SPRING BEYOND THE WINTER OF STARVATION'S CONCENTRATION CAMP

Camus said, in so many words, that he had discovered in the midst of winter an invincible spring within himself. The eating disordered patient is, in many ways, in the midst of a metabolic and psychological winter. When eating disorder symptoms are seen as personally meaningful events in psychological functioning, they may eventually become the source of a new springtime for psychololgical maturation and personal development. Unless patients come to understand that their eating disorders have served an existential purpose in their life and, in fact, cannot be taken away but only traded in for a better way of life, they will generally resist treatments that appear to threaten the role of the eating disorders as pseudo-solutions to issues in living.

Victor Frankl, in the concentration camp, was able to see beyond his temporary, severe suffering to a greater meaning and purpose in life. Eating disordered patients reside in a self-imposed, although societally sponsored and endorsed, concentration camp. A concluding phase of treatment, especially after cognitive–behavioral and psychodynamic efforts have been under way for some time, involves dealing with the essential questions of the meaning of life and the purpose of suffering. Chronic eating disordered patients often develop an existential identity in which the eating disorder takes on a professional and vocation-giving way of life. Eating disorders provide rituals for everyday life, reasons for living, methods for interacting, and boundaries on behaviors, much like religion and philosophy do. Eating disorders in their broadest understanding come from the search for meaning, diverted into the Faustian promise of happiness through slimming.

REPRODUCTION: PSYCHOLOGICAL AND PHYSICAL

There exist both psychological and physiological reproduction. The dictum of Santayana that those who do not understand history are condemned to repeat it applies well to eating disordered patients. Where early sexual or physical abuse are involved, patients are prone to repeating these patterns of behavior unless they are understood and changed through treatment. The harshness and bleakness of their early childhood may be reinfected upon themselves through their internalized "bad objects" such that self-nuturing capacity is difficult or impossible. Patients may identify vividly with Anna Freud's description of the mechanism of "identification with the aggressor", when the therapist interprets their repeating of dysfunctional parental patterns.

Physical reproduction in eating disorders may be altered in a number of ways. In anorexia nervosa, Professor Russell has expressed concern that prolonged amenorrhea during critical developmental years may lead to long-term delay or failure in sexual maturation and reproductive capacity. Brinch, Isager and Tolstrup (1988) have documented that anorexic patients are several times as likely to deliver infants with neonatal death, but after that, the children appear to do well.

Bulimic patients, on the other hand, may be prone to unwanted pregnancies, especially if they have comorbid impulsive traits. Also, because of their emotional lability and sometimes narcissistic immaturity, they find it difficult to give the necessary time and attention to an infant, or meet the needs of developing children, failing to provide the nurturing environment that Winnicott described as necessary to normal development (Philips, 1989). Timely exploration of sexual issues, reproductive consequences of the eating disorders, and the goals of intimacy and generativity, all will generally enhance cooperation with patients, whereas reliance on outmoded psychosexual motifs (fear of oral impregnation), or neglect of the issues of sexuality, will generally increase conflict.

RESEARCH AND PREVENTION

Professor Russell has said that every eating disordered patient is a potential research subject. Each case of anorexia nervosa is a natural experiment in the extremes of physiology. The surprising fact is not how poorly these patients do, but how well they do. Clinicians in practice, without any high technology research resources, but with research thinking, can make significant contributions to the understanding and treatment of eating disorders. A number of clinicians, including myself, could undoubtedly have described bulimia nervosa as a new syndrome contemporaneously with Professor Russell if only we had observed more carefully the clinical symptomatology in front of us every day. Discovery favors the prepared and observant mind, however.

Is Prevention Realistic?

Whether or not primary or secondary prevention is possible in the field of eating disorders remains a source of controversy. At a recent conference on eating disorders at the University of Iowa, I took the position that primary intervention in school systems is possible and necessary while Professor Fairburn vigorously challenged my view, and advocated instead the more realistic goal of early identification and prompt comprehensive treatment. Just as the powerful present sociocultural forces encouraging slimness represent an integral derived over time from many small changes leading to the large current sum total, so prevention may be seen as a feasible but multifactorial integral to be constructed from a large number of individually small changes, rather than from a single dramatic intervention.

Perhaps the critical time for prevention is with the 5–12 year old age-group. Where the development of self-esteem is tied, inappropriately, to the attachment of excessively thin body weight and currently favored shape, then dieting behavior usually follows. Individuals who are encouraged to develop healthy weight, independent self attitudes and healthy eating and exercise behaviors during the critical period of preadolescent development will, we hope, go through puberty and later adolescence with more adequate psychological and social tools to defend themselves against the relentless sociocultural pressures promoting thinness.

Some essential factors in prevention of eating disorders logically include the heightening of the family's role in functioning as a selective screen of sociocultural norms, teaching of alternatives to slimming as sources of self-esteem, the pairing of unnecessary slimness with negative, not positive, emotional reinforcements, and the endowment of individuals with a repertoire of coping behaviors and good stress management techniques.

CONCLUSION

Professor Russell stands in the tradition of the great clinicians in the field of eating disorders, combining the wisdom of Professor Gull with that of Dr Lasegue of the mid-nineteenth century. He has demonstrated the effectiveness of a team-oriented, multidisciplinary inpatient programme for anorexia nervosa. He was the first to identify, describe and treat a whole new category of patients, those with bulimia nervosa. He has contributed to understanding the psychology and psychophysiology of starvation, formulated enduring diagnostic criteria, demonstrated effective long-term treatments and conducted long-term follow-up studies. He has taught and practised through a combination of strict scientific research methods with humane personal understanding of patients and unexcellent phenomenological descriptions. His principles and practices constitute the foundation for the effective treatment of patients with eating disorders today throughout the world.

DEDICATION

In many ways, I owe my career in eating disorders to Professor Gerald Russell. He was the right person at the right time in my career development. Professor Russell introduced me into the basics of treatment of anorexia nervosa patients through a visit to the Johns Hopkins Hospital in the mid 1970s. There are few other fields within medicine where one can simultaneously be interested in neuroendocrine and biochemical mechanisms along with the broadest of sociocultural trends, all interacting with the psychosocial development of individual human beings as they deal with age-old developmental questions of self-esteem, identity, mood regulation, and family functioning. Therefore, it is fitting to dedicate this descriptive overview of the sequence of treatment decision-making to Professor Russell, acknowledging his role for any wisdom and mine or for any deficiencies.

REFERENCES

Andersen, A.E. (1990). A proposed mechanism underlying eating disorders and other disorders of motivated behavior. In: A.E. Andersen (Ed.), *Males with Eating Disorders*. New York: Brunner/Mazel.

Andersen, A.E. (1992). Analysis of treatment experience and outcome from the Johns Hopkins eating disorders program 1975–90. In: K. Halmi (Ed.), *Psychobiology and Treatment of Anorexia Nervosa and Bulimia Nervosa*. Washington, DC: American Psychiatric Press.

Andersen, A.E. and LaFrance, N. (1990). Persisting osteoporosis in bulimia nervosa patients with past anorexia nervosa. Presented at the Fourth International Conference on Eating Disorders, New York, 27–29 April.

Anderson, I.M., et al (1990). Dieting reduces plasma tryptophan and alters brain 5-HT function in women. *Psycho. Med.,* **20**, 785–791.

APA (1994). *DSM-IV*. Washington, DC: APA.

Brinch, M., Isager, T. and Tolstrup (1988). Anorexia nervosa and motherhood: reproduction pattern and mothering behavior of 50 women. *Acta Psych. Scand.,* **77**, 611–617.

Bruch, H. (1979). *The Golden Cage: The Enigma of Anorexia Nervosa*. New York: Random House.

Fairburn, C.G., Jones, R., Peveler, R.C. et al (1991a). Three psychological treatments for bulimia nervosa: a comparative trial. *Arch. Gen. Psych.,* **48**, 463–469.

Fairburn, C.G., Peveler, R.C., Davies, B., et al (1991b). Eating disorders in young adults with insulin dependent diabetes mellitus: a controlled study. *Br. Med. J.,* **303**, 17–20.

Freud, Anna (Ed.) (1966). *The Ego and the Mechanisms of Defense*, Vol. 2. New York: International Universities Press.

Gull, W.W.G. (1868). Anorexia nervosa (apepsia hystrica, anorexia hysterica). *Lancet,* August, 22–28.

Hedblom, J.E., Hubbard, F.A. and Andersen, A.E. (1981). Anorexia nervosa: a multidisciplinary treatment program for patient and family. *Social Work in Health Care,* **7**, 67–86.

Margolis, R., Spencer, W., De Paulo, R.J., et al (1994). Psychiatric comorbidity in eating disorder patients: a quantitative analysis by diagnostic subtype (in press).

Mecklenburg, R.S., Loriaux, D.L., Thompson, R.H., Andersen, A.E. and Lipsett, M.B. (1974). Hypothalamic dysfunction in patients with anorexia nervosa. *Medicine,* **53**, 147–159.

Mickalide, A.E. and Andersen, A.E. (1985). Subgroups of anorexia nervosa and bulimia: validity and utility. *J. Psych. Res.,* **19**(2/3), 121–128.

Minuchin, S., Rosman, B. and Baker, L. (1978). *Psychosomatic Families*. Cambridge, Mass: Harvard University Press.

Philips, A. (1989). Winnicott: an introduction. *Br. J. Psych.,* **155**, 612–618.

Russell, R.M., et al (1992). Chapter 12 in: K. Halmi (Ed.), *Psychobiology and Treatment of Anorexia Nervosa and Bulimia Nervosa*. Washington, DC: American Psychiatric Press.

Vandereycken, W., Kog, E. and Vanderlinden, J. (Eds) (1989). *The Family Approach to Eating Disorders*. New York: PMA Publishing.

Waldholtz, B.D. and Andersen, A.E. (1990). Gastrointestinal symptoms in anorexia nervosa: a prospective study. *Gastroenterology,* **98**, 1415–1419.

Yager, J., et al (1993). American Psychiatric Association Practice Guidelines for Eating Disorders. *Am. J. Psych.,* **150**, 207–228.

Part V

Prevention

Introduction to Part V

Only recently has there been serious discussion concerning the prevention of eating disorders. Professor Slade has been one of the major instigators. After persuading us that the eating disorders pose a significant health burden to our society, he presents a stimulating overview of the possibilities for "primary prevention" (aimed at preventing the disorder developing at all) and "secondary prevention" (early recognition and intervention, preventing its further development).

Slade's contribution helps towards the establishment of a conceptual framework for prevention of eating disorders, which includes a consideration of predisposing versus precipitating factors, of high-risk populations versus high-risk situations (or behaviours), and of ameliorating risk-factors versus improving coping responses or strengthening natural support systems. He raises important questions:

- Do we now have an adequate knowledge base for prevention?
- Do we have sufficiently well-defined targets?
- Do we have the models or tools for evaluation?
- Will support be forthcoming for the long-term studies necessary to show effectiveness?

Professor Slade takes us to our often uncertain limits in what we know about the development of eating disorders in proposing a range of interventions for both primary and secondary prevention. Whether the high-risk groups or high-risk behaviours he discusses have sufficient "sensitivity" and "specificity" (aspects of predictive power) to make primary prevention effective, predictable, or cost-efficient will be seen by many as questionable. Proposals for secondary prevention seem at this stage more likely to be successful, but even here adequate screening and effective early interventions remain to be demonstrated. We need also to consider whether, as in some other well-intentioned attempts at prevention, we might make matters worse by inadvertently creating new problems.

21

Prospects for Prevention

PETER SLADE
School of Health Sciences, University of Liverpool, UK

INTRODUCTION

This chapter is a review of ideas, proposals and suggestions for preventing the two eating disorders, anorexia nervosa and bulimia nervosa. As far as the writer is aware there are as yet no published accounts of the efficacy of prevention programmes in this area. Before commencing the review it is worth rehearsing some of the major reasons for taking the issue of prevention seriously.

The Size and Impact of the Problem

Although figures vary to some extent (see the review by Fairburn, 1990), 1–2% of adolescent and young adult females in developed societies develop one or other form of eating disorder. Indeed, in the USA according to Lucas (1989), anorexia nervosa is the third most common adolescent illness, while Fairburn (1991) has recently described bulimia nervosa as a "major public health problem". However, it is not just the size of the problem that is important but also its impact. An eating disorder causes long-term distress not only to the sufferer but also to her or his family, friends, employers and others. In addition it disrupts every aspect of the sufferer's life (personal, emotional, social, sexual, occupational, etc.) and that of the close family and friends. Such distress and disruption usually persist for years rather than months.

Handbook of Eating Disorders: Theory, Treatment and Research.
Edited by G. Szmukler, C. Dare and J. Treasure.
© 1995 John Wiley & Sons Ltd.

Treatability and Outcome

Treatment is often extremely difficult in the short term and the chance of relapse is high. While normal-weight bulimics often respond well to a structured psychological approach, restrictive anorectics are more difficult to treat, and those with a combination of the two often prove highly resistant. While medium-term follow-up studies (up to 10 years) generally reveal a 5–10% mortality rate, 20-year follow-up studies are now revealing a much higher mortality rate of around 20% (e.g. Steinhausen and Glanville, 1983; Herzog, Keller and Lavori, 1988). Moreover, specialist clinicians are now very familiar with the phenomenon of the "chronic, stuck, untreatable patient with a high mortality risk".

Irreversible Physical Consequences

For both anorexia nervosa and bulimia nervosa the physical complications are numerous during the illness, but surprisingly limited following recovery. Among the more persisting physical consequences are dental tooth wear (Milosevic and Slade, 1989) and osteoporosis (Carmichael, 1990).

Implications For Reproduction and Childbearing

In anorexia nervosa, markedly reduced fertility rates have been found in long-term follow-up studies (Brinch, Isager and Tolstrup, 1988). Moreover, when they do conceive, anorexics are likely to give birth to low-weight babies, with the consequent complications. Brinch and coworkers traced 50 anorexic mothers who had given birth to 86 infants and found that 7 babies had died within one week of delivery. This perinatal mortality rate was six times the national average at the time. In bulimia nervosa, various obstetric complications have been reported, including an increased risk of miscarriage (Mitchell et al, 1991) and an increased risk of fetal abnormality (Lacey and Smith, 1987). For a more detailed review of the evidence in this area the reader is referred to an editorial by Fahy and O'Donoghue (1991) and Chapter 11 in this volume.

There is some disturbing evidence that mothers who have an eating disorder may have special problems in feeding their children properly. Brinch and coworkers found that 17% of the infants born to the 50 anorexic mothers exhibited a "failure to thrive" during their first year of life. Similarly, van Wezel-Meijler and Wir (1989) reported on seven children of anorexic mothers with stunting of growth and concluded that the children were undernourished and had suffered psychosocial deprivation. Similar concerns have been raised about the children of bulimic mothers (Stein and Fairburn, 1989).

Conclusions

The conclusions from the above which render attempts at prevention of crucial importance are:

1. A sizeable minority of young women develop an eating disorder (either anorexia or bulimia nervosa) which causes severe distress and disruption to their lives and those of their close associates.
2. These disorders are often difficult to treat and, in the longer term, carry a high mortality.
3. These disorders also entail physical complications, the most persistent of which are dental tooth wear and osteoporosis.
4. Young women who develop an eating disorder either do not reproduce, or experience difficulties in doing so, or experience problems in nurturing their offspring appropriately. Clearly these are problems of extreme importance for society as a whole. We must therefore look carefully at all possible ways of preventing or minimising these pernicious disorders.

PROSPECTS FOR PRIMARY PREVENTION

Primary prevention refers to attempts at intervention prior to the development of a disorder and generally involves trying to alter "risk" factors. Thus, in the case of coronary heart disease, primary prevention involves efforts directed at changing peoples' diet and smoking behaviour, increasing their exercise and fitness levels, and modifying type-A behaviour patterns. The main strategy used in primary prevention is an educative one.

In anorexia nervosa and bulimia nervosa there are a number of potential targets for primary prevention. One of these is the "desire for thinness" (and the associated attempt at dieting), which is so prominent at present among adolescent and young adult females in developed societies. Crisp (1985), in a UK study, reported that over 60% of 17–18 year olds were attempting to change their shape and weight because they felt fat. These findings are very similar to those reported by Nylander (1971) in a much earlier Scandinavian survey. More recently, the results of a very large US survey were reported, which found that 64% of 16-year-old and 69% of 17-year-old girls admitted to "dieting" in the past year (Whitaker et al, 1989). There is a clear consensus that the majority of young females in developed societies are sufficiently weight-conscious to attempt to intervene to change their body size and shape through dietary restriction. This general concern about body size, shape and weight and the "desire for thinness" has been termed the "thin body cult". Moreover, a recent review paper has established a clear connection between societies which have the thin body cult and the prevalence of eating disorders in those societies (McCarthy, 1990). Thus, although not the whole story, living in a society which apparently values "slimness" and abhors "fatness" would appear to increase greatly the risk of anyone, particularly a female, developing an eating disorder.

For the first time, objective evidence is beginning to appear of a direct link between exposure to media presentations of female slimness and body image distortion. Hamilton and Waller (1992) asked anorectic and bulimic females, and a comparison group, to make judgements about their own body size following exposure to magazine pictures of either neutral images or of fashion models. The comparison women were unaffected by the manipulation; those with an eating disorder overestimated their body sizes to a significantly greater extent following exposure to the photographs of slim fashion models. Of course, we cannot know whether this specific sensitivity on the part of those with an established history of eating disorder was or was not present before they became ill. However, at the very least, the media effect may be one of helping to maintain and reinforce the appeal of slimness and thereby the eating disorder once it has been established. This alone is sufficient to justify attempts at primary prevention.

How might we attempt to intervene? One possibility would be to attempt to persuade critical parts of the media—for example women's magazines in general and fashion magazines particularly—to include a wider range of female shapes and sizes than at present. The crucial message to put across is not that "thinness is bad" but rather that a wide range of shapes and forms are acceptable and even desirable in our society. The associated message is one that stresses the value of "individuality" and "self-acceptance" as opposed to conformity to a "thin ideal". A second possibility which has been advocated by both Salmons (1987) and Hamilton and Waller (1992) is to use a Health Education approach in schools. It is proposed that schoolchildren could be given instruction in how to critically appraise the messages given out by women's magazines and how to resist them when appropriate.

A second potential target for primary prevention is the knowledge of the general public concerning the nature and severity of the eating disorders themselves. Although studies have found that members of the general public have heard of these disorders, particularly anorexia nervosa, and are familiar with their major behavioural features (e.g. Chiodo, Stanley and Harvey, 1984; Smith et al, 1986; Huon, Brown and Morris, 1988; Murray, Toyuz and Beumont, 1990), a study by Butler, Slade and Newton (1990) found that the general public were unsure about many important aetiological, treatment and prognostic features.

In the latter study, 56 experts in the area of eating disorders and 1052 members of the general public completed a 40-item questionnaire measuring knowledge of, and attitudes towards, anorexia nervosa and bulimia. The two samples were found to differ significantly on 29 out of the 40 items, indicating a greater level of disagreement than agreement. This was largely due to the fact that on many issues the experts had a clear view, while the general public were uncertain and divided. For example, in response to the statement "Dieting leads to anorexia nervosa", 86% of the experts said that this was false, while 46% of the general public said it was true, 39% said it was false and 14% were unsure. A second example concerns responses to the statement "Most anorectics starve to death", where 96% of experts said that this was false, while 35% of the general public said it was true, 48% said it was false and 17% were unsure. A third example involves responses to the statement "Most anorectics recover in a few months", where 93% of experts said this was false, while 24% of the general public said this was true, 37% said it was false and 39% were unsure. Our main findings were that, compared with the experts, the general public were *uncertain* about:

- whether dieting leads to anorexia nervosa and whether anorexia nervosa leads to death (the myth of the "slimmers disease")
- whether drugs have a role to play in treatment

- the length of time necessary for recovery
- the nature of bulimia.

The principal conclusion was that despite—or perhaps because of—the considerable media coverage given to the eating disorders, there remains a "knowledge gap;". In the UK organisations such as the Eating Disorders Association are now working hard to educate the general public about the nature of these disorders and to correct many of the unhelpful ideas and attitudes that are prevalent.

A third potential target for primary prevention is the highest-risk group itself, namely adolescents and young adults. Crisp (1988) has suggested that intervention might be directed at children in schools and might take three forms, namely:

1. The giving of information—facts and concepts; for example, knowledge about risk factors and the natural history of eating and body weight and shape disorders.
2. The giving of advice and the teaching of relevant skills by direct behavioural techniques.
3. The provision of personal/experiential opportunities for young people to learn about themselves.

I wholeheartedly concur with the general educational and preventive value of all three of these but would single out the last for special attention. My experience of working with eating disordered clients over many years has been that, while they usually come from enriched environments, they often appear emotionally and personally deprived, with little clear idea of where they are coming from and who they are.

The idea of targeting a preventive programme at schoolchildren is not new. In Canada, Barbara Carney (1986) introduced a structured preventive curriculum for anorexia nervosa and bulimia nervosa which is based on a mixture of group discussion and experiential learning. The structured learning materials which are used in the classroom cover the following topics:

- an overview (for teachers)
- diet and eating disorders
- male concerns with eating disorders
- sociocultural background of anorexia nervosa and bulimia in North America
- sociocultural influences which promote eating disorders and how to forestall them.

The aims of Carney's preventive curriculum are "to change attitudes towards slimness, dieting, competition and the roles of adolescent girls and of women in our society".

All three of the suggestions for primary prevention described so far involve an attempt to make changes in the present. However, another approach to primary prevention is to attempt to intervene in the natural history of the development of the disorders. To date, no prospective studies of high-risk groups have produced sufficient numbers of cases, nor studied them over a sufficient period of time prior to their developing an eating disorder, to reveal clear and unambiguous markers of formative experiences. We are therefore left with retrospective findings and clinical observations as our sole source of evidence about such experiences, particularly child-rearing practices. For example, there have been a number of studies using the Parental Bonding Instrument (Parker, Tupling and Brown, 1979) in which eating disordered and comparison subjects were asked to rate the behaviour of their parents, separately, towards them on items forming two scales, one of "warmth" and one of "protectiveness". In general, eating disordered patients tend to rate their parents as lower in "warmth" and higher in "protectiveness", although the latter finding is equivocal (Palmer, Oppenheimer and Marshall, 1988; Pole et al, 1988; Calam et al, 1990). While of interest because of the consistent picture they reveal, such studies are clearly prone to retrospective memory bias.

However, it must be useful for experienced clinicians to share their insights into common formative experiences in the histories of their patients, which may in the future contribute to a revealing large-scale prospective study. I attempted this myself some years ago in the form of a functional–analytical model which still directs my clinical approach and my research (Slade, 1982). More recently I have been thinking about the advice I would wish to give parents in an effort to prevent their children developing an eating disorder. On the basis of the literature and my own clinical experience, I have formulated the following set of 10 suggestions to parents (which I have termed the Ten Commandments):

1. Do not physically abuse your child.
2. Do not sexually abuse your child.
3. Do not make a big issue about food or eating.
4. Do not make a big issue about weight or body shape.
5. Show your child love and affection without being overprotective or overcontrolling.
6. Do not set impossible or difficult standards for your child.
7. Do not insist on perfect behaviour all the time.
8. Reward small attainments in the present rather than emphasising major goals in the future.
9. Encourage independence in your child.
10. Encourage your child to be sociable and to mix with other children.

These suggestions are based on observed formative experiences which are neither specific to the development of an eating disorder (e.g. physical or sexual abuse), nor essential for its prevention (e.g. encouraging independence and sociability). However, I suspect that if parents were able to follow these Ten Commandments, their children would have only a low risk of developing a serious eating disorder. Other specialists might want to give parents different advice.

PROSPECTS FOR SECONDARY PREVENTION

Secondary prevention refers to attempts to inhibit the development of a full-blown disorder/illness and involves early recognition and intervention. Although clearly beset by problems, it has been suggested that, in the field of eating disorders, secondary prevention is a more realistic target than primary prevention (Vandereycken and Meerman, 1984).

There are two logical requirements for successful approaches to secondary prevention. The first is that there should be simple, sensitive and reliable screening procedures for identifying the early signs and symptoms of the disorder or for identifying the high-risk candidate. The second requirement is that there should be established methods of therapy which are likely to prove effective when used as early interventions.

Early Recognition and Identification

There are two possible approaches to early recognition, the first focusing on early signs and symptoms and the second on the distinctive features of the high-risk candidate.

The Eating Attitudes Test. The most widely used screening measure is the *Eating Attitudes Test* (EAT), which was developed by Garner and Garfinkel (1979; see also Garner et al, 1982) as a measure of the symptoms of anorexia nervosa. This 40-item questionnaire has been used in a number of subsequent studies to screen for abnormal eating attitudes and behaviour among normal populations (e.g. Button and Whitehouse, 1981; Mann et al, 1983; Eisler and Szmukler, 1986; Johnson-Sabine et al, 1988; Patton et al, 1990). The main finding from such studies has been that, while the instrument has good "sensitivity" (i.e. the majority of eating disordered patients score well above the cutoff level), its "specificity" is rather low (i.e. many normal dieters also score above the cutoff level). For example, Mann et al, 1983 found that 83 (8.2%) of their sample of 1012 schoolchildren scored above their established cutoff point of 21, while only 4 (4.8%) of these were found to meet the criteria for a clinical eating disorder at interview. Similarly, Eisler and Szmukler (1986) found that of their sample of 1331 private-school girls, 65 (4.9%) scored above cutoff on the EAT, while at interview only 8 (0.6%) were deemed to be suffering from anorexia nervosa. When the interview criteria were expanded to include "partial syndrome" cases, the latter figure increased to 38 (2.85%) which is still only about a half of the number scoring above the cutoff mark. Eisler and Szmukler also found that responses to the EAT were affected by the social class of the respondent.

Despite the problems described above, the Eating Attitudes Test is still a useful tool, in both research and clinical work, for identifying abnormal attitudes to eating which may reflect the early signs of an eating disorder.

Identification of high-risk candidates. The alternative focus for early detection and intervention is the high-risk candidate. While many specialists in the field have put forward suggestions concerning the premorbid characteristics of those who develop an eating disorder, only a couple of us have specifically discussed these in relation to the issue of prevention.

Crisp (1986), in discussing primary prevention, presented a list of risk factors for the development of anorexia nervosa, namely:

- a high growth rate and a high "set point" for body weight
- premorbid obesity
- bulimia
- cognitive rigidity
- an inability to tolerate uncertainty and adolescent dysphoria at normal body weight
- poor self-esteem
- lack of social skills
- a tendency for avoidance behaviour—possibly partly genetic
- associated lack of communication skills

Incidentally, the first of these features has received independent support in a recent community-based sample of adolescent girls, in which the more developmentally advanced girls were found to have a substantially increased risk of developing an eating disorder (Killen et al, 1992).

Considering the list as a whole, many of these putative "risk" factors would seem to lend themselves to periodic monitoring by doctors, schoolteachers and parents. They could therefore provide the basis for early detection of the high-risk individual.

My own approach to the identification of the high-risk candidate (Slade, 1988) begins with *demography*. There is general agreement that the highest-risk category is that of adolescent and young adult females in developed societies. If we make this the target group for secondary prevention, how many people are we talking about? The UK census figures for 1981 showed that, of the total population of just over 54 million, 7% (about 3.8 million) were females between the ages of 16–24 years. In Liverpool, of the total population of about 510 000, 8% were females between the ages of 16 and 24 years. Thus, this "age–sex" high-risk target group amounts to 7–8% of the total population and is very sizeable numerically as these figures show. At issue is whether we can identify a subgroup of this "age–sex' group who have a particular vulnerability to the development of an eating disorder, and in recent years much of my research has been concerned with the development of simple screening procedures for this purpose.

The starting point for this was my original model of anorexia nervosa (Slade, 1982), a much simplified version of which is presented in Figure 21.1. In this model, I propose that the setting conditions (predisposing factors) for the development of anorexia nervosa involve a combination of perfectionist tendencies and general dissatisfaction. That is, the prospective sufferer has a set of high expectations for herself and her life, which she feels she is failing to live up to. In consequence she experiences a strong need to control completely some aspect of her life. Given that there are relatively few areas of ones life that one can hope to have complete control over (immediately excluded is anything to do with other people), the person is directed towards control over "self in general" and "their body in particular". If the individual then attempts to lose weight through dieting, and is successful even for a short period of time, the immediate feelings of "success" and "being in control" provide powerful reinforcement for the weight-control behaviour. In other words, the individual who feels a failure in every area of her life suddenly discovers that there is one thing she is good at, namely "weight control". She is therefore likely to devote her life to it. It is suggested that she then engages in further dieting and weight loss which eventually becomes an obsession. This obsession leads to her withdrawing from all normal activities, which in turn enables her to avoid the major problems in her life which made her dissatisfied in the first place. My contention is that, because of the nature of the setting conditions/predisposing factors, weight-control behavior is maintained by a combination of positive reinforcement (feelings of success) and negative reinforcement (avoidance of problems).

From the above model it follows that the high-risk candidate is someone who exhibits the characterstics of "perfectionist tendencies" combined with "general dissatisfaction". This combination has been described by Hamachek (1978) as "neurotic perfectionism".

A questionnaire (SCANS) has been developed to tap the hypothesised "setting conditions" (Slade and Dewey, 1986), and Slade et al (1990) reported on the group discrimination of this quetionnaire on an extended sample of 105 eating disordered patients and 1137 normal comparison subjects. The sensitivity of the 22-item measure was 87%, while its specificity was 92%. Moreover, the proportion of normal subjects scoring above the cutoff level was between 7% and 9% for each of the three subsamples (schoolgirls, college students and nursing students), suggesting a fairly stable level of "at-riskness" within the "age–sex" target group. In another study (Kiemle, Slade and Dewey, 1987), a sample of 424 college students were screened with the SCANS, of whom 36 (8.5%) scored above cutoff. Eighteen of these were interviewed, of whom 4 (22%) were deemed to be suffering from a partial syndrome of anorexia nervosa.

In another study carried out at the University of Texas (R. Ryan, personal communication 1991), the SCANS was administered to 101 "elite athletes". On average the athletes scored high on perfectionism and low on dissatisfaction, indicating that in general they are a normal or satisfied perfectionist group. However, a subgroup of 18 (18%) scored above both cutoffs, putting them in the "neurotic perfectionist" range. Of this subgroup, 12 have apparently been treated for an eating disorder while the other 6 are closely monitored for other reasons (e.g. high stress, poor grades, etc.).

Early Intervention

Evidence from follow-up studies shows that longer duration of symptoms prior to treatment is associated with a generally poorer outcome, while shorter duration of illness tends to be associated with a more favourable response to treatment (see reviews by Steinhausen and Glanville, 1983; Herzog, Keller and Lavori, 1988). This is consistent with my experience with the few individuals referred to me at a very early stage who responded well to simple advice and counselling.

There are good reasons to think that early intervention could be effective, but who should do it, when should it be contemplated, and how should it be done?

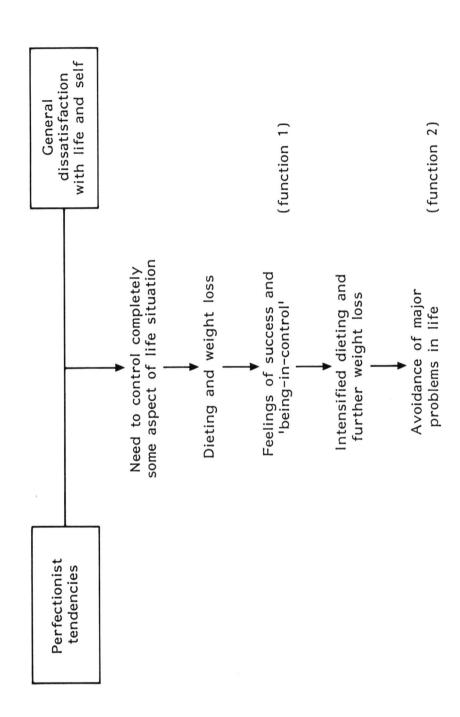

FIGURE 21.1   A simplified version of a model of anorexia nervosa.

There is also the problem raised by Vandereycken and Meerman (1984) and Crisp (1988) of the reluctance of some sufferers to accept help. However, it is my impression that this is only a problem *after* the individual has become stuck in the anorectic role. Early intervention should occur before this point is reached.

The persons best placed to identify high-risk candidates for an eating disorder (and to recognise the early signs and symptoms) are parents, friends, schoolteachers and general practitioners. The latter professionals might indeed have a statutory responsibility to monitor the high-risk "age–sex" group on a regular basis. The first indication of a potential problem is likely to be a combination of general emotional problems and social isolation/withdrawal during adolescence. The former may be disguised by the potential sufferer, while the latter will not. At this stage general and sensitive counselling by a teacher or general practitioner may be precisely what is required. If the potential sufferer moves on to using strict dieting, and is clearly successful in achieving significant weight loss, the individual may need to be referred to a specialist counsellor or mental health professional. The latter may intervene in one of two ways, namely through individual or family therapy.

Individual therapy/counselling will need to be educative in nature and include a discussion of the following issues:

1. The long-term negative consequences/dangers of an "eating disorder" career. This is important because anorexia nervosa can be perceived as glamorous by teenagers.
2. The possibility of alternative solutions to current problems (i.e. rather than anorexia).
3. The fact that "weight" and "happiness" are not correlated. Attention might be drawn to (a) the happy endomorph, and (b) the negative effects of semistarvation (e.g. the study of Keyes et al, 1950).
4. Common adolescent problems.
5. Common fears and problems in establishing an individual identity.

Family therapy is likely to be important for the following reason. Gerald Russell and colleagues (Russell et al, 1987) found that "family therapy" was more effective than individual therapy for a particular subset of their eating disordered patients, namely those below the age of 19 years, with a history of symptoms of less than 3 years. This is the group who should be the focus for early intervention. Thus, family therapy would appear to be the intervention of choice for secondary prevention at the present time.

SUMMARY AND CONCLUSIONS

The above review of the literature has established the following points:

1. The eating disorders are common and sometimes intractable problems. They produce physical changes, including tooth wear and osteoporosis, and they affect reproduction and child-rearing capabilities. There are some potent reasons for attempting to prevent the development and spread of eating disorders.

2. There are a number of potential targets for *primary prevention*. These include societal concerns with female thinness, the knowledge of the general public about the dangers of dieting and of "anorexia nervosa", and the emotional problems of the group at highest risk, namely adolescent and young female adults.
3. The efficacy of *secondary prevention* is predicated on the dual objectives of successful early recognition and effective early intervention. Various potential means of achieving these objectives have been discussed.

Finally, it is clear that prevention will not be an easy task. What is needed in the first instance, as Crisp (1986) has pointed out, is a series of properly evaluated and focused preventive studies. In order for this to happen the specialist scientific and research committee will need to give the philosophy of prevention its fullest support.

DEDICATION

This chapter is dedicated to Gerald Russell who first stimulated (fathered) my clinical and research interest in anorexia nervosa. The content and quality of this chapter inevitably fall below the high standards he set for his students and for himself. Given his potent influence it is not difficult to understand why I am currently interested in the processes underlying perfectionism. Personally, I know him as a kind, considerate and totally loyal supporter of his colleagues and students. His active presence will be sadly missed by many, and I wish him a happy and enjoyable retirement.

REFERENCES

Brinch, M., Isager, T. and Tolstrup, K. (1988). Anorexia nervosa and motherhood: reproduction pattern and mothering behaviour of 50 women. *Acta Psychiat. Scand.*, **77**, 98–104.

Butler, N., Slade, P. and Newton, T. (1990). Attitudes towards anorexia nervosa and bulimic disorders: expert and lay opinion. *Brit. Rev. Bulim. Anor. Nerv.*, **4**, 61–69.

Button, E.J. and Whitehouse, A. (1981). Subclinical anorexia nervosa. *Psychol. Med.*, **11**, 509–516.

Calam, R., Waller, G., Slade, P. and Newton, T. (1990). Eating disorders and perceived relationships with parents. *Int. J. Eat. Dis.*, **9**, 479–485.

Carmichael, K.A. (1990). How self-starvation damages bone structure. *BASH Magazine*, **9**, 13–15.

Carney, B. (1986). A preventive curriculum for anorexia nervosa and bulimia. BANA, Faculty of Human Kinetics, University of Windsor, Ontario, Canada.

Chiodo, J., Stanley, M. and Harvey, J.H. (1984). Attributions about anorexia nervosa and bulimia. *J. Soc. Clin. Psychol.*, **2**, 280–285.

Crisp, A.H. (1985). Regulation of the self in adolescence with particular reference to anorexia nervosa. *Trans. Med. Soc. Lond.*, **100**, 67–74.

Crisp, A.H. (1986). The integration of "self-help" and "help" in the prevention of anorexia nervosa. *Br. Rev. Bulim. Anor. Nerv.*, **1**, 27–38.

Crisp, A.H. (1988). Some possible approaches to prevention of eating and body weight/shape disorders, with particular reference to anorexia nervosa. *Int. J. Eat. Dis.*, **7**, 1–17.

Eisler, I. and Szmukler, G.I. (1986). Social class as a confounding variable in the eating attitudes test. In: G.I. Smukler et al (Eds), *Anorexia Nervosa and Bulimic Disorders*; Oxford: Pergamon Press.

Fahy, T.A. and O'Donaghue, G. (1991). Editorial: Eating disorders in pregnancy. *Psychol. Med.*, **21**, 577–580.

Fairburn, C.G. (1991). Paper presented at the International Conference on Eating Disorders, Paris, 17–19 April.

Fairburn, C.G. and Beglin, S.J. (1990). Studies of the epidemiology of bulimia nervosa. *Am. J. Psychiat.*, **147**, 401–408.

Garner, D.M. and Garfinkel, P.E. (1979). The Eating Attitudes Test: an index of the symptoms of anorexia nervosa. *Psychol. Med.*, **9**, 273–279.

Garner, D.M., Olmstead, M.P., Bohr, Y. and Garfinkel, P.E. (1982). The Eating Attitudes Test: psychometric features and clinical correlates. *Psychol. Med.*, **12**, 871–878.

Hamacheck, D.E. (1978). Psychodynamics of normal and neurotic perfectionism. *Psychol.*, **15**, 27–33.

Hamilton, K. and Waller, G. (1992). Media influences on body size estimation in anorexia and bulimia: an experimental study. *Br. J. Psychiat.*, **162**, 837–840.

Herzog, D.B., Keller, M.B. and Lavori, P.W. (1988). Outcome in anorexia nervosa and bulimia nervosa: a review of the literature. *J. Nerv. Ment. Dis.*, **176**, 131–143.

Huon, G.F., Brown, L.B. and Morris, S.E. (1988). Lay beliefs about disordered eating. *Int. J. Eat. Dis.*, **7**, 239–253.

Johnson-Sabine, E., Wood, K., Patton, G., et al (1988). Abnormal eating attitudes in London schoolgirls: a prospective epidemiological study. Factors associated with abnormal response on screening questionnaires. *Psychol. Med.*, **18**, 615–622.

Keyes, A., Brozek, J., Henschel, A., Mickelsen, O. and Taylor, H.L. (1950). *The Biology of Human Starvation*. Minneapolis: University of Minnesota Press.

Kiemle, G., Slade, P.D. and Dewey, M.E. (1987). Factors associated with abnormal eating attitudes and behaviours: screening individuals at risk of developing an eating disorder. *Int. J. Eat. Dis.*, **6**, 713–724.

Killen, J.D., Hayward, C., Litt, I., Hammer, L.D., Wilson, D.M., Miner, B., Taylor, C.B., Varady, A. and Shisslak, C. (1992). Is puberty a risk factor for eating disorders? *Am. J. Dis. Child*, **146**?, 323–325.

Lacey, J.H. and Smith, G. (1987). Bulimia nervosa: the impact of pregnancy on mother and baby. *Br. J. Psychiat.*, **150**, 777–781.

Lucas, A. (1989). Paper presented at BASH 7, St. Louis, Missouri, USA.

Mann, A.H., Wakeling, A., Wood, K., Monck, E., Dobbs, R. and Szmukler, G.I. (1983). Screening for abnormal eating attitudes and psychiatric morbidity in an unselected population of 15-year-old schoolgirls. *Psychol. Med.*, **13**, 573–580.

McCarthy, M. (1990). The thin ideal, depression and eating disorders in women. *Behav. Res. Ther.*, **28**, 205–216.

Milosevic, A. and Slade, P.D. (1989). The orodental status of anorexics and bulimics. *Br. Dent. J.*, **1**, 66–70.

Mitchell, J.E., Seim, H.C., Glotter, D., Soll, E.A. and Pyle, R.L. (1991). A retrospective study of pregnancy in bulimia nervosa. *Int. J. Eat. Dis.*, **10**, 209–214.

Murray, S.A., Touyz, S. and Beumont, P. (1990). Knowledge about eating disorders in the community. *Int. J. Eat. Dis.*, **9**, 87–93.

Nylander, I. (1971). The feeling of being fat and dieting in a school population. *Acta Sociol. Scand.*, **3**, 17–26.

Palmer, R.L., Oppenheimer, R. and Marshall, P.D. (1988). Eating-disordered patients remember their parents: a study using the Parental Bonding Instrument. *Int. J. Eat. Dis.*, **7**, 101–106.

Parker, G., Tupling, H. and Brown, L.B. (1979). A parental bonding instrument. *Br. J. Med. Psychol.*, **52**, 1–10.

Patton, G.C., Johnson-Sabine, E., Wood, K., Mann, A.H. and Wakeling, A. (1990). Abnormal eating attitudes in London schoolgirls: a prospective epidemiological study. Outcome at twelve-month follow-up. *Psychol. Med.*, **20**, 383–394.

Pole, R., Waller, D.A., Stewart, S.M. and Parkin-Feigenbaum (1988). Parental caring versus overprotection in bulimia. *Int. J. Eat. Dis.*, **7**, 601–606.

Russell, G.F.M., Szmukler, G.I., Dare, C. and Eisler, I. (1987). An evaluation of family therapy in anorexia nervosa and bulimia nervosa. *Arch. Gen. Psychiat.*, **44**, 1047–1056.

Salmons, P.H. (1987). Anorexia nervosa and related conditions in schoolchildren. *Nutr. Health*, **4**, 217–225.

Slade, P.D. (1982). Towards a functional analysis of anorexia nervosa and bulimia nervosa. *Br. J. Clin. Psychol.*, **21**, 167–179.

Slade, P.D. (1988). Early recognition and prevention: is it possible to screen people at risk of developing an eating disorder?' In: D. Hardoff and E. Chigier (Eds), *Eating Disorders in Adolescents and Young Adults*. London: Freund Publishing House.

Slade, P.D. and Dewey, M.E. (1986). Development and preliminary validation of SCANS: a screening instrument for identifying individuals at risk of developing anorexia and bulimia nervosa. *Int. J. Eat. Dis.*, **5**, 517–538.

Slade, P.D., Dewey, M.E., Kiemle, G. and Newton, T. (1990). Update on SCANS: a screening instrument for identifying individuals at risk of developing an eating disorder. *Int. J. Eat. Dis.*, **9**, 583–584.

Smith, M.C., Pruitt, J.A., Mann, L.M. and Thelen, M.H. (1986). Attitudes and knowledge regarding bulimia and anorexia nervosa. *Int. J. Eat. Dis.*, **5**, 545–553.

Stein, A. and Fairburn, C. (1989). Children of mothers with bulimia nervosa. *Br. Med. J.*, **299**, 777–778.

Steinhausen, H.C. and Glanville, K. (1983). Editorial: Follow-up studies of anorexia nervosa: a review of the research findings. *Psychol. Med.*, **13**, 239–249.

Vandereycken, W. and Meerman, R. (1984). Anorexia nervosa: is prevention possible? *Int. J. Psychiat. Med.*, **14**, 191–205.

van Wezel-Meijler, G. and Wir, J.M. (1989). The offspring of mothers with anorexia nervosa: a high-risk group for undernutrition and stunting. *Eur. J. Paediat.*, **149**, 130–135.

Whitaker, A., Davies, M., Shaffer, D., Johnson, J., Abrams, S., Walsh, T. and Kalikow, K. (1989). The struggle to be thin: a survey of anorexic and bulimic symptoms in a non-referred adolescent population. *Psychol. Med.*, **19**, 143–163.

Part VI

Acknowledgement of the Contribution of
G.F.M. Russell

22

Food for Thought: Gerald Russell's Writings on Eating Disorders

WALTER VANDEREYCKEN
University of Leuven, Belgium

On 5 May 1972 a symposium on anorexia nervosa and obesity was organised by the Royal College of Physicians of Edinburgh. Gerald Russell, by then Professor of Psychiatry at the Royal Free Hospital School of Medicine in London, was invited to speak about "The management of anorexia nervosa". With great clarity and a special sense for clinical pragmatism he described his experiences. Because of the extraordinary quality of the paper and the fact that its publication in the proceedings of the Edinburgh symposium had only limited circulation, we would like to quote extensively from this article, starting with the entire introduction:

> In this article the approach to the management of anorexia nervosa will be essentially empirical: the treatments described will be those which have been found to be effective in practice. A rational approach, based on knowledge of the causes or abnormal mechanisms underlying the illness, would clearly be preferable but is not yet available. The causation of anorexia nervosa remains unknown, and theories so far formulated in attempts to understand this illness have proved at the best simplistic, and at the worst frankly misleading. In adopting an empirical approach, however, it becomes necessary to assess the efficacy of the treatments chosen. It will be shown that this is possible only to a limited extent and some of the most important questions about the outcome of treatment remain unanswered. This is not to say, however, that one need be pessimistic about treating patients with anorexia nervosa. The patient's response to therapeutic efforts can seldom be accurately predicted, but it is usually highly rewarding (Russell, 1973, p. 44).

Handbook of Eating Disorders: Theory, Treatment and Research.
Edited by G. Szmukler, C. Dare and J. Treasure.
© 1995 John Wiley & Sons Ltd.

Twenty years later, these sentences can still be used as an introduction to a publication on the treatment of anorexia nervosa! As a quotation it also most typically reflects the spirit of Gerald Russell's work.

PRAGMATIC ASPECTS AND NONSPECIFIC FACTORS

Most apparent from Russell's (1973) article is his therapeutic pragmatism or the attitude of the practitioner who does not want his treatment approaches being rigidly determined by theoretical formulations.

> Instead, remedies which have been found in practice to be effective should be further developed and refined. Only when the efficacy of such remedies is established, and their mode of action clearly understood, would it seem worth while elaborating a theory aimed at explaining success in terms of possible causation. Similarly, until we know more about the aetiology of anorexia nervosa, we should guard against limiting our treatment according to our favourite theories (Russell, 1973, pp. 46–47).

Discussing the many different therapeutic approaches available in those days, Russell displays a kind of scepticism which characterises much of his clinical work. He addresses two crucial questions as to the long-term efficacy of a treatment:

1. Does the treatment influence the natural course of the illness?
2. How do the results compare with those of other forms of treatment?

Russell's attempt to answer the first question has led him to a series of follow-up studies which we will discuss further on. On the other hand, it would take several years (see below) before Russell carried out the type of research aimed at answering the second question, as he had put forward in an earlier publication: "It is obvious that therapeutic success can only be gauged by controlled studies taking into account the variable course of the illness and the overriding importance of processes of selection" (Russell, 1970, p. 151). His first approach to this issue was to critically question the specificity of so-called efficacious therapies: ". . . it must be conceded that no specific treatment has yet emerged" (Russell, 1970, p. 157), and if a treatment seems successful—even in the short run—one should wonder why it does work.

With regard to the available therapeutic approaches Russell (1973) asked the question "whether the setting in which they are conducted might be a common factor which accounts for the successes attributed to them" (p. 47). Especially focusing on inpatient treatment, he stresses that the success of several psychological methods—ranging from behavioural therapy to "educational" treatment—is brought about by "general nursing care", which he considers as "being probably the most important component" (p. 55). Here we see how Russell's therapeutic pragmatism is closely linked to his belief in what we would call now the "nonspecific" factors in treatment. No wonder, he emphasizes the importance of the nurse–patient relationship: "It is not simply the techniques of nursing care which are important, but the spirit in which they are applied" (Russell, 1973, p. 49).

At the multidisciplinary conference on anorexia nervosa held on 13–15 October 1976 at the National Institutes of Health in Bethesda (Maryland), Russell further elaborated on these themes. First he criticises the narrow-minded definition of success in some studies: "The criteria for a fundamental improvement in the course of the illness require much more radical change in the patient than gain in weight over the course of a few weeks" (Russell, 1977, p. 277). In a second step he shows "how the patients' weight can be quickly restored to normal with comparative ease and without any 'specific' method of treatment" (p. 278). After the description of the "general management" in the hospital, he refers to the reports on "impressive short-term therapeutic benefits, but none that are clearly superior to the nursing regime that is described here and makes no claims to specificity" (Russell, 1977, pp. 283–284.

Finally comes the hypothesis that "so far, no effective long-term treatment for patients with anorexia nervosa has been discovered" and that "both the patient and her therapist remain at the mercy of the natural course of the illness". Russell then briefly reports his 4-year follow-up study of 41 patients he had already described in detail elsewhere (Morgan and Russell, 1975). Typically for the caution and modesty of the author, the results are not presented as being particularly good or bad.

> If the general nursing treatment and the supportive psychotherapy that were given are considered nonspecific, the outcome can be seen to reflect the natural course of the illness, influenced only by the general care and management given to the patients. . . . This study may therefore be taken as a base line showing the long-term natural outcome of anorexia nervosa, the patients being representative of a wide spectrum of severity of the illness, and the treatment given being of a nonspecific supportive type. Any new treatments that are introduced and claimed to be specific for anorexia nervosa should be compared with this base line (Russell, 1977, p. 288).

Moreover, the criteria of success have to be based, according to the author, on the outcome after at least 4 years. No wonder Russell concludes his paper at the Bethesda conference with the ironical statement that this type of study "presents a daunting prospect to a would-be investigator" (p. 289).

CARTESIAN DISCUSSIONS

At the aforementioned Bethesda conference, more than half of the papers were reporting on biological studies. This reflects the revival of biological psychiatry in general and its growing interest for anorexia nervosa in particular. Due to a misinterpretation of Simmonds' disease as "pituitary cachexia", before the Second World War many clinicians believed that anorexia nervosa was just a form of endocrine deficiency. This viewpoint, implying the use of hormonal treatment, proved to be wrong and after 1945 the strong belief in the psychogenesis of anorexia nervosa brought the syndrome back into the handbooks of psychiatry. But one symptom kept intriguing clinicians and researchers alike: amenorrhoea.

Gerald Russell belonged to the first investigators who stimulated renewed biological interest in the disorder. He demonstrated the connection between low body weight and endocrine dysfunction, in particular decreased gonadotrophin and oestrogen excretion (Russell et al, 1965; Russell and Beardwood, 1968). But an early onset of amenorrhoea in anorexics, often occurring before any appreciable weight loss, as well as the persistence of menstrual dysfunction after recovery, remained to be explained. Russell began to speculate that some endocrine disturbances in anorexia nervosa were primary of nature, "not as a sequel of malnutrition but as a more fundamental feature of the illness" (Russell and Beardwood, 1970, p. 361). Hence, he hypothesised a failure of the anterior hypothalamic mechanisms concerned with the control of rhythmic gonadotrophin secretion.

Practically all of Russell's studies and reports in the 1960s had to do with biological facets of anorexia nervosa. Beside the endocrinological studies already discussed, he published on nutritional and metabolic aspects (e.g. Russell, 1965; Russell and Bruce, 1966; Russell, 1967). Finally, with the description of disturbances in the regulation of body temperature (Wakeling and Russell, 1970) he seemed to have paved the way for the "primary hypothalamic dysfunction theory" that would dominate the research from the 1970s on. Although convincing evidence for the theory is clearly lacking, still many biological researchers are adhering to it in one form or another. History, however, should teach them a lesson in modesty, as we have put it elsewhere: "Within less than a century, the Cartesian 'seat' of anorexia nervosa has moved a few centimetres upwards, from pituitary to hypothalamus" (Vandereycken and Meermann, 1984, p. 51).

It is most characteristic for this episode that Russell gave his chapter in an annual review of medicine the following title: "Metabolic, endocrine and psychiatric aspects of anorexia nervosa" (Russell, 1969). So, at that time the psychiatrist was not even playing second fiddle! But then something strange happened in Russell's scientific career. Instead of pursuing the biological track, his publications in the 1970s show a remarkable shift to psychological subjects. Retrospectively, one can already read it between the lines of his excellent discussion on the "identity" of anorexia nervosa (Russell, 1970), but especially two papers from 1972 typify this change: "Psychological and nutritional factors in disturbances of menstrual function and ovulation" and "Premenstrual tension and 'psychogenic' amenorrhoea: psychophysical interactions". The latter, especially, seems to reflect some ambivalence or hesitation in discussing "psychogenesis". The following years, however, don't leave any doubt: the clinical psychiatrist is back . . .

THE CLINICIAN'S EYE

While he still believed in a primary endocrine disorder, Russell (1970) started to discuss several other themes on which he would pursue research in the following two decades: course and prognosis, familial factors, psychogenesis, and treatment. His collaboration with the psychologist Peter Slade led to pioneering attempts to assess the body image disorder in eating disordered patients (Slade and Russell, 1973a,b). With this milestone started an era of "experimental studies on the nature of the psychological disorder in anorexia nervosa" (Russell, Campbell and Slade, 1975).

Another landmark is the aforementioned follow-up study of 41 anorexia nervosa patients treated at the Maudsley Hospital, all under Russell's care, between 1959 and 1966 (Morgan and Russell, 1975). It showed how difficult it is to predict the long-term outcome and how important to assess the course of the disorder over several years. Together with Theander's (1970) pioneering work, this investigation inspired the rapidly growing number of follow-up studies in the next 15 years (see Herzog, Deter and Vandereycken, 1992).

In a brief review on the status of anorexia nervosa in 1977, Russell emphasised that the disorder "allows the researcher to study simultaneously disturbances of mental and bodily function, so enabling him to observe their complex interaction" (p. 363). He is now more cautious in his discussion of an eventual "primary hypothalamic defect of unknown aetiology" and concludes that "self-perpetuating disturbances play an important part in anorexia nervosa" (p. 366). Against the background of Russell's own investigations it is most interesting to read the editorial in *The Lancet* of 15 September 1979. Officially anonymous, it had been written by Gerald Russell himself, who addressed the question whether there exists a conflict between treating the patient and investigating her endocrine status. Though avoiding a clear-cut answer, the author indirectly criticised investigations which "may be time-consuming and may delay the start of correct treatment" (Editorial, 1979, p. 563). No doubt, one recognises Russell's clinical pragmatism in the following sentence: "As the basic cause of anorexia nervosa is unknown the best approach to treatment is an empirical one" (p. 564).

Though he would always remain sceptical as to the efficacy and specificity of particular forms of therapy for eating disorders, less than ten years later he published the first controlled study of family therapy in these patients (Russell et al., 1987). But from the way he has lectured all over the world on the results of this most rewarding collaboration with George Szmukler, Christopher Dare and Ivan Eisler, one may conclude that Russell has never closed the eye of the clinician. The same applies also to his studies with fenfluramine in bulimic patients: he quickly realised "the limited role" of drugs in the treatment of eating disorders (Russell, 1985b; Russell, Checkley and Robinson, 1986).

LIMNER OF A "NEW" SYNDROME

As part of a series of Dahlem Conferences in Berlin, a special "Workshop on appetite and food intake" took place in 1975. The participants, a small but exquisite selection of clinicians and researchers, discussed the definition and classification of eating disorders. Just like politicians agreeing on a communiqué as the final result of the negotiations, a report was published reflecting the consensus among the discussants (Garrow, 1976). The presented criteria for anorexia nervosa echo very much Russell's (1970) viewpoint, although the report now speaks about a "secondary endocrine disorder". Then, as a separate clinical entity, the Dahlem group discussed "overeating and vomiting". As clinical features they mention:

> One group of subjects with chronic anorexia nervosa exemplify many aspects of addiction; they habitually/constantly ingest and vomit food in large quantities. They

frequently do this covertly. They are usually restless, preoccupied with food and its ingestion, and with an associated disgust at the thought and experience of weight gain. . . . This behavior, in less severe form, can characterize subjects of more normal weight and who retain menstrual function. Such individuals may previously have been of very low weight due to unequivocal anorexia nervosa or may have been overweight previously (Garrow, 1976, pp. 407–408).

We consider this quotation as historically important because it "announces" a new syndrome by a group of experts including—no surprise anymore—Gerald Russell. Around the same time, several other clinicians described a similar clinical picture using different names for it such as bulimarexia, compulsive eating, dietary chaos syndrome, and hyperorexia nervosa (Vandereycken, 1994). But only one name has become widely accepted now: *bulimia nervosa*, as proposed by Russell in 1979. His report on this "ominous variant of anorexia nervosa" is no doubt the most often quoted publication on this subject.

The fact that Russell's description—even after several years of confusion with the American "bulimia" as described in DSM-III (see Russell, 1985a)—is looked upon as the landmark publication cannot be attributed just to his fortunate choice of the term bulimia nervosa. The systematic description of the features of his 30 patients (seen between 1972 and 1978) reminds us of Lasègue's remarkable report on "hysterical anorexia" (Vandereycken and Van Deth, 1990). More than ten years after its apperance, everyone wanting to know what bulimia nervosa is can be recommended to read Russell's (1979b) article. It is and will remain a "classic" because of its clinical acuteness and plain clarity.

SCIENTIST–PRACTITIONER

In this short overview it is possible to highlight only the most significant facts of Gerald Russell's *oeuvre*. The most interesting aspect is his recurring struggle with his identity as psychiatrist. As such his career reflects much of what psychiatry in general had to come to terms with at least since its establishment as a specialty in the nineteenth century: a scientific discipline or a clinical art? Marrying the two is probably what makes this profession so fascinating and enriching. In Russell's work on eating disorders the practitioner has overshadowed the scientist in a creative and stimulating way. He not only described the history of the changing nature of eating disorders (Russell, 1985c; Russell and Treasure, 1989); he became an important part of it.

REFERENCES

Garrow, J.S. (Rapporteur) (1976). Pathology of eating group. In: T. Silverstone (Ed.), *Report on the Dahlem Workshop on Appetite and Food Intake*, pp. 405–416. Berlin: Life Sciences Research Report 2.
Herzog, W., Deter, H.C. and Vandereycken, W. (Eds) (1992). *The Course of Eating Disorders: Long-Term Follow-up Studies of Anorexia and Bulimia Nervosa*. Berlin–New York: Springer-Verlag.

Morgan, H.G. and Russell, G.F.M. (1975). Value of family background and clinical features as predictors of long-term outcome in anorexia nervosa: four-year follow-up study of 41 patients. *Psychological Medicine,* **5**, 355–371.

Russell, G.F.M. (1965). Metabolic aspects of anorexia nervosa. *Proceedings of the Royal Society of Medicine,* **58**, 811–814.

Russell, G.F.M. (1967). The nutritional disorder in anorexia nervosa. *Journal of Psychosomatic Research,* **11**, 141–149.

Russell, G.F.M. (1969). Metabolic, endocrine and psychiatric aspects of anorexia nervosa. In: *The Scientific Basis of Medicine Annual Reviews,* pp. 236–255. London: Athlone Press.

Russell, G.F.M. (1970). Anorexia nervosa: its identity as an illness and its treatment. In: J.H. Price (Ed.), *Modern Trends in Psychological Medicine,* Vol. 2, pp. 131–164. London: Butterworth.

Russell, G.F.M. (1973). The management of anorexia nervosa. In: R.F. Robertson (Ed.), *Symposium: Anorexia Nervosa and Obesity,* pp. 44–62. Edinburgh: Royal College of Physicians.

Russell, G.F.M. (1977). General management of anorexia nervosa and difficulties in assessing the efficacy of treatment. In: R.A. Vigersky (Ed.), *Anorexia Nervosa,* pp. 277–289. New York: Raven Press.

Russell, G.F.M. (1979a). Editorial: Anorexia nervosa: to investigate or to treat? *Lancet,* **2**, 563–564.

Russell, G.F.M. (1979b). Bulimia nervosa: an ominous variant of anorexia nervosa. *Psychological Medicine,* **9**, 429–448.

Russell, G.F.M. (1985a). Bulimia revisited. *International Journal of Eating Disorders,* **4**, 681–692.

Russell, G.F.M. (1985b). Do drugs have a place in the management of anorexia nervosa and bulimia nervosa? In: M. Sandler and T. Silverstone (Eds.), *Psychopharmacology and Food,* pp. 146–161. Oxford: University Press.

Russell, G.F.M. (1985c). The changing nature of anorexia nervosa. *Journal of Psychiatric Research,* **19**, 101–109.

Russell, G.F.M. and Beardwood, C.J. (1968). The feeding disorders, with particular reference to anorexia nervosa and its associated gonadotrophin changes. In: R.P. Michael (Ed.), *Endocrinology and Human Behaviour,* pp. 310–329. London: Oxford University Press.

Russell, G.F.M. and Beardwood, C.J. (1970). Amenorrhoea in the feeding disorders: anorexia nervosa and obesity. *Psychotherapy and Psychosomatics,* **18**, 359–364.

Russell, G.F.M. and Bruce, J.T. (1966). Impaired water diuresis in patients with anorexia nervosa. *American Journal of Medicine,* **40**, 38–48.

Russell, G.F.M., Campbell, P.G. and Slade, P.D. (1975). Experimental studies on the nature of the psychological disorder in anorexia nervosa. *Psychoneuroendocrinology,* **1**, 45–56.

Russell, G.F.M., Checkley, S.A. Robinson, P.H. (1986). The limited role of drugs in the treatment of anorexia and bulimia nervosa. In: M.O. Carruba and J.E. Blundell (Eds.), *Pharmacology of Eating Disorders: Theoretical and Clinical Developments,* pp. 151–167. New York: Raven Press.

Russell, G.F.M., Loraine, J.A., Bell, E.T. and Harkness, R.A. (1965). Gonadotrophin and oestrogen excretion in patients with anorexia nervosa. *Journal of Psychosomatic Research,* **9**, 79–85.

Russell, G.F.M., Szmukler, G.I., Dare, C. and Eisler, I. (1987). An evaluation of family therapy in anorexia nervosa and bulimia nervosa. *Archives of General Psychiatry,* **44**, 1047–1056.

Russell, G.F.M. and Treasure, J. (1989). The modern history of anorexia nervosa: an interpretation of why the illness has changed. *Annals of the New York Academy of Sciences,* **575**, 13–3-.

Slade, P.D. and Russell, G.F.M. (1973a). Awareness of body dimensions in anorexia nervosa: cross-sectional and longitudinal studies. *Psychological Medicine,* **3**, 188–199.

Slade, P.D. and Russell, G.F.M. (1973b). Experimental investigations of bodily perception in anorexia nervosa and obesity. *Psychotherapy and Psychosomatics,* **22**, 359–363.

Theander, S. (1970). Anorexia nervosa: a psychiatric investigation of 94 female cases. *Acta Psychiatrica Scandinavica,* Suppl. 214.

Vandereycken, W. and Meermann, R. (1984). *Anorexia Nervosa: A Clinician's Guide to Treatment.* Berlin–New York: Walter de Gruyter.

Vandereycken, W. and Van Deth, R. (1990). A tribute to Lasègue's description of anorexia nervosa (1873), with a completion of its English translation. *British Journal of Psychiatry,* **157**, 902–908.

Vandereycken, W. (1994). Emergence of bulimia nervosa as a separate diagnostic entity: Review of the literature from 1960 to 1979. *International Journal of Eating Disorders*, **16** (in press).

Wakeling, A. and Russell, G.F.M. (1970). Disturbances in the regulation of body temperature in anorexia nervosa. *Psychological Medicine,* **1**, 30–39.

Index

Index compiled by Liz Granger

Wiley Titles of Related Interest

EATING DISORDERS
Personal Construct Therapy and Change
Eric J. Button

Concerned with the personal meaning which underlies the eating disorders anorexia nervosa and bulimia nervosa, this book gives a general overview of the nature and treatment of eating disorders and outlines a personal construct approach to treatment.
0-471-94094-1 paper 264pp 1993

BULIMIA NERVOSA
Basic Research, Diagnosis and Therapy
Edited by Manfred M. Fichter

"...valuable to all psychiatrists, clinical psychologists, and any physician that has to cope with the rising tide of young women with this disorder." *Behaviour Research and Therapy*
0-471-92405-9 cased 376pp 1990

EXCESSIVE APPETITES
A Psychological View of Addictions
Jim Orford

Presents a comprehensive framework for understanding a whole range of addictive behaviours and the whole developmental process. The addictions covered are drinking, drug taking, eating, gambling and sexuality.
0-471-93613-8 paper 378pp 1992

IMPROVING THE LONG-TERM MANAGEMENT OF OBESITY
Theory, Research and Clinical Guidelines
Michael G. Perri, Arthur M. Nezu *and* Barbara J. Viegener

Designed to help confront the weight-loss maintenance problem head on by reviewing the effectiveness of various treatments currently in use for obesity.
0-471-52899-4 cased 320pp 1992

EUROPEAN EATING DISORDERS REVIEW
The Journal of the Eating Disorders Association

Provides practical help and new ideas for all those professionals who, as part of their routine work, have either to treat or care for anyone who suffers from bulimia or anorexia nervosa or related eating disorders.
ISSN: 1067–1633

INTERNATIONAL JOURNAL of EATING DISORDERS

Covers the scope of treatment, symptoms, causation, and long-term effects for such disorders as anorexia nervosa, bulimia, obesity and infantile rumination.
ISSN: 0276–3478